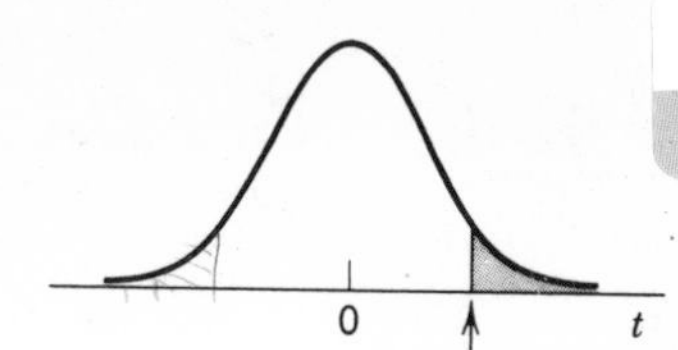

Critical point. For example: $t_{.025}$ leaves .025 probability in the tail.

TABLE V *t* Critical Points

d.f.	$t_{.25}$	$t_{.10}$	$t_{.05}$	$t_{.025}$	$t_{.010}$	$t_{.005}$	$t_{.0025}$	$t_{.0010}$	$t_{.0005}$
1	1.00	3.08	6.31	12.7	31.8	63.7	127	318	637
2	.82	1.89	2.92	4.30	6.96	9.92	14.1	22.3	31.6
3	.76	1.64	2.35	3.18	4.54	5.84	7.45	10.2	12.9
4	.74	1.53	2.13	2.78	3.75	4.60	5.60	7.17	8.61
5	.73	1.48	2.02	2.57	3.36	4.03	4.77	5.89	6.87
6	.72	1.44	1.94	2.45	3.14	3.71	4.32	5.21	5.96
7	.71	1.41	1.89	2.36	3.00	3.50	4.03	4.79	5.41
8	.71	1.40	1.86	2.31	2.90	3.36	3.83	4.50	5.04
9	.70	1.38	1.83	2.26	2.82	3.25	3.69	4.30	4.78
10	.70	1.37	1.81	2.23	2.76	3.17	3.58	4.14	4.59
11	.70	1.36	1.80	2.20	2.72	3.11	3.50	4.02	4.44
12	.70	1.36	1.78	2.18	2.68	3.05	3.43	3.93	4.32
13	.69	1.35	1.77	2.16	2.65	3.01	3.37	3.85	4.22
14	.69	1.35	1.76	2.14	2.62	2.98	3.33	3.79	4.14
15	.69	1.34	1.75	2.13	2.60	2.95	3.29	3.73	4.07
16	.69	1.34	1.75	2.12	2.58	2.92	3.25	3.69	4.01
17	.69	1.33	1.74	2.11	2.57	2.90	3.22	3.65	3.97
18	.69	1.33	1.73	2.10	2.55	2.88	3.20	3.61	3.92
19	.69	1.33	1.73	2.09	2.54	2.86	3.17	3.58	3.88
20	.69	1.33	1.72	2.09	2.53	2.85	3.15	3.55	3.85
21	.69	1.32	1.72	2.08	2.52	2.83	3.14	3.53	3.82
22	.69	1.32	1.72	2.07	2.51	2.82	3.12	3.50	3.79
23	.69	1.32	1.71	2.07	2.50	2.81	3.10	3.48	3.77
24	.68	1.32	1.71	2.06	2.49	2.80	3.09	3.47	3.75
25	.68	1.32	1.71	2.06	2.49	2.79	3.08	3.45	3.73
26	.68	1.31	1.71	2.06	2.48	2.78	3.07	3.43	3.71
27	.68	1.31	1.70	2.05	2.47	2.77	3.06	3.42	3.69
28	.68	1.31	1.70	2.05	2.47	2.76	3.05	3.41	3.67
29	.68	1.31	1.70	2.05	2.46	2.76	3.04	3.40	3.66
30	.68	1.31	1.70	2.04	2.46	2.75	3.03	3.39	3.65
40	.68	1.30	1.68	2.02	2.42	2.70	2.97	3.31	3.55
60	.68	1.30	1.67	2.00	2.39	2.66	2.92	3.23	3.46
120	.68	1.29	1.66	1.98	2.36	2.62	2.86	3.16	3.37
∞	.67 $= z_{.25}$	1.28 $= z_{.10}$	1.64 $= z_{.05}$	1.96 $= z_{.025}$	2.33 $= z_{.010}$	2.58 $= z_{.005}$	2.81 $= z_{.0025}$	3.09 $= z_{.0010}$	3.29 $= z_{.0005}$

INTRODUCTORY STATISTICS FOR BUSINESS AND ECONOMICS

INTRODUCTORY STATISTICS FOR BUSINESS AND ECONOMICS

FOURTH EDITION

Thomas H. Wonnacott
University of Western Ontario

Ronald J. Wonnacott
University of Western Ontario

JOHN WILEY & SONS

New York Chichester Brisbane Toronto Singapore

To our parents

COVER ILLUSTRATION BY LARRY ROSS

Library of Congress Cataloging in Publication Data:

Wonnacott, Thomas H., 1935–
Introductory statistics for business and economics Thomas H. Wonnacott, Ronald J. Wonnacott.
p. cm.—(Wiley series in probability and mathematical statistics)
Bibliography: p.
Includes index.

1. Social sciences—Statistical methods. 2. Statistics.
3. Commercial statistics. 4. Economics—Statistical methods.
I. Wonnacott, Ronald J. II. Title. III. Series.
HA29.W622 1990 89-33083
519.5—dc20

Printed in the Republic of Singapore

10 9 8 7 6 5

WILEY SERIES IN PROBABILITY AND MATHEMATICAL STATISTICS

ESTABLISHED BY WALTER A. SHEWHART AND SAMUEL S. WILKS

EDITORS

Vic Barnett, Ralph A. Bradley, J. Stuart Hunter, Joseph B. Kadane, David G. Kendall, Rupert G. Miller, Jr., Adrian F. M. Smith, Stephen M. Stigler, Geoffrey S. Watson

Probability and Mathematical Statistics

Adler The Geometry of Random Fields
Anderson The Statistical Analysis of Time Series
Anderson An Introduction to Multivariate Statistical Analysis, *Second Edition*
Arnold The Theory of Linear Models and Multivariate Analysis
Barnett Comparative Statistical Inference, *Second Edition*
Bernardo and Smith Bayesian Statistical Concepts and Theory
Bhattacharyya and Johnson Statistical Concepts and Methods
Billingsley Probability and Measure, *Second Edition*
Bollen Structural Equations with Latent Variables
Borovkov Asymptotic Methods in Queuing Theory
Bose and Manvel Introduction to Combinatorial Theory
Caines Linear Stochastic Systems
Cassel, Sarndal, and Wretman Foundations of Inference in Survey Sampling
Chen Recursive Estimation and Control for Stochastic Systems
Cochran Contributions to Statistics
Cochran Planning and Analysis of Observational Studies
Constantine Combinatorial Theory and Statistical Design
Doob Stochastic Processes
Dudewicz and Mishra Modern Mathematical Statistics
Eaton Multivariate Statistics: A Vector Space Approach
Ethier and Kurtz Markov Processes: Characterization and Convergence
Fabian and Hannan Introduction to Probability and Mathematical Statistics
Feller An Introduction to Probability Theory and Its Applications, Volume I, *Third Edition,* Revised; Volume II, *Second Edition*
Fuller Introduction to Statistical Time Series
Fuller Measurement Error Models
Grenander Abstract Inference
Groves Survey Errors and Costs
Guttman Linear Models: An Introduction
Hald A History of Probability and Statistics and Their Applications before 1750
Hall Introduction to The Theory of Coverage Processes
Hampel, Ronchetti, Rousseeuw, and Stahel Robust Statistics: The Approach Based on Influence Functions
Hannan Multiple Time Series
Hannan and Deistler The Statistical Theory of Linear Systems
Harrison Brownian Motion and Stochastic Flow Systems
Hettmansperger Statistical Inference Based on Ranks
Hoel Introduction to Mathematical Statistics, *Fifth Edition*
Huber Robust Statistics
Iman and Conover A Modern Approach to Statistics
Iosifescu Finite Markov Processes and Applications
Johnson and Bhattacharyya Statistics: Principles and Methods, *Revised Printing*
Laha and Rohatgi Probability Theory
Larson Introduction to Probability Theory and Statistical Inference, *Third Edition*
Lehmann Testing Statistical Hypotheses, *Second Edition*
Lehmann Theory of Point Estimation
Matthes, Kerstan, and Mecke Infinitely Divisible Point Processes
Muirhead Aspects of Multivariate Statistical Theory
Press Bayesian Statistics: Principles, Models, and Applications
Puri and Sen Nonparametric Methods in General Linear Models
Puri and Sen Nonparametric Methods in Multivariate Analysis
Puri, Vilaplana, and Wertz New Perspectives in Theoretical and Applied Statistics
Randles and Wolfe Introduction to the Theory of Nonparametric Statistics
Rao Linear Statistical Inference and Its Applications, *Second Edition*
Rao Real and Stochastic Analysis
Rao and Sedransk W. G. Cochran's Impact on Statistics
Rao Asymptotic Theory of Statistical Inference
Robertson, Wright and Dykstra Order Restricted Statistical Inference
Rogers and Williams Diffusions, Markov Processes, and Martingales, Volume II: Ito Calculus
Rohatgi An Introduction to Probability Theory and Mathematical Statistics
Rohatgi Statistical Inference
Ross Stochastic Processes
Rubinstein Simulation and The Monte Carlo Method
Ruzsa and Szekely Algebraic Probability Theory
Scheffe The Analysis of Variance
Seber Linear Regression Analysis
Seber Multivariate Observations
Seber and Wild Nonlinear Regression
Sen Sequential Nonparametrics: Invariance Principles and Statistical Inference
Serfling Approximation Theorems of Mathematical Statistics

Probability and Mathematical Statistics (Continued)

Shorack and Wellner Empirical Processes with Applications to Statistics
Stoyanov Counterexamples in Probability

Applied Probability and Statistics

Abraham and Ledolter Statistical Methods for Forecasting
Agresti Analysis of Ordinal Categorical Data
Aickin Linear Statistical Analysis of Discrete Data
Anderson and Loynes The Teaching of Practical Statistics
Anderson, Auquier, Hauck, Oakes, Vandaele, and Weisberg Statistical Methods for Comparative Studies
Arthanari and Dodge Mathematical Programming in Statistics
Asmussen Applied Probability and Queues
Bailey The Elements of Stochastic Processes with Applications to the Natural Sciences
Barnett Interpreting Multivariate Data
Barnett and Lewis Outliers in Statistical Data, *Second Edition*
Bartholomew Stochastic Models for Social Processes, *Third Edition*
Bartholomew and Forbes Statistical Techniques for Manpower Planning
Bates and Watts Nonlinear Regression Analysis and Its Applications
Beck and Arnold Parameter Estimation in Engineering and Science
Belsley, Kuh, and Welsch Regression Diagnostics: Identifying Influential Data and Sources of Collinearity
Bhat Elements of Applied Stochastic Processes, *Second Edition*
Bloomfield Fourier Analysis of Time Series: An Introduction
Bollen Structural Equations with Latent Variables
Box R. A. Fisher, The Life of a Scientist
Box and Draper Empirical Model-Building and Response Surfaces
Box and Draper Evolutionary Operation: A Statistical Method for Process Improvement
Box, Hunter, and Hunter Statistics for Experimenters: An Introduction to Design, Data Analysis, and Model Building
Brown and Hollander Statistics: A Biomedical Introduction
Bunke and Bunke Statistical Inference in Linear Models, Volume I
Bunke and Bunke Nonlinear Regression, Functional Relations and Robust Methods: Statistical Methods of Model Building
Chambers Computational Methods for Data Analysis
Chatterjee and Hadi Sensitivity Analysis in Linear Regression
Chatterjee and Price Regression Analysis by Example
Chow Econometric Analysis by Control Methods
Clarke and Disney Probability and Random Processes: A First Course with Applications, *Second Edition*
Cochran Sampling Techniques, *Third Edition*
Cochran and Cox Experimental Designs, *Second Edition*
Conover Practical Nonparametric Statistics, *Second Edition*
Conover and Iman Introduction to Modern Business Statistics
Cornell Experiments with Mixtures: Designs, Models and The Analysis of Mixture Data
Cox Planning of Experiments
Cox A Handbook of Introductory Statistical Methods
Daniel Biostatistics: A Foundation for Analysis in the Health Sciences, *Fourth Edition*
Daniel Applications of Statistics to Industrial Experimentation
Daniel and Wood Fitting Equations to Data: Computer Analysis of Multifactor Data, *Second Edition*
David Order Statistics, *Second Edition*
Davison Multidimensional Scaling
Degroot, Fienberg and Kadane Statistics and the Law
Deming Sample Design in Business Research
Dillon and Goldstein Multivariate Analysis: Methods and Applications
Dodge Analysis of Experiments with Missing Data
Dodge and Romig Sampling Inspection Tables, *Second Edition*
Dowdy and Wearden Statistics for Research
Draper and Smith Applied Regression Analysis, *Second Edition*
Dunn Basic Statistics: A Primer for the Biomedical Sciences, *Second Edition*
Dunn and Clark Applied Statistics: Analysis of Variance and Regression, *Second Edition*
Elandt-Johnson and Johnson Survival Models and Data Analysis
Fleiss Statistical Methods for Rates and Proportions, *Second Edition*
Fleiss The Design and Analysis of Clinical Experiments
Flury Common Principal Components and Related Multivariate Models
Fox Linear Statistical Models and Related Methods
Franken, König, Arndt, and Schmidt Queues and Point Processes
Gallant Nonlinear Statistical Models
Gibbons, Olkin, and Sobel Selecting and Ordering Populations: A New Statistical Methodology
Gnanadesikan Methods for Statistical Data Analysis of Multivariate Observations
Greenberg and Webster Advanced Econometrics: A Bridge to the Literature
Gross and Harris Fundamentals of Queueing Theory, *Second Edition*

Applied Probability and Statistics (Continued)

Groves, Biemer, Lyberg, Massey, Nicholls, and Waksberg Telephone Survey Methodology
Gupta and Panchapakesan Multiple Decision Procedures: Theory and Methodology of Selecting and Ranking Populations
Guttman, Wilks, and Hunter Introductory Engineering Statistics, *Third Edition*
Hahn and Shapiro Statistical Models in Engineering
Hald Statistical Tables and Formulas
Hald Statistical Theory with Engineering Applications
Hand Discrimination and Classification
Heiberger Computation for the Analysis of Designed Experiments
Hoaglin, Mosteller and Tukey Exploring Data Tables, Trends and Shapes
Hoaglin, Mosteller, and Tukey Understanding Robust and Exploratory Data Analysis
Hochberg and Tamhane Multiple Comparison Procedures
Hoel Elementary Statistics, *Fourth Edition*
Hoel and Jessen Basic Statistics for Business and Economics, *Third Edition*
Hogg and Klugman Loss Distributions
Hollander and Wolfe Nonparametric Statistical Methods
Hosmer and Lemeshow Applied Logistic Regression
Iman and Conover Modern Business Statistics
Jessen Statistical Survey Techniques
Johnson Multivariate Statistical Simulation
Johnson and Kotz Distributions in Statistics
Discrete Distributions
Continuous Univariate Distributions—1
Continuous Univariate Distributions—2
Continuous Multivariate Distributions
Judge, Hill, Griffiths, Lütkepohl and Lee Introduction to the Theory and Practice of Econometrics. *Second Edition*
Judge, Griffiths, Hill, Lütkepohl and Lee The Theory and Practice of Econometrics, *Second Edition*
Kalbfleisch and Prentice The Statistical Analysis of Failure Time Data
Kaufman and Rousseeuw Finding Groups in Data: An Introduction to Cluster Analysis
Kish Statistical Design for Research
Kish Survey Sampling
Kuh, Neese, and Hollinger Structural Sensitivity in Econometric Models
Keeney and Raiffa Decisions with Multiple Objectives
Lawless Statistical Models and Methods for Lifetime Data
Leamer Specification Searches: Ad Hoc Inference with Nonexperimental Data
Lebart, Morineau, and Warwick Multivariate Descriptive Statistical Analysis: Correspondence Analysis and Related Techniques for Large Matrices
Linhart and Zucchini Model Selection
Little and Rubin Statistical Analysis with Missing Data
McNeil Interactive Data Analysis
Magnus and Neudecker Matrix Differential Calculus with Applications in Statistics and Econometrics
Maindonald Statistical Computation
Mallows Design, Data, and Analysis by Some Friends of Cuthbert Daniel
Mann, Schafer and Singpurwalla Methods for Statistical Analysis of Reliability and Life Data
Martz and Waller Bayesian Reliability Analysis
Mason, Gunst, and Hess Statistical Design and Analysis of Experiments with Applications to Engineering and Science
Mike and Stanley Statistics in Medical Research: Methods and Issues with Applications in Cancer Research
Miller Beyond ANOVA, Basics of Applied Statistics
Miller Survival Analysis
Miller, Efron, Brown, and Moses Biostatistics Casebook
Montgomery and Peck Introduction to Linear Regression Analysis
Nelson Applied Life Data Analysis
Osborne Finite Algorithms in Optimization and Data Analysis
Otnes and Enochson Applied Time Series Analysis: Volume I. Basic Techniques
Otnes and Enochson Digital Time Series Analysis
Pankratz Forecasting with Univariate Box-Jenkins Models: Concepts and Cases
Platek, Rao, Sarndal and Singh Small Area Statistics: An International Symposium
Pollock The Algebra of Econometrics
Rao and Mitra Generalized Inverse of Matrices and Its Applications
Rényi A Diary on Information Theory
Ripley Spatial Statistics
Ripley Stochastic Simulation
Ross Introduction to Probability and Statistics for Engineers and Scientists
Rousseeuw and Leroy Robust Regression and Outlier Detection
Rubin Multiple Imputation for Nonresponse in Surveys
Rubinstein Monte Carlo Optimization, Simulation, and Sensitivity of Queueing Networks
Ryan Statistical Methods for Quality Improvement
Schuss Theory and Applications of Stochastic Differential Equations
Searle Linear Models
Searle Linear Models for Unbalanced Data
Searle Matrix Algebra Useful for Statistics
Skinner, Holt, and Smith Analysis of Data from Complex Surveys

Applied Probability and Statistics (Continued)

Springer The Algebra of Random Variables
Steuer Multiple Criteria Optimization
Stoyan Comparison Methods for Queues and Other Stochastic Models
Stoyan, Kendall and Mecke Stochastic Geometry and Its Applications
Thompson Empirical Model Building
Tijms Stochastic Modeling and Analysis: A Computational Approach
Titterington, Smith, and Makov Statistical Analysis of Finite Mixture Distributions
Upton The Analysis of Cross-Tabulated Data
Upton and Fingleton Spatial Data Analysis by Example, Volume I: Point Pattern and Quantitative Data
Upton and Fingleton Spatial Data Analysis by Example, Volume II: Categorical and Directional Data
Van Rijckevorsel and De Leeuw Component and Correspondence Analysis
Weisberg Applied Linear Regression, *Second Edition*
Whittle Optimization Over Time: Dynamic Programming and Stochastic Control, Volume I and Volume II
Whittle Systems in Stochastic Equilibrium
Williams A Sampler on Sampling
Wonnacott and Wonnacott Econometrics, *Second Edition*
Wonnacott and Wonnacott Introductory Statistics, *Fourth Edition*
Wonnacott and Wonnacott Introductory Statistics for Business and Economics, *Fourth Edition*
Woolson Statistical Methods for The Analysis of Biomedical Data

Tracts on Probability and Statistics

Ambartzumian Combinatorial Integral Geometry
Bibby and Toutenburg Prediction and Improved Estimation in Linear Models
Billingsley Convergence of Probability Measures
Devroye and Gyorfi Nonparametric Density Estimation: The L_1 View
Kelly Reversibility and Stochastic Networks
Raktoe, Hedayat, and Federer Factorial Designs
Toutenburg Prior Information in Linear Models

PREFACE

This book is a two-semester introduction to statistics for students in business and economics. It also is designed so that the first eight to twelve chapters can be used in a one-semester course. Our objective is to make statistics lively, practical, and clear.

TO THE STUDENT

Statistics is the intriguing study of how you can describe an unknown world by opening a few windows on it. You will discover the excitement of thinking in a way you have never thought before.

This book is not a novel, and it cannot be read that way. Whenever you come to a numbered example in the text, try first to answer it yourself. Only after you have solved it, or at least have given it a lot of hard thought, should you consult the solution we provide. The same advice holds for the exercise problems at the end of each section. These problems have been kept computationally as simple as possible, so that you can concentrate on insight rather than arithmetic. At the same time, we have tried to make them realistic by the frequent use of real data—or at least small subsets of real data. The point of going through the hand calculations in the text is *not* to become an expert at calculating, but to develop a feeling for what the concepts mean. For this purpose, small sets of numbers will do. (The much larger sets of real data are usually handled by computers anyway.)

Optional problems and sections are indicated by a star (*)—for example, some problems that require a computer package. We want students who like computers to see their power. But at the same time we keep these exercises optional, so that other students can master the text without using a computer themselves.

Brief answers to all odd-numbered problems are given in the back of the book. Their completely worked-out solutions are available in the *Student's Workbook*, along with 50 pages of new problems for review.

TO THE INSTRUCTOR

Throughout this book, we use examples to introduce new material; the general theory is presented only after the student has gained a clear, intuitive idea of the concepts. We give students the basic scientific understanding available only in more advanced texts, and use the simplest mathematics possible to achieve this. The only prerequisite is high school algebra. (Students who enjoy calculus can use it occasionally in the optional Appendixes at the back of the book.)

This book shows the logical relation between topics that often have appeared in texts as separate and isolated chapters. A few examples are the equivalence of confidence intervals and hypothesis testing; the *t* test and the *F* test; and analysis of variance and regression using dummy variables. In every case, our motivation has been to help students appreciate the underlying logic, so that they can arrive at answers to practical problems.

We have placed high priority on the regression model, not only because regression is widely regarded as the most powerful tool of the practicing statistician but also because it provides a good focal point for understanding such related techniques as correlation and analysis of variance. We give a great deal of coverage to nonlinear and multiple regression, and emphasize the value of multiple regression in reducing bias in observational studies.

This text is designed for maximum flexibility. Basic classical statistics are presented in the first fifteen chapters, while the last ten chapters include special but important topics such as nonparametric statistics, index numbers, decision trees, Bayesian inference, time series, and so on. The instructor can choose any combination of topics in these last ten chapters to complete the course.

To help instructors pick their way throughout the topics that best suit their classes, some chapters can be abbreviated or taught later, with little interruption to the continuity—by odd coincidence, the odd Chapters, 1, 3, 5, 7, and 9. And some sections, marked with a star, can be omitted entirely with no interruption whatsoever.

We have tried to keep the length of the book manageable by deleting about 50 topics (such as permutations and combinations, the Poisson distribution, confidence intervals for variances, game theory, and so on). To keep them accessible to instructors who need them for their course, however, we have retained them in the *Instructor's Manual*, where they can be easily photocopied for class use.

The *Instructor's Manual* also has the completely worked-out solutions to the even-numbered problems, to complement the odd-numbered solutions in the *Student's Workbook*.

As well as the *Instructor's Manual* and the *Student's Workbook*, a *Test Bank* of about a thousand questions is available, in both printed and disk form.

THIS NEW EDITION

As computers take over more of our routine and technical burdens, it becomes more and more important for students to develop the skills that only a human has—imagination and judgment. This has motivated most of the changes in this new edition, specifically:

i. If you want a quick taste of what's new, read the "Final Challenge" at the very end of each chapter. As the last Review Problem it makes an excellent assignment, since students can see how their new skills can be used to get imaginative solutions to practical problems—often real problems drawn from the literature, or simplified and manageable versions of them. This is only one of the many ways that we have tried to inject more of a real-life flavor.

ii. There is more emphasis on computing. To keep it simple as well as powerful, we extensively use MINITAB, one of the friendliest of the interactive packages.

In listing computer input and output, the text gives all students (including those who initially want to avoid computers) an easy familiarity with a tool that takes the drudgery out of statistics. (And as a byproduct, it relieves students from ever seeing complicated "calculating formulas.")

iii. We have expanded our advice about which techniques are appropriate—for example, the mean and median in Section 16-1, hypothesis testing in 9-6 and 10-3, simple and multiple regression in 13-5, and nonparametric and robust statistics in 16-7.

iv. We have added several new sections, ranging from a major section in Chapter 2 on graphs and common sense, to bootstrapping in Chapter 8.

v. *All* of the calculus and practically all of the proofs have been moved to the Appendixes at the back of the book, where they can easily be kept optional.

Over the past several editions, we have introduced many practical and modern topics in a brief and readable way. (If needed, their technical details can be looked up in Johnson, N. L. and S. Kotz (eds.) (1982–88), *Encyclopedia of Statistical Sciences*, Vols. 1–9, New York: Wiley—a work so comprehensive that it makes chapter-by-chapter reference lists obsolete.) Many of these topics are indispensible to practitioners, but are unavailable in introductory texts. A few are worth listing (in order of appearance, with a star indicating which are new to this edition):

- • Randomization to eliminate bias
- • Exploratory data analysis
- * Graphs and common sense
- * Expected value in bidding
- * The Bootstrap
- • Path analysis, to illuminate regression
- * Robust estimation, included with nonparametric statistics
- • Maximum likelihood estimation
- • Bayesian estimation and decisions
- • Decision trees
- • Box-Jenkins ARIMA forecasting
- • Proofs in the Appendix

ACKNOWLEDGMENTS

So many people have helped that it is impossible to thank them all. But special thanks go to David Bellhouse, Clayton Block, and our editors, Brad Wiley and Valerie Hunter.

We also warmly thank the many instructors and students who have forwarded suggestions to us based on their experience with earlier editions, especially the students of Business 306, Economics 135 and 255, and Statistics 135 here at the University of Western Ontario. Finally, we thank the reviewers of the manuscript, whose comments have greatly improved the final product:

Dr. Roger Even Bove
West Chester University

Professor John Hillas
Ohio State University

Professor Victor E. McGee
Amos Tuck School
Dartmouth College

Professor David Meredith
San Francisco State University

ABOUT THE AUTHORS

The authors both studied mathematics, statistics, and economics as undergraduates at the University of Western Ontario. Ron later received a Ph.D. in economics at Harvard, and Tom, a Ph.D. in statistics at Princeton. Between them, they have taught at Wesleyan University, the University of Minnesota, Duke University, and the University of California at Berkeley, and currently both teach at the University of Western Ontario.

Together they have written several other books for Wiley, including *Econometrics* and *Introductory Statistics*. Along with a third brother Paul, Ron has written several more books, including *Free-Trade Between the United States and Canada* (Harvard University Press), and *Economics* (now also published by Wiley). Tom has written numerous articles on statistical applications in medicine and social science.

The hobbies they share include Mozart, skiing, and tennis. Ron also plays golf while Tom enjoys touch football and quartet singing. Most important, each is fortunate to have a wife and family who provide a large measure of moral support.

RONALD J. WONNACOTT

THOMAS H. WONNACOTT

CONTENTS

PART I

Basic Probability and Statistics

CHAPTER 1

The Nature of Statistics

"It ain't so much the things we don't know that get us in trouble. It's the things we know that ain't so."

—ARTEMUS WARD

People often think of statistics as simply collecting numbers. Indeed, this was its original meaning: State-istics was the collection of population and economic information vital to the state. But statistics is now much more than this. It has developed into a scientific method of analysis widely applied in business and all the social and natural sciences. To illustrate the power of modern statistics, we will examine two typical applications—first, a pre-election poll, and second, the evaluation of a hospital routine.

1-1 RANDOM SAMPLING: A POLITICAL POLL

A—THE RELIABILITY OF A RANDOM SAMPLE

Before every presidential election, the Gallup poll estimates the percentage of the population that will vote for each candidate, and picks the winner. Clearly, canvassing the entire population would be an unrealistic task. Instead, a sample of voters is taken in the hope that the percentage of, say, Democrats that turns up in the sample will provide a good estimate of the percentage of Democrats in the population.

Just how should one select the individual Americans who will make up this sample? Some interesting lessons can be learned from past mistakes. For example, when polling was in its infancy in 1936, the editors of *Literary Digest* tried to predict the U.S. presidential election. But they used a sample of voters chosen from lists such as telephone books and club memberships—lists that tended to be more heavily Republican than the voting population at large. Even worse, only a quarter responded to their questionnaire and, as it turned out, they also tended to be more Republican than the nonrespondents. Altogether, this sample was so *biased* (i.e., lopsided, and not fairly representative of the population) that it led to a misleading prediction of a Republican victory. Election day produced a rude surprise: Less than 40% voted Republican, and the Democratic incumbent, Roosevelt, was elected by a landslide. The Republican candidate who woke up that morning expecting to become President—Alf Landon—is remembered now only by a few historians.

Other examples of biased samples are easy to find. Informal polls of people on the street are often biased because the interviewer may select people who seem civil and well dressed. Members of Congress cannot rely on unsolicited mail as an unbiased sample of their constituency, since it over-represents organized pressure groups and people with strong opinions.

From such bitter experience important lessons have been learned: To avoid bias, *every* voter must have a chance to be counted. To avoid slighting any voter, even unintentionally, the sample should be selected *randomly*. There are various ways of doing this, but the simplest to visualize is the following: Put each voter's name on a chip, stir the chips thoroughly in a large bowl, and draw out a sample of, say, a thousand chips. This gives the names of the thousand voters who make up what is called a *simple random sample* of size $n = 1000$.

Unfortunately, in practice simple random sampling is often very slow and expensive. For example, a random sample of American voters would include many in isolated areas who would be very difficult to track down. Much more efficient is *multistage sampling*: From the nation as a whole, take a random sample of a few cities (and counties); within each of these, take a random sample of a few blocks; finally, within each block, take a random sample of a few individuals. While methods like this are frequently used, for clarity we will go back to simple random sampling (as in drawing chips from a bowl).

A simple random sample will not reflect the population perfectly, of course. For example, if the sample includes only a few voters, the luck of the draw may be a big factor. To see why, suppose the population of voters is split 50–50 Democrat and Republican. How might a small sample of 10 voters turn out? The likeliest result would be 5 Democrats (and 5 Republicans), but the luck of the draw might produce 8 or 9 Democrats—just as 10 flips of a fair coin might produce 8 or 9 heads. In other words, in such a small sample, the proportion of Democrats might be 80% or 90%—a far cry from the population proportion of 50%.

In a larger sample, the sample proportion of Democrats (which we call P) will be a more reliable estimate of the population proportion (which we call π, the Greek equivalent of P. A list of Greek letters is given just before the Index.) In fact, the easiest way to show how well π is estimated by P is to construct a so-called *confidence interval:*

$$\pi = P \pm \text{sampling allowance} \tag{1-1}$$

with crucial questions being, "How small is this sampling allowance?" and "How sure are we that we are right?" Since this typifies the very core of the book, we state the answer more precisely, in the language of Chapter 8 (where you will find it fully derived):

For simple random sampling, we can state with approximately 95% confidence that

$$\pi = P \pm 1.96\sqrt{\frac{P(1-P)}{n}} \tag{1-2}$$

where π and P are the population and sample proportions, and n is the sample size.

We shall illustrate this confidence interval in Example 1-1 below. But first, we repeat a warning in the Preface: Every numbered example of this kind is an exercise you should first work out yourself, rather than just read. We therefore have put each example in the form of a question for you to answer; if you get stuck, then you can read the solution. But in all cases remember that *statistics is not a spectator sport*. You cannot learn it by watching, any more than you can learn to ride a bike by watching. You have to jump on and take a few spills.

EXAMPLE 1-1

THE GALLUP POLL CALLS A CLOSE ONE

Just before the 1988 presidential election, a Gallup poll of about 1500 voters showed 840 for Bush and the remaining 660 for Dukakis. Calculate the 95% confidence interval for the population proportion π of Bush supporters. (The Gallup poll combined multistage with other kinds of sampling that together provided about the same accuracy as simple random sampling. Thus equation (1-2) gives a good approximation.)

SOLUTION

The sample size is $n = 1500$ and the sample proportion is

$$P = \frac{840}{1500} = .56$$

Substitute these into equation (1-2):

$$\pi = .56 \pm 1.96 \sqrt{\frac{.56(.44)}{1500}}$$

$$\pi = .56 \pm .03 \tag{1-3}$$

That is, with 95% confidence, the proportion for Bush in the whole population of voters was between 53% and 59%. On election day, it turned out that Bush got 53.9% of the actual vote.

We must always remember that a confidence interval is an uncertain business. In equation (1-3) for example, we were only 95% confident. We must concede the 5% possibility that the "luck of the draw" turned up a misleading sample—just as flipping a coin 10 times may yield 8 or 9 heads.

A confidence interval can be made more precise, of course, by increasing sample size: As n increases in equation (1-2), the sampling allowance shrinks. For example, if we increased our sample tenfold to 15,000 voters, and continued to observe a proportion of .56 for Bush, the 95% confidence interval would shrink to the more precise value:

$$\pi = .56 \pm .01 \tag{1-4}$$

This is also intuitively correct: A larger sample contains more information about the population, and hence allows a more precise conclusion.

B—INDUCTION AND DEDUCTION

One of the major objectives of this book will be to construct confidence intervals like (1-3). Another related objective is to *test hypotheses*. For example, suppose a claim is made that 60% of the population supports Bush. In mathematical terms, this hypothesis may be written $\pi = .60$. It seems reasonable to reject this hypothesis, because it does not fall within the likely range (1-3). In general, there will always be this kind of relation: An hypothesis can be rejected if it lies outside the confidence interval.

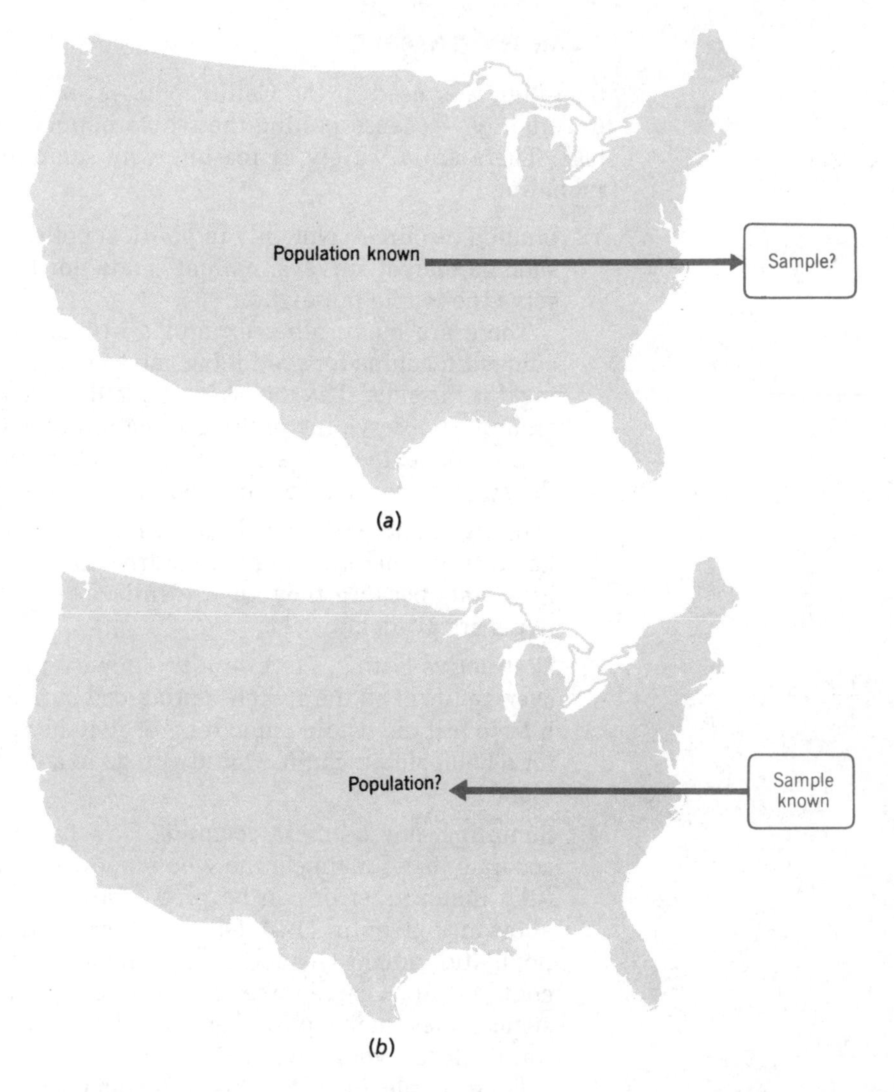

FIGURE 1-1
Deduction and induction contrasted. (a) Deduction (probability). (b) Induction (statistical inference).

Both confidence intervals and hypothesis tests are examples of *statistical inference* or *inductive* reasoning—using an observed sample to make a statement about the unknown population. In this text we will also study *probability theory* or *deductive* reasoning—arguing in the reverse direction, from a known population to the unknown sample. (In fact, this will be studied first because it is philosophically simpler and provides the necessary base for statistical inference later.) Figure 1-1 compares the two types of reasoning.

C—WHY SAMPLE?

Sampling was used in the Gallup poll—even though it involved some uncertainty—because polling the whole population is much too large a task. There are a variety of reasons why sampling is done in general, including:

1. *Limited resources.* Not only in political polls, but in many other cases such as market surveys, neither funds nor time are available to observe the whole population.

   There are many other examples in business. An allegedly more efficient machine for producing valves may be tested before purchasing, for instance. The manager of quality control simply cannot wait around to observe the entire population of valves that this machine will produce. Instead, a sample run is observed, and the decision on the machine is based on an inference from this sample.
2. *Scarcity.* Sometimes only a small sample is available. For example, in heredity versus environment controversies, identical twins provide ideal data because they have identical heredity. Yet very few such twins are available.
3. *Destructive testing.* For example, suppose that we wish to know the average life of all the switches produced by a factory. What use would it be to test the whole population of switches until they burn out? Or, for a hemoglobin count, would you go to a doctor who drew *all* your blood?
4. *Sampling may be more accurate.* How can a mere sample be more accurate than looking at the whole population? If the sample is carefully done, its error can be pretty well confined to the confidence allowance given in (1-2). On the other hand, a survey of the whole population might be such a gargantuan task that much worse errors could occur: A large force of inadequately trained personnel, for instance, may make measurement errors that a smaller and better trained force would avoid.

   For example, the U.S. Census Bureau conducts a monthly sample of about 100,000 Americans called the *Current Population Survey* (to determine unemployment, among other things). This is a model of careful work, and in some ways is more accurate than the complete census of all 250,000,000 Americans taken every 10 years.

PROBLEMS

1-1 Project yourself back in time to six recent U.S. presidential elections. In parentheses we give the results of the Gallup pre-election poll of 1500 voters. (As we mentioned already, each sample has about the same accuracy as a simple random sample. And we continue to ignore third parties.)

Year	*Democrat*	*Republican*
1968	Humphrey (50%)	Nixon (50%)
1972	McGovern (38%)	Nixon (62%)
1976	Carter (51%)	Ford (49%)
1980	Carter (48%)	Reagan (52%)
1984	Mondale (41%)	Reagan (59%)
1988	Dukakis (44%)	Bush (56%)

a. In each case, construct a 95% confidence interval for the proportion of Democratic supporters in the whole population.

b. Mark each case where the interval is wrong—that is, fails to include the true proportion π given in the following list of *actual* voting results:

1968	Humphrey	49.7%
1972	McGovern	38.2%
1976	Carter	51.1%
1980	Carter	44.7%
1984	Mondale	40.8%
1988	Dukakis	46.1%

1-2 In order to serve its advertisers better, a radio station specializing in FM music commissioned a market research survey of 500 listeners to determine their preference for classical or popular music. The survey results broken down by age and sex were as follows:

Numbers Who Prefer Classical

	Sex	
Age	*Male*	*Female*
under 25	19	26
25–50	38	34
over 50	48	60

Numbers Who Prefer Popular

	Sex	
Age	*Male*	*Female*
under 25	63	45
25–50	38	33
over 50	44	52

a. For each of the following, calculate the appropriate estimate and then a 95% confidence interval around it:

i. The percentage of young males (under 25) who prefer popular.

ii. The percentage of the young (under 25) who prefer popular.

iii. The percentage of males who prefer popular.

iv. The percentage of females who prefer popular.

v. The percentage of people who prefer popular. How is this answer related to the previous two?

b. What assumption did you make in part **a**?

1-3 Criticize each of the following sampling plans, pointing out some possible biases and suggesting how to reduce them.

a. In order to estimate how many of her constituents support a gun-control bill, a Senator found from her mail that 132 supported it while 429 opposed it.

b. In order to predict the vote on a municipal subsidy to child day-care centers, a survey selected every corner house and asked whoever answered the door which way they intended to vote. Out of 2180 corner homes canvassed between 9 a.m. and 5 p.m., 960 replies were obtained.

c. To estimate the average income of its MBA graduates 10 years later, a university questioned all those who returned to their tenth reunion. Of the 281 graduates, 56 returned to their reunion and 14 were willing to provide information on their income.

1-2 RANDOMIZED EXPERIMENTS: TESTING A HOSPITAL ROUTINE

Thus far we have seen how randomizing ensures a sample against bias. In this section we will see how randomization similarly frees an experiment of bias.

Is the emotional bond of a mother to her infant weakened by the traditional hospital routine (allowing the woman only a glimpse of her newborn and then keeping them apart for about eight hours)? To test this, a group of mothers were provided with a different treatment—*extended contact* with their infants. They were allowed a full hour with their baby just after birth, plus extra contact for the first three afternoons (Klaus and others, 1972).

A—TREATMENT VS. CONTROL GROUPS

Rather than giving the extended contact treatment to all 28 women selected for this study, half were kept in the traditional routine as a *control group* for comparison. The question was: Who should be given the new treatment, and who should be kept in the control group? The new treatment should not be given just to the women who requested it, since these women might inherently be the ones most interested in their children. Then, if the mother-child relationship thrived, how could one tell if it was because of the treatment, or because of this confounding factor—that is, because the women who got the treatment were initially better mothers?

In fact, there are probably many other confounding factors as well. For example, the woman's education, age, or marital status might also influence the bond with the infant. The most effective way to neutralize *all* these confounding factors at once is to randomize.

B—RANDOM ASSIGNMENT

To randomize, we could simply put the name of each of the 28 women on a chip, stir the chips in a bowl, and draw out half of them at random.[1] These will be assigned the new treatment, while the other half are assigned to the control group. Then the single women, for example, will on average be equally spread into the treatment group and control group.[2] Similarly, the treatment and control groups will on average be equal in terms of every other possible confounding factor—such as education, age, and so on (the list may be almost endless).

Thus random assignment tends to neutralize all confounding factors. If we observe that the group getting the treatment has a better result, we can therefore conclude it is *caused* by the treatment, rather than by something else.

C—BLIND AND DOUBLE-BLIND

To ensure a fair test of a treatment, the treatment and control groups must not only be initially *created* equal by random assignment, they must also be *kept* equal (except, of course, for the fact that one is getting the treatment and the other is not). To see how they might not be kept equal, suppose the doctor who finally evaluates the subjects (patients) knows who has received the new treatment and who has not; she might tend unconsciously to give a more favorable report to the treated subjects (especially if it is a treatment she herself has recommended). Consequently, the evaluator should be kept blind about who has been treated and, if possible, so should the nurses and anyone else who deals with the subjects.

Sometimes it is possible to keep even the subjects themselves blind[3], in a *double-blind* experiment. In drug trials, for example, the control subjects can be given sugar pills (a *placebo*) that they cannot distinguish from the treatment pill; then none of the participants know which group they are in.

---

[1] In the actual experiment, it was expedient to assign the patients to the treatment and control groups on alternating days of admission to hospital. Since onset of labor is pretty unpredictable, this roughly achieved randomized assignment.

[2] Suppose that, of the 28 women in this experiment, 10 are single. Then random assignment will on *average* put 5 of these single women in the treatment group (and 5 in the control group); but in the one experiment actually carried out, the luck of the draw may overload the treatment group with 6 or 7 of these single women.

One way to keep this from happening is to divide the 10 single women into 5 *matched pairs*. In each pair, one woman is assigned at random to the control group, with the other woman going into the treatment group. Then there will be the exact 5-5 split desired.

[3] In the mother-child experiment, the evaluators could be kept blind, but the subjects and many of the personnel providing the treatment could not: Every woman knew of course whether or not she was getting her baby immediately after birth, and so did the attending nurses.

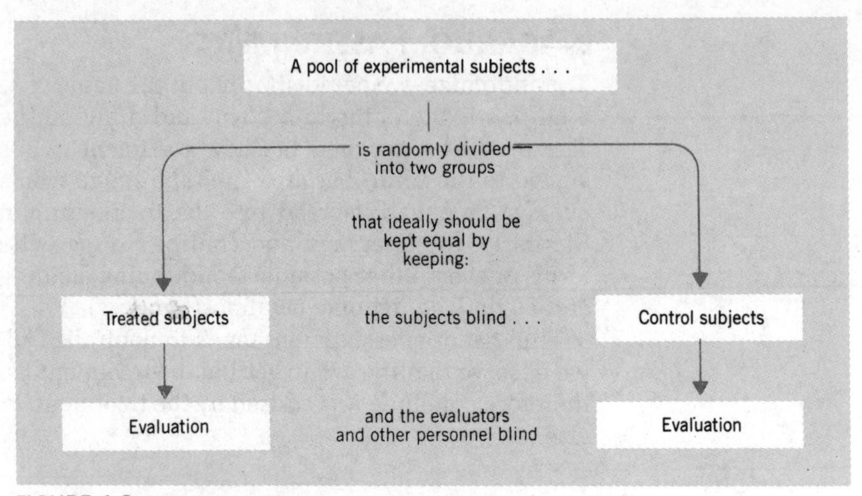

FIGURE 1-2
The logic of a randomized double-blind experiment.

In conclusion, an experiment should be rigorously controlled by being randomized and blind (double-blind, if possible). As shown in Figure 1-2, such experiments are the scientific ideal:

Randomized blind experiments ensure that on average the two groups are initially equal, and continue to be treated equally. Thus a fair comparison is possible.	(1-5)

D—THE RESULTS OF THE EXPERIMENT

The treated women acted differently: They scored higher on care and interest in the baby during the doctor's physical examination a month later. (See Problem 8-32 for details.) Even two years later, there were still differences: For example, in talking to their child, the treated women tended to use questions rather than commands. (Kennel, Voos, and Klaus, 1979)

In conclusion, this experiment suggested the importance of early contact of mothers with their infants. (Interestingly, the subjects of this study were relatively poor women with few social supports. Some similar experiments on other women have not shown such strong bonding effects.)

PROBLEMS

1-4 Underline the correct choice in each pair of brackets.

a. A "randomized controlled experiment" is an experiment where some of the subjects [have the new treatment deliberately withheld, are given random and unknown doses of the new treatment]—the so-called control group. Whether any given subject gets assigned to the treatment or control group is then determined by [chance, the expert judgment of the experimenter, the wishes of the subject].

b. The purpose of random assignment to treatment and control groups is to [keep, initially start] both groups equal, whereas the purpose of blind care throughout the experiment is to [keep, not keep, initially start] both groups equal.

At the end, the evaluator generally [should, should not] know whether the subject she is evaluating is in the treatment or control group. This is called being ["blind," "randomized"] and it prevents the evaluator from being [blind, biased]. This is especially important when the evaluation is [merely technical, a difficult judgment].

1-5 Give an example of some "treatment" whose full effects are still unknown (for example, alcohol, compulsory education, certain forms of psychotherapy). Suggest how you might conduct an experiment to evaluate its effects. Include in your discussion:

a. Who would be the subjects?

b. Who would get the treatment, and who would not?

c. Who would be kept blind?

d. How would the effects be evaluated?

1-6 To determine how well vitamin C prevents colds, a study divided volunteers randomly into two groups of about 400 each—a treatment group given vitamin C, and a control group given a placebo (a "dummy" pill that had no drug, but looked indistinguishable). The proportions who were free of colds during the winter were 26% and 18%, respectively. (Consumer Reports, 1976.)

a. What was the purpose of the placebo?

b. It is customary to imagine that the volunteers represent a random sample from a large hypothetical population, for which we can construct a 95% confidence interval. For the proportion of people treated with vitamin C who would be free of colds, construct this interval.

c. Repeat part **b** for the people treated with a placebo.

d. Write a brief verbal conclusion about the effect of vitamin C.

1-3 OBSERVATIONAL STUDIES VS. RANDOMIZED EXPERIMENTS

As we have seen, randomized assignment of subjects to the treatment or control group is what frees an experiment of bias. Sometimes, however, a treatment is studied less rigorously by simply observing how it has worked on those who happened to have got it: This is called a happenstance or *observational* study. Although such studies are often less satisfactory than randomized experiments, they are sometimes all that is possible or practical, for a number of reasons:

A—RANDOMIZATION IS SOMETIMES NOT POSSIBLE

Especially in the social sciences, there are often examples where random assignment is just not possible. For example, suppose we wish to determine whether sex affects college faculty salaries. Specifically, do women earn less simply because they are women?

In this case a randomized experiment would involve taking an initial pool of professors, and assigning a sex to each by some random process (heads you're a woman, tails you're a man), and then watching what happens to the salaries of women compared to men over the next 10 years. In this way we could remove the effect on salaries of confounding factors, such as years an individual has been teaching. (Because of randomization, about half of the most experienced teachers would be assigned to the male group, and half to the female group.)

But, of course, we cannot randomly assign sex. We just have to take professors as they come in an observational study.

B—RANDOMIZATION IS SOMETIMES NOT PRACTICAL

Suppose we wish to examine whether the crime rate is affected by whether people live in the city or in the country. Could we randomly assign half the subjects to the city and half to the country (regardless of where they are now living)? Obviously, people would be unwilling to move and change their way of life, just to assist in a statistical study. Again, we have to take people as they come—some in the city, and some in the country—in an observational study.

C—RANDOMIZATION IS SOMETIMES NOT DONE, EVEN WHEN PRACTICAL

Suppose we wish to evaluate the benefits of a free educational program for prekindergarten children. Since limited funds mean fewer available places than applicants, random assignment is a fair way of deciding which children should be allowed to participate. At the same time, such randomization satisfies the requirements of a valid scientific experiment. Unfortunately, randomization is not used often enough, and so the value of many such programs remains in dispute.

It is interesting to speculate on why randomization isn't used more often, even when it costs relatively little. Is it because some investigators just don't appreciate its importance? Or is it because some administrators cannot admit that a mere coin or a bowl of chips does a better job of assignment than they do?

Whatever the reason, randomization could be done more frequently; indeed, whenever practical, it should be undertaken. We cannot repeat this often enough, since it is one of the most important points we make: *Random assignment initially removes the influence of all the confounding factors.*

D—SOME ETHICAL ISSUES

Is it ethical to experiment with people? In our original example, for instance, was it ethical for the hospitals to experiment with mothers and infants? Since the new experimental treatment seemed to harm no one, it is hard to imagine any ethical objection to trying it out. In fact, a far more interesting question is this: Was it ethical to install the earlier routine measures (separation of mother and infant) *without* gathering careful experimental evidence?

In general, *every* time a new program is introduced—medical, educational, social, business, or whatever—at some stage it *has* to be tried on people for the first time; that is, an experiment has to be undertaken. So the real question is: Do we experiment carefully, or haphazardly? Do we experiment with randomized control and learn quickly, or do we run poor experiments that yield misinformation and hence result in policies and practices that cause unnecessary harm? The ethical problem has been nicely summarized by a surgeon (Peacock, 1972; via Tufte, 1974):

> One day when I was a junior medical student, a very important Boston surgeon visited the school and delivered a great treatise on a large number of patients who had undergone successful operations for vascular reconstruction. At the end of the lecture, a young student at the back of the room timidly asked, "Do you have any controls?" Well, the great surgeon drew himself up to his full height, hit the desk, and said, "Do you mean did I not operate on half of the patients?" The hall grew very quiet then. The voice at the back of the room very hesitantly replied, "Yes, that's what I had in mind." Then the visitor's fist really came down as he thundered, "Of course not. That would have doomed half of them to their death." . . It was absolutely silent then, and one could scarcely hear the small voice ask, "Which half?"

E—REDUCING BIAS IN OBSERVATIONAL STUDIES: REGRESSION

As already noted, the difficulty of randomized experiments in the social sciences often means that there is no alternative but to take individuals as they come, in an observational study. But in such a study how can we reduce the *bias* due to confounding factors? To use our earlier example in estimating the effect of sex on professors' income, how do we control for such confounding factors as years of experience? Fortunately, there is a general answer.

> **Along with the variables we are studying (such as sex and income) we also record whatever confounding factors we can (such as years of experience).**
>
> **Because we cannot hold these confounding factors constant by random assignment, we analyze our data in a compensating way that gives us, insofar as possible, the same answer *as if we had held them constant.* The technical method used to accomplish this is called *multiple regression analysis*, or just *regression* (which will be described in Chapter 13).** (1-6)

Although it does the best job possible under the circumstances, regression still cannot do a perfect job—it is just not possible to record or even identify the endless list of confounding factors. So we must recognize that no method of analyzing an observational study—not even regression—can *completely* compensate for a lack of random assignment.

Yet regression, in the hands of a good researcher who understands and carefully measures the most important confounding factors, can often make an observational study reliable. This is particularly important for social issues that are too important and complex to try to settle with just one piece of research. Instead, it is often wise to start with observational studies using multiple regression (or even more advanced techniques), which are relatively fast, inexpensive, and cost-effective. If their findings can be confirmed with randomized experiments, we then have a solid scientific basis to settle policy questions.

F—CONCLUSION

We have seen that when randomized experiments are not feasable, we have to be satisfied with observational studies that passively observe how the treatment happened to be given, rather than actively assign it randomly and fairly. The problem with such observational studies is that the effect of the treatment is often badly biased by confounding factors. Fortunately, the bias can be reduced by including as many of these factors as possible in a regression analysis.

Regression powerfully describes, in a single equation that is relatively free of bias, how one variable is related to many others—for example, how a professor's income is related to sex, age, teaching performance, research work, and so on. Regression may be the most important statistical tool you will ever use, so we will place heavy emphasis on it.

PROBLEMS

1-7 "To find out what happens when you change something, it is necessary to change it." (Box, Hunter, and Hunter, 1978, p. 495). What does this mean, in terms of randomized controlled experiments and observational studies?

1-8 Underline the correct choice in brackets:

a. In an observational study, it is [difficult, easy] to determine the effect of the treatment, because its effect is [confounded with, clarified by] the effects of all the other variables that happen to be changing at the same time.

b. Confounding is particularly serious if the effect we're looking for is relatively [large, small] and consequently easily [masked, double-blinded] by the confounding variables—as, for example, in a study that tried to measure the effect of [seat belts, capital punishment].

c. In an observational study, multiple regression can [reduce, completely eliminate] confounding if the confounding variables that can be measured are [included in the regression, held constant by the experimenter].

d. To be ethical, a human experiment to evaluate a potentially hazardous treatment ought to be [never done, done only if the potential good seems likely to outweigh the potential harm], and should be carried out first in [volunteers, people randomly selected from the population].

e. One difficulty with limiting an experiment to volunteers is that [it is unethical, the effect the treatment has on volunteers may not hold for the whole population]. Nevertheless, if the treatment turns out to be beneficial to the volunteers, it is likely that in later experiments [fewer, more] people would volunteer, so that the "volunteer bias" would be of [growing, decreasing] concern.

1-9 As we have seen, the outcome of an observational study may be influenced more by confounding variables than by the actual treatment given. Let us now look at another possible source of confusion: Cause-and-effect may run in the *opposite direction* to what is first supposed. For the following examples, underline the correct choice in brackets:

a. Death rates from respiratory disease are unusually high in Arizona. A foreigner might guess that this is caused by Arizona's terrible air. But any American knows that, on the contrary, Arizona's air is so dry and clean that it attracts people who suffer from respiratory disease. We therefore conclude that:

Arizona has a lot of people dying from respiratory disease [because Arizona causes the disease, because the disease causes these people to move to Arizona.]

The high death rate from respiratory disease in Arizona occurs because the effect of people with respiratory disease entering Arizona [overwhelms, is overwhelmed by] the good effects of the climate.

b. In Sri Lanka, a negative relation has been observed between population density and malaria; that is, low density is associated with a high malaria rate (Gourou, 1966). Two possible reasons for this are:

1. High malaria rates [drive out, attract] people, thus producing a relatively [low, high] population density in a district, or
2. A high population density might help [maintain, destroy] drainage and consequently [reduce, increase] the breeding grounds of malaria-carrying mosquitoes.

From the negative relation alone, it is [impossible, possible but difficult, quite easy] to tell which of these explanations are true.

c. Some studies have shown that states with capital punishment have *higher* murder rates.[4] Again, two possible reasons for this are:

1. Capital punishment [works, is counterproductive], causing the murder rate to be [lower, higher], or
2. States with [low, high] murder rates tend to be the most anxious to reduce them, by resorting to drastic measures such as capital punishment.

From the positive relation alone, it is [impossible, possible but difficult, easy] to tell which explanation is true.

1-10 To generalize 1-9, suppose an observational study shows Y related to X. Consider three possible ways this could occur:

i. X might cause Y.

ii. Some confounding factors might cause both X and Y.

iii. Y might cause X.

a. Match up these three phenomena with the following "path diagrams" (where the arrow indicates the direction of causation):

---

[4] Other studies have shown *lower* murder rates. So these studies prove nothing, because of the inherent limitations discussed in this question, and elaborated on by Fisher, 1980.

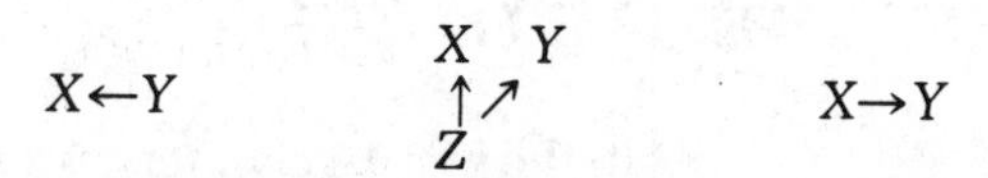

b. Is it possible that the relation of Y to X could be due to two or three of these phenomena in combination?

c. Is it possible for X to have a positive *effect* on Y, yet the *relation* of X and Y be negative? If not, why not? If so, how?

1-11 Naive studies earlier in this century showed a positive relation between population density and crime. (Higher density areas of cities had higher crime rates.) However, more careful studies using regression (Choldin, 1978 or Simon, 1981) have shown that for confounding factors kept constant, the relation often disappears or even becomes slightly negative.

a. Suggest some confounding factors that often accompany high density, and might be responsible for some of the crime.

b. Underline the correct choice:

i. This illustrates how [double-blindedness, observational studies, randomized experiments] can often be deceptive when analyzed naively.

ii. Specifically, the [confounding factors, confidence intervals, sociological theories] may be what produce some—or all—of the effects.

iii. We therefore say the effect of population density is [biased by, interchangeable with, multiplied by] the effect of the confounding factors.

1-12 An experiment was conducted to evaluate the relative benefits of a new welfare policy (the "negative income tax") in several American cities in the 1970s (Ferber and Hirsch, 1982). To determine which families would continue with the old program, and which would get this new program, random assignment was proposed. Underline the correct choice:

a. Random assignment permits a [less biased, perfectly accurate] evaluation of the new program.

b. Instead of being randomly assigned, suppose the group assigned to the new program included just those families who had been on welfare the longest, and therefore had greatest need of a new approach. In the final evaluation the new program would consequently [be more fairly compared, have its effect confounded with the effect of duration of welfare]. On the whole, this form of selection would therefore [slightly improve, greatly improve, invalidate] the comparison of the new and the old welfare programs.

1-4 BRIEF OUTLINE OF THE BOOK

In the first 10 chapters, we study how a random sample such as the Gallup poll can be used to make a statement about the underlying population from which the sample was drawn. The necessary foundation of deduction (probability theory) is laid in Chapters 3 to 6, so that induction (statistical inference) can be developed in Chapters 7 to 10. By the time we complete Chapter 10, we will be in a position to estimate a wide variety of things, such as the average air pollution in Cleveland, or the average quality of a product coming off an assembly line. Each of these is relatively simple to estimate, because just one variable is being considered.

In Chapters 11 to 15 we take up the even more interesting question of how one variable is related to several others. For example, how is the death rate in American cities related to air pollution, the average age of the population, and so on? It is in these chapters that we develop regression analysis, along with numerous applications.

Finally, from Chapter 16 to the end, we cover a wide variety of additional topics, including some of the most modern and challenging applications of statistics.

CHAPTER 1 SUMMARY

1-1 Statisticians can estimate a whole population just by looking at a sample that is properly drawn from it. To avoid bias, the sample must be *randomly* drawn. Then a confidence interval can be constructed, with an error allowance that shows the sampling uncertainty.

1-2 In an experiment to evaluate a new treatment, how can we avoid bias? We must *randomly* determine who gets the treatment and who gets left as a control. And anyone who might prejudice the results should be kept blind about who has received the treatment and who has not.

1-3 When random assignment of treatment in an experiment is not possible, we have to be satisfied with observational studies that simply observe who happens to get the treatment. Then the effect of the treatment may be badly biased by confounding factors. Fortunately, regression can reduce this bias.

As a whole, this chapter has illustrated a truth as old as science itself: *The way we collect data is at least as important as how we analyze it.* There are many excellent books that develop this vital issue further, including some entertaining and inexpensive paperbacks—by Campbell, Huff, Moore, Tanur and others, Slonim, Sprent, and Wallis and Roberts. Their titles are listed in the Reference Section at the back of the book.

REVIEW PROBLEMS

These review problems included at the end of each chapter give an overview of all the material. Because they do not fit neatly into a pigeonhole, they require more thought. Consequently, they provide the best preparation for meeting real life—and exams.

1-13 "The possession of such a degree as the MBA will double lifetime earnings as compared to those of a high school graduate." (Bostwick, 1977)

To back this up, suppose the author found out that MBAs' annual incomes are twice as high on average as high school graduates'. Is the author's conclusion accurate? Explain.

1-14 Do seat belts reduce injury and death? They definitely do, according to experiments that have been done, smashing up cars and measuring the damage to dummy passengers. It is also valuable to look for confirming evidence from real people, in observational studies. For example, in a study of accidents, we could compare injury rates of those who were wearing seat belts to those who were not. In order to keep confounding factors to a minimum, which of the two alternatives in each of the cases below would be better, and why?

a. Using data from all accidents, or from just those involving cars equipped with seat belts?

b. Using data on all the occupants, or on just the drivers?

c. Using data that lumps together all injuries, or that categorizes them into several levels of severity?

d. Having the doctor who evaluates the injury be informed, or not informed, of whether the patient had been wearing a seat belt?

1-15 The following data on seat belt usage and injury rates was collected in the 1970s from selected states that kept good records:

Belt Usage and Injury Rates for Accident-Involved Occupants With Safety Belts Available

		Injury Rate	
Seat Belt Usage	*Percent of All Occupants*	*Moderate Injury* ($2 \leq AIS < 3$)[a]	*Serious or Greater Injury* ($AIS \geq 3$)
Unbelted	85.9	.023	.013
Lap Belt	3.9	.011	.009
Lap-and-Shoulder Belt	7.8	.005	.004
Unknown	2.4	—	—

U.S. Dept. of Transportation, 1981

[a] AIS: Abbreviated Injury Scale 1980 Revision, Amer. Assoc. for Automotive Medicine.

a. Regard the data as a random sample of 100,000 accident-related occupants over the whole decade from the whole country. Construct a confidence interval for the rate of moderate injury among those wearing lap-and-shoulder belts. Then do the same for those wearing no seat belts.

b. Repeat part **a** for injury that is serious or worse.

c. What can you conclude about the value of lap-and-shoulder belts?

1-16 **a.** Of the 18,000 deaths in Arizona in 1977, 1440 were from respiratory disease. Assuming these deaths can be regarded as a random sample from a hypothetical population of millions who might have lived and died in Arizona, calculate a 95% confidence interval for the population proportion of deaths that are due to respiratory disease.

b. For the whole United States in 1977 calculate the corresponding proportion, given the data that out of 1,900,000 deaths, 110,000 were from respiratory disease.

c. To what extent does the data show that:

i. Arizona has a higher proportion of deaths from respiratory disease?

ii. Arizona's climate worsens respiratory disease?

1-17 U.S. unemployment statistics are obtained through the Current Population Survey, a sample of about 100,000 adults conducted monthly by the U.S. Census Bureau. Like the Gallup poll, it is a combination of multistage and other kinds of random sampling that altogether provide about the same accuracy as simple random sampling, so that equation (1-2) gives a good approximation. In July 1987, the sample gave roughly the following figures for the noninstitutional population aged 16 and over:

Employed	62,690
Unemployed	4,080
Outside the Labor Force	33,230
Total	100,000

(*U.S. Survey of Current Business*, November 1987.)

a. The "participation rate" is the proportion who are in the labor force, that is, who are employed or looking for employment (unemployed). Construct a 95% confidence interval for the participation rate for the entire U.S. population.

b. Construct a 95% confidence interval for the unemployment rate.

c. When an unemployment rate is quoted by the media, they don't bother with the confidence limits, of course. Nevertheless this uncertainty must be appreciated by anyone who tries to interpret unemployment figures carefully.

For example, if the quoted rate of unemployment went down from 5.8% to 5.7%, does this mean the actual *population* rate dropped 0.1%?

1-18 ***A Final Challenge: How Hard Was It In 1973 For Women To Get Into Berkeley?***

In that year, their Graduate School admitted 3700 out of 8300 men applicants, and 1500 out of 4300 women applicants (Bickel and O'Connell, 1975).

a. What is the difference in admission rates, between men and women? How good is this evidence of sex discrimination?

b. To find out where this difference arises, the data was broken down by faculty, as follows (although this breakdown is hypothetical, it preserves the spirit of the problem while simplifying the computations):

	Men		*Women*	
Faculty	*Number of Applicants*	*Number Admitted*	*Number of Applicants*	*Number Admitted*
Arts	2300	700	3200	900
Science	6000	3000	1100	600
Totals	8300	3700	4300	1500

Now what is the difference in admission rates between men and women, for Arts? And for Science?

c. Explain why your answers to parts **a** and **b** seem to be in conflict. (This is an example of *Simpson's paradox:* What is true for the parts may not be true for the whole.)

d. Underline the correct choice:

i. If faculty is kept constant, men and women are admitted about equally. However, there is a tendency for women to apply to the [easier, tougher] faculty, which may explain why their overall admission rate is considerably [lower, higher].

ii. In part **a,** the effect of sex on admissions could not be properly understood because there was a confounding factor (faculty) that wasn't being controlled. When appropriate control was introduced in part **b,** however, a more [incriminating, accurate] picture emerged.

iii. The analysis could be improved further by taking into account other confounding variables as well as faculty. For example, since we aren't sure the men and women were equally qualified, we could, to some extent, allow for different qualifications by using their graduate record exam scores in a [regression analysis, confidence interval, double-blind experiment].

CHAPTER 2

Descriptive Statistics

The average statistician is married to 1.75 wives who try their level best to drag him out of the house 2¼ nights a week with only 50 percent success.

He has a sloping forehead with a 2 percent grade (denoting mental strength), ⅝ of a bank account, and 3.06 children who drive him ½ crazy; 1.65 of the children are male.

Only .07 percent of all statisticians are ¼ awake at the breakfast table where they consume 1.68 cups of coffee—the remaining .32 dribbling down their shirt fronts. . . . On Saturday nights, he engages ⅓ of a baby-sitter for his 3.06 kiddies, unless he happens to have ⅝ of a mother-in-law living with him who will sit for ½ the price. . . .

W. F. MIKSCH (1950)

We already have discussed the primary purpose of statistics—to make an inference from a sample to the whole population. As a preliminary step, the sample must be simplified and reduced to a few descriptive numbers, called sample *statistics*.

For instance, in the Gallup poll of Example 1-1, the polltaker would record the answers of the 1500 people in the sample, obtaining a sequence such as D,R,R,D,D,R, . . . , where D and R represent Democrats and Republicans. An appropriate summary of this sample is the statistic P, the sample proportion of Republicans; this can be used to make an inference about π, the population proportion. Admittedly, this statistic P is trivial to compute. It requires merely counting the number of Rs and then dividing by the sample size, obtaining $P = 780/1500 = .52$.

Now we will take a look at some other samples, and calculate the appropriate statistics to summarize them.

2-1 FREQUENCY TABLES AND GRAPHS

A—DISCRETE EXAMPLE

Employee absenteeism is a major problem for some firms, and to deal with it the evidence must first be arranged in understandable form. For example, suppose a management consultant looked up the records of the 50 employees in the shipping department of a large firm in 1984. Let X denote the number of days an employee was absent over the year, excluding major medical episodes. For the 50 employees listed alphabetically, X turned out as follows (simplified version of Gandz, 1985):

$X =$ 6, 4, 4, 6, 0	6, 11, 5, 10, 8	4, 8, 4, 7, 7	3, 2, 3, 6, 2
4, 3, 6, 1, 3	2, 4, 6, 6, 6	6, 8, 3, 3, 6	2, 3, 2, 4, 0
8, 3, 6, 0, 1	6, 5, 13, 11, 6		

X is called a *discrete* random variable because it takes on a countable number of values (for example, 0, 1, 2, . . . ; but X does not take on the whole continuous set of values in between).

To simplify the data, in Table 2-1 we use dots (or strokes) to keep a running tally of X. In the next column we record each frequency, for example, $X = 0$ days absent occurred for 3 employees. Then the *relative* frequency was $3/50 = .06$ or 6%, and is recorded in the final column.

In Figure 2-1 we graph the frequency distribution—essentially just the tallies of Table 2-1 turned 90°. The *relative* frequency distribution in the last column can be shown on the same graph, using the different vertical scale on the right. To keep clear the meaning of this graph, always remember that each dot represents an employee. For example, the highest stack of dots represents the 13 employees who were absent 6 days. (To explain this curious popularity, a careful reading of the company's policy showed that full pay was given for up to 6 days absence per year.)

TABLE 2-1 Absenteeism in the Shipping Department

Number of Days Absent X	Tally of 50 Employees	Frequency f	Relative Frequency f/n
0	●●●	3	.06
1	●●	2	.04
2	●●●●●	5	.10
3	●●●●● ●●●	8	.16
4	●●●●● ●●	7	.14
5	●●	2	.04
6	●●●●● ●●●●● ●●●	13	.26
7	●●	2	.04
8	●●●●	4	.08
9		0	.00
10	●	1	.02
11	●●	2	.04
12		0	.00
13	●	1	.02
		$n = 50$	1.00✓

B—CONTINUOUS EXAMPLE

Suppose we take a sample of 200 American men, and record each height in inches. We call height X a *continuous* variable, since its possible values vary continuously (X could be 64, 65, 66, . . . , or *anywhere in between*, such as 64.328... inches). We no longer talk about the frequency of a specific value of X, since we will never again observe anyone exactly 64.328... inches tall. Instead, we can tally the frequency of heights within a cell, as in Table 2-2. (This time we tally each observation with a customary stroke, instead of a dot.)

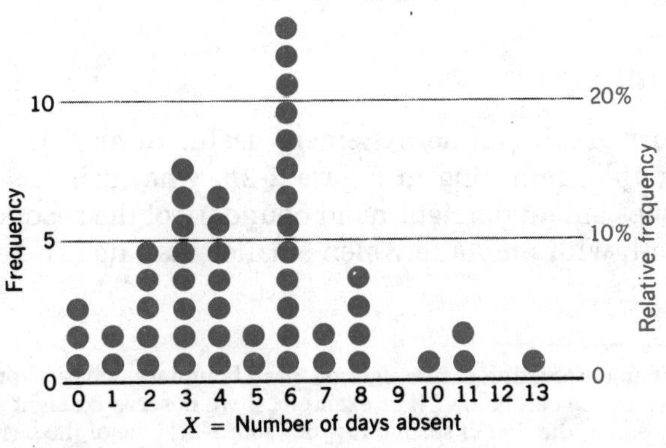

FIGURE 2-1
Distribution of absenteeism (as in Table 2-1).

TABLE 2-2 Frequency and Relative Frequency of 200 Heights

Cell Boundaries	*Cell Midpoint*	*Tally*	*Frequency f*	*Relative Frequency f/n*
58.5–61.5	60	||||	4	.02
61.5–64.5	63	~~||||~~ ~~||||~~ ||	12	.06
·	66	·	44	.22
·	69	·	64	.32
·	72	·	56	.28
73.5–76.5	75		16	.08
76.5–79.5	78	||||	4	.02
			n = 200	1.00

The cells have been chosen somewhat arbitrarily, but with the following conveniences in mind:

1. The number of cells is a reasonable compromise between too much detail and too little. Usually 5 to 15 cells is appropriate.
2. Each cell midpoint, which hereafter will represent all observations in the cell, is a convenient whole number.[1]

Figure 2-2 illustrates the grouping of the 200 heights into cells. In panel (*a*), the 200 men are represented by 200 tiny dots strung out along the X-axis. The grouped data can then be graphed in panel *b*. (Note how this is simply a graph of the frequency distribution in the second-to-last column of Table 2-2.) Bars are used to represent frequencies as a reminder that the observations occurred throughout the cell, and not just at the midpoint. Such a graph is called a *bar graph* or *histogram*.

Once more, to emphasize the meaning of this graph, we have represented each observation (man's height) by a dot. Thus the initial 4 dots represent the 4 shortest men, and so on.

C—PERCENTILES

A bar graph can be extremely useful in showing relative position. For example, returning to Figure 2-2*b*, what can we say about a man 64.5 inches tall (at the right-hand boundary of the second cell)? He is relatively small, with only a few men smaller than he. To be specific, only 8% are

[1] If an observation occurs right on a cell boundary, where should it be placed—in the cell above or the cell below? (For example, if we observe a height of 61.5 inches, should it be recorded in the first or second row of Table 2-2?) One of the best solutions is systematically to move the first such borderline observation up into the cell above, move the second such observation into the cell below, the third up, the fourth down, and so on. This procedure avoids the bias that would occur if, for example, all borderline observations were moved to the cell above.

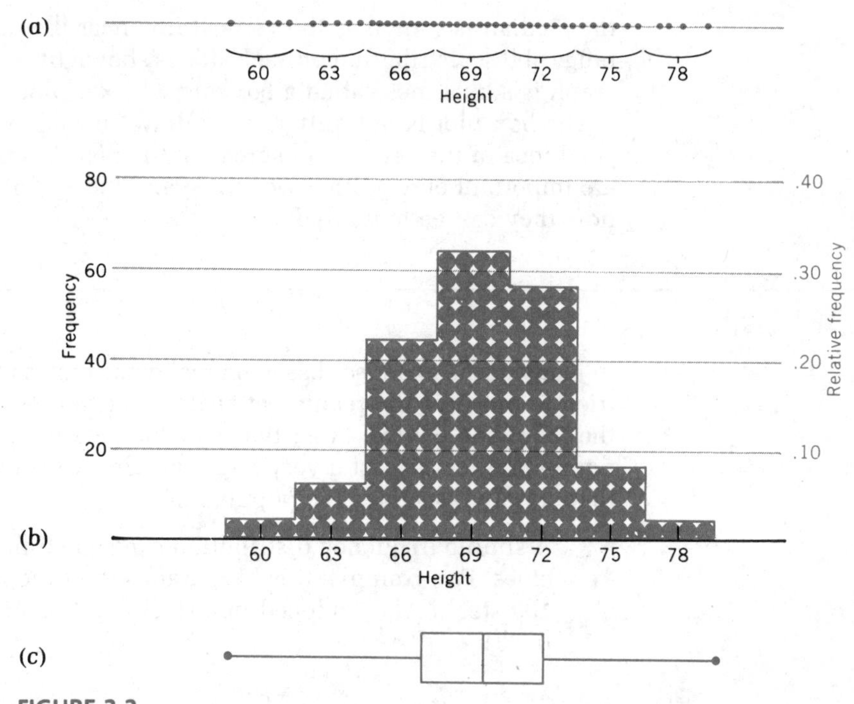

FIGURE 2-2
Different graphs of the same dots (heights of 200 American men). (a) The grouping of observations into cells, illustrating the first two columns of Table 2-2. (b) The bar graph for the grouped data. (c) The very brief box plot.

smaller. (From the last column of Table 2-2, we add up the first two cells: 2% + 6% = 8%.) His height is therefore said to be the 8th percentile. At the other end, a height of 73.5 inches would be the 90th percentile (since only 8% + 2% = 10% of the observations are higher).

The percentiles that cut the data up into four quarters have special names: The 25th percentile and 75th percentiles are called the *lower* and *upper* quartiles. The 50th percentile is called the *median*, because it is the middle value that cuts the data in half. In Figure 2-2, for example, we see (and confirm in Appendix 2-2) that:

Lower quartile $\simeq$ 67 inches
Median $\simeq$ 69.5 inches
Upper quartile $\simeq$ 72 inches

D—BOX PLOTS

The quartiles of a distribution can be very clearly shown with an alternative graph of the data called the *box plot* (Tukey, 1977). Panel (c) at the bottom of Figure 2-2 shows the box plot alternative to describe the distribution of men's heights. The two quartiles mark the ends of the box, while the median is shown as the vertical line near the middle of the box. The range of the distribution on each side is shown by an extended line, so the graph is sometimes called a *box and whisker* plot.

The box plot is not only easy to draw and understand; it also gives a good idea of the center and spread of the distribution. Center and spread are important enough that we will spend the rest of the chapter detailing how they can be measured.

PROBLEMS

In many of the exercises based on real data, such as Problem 2-2, we have tried to preserve the reality yet keep the arithmetic manageable by using the following device: From the available data (which usually is a whole population, or at least a very large sample) we construct a small sample that closely resembles the population.

2-1 A simple frequency distribution can sometimes provide remarkable clues. For example, this histogram shows the measured hardness of 100 steel coils produced in a steel plant about 1970 (Roberts 1974, p. 73):

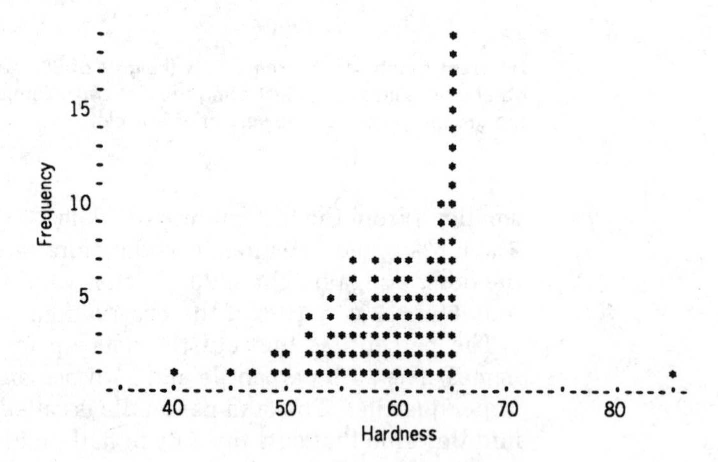

Clues in this histogram uncovered several troubles in the plant:

a. The employee who measured the hardness of each coil was aware of the maximum hardness the firm's managers would accept. What was she doing wrong, and what observations betrayed her?

b. Due to a scheduling error at the steel mill, one coil was made of the wrong kind of steel. Which observation showed this?

2-2 **a.** In a large American university, a random sample of female professors gave the following annual salaries (in thousands of dollars, reconstructed from Katz, 1973). Without sorting into cells, graph the salaries as dots along an X-axis.

9, 12, 8, 10, 16

b. Using the same scale, construct a similar graph for the following sample of 25 *male* professors' salaries:

13	11	19	11	22	22	13	11	17	13
27	14	16	13	24	31	9	12	15	15
21	18	11	9	13					

In your view, how good is the evidence that, over the whole university, men tended to earn more than women? (This issue will be answered more precisely later.)

2-3 Graph the data in Problem 2-2 as box plots. (Hints: In **a,** the median is the middle observation. For the quartiles, cut off 1/4 of $5 \simeq 1$ observation from each end. In **b,** the median is the middle observation, with 12 below and 12 above. For the quartiles, cut off 1/4 of $25 \simeq 6$ observations from each end.)

2-4 Sort the data of Problem 2-2**b** into cells with midpoints of 10, 15, 20, 25, 30, and draw the bar graph.

2-5 Using the 25 men's salaries plotted in Problem 2-2**b** (where each observation represents 4% of the data), what percentile is a salary of 10 thousand? 20 thousand? 30 thousand?

2-6 In 1990, the 789 million people in Europe lived in 25 different countries ranked as follows (in millions):

Russia	292	Yugoslavia	24	Bulgaria	9
West Germany	59	East Germany	17	Sweden	8
Italy	58	Czechoslovakia	16	Austria	8
Britain	56	Holland	15	Switzerland	6
France	56	Hungary	11	Denmark	5
Spain	39	Portugal	11	Finland	5
Poland	39	Belgium	11	Norway	4
Romania	24	Greece	9	Ireland	3
				Albania	3

a. Graph the relative frequency distribution (with cells centered at 5, 15, 25, . . .).

Note how well this graph emphasizes that one country is overwhelming in size.

b. Find the median and two quartiles. (Hint: Problem 2-3.)

c. Draw the box plot.

2-2 CENTER OF A DISTRIBUTION

There are many different ways to define the center of a distribution. We will discuss the three most popular—the mode, the median, and the mean—starting with the simplest.

A—THE MODE

Since *mode* is the French word for fashion, the mode of a distribution is defined as the most frequent (fashionable) value. In the example of men's heights, the mode is 69 inches, since this cell has the greatest frequency (highest bar) in Figure 2-2. That is, the mode is where the distribution peaks.

The mode is the most frequent value (2-1)

Although the mode is very easy to obtain—at a glance—it is not a very good measure of central tendency, since it often depends on the arbitrary grouping of the data. It is also possible to draw a sample where the largest frequency occurs twice (or more). Then there are two peaks, and the distribution is called *bimodal*.

B—THE MEDIAN

The median we have met already—the 50th percentile. To denote that it is the middle value that splits the distribution into two halves, we use the symbol $\overset{|}{X}$:

Median $\overset{|}{X} \equiv$ middle observation or 50th percentile (2-2)

where $\equiv$ means *equals, by definition*. (See the glossary just before the index for the list of such symbols.)

For example, suppose five rail shipments suffered the following damages (ordered by size of loss): \$10, \$20, \$30, \$50, \$90. Then the median loss would be the middle value, \$30. (When the sample size n is even, there are *two* middle values, and the median is defined as their midpoint. For example, suppose the damages to four shipments were: \$10, \$20, \$30, \$50. Then the median loss would be \$25, the midpoint of \$20 and \$30.)

If the array consists of a large number of observations grouped into cells, then the median can be approximated by covering the appropriate distance across the median cell. For example, in the distribution of men's heights in Table 2-2, we can first find the median cell by accumulating the relative frequency as we pass down the cells: 2%, 2% + 6% = 8%, 30%,

62%. That is, by the end of the fourth cell, we have accumulated more than 50% of the observations, and therefore have passed the median. Somewhere back within the fourth cell we will find the median itself. As a rough approximation, we can take the median as the midpoint of the cell, 69 inches. (For a more careful approximation, see Appendix 2-2.)

C—THE AVERAGE OR MEAN

The word *average* is derived from the Arabic root *awar* meaning "damaged goods." Even today, in marine law, average means the equal division of loss among the interested parties. For example, consider again the five shippers who suffered losses of \$10, \$20, \$30, \$50, and \$90. Their average loss is found by dividing the total loss among them equally:

$$\text{Average} = \frac{10 + 20 + 30 + 50 + 90}{5} = \frac{200}{5} = \$40$$

To generalize this, suppose a sample of n observations is denoted by X_1, $X_2, \ldots, X_n$. Then the average or mean, denoted by $\overline{X}$, is found by summing all values and dividing by the sample size n:

$$\text{Mean } \overline{X} \equiv \frac{1}{n}(X_1 + X_2 + \cdots + X_n) \tag{2-3}$$

The sum of all the X values is abbreviated[2] to ΣX (where Σ is sigma, the Greek equivalent of our S as in Sum.) Thus (2-3) can be written briefly as

$$\boxed{\textbf{Mean } \overline{X} \equiv \frac{1}{n} \Sigma X} \tag{2-4}$$

The average for our earlier sample of heights could be computed by summing all 200 observations and dividing by 200. However, this tedious calculation can be greatly simplified by using grouped data. Let us denote the first cell midpoint by x_1 and use it to approximate all the observations in the first cell (f_1 in number). Similar approximations hold for all the

[2] The sum ΣX could be written more formally as

$$\sum_{i=1}^{n} X_i$$

That is, the typical observation X_i is being summed over all its n values. When all our sums are over the range from 1 to n, however, we need not explicitly state this every time. The informal notation ΣX is quite adequate.

TABLE 2-3 Calculation of the Mean $\bar{X}$

(a) 5 shipping losses	(b) 200 men's heights (grouped, from Table 2-2) Given Data		Calculation of $\bar{X}$
X	x	f	xf
10	60	4	240
20	63	12	756
30	66	44	2904
50	69	64	4416
90	72	56	4032
	75	16	1200
	78	4	312
$\bar{X} = \frac{200}{5} = 40$		$n = 200$	$\bar{X} = \frac{13{,}860}{200} = 69.3$

other cells, too, so that

$$\bar{X} \simeq \frac{1}{n}\Big[\underbrace{(x_1 + x_1 + \cdots + x_1)}_{f_1 \text{ times}} + \underbrace{(x_2 + x_2 + \cdots + x_2)}_{f_2 \text{ times}} + \cdots\Big]$$

$$= \frac{1}{n}\left[x_1 f_1 + x_2 f_2 + \cdots\right] \qquad (2\text{-}5)$$

where $\simeq$ means *approximately equals.*[3] In brief notation,

$$\boxed{\text{For grouped data,} \quad \bar{X} \simeq \frac{1}{n}\Sigma\, xf} \qquad (2\text{-}6)$$

Using (2-6), we calculate the mean height in Table 2-3, part (b). The calculation is just like the ungrouped calculation in part (a), except that we carefully count each x with its frequency f.

[3] In approximating each observation by the midpoint of its cell, we sometimes err positively, sometimes negatively; but these errors will tend to cancel out, so that finally (2-6) should be a good approximation.

Note that cell midpoints are denoted by small x, to distinguish them from observed values X. If there are c cells altogether, then (2-6) could be written more formally as

$$\bar{X} \simeq \frac{1}{n}\sum_{i=1}^{c} x_i f_i$$

D—THE MEAN INTERPRETED AS THE BALANCING POINT

The 200 heights appeared in Figure 2-2*a* as points along the *X*-axis. If we think of each observation as a one-pound mass, and the *X*-axis as a weightless supporting rod, we might ask where this rod balances. Our intuition suggests "the center."

The precise balancing point, also called the center of gravity, is given in physics by exactly the same formula as the mean. Thus we may think of the sample mean as the "balancing point" of the data, symbolized by ▲ in our graphs.

E—RELATIVE POSITIONS OF THE MODE, MEDIAN, AND MEAN

Figure 2-3 shows a distribution that has a single peak and is symmetric. In this case the mode, median, and mean all coincide.

But what if the distribution is skewed? For example, panel (*a*) of Figure 2-4 shows a long tail to the right. Then will the median, for example, coincide with the mode? With so many observations strung out in the right-hand tail, we have to move from the peak value toward the right in order to pick up half the observations. Thus the median is to the right of the mode.

Finally, where will the mean lie? Near the median perhaps? In Figure 2-4, panel (*a*) shows what happens if we try to balance the distribution at the median. Half the observations lie on either side, but the observations on the right are farther out and exert more downward leverage. To find the actual balancing point (mean) we have to go farther to the right, as in panel (*b*). Thus the mean lies to the right of the median.

What then are the conclusions for a skewed distribution? *Relative to the mode, the median lies out in the direction of the long tail. And the mean lies even farther out.*

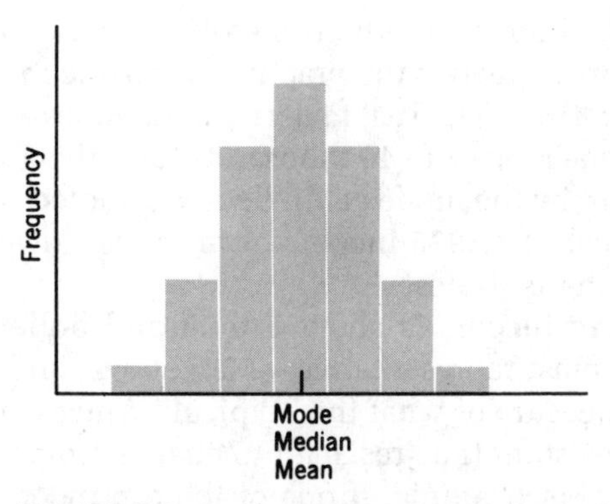

FIGURE 2-3
A symmetric distribution with a single peak. The mode, median, and mean coincide at the point of symmetry.

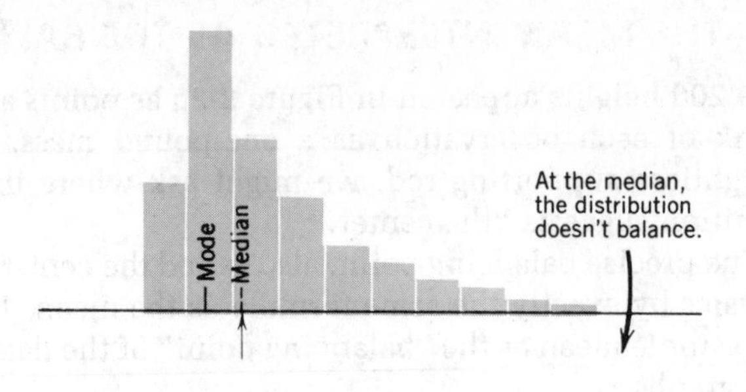

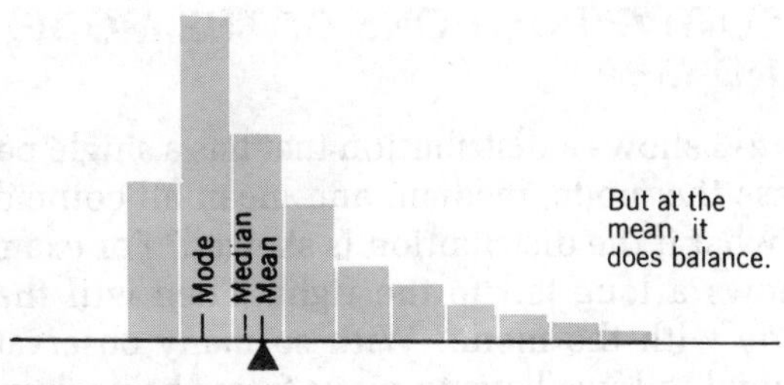

FIGURE 2-4
The mode, median, and mean of a distribution skewed to the right. (a) The median is to the right of the mode. (b) The balancing point (mean) is to the right of the median. (The distribution won't balance at the median because it will be tipped by the far-out observations on the right.)

F—WHICH CENTER IS APPROPRIATE—THE MODE, MEDIAN, OR MEAN?

For some purposes, one measure of center may be appropriate; for other purposes, another may be. To illustrate, consider the distribution of earned incomes of the 78 million American men in 1975 shown in Figure 2-5.

The mode is about 0, which merely reflects the fact that there was a concentration of men with practically no income—some of the unemployed and retired. The vast majority of incomes are scattered more thinly throughout the range 2 to 40 thousand—and this important information is not picked up by the mode at all. So if we quoted the mode of 0, we could not distinguish the 1975 income from the far lower 1875 income! In this case, the mode is useless.

The median income is about 8 thousand dollars, and this figure in a sense is the most representative—50% above, and 50% below. It perhaps is the best measure of what the "typical" American man earned. Furthermore, it is *resistant* (i.e., resistant to change from a wild swing in a single observation. For example, if one of the top incomes were increased tenfold, the median would stay unchanged.)

Finally, the mean is about 10 thousand dollars, a figure that was obtained by counting up every dollar—the pauper's and the millionaire's

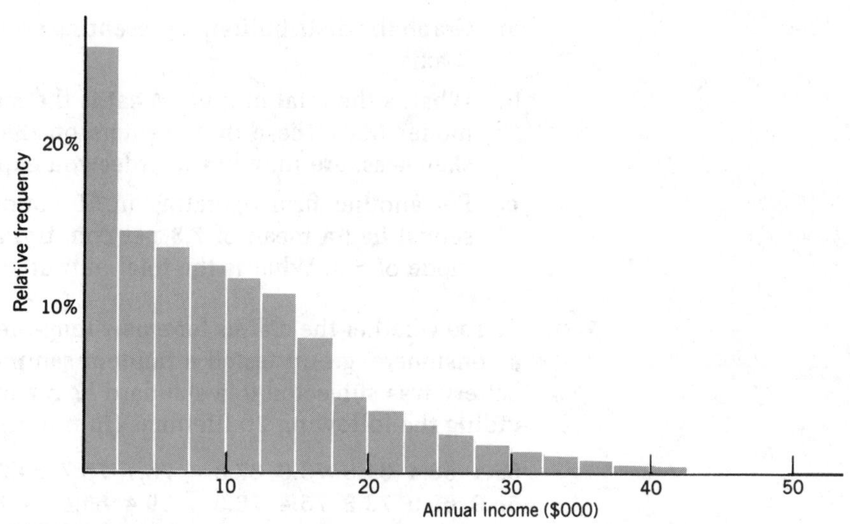

FIGURE 2-5
Incomes of American men, 1975. (Stat. Abst. of U.S., 1980, p. 462)

equally. This is both its advantage and disadvantage: it is the figure of most use to the tax department, since it gives the total income (78 million men × 10 thousand dollars = 780 billion dollars); yet it is not as good a measure of typical income as the median because it can be inflated by a few very large incomes (that is, it lacks the resistance of the median).

To sum up, we can conclude that the mode is the easiest, but the most inadequate measure of center. The median is more useful because it represents a more typical value, as many people understand the term. Finally, the mean is the only central measure that takes into account the total of all the observations. For this reason, the mean is often the most useful value in such fields as engineering, economics, and business. Since it has other advantages as well we will primarily use the mean for the rest of the book.

PROBLEMS

2-7 One of the most important calculations for business or economics is to find a total. To find the total sales of 200 agents, for example, would we multiply 200 by the mode, median, or mean sales?

2-8 Overheard in a Scottish pub: "When a Scotsman moves from Scotland to England, he improves the average IQ in both places."

a. How could this be possible (or is it impossible)?

b. What would you hear in an English pub?

2-9 The annual tractor output of a multinational firm in seven different countries was as follows (in thousands):

6, 8, 6, 9, 11, 5, 60,

a. Graph the distribution, representing each output as a dot on the X-axis.

b. What is the total output? What is the mean? The median? The mode? Mark these three centers on the graph. In view of the skewness, are they in the order you expect?

c. For another firm operating in 10 countries, output (in thousands) had a mean of 7.8 per country, a median of 6.5, and a mode of 5.0. What is the total output?

2-10 To see whether the claims for a new long-life battery were justified, a consumers' group tested a random sample of 20 batteries. Each battery was subjected to a standard heavy load until burnout, providing the following 20 lifetimes (in minutes):

65.1 58.4 64.9 76.0 67.8 75.1 76.7 64.2 74.9 77.6
58.0 68.0 73.3 75.4 76.0 59.4 65.4 74.7 76.6 81.3

Using a cell width of 5 minutes,

a. Graph the relative frequency distribution.

b. Approximately what are the mean and mode? Mark the mean as the balancing point ▲.

2-11 Sort the data of Problem 2-10 into three cells, whose midpoints are 60, 70, and 80 minutes. Then answer the same questions.

2-12 Summarize the answers to the previous two problems by completing the table below.

Grouping	*Mean*	*Mode*
Original Data	70.4	Not Defined
Fine Grouping (Problem 2-10)		
Coarse Grouping (Problem 2-11)		

a. Why is the mode not a good measure?

b. Which gives a closer approximation to the mean of the original data: the coarse or the fine grouping?

2-13 A manufacturer of pocket calculators, bothered by persistently poor quality, tried slowing down the assembly line. The improvement in quality and profitability per calculator seemed to make up for the smaller quantity. In fact, several slower speeds were tried, as follows:

Speed	*Weekly Production*	*Average Profitability*	*Median Profitability*
Standard	10,000	\$ .50	\$.50
20% slower	8,000	\$ .80	\$.60
40% slower	6,000	\$1.00	\$.85
50% slower	5,000	\$1.10	\$.90

What is the best speed, in order to maximize total profit?

2-14 **a.** Two samples had means of $\overline{X}_1 = 100$ and $\overline{X}_2 = 110$. Then the samples were pooled into one large sample, for which the mean $\overline{X}$ was calculated. What is $\overline{X}$ if the sample sizes are:

i. $n_1 = 30, \quad n_2 = 70$?

ii. $n_1 = 80, \quad n_2 = 20$?

iii. $n_1 = 50, \quad n_2 = 50$?

iv. $n_1 = 15, \quad n_2 = 15$?

b. Answer true or false; if false, correct it.
We can express the average in general as:

$$\overline{X} = \frac{n_1\overline{X}_1 + n_2\overline{X}_2}{n_1 + n_2} \tag{2-7}$$

2-15 **a.** Calculate the mean of the following 5 numbers:

3, 7, 8, 12, 15

b. Calculate the five deviations from the mean, $X - \overline{X}$ (keeping the + or − sign). Then calculate the average of these deviations.

c. Write down any set of numbers. Calculate their mean, and then the average deviation from the mean.

d. Prove that, for every possible sample of n observations, the average deviation from the mean is exactly zero. Is this also true for deviations from the median?

2-3 SPREAD OF A DISTRIBUTION

Although the average may be the most important single statistic, it is also important to know how spread out or varied the observations are. As with measures of center, there are several measures of spread. Two commonly used are the inter-quartile range and the standard deviation. Several others will also be considered because of the way they illuminate these two.

A—THE RANGE

The range is simply the distance between the largest and smallest value:

$$\text{Range} \equiv \text{largest} - \text{smallest observation}$$

For the heights in Figure 2-2, the range is 79 − 59 = 20 inches. The trouble with the range is that it depends entirely upon two observations—the largest and smallest. If, for example, the tallest person happens to be 3 inches taller, the range would be 3 inches more.

B—THE INTER-QUARTILE RANGE (IQR)

As an alternative to the two end observations, let us take the two quartiles. In Figure 2-2c, for example, they were already shown in the box plot as about 67 inches and 72 inches. The distance between the quartiles then measures the spread of the middle half of the observations. It is therefore called the *inter-quartile range* (IQR), or *midspread:*

$$\boxed{\text{IQR} \equiv \text{upper quartile} - \text{lower quartile}} \tag{2-8}$$

For the heights in Figure 2-2, the IQR is about 72 − 67 = 5 inches. Note that the IQR is just the *length of the box* in panel (c).

Because it uses only two key observations, the IQR is easy to calculate and is *resistant* like the median (i.e., resistant to change from a wild swing in a single observation. For example, if one of the largest heights were increased a foot, the IQR would stay unchanged.)

For many purposes, however, it is important to use all the observations to measure spread. To achieve this, we will embark on a new course that will eventually take us to the standard measure of spread (the "standard deviation").

C—MEAN ABSOLUTE DEVIATION

To incorporate all the observations, we first list them in a table; for example, in Table 2-4 we show again the five shipment losses X, and their average $\overline{X} = 40$. In the next column, we calculate all five *deviations from the mean* $(X - \overline{X})$. Some are positive, and some are negative; since these cancel out, their total is exactly zero, and so is their average.[4] The average

[4] To prove this, we first total all the deviations:

$$\begin{aligned}\Sigma(X - \overline{X}) &\equiv (X_1 - \overline{X}) + (X_2 - \overline{X}) + \cdots \\ &= (X_1 + X_2 + \cdots) - (\overline{X} + \overline{X} + \cdots) \\ &= \Sigma X - n\overline{X} \\ &= \Sigma X - n\left(\frac{1}{n}\Sigma X\right) \\ \Sigma(X - \overline{X}) &= 0\end{aligned} \tag{2-9}$$

$$\text{Average deviation} = \frac{\text{total}}{n} = \frac{0}{n} = 0$$

TABLE 2-4 Various Measures of Deviation, Leading Up to the Standard Deviation s

(1) Data X	(2) Deviations $(X-\bar{X})$	(3) Absolute Deviations $\lvert X-\bar{X}\rvert$	(4) Squared Deviations $(X-\bar{X})^2$	(5) Once again $(X-\bar{X})^2$
10	−30	30	900	900
20	−20	20	400	400
30	−10	10	100	100
50	10	10	100	100
90	50	50	2500	2500
$\bar{X}=\frac{200}{5}=40$	0	$MAD=\frac{120}{5}=24$	$MSD=\frac{4000}{5}=800$	$s^2=\frac{4000}{4}=1000$
				$s=32$

deviation is therefore a useless measure of spread. It is *always* zero no matter how spread out the distribution may be.

We can solve this problem of "cancelling signs" by ignoring all negative signs. In other words, take the average of the *absolute* values of the deviations:

$$\text{Mean Absolute Deviation, MAD} \equiv \frac{1}{n}\Sigma|X-\bar{X}|$$

This is calculated in column (3) of Table 2-4.

D—MEAN SQUARED DEVIATION (MSD)

Another way to avoid "cancelling signs" is to *square* each deviation:

$$\text{Mean Squared Deviation, MSD} \equiv \frac{1}{n}\Sigma(X-\bar{X})^2 \tag{2-10}$$

Calculated in column (4) of Table 2-4, MSD is mathematically better behaved than MAD, as we shall see.

E—VARIANCE AND STANDARD DEVIATION

For certain technical reasons described in part F below, it is customary in (2-10) to use the divisor $n-1$ instead of n. This gives a slightly different measure of spread:

$$\text{Variance, } s^2 \equiv \frac{1}{n-1}\Sigma\,(X-\bar{X})^2 \tag{2-11}$$

For grouped data, we must as usual modify this formula, by counting each deviation with the frequency f that it occurs. Then the variance becomes:

$$\text{Variance for grouped data, } s^2 \simeq \frac{1}{n-1} \Sigma (x - \bar{X})^2 f \tag{2-12}$$

To compensate for having squared the deviations, let us finally take the square root. This will give us the standard way to measure the deviation from the mean—so it is called the *standard deviation*, s:

$$\text{Standard deviation, } s \equiv \sqrt{\text{variance}} \tag{2-13}$$

$$\text{For grouped data, } s \simeq \sqrt{\frac{1}{n-1} \Sigma (x - \bar{X})^2 f} \tag{2-14}$$

In the last column of Table 2-4, we calculate the variance and standard deviation. The variance is huge (1000)—because of the squaring. By taking the square root, we obtain s = 32, a more suitable measure of deviation. After all, if we look at the individual deviations in column (3), they range from 10 to 50. Since the standard deviation s = 32 lies in between, it may therefore be viewed as the typical deviation.

The standard deviation s is the typical deviation,[5] lying somewhere between the smallest and largest deviation $|X - \bar{X}|$. (2-15)

Table 2-5 shows the calculation of the standard deviation for grouped data—specifically, the grouped data on men's heights from Table 2-2. (Note that here, or anywhere else we use grouped data, n is the *sample size*, not the number of rows in the table. And note that rounding $\bar{X}$ makes the calculations easier, with negligible loss in accuracy.)

The calculated value s = 3.6 is indeed the typical deviation, lying between the smallest and largest deviation (0 and 9). To emphasize this, in Figure 2-6 we mark the standard deviation s as a bar extending on either side of the mean.

In conclusion, Figure 2-6 has shown how a large sample can be summarized by the frequency distribution, and further condensed to a couple of

[5] This rule of thumb would be invariably true (a theorem) if s^2 had a divisor of n. (Even with s^2 having a divisor of n − 1, however, the rule still is valid for every distribution we shall encounter.)

TABLE 2-5 Calculation of Standard Deviation of 200 Men's Heights

Given Data		*Calculation of s*		
x	f	$(x - \overline{X})$	$(x - \overline{X})^2$	$(x - \overline{X})^2 f$
60	4	−9	81	324
63	12	−6	36	432
66	44	−3	9	396
69	64	0	0	0
72	56	3	9	504
75	16	6	36	576
78	4	9	81	324

$n = 200$

Recall:

$\overline{X} = 69.3$
$\simeq 69$

$$s^2 = \frac{2556}{199} = 12.8$$

$$s = \sqrt{12.8} = 3.6$$

numbers that measure the center and spread—the mean $\overline{X}$ and standard deviation s. ($\overline{X}$ and s^2 are called the first and second *moments* of the sample.)

F—DEGREES OF FREEDOM (d.f.)

The MSD was a good measure of spread, provided we only want to describe the sample. But typically we want to go one step further, and make a statistical inference about the underlying population. For this purpose the sample variance is better, as the following intuitive argument indicates.

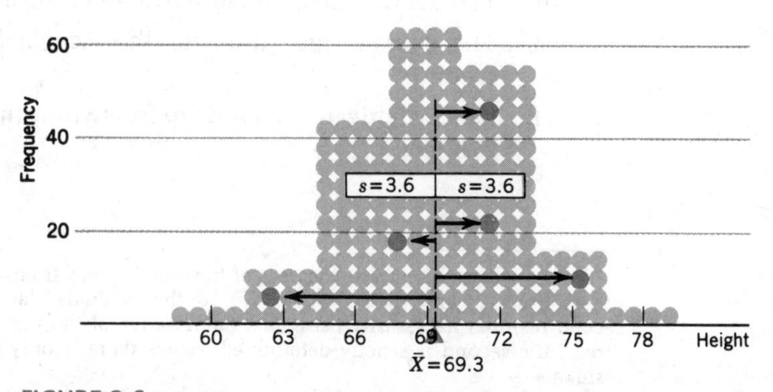

FIGURE 2-6
The standard deviation s is the typical deviation—some deviations are smaller and some are larger, as shown. (Same distribution as Figure 2-2.)

If only $n = 1$ observation were available, this observation would be the sample mean and would give us some idea of the underlying population mean. Since there is no spread in the sample, however, we would have absolutely no idea about the underlying population spread. For example, suppose we observe only one basketball player, and his height is 6′6″. This provides us with an estimate of the *average* height of all players, but no information whatever about how spread out their heights may be (6′4″ to 6′8″? Or 5′ to 8′? From this single observation, we have no clue whatsoever.)

Only to the extent that n exceeds 1 can we get information about the spread. That is, there are essentially only $(n - 1)$ pieces of information for the spread, and this is the appropriate divisor for the variance. Customarily, pieces of information are called *degrees of freedom* (d.f.),[6] and our argument is summarized as:

For the variance, there are $n - 1$ d.f. (degrees of freedom, or pieces of information).	(2-16)

PROBLEMS

2-16 Often the mean is a typical value; but if there is a large standard deviation, it may not be typical at all. In which of the following cases is the mean not typical?

- **a.** My wife and I are very athletic. Between us, we jog an average of 5 miles a day. My wife jogs 10.
- **b.** In freeway driving, my car averages 32 miles per gallon.
- **c.** Last year my car repairs averaged \$48 per month.
- **d.** The average statistician has 3.46 children.
- **e.** The average fuse time for the army's hand grenades is 4.0 seconds.
- **f.** Lake Michigan is a bit deep for swimming. Its average depth is 279 feet.

[6] To see where the phrase "degrees of *freedom*" comes from, consider a sample of $n = 2$ observations, 21 and 15, say. Since $\bar{X} = 18$, the residuals (deviations) are +3 and −3, the second residual necessarily being just the negative of the first. While the first residual is "*free*," the second is strictly determined. Hence there is only 1 degree of freedom in the residuals.

Generally, for a sample of size n, the first $n - 1$ residuals are free. However, the last residual is strictly determined by the requirement that the sum of all residuals be zero—that is, $\Sigma(X - \bar{X}) = 0$, as shown in (2-9).

2-17 Recall that the women's salaries in Problem 2-2 ranked in order were

8, 9, 10, 12, 16

a. Find the range and IQR. (*Hint:* Read them off the box plot in Problem 2-3.)

b. Calculate the MAD, MSD, variance, and standard deviation.

2-18 Recall that the 25 men's salaries in Problem 2-2 were:

X	*f*
10	7
15	10
20	5
25	2
30	1

a. Find the IQR. (*Hint:* Read it off the box plot in Problem 2-3.)

b. Calculate the standard deviation s.

2-19 In a test of the reliability of his machine, a technician repeatedly measured the viscosity of a specimen of crude oil. On each of three days, he took 50 measurements:

Viscosity	*Frequency*		
X	*Day 1*	*Day 2*	*Day 3*
60	0	1	0
65	2	7	5
70	15	22	38
75	19	18	6
80	11	2	1
85	3	0	0
	50	50	50

a. Graph the 3 sets of data, side by side. Do you discern any trends from day to day?

b. For each of the 3 days, calculate the mean and standard deviation. Do these calculations show the same trends you observed in part **a**?

c. For the complete set of 150 observations, calculate the mean and standard deviation. How are they related to the means and standard deviations found in part **b**?

2-20 Suspecting that your company's new scales for ready-mix concrete are registering too heavy, you rent a standard ton weight and weigh it on your scales under a variety of conditions of temperature and humidity. Your scales yield the following five readings:

1.004, 1.007, 1.013, 1.012, 1.004

The next time you weigh this standard ton, you would expect the scales to read about ____, plus or minus about ____.

2-4 STATISTICS BY COMPUTER

Statistical studies are customarily analyzed by computer, using software that is either *batch* or *interactive*. In a *batch* system, all data and commands are typed up ahead of time, run through the computer, and then all the output is printed up for the user to sort out.

On the other hand, in an *interactive* system, the computer carries on a running conversation with the user, who gives one command at a time. Depending on the computer's reply, the user can then choose the next command. If a mistake is made, it is easily corrected, and interactive systems are so forgiving that they are ideal for amateurs. One of the most popular interactive systems is Minitab[7] (Ryan, Joiner, Ryan, 1985), and we will use it throughout the text to illustrate how the computer works.

For example, Table 2-6 shows how Minitab handles the data on 200 men's heights. To understand who is typing—the user or the computer—it is important to look for the symbol MTB > that Minitab has the computer write, to mean "Your turn, user." For example, MTB > appears at the very beginning of Table 2-6. In response, the user types READ 'X', which commands the computer to prepare to read the data into a column denoted by 'X'. In reply, the computer requests the data by typing DATA >. The user then types in the 200 heights.

Next, with the command HISTOGRAM OF 'X' . . . the user gets a histogram as a series of asterisks.

Then, with the command BOXPLOT OF 'X', the user gets a box-and-whisker alternative to the histogram.

Finally, with the commands MEAN OF 'X' and STANDARD DEVIATION OF 'X', the user gets the exact values, which are slightly different from the approximate answers in Tables 2-3 and 2-5. (The computer is so fast that it doesn't have to bother with grouping data. Thus it calculates the exact mean from all of the original 200 observations, whereas the approximate mean in Table 2-3 was based on grouped data.)

---

[7] MINITAB is a registered trademark of Minitab, Inc., 3081 Enterprise Drive, State College, PA 16801. Phone (814) 238-3280, Telex 881612. The authors gratefully acknowledge Minitab's co-operation in replacing much of the drudgery of calculation with a user-friendly computing system.

TABLE 2-6 MINITAB Computations for the 200 Heights in Table 2-2: The Histogram, Box Plot, Mean, and Standard Deviation

```
MTB > READ 'X'
DATA> 64.3
DATA> 74.1
DATA> 68.7
DATA> 69.5
DATA>   .
DATA>   .
DATA>   .
DATA> 70.7
DATA> END
     200 ROWS READ
```

```
MTB > HISTOGRAM OF 'X',FIRST MIDPOINT AT 60, CELLWIDTH 3

HISTOGRAM OF X    N = 200
EACH * REPRESENTS 2 OBS.

MIDPOINT    COUNT
   60.00        4  **
   63.00       12  ******
   66.00       44  **********************
   69.00       64  ********************************
   72.00       56  ****************************
   75.00       16  ********
   78.00        4  **
```

```
MTB > BOXPLOT OF 'X'
```

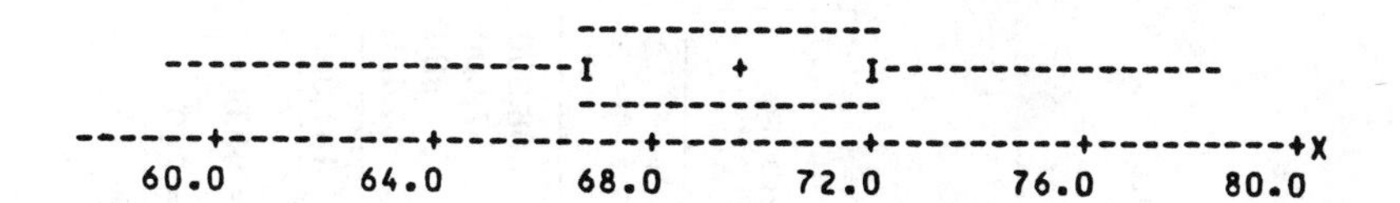


```
MTB > MEAN OF 'X'
   MEAN     =         69.372
MTB > STANDARD DEVIATION OF 'X'
   ST.DEV. =          3.4278
```

2-5 LINEAR TRANSFORMATIONS

A—CHANGE OF ORIGIN

For four midwestern states of about the same size, Table 2-7*a* gives the elevation X, in feet above sea level. The mean elevation $\overline{X}$ and standard deviation *s* are then calculated.

TABLE 2-7 Altitudes of Four Midwestern States

	(a) Altitude in Feet Above Sea Level			*(b) Altitude in Feet Above Lake Superior*			*(c) Altitude in Yards Above Sea Level*		
State	given X	$(X - \bar{X})$	$(X - \bar{X})^2$	$X' = X - 600$	$(X' - \bar{X}')$	$(X' - \bar{X}')^2$	$X^* = X/3$	$(X^* - \bar{X}^*)$	$(X^* - \bar{X}^*)^2$
Illinois	600	−330	108,900	0	−330	108,900	200	−110	12,100
Iowa	1,170	240	57,600	570	240	57,600	390	80	6,400
Michigan	900	−30	900	300	−30	900	300	−10	100
Wisconsin	1,050	120	14,400	450	120	14,400	350	40	1,600
	$\bar{X} = \frac{3,720}{4} = 930$		$s_X^2 = \frac{181,800}{3} = 60,600$	$\bar{X}' = \frac{1,320}{4} = 330$		$s_{X'}^2 = \frac{181,800}{3} = 60,600$	$\bar{X}^* = \frac{1,240}{4} = 310$		$s_{X^*}^2 = \frac{20,200}{3} = 6,733$
			$s_X = 246$			$s_{X'} = 246$			$s_{X^*} = 82$

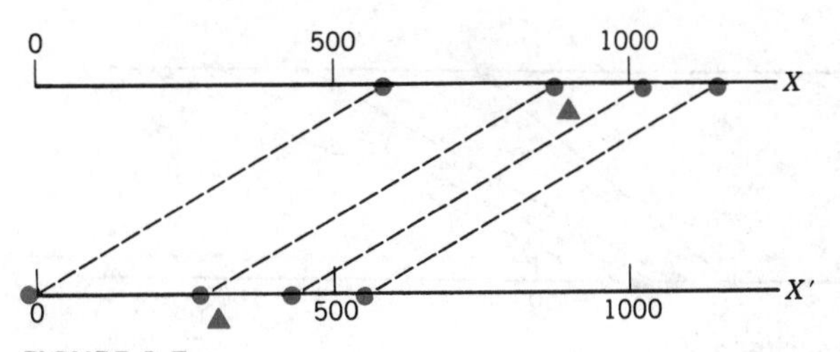

FIGURE 2-7
Change of origin (shift).

It often happens that a new reference level is more convenient—for example, Lake Superior, which is 600 feet above sea level. Table 2-7b, therefore shows X', the elevation in feet above Lake Superior. Of course, each new elevation will be 600 feet less than the old:

$$X' = X - 600$$

Now what will the new mean elevation $\overline{X}'$ be? It will, of course, be 600 feet less than the old mean $\overline{X}$:

$$\overline{X}' = \overline{X} - 600$$

On the other hand, the spread of the new elevations will be exactly the same as the old:

$$s_{X'} = s_X$$

These two equations are easy to verify by actual calculation: In Table 2-7b, we find that $\overline{X}' = 330$, which indeed is 600 feet less than $\overline{X} = 930$. We also find that $s_{X'} = 246 = s_X$.

These issues are illustrated in Figure 2-7, and generalized in the following theorem:

$$\boxed{\begin{aligned}\text{If } X' &= X + a\\ \text{then } \overline{X}' &= \overline{X} + a\\ \text{and } s_{X'} &= s_X\end{aligned}} \tag{2-17}$$

B—CHANGE OF SCALE

Sometimes a new scale of measurement is more convenient—for example, yards instead of feet. Table 2-7c therefore shows X^*, the elevation in yards above sea level. Of course, each new elevation will be 1/3 of the old:

$$X^* = \tfrac{1}{3}X$$

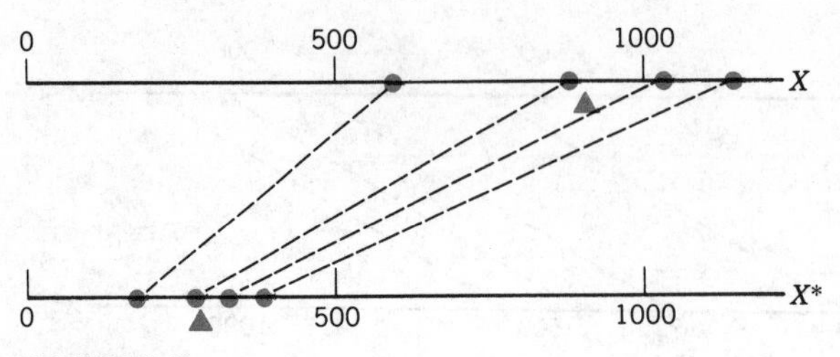

FIGURE 2-8
Change of scale (shrink or stretch).

What will the new mean elevation $\overline{X}^*$ be? It will, of course, be 1/3 of the old mean $\overline{X}$:

$$\overline{X}^* = \tfrac{1}{3}\overline{X}$$

Similarly, the spread of the new elevations will be 1/3 of the old:

$$s_{X^*} = \tfrac{1}{3}s_X$$

These two equations again are easy to verify by actual calculation: In Table 2-7(c), we find that $\overline{X}^* = 310$, which indeed is 1/3 of $\overline{X} = 930$. We also find that $s_{X^*} = 82$, which is 1/3 of $s_X = 246$.

These issues are illustrated in Figure 2-8, and generalized in the following theorem:[8]

$$\boxed{\begin{aligned} \text{If } X^* &= bX \\ \text{then } \overline{X}^* &= b\overline{X} \\ \text{and } s_{X^*} &= |b|s_X \end{aligned}} \qquad (2\text{-}18)$$

C—GENERAL LINEAR TRANSFORMATION

It now is appropriate to combine the above two cases into one, by considering $Y = a + bX$. (Because the graph of Y is a straight line, this is called a *linear* transformation.) We find the mean and standard deviation are transformed just as we would expect:

$$\boxed{\begin{aligned} \text{If } Y &= a + bX \\ \text{then } \overline{Y} &= a + b\overline{X} \\ \text{and } s_Y &= |b|s_X \end{aligned}} \qquad (2\text{-}19)$$

---

[8] Since b can be either positive or negative, we must use its absolute value $|b|$ in equation (2-18).

Incidentally, if $|b| < 1$, the transformation is a shrinking, as in Figure 2-8. If $|b| > 1$, then it is a stretching.

This theorem is proved in Appendix 2-5, and may be interpreted very simply: If the *individual* observations are linearly transformed, then the *mean* observation is transformed in exactly the same way, and the *standard deviation* is changed by the factor $|b|$, with no effect from a.

PROBLEMS

2-21 The temperature inside an experimental solar heater was measured in four different spots (degrees Fahrenheit): 238, 227, 220, 235.

a. Calculate the mean and standard deviation.

b. If the temperatures had been measured in degrees centigrade, what would the mean and standard deviation be? [Hint: If F and C represent a given temperature in Fahrenheit and Centigrade, then $C = (F - 32) \times 5/9$]

2-22 The altitudes of four mountain states of about the same size are approximately as follows (feet above sea level):

Arizona	4100
Nevada	5500
Colorado	6900
Wyoming	6700

a. To calculate the mean and standard deviation, it would be natural to just drop the last two zeros. Would this give you the right answer? Why or why not?

Then calculate the mean altitude and standard deviation.

b. What are the mean and standard deviation in *yards* above sea level?

2-23 An agricultural experimental station has five square plots, whose lengths (in feet) are:

10, 20, 30, 50, 90

a. What is the average length?

b. What is the total area? The average area?

c. Can you calculate the average area by squaring the average length? Why, or why not?

2-24 The following is the grouped frequency table for the actual weight (in ounces) of 50 "6 ounce" bags of cashews that a supermarket clerk filled from bulk stock.

Actual Weight	*Number of Bags*
5.9	2
6.0	16
6.1	22
6.2	10

a. Calculate $\overline{X}$, s, and the relative standard deviation (or coefficient of variation) defined as $CV = s/\overline{X}$.

b. If the weights were in pounds instead of ounces, what would be the answers in **a**?

c. Each bag costs the supermarket 42¢ per ounce plus 24¢ (for the cashews plus labor). Find the mean and standard deviation of the costs.

2-6 CALCULATIONS USING RELATIVE FREQUENCIES

Sometimes original data is not available and only a summary is given in the form of the relative frequency distribution. (For example, suppose the original information in the middle columns of Table 2-1 has been discarded, and only the relative frequency distribution in the first and last columns is available.) From this, how can we calculate $\overline{X}$ and s?

To derive the appropriate formula for $\overline{X}$, recall that for grouped data,

$$\overline{X} \simeq \frac{1}{n}\left(x_1 f_1 + x_2 f_2 + \cdots\right) \qquad \text{(2-5) repeated}$$

$$= x_1\left(\frac{f_1}{n}\right) + x_2\left(\frac{f_2}{n}\right) + \cdots$$

$$\boxed{\overline{X} \simeq \Sigma x\left(\frac{f}{n}\right)} \qquad \text{(2-20) like (2-6)}$$

That is, $\overline{X}$ is just the sum of the x values weighted according to their relative frequencies f/n. In the same way the MSD can also be calculated from the relative frequencies:

$$\boxed{\text{MSD} \simeq \Sigma\,(x - \overline{X})^2\left(\frac{f}{n}\right)} \qquad \text{(2-21) like (2-10)}$$

Finally, we can easily calculate s^2 from the MSD, by comparing divisors in the definitions (2-10) and (2-11):

$$\text{Variance, } s^2 = \left(\frac{n}{n-1}\right)\text{MSD} \qquad \text{(2-22)}$$

For large n, the factor $n/(n - 1)$ is practically 1. (For example, when $n = 1000$, it is 1.001.) Then

$$\text{Variance, } s^2 \simeq \text{MSD} \qquad \text{(2-23)}$$

TABLE 2-8 Calculation of Mean and Standard Deviation from the Relative Frequency Distribution (n = 200 observations)

Given Data		Calculating $\overline{X}$ with (2-20)	Calculating MSD with (2-21)		
Height x	Weighting $\frac{f}{n}$	Weighted Height $x\left(\frac{f}{n}\right)$	Deviation $(x - \overline{X})$	Sq. Dev. $(x - \overline{X})^2$	Weighted Sq. Dev. $(x - \overline{X})^2\left(\frac{f}{n}\right)$
60	.02	1.20	−9	81	1.62
63	.06	3.78	−6	36	2.16
66	.22	14.52	−3	9	1.98
69	.32	22.08	0	0	0
72	.28	20.16	3	9	2.52
75	.08	6.00	6	36	2.88
78	.02	1.56	9	81	1.62
		$\overline{X}$ = 69.30 ≃ 69			MSD ≃ 12.78

$$\text{by (2-22), } s^2 = \left(\frac{200}{199}\right) 12.78 = 12.84$$

$$s = \sqrt{12.84} = 3.6$$

Table 2-8 shows how these formulas can be used to calculate $\overline{X}$ and s. Note that the answers agree, of course, with the previous answers in Tables 2-3 and 2-5.

PROBLEMS

2-25 Compute the mean and standard deviation of the following sample of 25 salaries ($000 annually, as in Problem 2-18).

Salary (Midpoint of Cell)	Relative Frequency
10	.28
15	.40
20	.20
25	.08
30	.04
	1.00

2-7 THE USE AND MISUSE OF GRAPHS

A picture is worth a thousand words. And as computers draw them better and better, graphs will become a more and more effective way of providing information. But beware: They can be used to mislead as well as inform. In this last section of relatively light and optional reading, we will show how to recognize some standard scams—often called "Gee Whiz" graphs. (For more good reading, see for example Huff 1954, and Tufte 1983; and Cleveland 1985 for computer graphics.)

A—THE DISAPPEARING BASELINE

Look at Figure 2-9 closely. (Each time you encounter a graph such as this, look it over carefully to form your own judgment first, before you read our criticism. Be *especially* careful to cover up our redrawn version on the right.)

Figure 2-9 seems to illustrate what its headline trumpets—the "soaraway" *Post*, climbing from obscurity. But did the *Post* really increase from next-to-nothing? A close look at the vertical scale shows a "disappearing baseline": the *Post* started out not near 0, but instead near 500,000.

Furthermore, a close look at the middle of the vertical scale uncovers a really cheap trick. All the numbers from 900,000 to 1,400,000 were cut out in order to close the gap between the Post and the *News*.

When the numbers are plotted on a complete vertical axis, without distortion in Figure 2-10, we see that the *Post* still had a long way to go.

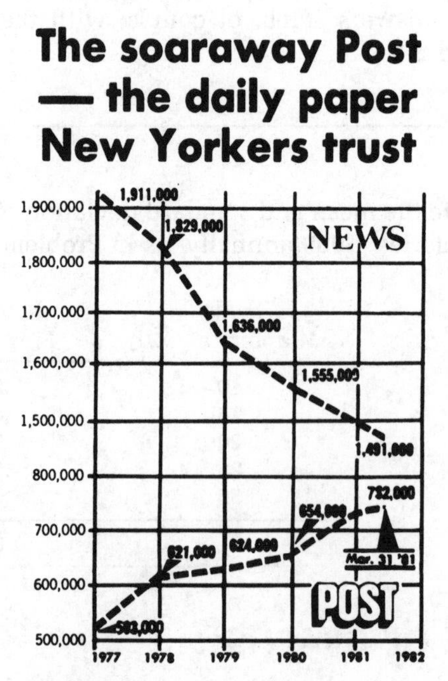

FIGURE 2-9
The *Post's* spectacular climb from obscurity. (*New York Post,* 1981, via Wainer, 1984.)

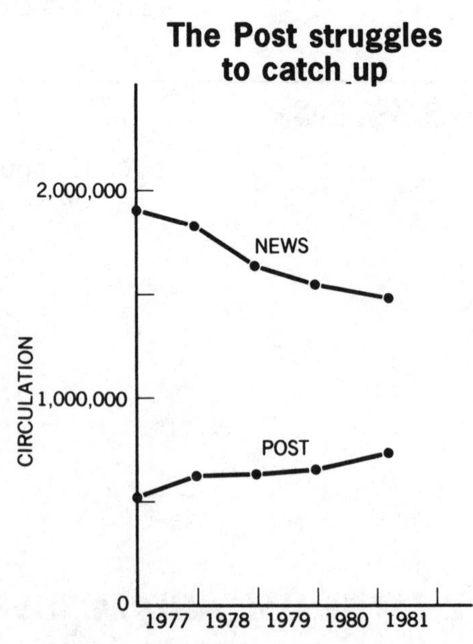

FIGURE 2-10
Restoring the complete *y*-axis in Figure 2-9 shows a much more modest performance for the *Post,* with the *News* still well in the lead.

B—THE GIANT OIL DRUM

Figure 2-11 shows the spectacular rise in the price of oil after 1973. Since the final price of \$13.34 is about 6 times as high as the initial price of \$2.41, the artist made the final oil drum about 6 times as high as the first. But it is 6 times as wide too. And we imagine it 6 times as deep. Accounting for all 3 dimensions, that big drum holds about $6^3 = 216$ times as much oil as the little one. Exaggeration seems too kind a word for it. Tufte (1983) calls it a "lie factor" of $6^2 = 36$.

Figure 2-11 is misleading in another, more subtle way. Much of the increase in oil price was offset by inflation—specifically, a near doubling of the cost of living index between 1973 and 1979. When the price of oil is expressed in constant buying power (1972 dollars), its increase is not 6-fold but only about $3\frac{1}{2}$-fold. Thus, a much more accurate picture is shown in Figure 2-12: after this spectacular $3\frac{1}{2}$-fold rise in 1973, the real price of oil slowly sank for the next few years before starting another rise in 1979.

C—MISLEADING COMPARISONS

Figure 2-13 shows what happens if we naively graph U.S. government expenditures over time—a simple unadjusted "time series." It shows gov-

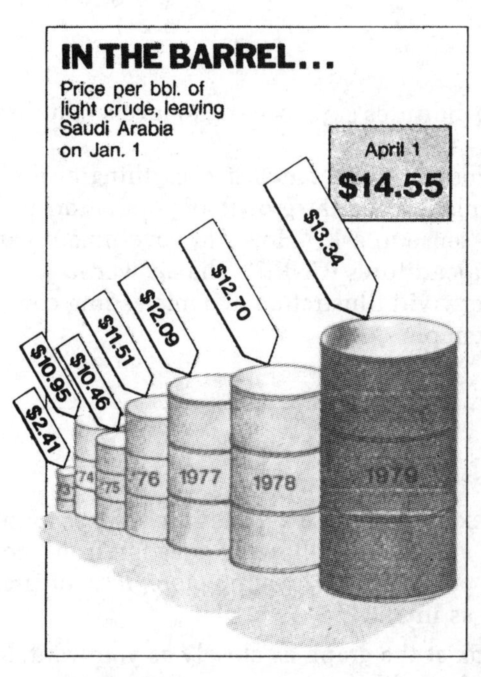

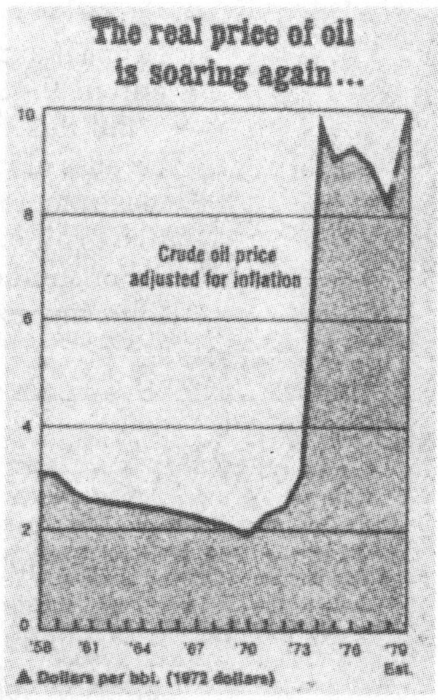

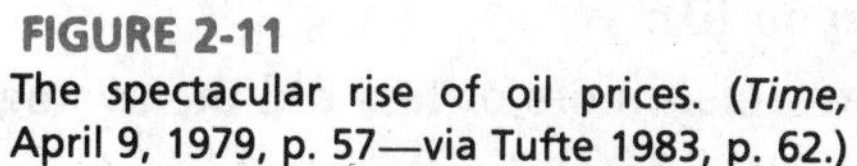

FIGURE 2-11
The spectacular rise of oil prices. (*Time*, April 9, 1979, p. 57—via Tufte 1983, p. 62.)

FIGURE 2-12
The real rise of oil prices. Just look at the years 1973–79 and compare to Figure 2-11. (*Business Week*, April 9, 1979, p. 99—via Tufte 1983, p. 63.)

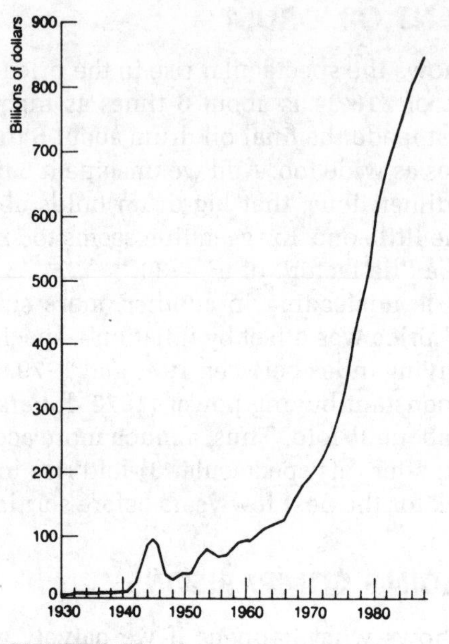

FIGURE 2-13
U.S. Government Expenditures, 1930–80.

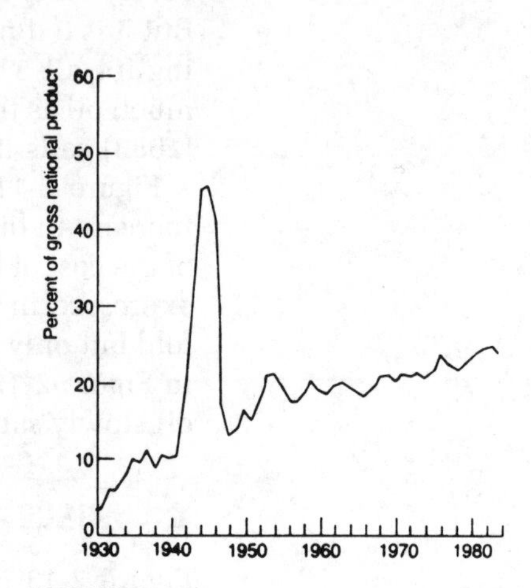

FIGURE 2-14
Relative U.S. Government Expenditures (as a % of GNP), 1930–80 (Wonnacott 1986, p. 24.)

ernment expenditures skyrocketing to levels that dwarf the little wartime blip in 1941–1945.

But this doesn't mean much if everything else was skyrocketing too, because of inflation and the growth of population and income. It therefore makes more sense to ask: "How did government expenditure grow relative to all expenditures (GNP)?" The answer is given in Figure 2-14.

For another vivid illustration of a misleading comparison, consider the following example.

EXAMPLE 2-1 HOW WELL ARE WE EATING?

a. Briefly examine Figure 2-15 for 20 or 30 seconds. Then cover it up, and answer the following question from memory: "Was the average person in 1974 eating *more*, *less*, or practically the *same* amount as in 1954?"

b. Now look at the graph as closely as you want, and change your answer if you like.

c. About *how much* more or less did the average person eat?

d. What would the graph have looked like if *total* (rather than per capita) production had been graphed?

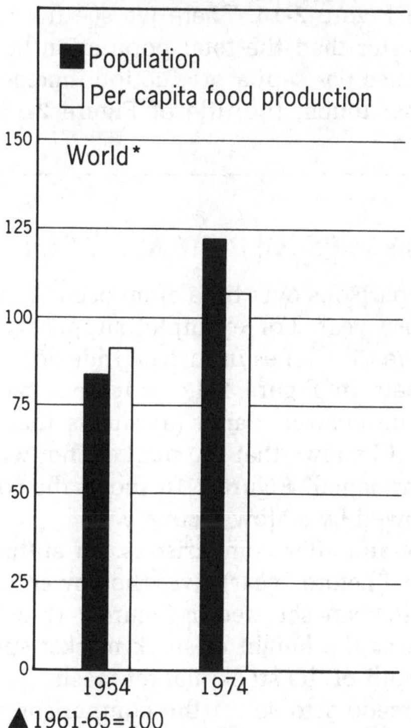

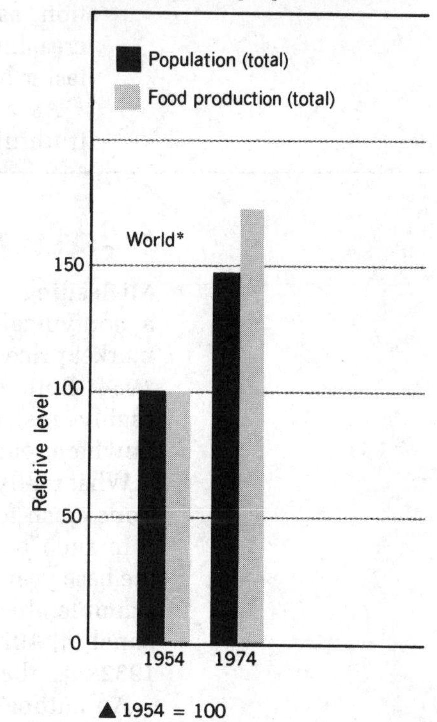

FIGURE 2-15
The disproportions of people and food. (*Business Week,* June 16, 1975, p. 65, via Simon 1981, p. 60.)

*To avoid clutter, we have blanked out the similar graphs that were drawn for the developed countries and the developing countries, separately.

FIGURE 2-16
A cleaned-up version of Figure 2-15.

SOLUTION

a. Because the shaded *population* bar is growing faster in this figure than the white *production* bar, most readers are led to the conclusion that we were running out of food and the average person was eating less and less. To make sure we get the point, the caption warns, "The disproportions of people and food".

b,c. But quite the opposite was true. Note carefully that the white bar represents not total production, but *per capita* production (average production per person). Since it was growing, the average person was eating *more*, not less. Specifically, the white bar rose from an index of about 90 in 1954 to about 105 in 1974, an increase of about 15%.

d. This good news would have been clear if *Business Week* had graphed *total* production as a natural companion to total population, as in Figure 2-16. There we see the total production bar increasing faster than the total population bar. (It must have grown faster because per capita production increased.)

As a final touch, the title of Figure 2-16 has been made more truthful too.

D—SELECTING A PECULIAR BASE YEAR

Misleading comparisons over time often occur because of the selection of a nontypical base year. For example, suppose we ask how U.S. stock market prices (the Dow Jones industrial index or average) increased up to 1954. Both panels in Figure 2-17 provide a technically accurate, but highly misleading answer. Panel (a) shows that the market was going nowhere; panel (b) shows that the market shot way up.

What really happened? Figure 2-18 shows the complete story—a disastrous crash followed by a slow recovery.

In such before-and-after comparisons, an author's freedom to choose the base year (the "before" year) gives the power to seriously mislead. For example, the base years selected in Figure 2-17 were not at all typical: In panel (a) 1929 was the height of stock market speculation; in panel (b) 1932 was the depth of the stock market crash.

An author's freedom to select the comparison year (the "after" year) also gives the power to mislead. To illustrate, suppose the question is, "What happened after 1920?" If the comparison year is 1929, the market

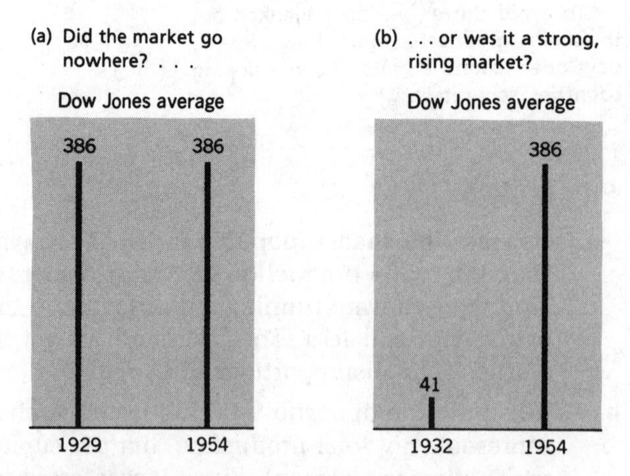

FIGURE 2-17
How the New York Stock Market compared in 1954 with earlier years.

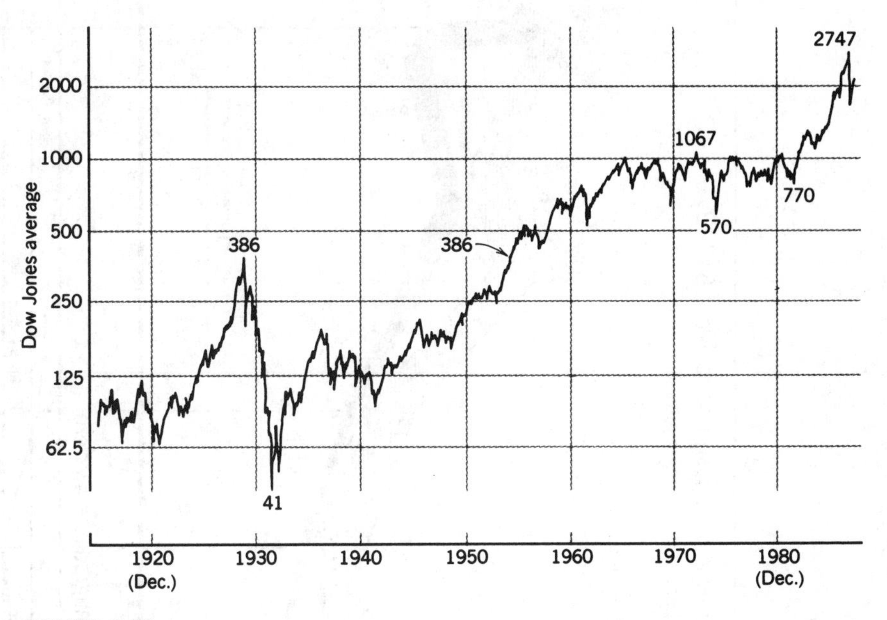

FIGURE 2-18
The full story of the Stock Market: A rapid collapse, followed by a long recovery.

rose dramatically. On the other hand, if the comparison year chosen is 1932, the market fell.

These few examples of how to lie with statistics are not rare cases unfortunately. The Problems give several more, and your everyday reading will provide you with a lifetime of similar challenges.

E—HOW TO TELL THE TRUTH WITH STATISTICS

We end this section on a positive note. With a little imagination, a graph can hit us over the head with the truth more powerfully than words. And at the same time, it can provide many detailed facts to back it up. For example, Tufte (1983) reproduces what he says "may well be the best statistical graphic ever drawn." Translated from French in Figure 2-19, it shows Napoleon's 1812 Russian campaign, as drawn 50 years later by one of his officers.

It shows how a vast army of over 400,000 men was reduced to 100,000 by the time they had fought their way to Moscow (gray band). Finding Moscow sacked, they retreated through the snow, till a mere 10,000 straggled back to the Polish border (black band). Of every 40 men who started out on that June morning of 1812, only one returned, nearly frozen to death six months later.

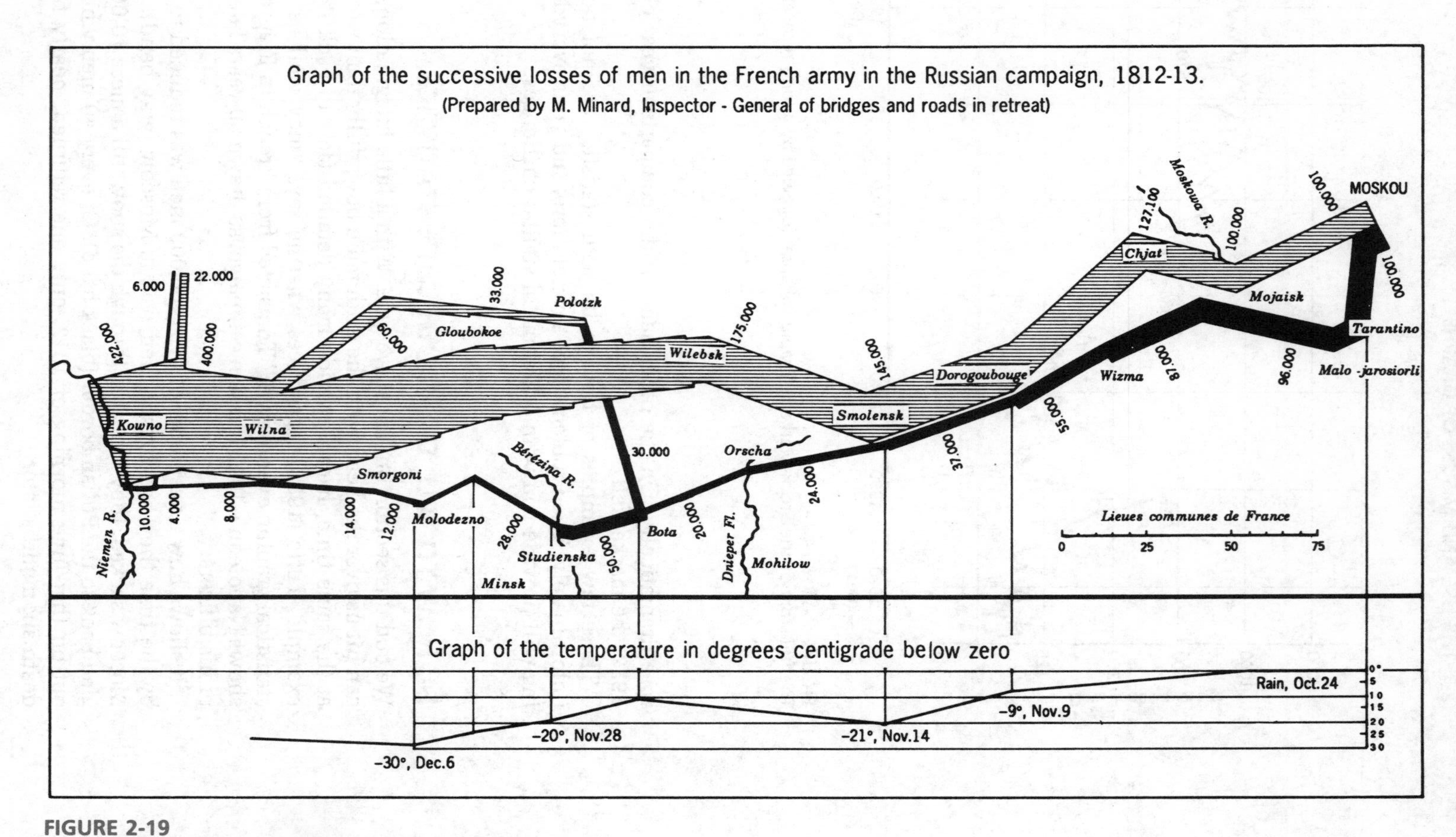

FIGURE 2-19
Napoleon's Russian Campaign (Marey 1885, via Tufte, 1983, p. 41).

PROBLEMS

2-26 **a.** In Figure 2-18, considering the stock market since 1965, say, let us see how selecting both the before and after years can show almost anything we want.

For example, what period of two years or more would you select to show a gloomy picture? A rosy picture?

b. In a sentence or two, give an unbiased summary of the stock market behaviour from 1965 to 1988, somewhere between the two extremes of **a**.

2-27 Criticize this graph (*Washington Post*, Oct. 25, 1978, p. 1, via Wainer, 1984). Then sketch an improved version.

2-28

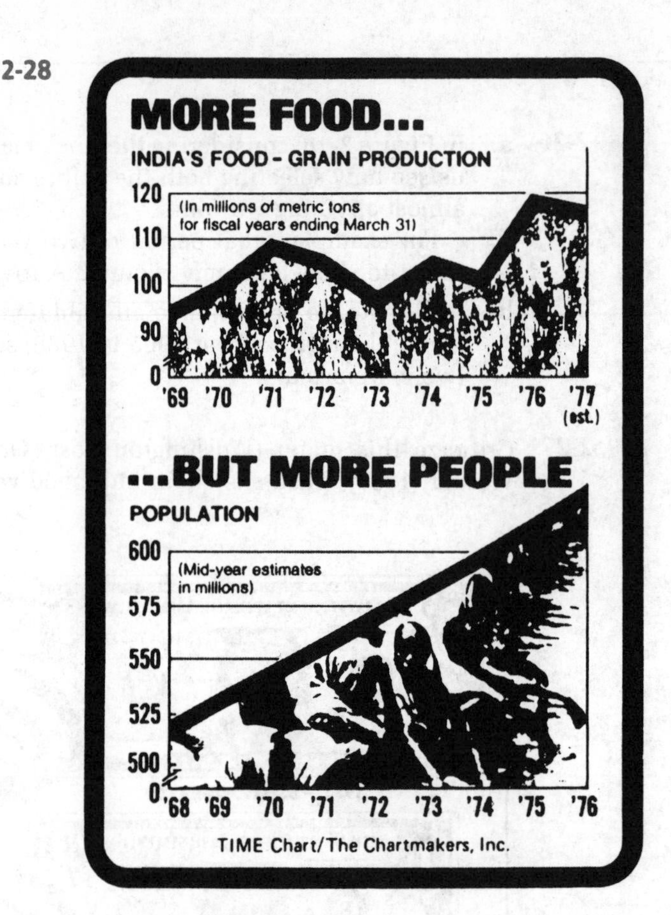

a. On the basis of a quick glance, underline the correct choice: India is producing more grain, but its population is growing [slower, faster]. This means that the average Indian is eating [more, less].

b. Now take the time to calculate the numbers to confirm your answers to **a**. What do you find?

c. Write a few words stating why the graph is appropriate, or else criticize it and redraw it appropriately.

2-29 As well as showing the terrible cruelty of war, the graph of Napoleon's Russian Campaign in Figure 2-19 gives a great deal of historical detail. For example:

a. What river crossing cost Napoleon half his men? About how cold was it then? (This was a battle made famous in Tolstoy's *War and Peace*.)

b. Of the 10,000 French soldiers who finally made it back to Poland, only a fraction had actually returned from Moscow. Where did the others come from?

c. Of all the soldiers who started out for Moscow, what proportion made it there? That is, what was the chance that a soldier would make it to Moscow? What was the chance that a soldier returning from Moscow would make it back to Poland?

2-30 As another example of how effective good graphs can be, these two "population pyramids" compare the United States and Brazilian populations in 1985 (Stat. Abst. of U.S., 1987, p. 18). If we examine them carefully, they will give us great insight into the past, and even into the future. First let us begin with the most obvious points:

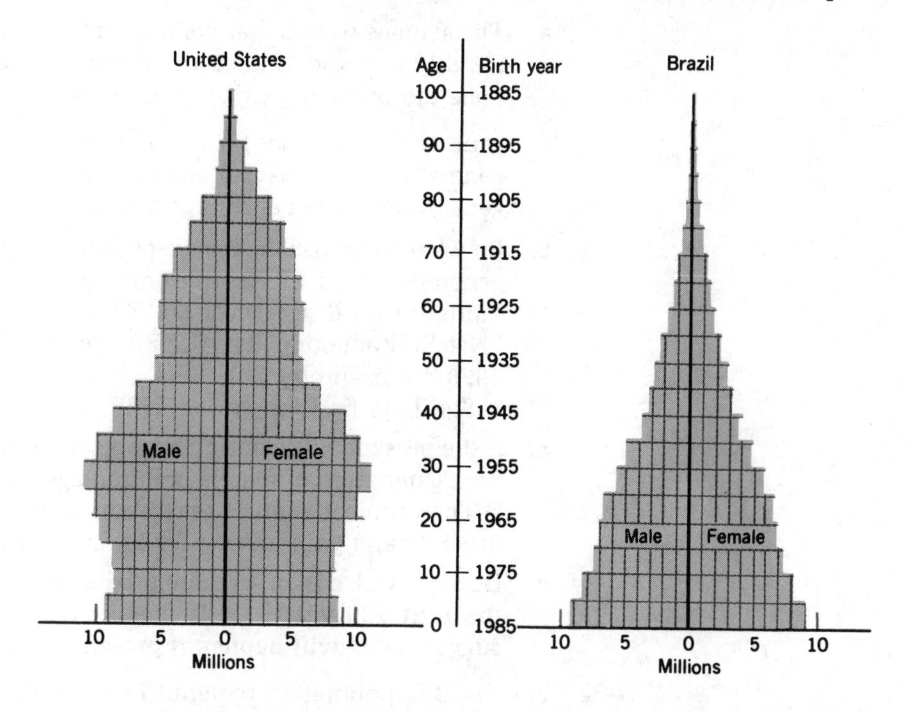

a. Approximately how many times larger is the U.S. population than Brazil's?

b. Aside from sheer size, what is the main difference between the U.S. and Brazilian population?

c. Both pyramids taper off at the top. Why?

d. The population "pyramid" for the United States, like other developed countries, is rather like a carved table leg. It shows there was a "baby boom" that peaked about ____, producing a large number of people (the "baby boomers") aged ____ in 1985.

It also shows the first "baby bust" that peaked about ____, and a much larger one about ____.

e. The baby bust helps to explain some important economic and social phenomena, such as (underline the correct choice):

Over the next two decades, the average age of Americans will very likely [decrease, increase].

In about 30 or 40 years, there will likely be a large [increase, decrease] in the social security burden to fund retirement, as the relative number of people under 65 paying for it shows a large [increase, decrease].

2-31 From the U.S. population pyramid in Problem 2-30, we can find some interesting clues about growth rates. For simplicity, we will concentrate on just the female half of the pyramid.

a. The average woman has her children around age 25, so this can roughly be taken as the age between generations. Roughly estimate the population size for these female generations:

generation 1, the bar for age 50 to 55
generation 2, the bar for age 25 to 30
generation 3, the bar for age 0 to 5

b. By what factor did the female population grow in the past, from generation 1 to 2? Assume immigration was negligible, also mortality until age 50 or 60. Then this factor is roughly the "Net Reproduction Rate," NRR (detailed in Haupt and Kane 1978, for example).

Similarly find the present NRR, from generation 2 to 3.

c. If the present NRR continues, project the size in 25 years of the next generation of female children aged 0–5.

Then project another generation later, and another, and another. Graph your answer for all four generations (100 years).

d. Do you think **c** is an accurate prediction of what will happen in the next 100 years? Or is it more useful as a policy tool to suggest what will happen *if* present trends continue?

2-32 For the U.S. population pyramid in Problem 2-30, let us compare the two halves—the males and females.

a. What is the ratio of males to females for babies (age 0–5)? For the old (over 75)?

What does this imply about the mortality rate for men compared to women?

b. About what age does the sex ratio become 1.00?

CHAPTER 2 SUMMARY

2-1 Data can be easily understood by graphing the frequency distribution. Alternatively, the box plot gives less detail but three useful summaries—the median and two quartiles.

2-2 To define the center of a distribution, the most common measures are the median $\tilde{X}$ (middle value) and the mean $\overline{X}$ (balancing point).

2-3 To define the spread of a distribution, the most common measures are the interquartile range IQR and the standard deviation s.

2-4 To illustrate how easily data can be analyzed on a computer (using an interactive system such as MINITAB), we summarized some data by computing its frequency distribution, box plot, $\overline{X}$ and s.

2-5 If a sample of observations are linearly transformed (shifted, and shrunk or stretched), then the mean is transformed exactly the same way. The standard deviation is similarly shrunk or stretched, but not shifted.

2-6 The mean and standard deviation can be calculated from the *relative* frequency distribution just as easily as from the frequency distribution itself.

2-7 A good graph can highlight a key idea, and provide rich detail to support it. In contrast, there are bad graphs that have misleading or downright dishonest messages—and it's important to be able to recognize them.

REVIEW PROBLEMS

2-33 To order a screen door, you carefully measured the width of your doorway in three randomly chosen places:

$34\frac{7}{16}''$, $34\frac{2}{16}''$, $34\frac{3}{16}''$

If you took another measurement, you would expect it to be about ____, give or take about ____.

2-34 The incomes of American households in 1984 were distributed around a mean of $27,000 and a median of $22,000 (*Stat. Abst. of U.S.*, 1987, p. 431).

a. What can you say about the symmetry of the distribution?

b. What is the total income for the whole country (all 87 million households)?

2-35 *Dollar-cost averaging.* In each quarter of this year, John Villani buys 100 shares of a mutual fund at the following prices:

Quarter	*Price per Share*
1	$ 8
2	$ 8
3	$10
4	$ 5

a. How much does the average share cost John ("straight" average)?

b. Susan York buys under a different plan. Every quarter she sets aside $800 to buy as many stocks as she can at the going price. How much does the average share cost Susan ("dollar-cost" average)?

c. Which gives the lower average price—straight averaging or dollar-cost averaging?

d. Next year, Susan wants to *sell* a little stock every quarter, and wants the price per share to be relatively *high*. Now what should her strategy be—sell off 20 shares per quarter, or $160 worth per quarter?

2-36 In the summer of 1983, several dozen economic forecasters gave widely varying predictions of the inflation rate for the next year, as follows:

Inflation Rate (range of forecast)	*Proportion of Forecasters*
2–4%	.12
4–6%	.60
6–8%	.23
8–10%	.05

AMSTAT News, Nov. 1983, p. 6

a. What is the average forecast? How does it compare to the inflation rate of 3.9% that actually occurred?

b. What is the standard deviation?

2-37 The 1980 U.S. population of 222 million was widely distributed among the 50 states—from Alaska (0.4 million) to California (23 million) as shown by this box plot:

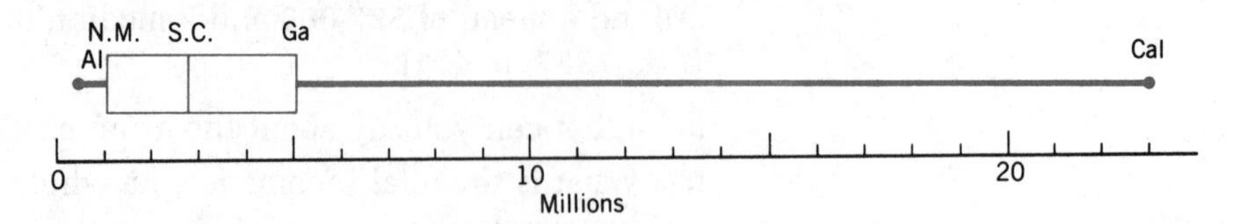

Roughly estimate:

a. The median state population.

b. The mean state population.

c. The IQR.

d. The approximate percentile ranking of Louisiana (population 4.0 million).

2-38 Five states were randomly sampled, and gave the following areas (in thousands of square miles):

Montana	147	Utah	85
Minnesota	84	California	159
W. Virginia	24		

a. Calculate the mean $\overline{X}$, and standard deviation s.

b. On the basis of this sample of 5 states, estimate the area for the whole country (50 states).

2-39 Repeat Problem 2-38 for another random sample of 5 states, that turned out this time to be:

Maryland	11	Idaho	84
Ohio	41	New Jersey	8
Nebraska	77		

Note that the estimated area of the country is different—of course, since the sample is different. This illustrates the inherent variability in statistical estimation. (The true area of the country is 3620 thousand square miles.)

2-40 In the 1970s, the U.S. unemployment rate was as follows:

Year	*Unemployment*	*Year*	*Unemployment*
1970	4.9%	1975	8.5%
1971	5.9	1976	7.7
1972	5.6	1977	7.0
1973	4.9	1978	6.0
1974	5.6	1979	5.7

(*Stat. Abst. of U.S.*, 1981.)

Calculate the average and standard deviation:

a. For the first 5 years, 1970–1974.

b. For the last 5 years, 1975–1979.

c. For all 10 years. How is this answer related to the answers in parts **a** and **b**?

2-41 At the local university there are three sections of the basic accounting course, with 8, 12, and 120 students.

a. For the three instructors who teach this course, what average class size do they face?

b. Do the 140 students who are taking this course have a different view? Calculate the average class size that they sit in.

2-42 *A Final Challenge: To Maximize Profit, We Need the Right Figures.*

The manager of a large ranch in Montana currently finishes 600 Charolais cattle. He is thinking of switching to a smaller hybrid breed that would eat less, so that he could finish 750 every year on the same pasture. The main drawback of the hybrids is their smaller profit margin, as the following comparison shows:

Distribution of Net Profit per Head

	Current Cattle (Charolais)		*Proposed Cattle (Hybrid)*
Net Profit	*Frequency*	*Relative Frequency*	*Relative Frequency*
−$200	36	6%	1%
0	12	2%	2%
$200	185	31%	57%
$400	367	61%	40%
	600	100%	100%

	Current	Proposed
median	= $336	= $265
mean	= $294	=
st. dev.	= $161	=

a. For the proposed hybrid cattle, calculate the mean and standard deviation of profit.

b. Which breed of cattle should the manager choose? Why?

c. (Sensitivity Analysis) The figures in the last column are just rough estimates of what the manager expects would happen. In fact, the profit figures for the hybrids might turn out to be a little better or worse. Just how much better or worse would the hybrids have to perform in order to change the decision in **b**?

CHAPTER 3

Probability

The urge to gamble is so universal and its practice so pleasurable that I assume it must be evil.

HEYWOOD BROUN

3-1 INTRODUCTION

In the next four chapters, we will make deductions about a sample from a known population. For example, if the population of American voters is 55% Democrat, we can hardly hope to draw exactly that same percentage of Democrats in a random sample. Nevertheless, it is "likely" that "close to" this percentage will turn up in our sample. Our objective is to define "likely" and "close to" more precisely, so we can make useful predictions. First, however, we must lay a good deal of groundwork. Predicting in the face of uncertainty requires a knowledge of the laws of *probability*, and this chapter is devoted to their development. We shall begin with the simplest example—rolling dice—which was also the historical beginning of probability theory, several hundred years ago.

EXAMPLE 3-1
RELATIVE FREQUENCIES SETTLE DOWN TO PROBABILITIES

Throw a single fair die 50 times. Or simulate this by consulting the random numbers in Appendix Table I at the back of the book, disregarding the digits 7, 8, 9, and 0. Since the remaining digits 1, 2, . . . , 6 will of course still be equally likely, they will provide an accurate simulation of a die.

Graph the relative frequency distribution:

a. After 10 throws.

b. After 50 throws.

c. After zillions of throws (guess).

SOLUTION

Since we don't have a die at hand, we will simulate (it's also faster). Although it would be best to start at a random spot in Table I, we will start at the beginning so that our work will be easy to follow. The first few digits in Table I are

3~~9~~65~~7~~645451~~990~~6~~9~~ . . .

with the irrelevant digits stroked out.

The first sample ($n = 10$ throws) is summarized in Table 3-1 in column (*a*). The second sample (with n increased to 50 throws) is shown in column (*b*). The emerging picture confirms what we might guess would eventually happen: In the long run, the six relative frequencies will approach equality (the very definition of a "fair" die). And since all six must add up to 1.00 (or 100%), each relative frequency must approach ⅙—which we record in column (*c*).

TABLE 3-1 Relative Frequency Distributions for a Die, Using Various Sample Sizes

X Number of Dots	Relative Frequency $= \frac{f}{n}$ (a) $n = 10$	(b) $n = 50$	(c) $n = \infty$
1	.10	.22	1/6 = .167
2	0	.12	1/6 = .167
3	.10	.14	1/6 = .167
4	.20	.14	1/6 = .167
5	.30	.14	1/6 = .167
6	.30	.24	1/6 = .167
	1.00✓	1.00✓	1.00✓

Figure 3-1 shows this graphically. We note in the first graph how relative frequency fluctuates wildly when there are few observations in the sample. Yet as the sample becomes larger and larger, relative frequency eventually settles down. And the limiting value is called the *chance* or *probability:*

$$\text{Probability} \equiv \text{limiting relative frequency} \tag{3-1}$$

Or, in symbols,

$$\text{Pr} \equiv \lim \left(\frac{f}{n}\right) \tag{3-2}$$

Of course, if we rolled a loaded die, we could no longer guess that the probability of each face would be 1/6. Instead, we would have to rely on the definition (3-1), and estimate the probabilities by rolling the die over and over.

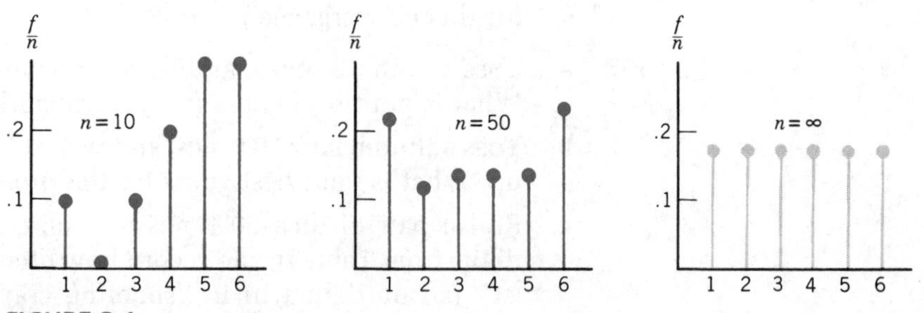

FIGURE 3-1
Relative frequency distributions for a die, using various sample sizes.

PROBLEMS

3-1 Fill in the blanks:

a. We define probability or chance as _____.

b. To estimate the chance that a loaded die comes up 1, we could _____.

c. To estimate the chance that it will snow in Boston next Christmas day, we could _____.

d. Referring to the data in Problem 2-1, suppose a coil was randomly sampled from the same production run. Then the chance that its hardness would be 50 or less is approximately _____.

3-2 To see how random fluctuation settles down consistently in the long run, repeat Example 3-1. That is, throw a die 50 times (or simulate with random digits, starting at a random spot in Appendix Table I).

a. Graph the relative frequency distribution after 10 throws, after 50 throws, and finally after zillions of throws (guess).

b. These graphs can alternatively be condensed onto a time axis. That is, in the following graph, above $n = 10$ plot all six relative frequencies. Similarly, show the relative frequencies for $n = 50$ and $n = \infty$.

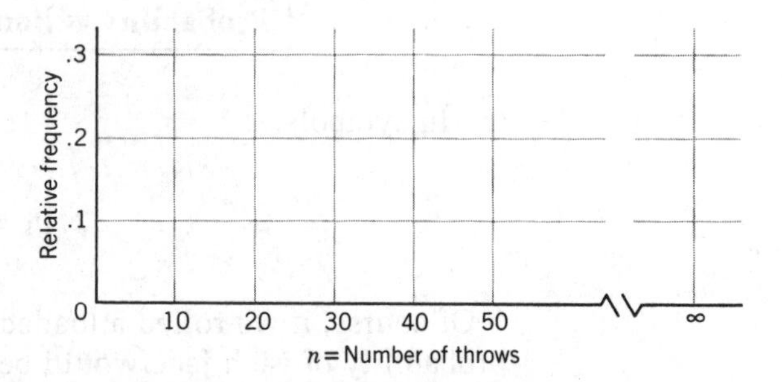

To make the graph more complete, also graph the relative frequencies at $n = 5$ and $n = 20$. Then note how the relative frequencies converge. (In Chapter 6 we will get a precise formula for this convergence.)

3-3 **a.** Toss a coin 50 times, and record how often it comes up heads. What is your best guess for the *probability* of a head?

b. Toss a thumb tack 50 times, and record how often it comes point up. What is your best guess for the *probability* of this?

c. Roll a pair of dice 50 times (or simulate by drawing pairs of digits from Table I), and record how often you get a "total of 7 or 11" (an outright win in "shooting craps"). What is your best guess for the *probability*?

3-2 PROBABILITY MODELS

A—THE VALUE OF A MODEL

In the previous section, the die example was an experiment in which the 6 outcomes (faces) were extremely simple. Usually, an experiment has a more complex set of outcomes.

For example, suppose the "experiment" consists of having a family of three children. A typical outcome might be BGB, that is, a boy, then a girl, finally another boy. How can we find the probability of this outcome?

One answer, in theory, would be to carry out the experiment zillions of times, and record the proportion of the times we get BGB, that is, the relative frequency of BGB. But since this is impossible, we could, as a good approximation, look at the few million American families who have actually had three children, and calculate the proportion of these families that are BGB.

An even simpler approach is to use a *thought experiment*, or *mathematical model*. The value of models—nonmathematical ones at least—is familiar. For example, when a new airplane is designed, a small-scale model is first tested out in a wind tunnel. It is relatively cheap and easy to test and modify. If it is a good model, there will be few surprises when the full-scale plane is built. In the same way, a mathematical model—in our head, or in a computer—provides a wonderfully simple way to calculate probabilities, as we illustrate next.

B—THE TREE MODEL

To find the probability of getting BGB in a family of three children, a simple model can be used: Just imagine a million couples performing the experiment. A systematic breakdown, birth by birth, is shown in Figure 3-2. At the left we imagine the million couples starting out, forming the trunk of what will soon become a tree. At the first birth, half the couples have B and the other half have G—as indicated by the first branching in Figure 3-2.

At the second birth, one-half would again report B and the other half would report G. This is illustrated by the further branching of the tree. When all such possible branchings are shown, we obtain a tree with $2 \times 2 \times 2 = 8$ branches (outcomes) altogether.

Each path, from beginning to end, represents a complete outcome (family of three children). The outcome BGB, for example, is the path marked in Figure 3-2. What is its probability? Of the millions of couples who start out, only one-half have a boy initially. Of these, only one-half have a girl next, and of these, only one-half finally have a boy. Thus the proportion of the couples who would report the complete outcome BGB is

$$\frac{1}{2} \text{ of } \frac{1}{2} \text{ of } \frac{1}{2} = \frac{1}{8} = .125 \tag{3-3}$$

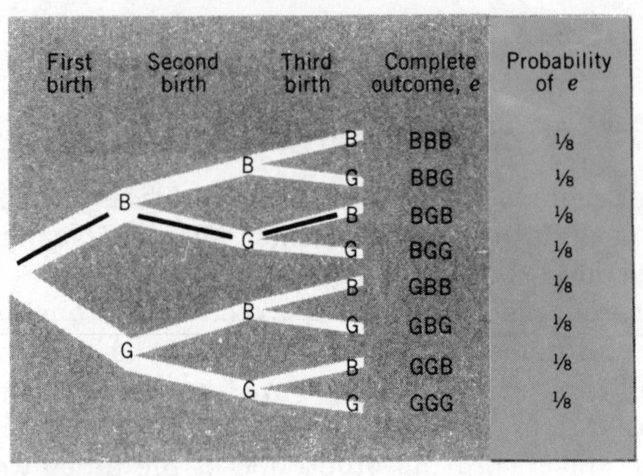

FIGURE 3-2
The probability tree for a family of three children.

This long-run proportion, or probability, is duly recorded in Figure 3-2 in the last column. Similarly, we calculate and record the probability for every one of the 8 possible outcomes. Since boys and girls are equally likely, each probability in this example is the same (1/8).

In general, trees provide a very powerful way of analyzing any step-by-step experiment—even when there are more than two branchings at each step, or the probabilities are unequal. Another example will illustrate.

EXAMPLE 3-2
THE THREE-CHILD FAMILY—A MORE REALISTIC MODEL

Suppose on every birth the probability of a boy is 52% and a girl is 48%. (According to U.S. birth statistics, this is a more realistic assumption than our earlier .50-.50 assumption.) Calculate the probability tree for a couple having three children.

SOLUTION

The tree will be similar to Figure 3-2. But now the branchings are asymmetric, with 52% of the couples having B at each birth. This will affect the final probabilities. For example, what proportion of the couples will finally attain the outcome BGB?

$$\begin{aligned} \Pr(BGB) &= 52\% \text{ of } 48\% \text{ of } 52\% \\ &= .52 \times .48 \times .52 = .13 \end{aligned} \tag{3-4}$$

Continuing in this way, we obtain the tree shown in Figure 3-3.

We have found that the probability of BGB is 13%, rather than the 12½% approximation calculated from the less precise model in Figure

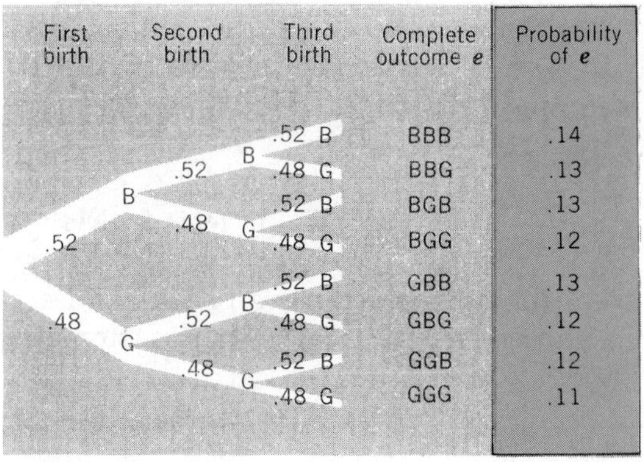

First birth	Second birth	Third birth	Complete outcome e	Probability of e
.52 B	.52 B	.52 B	BBB	.14
		.48 G	BBG	.13
	.48 G	.52 B	BGB	.13
		.48 G	BGG	.12
.48 G	.52 B	.52 B	GBB	.13
		.48 G	GBG	.12
	.48 G	.52 B	GGB	.12
		.48 G	GGG	.11

FIGURE 3-3
The probability tree for a family of three children, if the probability of a boy on each birth is 52%.

3-2. While the model of Figure 3-2 is adequate for many purposes, the refined model of Figure 3-3 would sometimes be a worthwhile improvement.

C—OUTCOME SETS AND EVENTS

We have seen how a probability tree is one of the most effective ways to get a complete list of outcomes and their probabilities. For example, Figure 3-4 repeats the information for the simple model of a three-child family. Since we will often be referring to these eight elementary outcomes $e_1, e_2, \ldots, e_8$, each is shown as a *point* in this figure. All of these points then make up the *outcome set* S (shown as the shaded area in

Outcome Set S		Probabilities
BBB	• e_1	1/8
BBG	• e_2	1/8
BGB	• e_3	1/8
BGG	• e_4	1/8
GBB	• e_5	1/8
GBG	• e_6	1/8
GGB	• e_7	1/8
GGG	• e_8	1/8

FIGURE 3-4
Outcome Set for three-child family, with probabilities (assuming boys and girls are equally likely).

Figure 3-4). This is also called the sample space, since statisticians are mostly interested in outcome sets in sampling contexts.

In planning three children, suppose that a couple is hoping for the event

$$E: \quad \text{at least 2 girls} \tag{3-5}$$

This event includes outcomes e_4, e_6, e_7, and e_8, illustrated in the *Venn diagram* shown in Figure 3-5. This is customarily written:

$$E = \{e_4, e_6, e_7, e_8\}$$

In fact, this method provides a convenient way to define an event in general:

$$\boxed{\textbf{An event } E \textbf{ is a subset of the outcome set } S} \tag{3-6}$$

Now, the interesting question is: What is the probability of E? If we imagine many families carrying out this experiment, 1/8 of the time e_4 will occur; 1/8 of the time e_6 will occur; and so on. Thus, in one way or another, E will occur $1/8 + 1/8 + \cdots = 4/8$ of the time; that is,

$$\Pr(E) = \frac{1}{8} + \frac{1}{8} + \frac{1}{8} + \frac{1}{8} = \frac{4}{8} = .50$$

The obvious generalization is that the probability of an event is the sum of the probabilities of all the points (or outcomes) included in that event. That is,

$$\boxed{\Pr(E) = \sum \Pr(e)} \tag{3-7}$$

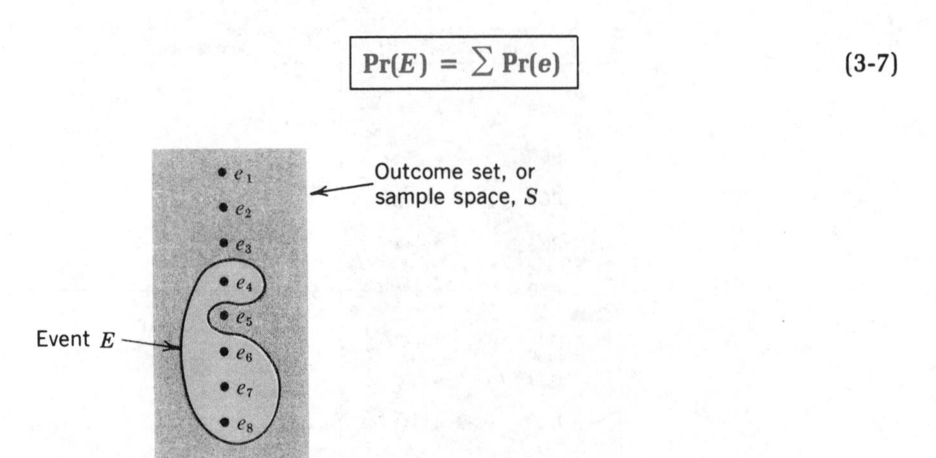

FIGURE 3-5
Venn diagram: An event as a subset (same outcome set as in Figure 3-4).

where we sum over just those elementary outcomes e that are in E. There is a nice analogy between mass and probability: The mass of an object is the sum of the masses of all the atoms in that object; the probability of an event is the sum of the probabilities of all the outcomes included in that event.

EXAMPLE 3-3
OTHER EVENTS IN A THREE-CHILD FAMILY

Refer again to the planning of three children in Figure 3-4.

a. Make a Venn diagram to show the event:

$$F = \text{last two children are girls}$$

Then calculate its probability.

b. Calculate the probabilities for each of the following events:

G = less than 2 girls
H = all the same sex
K = less than 2 boys
I = no girls
I_1 = exactly 1 girl
I_2 = exactly 2 girls
I_3 = exactly 3 girls

SOLUTION

a. Using the sample space of Figure 3-4, we scan the points one by one. We find that there are two points in the event F. And so its probability is 2/8.

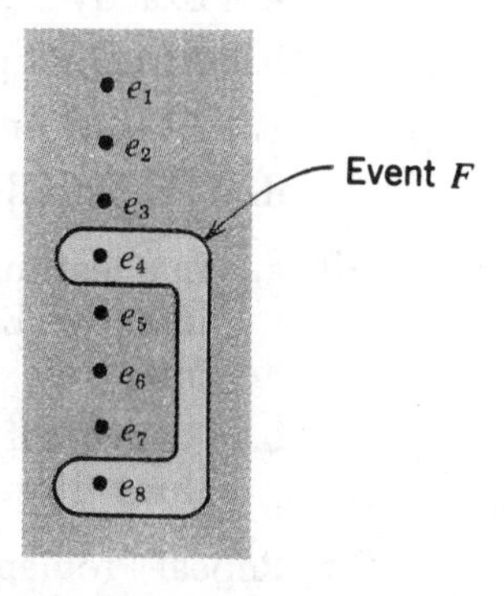

b. The probability of each event simply requires counting up the outcomes in it—because every outcome has the same probability, 1/8. Table 3-2 gives the answers (and for completeness, also lists the events E and F discussed earlier.)

TABLE 3-2 Several Events in Planning 3 Children

Three Alternative Ways of Naming an Event			
(1) *Arbitrary Symbol for Event*	(2) *Verbal Description*	(3) *Outcome List*	(4) *Probability*
E	At least 2 girls	$\{e_4, e_6, e_7, e_8\}$	4/8
F	Last two are girls	$\{e_4, e_8\}$	2/8
G	Less than 2 girls	$\{e_1, e_2, e_3, e_5\}$	4/8
H	All the same sex	$\{e_1, e_8\}$	2/8
K	Less than 2 boys	$\{e_4, e_6, e_7, e_8\}$	4/8
I	No girls	$\{e_1\}$	1/8
I_1	Exactly 1 girl	$\{e_2, e_3, e_5\}$	3/8
I_2	Exactly 2 girls	$\{e_4, e_6, e_7\}$	3/8
I_3	Exactly 3 girls	$\{e_8\}$	1/8

The first three columns of Table 3-2 show three different ways to name or specify an event. The value of specifying an event the third way—by its outcome list—is evident when we look at the event K (less than 2 boys). The list for K is the same as the list for the first event E (at least 2 girls). That is, K = E, an equality that is not so evident from the verbal description.

PROBLEMS

3-4 Using Figure 3-3, find the chance that in a family of three children, there will be:

a. Exactly 2 girls?

b. At least 2 girls?

c. At least one child of each sex?

d. The middle child opposite in sex to the other two?

3-5 **a.** In a learning experiment, a subject attempts a certain task twice in a row. Each time his chance of failure is .40. Draw the probability tree, and then calculate the chance of exactly one failure.

b. Repeat **a** if the subject attempts his task once more, for a total of three tries.

3-6 Repeat Problem 3-5**b**, if the subject makes three tries and he learns from his previous trials, especially his previous successes, as follows: His chance of failure is still .40 at the first trial. However, for later trials his chance of failure drops to .30 if his previous trial was a failure, and drops way down to .20 if his previous trial was a success.

3-7 **a.** (Acceptance sampling) The manager of a small hardware store buys electric clocks in cartons of 12 clocks each. To see whether each carton is acceptable, 3 clocks are randomly selected and thoroughly tested. If all 3 are of acceptable quality, then the carton of 12 is accepted.

Suppose in a certain carton, unknown to the hardware manager, only 8 of the 12 are of acceptable quality. What is the chance that the sampling scheme will inadvertently accept the carton?

b. Repeat part **a,** if the given carton of 12 clocks has only 6 of acceptable quality.

3-8 When a penny and a nickel are tossed, the outcome set could be written as a tree or as a rectangular array:

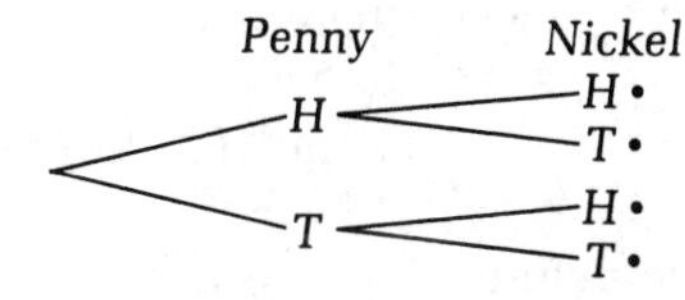

Penny \ Nickel	H	T
H	• (H H)	• (H T)
T	• (T H)	• (T T)

Draw up the same two versions of the outcome set when a pair of dice are thrown—one red, one white. Then, using whichever version is more convenient, calculate the probability of:

a. A total of 4 dots.

b. A total of 7 dots.

c. A total of 7 or 11 dots (as in Problem 3-3**c**).

d. A double (the same value on both dice).

e. A total of at least 8 dots.

f. A 1 on one die, 5 on the other.

g. A 1 on both dice ("snake eyes").

h. Would you get the same answers if both dice were painted white? In particular, would you get the same answers as before, for parts **f** and **g**?

3-3 COMPOUND EVENTS

A—DEFINITIONS

In planning their three children, suppose that the couple would be disappointed if there were fewer than two girls, or if all were the same sex. Referring to Table 3-2, you can see that this is the event "*G* or *H*." From the lists of Table 3-2, we can pick out the points that are in G or in H, and so obtain:

$$G \text{ or } H = \{e_1, e_2, e_3, e_5, e_8\}$$

And in general, we define:

$$\boxed{G \text{ or } H \equiv \text{set of points that are in } G, \text{ or in } H, \text{ or in both.}} \quad (3\text{-}8)$$

Figure 3-6*a* illustrates this definition. Since five outcomes are included in G or H, its probability is 5/8.

The couple would be doubly disappointed if there were fewer than two girls *and* if all children were the same sex—the event "G *and* H". From the lists of Table 3-2, we see there is only one point both in G and in H:

$$G \text{ and } H = \{e_1\}$$

And in general, we define:

$$\boxed{G \text{ and } H \equiv \text{set of points that are both in } G \text{ and in } H} \quad (3\text{-}9)$$

Figure 3-6*b* illustrates this definition. Since only one outcome is included in G and H, its probability is 1/8.

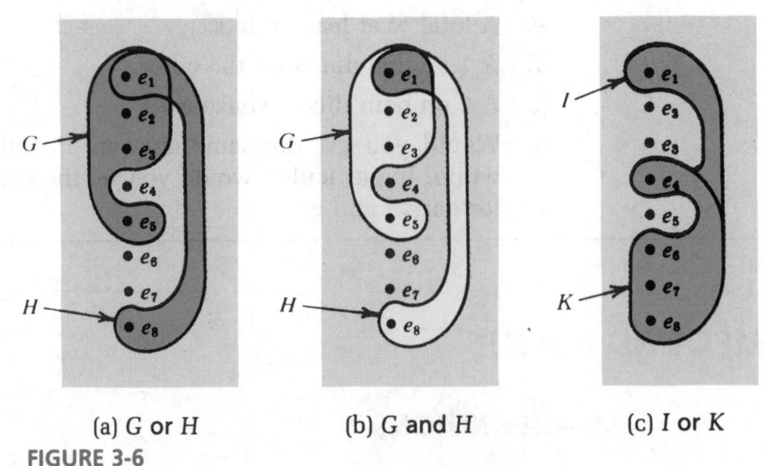

FIGURE 3-6
Venn diagrams, illustrating compound events with dark coloring. (*a*) "G or H" shaded. (*b*) "G and H" shaded. (*c*) "I or K" shaded.

EXAMPLE 3-4
COMPOUND EVENTS IN A THREE-CHILD FAMILY

From the lists in Table 3-2, construct the lists for the following compound events and hence find their probability.

F or H, F and H, I or K, I and K

SOLUTION

F or $H = \{e_1, e_4, e_8\}$
F and $H = \{e_8\}$
I or $K = \{e_1, e_4, e_6, e_7, e_8\}$
I and $K = \{\}$

Hence Pr(F or H) = 3/8
Pr(F and H) = 1/8
Pr(I or K) = 5/8
Pr(I and K) = 0

B—PROBABILITY OF *G* OR *H*

We already have shown how Pr(G or H) may be found from the Venn diagram in Figure 3-6. Now we will develop a formula. First, consider a pair of events that do not have any points in common, such as the event I and the event K from Table 3-2. Because these events do not overlap, they are called mutually exclusive—that is, if one occurs, the other cannot. From Figure 3-6c, it is obvious that:

$$\Pr(I \text{ or } K) = \Pr(I) + \Pr(K) \tag{3-10}$$

$$\frac{5}{8} = \frac{1}{8} + \frac{4}{8}$$

But this simple addition does not always work. For example:

$$\Pr(G \text{ or } H) \neq \Pr(G) + \Pr(H) \tag{3-11}$$

$$\frac{5}{8} \neq \frac{4}{8} + \frac{2}{8}$$

What has gone wrong in this case? In summing Pr(G) and Pr(H) we double counted the overlap, G and H. Subtracting Pr(G and H) eliminates this double counting. Accordingly, it is generally true that:

$$\boxed{\Pr(G \text{ or } H) = \Pr(G) + \Pr(H) - \Pr(G \text{ and } H)} \tag{3-12}$$

In our example:

$$\frac{5}{8} = \frac{4}{8} + \frac{2}{8} - \frac{1}{8}$$

Formula (3-12) also applies in cases like (3-10), where I does not overlap K, that is, Pr(I and K) = 0, and so the last term in (3-12) disappears. Then we obtain the special case:

If I and K are mutually exclusive,

$$\Pr(I \text{ or } K) = \Pr(I) + \Pr(K) \qquad \text{(3-13)}$$

C—COMPLEMENTS

In Table 3-2, note that G consists of exactly those points that are not in E. We therefore call G the "*complement of* E," or "*not* E," and denote it by $\bar{E}$. In general, for any event E:

$$\bar{E} \equiv \text{set of points that are } \textit{not} \text{ in } E \qquad \text{(3-14)}$$

Since the points in E plus the points in $\bar{E}$ make up 100% of the outcomes,

$$\Pr(E) + \Pr(\bar{E}) = 1.00$$

This gives us a very useful formula:

$$\Pr(E) = 1 - \Pr(\bar{E}) \qquad \text{(3-15)}$$

EXAMPLE 3-5
WILL HAVING FIVE CHILDREN GUARANTEE A BOY?

To make sure that they get at least one boy, a couple plans on having five children. What is their chance of success?

SOLUTION

Since it would be tedious to list the sample space and pick out the event of at least one boy, let's try using the complement.

Let E = at least one boy

then $\bar{E}$ = no boys; that is, all girls.

We see that $\Pr(\bar{E})$ is much easier to calculate. The probability of getting a girl every time is:

$$\Pr(\bar{E}) = \frac{1}{2} \times \frac{1}{2} \times \frac{1}{2} \times \frac{1}{2} \times \frac{1}{2} = \frac{1}{32}$$

Finally, we can obtain the required probability of E (at least one boy) as the complement:

$$\Pr(E) = 1 - \Pr(\bar{E}) \qquad \text{(3-15) repeated}$$

$$= 1 - \frac{1}{32} = \frac{31}{32} = .97$$

In other words, the probability is 97% that they will get at least one boy in five births.

In this example, we have seen how complements sometimes provide the easiest way to calculate the required probability. You should be on the alert for similar problems: The key words to watch for are "at least," "more than," "less than," "no more than," and so on.

EXAMPLE 3-6
A RANDOM INTERVIEW

In a certain college, the students engage in recreational sports in the following proportions:

Football (F), 20%
Basketball (B), 50%
Both football and basketball, 15%

What is the chance that a student selected at random will:

a. Play football or basketball?
b. Play neither sport?

SOLUTION

a. $\Pr(F \text{ or } B) = \Pr(F) + \Pr(B) - \Pr(F \text{ and } B)$ like (3-12)
$\qquad = .20 + .50 - .15 = .55$

b. $1 - P(F \text{ or } B) = 1 - .55 = .45$

PROBLEMS

3-9 The chance that a factory's sprinkler system will fail is 20%; the chance that its alarm system will fail is 10%; and the chance that both will fail is 4%. What is the chance that:

a. At least one will work?

b. Both will work?

3-10 Of the U.S. population in 1980,

10% were from California
6% were of Spanish origin
2% were from California and of Spanish origin

If an American was drawn at random, what is the chance she would be:

a. From California or of Spanish origin?

b. Neither from California nor of Spanish origin?

c. Of Spanish origin, but not from California?

3-11 In a family of 10 children (assuming boys and girls are equally likely), what is the chance there will be:

a. At least one boy?

b. At least one boy and one girl?

3-12 Suppose that a class of 100 students consists of four subgroups, in the following proportions:

	Men	*Women*
Taking economics	17%	38%
Not taking economics	23%	22%

If a student is chosen by lot to be class president, what is the chance that the student will be:

a. A man?

b. A woman?

c. Taking economics?

d. A man, or taking economics?

e. A man, and taking economics?

f. If the class president in fact turns out to be a man, what is the chance that he is taking economics? not taking economics?

3-13 The men in a certain college engage in various sports in the following proportions:

Football, 30% of all men	Both football and basketball, 5%
Basketball, 20%	Both football and soccer, 10%
Soccer, 20%	Both basketball and soccer, 5%

All three sports, 2%

If a man is chosen by lot for an interview, use a Venn diagram to calculate the chance that he will be:

a. An athlete (someone who plays at least one sport).

b. A football player only.

c. A football player or a soccer player.

If an *athlete* is chosen by lot, what is the chance that he will be:

d. A football player only?

e. A football player or a soccer player?

3-14 A salesman makes 12 calls per day, and on each call has a 20% chance of making a sale.

a. What is the chance he will make no sales at all on a given day?

b. What is the chance he will make at least one sale?

c. If he sells for 200 days of the year, about how many of these days will he make at least one sale?

3-4 CONDITIONAL PROBABILITY

A—DEFINITION

Conditional probability is just the familiar concept of limiting relative frequency, but with a slight twist—the set of relevant outcomes is restricted by a condition. An example will illustrate.

EXAMPLE 3-7
PROBABILITY AFTER A CONDITION (EVENT) IS KNOWN

In a family of 3 children, suppose it is known that G (fewer than two girls) has occurred. What is the probability that H (all the same sex) has occurred? That is, if we imagine many repetitions of this experiment and consider just those cases in which G has occurred, how often will H occur? This is called the *conditional probability of H, given G*, and is denoted $\Pr(H|G)$.

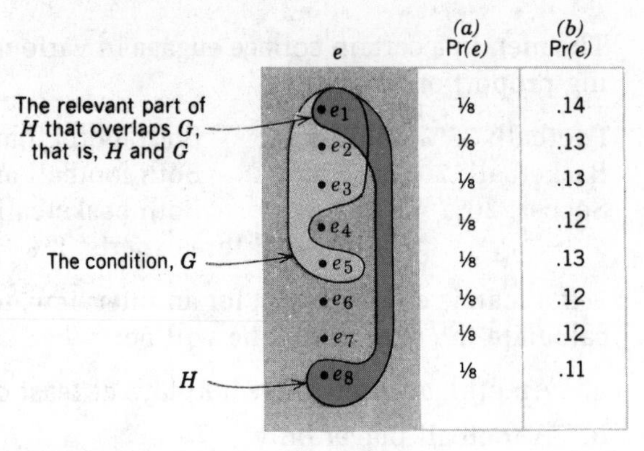

FIGURE 3-7
(a) If Pr(Boy) = .50 (b) If Pr(Boy) = .52
Venn diagram to illustrate the conditional probability Pr (H|G).

Answer in two different cases, where the probability of a boy is:

a. 50% (as in Figure 3-2).
b. 52% (as in Figure 3-3).

SOLUTION

a. As shown in Figure 3-7, there are four outcomes in G, and only one of them is in *H*. Thus, when all outcomes are equally likely:

$$\Pr(H|G) = \frac{1}{4} = .25$$

b. When the outcomes are not equally likely, we must be more subtle. Suppose, for example, that the experiment is carried out 100 million times. Then how often will G occur? The answer is about 53 million times (from the last column of Figure 3-7, Pr(G) = .14 + .13 + .13 + .13 = .53). Of these times, how often will *H* occur? The answer is about 14 million times. Thus, from our fundamental notion of probability as relative frequency:

$$\Pr(H|G) = \frac{14 \text{ million}}{53 \text{ million}} = .26 \tag{3-16}$$

Now let us express our answer in general terms. The ratio in (3-16) is Pr(*H* and G) divided by Pr(G). Thus:

$$\boxed{\Pr(H|G) = \frac{\Pr(H \text{ and } G)}{\Pr(G)}} \tag{3-17}$$

B—AN APPLICATION OF CONDITIONAL PROBABILITY

Formula (3-17) can be reexpressed. Let us cross-multiply by Pr(G), and note of course that Pr(H and G) = Pr(G and H). Then:

$$\boxed{\Pr(G \text{ and } H) = \Pr(G)\Pr(H|G)} \quad (3\text{-}18)$$

This formula breaks Pr(G and H) into two easy steps: Pr(G) and then Pr($H|G$). An example will show how useful it is.

EXAMPLE 3-8
SAMPLING FROM A SMALL POPULATION

Three defective light bulbs inadvertently got mixed with 6 good ones. If 2 bulbs are chosen at random for a ceiling lamp, what is the probability that they both are good?

SOLUTION

We can break down this problem very naturally if we imagine the bulbs being picked up one after the other. Then let us denote:

$$G_1 = \text{first bulb is good}$$
$$G_2 = \text{second bulb is good}$$

Thus:

$$\begin{aligned}\Pr(\text{both good}) &= \Pr(G_1 \text{ and } G_2)\\ &= \Pr(G_1)\Pr(G_2|G_1) \qquad \text{like (3-18)}\end{aligned}$$

Now on the first draw, there are 6 good bulbs among 9 altogether, so that the probability of drawing a good bulb is Pr(G_1) = 6/9. After that, however, there are only 5 good bulbs among the 8 left, so that Pr($G_2|G_1$) = 5/8. Thus:

$$\Pr(G_1 \text{ and } G_2) = \frac{6}{9} \times \frac{5}{8} = \frac{5}{12} = .42 \quad (3\text{-}19)$$

REMARKS

This problem could have been solved just as well using a tree. If this experiment were repeated many times, 6/9 of the time there would be a good bulb drawn first; of these times, 5/8 of the time there would be another good bulb drawn second. Thus, the probability of drawing two good bulbs together would be:

$$\frac{5}{8} \text{ of } \frac{6}{9} = \frac{5}{12} \qquad \text{(3-19) confirmed}$$

Thus, the product formula (3-18) has a strong intuitive basis.

PROBLEMS

3-15 The table below shows the percentages of the 1985 U.S. labor force, classified by sex and employment status (*Stat. Abst. of U.S.*, 1987, p. 378):

	Sex		
	M (male)	*F (female)*	*Totals*
E (employed)	51.9%	40.9%	92.8%
U (unemployed)	3.9%	3.3%	7.2%
Totals	55.8%	44.2%	100.0%

a. What is the unemployment rate? That is, what is $\Pr(U)$, the chance that a worker drawn at random will be unemployed?

b. What is $\Pr(U|M)$? What is this called?

c. What is $\Pr(U|F)$? What is this called?

3-16 In the U.S. in 1974, the population was classified as male or female, and as favoring or opposing abortion.[1] The proportions in each category were approximately as follows (note that all the proportions add up to 1.00 = 100% of the population):

	Favor	*Opposed*
Male	.27	.21
Female	.24	.28

What is the probability that an individual drawn at random would be:

a. In favor of abortion?

b. In favor of abortion, if male?

c. In favor of abortion, if female?

---

[1] The *Gallup Opinion Index*, April 1974, p. 24. The exact question was, "The U.S. Supreme Court has ruled that a woman may go to a doctor to end pregnancy at any time during the first 3 months of pregnancy. Do you favor or oppose this ruling?" The 10% who had no opinion are not included.

3-17 In a family of three children, what is the chance of:

a. At least one girl?
b. At least two girls?
c. At least two girls, given at least one girl?
d. At least two girls, given that the eldest child is a girl?

3-18 Suppose that 4 defective light bulbs inadvertently have been mixed up with 6 good ones.

a. If 2 bulbs are chosen at random, what is the chance that they both are good?
b. If the first 2 are good, what is the chance that the next 3 are good?
c. If we started all over again and chose 5 bulbs, what is the chance they all would be good?

3-19 A student of statistics, so we're told, once heard that there was one chance in a million of a bomb being on an aircraft. He calculated there would be only one chance in a million million (trillion) of there being two bombs on an aircraft. In order to enjoy these longer odds, therefore, he always carried a bomb on with him (carefully defused, of course—he was no fool.)

Comment.

3-20 Two dice are thrown and we are interested in the following events:

E: first die is 5
F: total is 7
G: total is 10

By calculating the probabilities using Venn diagrams, show that:

a. $\Pr(F|E) = \Pr(F)$.
b. $\Pr(G|E) \neq \Pr(G)$.
c. Is the following a correct verbal conclusion? If not, correct it.
If I'm going to bet on whether the dice show 10, it will help (change the chances) to peek at the first die to see whether it is a 5. But if I'm going to bet on whether the dice show 7, a peek won't help.

3-5 INDEPENDENCE

A—DEFINITION

Independence is a very precise concept that we define in terms of certain probabilities. An example will illustrate.

EXAMPLE 3-9
IS OPINION ABOUT ABORTION DEPENDENT ON RACE?

In the U.S. in 1974, a Gallup poll classified the population as white or nonwhite, and as favoring or opposing abortion. The proportions in each category were approximately as follows (note that all the proportions add up to 1.00 = 100% of the population).

	Favor (F)	*Opposed (O)*
White (*W*)	.459	.441
Nonwhite (*B*)	.051	.049

(Same source as Problem 3-16)

If a person is drawn at random, what is:

a. $\Pr(F)$?

b. $\Pr(F|W)$?

SOLUTION

a. $$\Pr(F) = .459 + .051 = .51 \qquad \text{like (3-13)}$$

b. $$\Pr(F|W) = \frac{\Pr(F \text{ and } W)}{\Pr(W)} \qquad \text{like (3-17)}$$

$$= \frac{.459}{.459 + .441} = .51$$

Since both these probabilities are the same, the probability of being *F* is not in any way affected by being *W*. This kind of independence, defined in terms of probability, is called *statistical independence*. We can state the exact definition.

> **F is called *statistically independent* of E if**
>
> $$\Pr(F|E) = \Pr(F) \qquad (3\text{-}20)$$

Of course, if $\Pr(F|E)$ is different from $\Pr(F)$, we call F statistically *dependent* on E. Statistical dependence is the usual case, since it is much easier for two probabilities to be somewhat unequal than to be exactly equal. For example, in Problem 3-16 we found that being in favor of abortion was statistically dependent on being male.[2]

[2] And if, in Example 3-9, the *exact* probabilities for the U.S. were quoted instead of the approximate probabilities, $\Pr(F|W)$ would turn out to be slightly different from $\Pr(F)$; that is, *F* would be slightly dependent on *W*.

So far we have insisted on the phrase "*statistical* independence," in order to distinguish it from other forms of independence—philosophical, logical, or whatever. For example, we might be tempted to say that for the dice of Problem 3-20, F was "somehow" dependent on E because the total of the two tosses depends on the first die. Although this vague notion of dependence is not used in statistics and will be considered no further, we mention it as a warning that *statistical* independence is a very precise concept, defined by probabilities in (3-20).

Now that we clearly understand statistical independence and agree that it is the only kind of independence we will consider, we can be informal and drop the word "statistical."

B—IMPLICATIONS

If an event F is independent of another event E, we can develop some interesting logical consequences. According to (3-18), it is always true that

$$\Pr(E \text{ and } F) = \Pr(E)\,\Pr(F|E)$$

When we substitute (3-20), this becomes the simple multiplication rule:

For independent events,

$$\Pr(E \text{ and } F) = \Pr(E)\,\Pr(F) \tag{3-21}$$

Furthermore, by dividing (3-21) by $\Pr(F)$ we obtain

$$\frac{\Pr(E \text{ and } F)}{\Pr(F)} = \Pr(E)$$

that is,

$$\Pr(E|F) = \Pr(E) \tag{3-22}$$

That is, E is independent of F. In other words:

Whenever F is independent of E, then E must be independent of F (3-23)

In view of this symmetry, we can simply state that E and F are *independent of each other* whenever any of the three logically equivalent statements (3-20), (3-21), or (3-22) is true. Often the multiplicative form (3-21) is the preferred form, because of its symmetry—in fact, it is sometimes used as the very definition of statistical independence.

TABLE 3-3 Review of Probability Formulas

	Pr(E or F)	Pr(E and F)
General Theorem	$= \Pr(E) + \Pr(F) - \Pr(E \text{ and } F)$	$= \Pr(E)\Pr(F\|E)$
Special Case	$= \Pr(E) + \Pr(F)$ if E and F are mutually exclusive; i.e., if $\Pr(E \text{ and } F) = 0$	$= \Pr(E)\Pr(F)$ if E and F are independent; i.e., if $\Pr(F\|E) = \Pr(F)$

C—CONCLUSION

Now we have completed our development of the most important formulas of probability. To review them, Table 3-3 sets out our basic conclusions for Pr(E or F) and Pr(E and F).

PROBLEMS

3-21 The 1980 U.S. population, broken down by region and attitude to legalization of marijuana, roughly turned out as follows (note that all proportions add up to 100%):

	In Favor (F)	*Opposed* ($\bar{F}$)
East (E)	7.8%	22.2%
All except East ($\bar{E}$)	18.2%	51.8%

a. What is Pr(F) (the probability that an individual drawn at random will be in favor of legalization?

b. What is $\Pr(F|E)$?

c. Is F independent of E?

3-22 In Problem 3-21, we found that F was independent of E.

a. Can you guess, or better still, state for certain on the basis of theoretical reasoning:

i. Whether E will be independent of F?

ii. Whether E will be independent of $\bar{F}$?

b. Calculate the appropriate probabilities to verify your answers in part (a).

3-23 The table below classifies the 115.5 million civilians in the 1985 U.S. labor force by age and employment status (*Stat. Abst. of U.S.*,

1987, p. 378):

	Age		
	Y (*young, under 25*)	*O* (*older, 25 and over*)	Totals
E (*employed*)	20.4	86.8	107.2
U (*unemployed*)	3.2	5.1	8.3
Totals	23.6	91.9	115.5 million

a. What is $\Pr(U)$, the probability that a worker drawn at random will be unemployed? That is, find the unemployment rate.

b. What is $\Pr(U|Y)$?

c. Is unemployment independent of age?

3-24 If E and F are two mutually exclusive events, what can be said about their independence? [*Hint:* What is $\Pr(E \text{ and } F)$? Then, using (3-17), what is $\Pr(E|F)$? Does it equal $\Pr(E)$?]

3-6 BAYES THEOREM: TREE REVERSAL

An important branch of applied statistics called *Bayes Analysis* can be developed out of conditional probability and trees. An example will illustrate.

EXAMPLE 3-10
HOW TO BUY A USED CAR

I am thinking of buying a used Q-car at Honest Ed's. In order to make an informed decision, I look up the records of Q-cars in an auto magazine, and find that, unfortunately, 30% have faulty transmissions.

To get more information on the particular Q-car at Honest Ed's, I hire a mechanic who can make a shrewd guess on the basis of a quick drive around the block. Of course, he isn't always right; but he does have an excellent record: Of all the faulty cars he has examined in the past he correctly pronounced 90% "faulty"; in other words, he wrongly pronounced only 10% "OK." He has almost as good a record in judging good cars: He has correctly pronounced 80% "OK," while he wrongly pronounced only 20% "faulty." (We emphasize that "*faulty*" in quotation marks describes the mechanic's opinion, while *faulty* with no quotation marks describes the actual state of the car.)

What is the chance that the Q-car I'm thinking of buying has a faulty transmission:

a. Before I hire the mechanic?

b. If the mechanic pronounces it "faulty"?

c. If the mechanic pronounces it "OK"?

SOLUTION

a. Before any mechanical examination, the chance this car is faulty is 30% (the proportion of all Q-cars that are faulty—the only information I have).

b. Imagine running hundreds of Q-cars past the mechanic to see how he judges them. The first branching of the tree in Figure 3-8 shows the 30% of the cars that *actually* are faulty, and the 70% that are OK. As we move to the right, the second branching shows how well the mechanic is able to *judge* them: For example, in the top branch we see that if a car is faulty, he's 90% sure of correctly judging it "faulty." So 90% of 30% = 27% of all cars are actually faulty and then correctly identified as such, and we mark this 27% in the right-hand column.

Looking down to the third number in the right-hand column, we similarly find that 20% of 70% = 14% of all cars are *good* cars that are judged "faulty."

Thus altogether 27% + 14% = 41% of the cars are judged "faulty," and are encircled in blue in Figure 3-8. Of these cars, about two-thirds (27/41) are actually faulty. Once the mechanic says "faulty," therefore, the probability is about ⅔ that the car actually is faulty. This conditional probability can be calculated more formally from (3-17):

$$\text{Pr(faulty/"faulty")} = \frac{.27}{.41} = .66 \qquad \text{(3-24)}$$

To sum up: Once the car has been pronounced "faulty" by the mechanic, the chance that it is actually faulty rises from the original 30% (calculated in part **a**) up to 66%.

c. Once the mechanic says "OK," now we know it must be one of the cars in the complementary event—also encircled at the right of Figure 3-8. And only a very small proportion of these cars actually are faulty:

$$\text{Pr(faulty/"OK")} = \frac{.03}{.59} = .05 \qquad \text{(3-25)}$$

This also makes good intuitive sense: Once the car has been pronounced "OK," the chance that it actually is faulty drops from 30% down to 5%.

The calculations in Figure 3-8 can be clearly summarized in another tree, the *reverse tree* in Figure 3-9. (We emphasize that this involves no new calculations; it is only a way of conveniently *displaying* the calculations already done.) Notice the reverse order in Figure 3-9: The first branching now shows the test opinion of the mechanic. (The 41% "faulty" and the 59% "OK" appeared as the two encircled events on the right of Figure 3-8.)

Moving to the right in Figure 3-9, the second branching shows the actual condition of the cars—and the answers to our questions. For example, the top branch displays the answer calculated earlier in (3-24): Once the car is judged "faulty" the chance that it actually turns out faulty is .66. And the third branch from the top displays the answer calculated in (3-25): Once the car is judged "OK," the chance that it actually is faulty is just .05. (To complete the tree, the complementary probability .95 is shown on the final branch.)

Alternatively, this whole problem could have been illustrated with a rectangular sample space instead of a pair of trees, as Figure 3-10 shows.

No matter how we represent it—whether Figure 3-10 or Figure 3-9—this technique is called *Bayes Theorem*. The initial probabilities *before*

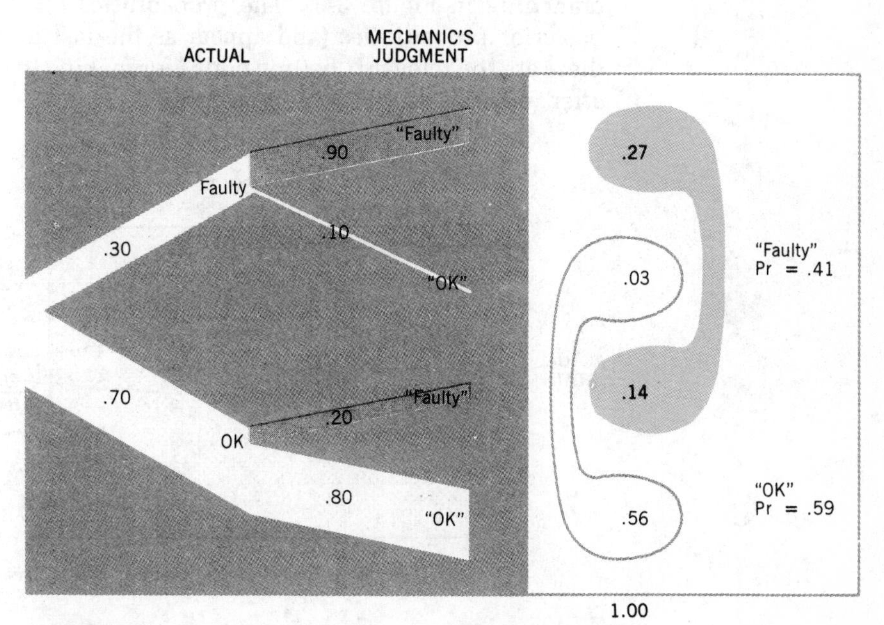

FIGURE 3-8
Calculation of the tree and conditional probabilities.

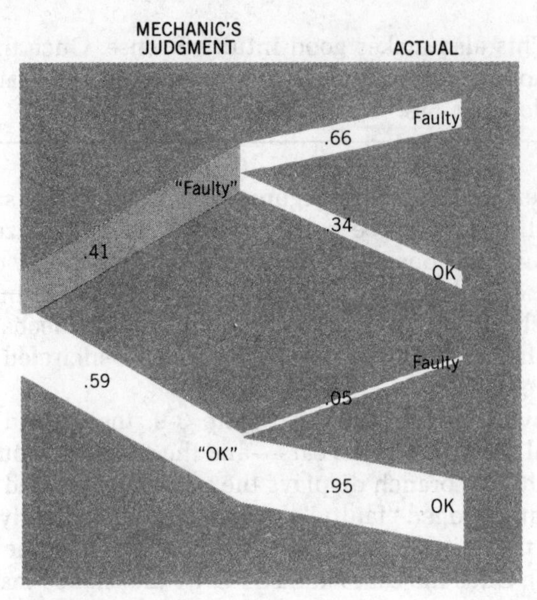

FIGURE 3-9
Bayes Theorem (tree reversal). The results of Figure 3-8 displayed as a reverse tree. The last branching gives the posterior probabilities.

any testing are called the *prior probabilities* (and appear at the first branching in Figure 3-8). The probabilities *after* testing are called the *posterior probabilities* (and appear as the last branching in Figure 3-9); these are the relevant "betting odds" for making the decision about the car *after* we have the mechanic's opinion.

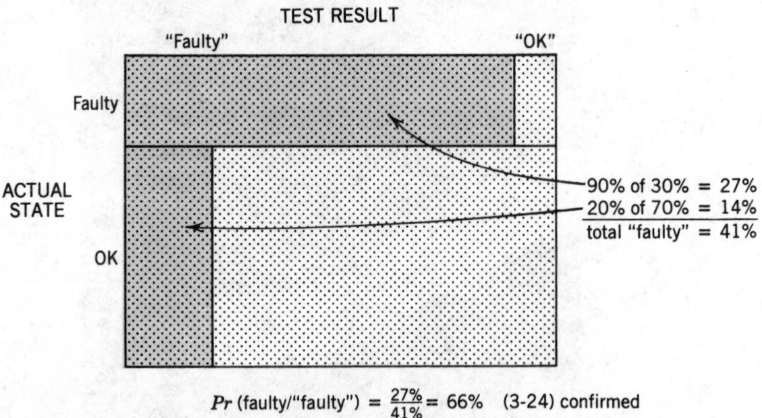

FIGURE 3-10
Alternative to tree reversal: Bayes Theorem illustrated in a rectangular Venn diagram. Each of the hundreds of possible cars is shown as a dot, and those that test out "faulty" are shaded.

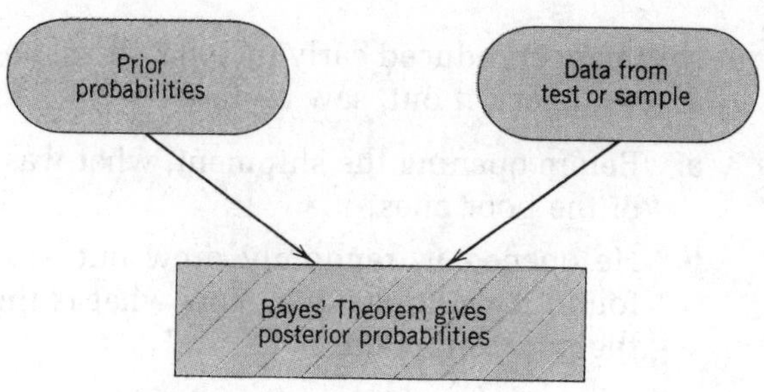

FIGURE 3-11
The logic of Bayes Theorem.

The point of Bayes Theorem may be stated more generally: Prior probabilities, combined with some sort of information such as a test or sample, yield posterior probabilities (the relevant betting odds). Figure 3-11 shows this schematically.

PROBLEMS

3-25 An incipient form of cancer occurs in three out of every 1000 Americans. To provide early detection, a screening test has been developed that rarely errs. Among healthy patients, only 5% get a + reaction (false alarm). Among patients with this incipient cancer, only 2% get a − reaction (missed alarm).

If this test is used to screen the American public, all those who get a + reaction will be hospitalized for exploratory surgery. What proportion of these people who are thought to have cancer, will *actually* have cancer?

3-26 A barometer manufacturer, in testing a very simple model, found that it sometimes erred: on rainy days it erroneously predicted "no rain" 10% of the time; and on the days when it didn't rain, it erroneously predicted "rain" 30% of the time.

In a small town on the Oregon coast, it rains 40% of the days in September. This is roughly the chance it will rain next Labor Day, for example.

As Labor Day approaches, its barometer prediction turns out to be "rain." Now what is the chance it will actually rain?

3-27 The chain saws produced by a large manufacturer for the first three months of 1990 were of poor quality. In each of the 300 shipments, 40% of the saws were defective. After tightening up quality control, however, this figure was reduced to 10% defective in each of the 900 shipments produced in the last nine months.

The manager of a large hardware store was sent a shipment of the 1990 model, and wanted to know whether it was one of the poor shipments produced early in 1990. (If so, he wanted to return it, or at least check it out, saw by saw.)

a. Before opening the shipment, what was the chance it was one of the poor ones?

b. He opened it, randomly drew out a saw, and tested it, and found it was defective. Now what is the chance it was one of the poor shipments?

***[3]3-28** Continuing Problem 3-27, calculate the chance it is one of the poor shipments if he:

a. Draws a second defective saw?

b. Draws a third defective saw?

***3-29** A small plane has gone down, and the search is organized into three regions. Starting with the likeliest, they are:

Region	*Initial Chance Plane is There*	*Chance of Being Overlooked in the Search*
Mountains	.50	.30
Prairie	.30	.20
Sea	.20	.90

The last column gives the chance that if the plane is there, it will not be found. For example, if it went down at sea, there is 90% chance it will have disappeared, or otherwise not be found.

Since the pilot is not equipped to long survive a crash in the mountains, it is particularly important to determine the chance that the plane went down in the mountains.

a. Before any search is started, what is this chance?

b. The initial search was in the mountains, and the plane was not found. Now what is the chance the plane is nevertheless in the mountains?

c. The search was continued over the other two regions, and unfortunately the plane was not found anywhere. Finally now what is the chance that the plane is in the mountains?

d. Write a few lines describing how and why the chances changed from **a** to **b** to **c.**

---

[3] As mentioned in the Preface, a star indicates a problem is more challenging, or requires optional starred material.

3-7 OTHER VIEWS OF PROBABILITY

In Section 3-1, we regarded probability as the limit of relative frequency. There are several other possible approaches, including *symmetric* probability, *axiomatic* probability, and *subjective* probability, which we shall treat in historical order.

A—SYMMETRIC PROBABILITY

Symmetric probability was first developed for fair games of chance such as dice, where the outcomes were equally likely. This permitted probabilities to be calculated even before the dice were thrown; the empirical determination (3-1) was not necessary, although it did provide a reassuring confirmation.

EXAMPLE 3-11
FAIR DICE: A CLASSIC CASE OF SYMMETRIC PROBABILITY

In throwing a single die, what is the probability of getting 3 or more?

SOLUTION

We already showed in Example 3-1 that since the die is symmetric, each outcome must have the same probability, ⅙. Thus:

$$\Pr(3 \text{ or more}) = \Pr(3 \text{ or } 4 \text{ or } 5 \text{ or } 6)$$

$$= \frac{1}{6} + \frac{1}{6} + \frac{1}{6} + \frac{1}{6} = \frac{4}{6} = .67$$

It is easy to generalize. Suppose an experiment has N equally probable outcomes altogether, and M of them constitute event E. Then

$$\boxed{\Pr(E) = \frac{M}{N}} \qquad (3\text{-}26)$$

Symmetric probability theory begins with (3-26) as the very definition of probability, and it is a little simpler than the relative frequency approach. However, it is severely limited because it lacks generality—it cannot even handle crooked dice.

Symmetric probability theory also has a major philosophical weakness. Note how the preamble to the definition (3-26) involved the phrase "equally probable." In using the word "probable" in defining probability, we are guilty of circular reasoning.

Our own relative frequency approach to probability suffers from the same philosophical weakness, incidentally. What sort of limit is meant in equation (3-2)? It is *logically* possible that the relative frequency f/n behaves badly, even in the limit; for example, no matter how often we toss a die, it is just conceivable that the ace will keep turning up every time, making $\lim f/n = 1$. Therefore, we should qualify equation (3-2) by stating that the limit occurs with high *probability*, not logical certainty. But then we would be using the concept of probability to define probability in (3-2)—circular reasoning again. To break such a circle, we shall turn next to an axiomatic approach.

B—AXIOMATIC PROBABILITY

All attempts so far to define probability have been weak because they require using probability itself within the definition of probability. The only philosophically satisfactory way to break this circular reasoning is to let probability be a basic undefined term. In such a mathematical model, we make no attempt to say what probability *really* is. We simply state the rules (*axioms*) that it follows.

Perhaps an analogy from chess will help. In chess, no attempt is made to define what a queen, for example, *really* is. Instead, a queen is merely characterized by the set of rules (axioms) she must obey: She can move any number of spaces, in any straight direction. She is no more and no less than this. Similar rules (axioms) are made for the other pieces, to complete the definition of the game. It is then possible to draw some conclusions (prove theorems) such as: A king and a rook can win against a king alone; a king and a knight cannot.

Axiomatic probability theory is like the game of chess. It starts with basic undefined terms and axioms, and from them draws conclusions (proves theorems), such as a carefully stated version of equation (3-2)—which is known as the theorem or law of large numbers. An example of how this "game of probability" works is illustrated in Appendix 3-7 at the end of the book.

In its intellectual content, of course, axiomatic probability theory is much richer than chess. Moreover, it leads to theorems that are useful in dealing with practical problems. These are, in fact, the same theorems that we have derived earlier in this chapter using our less abstract approach—and that we will find so useful in the rest of this book.

C—PERSONAL PROBABILITY

Personal or *subjective* probability is an attempt to deal with unique historical events that cannot be repeated, and therefore cannot be given any frequency interpretation. For example, consider events such as a doubling of the stock market average within the next decade, or the overthrow of a certain government within the next month. These events are described as "likely" or "unlikely," even though there is no hope of estimating this by observing their relative frequency. Nevertheless, their likelihood vitally influences policy decisions, and as a consequence must be estimated in some way. Only then can wise decisions be made on what risks are worth taking.

The key question, of course, is: How might we estimate, for example, Mary Smith's subjective probability that the stock market (Dow-Jones average) will double in the next decade? To answer this question, we could get her to compare her subjective probability of this event with some other well-defined *objective* probability. For example, which bet would she prefer: the bet that the stock market will double or that a penny will turn up heads? If she prefers to bet on the stock market doubling then her personal probability of this happening is clearly more than .50. This general approach can be used to "pin her down" even further, as we illustrate in the Problems.

D—ODDS

Instead of presenting yet another kind of probability, we will finally show how any kind of probability can be expressed as *odds*. In throwing a die, for example, recall that the probability of an ace is one in six:

$$\text{probability, } p = \frac{1}{6} = .167$$

The *odds* for an ace are defined as one to five:[4]

$$\text{odds, } d = \frac{1}{5} = .20$$

Note how the denominator has been changed from the six possible outcomes to the five outcomes *complementary* to an ace. In general, odds can be defined as:

$$\boxed{\textbf{odds, } d \equiv \frac{p}{1-p}} \qquad (3\text{-}27)$$

[4] For gamblers, odds occur naturally as the stakes in a fair wager, as an example will illustrate. Suppose I bet you that a die will turn up an ace. If I put $1 on the table, how much should you put up to make it fair? Since you would win the table 5 times as often in the long run, you ought to put up 5 times as much. So the stakes we put up should be in the ratio 1 to 5, that is, the odds for an ace.

Actually, gamblers customarily quote the odds the other way around. They say the odds *against* an ace (or a horse) are 5 to 1, and this means I should win $5 for every $1 bet.

Note that this does indeed give us the odds in our example, that is,

$$\text{the odds of getting an ace, } d = \frac{1/6}{1 - 1/6} = \frac{1}{5}$$

Of course, we can algebraically solve (3-27) to express p in terms of d:

$$p = \frac{d}{d+1} \tag{3-28}$$

In our example, knowledge that the odds for an ace are $d = 1/5$ would allow us to solve (3-28) for the probability of an ace, that is,

$$p = \frac{1/5}{1 + 1/5} = \frac{1}{6}$$

PROBLEMS

3-30 **a.** If you had your choice today between the following two bets, which would you take?
Election Bet: If the Democratic candidate wins the next presidential election, you will then win a $100 prize (and win nothing otherwise).
Jar Bet: A chip will be drawn at random from a jar containing 1 black chip and 999 white chips. If the chip turns out black, you will then win the $100 prize (and win nothing otherwise).

b. Repeat choice **a**, with a change—make the composition of the jar the opposite extreme: 999 black chips and 1 white chip.

c. Obviously, your answers in parts **a** and **b** depended on your subjective estimate of American politics; there were no objective "right answers." However, the number of chips in the urn were so lopsided that there undoubtedly is widespread agreement in part **a** to prefer the election bet, and in part **b** to prefer the jar bet. The question is: as you gradually increase the black chips from 1 to 999, at what point do you become indifferent between the two bets? Is it reasonable to call this your personal probability of a Democratic win?

3-31 Using the "calibrating jar" of Problem 3-30, roughly evaluate your personal probability that:

a. The Dow Jones average (of certain stock market prices) will advance at least 10% in the next twelve months.

b. U.S. population will increase at least 1% next year.

c. U.S. inflation will be at least 5% next year.

d. The next vice president of the U.S. will be a female.

e. The next president of your student council will be a female.

f. The next president of your student council will be a female, if the president is a senior student chosen at random.

g. At the next Superbowl game, the coin that is flipped (to determine the kickoff) will turn up heads.

h. Suppose you go to the largest Ford dealer in town, pick out a three-year-old used car, and offer 90% of the sticker price—cash, take it or leave it. What is your subjective probability that after a certain amount of huffing and bluffing, the dealer will finally accept your offer?

3-32 In Problem 3-31, for which answers do you think there will be least agreement among the students in your class? Most agreement? Which questions are amenable to a brief investigation that would result in everyone agreeing? (If you have time in class, check out your answers.)

3-33 Do you think the following conclusions are valid? If not, correct them:

i. Certain probabilities (as in part g of Problem 3-31) are agreed upon by practically everybody; we may call them "objective probabilities."

ii. Other probabilities (as in parts **a** or **c**) are disagreed upon, even by experts; we may call them "subjective probabilities."

iii. But in between, there is a continuous range of probabilities that are subjective to a greater or lesser degree.

3-34 From a deck of 52 cards you are dealt one face down. What is **(i)** the chance and **(ii)** the odds that the card will turn out to be:

a. A club?

b. A black card?

c. An ace?

d. An honor card (A, K, Q, or J)?

e. The same denomination as the next card to be dealt (for example, a Queen followed by another Queen)?

***f.** A higher denomination than the next card to be dealt?

CHAPTER 3 SUMMARY

3-1 Probability is just the proportion that emerges in the long run, as the experiment is endlessly repeated (the sample size n grows larger and larger). The abbreviation Pr can therefore be thought of as representing *proportion* or *percentage*, as well as *probability*.

3-2 Probability trees break a complex experiment into small manageable stages. At each stage, the various outcomes are represented by branches, and so the tree eventually represents the whole outcome set.

3-3 An event is just a collection of individual outcomes, and its probability is just the sum of the individual probabilities. From this first principle, we can easily find the probability of G or H by addition:

$$\Pr(G \text{ or } H) = \Pr(G) + \Pr(H) - \Pr(G \text{ and } H)$$

3-4 The probability of G and H is obtained by multiplication:

$$\Pr(G \text{ and } H) = \Pr(G)\,\Pr(H|G)$$

This multiplication principle is so natural, in fact, that it was used in probability trees without formal introduction.

3-5 An event F is called independent of another event E, if the probability of F remains the same after E has occurred:

$$\Pr(F|E) = \Pr(F)$$

3-6 Bayes Theorem is simply a clever use of conditional probability to reverse probability trees. It combines prior probabilities with sample information (in the original tree) to obtain the posterior probabilities (in the reversed tree).

3-7 As well as the relative-frequency view, other views of probability are of interest: symmetric probability in fair games; axiomatic probability in mathematics; and subjective probability, which is increasingly important whenever human judgment is required—as in business or social science.

REVIEW PROBLEMS

3-35 Suppose that A and B are independent events, with $\Pr(A) = .6$ and $\Pr(B) = .2$. What is:

a. $\Pr(A|B)$?

b. $\Pr(A \text{ and } B)$?

c. $\Pr(A \text{ or } B)$?

3-36 Repeat Problem 3-35 if A and B are mutually exclusive instead of independent.

3-37 Kevin Stern, marketing VP for a corporation manufacturing small pleasure craft, must decide whether or not to enter the sailboard market with an inexpensive new model. The high initial cost of its development and promotion can only be justified if it captures 10% or more of the market.

To estimate the potential market share, he contacts a random survey of 200 potential buyers, who are given a hypothetical choice between buying this model at $950, or an alternative. Their responses are classified in the first column of the table below.

Response	Frequency of Response	Estimated Probability of Buying
"Would definitely buy it"	24	40%
"Would probably buy it"	46	20%
"Would maybe buy it"	34	8%
"Would not buy it"	96	1%
	$n = 200$	

From bitter experience with similar surveys, Kevin has learned that of all those who say they will "definitely buy it," only 40% actually do. This estimated probability of buying is listed in the last column, varying from 40% at the top to 1% at the bottom. (For similar examples, see Schwarz 1978.)

a. Estimate the market share (i.e., the proportion who would actually buy the model). Does it surpass the 10% target?

b. Of those who buy it, what proportion had earlier felt they would "definitely buy it?"

3-38 To reduce theft, suppose a company proposes to screen its workers with a lie-detector test that has been proven correct 90% of the time (for guilty subjects, and also for innocent subjects). The company would fire all the workers who fail the test. Suppose also that 5% of the workers steal from time to time.

a. Of the fired workers, what proportion would actually be innocent?

b. Of the remaining workers not fired, what proportion would still steal from time to time?

3-39 A national survey of couples showed that 30% of the wives watched a certain TV program, and 50% of the husbands. Also, if the wife watched, the probability that the husband watched increased to 60%. For a couple drawn at random, what is the probability that:

a. The couple both watch?

b. At least one watches?

c. Neither watches?

d. If the husband watches, the wife watches?

e. If the husband does not watch, the wife watches?

f. Answer True or False; if false correct it: The unconditional probability that the wife watches is somewhere between the two conditional probabilities given in parts **d** and **e.**

3-40 For various forms of transportation, the 1975–78 U.S. death rates were approximately as follows (deaths per billion passenger miles):

Car	16
Train	0.84
Scheduled airline	0.35

a. Graph these rates.

b. Suppose you travel about 20,000 miles per year. Over a remaining lifetime of 60 years, what is your approximate chance of being killed in an accident if you traveled:

i. Always by car?
ii. Always by plane?
iii. By car or plane, 50-50?

c. What assumptions did you make in **b**?

3-41 Yesterday I bought a packet of inexpensive videotapes and wondered whether they might be defective. I learned that 20% of the packets in the store came from a now-bankrupt wholesaler, with an appalling record of supplying 15% defective tapes. The remaining packets came from a new wholesaler, with a much improved record of only 1% defective tapes.

a. What is the chance that the first videotape I draw from the packet is defective?

b. As luck would have it, the first tape was indeed defective. Now what is the chance that the second tape I draw from the packet is defective?

3-42 Suppose that the last three men out of a restaurant all lose their hat checks, so that the hostess hands back their three hats in random order. What is the probability:

a. That no man will get the right hat?

b. That exactly one man will?

c. That exactly two men will?

d. That all three men will?

3-43 Find (without bothering to multiply out the final answer) the probability that:

a. A group of 3 people (picked at random) all have different birthdays?

b. A group of 30 people all have different birthdays?

c. In a group of 30 people there are at least two people with the same birthday?

d. What assumptions did you make above?

3-44 On November 24, 1968, two hijackings occurred on the same day, and made the front page of the *New York Times*. How unusual and newsworthy is such a coincidence? (Glick, 1970) To answer this question, the following data are relevant: During the 4 winter months November–February, there are 120 days, and it turns out that there were 22 hijackings. If we assume that the hijackings are independent and apt to occur equally likely on any day, what is the probability that in a 120-day period with 22 hijackings, there will be some day when two or more hijackings occur? (Hint: do Problem 3-43 first.)

3-45 True or False? If false, correct it:

a. When two events are independent, the occurrence of one event will not change the probability of the second event.

b. Two events are mutually exclusive if they have no outcomes in common.

c. A and B are mutually exclusive if $\Pr(A \text{ and } B) = \Pr(A)\Pr(B)$.

d. If a fair coin has been fairly tossed 5 times and has come up tails each time, on the sixth toss the conditional probability of tails will be $1/64$.

3-46 ***A Final Challenge: How to Guarantee Questionnaire Security***

In Chapter 1, we saw how random selection guaranteed fairness. Now let us look at yet another ingenious use of randomization—to guarantee anonymity in a sensitive area of survey sampling.

Suppose, for example, that we are taking a survey to determine what proportion of executives have ever engaged in "inside trading" (using privileged information about a company's financial position to gain an illegal advantage in trading its stock). What executive would truthfully admit to this without an absolute guarantee of being untraceable (anonymous)?

Let us therefore phrase our survey with airtight protection. Each executive interviewed could be asked to privately flip a coin, and then:

i. If it turns up tails, answer the question "Have you ever engaged in inside trading?"

ii. If it turns up heads, flip it again and now answer "Did the coin come up heads this second time?"

Suppose the executive returns with the answer "Yes." There is no possible way for the interviewer to know whether this came from inside trading, or merely a second head. Thus anonymity is guaranteed. This is not only good ethics, but good science too, since allowing people to be honest eliminates bias.

Although it is impossible for us to ascertain anything about the individual, can we nevertheless find out what we need to know about the population? Let us see.

a. Suppose the proportion of executives who had actually engaged in inside trading is $A = 20\%$, for example. What proportion Y would answer "Yes" to the interviewer?

b. Find the equation relating Y to A in general. Then solve for A in terms of Y.

c. In the actual survey, suppose 30% answered "Yes" to the interviewer. Estimate the proportion of all executives who have actually engaged in inside trading.

d. What assumptions are you making to get the answers above?

CHAPTER 4

Probability Distributions

The
normal
law of error
stands out in
the experience of
mankind as one of the
broadest generalizations of
natural philosophy. It serves
as the guiding instrument in
researches in the physical and social
sciences and in medicine, agriculture,
and engineering. It is an indispensable
tool for the analysis and the interpretation of the
basic data obtained by observation and experiment.

W. J. YOUDEN

4-1 DISCRETE RANDOM VARIABLES

A—PROBABILITY DISTRIBUTIONS

Suppose a couple plan to have 3 children, and are interested in the number of girls they might have. This is an example of a *random variable* and is customarily denoted by a capital letter:

$$X = \text{the number of girls}$$

The possible values of X are 0, 1, 2, 3; however, they are not equally likely. To find what the probabilities are, we must examine the original sample space. Already calculated in Figure 3-3, it is repeated in Figure 4-1 (taking the more accurate model where the probability of a boy on each birth is .52). Thus, for example, the event "exactly one girl" ($X = 1$) consists of three outcomes, each having probability .13; hence its probability is

$$.13 + .13 + .13 = 3(.13) = .39 \tag{4-1}$$

Similarly, the probability of each of the other events is computed. Thus, in Figure 4-1 we obtain the *probability distribution* of X shown on the right. This illustrates the key idea of a random variable:

A discrete random variable takes on various values x with probabilities specified by its probability distribution *p*(x).	(4-2)

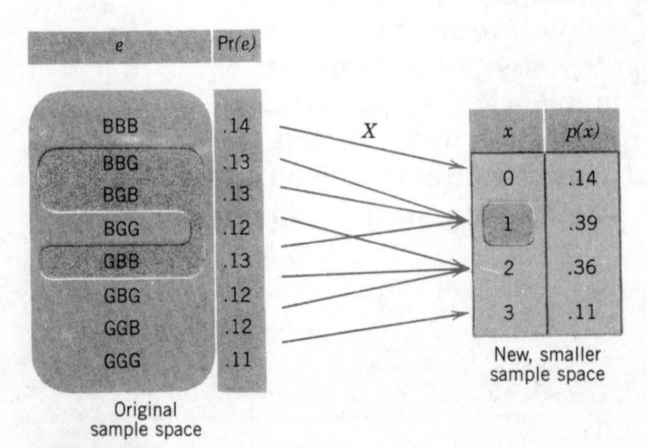

FIGURE 4-1
The random variable X = number of girls.

In Figure 4-1, the original sample space on the left has been reduced to a new, more convenient numerical sample space on the right. The original sample space was introduced to enable us to calculate the probability distribution $p(x)$ for the new space; having served its purpose, the old unwieldy space is then forgotten. The interesting questions can be answered very easily in the new space. For example, referring to Figure 4-1, what is the probability of fewer than 2 girls? We simply add up the relevant probabilities in the new sample space:

$$\begin{aligned}\Pr(X < 2) &= p(0) + p(1) \\ &= .14 + .39 = .53\end{aligned} \tag{4-3}$$

Figure 4-2 illustrates this calculation.

*B—A MORE RIGOROUS TREATMENT

Although the intuitive definition of a random variable in (4-2) is usually good enough, in this brief optional section we give a more careful definition. As Figure 4-1 shows, the random variable X associates each outcome e with a number x. This relation is shown by the blue arrows, and is a kind of function. In fact, a random variable is mathematically defined just this way—as a *numerical-valued function defined over a sample space.*

This definition stresses the random variable's relation to the original sample space. Thus, for example, the random variable Y = the number of boys, is clearly a different function (random variable) than X = the number of girls. Yet, if boys and girls were equally likely on each birth, X and Y would have the *same probability distribution*, and anyone who used the loose definition (4-2) might be deceived into thinking that they were the *same random variable*. In conclusion, there is more to a random variable than its probability distribution.

These ideas will be easier to keep in mind if we use appropriate notation. A *capital* letter such as X represents a random variable, while small x represents a specific value that it may take. If these values are 0, 1, 2, . . . , then they form the new small sample space. Their probabilities are denoted $p(0)$, $p(1)$, $p(2)$, . . . , or $p(x)$ in general. This notation, like any

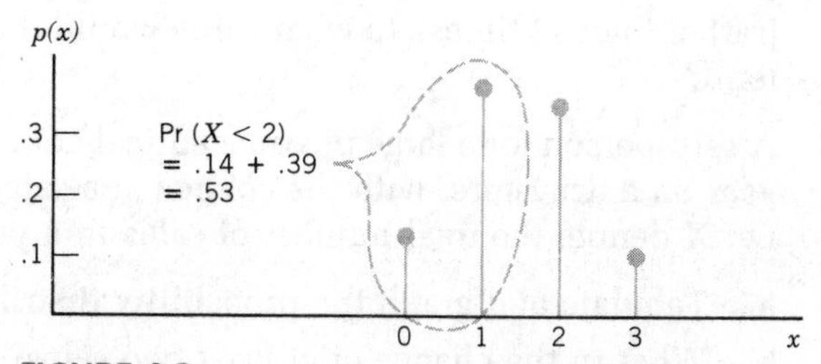

FIGURE 4-2
The graph of the probability distribution in Figure 4-1.

other, may be regarded simply as an abbreviation for convenience. Thus, for example, to denote "the probability of one girl" we can write:

$$\Pr(X = 1) \text{ or just } p(1)$$

Finally, we emphasize the difference between *discrete* and *continuous* variables. A random variable is called *discrete* if it has just a finite (or "countably infinite") set of values. For example, when X = the number of heads in 3 tosses of a coin, then its values are 0, 1, 2, 3—a finite set. Or if X = the number of tosses required to get the first head, then its values are 1, 2, 3, 4, 5, . . .—a "countably infinite" set.

By contrast, a *continuous* random variable takes on a continuum of values. For example, if X = the number of gallons that pass hourly through a meter with a capacity of 50 gallons per hour, then its value could be *any* number between 0 and 50—for example, 17.2 or 39.826. The mathematics required for continuous random variables is more advanced, requiring integration (the analog of summation in calculus).

PROBLEMS

4-1 In planning a family of 3 children, assume boys and girls are equally likely on each birth. Find the probability distribution of:

a. X = the number of girls

b. Y = the number of runs (where a "run" is a run or string of children of the same sex. For example Y = 2 for the outcome BGG).

4-2 Simulate the experiment in Problem 4-1 by using the random numbers in Appendix Table I (even number = heads, odd = tails). Repeat this experiment 50 times, tabulating the frequency of X. Then calculate:

a. The relative frequency distribution.

b. The mean $\overline{X}$.

c. The variance s^2.

4-3 If the experiment in Problem 4-2 were repeated millions of times (rather than 50 times), to what value would the calculated quantities tend?

4-4 A salesperson for a large pharmaceutical company makes 3 calls per year on a drugstore, with the chance of a sale each time being 80%. Let X denote the total number of sales in a year (0, 1, 2, or 3).

a. Tabulate and graph the probability distribution p(x).

b. What in the chance of at least two sales?

4-5 Repeat Problem 4-4 under the different assumption that "nothing succeeds like success." Specifically, while the chance of a sale on the first call is still 80%, the chance of a sale on later calls depends on what happened on the previous call, being 90% if the previous call was a sale, or 40% if the previous call was no sale.

4-2 MEAN AND VARIANCE

In Chapter 2 we calculated the mean $\overline{X}$ and variance s^2 of a sample of observations from its relative frequency distribution (f/n). In the same way, it is natural to calculate the mean and variance of a random variable from its probability distribution $p(x)$:

$$\text{Mean } \mu \equiv \Sigma x p(x) \quad (4\text{-}4) \text{ like (2-20)}$$

$$\text{Variance } \sigma^2 \equiv \Sigma(x - \mu)^2 p(x) \quad (4\text{-}5) \text{ like (2-21) and (2-23)}$$

Here we are following the usual custom of reserving Greek letters for theoretical values (μ is the Greek letter mu, equivalent to m for mean, and σ is the Greek letter sigma, equivalent to s for standard deviation). Of course, probabilities can be viewed as just the long-run relative frequencies from the population of all possible repetitions of the experiment. Thus we often call μ and σ^2 the *population* moments, to distinguish them from the *sample* moments $\overline{X}$ and s^2 that are calculated for a mere sample. Table 4-1 makes this clear.

TABLE 4-1 A Comparison of Sample and Population Moments

Sample Moments *Use Relative Frequencies f/n*	*Population Moments (in Greek)* *Use Probabilities p(x)* *(long-run f/n)*
Sample Mean	Population Mean
$\overline{X} = \Sigma x \left(\frac{f}{n}\right)$	$\mu \equiv \Sigma x p(x)$
Sample Variance	Population Variance
$s^2 \simeq \text{MSD} = \Sigma(x - \overline{X})^2 \left(\frac{f}{n}\right)$	$\sigma^2 \equiv \Sigma(x - \mu)^2 p(x)$

The calculation of σ^2 can often be simplified by using an alternative formula developed in Appendix 4-2:

$$\sigma^2 = \Sigma x^2 p(x) - \mu^2 \tag{4-6}$$

EXAMPLE 4-1

HOW MANY GIRLS IN THE AVERAGE FAMILY?

Again consider X = the number of girls in a family of 3 children. Using its probability distribution derived in Figure 4-1, calculate the mean, variance, and standard deviation of X.

SOLUTION

The computations are similar to Table 2-8, and are set out in Table 4-2.

REMARKS

To calculate σ^2, the alternative formula (4-6) was easier. It required calculating just the last column of Table 4-2, instead of the previous three columns required by the definition (4-5).

Also note that $\sigma = \sqrt{.75} = .87$ is indeed the typical deviation, lying between the largest deviation 1.56 and smallest deviation .44 (found in the fourth column).

Since the definitions of μ and σ are similar to those of $\overline{X}$ and s, we find similar interpretations. We continue to think of the mean μ as the balanc-

TABLE 4-2 Calculation of the Mean and Variance of X = number of girls

Given Probability Distribution		*Calculation of μ using (4-4)*	*Calculation of σ^2 Using (4-5)*			*Or, Easier Calculation of σ^2 Using (4-6): Multiply 1st and 3rd Columns*
x	$p(x)$	$xp(x)$	$(x-\mu)$	$(x-\mu)^2$	$(x-\mu)^2p(x)$	$x^2p(x)$
0	.14	0	−1.44	2.07	.29	0
1	.39	.39	− .44	.19	.08	.39
2	.36	.72	.56	.31	.11	1.44
3	.11	.33	1.56	2.43	.27	.99
		$\mu = 1.44$			$\sigma^2 = .75$	$\Sigma x^2p(x) = 2.82$ $\mu^2 = 2.07$ Difference $\sigma^2 = .75\checkmark$

ing point—a weighted average using probability weights rather than relative frequency weights. And the standard deviation σ is the typical deviation.

We emphasize that the distinction between sample and population moments must not be forgotten: μ is called the population mean since it is based on the population of all possible repetitions of the experiment; on the other hand, we call $\overline{X}$ the sample mean since it is based on a mere sample drawn from the parent population.

PROBLEMS

4-6 Compute μ and σ for each of the following distributions (from Problems 4-4 and 4-5). Graph each distribution, showing the mean as the balancing point, and the standard deviation as a typical deviation (like Figure 2-6).

a.

x	p(x)
0	.01
1	.10
2	.38
3	.51

b.

x	p(x)
0	.07
1	.10
2	.18
3	.65

4-7 On the basis of past experience, the buyer for a large sports store estimates that the number of 10-speed bicycles sold next year will be somewhere between 40 and 90—with the following distribution:

Number of Bicycles Sold x	*Probability* p(x)
40	.05
50	.15
60	.41
70	.34
80	.04
90	.01

a. What is the mean number sold? What is the standard deviation?

b. If 60 are ordered, what is the chance they will all be sold? What is the chance some will be left over (undesired inventory)?

c. To be almost sure (95%) of having enough bicycles, how many should be ordered?

4-8 In planning a huge outdoor concert for June 16, the producer estimates the attendance will depend on the weather according to the following table. He also finds out from the local weather office what the weather has been like, for June days in the past 10 years.

Weather	*Attendance*	*Relative Frequency*
wet, cold	5,000	.20
wet, warm	20,000	.20
dry, cold	30,000	.10
dry, warm	50,000	.50

a. What is the expected (mean) attendance?

b. The tickets will sell for $9 each. The costs will be $2 per person for cleaning and crowd control, plus $150,000 for the band, plus $60,000 for administration (including the facilities). Would you advise the producer to go ahead with the concert, or not? Why?

4-9 In Problem 4-8, suppose the producer has gone ahead with his plans, and on June 10 has obtained some rather gloomy long-run weather forecasts: The 4 weather conditions now have probabilities .30, .20, .20, and .30, respectively.

If he cancels the concert, he will still have to pay half of the $60,000 administration cost, plus a $15,000 cancellation penalty to the band.

Would you advise him to cancel or not?

4-3 THE BINOMIAL DISTRIBUTION

A—THE BINOMIAL ASSUMPTIONS AND FORMULA

There are many types of discrete random variables, and the commonest is called the *binomial*. The classical example of a binomial variable is:

$$S = \text{number of heads in several tosses of a coin.}$$

There are many random variables of this binomial type, a few of which are listed in Table 4-3. (We have already encountered not only the coin-tossing example, but also another: the number of girls in a family of three children.) To handle all such cases, it will be helpful to state the basic assumptions in general notation:

1. We suppose there are n *trials* (tosses of the coin).
2. In each trial, a certain event of interest can occur, or fail to occur; then we say a *success* (head) or *failure* (tail) has occurred. Their respective

TABLE 4-3 Examples of Binomial Variables

Trial	*"Success"*	*"Failure"*	π	n	S
Tossing a fair coin	Head	Tail	1/2	Number of tosses	Number of heads altogether
Birth of a child in a family	Girl	Boy	.48 ≃ 1/2	Number of children	Number of girls in the family
Pure guessing on a multiple choice question (with 5 choices, say)	Correct	Wrong	1/5	Number of questions on exam	Number of correct answers
Randomly drawing a voter in a poll	Republican	Democrat or other non-Republican	Proportion of Republicans in the population	Size of poll	Number of Republicans in the sample
Randomly drawing an item from a day's production	Item is satis-factory	Item is defective	Proportion of satis-factory items in the day's output	Size of sample	Number of satis-factory items in the sample

probabilities are denoted by π and $(1 - \pi)$, and these do not change from trial to trial.

3. Finally, we assume the trials are *statistically independent.*

Then S, the total number of successes in n trials, is called a binomial variable. A formula for its probability distribution p(s) can be easily derived—as we already found in Figure 4-1: When each child has a .48 chance of being a girl, the probability of exactly 1 girl in a family of 3 children was:

$$p(1) = 3(.48)^1(.52)^2 = .39 \tag{4-7}$$

like (4-1) and (3-4)

The general binomial formula is similar (a formal derivation is given in Appendix 4-3): When each trial has probability π of success, the probability of exactly s successes in n trials is

Binomial distribution

$$p(s) = \binom{n}{s} \pi^s(1 - \pi)^{n-s} \tag{4-8}$$

The *binomial coefficient* $\binom{n}{s}$ is defined by[1]

$$\boxed{\binom{n}{s} \equiv \frac{n!}{s!(n-s)!}} \qquad (4\text{-}9)$$

where, in turn, the *factorial* n! is given by

$$\boxed{n! \equiv n(n-1)(n-2) \cdots 1} \qquad (4\text{-}10)$$

For example, the binomial coefficient $\binom{3}{1}$ is:

$$\binom{3}{1} = \frac{3!}{1!2!}$$
$$= \frac{3 \cdot 2 \cdot 1}{(1)(2 \cdot 1)} = 3$$

We can confirm that the general binomial formula does indeed cover the probability of exactly 1 girl in (4-7) as a special case. We simply substitute $n = 3$, $\pi = .48$, and $s = 1$ into (4-8):

$$p(1) = \binom{3}{1} (.48)^1(.52)^2$$
$$= 3(.13) = .39 \qquad (4\text{-}7) \text{ verified}$$

In using (4-8), we must emphasize the most important assumption: The binomial distribution is appropriate only if the trials are *independent*. As an example of independence, knowing that the first toss of a coin has come up heads will not affect the probability of a head on the second toss, if the coin is properly tossed.

However, if the coin is poorly tossed (e.g., tossed so that it is likely to do just one complete flip), then knowing that the first toss is heads will increase the probability of heads on the second toss; this is an example of dependence.

As another example of independence, suppose you are drawing two cards from a deck and you *replace* the first before drawing the second. Then the chance of, say an ace on the second draw is 4/52, independent of whatever the card on the first draw happened to be.

---

[1] $\binom{n}{s}$ is the number of combinations of n things taken s at a time. The special cases $\binom{n}{n}$ and $\binom{n}{0}$ are not covered by (4-9), but are independently defined to equal 1. This enables (4-8) to give the correct answer even when $s = n$ or $s = 0$.

On the other hand, if you *keep out* the first card, your chances on the second draw are altered, since you can't get that first card again. Thus if the first card is an ace, the chance of the second card being an ace is reduced to 3/51; if the first card is a non-ace, the chance of the second card being an ace is increased to 4/51. This is another example of dependence, where the binomial (4-8) cannot be applied.

B—SAMPLING FROM A LARGE POPULATION

To see how extraordinarily useful the binomial model can be, here is another very common example.

EXAMPLE 4-2

QUALITY CONTROL FOR MICROWAVE OVENS

Suppose that a production run of 40,000 microwave ovens includes 32,000 (80%) that are flawless, requiring absolutely no adjustments. But the quality control department, not knowing this 80% figure, takes a random sample of 10 ovens to estimate the overall quality.

What is the chance that the sample will be evenly split—5 flawless, 5 not?

SOLUTION

Let's see if we can apply the binomial formula. Each of the 10 successive ovens in the sample can be considered a "trial," so $n = 10$.

For the first oven, the probability of "success" (a flawless oven) is 32,000/40,000 = .800. Depending on whether this first oven was a success or not, the second oven then has a probability of success equal to 31,999/39,999 or 32,000/39,999. But to three decimals, we get .800 either way. So the second trial is *practically* independent of the first, and has the same probability of success, $\pi = .800$.

This kind of argument holds for the rest of the 10 ovens too, so that we do indeed have, for all practical purposes, a binomial distribution. We therefore substitute $n = 10$, $\pi = .80$ and $s = 5$ into (4-8):

$$\begin{aligned} p(5) &= \binom{10}{5}(.80)^5(.20)^5 \\ &= \frac{10 \times 9 \times 8 \times 7 \times 6 \times 5 \times 4 \times 3 \times 2 \times 1}{(5 \times 4 \times 3 \times 2 \times 1)(5 \times 4 \times 3 \times 2 \times 1)}(.80)^5(.20)^5 \\ &= 252(.000105) = .026 \simeq 3\% \end{aligned} \tag{4-11}$$

That is, in a random sample of 10 ovens, there is a 3% chance that 5 will be flawless and 5 will not.

In our earlier example of cards, we found that successive draws were *not* independent, because the population was small (52 cards in the deck); the probability of drawing an ace *did* depend on what we had drawn before.

But in Example 4-2, we are drawing from such a large population (40,000 microwave ovens) that each draw is *practically*—though not perfectly—independent of the others; π remains practically .800, no matter what we may have drawn before.

This independence of successive draws from a *large* population is a common theme—recurring again, for instance, in Example 4-3 below.

C—A SHORTCUT: USE BINOMIAL TABLES

In practice, it is a nuisance calculating binomial coefficients and binomial probabilities by hand. Why not let the computer do them once and for all? In Appendix Table IIIa we give the printout for some binomial coefficients$\binom{n}{s}$. And in Table IIIb we give the printout for some binomial probabilities $p(s)$ computed from (4-8). With these, we could find the answer in Example 4-2 very easily. In Table IIIb we simply look up $n = 10$, $\pi = .80$, and $s = 5$. This immediately gives .026 as the probability for a 5-5 split, which confirms (4-11).

Incidentally, wouldn't the sample be more likely to split 8-2 (the same 80%—20% split as the population)? This is the kind of "representativeness" that would make random sampling attractive. A quick glance down Table IIIb confirms this conjecture: The most likely number of flawless is indeed $s = 8$, where $p(s)$ has a peak value of .302.

Another example will show how useful binomial tables can be.

EXAMPLE 4-3

HOW RELIABLE IS A SMALL POLL?

A sample of 5 voters is to be randomly drawn from the U.S. population, when 60% vote Republican (as in the 1984 U.S. presidential election, for example, when Reagan defeated Mondale).

a. The number of Republican voters in this sample of 5 can vary anywhere from 0 to 5. Tabulate its probability distribution.

b. Calculate the mean and standard deviation.

c. What is the probability of exactly 3 Republican voters in the sample?

d. Calculate the probability that the sample will have a majority of Republican voters (that is, at least 3) and thus will correctly reflect the population majority.

e. Graph your answers above.

SOLUTION

a. Each voter who is drawn constitutes a trial. On each such trial, the probability of a Republican voter (success) is $\pi = .60$. In a total of $n = 5$ trials, we want the probability of S successes, where $S = 0, 1, \ldots, 5$. So we simply look up Appendix Table IIIb and copy down the distribution for $n = 5$ and $\pi = .60$.

(a) Distribution		*(b) Mean*	*Standard Deviation*		
s	$p(s)$	$sp(s)$	$s - \mu$	$(s - \mu)^2$	$(s - \mu)^2 p(s)$
0	.010	0	−3	9	.090
1	.077	.077	−2	4	.308
2	.230	.460	−1	1	.230
3	.346	1.038	0	0	0
4	.259	1.036	1	1	.259
5	.078	.390	2	4	.312
	1.000	$\mu = 3.00$			variance $\sigma^2 = 1.20$ st. dev. $\sigma = 1.10$

c. From the table, we find:

$$p(3) = .346 \simeq 35\%$$

d. From the table, we add up:

$$p(3) + p(4) + p(5) = .346 + .259 + .078 = .683 \simeq 68\% \tag{4-12}$$

e.

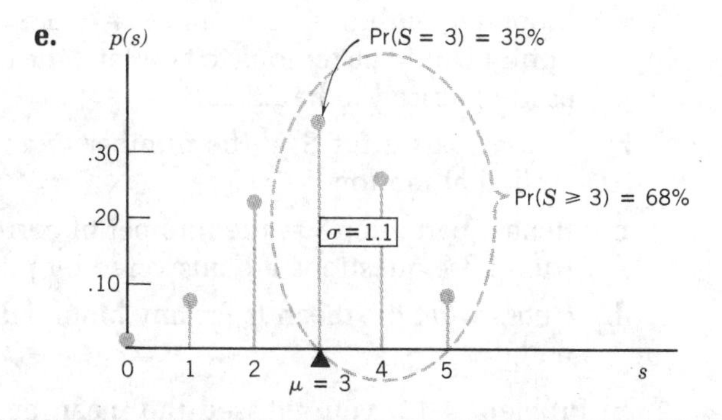

In practice, we often want to add up a string of probabilities as in Example 4-3. Again, why not let the computer do it once and for all? In Appendix Table IIIc, we give the computer output for the sum of the probabilities in the right-hand tail—called the *cumulative* binomial probability. For instance, we could find the answer in Example 4-3**d** very easily. In Table IIIc we simply look up $n = 5$, $\pi = .60$, and $s_0 = 3$. This immediately gives the answer .683, which confirms (4-12).

PROBLEMS

4-10 In families with 6 children, let X = the number of boys. For simplicity, assume that births are independent and boys and girls are equally likely.

a. Graph the probability distribution of X.

b. Calculate the mean and standard deviation, and show them on the graph.

c. Of all families with 6 children, what proportion have:

i. Exactly an even split between the sexes (3-3)?

ii. Nearly an even split (3-3, or 4-2)?

iii. 3 or more boys?

4-11 In a desperate gamble, Wildcat Oil Exploration has committed all its remaining funds to finance a sequence of 12 drillings. Each drilling in this region has a 20% chance of successfully producing oil, independent of the other drillings.

To avoid bankruptcy, three or more drillings must produce oil. What is the chance of this?

4-12 **a.** One hundred coins are spilled at random on the table, and the total number of heads S is counted. The distribution of S is binomial, with $n =$ ____ and $\pi =$ ____. Although this distribution would be tedious to tabulate, the *average* (mean) of S is easily guessed to be ____.

b. Repeat part **a** for S = the number of aces when 30 dice are spilled at random.

c. Repeat part **a** for S = the number of correct answers when 20 true–false questions are answered by pure guessing.

d. Guess what the mean is for *any* binomial variable, in terms of n and π.

4-13 In Problem 4-12, you guessed the mean of a binomial variable. There is also a formula for the standard deviation (both formulas will be proved later, in Problem 6-23):

$$\textbf{Binomial mean: } \mu = n\pi \qquad \textbf{Standard deviation: } \sigma = \sqrt{n\pi(1-\pi)} \tag{4-13}$$

Now that you understand these formulas, you can use them whenever it is convenient. For example,

a. Verify μ and σ found earlier in Problem 4-10.

b. Calculate μ and σ for Problem 4-11.

4-14 A multiple choice exam consists of 12 questions, each having 5 possible answers. To pass, you must answer at least 8 out of 12 questions correctly. What is the chance of this, if:

a. You go into the exam without knowing a thing, and have to resort to pure guessing?

b. You have studied enough so that on each question, 3 choices can be eliminated. But then you have to make a pure guess between the remaining 2 choices.

c. You have studied enough so that you know *for sure* the correct answer on 2 questions. For the remaining 10 questions you have to resort to pure guessing.

4-15 a. Suppose a warship takes 10 shots at a target, and it takes at least 4 hits to sink it. If the warship has a record of hitting with 20% of its shots in the long run, what is the chance of sinking the target?

b. What crucial assumptions did you make in part **a**? Why might they be questionable?

c. To appreciate these crucial assumptions, put yourself in the position of the captain of the British battleship *Prince of Wales* in World War II. The gunners on the German *Bismark* have just homed in on the British *Hood*, and sunk it after several shots. They now turn their fire on you, and after an initial miss they make a direct hit. Do you leave the probability they will hit you on the next shot unchanged, or do you revise it? (In that actual situation, the captain of the *Prince of Wales* broke off the action, and the *Bismark* was sunk by the British a few days later.)

***4-16 a.** The governing board of a small corporation consists of the chairman and six other members, with a majority vote among these seven deciding any given issue. Suppose that the chairman wants to pass a certain motion, but is not sure of its support. Suppose the other six members vote independently, each with probability 40% of voting for the motion. What is the chance that it will pass?

b. If the chairman had two firm allies who were certain to vote for the motion, how would that improve the chances of its passing? [Assume that the other four members are the same as in part **a**.]

c. Go back to the same model as in part **a**, except now assume that two board members are political allies of the chairman, and gather privately with him beforehand. All three agree to vote within their private group to determine their majority position, and then go into the general meeting with a solid block of three votes to support that position. Does this help or hinder the chances of the chairman's motion passing? How much?

d. Does this illustrate the motto "united we stand, divided we fall"? Why?

e. Do you think this helps the democratic process? Why?

4-4 CONTINUOUS DISTRIBUTIONS

In Figure 2-2 we saw how a continuous variable such as men's height could be represented by a bar graph showing relative frequencies. This graph is reproduced in Figure 4-3*a* (with men's height now measured in feet rather than inches; furthermore, the Y-axis has been shrunk to the same scale as the X-axis). The sum of all the relative frequencies (i.e., the sum of all the *lengths* of the bars) in Figure 4-3*a* is of course 1, as first noted in Table 2-2.

We now find it convenient to change the vertical scale to relative frequency *density* in panel (*b*), a rescaling that makes the total area (i.e., the

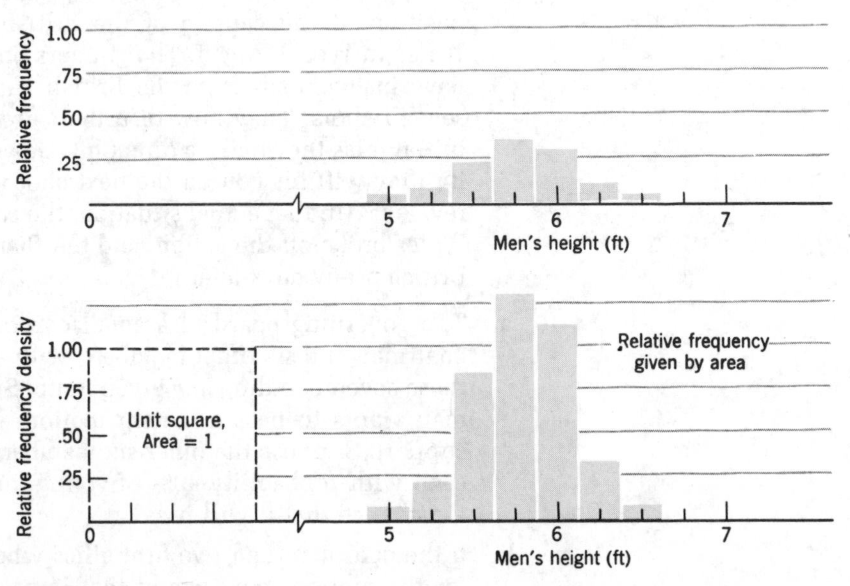

FIGURE 4-3
(a) Relative frequency histogram with the sum of the lengths of the bars = 1. (b) Rescaled into relative frequency density, making the sum of the areas of the bars = 1.

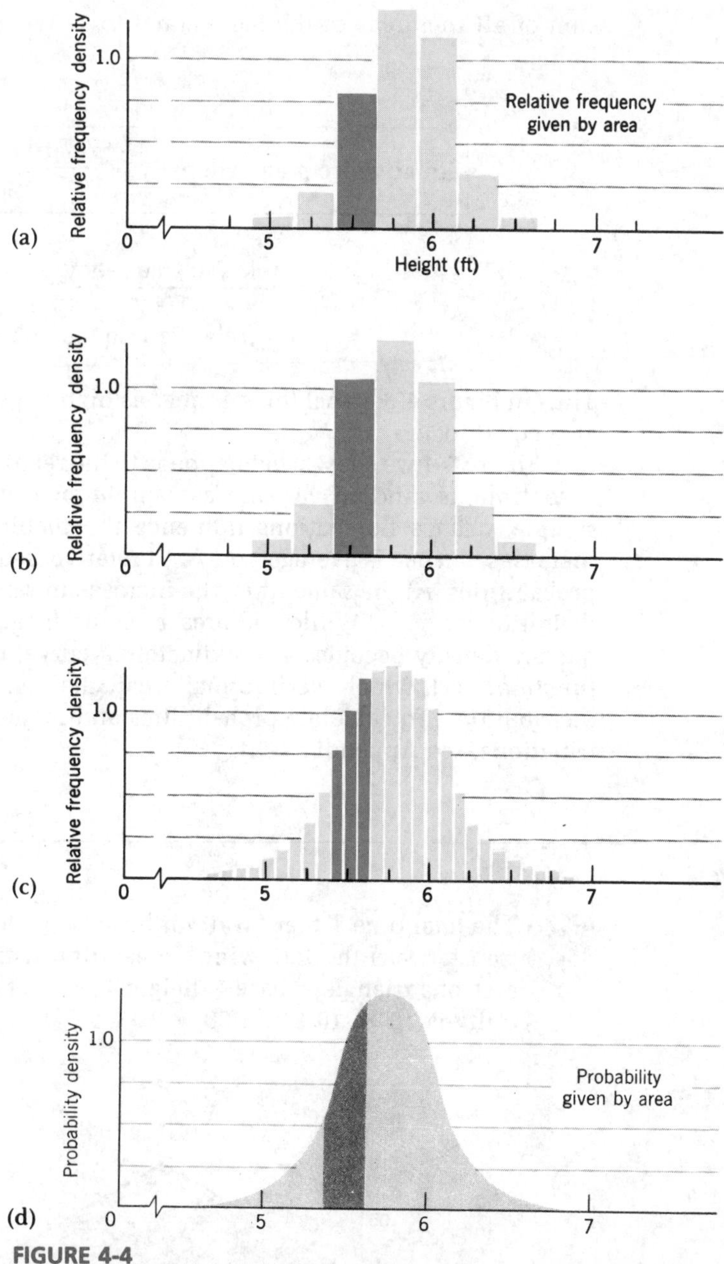

FIGURE 4-4

How relative frequency density may be approximated by a probability density as sample size increases, and cell size decreases. (a) Small n, as in Figure 4-3b. (b) Large enough n to stabilize relative frequencies. (c) Even larger n, to permit finer cells while keeping relative frequencies stable. (d) For very large n, this becomes (approximately) a smooth probability density curve.

sum of all the *areas* of the bars) equal to 1. We accomplish this by defining:

$$\boxed{\text{Relative frequency density} \equiv \frac{\text{relative frequency}}{\text{cell width}}} \tag{4-14}$$

$$= \frac{\text{relative frequency}}{1/4}$$
$$= 4\ (\text{relative frequency}) \tag{4-15}$$

Thus in Figure 4-3, panel (*b*) is 4 times as high as panel (*a*) and now has an area equal to 1.

In Figure 4-4 we show what happens to the relative frequency density of a continuous random variable as sample size increases. With a small sample, chance fluctuations influence the picture. But as sample size increases, chance is averaged out, and relative frequencies settle down to probabilities. At the same time, the increase in sample size allows a finer definition of cells. While the area remains fixed at 1, the relative frequency density becomes approximately a curve, the *probability density function*, p(x), which we informally call the *density*, or the *probability distribution*. (To calculate probabilities and moments of continuous distributions, see Appendix 4-4.)

PROBLEMS

4-17 The total time T that I wait for buses, on a long trip that includes a transfer, has the following probability distribution: Note that the area of a triangle = base × height/2, so that the total area or probability is 20 × .10/2 = 1.00.

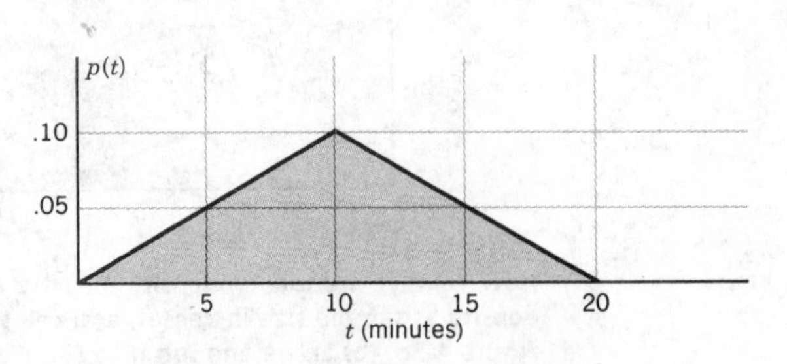

a. If I wait more than 15 minutes, I will be late for my appointment. What is the chance of this?

b. What is the mean waiting time?

4-18 At a busy switchboard, the waiting time T between one incoming call and the next was recorded thousands of times, as follows:

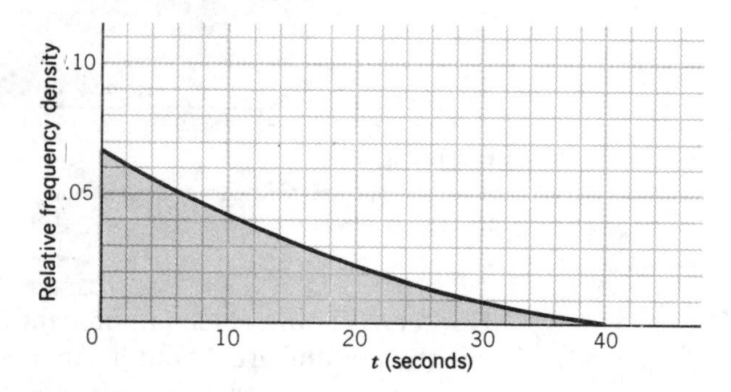

a. Estimate the probability that T exceeds 30 seconds.

b. Find the modal time and the median time. In relation to these two, where would the mean be?

4-5 THE NORMAL DISTRIBUTION

For many random variables, the probability distribution is a specific bell-shaped curve, called the *normal* curve, or *Gaussian* curve (in honor of the great German scientist Karl Friedrick Gauss, 1777–1855). This is the most common and useful distribution in statistics. For example, errors made in measuring physical and economic phenomena often are normally distributed. In addition, many other probability distributions (such as the binomial) often can be approximated by the normal curve.

A—STANDARD NORMAL DISTRIBUTION

The simplest of the normal distributions is the *standard normal* distribution shown in Figure 4-5, and discussed in detail in Section C. Called the Z distribution, it is distributed around a mean $\mu = 0$ with a standard deviation $\sigma = 1$. Thus, for example, the value $Z = 1.5$ is one-and-a-half standard deviations above the mean, and in general:

Each Z value is *the number of standard deviations* away from the mean.	(4-16)

We often want to calculate the probability (i.e., the area under the curve) beyond a given value of Z, like the value $Z = 1.5$ in Figure 4-5.

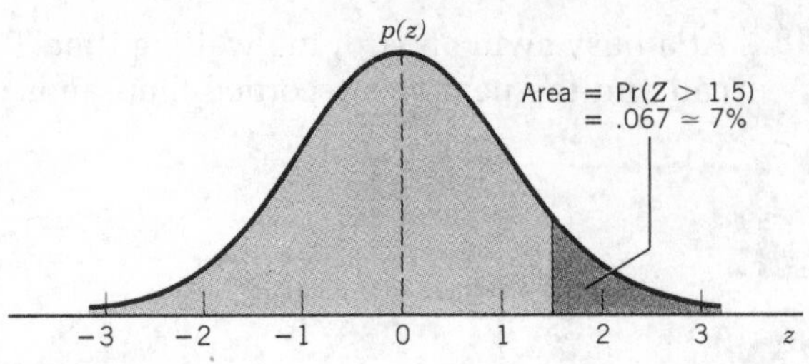

FIGURE 4-5
Standard normal distribution, illustrating the tabulated probability beyond a given point.

This, and all other such tail probabilities, have already been calculated by statisticians and are set out in Appendix Table IV (which is very similar to the binomial tail probabilities in Table IIIc).[2]

EXAMPLE 4-4

If Z has a standard normal distribution, find:

a. $\Pr(Z > 1.64)$
b. $\Pr(Z < -1.64)$
c. $\Pr(1.0 < Z < 1.5)$
d. $\Pr(-1 < Z < 2)$
e. $\Pr(-2 < Z < 2)$

SOLUTION

Since the normal probabilities in Appendix Table IV are so useful, we record them also inside the front cover where they are easy to find. Using them, we calculate each probability and illustrate it in the corresponding panel of Figure 4-6.

a. $\Pr(Z > 1.64) = .051 \simeq 5\%$
b. By symmetry,

$$\begin{aligned}\Pr(Z < -1.64) &= \Pr(Z > 1.64) \\ &= .051 \simeq 5\%\end{aligned} \tag{4-18}$$

[2] There is one new feature, however, in looking up probabilities for a continuous variable: The probability of a single point is zero (since the "area" above a single point reduces to a line of zero width). It therefore makes no difference whether we include or exclude any single point—call it c:

$$\text{If } X \text{ is continuous, } \Pr(X \geq c) = \Pr(X > c) \tag{4-17}$$

In other words, $\geq$ and $>$ can be used interchangeably for any continuous random variable including the standard normal Z.

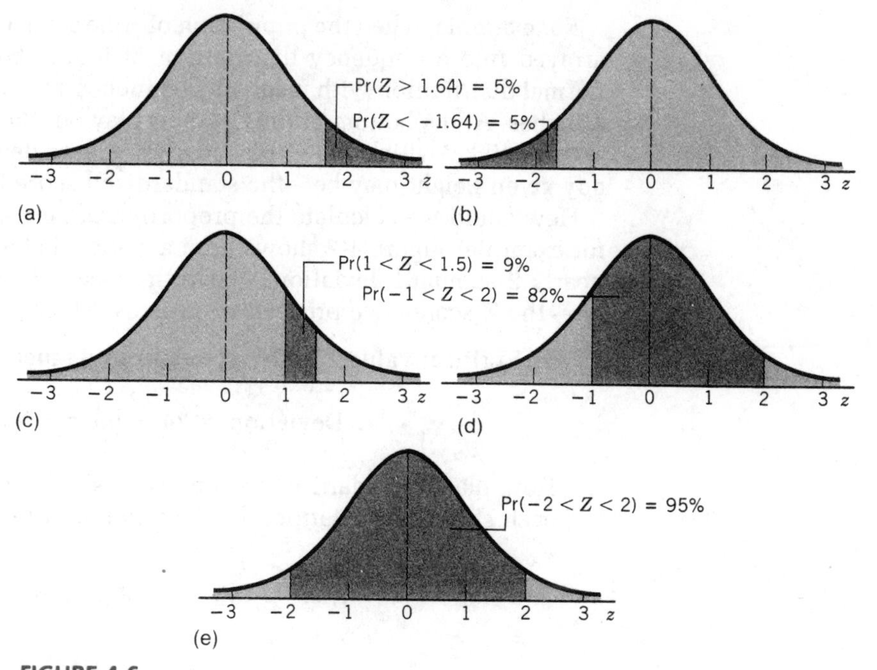

FIGURE 4-6

Standard normal probabilities illustrated.

c. Take the probability above 1.0, and subtract from it the probability above 1.5:

$$\begin{aligned} \Pr(1.0 < Z < 1.5) &= \Pr(Z > 1.0) - \Pr(Z > 1.5) \\ &= .159 - .067 \\ &= .092 \simeq 9\% \end{aligned} \tag{4-19}$$

d. Subtract the two tail areas from the total area of 1:

$$\begin{aligned} \Pr(-1 < Z < 2) &= 1 - \Pr(Z < -1) - \Pr(Z > 2) \\ &= 1 - .159 - .023 \\ &= .818 \simeq 82\% \end{aligned} \tag{4-20}$$

e.

$$\begin{aligned} \Pr(-2 < Z < 2) &= 1 - \Pr(Z < -2) - \Pr(Z > 2) \\ &= 1 - 2(.023) \\ &= .954 \simeq 95\% \end{aligned}$$

B—GENERAL NORMAL DISTRIBUTION

So far we have considered only a very special normal distribution—the standard normal Z with mean zero and standard deviation 1. But in general, a normal distribution may have any mean μ, and any standard deviation σ.

For example, when the population of American men have their height X arrayed into a frequency distribution, it looks about like Figure 4-7—a normal distribution with mean $\mu = 69$ inches, and standard deviation $\sigma = 3$ inches. At the bottom of the figure, we lay out the standard deviation as a "yardstick," which shows how many standard deviations from the mean any given height may be—the standardized score Z.

How could we calculate the proportion of men above 6′2″ (74 inches), for example? Figure 4-7 shows us at a glance that a height of 74 inches is nearly 2 standard deviations above the mean. To calculate exactly how far—the Z score—we proceed in two easy steps:

1. The critical value $X = 74$ differs from its mean $\mu = 69$ by:

$$\text{Deviation} = 74 - 69 = 5 \text{ inches} \tag{4-21}$$

2. How many standard deviations is this? Since there are 3 inches in each standard deviation, the deviation of 5 inches represents:

$$Z = \frac{5}{3} = 1.67 \text{ standard deviations} \tag{4-22}$$

Finally we can refer this to Table IV to get the required probability:

$$\Pr(Z > 1.67) = .047 \simeq 5\%$$

That is, the proportion is about 5%, which is graphed in Figure 4-7.

To formalize how we derived the Z value of 1.67 in (4-22), we first calculated the deviation $(X - \mu)$, and then compared it to the standard deviation σ.

$$\boxed{Z = \frac{X - \mu}{\sigma}} \tag{4-23}$$

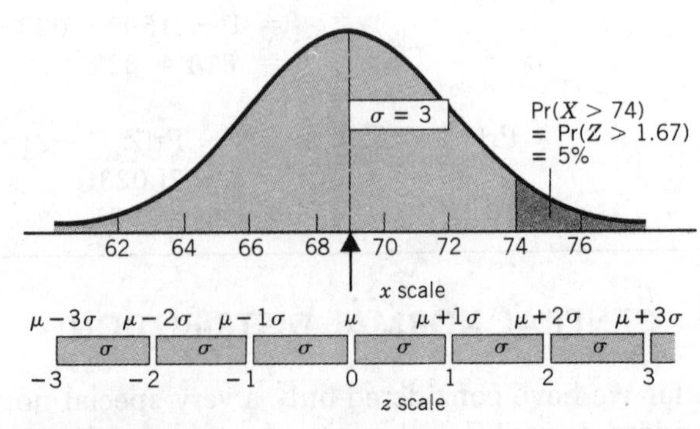

FIGURE 4-7
Standardization: A general normal variable (men's heights) rescaled to a standard normal.

That is, the Z value gives the number of standard deviations away from the mean—as we first saw in (4-16).

EXAMPLE 4-5

Suppose the yearling trout in a lake have lengths that are approximately normally distributed, about a mean $\mu = 9.5''$ with a standard deviation $\sigma = 1.4''$. What proportion of them:

a. Exceed 12″ (the legal length for keeping a catch)?

b. Exceed 10″ (the newly proposed legal length)?

SOLUTION

a. As shown in Figure 4-8, we first must *standardize* the score $X = 12$ (that is, express it as a standard Z value):

$$Z = \frac{X - \mu}{\sigma} \qquad \text{(4-23) repeated}$$

$$= \frac{12.0 - 9.5}{1.4} = \frac{2.5}{1.4} = 1.79$$

Thus

$$\Pr(X > 12) = \Pr(Z > 1.79)$$
$$= .037 \simeq 4\% \qquad \text{(4-24)}$$

b. Now

$$Z = \frac{10.0 - 9.5}{1.4} = \frac{0.5}{1.4} = 0.36$$

Thus

$$\Pr(X > 10) = \Pr(Z > .36)$$
$$= .359 \simeq 36\%$$

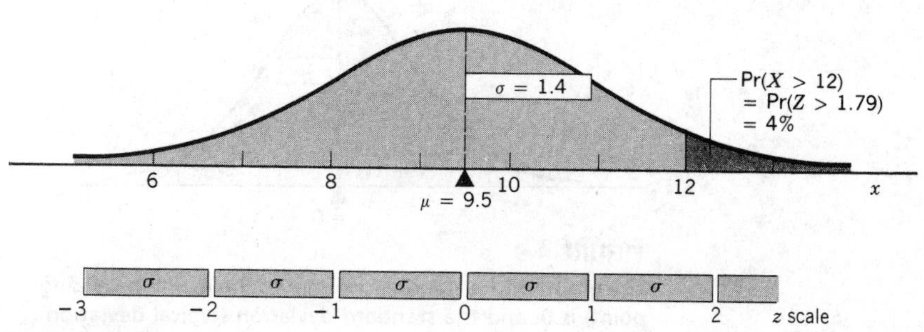

FIGURE 4-8
General normal rescaled to a standard normal.

As these examples have shown, we can always calculate probabilities for a normal distribution, by first finding the standard Z value.

*C—FORMULAS AND GRAPHS

This optional section sets out some of the details. First, the standard normal distribution has the probability function (density):

$$p(z) = \frac{1}{\sqrt{2\pi}} e^{-\frac{1}{2}z^2} \tag{4-25}$$

The constant $1/\sqrt{2\pi}$ is a scale factor required to make the total area 1. The symbols π and e denote important mathematical constants, approximately 3.14 and 2.72, respectively.

The graph of (4-25) is shown in Figure 4-9, and has the following features:

1. As we move to the left or right of 0, z^2 increases in the negative exponent. Therefore, $p(z)$ decreases, approaching 0 symmetrically in both tails.
2. The mean is 0—the balancing point is the center of symmetry.
3. The standard deviation is 1. This can be rigorously proved by advanced calculus. Or, the intuitive reason is shown in Figure 4-9. Six typical values of Z are shown as dots. Their deviations from the mean are sometimes less than 1, sometimes more than 1. Thus 1 seems to be the typical deviation, or standard deviation.

For occasional theoretical purposes, we also need the formula for the *general* normal distribution:

$$p(x) = \frac{1}{\sqrt{2\pi}\sigma} e^{-\frac{1}{2}\left(\frac{x-\mu}{\sigma}\right)^2} \tag{4-26}$$

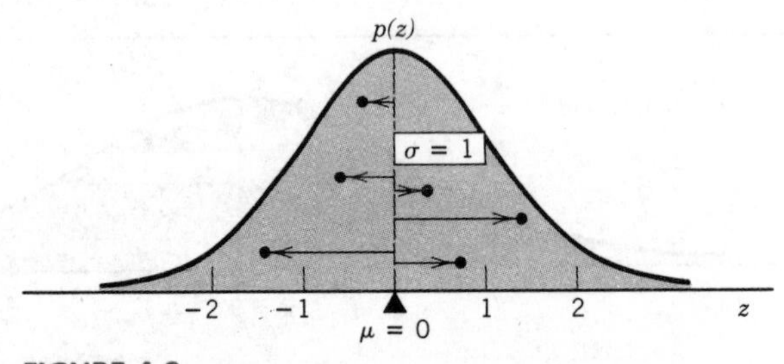

FIGURE 4-9

The graph of the standard normal Z. The mean (balancing point) is 0, and the standard deviation (typical deviation) is 1.

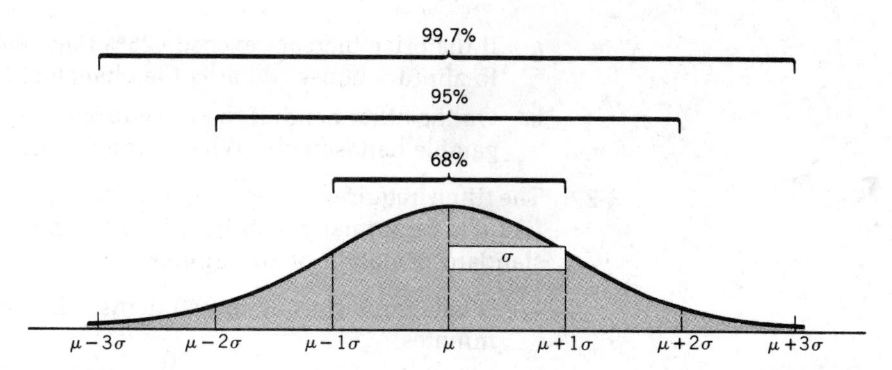

FIGURE 4-10
To graph a normal distribution, it helps to know that nearly all (99.7%) of its probability is within three standard deviations of the mean.

In the exponent we find the familiar $z = (x - \mu)/\sigma$ as in (4-23). The shape of this distribution is therefore the same bell shape as the standard normal—being centered at μ, and spread out by the factor σ.

To graph the normal distribution, it helps to know that nearly all of the area or probability lies within 3 standard deviations of the mean. (By looking up $z = 3$ in the standard normal table, we find the probability is 99.7%.) This is shown, along with several other areas, in Figure 4-10.

PROBLEMS

Recall that Table IV is repeated inside the front cover where it is easy to find.

4-19 If Z is a standard normal variable, calculate:

a. $\Pr(Z > 1.60)$
b. $\Pr(1.60 < Z < 2.30)$
c. $\Pr(Z < 1.64)$
d. $\Pr(-1.64 < Z < -1.02)$
e. $\Pr(0 < Z < 1.96)$
f. $\Pr(-1.96 < Z < 1.96)$
g. $\Pr(-1.50 < Z < .67)$
h. $\Pr(Z < -2.50)$

4-20 If X is normally distributed around a mean of 16 with a standard deviation of 5, find

a. $\Pr(X > 20)$
b. $\Pr(20 < X < 25)$
c. $\Pr(X < 10)$
d. $\Pr(12 < X < 24)$

4-21 Phil and Kim Bell don't know whether to buy a house now or wait a year, in which case a price increase may put a house beyond their reach. Their best guess is that, if they wait a year, the price increase will be approximately normal, with a mean of 8% and, reflecting the uncertainty of the market, a standard deviation of 10%.

a. If the price increase exceeds 25% they feel they will be unable to afford a house. What is the chance of this?

b. On the other hand, if the price drops, they will have won their gamble handsomely. What is the chance of this?

4-22 The time required to complete a college achievement test was found to be normally distributed, with a mean of 110 minutes and a standard deviation of 20 minutes.

a. What proportion of the students will finish in 2 hours (120 minutes)?

b. When should the test be terminated to allow just enough time for 90% of the students to complete the test?

4-23 Wearever tires have a track record of lasting 56,000 miles on average, with a standard deviation of 8,000 miles, and a normal distribution.

a. What is the chance that a given tire will last 50,000 miles?

b. What is the chance that all four Wearever tires on my car will last 50,000 miles?

c. State the assumptions made in **b**, and how more realistic assumptions would change your answer.

4-6 A FUNCTION OF A RANDOM VARIABLE

A—FUNCTIONS IN GENERAL

Consider again the planning of a family of three children. Suppose the annual cost of clothing (R) is a function of the number of girls (X) in the family, that is:

$$R = g(X) \tag{4-27}$$

Specifically, suppose $R = -100X^2 + 300X + 500$. Then, for each X, the

TABLE 4-4 Annual Clothing Cost *R* as a Function of *X*.

Number of Girls x	*Probability* $p(x)$	*Clothing Cost* $r = g(x)$
0	.14	$500
1	.39	$700
2	.36	$700
3	.11	$500

Why is clothing cost R lower if $X = 0$ or 3, that is, if all children are the same sex? The answer is that they will be better able to re-use the same clothes.

TABLE 4-5 Calculation of the Distribution and Mean of *R*.

x	p(x)	r	p(r)	rp(r)
0	.14	$500	.25	$125
1	.39	$700	.75	$525
2	.36			
3	.11			μ_R = $650

corresponding value for R can be calculated, and is given in the last column of Table 4-4. How can we get the probability distribution of R?

The values of R—$500 and $700—are customarily rearranged in order as shown in the middle column of Table 4-5. Furthermore, the values of R have certain probabilities that can be deduced from the probabilities of X (just as the probabilities of X were deduced from the original sample space, as in Figure 4-1).

For example, when does R = $500? The answer is when X = 0 (14% of the time) or when X = 3 (11% of the time), for a total of 25% of the time.

Once the distribution of R has been derived in this way in Table 4-5, we can, in the last column, calculate its average μ_R = $650.

An easier calculation of average cost μ_R is possible, using the data in Table 4-4 directly. We simply add up the costs g(x) weighted with the probabilities p(x):

$$\mu_R = \Sigma\, g(x)p(x) \tag{4-28}$$

This is illustrated in Table 4-6, where we find μ_R = $650. This agrees with our earlier answer in Table 4-5, and it is easy to see why. In a disguised way, we are calculating μ_R with the same numbers as in Table 4-5. For example, the two rows for X = 0 and X = 3 in Table 4-6 appear condensed together as the single row for R = $500 in Table 4-5. Similarly, the other two rows in Table 4-6 correspond to the single row for R = $700 in Table 4-5, so that both tables yield the same value for μ_R. The only difference, really, is that Table 4-6 is ordered according to X values, while Table 4-5 is ordered (and condensed) according to R values.

An example will illustrate the usefulness of formula (4-28).

TABLE 4-6 Easier Calculation of the Mean of *R*, Directly from *p*(*x*).

x	p(x)	r = g(x)	g(x)p(x)
0	.14	$500	$ 70
1	.39	$700	$273
2	.36	$700	$252
3	.11	$500	$ 55
			$\mu_R = \Sigma\, g(x)p(x)$ = $650

EXAMPLE 4-6
WEAR AND TEAR ON THE RAILROAD

The wear on the axle of a railroad car increases as the load on it increases. Roughly speaking, a doubling of the load X quadruples the wear R, and in general,

$$R = X^2$$

Now suppose the car passes over an irregular section of track, so that the weight on each axle fluctuates widely according to the following distribution:

Load x	Proportion of Time $p(x)$
8	.25
20	.70
80	.05

a. Calculate the average load, μ_X
b. Calculate the average wear, μ_R
c. If the railroad was perfectly smooth (so the load on each axle was always exactly 20 tons), would the wear on the axles be reduced?

SOLUTION

Given		a. μ_X	b. μ_R	
x	$p(x)$	$xp(x)$	$g(x) = x^2$	$g(x)p(x)$
8	.25	2	64	16
20	.70	14	400	280
80	.05	4	6400	320
		$\mu_X = 20$		$\mu_R = 616$

c. With a constant load of $X = 20$ tons on each axle, the wear would be $20^2 = 400$. This is 216 less than before—a substantial reduction.

B—LINEAR FUNCTIONS

When we say that R is a function of X, there are many forms this relationship may take. For example, we have already met $R = -100X^2 + 300X + 500$, and $R = X^2$. The simplest form is a *linear function:*

$$R = a + bX$$

where a and b are constants. In this case, there is an extremely simple formula to calculate the mean μ_R, and an equally simple formula for the standard deviation σ_R:

$$\boxed{\begin{aligned} &\text{If } R = a + bX \\ &\text{then } \mu_R = a + b\mu_X \\ &\text{and } \sigma_R = |b|\,\sigma_X \end{aligned}} \qquad \begin{matrix}(4\text{-}29)\\ \text{like } (2\text{-}19)\end{matrix}$$

An example will illustrate.

EXAMPLE 4-7 EXPECTED COST OF REPAIR

Johnson's Sports will have to repair some of their most badly damaged sailboats this fall, after two seasons of heavy rentals. Past experience indicates that each of the 5 boats in their rental fleet has a 50% chance of requiring repair, independent of the others. Thus the total number of boats requiring repair (X) will vary according to the binomial distribution, with $n = 5$ and $\pi = .50$.

Each repair job—replacing the fiberglass on the hull—costs \$600, so the total cost of repairs is $R = 600X$. Find the expected cost of repair in two ways:

a. The hard way, by first tabulating the distribution of X, and using (4-28).

b. The easy way, exploiting the linearity formula (4-29).

SOLUTION

a. The binomial distribution $p(x)$ can be copied down from Table IIIb with $n = 5$ and $\pi = .50$. Then we calculate the mean from $\Sigma g(x)p(x)$:

x	p(x)	cost, g(x) = 600x	g(x)p(x)
0	.031	0	0
1	.156	\$ 600	\$93.6
2	.313	\$1200	\$375.6
3	.313	\$1800	\$563.4
4	.156	\$2400	\$374.4
5	.031	\$3000	\$93.0
			\$1500

b. Since $R = 600X$,

$$\mu_R = 600\mu_X \qquad \text{like (4-29)}$$

$$= 600(n\pi) \qquad \text{like (4-13)}$$

$$= 600(5)(.5) = \$1500 \qquad (4\text{-}30)$$

This $1500 is the same answer for expected cost that we found in **a**. But it's a lot less work.

C—NOTATION FOR THE MEAN

Since means play a key role in statistics, they have been calculated by all sorts of people, who sometimes use different names for the same concept. For example, geographers use the term "*mean* annual rainfall," teachers use the term "*average* grade," and gamblers and economists use the term "*expected* profit." Thus all the following terms have exactly the same mathematical meaning:

$$\mu_T = \text{mean of } T$$
$$= \text{average of } T$$
$$= \text{expected value of } T\text{, or } E(T)$$

Thus we can rewrite (4-28) as:

$$E(R) = \Sigma\, g(x)p(x) \qquad (4\text{-}31)$$

This expected value symbol E is often used as a reminder that it represents a weighted sum (E looks like Σ).

Finally, since we recall that R was just an abbreviation for $g(X)$, we can rewrite (4-31) as:

$$\boxed{E[g(X)] = \Sigma\, g(x)p(x)} \qquad (4\text{-}32)$$

As an example, one possible form of the function $g(X)$ is:

$$g(X) = (X - \mu)^2$$

Then (4-32) becomes:

$$E(X - \mu)^2 = \Sigma(x - \mu)^2 p(x) \qquad (4\text{-}33)$$

That is, noting (4-5):

$$\boxed{E(X - \mu)^2 = \sigma^2} \tag{4-34}$$

This emphasizes that σ^2 *may be regarded as just a kind of expected value—the expected squared deviation* [like the mean squared deviation in (2-10)]. In this new E notation, we also can rewrite (4-6) as:

$$\boxed{\sigma^2 = E(X^2) - \mu^2} \tag{4-35}$$

Sometimes we find it useful to solve this for $E(X^2)$:

$$E(X^2) = \mu^2 + \sigma^2 \tag{4-36}$$

The E notation is so useful that we shall continue to use it throughout the book.

PROBLEMS

4-24 **a.** If X is a random variable, then a function of X, say g(X), will be a random variable too. What is the easiest way to find its mean

i. If g(X) is linear?

ii. If g(X) is nonlinear?

b. Classify as linear or nonlinear:

i. $g(X) = 2X + 4$

ii. $g(X) = (X + 2)(X - 4)$

iii. $g(X) = 5(X - 32)/9$

iv. $g(X) = (X + 7)/3$

v. $g(X) = 3/(X + 7)$

vi. $g(X) = \sqrt{X^2 + 4}$

4-25 In her new job of selling computers, Dawn Elliot faces uncertain prospects next year. She guesses that her taxable income X might be anywhere from 20 to 50 thousand dollars according to her schedule of personal probabilities p(x) given below. The corresponding tax is given in the final column.

Income x ($000)	*Probability* p(x)	*Tax* t(x) ($000)
20	.10	4
30	.30	6
40	.40	9
50	.20	13

a. Calculate her expected income.

b. Calculate her expected tax.

c. Calculate her expected disposable income (after tax) in two ways:

  i. Calculate first the table of disposable incomes, and then take their expected value.

  ii. As an easier way, just use the answers in **a** and **b**.

4-26 To fill up the last week of the season, Larry's Paving bids on 6 similar but statistically independent small jobs. Larry has a 40% chance of getting each contract, and will earn $200 on each contract he gets. However, he has a $300 expense in preparing all 6 bids.

a. What is the expected number of contracts he will get?

b. What is the expected profit $E(P)$?

c. What is the chance he will make a (positive) profit? And the chance he will lose?

4-27 Now let's change Problem 4-26. Suppose the more contracts Larry wins (X), the more overtime he must pay, so that his profit is now:

$$P = \$200X - \$300 - \$20X^2$$

with this last quadratic term being the downward adjustment in his profit for overtime pay. Now answer the same questions as before.

4-28 Larry's accountant in Problem 4-27 pointed out that Larry was perhaps unwise to submit that sixth bid. After all, if he won all his bids he would be so busy paying overtime that he would *lose* money on that sixth contract.

Larry has asked you, as a consultant, to check out whether his accountant is right. (Assume that it still costs $300 to prepare the bids, whether 6 or fewer.)

4-29 Suppose that X is a very simple discrete random variable, distributed as follows:

x	p(x)
2	.50
4	.50

For each of the following, state True or False, and back up your answer either by calculating both sides of the equation, or by appealing to a general theorem.

a. $E(X + 10) = E(X) + 10$

b. $E(X/10) = E(X)/10$

c. $E(10/X) = 10/E(X)$

d. $E(X^2) = [E(X)]^2$

e. $E(5X + 2)/10 = (5E(X) + 2)/10$

*4-7 EXPECTED VALUE IN BIDDING[3]

Bidding and negotiating are always chancy. You never know at the beginning what package you will get at the end. So this is one of the most interesting applications of probability and expected value.

Negotiating skills are essential for business and labor leaders in their collective bargaining over wages and benefits; for government officials in negotiating arms limitations or trade agreements; and for individuals negotiating a salary or the price of a car. One of the simplest negotiating problems arises in bidding, as an example will show.

EXAMPLE 4-8
HOW HIGH SHOULD YOU BID?

You are thinking of buying a summer cottage listed for $40,000. Since it has been listed unsold for six months, the owner is offering it for public auction during the regatta weekend—with the cottage going to the highest sealed bid.

You feel you might possibly get it for as little as $30,000 or $32,000, and you are almost certain to get it for $38,000 or $40,000. In fact, you estimate that the chance of winning increases as the bid increases, roughly as shown in Figure 4-11.

What should you bid?

SOLUTION

You don't have sufficient information yet. In negotiating any price, two things are vital to know:

1. What do your opponents—in this case, the competitive bidders—think it is worth? This is the information that has already been captured in Figure 4-11.

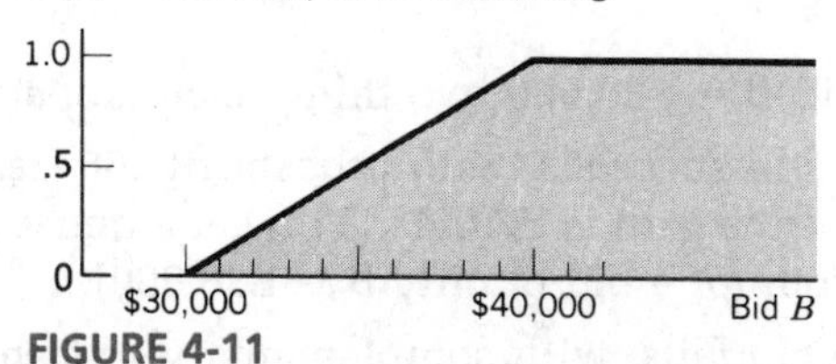

FIGURE 4-11
Higher bids give a higher probability of winning.

[3] The star means this is an optional section that is not needed in later chapters.

2. What do you think it is worth yourself? This is what you haven't yet determined.

For example, if you feel it is worth only \$31,000 then you would be crazy to submit a bid as high as \$33,000. You might possibly win it, and essentially lose the \$2,000 difference.

On the other hand, if you feel the cottage is worth \$60,000, you would be unwise to submit a bid as low as \$33,000: You would probably lose it, and regret that you hadn't bid the full \$40,000 that would have assured you of winning—and being ahead by \$20,000 (the amount you value it above its price).

Thus you can't make a sensible decision unless you first decide what the cottage is worth to you. Let's call this value V. It is the price that would leave you indifferent about getting the cottage—that is, the price that would leave you equally happy, whether you get the cottage or not.

EXAMPLE 4-9 THE BIDDING FINISHED

After consulting with your family, and looking at alternative cottages for sale, suppose you decide that your value for this cottage is $V = \$38{,}000$. Using also the information in Figure 4-11, determine the best bid in three steps:

a. Calculate your expected gain if you bid $B = \$36{,}000$. (Hint: What is the chance you will win? And if you win, what gain will you make, that is, how much less will you pay than what the cottage is worth to you?)

b. Similarly calculate the expected gain when $B = \$35{,}000$. And then $B = \$37{,}000$. And so on.

c. Which bid gives the greatest expected gain?

SOLUTION

a. If you bid $B = \$36{,}000$ two things can happen:

i. The bid succeeds, with probability .60 (read off Figure 4-11). Then the gain is \$2,000. (You get a house worth $V = \$38{,}000$ to you, for a bid of only $B = \$36{,}000$).

ii. The bid fails, with complementary probability .40. Then the gain is 0; you are right back where you started from. We can summarize these two probabilities in a table, and so calculate expected gain:

	Gain	Probability	Weighted Gain
i.	$2000	.60	$1200
ii.	0	.40	0
		Expected Gain =	$1200

b. For B = $35,000, we have a similar calculation: A lower chance of succeeding (.50), but a higher gain if successful ($3,000). So the expected gain is $1500—an overall improvement.

All such reasonable bids are displayed in Table 4-7 below. (A bid below $30,000 is not reasonable, because it's sure to fail, while a bid above $38,000 is unreasonable because that is more than the house is worth to you.)

c. This table shows the highest expected gain comes from the optimal bid B_O = $34,000. This figure nicely balances your desire to bid low enough to get a big bargain, but still high enough to give yourself a good chance of getting the cottage.

TABLE 4-7 Various Bids Produce Various Expected Gains

(1) Possible Bid B	(2) Gain $38,000 − B	(3) Probability P(B) (from Fig. 4-11)	(4) Expected Gain (2) × (3)
$30,000	$8,000	0	0
$31,000	$7,000	.1	$700
$32,000	$6,000	.2	$1200
$33,000	$5,000	.3	$1500
$34,000	$4,000	.4	$1600 ← max.
$35,000	$3,000	.5	$1500
$36,000	$2,000	.6	$1200
$37,000	$1,000	.7	$700
$38,000	0	.8	0

We can easily generalize the lessons from this example. The $30,000 that is so low that it just ceases to have any chance of success, will be called the low bid L. Similarly, the $40,000 bid that is so high that it is certain to succeed, will be called the high bid H. The value to the buyer will continue to be called V.

In Example 4-9, you chose the bid to maximize expected gain. Note that either bid L or V would drive the expected gain down to zero: for a bid as low as L = $30,000 there was no chance of success; for a bid as high as V = $38,000 there was no gain to be achieved. The optimal bid lay exactly halfway between, at $34,000. And with one simple exception, this is generally true (as proved in Problem 4-33), assuming the probability of accepting a bid $P(B)$ is a straight line as in Figure 4-11. That is,

$$\text{optimal bid } B_O = \frac{L+V}{2} \tag{4-37}$$

To see the simple exception to this rule, suppose that V, the buyer's valuation of what the house is worth in Example 4-9, were much higher, say \$52,000. Then (4-37) would tell us that the buyer should bid higher:

$$B_O = \frac{L+V}{2} = \frac{\$30{,}000 + \$52{,}000}{2} = \$41{,}000 \tag{4-38}$$

But \$41,000 is too high. A bid of H = \$40,000 is enough to guarantee winning the bid, so it makes no sense to throw money away by bidding higher. Thus (4-37) must be modified:

$$\boxed{\begin{aligned}\textbf{optimal bid } B_O &= \frac{L+V}{2}\\ \textbf{except} &= H, \textbf{ if } H \textbf{ is smaller}\end{aligned}} \tag{4-39}$$

Because it involves no interaction between buyer and seller, the bidding we have studied so far was easily modelled. And it was solved with the remarkably simple but effective formula (4-39).

What happens, however, when there is interaction—that is, when the two parties must negotiate with each other, as for example, in a wage dispute between labor and management? This is a much more complex problem of offer and counteroffer, rather than a single bid. At first glance it looks like a "zero-sum game"—whatever labor loses, management gets. But it is very dangerous to treat it this way. If both sides are not careful, negotiations may fail and they *both* would lose in a strike. In fact, simulation experiments at the Harvard Business School (Raiffa 1982) showed that students representing the two sides were often too greedy: In trying to get more for themselves at the expense of the other party, they often failed to reach any agreement at all.

The lesson is clear: Better a share of a pie than no pie at all. In negotiations of every sort—for wages, trade liberalization, or arms reduction—we should avoid mutually hardened positions that produce no chance of agreement.

*PROBLEMS

4-30 **a.** In Example 4-9, continue to assume L = \$30,000 and V = \$38,000. What would be the optimal bid B_O if the high bid H was not \$40,000, but instead:

i. $H = \$44,000$ iii. $H = \$36,000$
ii. $H = \$60,000$ iv. $H = \$33,000$

b. Answer True or False; if false, correct it:

i. To determine the optimal bid B_O the most important figure is V, the value of the house to you.

ii. If V is somewhere between the low and high bids L and H, then an equally important figure is the high bid H.

4-31 In looking for a used car, I find what I'm looking for—a three-year old Toyota Tercel for \$5000. A brief talk with the seller plus some market information suggests that any bid less than \$4200 would have no chance whatsoever of striking a deal.

a. What advice would you give me about what to bid?

b. Suppose I tell you that any bid over \$4800 is certain to be accepted by the seller. And the value of the car to me is \$5600—it's exactly what I want, at a price I didn't expect to find. Now what would you advise me to bid?

c. On the other hand, suppose the value to me is not \$5600, but only \$4600. Now what should I bid?

4-32 Bidding not to buy, but to sell (tendering).

Suppose you are bidding to *sell* something, instead of to buy. For example, as vice-president of a construction firm, suppose you are bidding to sell the city of Seattle a new overpass. Now it is a *low* bid that has the best chance of succeeding. For example, the probability of your bid succeeding may be 1 if you bid 4.0 million dollars, and gradually fall (linearly) to 0 if you bid 6.0 million dollars.

Suppose finally that V, your cost of building this project, is 5.2 million. Thus, for example, if you successfully bid 5.5 million, you would make a profit of 0.3 million.

a. The formula for the optimal bid is now the mirror image of (4-39). Write it down.

b. Calculate the optimal bid in this case.

c. If I bid .2 million higher than the optimal figure in **b**, would it be almost as good?

***d.** Can you think of any circumstances where you would be willing to bid slightly less than the answer in **b**?

4-33 **a.** Graph the expected gain $E(G)$ in the last column of Table 4-7, as a function of the possible bid B.

b. Is $E(G)$ a parabola? Why?

c. True or False: If false, correct it: Since $E(G)$ is a symmetric parabola, its maximum value must occur halfway between its zero values (at the low bid $L = 30$ and at the buyer's value $V = 38$). This rigorously proves that (4-38) is true.

4-34 In Table 4-7 again, suppose you put a much higher value on the cottage—say $V = \$60{,}000$ instead of \$38,000. Since this makes greater gains possible, tabulate the new expected gain $E(G)$ in the last column. Then answer the same questions as in Problem 4-33.

CHAPTER 4 SUMMARY

4-1 A random variable has a probability distribution that can often be derived from the original sample space of elementary outcomes.

4-2 The mean μ and standard deviation σ are defined for a probability distribution in the same way as $\overline{X}$ and s were defined for a relative frequency distribution in Chapter 2. The Greek letters emphasize their theoretical nature.

4-3 When an experiment consists of *independent* trials with the *same* chance π of success on each trial, the total number of successes S is called a binomial variable. Its probability distribution can be easily found from a formula, or Table IIIb.

4-4 For random variables that vary continuously, probabilities are given by areas under a continuous distribution (probability density curve).

4-5 The commonest continuous distribution is the bell-shaped normal (Gaussian) distribution. To measure the number of standard deviations from the mean, we calculate:

$$Z = \frac{X - \mu}{\sigma}$$

We can then use this calculated value of Z to read off probabilities from the standard normal table (Table IV, inside the front cover).

4-6 Whatever the name—average, mean, expected value, or E—they all have exactly the same meaning. A new random variable obtained from X, say g(X), can have its mean directly calculated from the distribution $p(x)$:

$$E[g(X)] = \Sigma\, g(x)p(x)$$

If $g(X) = a + bX$, then calculating its mean is even easier: We just transform the mean of X in the same linear way, that is,

$$E(a + bX) = a + bE(X)$$

***4-7** Expected gain from bidding is often maximized for a bid that splits the difference between V, the value to the buyer, and L, the lowest bid he could possibly hope to get the item for.

REVIEW PROBLEMS

4-35 In the 1984 U.S. presidential election, approximately 60% voted Republican and 40% voted Democratic. Calculate the probability that a random sample would correctly forecast the election winner—that is, that a majority of the sample would be Republicans, if the sample size were:

a. $n = 1$

b. $n = 3$

c. $n = 9$

Note how the larger sample increases the probability of a correct forecast.

4-36 A manufacturer needs washers between .1180 and .1220 inches thick; any thickness outside this range is unusable. One machine shop will sell washers at $3.00 per 1000. Their thickness is normally distributed with a mean of .1200 inch and a standard deviation of .0010 inch.

A second machine shop will sell washers at $2.60 per 1000. Their thickness is normally distributed with a mean of .1200 inch and a standard deviation of .0015 inch.

Which shop offers the better deal? (Use the price per usable washer as the criterion. The costs for sorting the washers can be assumed about the same in both cases.)

4-37 American women born in 1950 have completed their families by now, as follows:

Number of Children	*Relative Frequency*
0	17%
1	19%
2	36%
3	17%
4	7%
5 (or more)	4%
Total	100%

Estimates based on *Stat. Abst. of U.S.*, 1987, pp. 59, 64.

a. Find the average number of children per woman. Also the median, mode, and standard deviation.

To determine population growth, which of these measures is most appropriate?

b. Graph the relative frequency distribution. Mark the average as the balancing point. Show the standard deviation as the unit of scale as in Figure 2-6.

4-38 How many Americans would there be a generation later if American women continued to reproduce at the rate shown in Problem 4-37? Let us see how the average produces the key to the answer.

a. To start, the average number of children born per woman was found to be 1.90. But to get to the next generation of women, we must allow that only 48.8% of these children are girls (slightly less than half) and only 97% will survive to adulthood (projecting the present 3% mortality rate). These reductions leave an average of how many females surviving to the next generation?

This figure is called the "net reproduction rate," NRR. Is it consistent with your answer to Problem 2-31?

b. Suppose the NRR doesn't change. And suppose we ignore the relatively minor effects of immigration, change in life expectancy, and other changes in age distribution. Then we can get a simple *projection* of America's future population.

Starting from 250 million in 1980, roughly graph America's population as far as four generations (about 100 years). How useful do you think this projection is? Why might the NRR change?

4-39 Hawaii contains 1,100,000 people, 60% of whom are Asian, 39% white, and 1% black. If a random sample of 7 persons is drawn:

a. What is the chance that a majority will be Asians?

b. What is the chance that none will be black?

c. For the number of Asians in the sample, what is the expected value? And the standard deviation?

4-40 Mercury Mufflers guarantees its mufflers for 3 years. On each muffler, they make a profit of $15. However, they must pay $50 for any replacement under the guarantee. (If this replacement also burns out within 3 years, they are *not* committed to a second replacement.)

Their muffler life is approximately normally distributed around a mean of 4.2 years, with a standard deviation of 1.8 years.

a. What is the average profit per sale (net, after paying for a possible replacement under the guarantee)?

b. If they want this average profit per sale to be $5, by how much should they reduce the time period of the guarantee?

4-41 A family has four smoke alarms in their home, all battery operated and working independently of each other. Each has a reliability of 90%—that is, has a 90% chance of working. If fire breaks out that engulfs all four in smoke, what is the chance that at least one of them will sound the alarm?

***4-42** In a large New England college, there are 20 classes of introductory statistics with the following distribution of class size.

Class Size	*Relative Frequency*
10	.50
20	.30
90	.20
Total	1.00

The student newspaper reported that the average statistics student faced a class size "over 50." Alarmed, the Dean asked the 20 professors to calculate their average class size, and they reported, "under 30." Who's telling the truth? Or are there two truths? Specifically, calculate:

a. What class size does the average professor have?

b. What class size does the average student have? (Hint: Problem 2-41)

4-43 (The *Sign Test*) Eight volunteers are to have their breathing capacity measured before and after a new treatment for asthma, with the data recorded in a layout like the following:

	Breathing Capacity		
Person	*Before*	*After*	*Improvement*
H.J.	750	850	+100
K.L.	860	880	+20
M.M.	950	930	−20
·	·	·	·
·	·	·	·
·	·	·	·

a. Ignore the actual numbers in the table, and instead suppose that the treatment has *no effect whatever*. Then the "improvements" will be mere random fluctuations (resulting from minor variations in people's performance, and as likely to be negative as positive. Also assume that measurement is so precise that an improvement of exactly zero is never observed.)

What is the probability that seven or more signs will be +?

b. If it actually turned out that seven of the eight signs were +, would you question the hypothesis in part **a** that the treatment has no effect whatever?

4-44 In the 1984 presidential election, 60% voted for Reagan (Republican). A small random sample of 5 voters was simulated, and the number who voted Republican turned out to be $R = 4$. This simulation was repeated by each of 50 students in an econometrics course. Usually R turned out to be 2, 3, or 4, but occasionally as extreme as 5 or 1 or even 0. The results were arrayed in the following table:

r	*Frequency*
0	1
1	3
2	9
3	15
4	16
5	6
	50

a. Graph the relative frequency distribution of R, and calculate the mean and standard deviation.

b. If the sampling simulation were repeated millions of times (not merely 50), what would be your answers to part **a**?

c. Do this simulation yourself 10 more times, using the random digits in Appendix Table I.

***4-45** A small plumbing contractor specializing in home repairs employs five plumbers on a full-time basis—that is, 40 hours a week each. Business is so good that he has to turn away customers occasionally, and so he wonders whether adding a sixth plumber would be profitable.

A new full-time plumber would cost the contractor $800 per week ($20/hour). Yet the additional revenue generated would be uncertain. Past records indicate that the total weekly demand (X) in hours would vary as follows:

x	*Relative Frequency*
180–190	.03
190–200	.09
200–210	.12
210–220	.15
220–230	.22
230–240	.21
240–250	.13
250–260	.05

a. If the revenue from this work is $30 per hour, will it pay to hire the extra plumber,

i. assuming inflexible hours (i.e., no overtime is possible).

ii. assuming each plumber could work overtime up to 5 hours per week, at a cost of $25 per hour to the contractor.

b. How much is it worth to the contractor to be able to hire plumbers overtime?

4-46 *A Final Challenge: Estimating the Chances of "No Shows"*

Transamerican Airlines has opened a new daily flight from Chicago to Boise, Idaho. It is so popular that its 75 seats have all been reserved in its first 20 flights. Unfortunately, in each flight some of the passengers failed to show up, so that the plane left with some empty seats and lost revenue.

The number of "no shows" varied from 2 on the best flight to 11 on the worst flight. Here are the details:

Number of "No Shows," x	*Frequency*
2	1
3	4
4	0
5	4
6	2
7	5
8	1
9	1
10	0
11	2
	20 Flights

To reduce the number of empty seats, the airline can sell more than 75 reservations, of course. But that introduces a new risk of overbooking, if more than 75 people show up with reservations. In order to properly balance its risks, the airline needs to estimate the chances of various "no shows." We therefore imagine collecting data for many many flights (under similar conditions) so that the relative frequencies would settle down to probabilities $p(x)$. Let us estimate one of these probabilities—for example, the chance of exactly *3* "no shows," $p(3)$.

a. To estimate this long-run relative frequency $p(3)$, the short-run relative frequency in the table above is $4/20 = .20$. Do you think this estimate is too high, or too low? Why?

b. Graph the relative frequency distribution of X from the table above. Sketch a smooth curve through it—a crude probability model. What is its height at $X = 3$? Do you think this is a better estimate of the probability of $p(3)$?

c. For a more refined model, let π denote the proportion of passengers who are "no shows." Then assume that a flight consists of $n = 75$ *randomly* chosen passengers, so that X has a binomial distribution.

To estimate π, how many passengers were there altogether in the 20 flights? And how many "no shows"? So what is your estimate of π?

d. Now estimate $p(3)$ using the binomial distribution. Graph it alongside your other estimates for comparison.

CHAPTER 5

Two Random Variables

If you bet on a horse, that's gambling. If you bet you can make three spades, that's entertainment. If you bet cotton will go up three points, that's business. See the difference?

5-1 DISTRIBUTIONS

This first section is a simple extension of the last two chapters. The main problem will be to recognize the old ideas behind the new names. We therefore give an outline in Table 5-1, both as an introduction and a review.

A—JOINT DISTRIBUTIONS

In the planning of three children, let us define two random variables:

$$X = \text{number of girls}$$
$$Y = \text{number of runs}$$

where a *run* is an unbroken string of children of the same sex. For example, $Y = 1$ for the outcome BBB, while $Y = 2$ for the outcome BBG.

Suppose that we are interested in the probability that a family would have 1 girl and 2 runs. As usual, we refer to the sample space of the experiment, copied down from Figure 4-1 into Figure 5-1. These two events are colored, and their intersection has probability:

$$\Pr(X = 1 \text{ and } Y = 2) = .13 + .13 = .26 \tag{5-1}$$

which we simply denote by $p(1, 2)$.

Similarly, we could compute $p(0, 1)$, $p(0, 2)$, $p(0, 3)$, $p(1, 2)$, . . . , obtaining the *joint* (or *bivariate*) *probability distribution of* X and Y. Actually, the easiest way to derive the joint distribution is to run down the columns of X and Y values, tabulating all this information line by line into the appropriate cell on the right of Figure 5-1—as shown by the two typical arrows.

The distribution $p(x, y)$ may be graphed, as shown in Figure 5-2. Each probability can be represented by an appropriately sized dot as shown in panel (*a*), or by a height as shown in panel (*b*).

TABLE 5-1 Outline of Section 5-1

Old Idea		*New Terminology*	
Pr(G and H) applied to: $\Pr(X = 1 \text{ and } Y = 2)$ $\Pr(X = x \text{ and } Y = y)$ in general	(3-9)	Joint distribution: $p(1, 2)$ $p(x,y)$ in general	(5-2)
Event E is independent of F if: $\Pr(E \text{ and } F) = \Pr(E)\Pr(F)$	(3-21)	Variable X is independent of Y if, for all x and y: $p(x, y) = p(x)p(y)$	(5-6)

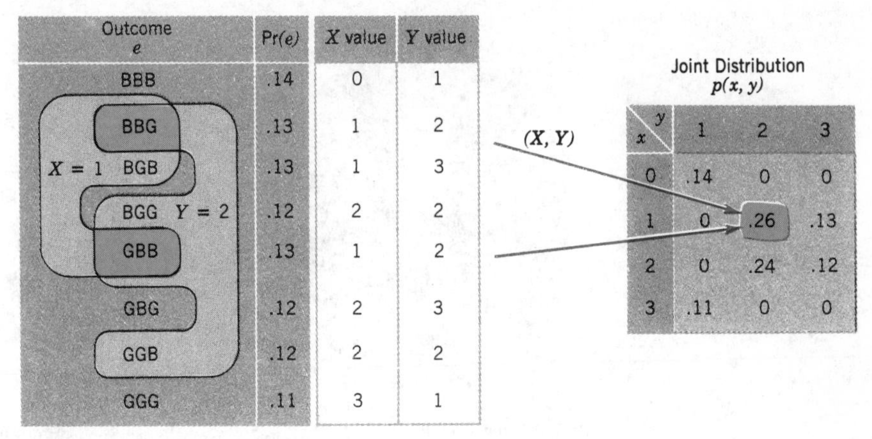

FIGURE 5-1
Two random variables defined on the same sample space.

The formal definition of the joint probability distribution is:

$$p(x, y) \equiv \Pr(X = x \quad \text{and} \quad Y = y) \tag{5-2}$$

The general case is illustrated in Figure 5-3. The events $X = 0$, $X = 1$, $X = 2, \ldots$, are shown schematically as a horizontal slicing. Similarly, the events $Y = 0$, $Y = 1, \ldots$, are shown as a vertical slicing. The intersection of the slice $X = x$ and the slice $Y = y$ is the event ($X = x$ and $Y = y$). Its probability is collected into the table, and denoted $p(x, y)$.

B—MARGINAL DISTRIBUTIONS

Suppose that we are interested only in X, yet have to work with the joint distribution of X and Y. Specifically, suppose we are interested in the event $X = 2$, which is a horizontal slice in the schematic sample space of

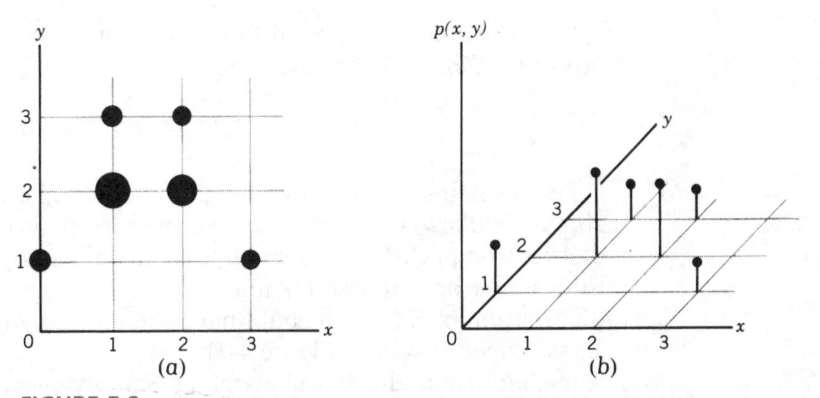

FIGURE 5-2
Two graphic presentations of the joint distribution in Table 5-2. (*a*) p(x, y) is represented by the size of the dot. (*b*) p(x, y) is represented by height.

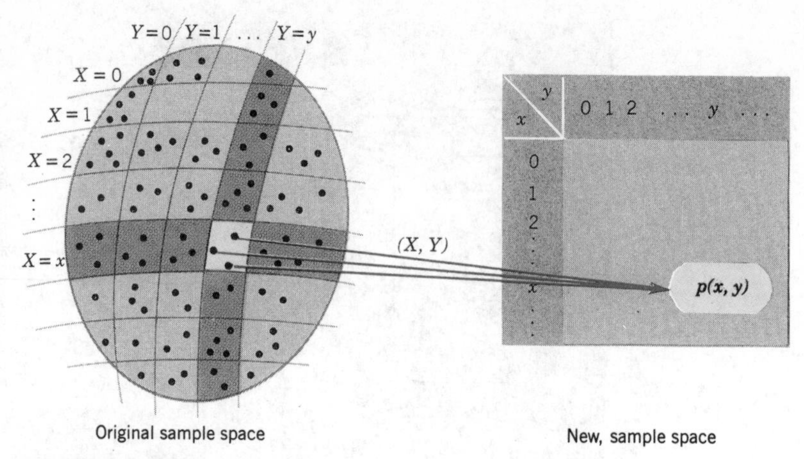

FIGURE 5-3
Two random variables (X, Y), showing their joint probability distribution derived from the original sample space (compare with Figure 5-1).

Figure 5-3. Of course, its probability $p(2)$ is the sum of the probabilities of all those chunks comprising it:

$$\begin{aligned} p(2) &= p(2, 0) + p(2, 1) + p(2, 2) + p(2, 3) \\ &\quad + \cdots + p(2, y) + \cdots \\ &= \sum_y p(2, y) \end{aligned} \tag{5-3}$$

and, in general, for any given x:

$$\boxed{\mathbf{p(x) = \sum_y p(x, y)}} \tag{5-4}$$

This idea may be applied to the distribution in Figure 5-1, which we repeat in Table 5-2. For example,

$$p(2) = 0 + .24 + .12 = .36 \tag{5-5}$$

We place this row sum in the right-hand margin. When all the other row sums are likewise recorded in the margin, they make up the complete distribution $p(x)$. This is sometimes called the *marginal* distribution of X, to describe how it was obtained. But, of course, it is just the ordinary distribution of X (which could have been found without any reference to Y, as indeed it was in Figure 4-1).

In conclusion, the word "marginal" merely describes how the distribution of X can be calculated from the joint distribution of X and another variable Y; row sums are calculated and placed "in the margin."

TABLE 5-2 The Marginal Distributions Obtained by Summing Rows and Columns of the Joint Distribution

x	y = 1	y = 2	y = 3	p(x)
0	.14	0	0	.14
1	0	.26	.13	.39
2	0	.24	.12	.36
3	.11	0	0	.11
p(y)	.25	.50	.25	1.00✓

Of course, the distribution of Y can be calculated in a similar way. The sum of each column is placed in the bottom margin, giving us the marginal distribution $p(y)$.[1]

C—INDEPENDENCE

Two random variables X and Y are called independent if the events $(X = x)$ and $(Y = y)$ are independent. That is,

X and Y are independent if
$$p(x, y) = p(x)p(y) \tag{5-6}$$
for all x and y — like (3-21)

For example, for the distribution in Table 5-2, are X and Y independent? For independence, (5-6) must hold for every (x, y) combination. We ask whether it holds, for example, when $x = 0$ and $y = 1$. In other words, is it true that:

$$p(0, 1) \stackrel{?}{=} p(0)p(1)$$

The answer is no, because

$$.14 \neq (.14)(.25)$$

Thus X and Y fail to be independent; that is, they are *dependent*.

Another example will illustrate further.

---

[1] Strictly speaking, $p(y)$ is not an adequate notation, and may cause ambiguity on occasion. For example, from Table 5-2 we can find any particular value for the marginal distribution of Y; when $y = 2$, for example, we find $p(2) = .50$. This seems to contradict (5-5), where we wrote $p(2) = .36$. (There, of course, we were referring to X, not Y, but the notation did not distinguish.) We could resolve this contradiction by more careful notation:

$$p_Y(2) = .50 \text{ whereas } p_X(2) = .36$$

Such subscripts are so awkward, however, that we will avoid them unless they are absolutely necessary.

EXAMPLE 5-1
HOW TO CHECK FOR INDEPENDENCE

Suppose that X and Y have the following joint distribution $p(x, y)$:

x	y: 10	20	40	80
20	.04	.08	.08	.05
40	.12	.24	.24	.15

Are X and Y independent?

SOLUTION

To check the condition for independence (5-6), we first calculate the marginal distributions $p(x)$ and $p(y)$:

x	y: 10	20	40	80	p(x)
20	.04	.08	.08	.05	.25
40	.12	.24	.24	.15	.75
p(y)	.16	.32	.32	.20	1.00√

Then we systematically multiply $p(x)p(y)$, which is easiest to do in a table again:

Table of $p(x)p(y)$

x	y: 10	20	40	80
20	(.25)(.16) = .04	(.25)(.32) = 0.08	(.25)(.32) = .08	(.25)(.20) = .05
40	(.75)(.16) = .12	(.75)(.32) = .24	(.75)(.32) = .24	(.75)(.20) = .15

Since this table of $p(x)p(y)$ agrees everywhere with the original table of $p(x, y)$, we have proved that (5-6) is true, and so X and Y are indeed independent.

In Example 5-1, an interesting pattern is evident. The rows are proportional (the second row is 3 times the first). The columns too are proportional (the second column is 2 times the first, etc.). And this pattern is generally true.

Whenever X and Y are independent, then the rows of the table $p(x, y)$ will be proportional, and so will the columns.	(5-7)

PROBLEMS

5-1 The approximately 100 million adult Americans (age 25 and over in 1985) were roughly classified by education X and age Y as follows (Stat. Abst. of U.S., 1987, p. 122. Actually there were 144 million, but we have conveniently scaled down to 100 million).

Education X (*last completed school*)		Age Y (25–35) 30	(35–55) 45	(55–100) 70
none	0	1,000,000	2,000,000	5,000,000
primary	1	3,000,000	6,000,000	10,000,000
secondary	2	18,000,000	21,000,000	15,000,000
college	3	7,000,000	8,000,000	4,000,000

Suppose the Gallup poll draws an adult American at random.

a. What is the probability of getting a 30-year-old college graduate ($X = 3$ and $Y = 30$, in the lower left cell)? And what is the probability of getting each of the 12 possible combinations of education and age? That is, tabulate the joint probability distribution $p(x, y)$.

b. Calculate $p(x)$ and $p(y)$.

c. Are X and Y independent?

d. Calculate μ_X and σ_X.

e. Graph the joint distribution, as in Figure 5-2.

5-2 **a.** Continuing Problem 5-1, look at just those Americans aged 30. Tabulate their distribution of education X—call it the *conditional* distribution $p(x|y)$ for $Y = 30$. Then calculate their average education—call it $E(X|Y = 30)$.

b. Similarly calculate $E(X|Y = 45)$, and $E(X|Y = 70)$. Mark them all on the graph of $p(x, y)$. Describe in words what this shows.

c. In view of part **b**, would you say education X is independent of age Y? Is this consistent with your answer to Problem 5-1**c**?

5-3 What we calculated in Problem 5-2 can alternatively be done with formulas. The conditional distribution of X is defined as:

$$p(x|y) \equiv \frac{p(x, y)}{p(y)} \qquad \text{like (3-17)}$$

Use this to calculate $p(x|y)$ for $Y = 30$. Does it agree with your answer in Problem 5-2**a**?

5-4 For which of the following joint distributions are X and Y independent?

a.

x	y = 1	y = 2
1	.10	.20
2	.30	.40

b.

x	y = 0	y = 1	y = 2
0	.10	.20	.10
1	.15	.20	.25

c.

x	y = 0	y = 1	y = 2
1	0	.1	.1
2	.1	.4	.1
3	.1	.1	0

d.

x	y = 1	y = 2	y = 3	y = 4
1	.12	.03	.06	.09
2	.20	.05	.10	.15
3	.08	.02	.04	.06

5-5 Using the table in Problem 5-4**c**, calculate and tabulate $p(x|y)$ for $Y = 1$. Is it the same as the unconditional distribution $p(x)$? What does this indicate about the independence of X and Y? Is this consistent with your earlier answer?

5-6 Repeat Problem 5-5, using the table in Problem 5-4**d**.

5-7 A salesman has an 80% chance of making a sale on each call. If three calls are to be made next month, let

$$X = \text{total number of sales}$$

$$Y = \text{total profit from the sales}$$

where the profit Y is calculated as follows: Any sales on the first two calls yield a profit of \$100 each. By the time the third call is made, the original product has been replaced by a new product whose sale yields a profit of \$200. Thus, for example, the sequence (sale, no sale, sale) would give $Y = \$300$.

List the sample space, and then:

a. Tabulate and graph the bivariate distribution.

b. Calculate the marginal distribution of X and of Y. Does the distribution of X agree with Problem 4-4?

c. What is the mean of X and of Y?

d. Are X and Y independent?

5-2 A FUNCTION OF TWO RANDOM VARIABLES

Again consider the planning of a 3 child family. Suppose the cost of clothing R depends upon both the number of girls X and the number of runs Y; that is:

$$R = g(X, Y)$$

What will be the average cost, μ_R? The answer is very similar to what we worked out in Section 4-6; there are two alternatives:

a. We could tabulate the distribution of R, and then calculate

$$E(R) = \Sigma r p(r) \tag{5-8}$$

b. An alternative one-step method is to use the distribution $p(x, y)$ directly:

$$\boxed{E[g(X, Y)] = \sum_x \sum_y g(x, y) p(x, y)} \tag{5-9}$$

Note how similar this is to the earlier formula:

$$E[g(X)] = \sum_x g(x) p(x) \qquad \text{(4-32) repeated}$$

A example will illustrate that methods **a** and **b** are equivalent.

EXAMPLE 5-2

In planning the 3 child family, suppose specifically that annual clothing costs are:

$$R = g(X, Y) = 10 + X + Y$$

Calculate the expected cost $E(R)$ in the two alternative ways:

a. Using (5-8).

b. Using (5-9).

SOLUTION

a. In Table 5-3 below, we first derive the distribution of R. (Compare to Table 4-5). For example, the three arrows represent the three ways that $R = 10 + X + Y$ can equal 14: When X and Y are 3 and 1; or 2 and 2; or 1 and 3. Finally, on the extreme right,

TABLE 5-3 Mean of *R* Calculated by First Deriving the Distribution of *R*

x	y: 1	2	3	Distribution of R: $r = g(x, y) = 10 + x + y$	$p(r)$	E(R): $rp(r)$
0	.14	0	0	11	.14	1.54
1	0	.26	.13	12	0	0
2	0	.24	.12	13	.26	3.38
3	.11	0	0	14	.48	6.72
				15	.12	1.80
						$E(R) = 13.44$

TABLE 5-4 Mean of *R* Calculated Directly from *p(x, y)*

x	y: 1	2	3
0	$(10 + 0 + 1).14 = 1.54$	0	0
1	0	$(10 + 1 + 2).26 = 3.38$	$(10 + 1 + 3).13 = 1.82$
2	0	$(10 + 2 + 2).24 = 3.36$	$(10 + 2 + 3).12 = 1.80$
3	$(10 + 3 + 1).11 = 1.54$	0	0

Overall Sum = $E(R) = 13.44\checkmark$

we calculate the expected value as usual, weighting each value of r with its probability.

b. In Table 5-4 above, we calculate $E(R)$ directly by calculating $g(x, y)p(x, y)$ for every combination of x and y. (Compare to Table 4-6). For example, in the first cell, when $x = 0$ and $y = 1$, we calculate $g(x, y) = 10 + x + y = 10 + 0 + 1$, and multiply by its probability $p(x, y) = .14$, to get 1.54. We sum these values in all the rows and columns (over all x and y) to finally obtain $E(R) = 13.44$. This agrees with the answer to part **a** as promised.

PROBLEMS

5-8 Suppose $R = X^2 + Y^2$, where X and Y have the following joint distribution:

x	y: 0	2	4
0	.1	.1	0
2	.1	.4	.1
4	0	.1	.1

a. Find $E(R)$ by first finding its distribution $p(r)$ and then calculating $\Sigma rp(r)$, as in (5-8).

b. Find $E(R)$, that is, $E(X^2 + Y^2)$, by using $\Sigma\Sigma g(x, y)p(x, y)$, as in (5-9).

c. Find the following expected values any way you like:

i. $E(X - 2)(Y - 2)$

ii. $E(X - 2)^2$

iii. $E(4X + 2Y)$

5-9 In a stand of 380 hardwood trees of marketable size, the diameter at waist height (D) and usable height (H) of each tree was measured (in feet). The 380 pairs of measurements were tallied in the following table, and then converted to relative frequency:

d	h: 20	25
1.0	.16	.09
1.25	.15	.30
1.50	.03	.17
1.75	.00	.10

Since a tree trunk is roughly a cylinder, the volume V of usable wood that it contains is given approximately by:

$$V = .4D^2H$$

a. Calculate the average volume per tree $E(V)$.

b. Calculate the standard deviation of V.

c. What is the total volume in the whole stand of 380 trees?

d. Calculate the average diameter $E(D)$ and the average height $E(H)$. Is it true that *average* volume obeys the same formula as volume itself, namely $E(V) = .4[E(D)]^2[E(H)]$?

5-10 In a certain gambling game, a pair of dice have their faces renumbered: The sides marked 4, 5, and 6 are renumbered with 1, 2, and 3, so that each die can have only three outcomes—each with the same probability $2/6 = 1/3$.

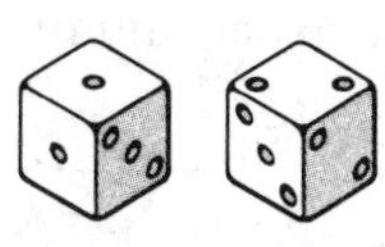

If the two dice are thrown independently, tabulate the joint distribution of:

X = number on the first die

Y = number on the second die

Then find the mean, variance, and standard deviation for each of the following:

a. X

b. Y

c. The total number of dots, $S = X + Y$

d. Note that S is just the sum of X and Y. Is the mean of S similarly just the sum of the means? Is the variance just the sum of the variances? And is the standard deviation just the sum of the standard deviations?

5-11 Suppose the two dice in Problem 5-10 have their faces renumbered, so that now the probabilities for X and Y are as follows:

x	p(x)
1	1/6
2	2/6
3	3/6

y	p(y)
1	3/6
2	1/6
3	2/6

Answer the same questions as before.

5-3 COVARIANCE

A—COVARIANCE IS LIKE VARIANCE

In this section we will develop the *covariance* to measure how two variables X and Y vary together, using the familiar concept of $E[g(X, Y)]$.

First recall our measure of how X alone varies: We started with the deviations $X - \mu$, squared them, and then took the expectation:

$$\sigma_X^2 = \text{Variance of } X \equiv E(X - \mu)^2 \qquad \text{(4-34) repeated}$$

To measure how two variables X and Y vary together, we again start with the deviations, $X - \mu_X$ and $Y - \mu_Y$. We multiply them, and then take the expectation:

$$\boxed{\sigma_{X,Y} = \textbf{Covariance of } X \textbf{ and } Y \equiv E(X - \mu_X)(Y - \mu_Y)} \qquad \text{(5-10)}$$

An example will show how similar the covariance is to the variance. (Incidentally, if you have done Problem 5-8**c**, you have already calculated a covariance as well as a variance, without even realizing it.)

EXAMPLE 5-3
COVARIANCE IS CALCULATED LIKE VARIANCE

Suppose a population of working couples has the bivariate distribution of income shown in Table 5-5.

a. Calculate the variance of X, and of Y.

b. Calculate the covariance of X and Y.

SOLUTION

a. The calculation of σ_X^2 is based on $p(x)$—the marginal distribution of X in the last column of Table 5-5 below. We first find $\mu_X = 20$, and then:

Given		*Variance*
x	p(x)	$(x-\mu)^2 p(x)$
10	.25	$(-10)^2 .25 = 25$
20	.55	$0^2 .55 = 0$
30	.15	$(10^2 .15 = 15$
40	.05	$(20)^2 .05 = 20$
		sum $= \sigma_X^2 = 60$

Similarly, using the marginal distribution of Y along the bottom row of Table 5-5, we would find $\mu_Y = 20$, and then $\sigma_Y^2 = 70$. We have gone through the familiar calculations for σ^2 in this explicit form in order to clarify the calculation in part **b**.

b. The covariance calculation is much the same, except that we now use the whole bivariate distribution (rather than just the marginal distribution that we used in part **a**.) The calculations are shown in Table 5-6. For example, in the northeast cell, where $x = 10$ and $y = 30$, we calculate $(x - \mu_X)(y - \mu_Y)p(x, y) =$

TABLE 5-5 Joint Distribution of Husband's Income *X* and Wife's Income *Y* ($000 Annually)

x	y = 10	20	30	40	p(x)
10	.20	.04	.01		.25
20	.10	.36	.09		.55
30		.05	.10		.15
40				.05	.05
p(y)	.30	.45	.20	.05	

TABLE 5-6 Sum of $(x - \mu_X)(y - \mu_Y)p(x, y)$ Yields Covariance $\sigma_{X,Y}$

x	y: 10	20	30	40
10	(−10)(−10).20 = +20	(−10)(0).04 = 0	(−10)(10).01 = −1	
20	(0)(−10).10 = 0	(0)(0).36 = 0	(0)(10).09 = 0	
30		(10)(0).05 = 0	(10)(10).10 = +10	
40				(20)(20).05 = +20

Overall sum $= \sigma_{X,Y} = 49$

$(10 - 20)(30 - 20)(.01) = -1$. We sum all such values, to finally obtain $\sigma_{XY} = 49$.

The calculation of the covariance can often be simplified by using an alternative formula:

$$\boxed{\sigma_{X,Y} = E(XY) - \mu_X\mu_Y} \tag{5-11}$$

like (4-35)

B—THE COVARIANCE OF *X* AND *Y* INDICATES HOW THEY ARE RELATED

The mean levels of X and Y in Table 5-6 were shown by dotted lines, which break the table into four quadrants. When large values of X and of Y occur together (in the southeast quadrant), the deviations $(X - \mu_X)$ and $(Y - \mu_Y)$ are both positive, and so their product is positive. Similarly, when small values of X and of Y occur together (in the northwest quadrant), both deviations are negative, so that their product is positive in this case as well.

In Table 5-6, most of the probability is in these two quadrants. Therefore, the sum of all the calculated values—the covariance—is positive, and nicely summarizes the positive relation between the two variables (when one is large, the other tends to be large also).

But now consider the other two quadrants, where one deviation is negative and the other is positive—and hence their calculated product is negative. If most of the probability were in these two quadrants, then the sum of all the calculated values—the covariance—would be negative, and would nicely summarize the negative relation between the two variables (when one is large, the other tends to be small).

Finally, what if all four corners of the table had substantial probabilities so that the positive and negative calculations cancelled each other out? The covariance $\sigma_{X,Y}$ would be zero, and X and Y would be called *uncorrelated*. One way this can happen is for X and Y to be independent. Stated more formally (and proved in Appendix 5-3):

If X and Y are independent, then they are uncorrelated ($\sigma_{X,Y} = 0$). (5-12)

C—CORRELATION: THE COVARIANCE RESCALED

We have seen how the covariance can indicate whether X and Y have a positive, negative, or zero relation. Yet $\sigma_{X,Y}$ can still be improved, because it depends upon the units in which X and Y are measured. If X, for example, were measured in inches instead of feet, each X deviation in (5-10), and hence $\sigma_{X,Y}$ itself, would unfortunately increase by 12 times. To eliminate this difficulty, we define the correlation ρ (rho, the Greek equivalent of r for relation):

$$\text{Correlation, } \rho \equiv \frac{\sigma_{X,Y}}{\sigma_X \sigma_Y} \tag{5-13}$$

This does, in fact, work: Measuring X in terms of inches rather than feet still increases $\sigma_{X,Y}$ in the numerator by 12 times, but this is exactly cancelled by the same 12 times increase in σ_X in the denominator. Similarly, (5-13) neutralizes any change in the scale of Y; thus correlation is completely independent of the scale in which either X or Y is measured.

Another reason that ρ is a very useful measure of the relation between X and Y is that it is always bounded:

$$-1 \leq \rho \leq +1 \tag{5-14}$$

Now suppose X and Y have a perfect positive linear relation. For example, suppose they always take on the same values, so that $X = Y$. In this case, all the probabilities in Table 5-6 would lie along the northwest–southeast diagonal of the table (e.g., some probability that $X = 30$ and $Y = 30$, but no probability that $X = 30$ and $Y = 20$). Then it is easy to show that ρ takes on the limiting value of +1.[2] Similarly, if there is a perfect negative linear relation, then ρ would be -1.

To illustrate these bounds, we can calculate ρ for the data in Example 5-3.

$$\rho = \frac{49}{\sqrt{60}\sqrt{70}} = .76$$

This is indeed less than the upper bound of 1.

PROBLEMS

5-12 For each of the following joint distributions, calculate σ_{XY} from the definition (5-10), and from the easier formula (5-11). Then calculate ρ_{XY}.

a.

x \ y	0	1
0	.2	0
1	.4	.2
2	0	.2

b.

x \ y	0	5	10
2	0	.1	.1
4	.1	.4	.1
6	.1	.1	0

c.

x \ y	1	2
0	.06	.04
1	.30	.20
2	.24	.16

d.

x \ y	1	2	3
0	1/8	0	0
1	0	2/8	1/8
2	0	2/8	1/8
3	1/8	0	0

5-13 **a.** In Problem 5-12, parts **c** and **d**, what is ρ? Are X and Y independent?

b. Looking beyond these particular examples, which of the following statements are true for *any* X and Y?

1. If X and Y are independent, then they must be uncorrelated.
2. If X and Y are uncorrelated, then they must be independent.

5-14 Does money make you happy?

Americans were asked in 1971 to rank themselves on a "happiness index" as follows: $H = 0$ (not happy), $H = 1$ (fairly happy), or

[2] Since $X = Y$, (5-10) becomes

$$\sigma_{X,Y} = E(X - \mu_X)(X - \mu_X)$$
$$= E(X - \mu_X)^2 = \sigma_X^2$$

Also note that, since $X = Y$, $\sigma_X = \sigma_Y$. When we substitute all this into (5-13), ρ becomes $\sigma_X^2/\sigma_X\sigma_X = 1$.

$H = 2$ (very happy). Annual household income X (in thousands of dollars) was also recorded for each individual. Then the relative frequencies of various combinations of H and X were roughly as follows (Gallup, 1971):

Joint Distribution of Happiness *H* and Income *X*

x	h = 0	h = 1	h = 2
2.5	.03	.12	.07
7.5	.02	.13	.11
12.5	.01	.13	.14
17.5	.01	.09	.14

a. Calculate $E(H|X)$ for the various levels of X, and mark them on the graph of the bivariate distribution (as in Problem 5-2).

b. Calculate the covariance and correlation.

c. Answer True or False; if False, correct it:

i. As X increases, the average level of H increases. This positive relation is reflected in a positive correlation ρ.

ii. Yet the relation is just a *tendency* (H fluctuates around its average level), so that ρ is less than 1.

iii. This shows that the rich tend to be happier than the poor, that is, money tends to make people happier.

5-15 Does education make you happy?

In Problem 5-14, the amount of education was also measured for each individual: $X = 1$ (elementary school completed), $X = 2$ (high school completed), or $X = 3$ (college completed, or more). Thus X = number of schools completed. Then the relative frequencies of various combinations were roughly as follows (Gallup, 1971):

Joint Distribution of Happiness *H* and Education *X*

x	h = 0	h = 1	h = 2
1	.02	.08	.05
2	.02	.28	.25
3	.01	.13	.16

Repeat the same questions as in Problem 5-14 (with education substituted for income, of course).

5-4 LINEAR COMBINATION OF TWO RANDOM VARIABLES

Suppose that a couple is drawn at random from a large population of working couples. In thousand dollar units, let:

$$X = \text{man's income}$$
$$Y = \text{woman's income}$$

Then the couple's total income is the sum:

$$S = X + Y$$

Or, suppose their pension contribution is 10% of the man's income, and 20% of the woman's income. Then the couple's total pension contribution is a weighted sum (also called a linear combination):

$$W = .10X + .20Y \tag{5-15}$$

Of course, since X and Y are random variables, S and W are also. How can we find their moments easily?

A—MEAN

Continuing our example, suppose we know that the average man's income is 20, and the average woman's is 16; that is,

$$E(X) = 20 \quad \text{and} \quad E(Y) = 16$$

It is natural to guess that the average total income is:

$$E(S) = 20 + 16 = 36$$

This guess is correct because, as illustrated in Problems 5-10 and 5-11, and proved in Appendix 5-4, it is generally true that:

$$\boxed{E(X + Y) = E(X) + E(Y)} \tag{5-16}$$

Similarly, it is natural to guess that the average pension contribution is:

$$E(W) = .20(20) + .10(16) = 5.6$$

This guess also is correct, because it is generally true that:

$$\boxed{E(aX + bY) = aE(X) + bE(Y)} \tag{5-17}$$

like (4-29)

Statisticians often refer to this important property as the *additivity* or *linearity* of the expectation operator.

How helpful is it? Recall how complicated it was to calculate the average of the cost function $R = 10 + X + Y$ in Example 5-2. Now that we recognize it as a linear combination, we can apply (5-16):

$$E(R) = E(10 + X + Y)$$
$$= 10 + E(X) + E(Y)$$

From earlier calculations, we found $E(X) = 1.44$ and $E(Y) = 2.0$. Thus

$$E(R) = 10 + (1.44) + (2.0)$$
$$= 13.44 \qquad \text{(Table 5-4 confirmed)}$$

So the linearity property is very helpful indeed. It allows us to simply use the individual means $E(X)$ and $E(Y)$, instead of working through a whole bivariate table such as Table 5-4.

B—VARIANCE

The *variance* of a sum is a little more complicated, as we prove in Appendix 5-4:

$$\boxed{\text{var}(X + Y) = \text{var } X + \text{var } Y + 2 \text{ cov } (X, Y)} \qquad (5\text{-}18)$$

where var and cov are abbreviations for variance and covariance, of course. Similarly, for a weighted sum:

$$\boxed{\text{var}(aX + bY) = a^2 \text{ var } X + b^2 \text{ var } Y + 2ab \text{ cov } (X, Y)} \qquad (5\text{-}19)$$

It is helpful to briefly sketch just why the covariance term appears in these two formulas. It is because variance is defined by *squared* deviations. And, as everyone knows:

$$(x + y)^2 = x^2 + y^2 + 2xy \qquad (5\text{-}20)$$

A more intuitive reason for the covariance in (5-18) can be developed. Consider, for example, what happens if X and Y are positively related. When X is high, Y tends to be high as well, making the sum $(X + Y)$ very high. Similarly, when X is low, Y tends to be low, making the sum $(X + Y)$ very low. These extreme values of $(X + Y)$ make its variance large, and the formula for var$(X + Y)$ reflects this—by adding on the final term (cov X, Y).

An example will illustrate how the variance formulas work.

EXAMPLE 5-4
A COUPLE'S INCOME AND PENSION

In Example 5-3, we were given a joint distribution of income for husbands (X) and wives (Y), from which we calculated

$$\sigma_X^2 = 60 \qquad \sigma_Y^2 = 70 \qquad \sigma_{X,Y} = 49$$

Calculate the standard deviation of:

a. Total income $S = X + Y$

b. Total pension contribution $W = .10X + .20Y$

SOLUTION

a. Although it is the standard deviation σ we eventually want, it is the variance σ^2 that has the formula we can use:

$$\begin{aligned} \text{var}(X + Y) &= \text{var } X + \text{var } Y + 2\text{cov}(X, Y) \qquad \text{like (5-18)} \\ &= 60 + 70 + 2(49) = 228 \end{aligned}$$

$$\text{standard deviation} = \sqrt{228} = 15.1$$

b.

$$\begin{aligned} \text{var}(.20X + .10Y) &= (.20)^2 \text{ var } X + (.10)^2 \text{ var } Y \qquad \text{like (5-19)} \\ &\quad + 2(.20)(.10) \text{ cov}(X, Y) \\ &= (.20)^2(60) + (.10)^2(70) + 2(.20)(.10)(49) \\ &= 5.06 \end{aligned}$$

$$\text{standard deviation} = \sqrt{5.06} = 2.25$$

Finally, consider the very simple and common case that occurs when X and Y are uncorrelated—that is, $\text{cov}(X, Y) = 0$. Then (5-18) reduces to:

$$\text{var}(X + Y) = \text{var } X + \text{var } Y$$

Since independence assures us that X and Y are uncorrelated according to (5-12), we may finally conclude that:

If X and Y are independent:

$$\text{var}(X + Y) = \text{var } X + \text{var } Y \qquad (5\text{-}21)$$

Similarly:

$$\text{var}(aX + bY) = a^2 \text{ var } X + b^2 \text{ var } Y \qquad (5\text{-}22)$$

Two examples will illustrate how these formulas simplify an otherwise tedious task.

EXAMPLE 5-5

When a pair of dice are thrown, we are customarily interested in the total number of dots T. Calculate:

a. Its mean.

b. Its standard deviation.

SOLUTION

The hard way to solve this problem is with a tree, or, equivalently, a bivariate distribution. But we now have an easier way: Break down the problem into simple components by writing:

$$T = X_1 + X_2$$

where X_1 is the number of dots on the first die, and X_2 is the number of dots on the second die. For each die, the distribution (and hence the moments) are easy to calculate:

Fair Die		*Mean*	*Variance*
x	p(x)	xp(x)	$(x - \mu)^2 \, p(x)$
1	1/6	1/6	6.25/6
2	1/6	2/6	2.25/6
3	1/6	3/6	.25/6
4	1/6	4/6	.25/6
5	1/6	5/6	2.25/6
6	1/6	6/6	6.25/6
		21/6	17.50/6
		$E(X) = 3.5$	$\sigma^2 = 2.92$
			$\sigma = 1.71$

Now we can put these components together:

a. $E(X_1 + X_2) = E(X_1) + E(X_2)$
$= 3.5 + 3.5 = 7.0$ like (5-16)

b. Since the two dice are independent, (5-21) gives:

$$\begin{aligned} \text{var}(X_1 + X_2) &= \text{var}\, X_1 + \text{var}\, X_2 \\ &= 2.92 + 2.92 = 5.84 \end{aligned} \tag{5-23}$$

For the standard deviation (SD), we take the square root:

$$SD(X_1 + X_2) = \sqrt{5.84} = 2.42$$

REMARKS

We might have been tempted to calculate the standard deviation (SD) by a formula similar to (5-23), namely:

$$SD(X_1 + X_2) \stackrel{?}{=} SD(X_1) + SD(X_2)$$

We can easily confirm that this would not work:

$$2.42 \neq 1.71 + 1.71$$

In conclusion, then, it is *variances* that we add, not standard deviations.

EXAMPLE 5-6

Suppose a die is thrown 10 times, instead of just twice. For the total number of dots, calculate:

a. The mean.

b. The standard deviation.

SOLUTION

The hard way to do this problem is with a tenfold multivariate distribution—a preposterous task, even for a computer.

The easy way, once more, is to break down the problem into simple components. Again let X_1 be the number of dots on the first toss, X_2 the number on the second loss, and so on. Also note the mean and variance for each toss calculated in the previous example.

a. $$E(X_1 + X_2 + \cdots + X_{10}) = 3.5 + 3.5 + \cdots = 10(3.5) = 35$$

b. $$\text{var}(X_1 + X_2 + \cdots + X_{10}) = 2.92 + 2.92 + \cdots = 10(2.92) = 29.2$$

$$SD = \sqrt{10}\,\sqrt{2.92} = 5.40 \qquad (5\text{-}24)$$

The theorems of this chapter are summarized in Table 5-7.

TABLE 5-7 The Mean and Variance of Functions of *X* and *Y*

Function of X and Y	Mean	Variance
1. Any function $g(X, Y)$	$E[g(X, Y)] = \sum_x \sum_y g(x, y)p(x, y)$	
2. Linear combination $aX + bY$	$E(aX + bY) = aE(X) + bE(Y)$	$\text{var}(aX + bY) = a^2 \text{var } X + b^2 \text{var } Y + 2ab \text{ cov }(X, Y)$
3. Simple sum $X + Y$	$E(X + Y) = E(X) + E(Y)$	$\text{var}(X + Y) = \text{var } X + \text{var } Y + 2 \text{ cov}(X, Y)$

PROBLEMS

5-16 Following (5-20), it was explained why the formula for $\text{var}(X + Y)$ includes the covariance term—when the covariance was positive. Give a similar explanation when the covariance is negative.

5-17 A marriage counseling office consisted of 10 couples. The annual incomes (in thousands of dollars) of the men and women were as follows:

Couple	Man	Woman
MacIntyre	20	15
Sproule	30	35
Carney	30	25
Devita	20	25
Peat	20	25
Matias	30	15
Steinberg	40	25
Aldis	30	25
Yablonsky	40	35
Singh	40	25

A couple is drawn by lot to represent the office at a workshop on personal finances. Let X and Y denote the randomly drawn income of the man and woman. Then find:

a. The bivariate probability distribution, and its graph.

b. The distribution, mean, and variance of X. Also of Y.

c. The covariance $\sigma_{X,Y}$.

d. If S is the combined income of the couple, what is its mean and variance? Calculate two ways: from the distribution of S, as in (5-8), and then using the easy formulas for sums.

e. Suppose (not very realistically) that the couple's income after taxes is $W = .6X + .8Y$. What is its mean and variance?

f. To measure the degree of sex discrimination against wives, a sociologist measured the difference $D = X - Y$. What is its mean and variance?

g. How good a measure of sex discrimination is $E(D)$?

5-18 Continuing Problem 5-17, we shall consider some alternative schemes for collecting the tax T on the couple's income S. Find the mean and standard deviation of T,

a. If S is taxed at a straight 20%—that is,

$$T = .20S$$

b. If S is taxed at 50%, with the first 15 thousand exempt—that is,

$$T = .5(S - 15)$$

c. If S is taxed according to the following progressive tax table:

S	T	S	T
30	4	55	11
35	5	60	13
40	6	65	16
45	7	70	19
50	9	75	22

5-19 Compare the three tax schemes in Problem 5-18 in terms of the following criteria:

i. Which scheme yields the most revenue to the government?

ii. Which scheme is most egalitarian; that is, which scheme results in the smallest standard deviation in net income left after taxes?

CHAPTER 5 SUMMARY

5-1 A pair of random variables X and Y has a joint probability distribution $p(x, y)$, from which the distributions $p(x)$ and $p(y)$ can be found in the margin. X and Y are then called independent if the simple multiplication rule holds: $p(x, y) = p(x)p(y)$ for all x and y.

5-2 A new random variable $R = g(X, Y)$ has an expected value that can be calculated from the joint distribution $p(x, y)$:

$$E[g(X, Y)] = \Sigma\Sigma\, g(x, y)p(x, y).$$

5-3 Just as variance measures how much one variable varies, so covariance measures how much two variables vary together. Its standardized version is the correlation $\rho = \sigma_{XY}/\sigma_X\sigma_Y$, which measures the degree of linear relation between X and Y.

5-4 The sum $X + Y$ is a particularly convenient function. Its expected value is simply $E(X) + E(Y)$, and its variance is $\text{var}(X) + \text{var}(Y) + 2\,\text{cov}(X, Y)$.

REVIEW PROBLEMS

Problems 5-20 to 5-25 form a sequence that gives a summary of this chapter, with a more applied flavor.

5-20 The approximately 100 million adult Americans (age 25 or over, in 1980) were roughly classified by education X, and sex Z, as follows (U.S. Current Population Reports, Series P-20, No. 390, Mar 1981 and 1980. Actually there were 133 million, but we have conveniently rescaled down to 100 million.):

Education X (last completed school)		*Sex Z*	
		0 (male)	*1 (female)*
none	0	4,000,000	5,000,000
primary	1	10,000,000	12,000,000
secondary	2	23,000,000	29,000,000
college	3	10,000,000	7,000,000

Suppose the Gallup poll draws an adult American at random.

a. What is the chance of getting a college-graduate female ($X = 3$ and $Z = 1$, in the lower-right cell)? Similarly, what is the chance of getting each of the 8 possible combinations of education and sex? That is, tabulate the (joint) probability distribution of X and Z.

b. What is the chance of getting a college graduate ($X = 3$)? Similarly, what is the chance of getting each of the 4 possible levels of education? That is, tabulate the (marginal) probability distribution of X.

c. What is the chance of getting a person with at least secondary school graduation ($X \geq 2$)?

d. Calculate the mean education $E(X)$.

e. Similarly, tabulate the (marginal) probability distribution of sex Z. Then calculate $E(Z)$.

5-21 Continuing Problem 5-20.

a. If the person is male, what are the probabilities of the 4 possible levels of education? That is, find the conditional distribution of X, given $Z = 0$.

b. Is this conditional distribution of X different from the unconditional distribution of X found in Problem 5-20? Is education X therefore dependent or independent of sex Z?

c. Calculate the conditional mean $E(X|Z = 0)$. That is, find the mean education of males.

d. Similarly, calculate $E(X|Z = 1)$. That is, find the mean education of females. Is it higher or lower than for males?

e. How does the unconditional mean $E(X)$ found in Problem 5-20 compare to the two conditional means found above?

5-22 Continuing Problem 5-20, suppose (contrary to fact, fortunately) that each American drew a salary S that depended only upon education and sex as follows (annual salary in \$000):

$$S = 10 + 2X + 4Z$$

(that is, a basic 10 thousand, plus bonuses for education and sex).

a. What would the salary be for each of the 8 combinations (cells) in the given table?

To reorganize your answer, list the possible salaries in order, and tabulate the corresponding probabilities (the distribution of salary).

b. From the distribution of salary, calculate the expected salary $E(S)$.

c. Since $S = 10 + 2X + 4Z$, try calculating its expected value alternatively as:

$$E(S) = 10 + 2E(X) + 4E(Z)$$

where $E(X)$ and $E(Z)$ were found in Problem 5-20**d** and **e**.

d. Why does your answer to **c** agree with **b**? (Is it a fluke, or is it because S is a special function?)

5-23 Continuing Problem 5-22, now suppose salary S has a different formula, as given below. In each case, calculate $E(S)$ as easily as you can. (Hint: If S is linear, you can use the shortcut in part **c**

above. If S is nonlinear, you can still proceed as in parts **a** and **b** above.)

a. $S = 10 + 10XZ$

b. $S = 10 + 3X - 2Z$

c. $S = (2X + 40)/5$

d. $S = 10 + X^2$

5-24 The approximately 100 million adult Americans (age 25 or over in 1980) were roughly classified by age Y, as well as education X and sex Z, as follows (same source as Problem 5-20):

Education X (last completed school)		Sex Z: Z = 0 (male)			Z = 1 (female)		
		Age Y			Age Y		
		30	45	70	30	45	70
none	0	400,000	1,200,000	2,700,000	400,000	1,100,000	3,300,000
primary	1	1,600,000	3,300,000	4,700,000	1,700,000	3,600,000	6,300,000
secondary	2	8,400,000	9,100,000	5,600,000	9,300,000	11,500,000	8,600,000
college	3	3,700,000	4,200,000	2,100,000	3,000,000	2,800,000	1,400,000

a. If an adult American was drawn at random, what is the probability of drawing a female college graduate about age 30? In general, tabulate the probability for each of the 24 possible combinations of education, age, and sex.

b. Now suppose we did not need the detail of age. Instead, we just wanted the breakdown by education and sex. Find the probability of drawing a female college graduate. And in general, tabulate the probability for each of the 8 combinations of education and sex.

Round your table to two decimals (%), and see if it agrees with Problem 5-20.

c. Suppose we did not need the detail of sex. Instead, we just wanted the breakdown by education and age. Find the probability of drawing a college graduate about age 30. And in general, tabulate the probability for each of the 12 combinations of education and age.

Round your table to two decimals (%), and see if it agrees with Problem 5-1. (Read the table descriptions carefully.)

5-25 The detail (disaggregation) given in Problem 5-24 is often useful to clarify what is going on. For example, we noted in Problem 5-21**d** that the mean education for females was lower than for males. To track down the source of this difference,

a. Compare the mean education of males and females, for age 30.

b. Then repeat for age 45, and for age 70.

c. Summarize in a graph, and in words, what you have discovered.

d. Underline the correct choice:
In part (c) we found females had about .06 units of education less than males, at each age level. Earlier in Problem 5-21(d) the analysis that ignored age showed an overall difference that was [the same of course, surprisingly larger]. This confounding occurs because there are [more, fewer] older women than men, and it is the older people who tend to have [more, less] education.
To restate this point, suppose at each age women achieved the same education as men. Then women's average education overall would [still be somewhat less than men's, now be equal to men's].
Routinely and easily controlling for confounding factors—not just age, but any others as well—is what [multiple regressions, confidence intervals] do, and we will accordingly analyze this data again in Problem 14-8.

5-26 *A Final Challenge: How to Hedge Your Investment Bets*

You have $10,000 saved up to invest for a year, and are considering stocks and/or short-term Treasury bills. The returns from both sources are judged uncertain, of course, as the following personal probability table indicates:

Bivariate Probability Distribution for Annual Rates of Return on Stocks (*S*) and Treasury Bills (*T*)

	S			
T	−10%	0	10%	20%
6%	0	0	.10	.10
8%	0	.10	.30	.20
10%	.10	.10	0	0

a. Without calculating, state whether the covariance of S and T will be positive, zero, or negative. Now calculate the covariance to confirm.

b. If you invested your $10,000 entirely in stocks, what would be the expected value of your return? And the standard deviation?
Repeat, for investing entirely in Treasury bills, for splitting your investment 50-50, then finally for splitting 20-80. Then record your four answers in the following table:

Summary of the Returns from Four Possible Portfolios

Stocks/Treasury Bills Split	*Expected Value, μ*	*Standard Deviation, σ*
100/0		
0/100		
50/50		
20/80		

c. The two things you would like from an investment portfolio of course are high expected return (high μ) and low risk (low σ).
Which of the four portfolios listed in **b** gives the highest μ? And which gives the lowest σ?

d. In your best judgment, is there another possible portfolio that would give an even higher value of μ?

e. Can you prove your conjecture in **d**?

f. In your best judgment, is there another possible portfolio that would give an even lower value of σ?

*g. A proof of your conjecture in **f** will be much more difficult, of course, since the formulas for σ are more complex than for μ. Here is a theorem that will help (Wonnacott 1984, p 407):
The weights (split) that minimize σ are in the ratio

$$\frac{\sigma_T^2 - \sigma_{S,T}}{\sigma_S^2 - \sigma_{S,T}} \tag{5-25}$$

Calculate this ratio, and re-express it as two percentages that add up to 100% (i.e., 70/30, 60/40, or whatever).
For this split, what is the standard deviation? Is it indeed smaller than the four other values of σ found in part **b**?

h. To summarize, we found it [was, was not] possible to find an ideal portfolio that simultaneously maximizes expected profit μ and minimizes risk σ. In fact, the best portfolio for maximizing expected profit was ____, while the best portfolio for minimizing risk was ____.
This tension between the twin goals of portfolio theory is still one of the exciting areas of research—research that requires [careful evaluation of, a mathematical model that ignores] just how risk averse the investor is.

REVIEW PROBLEMS, CHAPTERS 1 TO 5

5-27 Circle the correct choice in each of the five following brackets. Note the following abbreviations:

$$RCE = \text{randomized controlled experiment}$$
$$OS = \text{observational study}$$

To really find out how effective a treatment is, a [*RCE*, *OS*] is better than a [*RCE*, *OS*], where feasible. This is because a [*RCE*, *OS*] actually makes the treatment and control groups equal on average in every respect—except for the treatment itself, of course; whereas a [*RCE*, *OS*] is usually cluttered up with confounding factors that bias the answer. To the extent these confounding factors can be measured and analyzed with a [*multiple regression*, *confidence interval*], however, bias can be reduced.

5-28 Suggest some plausible reasons for each of the following relations:

a. Over a period of several years, the relation between the number of colds reported weekly in a city and the amount of beer sold was found to be negative (low numbers of colds associated with high beer sales). Does beer prevent colds?

b. Over a period of 50 years, the relation between clergymen's annual salaries and annual alcohol sales in the U.S. was found to be positive. Would paying clergymen more increase alcohol sales?

c. The Irish humorist George Bernard Shaw once observed that there was a strong positive relation between a young man's income and clothes. His advice to a young man aspiring to be rich was therefore simple: Buy a black umbrella and top hat.

5-29 The distribution of the earned income of American men in 1975 was very roughly as follows:

Annual Income ($000)	*Proportion of Men Earning That Income*
0–5	36%
5–10	23%
10–15	20%
15–20	11%
20–25	5%
25–30	3%
30–35	2%

a. Graph this distribution.

b. Calculate the mean income, and the standard deviation, and show them on the graph.

c. What is the mode? Where will the median be in relation to the mean and mode?

d. What was the total earned income of the whole population of 78 million men?

5-30 A test consists of eight multiple-choice questions, each with a choice of 5 answers. Let X be the number of correct answers for a student who resorts to pure guessing.

a. Graph the distribution of X.

b. Calculate μ_X and σ_X and show them on the graph.

c. If the instructor calculates a rescaled mark $Y = 10X + 20$, what are μ_Y and σ_Y?

d. If the passing mark is $Y = 50$, what is the chance the student who resorts to pure guessing will pass?

5-31 To find out who won the Reagan-Carter TV debate before the 1980 Presidential election, ABC News conducted a phone-in survey. Nearly a million people volunteered to call in: 723,000 believed that Reagan had won the debate, and 244,000 believed Carter had (*New York Times*, Oct. 29, 1980).

CBS on the other hand conducted a very small sample survey. Of all the registered voters who had watched the debate, 1,019 were polled at random by telephone: 44% believed that Reagan had won the debate, 36% believed Carter had, 14% called it a tie, and 6% had no opinion.

Do these two polls agree, allowing for sampling fluctuation? Explain why, or why not. Include a critique of each poll.

5-32 A firm specializing in political polling took a preliminary random sample of a dozen voters from a suburb that is 60% Republican, 20% Democratic, and 20% Independent. What is the chance that a majority in the sample are Republican (6 or more)?

5-33 The following table gives, for a thousand newborn American baby boys (white U.S. males, 1970), the approximate number dying, in successive decades:

a. The third column shows the number surviving at the beginning of each decade. Complete this tabulation of $L(x)$.

b. The mortality rate in the last column is just the number dying during the decade, relative to the number living at the beginning of the decade. Complete the tabulation of the mortality rate $m(x)$. Then answer True or False. If False, correct it.

i. The mortality rate is lowest during the first decade of life.

ii. Roughly speaking, the mortality rate nearly doubles every decade.

c. Ten-year term insurance is an agreement whereby a man pays the insurance company \$x (the "premium," which usually is spread throughout the decade in 120 monthly payments) in return for a payment of $1000 to the man's estate if he dies. In order for this to be a "fair bet" (and ignoring interest), what should the premium x be for a man:

i. In his 20s?

ii. In his 40s?

d. The work that we have done so far could be just as well expressed in probability terms. For example, find:

i. The probability of a man dying in his 40s.

ii. The probability of a man surviving to age 40.

iii. The conditional probability of a person dying in his 40s, given that he has survived to 40.

Age, x	n(x) = Number Dying Within the Decade	L(x) = Number Living to the Beginning of the Decade	Mortality Rate, Per Decade $m(x) = \frac{n(x)}{L(x)}$
0 to 10	26	1,000	.026
10 to 20	9	974	.009
20 to 30	18	965	.019
30 to 40	21	947	.022
40 to 50	49	.	.
50 to 60	117	.	.
60 to 70	219	.	.
70 to 80	282		
80 to 90	208		
90 to 100	51		
	Total = 1000		

5-34 Referring to the mortality table in Problem 5-33:

a. Find the mean age at death (i.e., mean length of life, also called life expectancy).

*b. If the mortality rate were 50% higher after age 40, how much would this reduce life expectancy? (Incidentally, heavy cigarette smoking—two or more packs per day—seems to be associated with roughly this much increase in mortality according to the U.S. Department of Health, Education, and Welfare, 1964.)

5-35 An apartment manager in Cincinnati orders three new refrigerators, which the seller guarantees. Each refrigerator has a 20% probability of being defective.

a. Tabulate the probability distribution for the total number of defective refrigerators, X.

b. What are the mean and variance of X?

c. Suppose that the cost of repair, in order to honor the guarantee, consists of a fixed fee (\$10) plus a variable component (\$15 per defective refrigerator). That is:

$$\begin{aligned} c(x) &= 0 && \text{if } x = 0 \\ &= 10 + 15x && \text{if } x > 0 \end{aligned}$$

Find the average cost of repair.

5-36 A company produces TV tubes with a length of life that is normally distributed with a standard deviation of 5 months. How large should the mean μ be in order that 90% of the tubes last for the guarantee period (18 months)?

5-37 A clinic plans to set up a mass testing program for diabetes using an inexpensive test of high reliability: Of all people with diabetes, 95% are correctly diagnosed positive (as having diabetes); of all people free of diabetes, 98% are correctly diagnosed negative (the remaining 2% being erroneously diagnosed positive).

The community served by the clinic has about 10,000 patients, and the undiagnosed diabetes rate runs at about 1%. The clinic director wants to know three things:

a. About how many patients will have diabetes and be missed (i.e., get a negative diagnosis)?

b. About how many patients will be diagnosed positive (and therefore require follow up)?

c. What proportion of the patients in part **b** will actually have diabetes?

d. The director cannot believe your answer to part **c.** Explain why it is so low, as simply as you can.

5-38 When is it true, or approximately true, that:

a. $E(X^2) = [E(X)]^2$?

b. $E(XY) = E(X)E(Y)$?

5-39 Because of unforeseen delays, the last two stages for manufacturing a complex plastic were of very uncertain duration. In fact, the times required for completion (X and Y, in hours) had the following probability distributions:

x	p(x)
1	.4
2	.2
3	0
4	.4

y	p(y)
0	.4
1	.2
2	0
3	0
4	.4

Two questions were of interest to management: (1) the total time T required; and (2) the cost C of running the first process, which was \$200 per hour, plus a fixed cost of \$300. In formulas,

$$T = X + Y$$

$$C = 200X + 300$$

Assuming X and Y are independent, tabulate the distribution of T, and of C, and then answer the following questions:

a. What are the medians $M(X)$, $M(Y)$, $M(T)$, and $M(C)$.

b. Is it true that $M(T) = M(X) + M(Y)$? That is,

$$M(X + Y) = M(X) + M(Y)?$$

c. Is it true that $M(C) = 200M(X) + 300$? That is,

$$M(200X + 300) = 200M(X) + 300?$$

5-40 Repeat Problem 5-39 for the means, instead of the medians.

PART II

Inference for Means and Proportions

CHAPTER 6

Sampling

You don't have to eat the whole ox to know that it is tough.
SAMUEL JOHNSON

In the last three chapters, we developed the mathematical tools—probability and random variables—so that we can now answer the basic deductive question in statistics: What can we expect of a random sample drawn from a known population?

Before pursuing this question, however, we must repeat an important warning: How we *collect* data is at least as important as how we analyze it. In particular, a sample should be *representative* of the population, and *random sampling* is often the best way to achieve this.

If a sample is not random, it may be so biased that it is worse than useless. In Chapter 1, for example, we already cited the infamous *Literary Digest* poll. As another example, consider a telephone survey of consumer attitudes toward fast foods. If a survey of residences is conducted from 9 to 5, it will miss the working population, the very people most likely to use and appreciate fast foods. Thus, even if the phone list were randomly selected, we see that the responses would still not be random—and this is what ultimately counts.

A better approach would be to select a smaller random sample of residences, and then phone back as often as necessary to get a complete, or at least a very high, response rate. A truly random sample of 20 replies like this might be much better than a biased sample ten times as large. Quality is more important than quantity.

In fact, quantity alone can be very deceptive. A large but biased sample may look good because of its size, but in fact, it just consists of the same bias being repeated over and over—the sort of mistake the *Literary Digest* repeated millions of times. By contrast, modern polling organizations like Gallup or Harris essentially use small random samples of about a thousand, and get far better answers: Their samples are unbiased, and can be analyzed by probability theory to ascertain how much sampling uncertainty they have.

It is precisely this issue of sampling uncertainty in random samples that will take up the next few chapters.

6-1 RANDOM SAMPLING

A—THE POPULATION

The word *population* has a very specific meaning in statistics: It is the total collection of objects or people to be studied, from which a sample is to be drawn. For example, if we wished to predict an election, the population of interest might be all the American voters. Or, for a market survey, it might be just the population of adults who own a car in New York State.

The population can be any size. For example, it might be only 100 students in a certain men's physical education class (if we wished to estimate their average height). To be specific, suppose this population of 100 heights has the frequency distribution shown in Table 6-1. When we

TABLE 6-1 A Population of 100 Students' Heights, and the Calculation of μ and σ

Population Distribution			Calculation of Mean μ	Calculation of Variance σ^2
Height x	Frequency	Relative Frequency, Also $p(x)$	$xp(x)$	$(x-\mu)^2p(x)$
60	1	.01	.60	.81
63	6	.06	3.78	2.16
66	24	.24	15.84	2.16
69	38	.38	26.22	0
72	24	.24	17.28	2.16
75	6	.06	4.50	2.16
78	1	.01	.78	.81
	$N = 100\surd$	$1.00\surd$	$\mu = 69.00$	$\sigma^2 = 10.26$ $\sigma = 3.20$

have a random observation, what is the chance it will be 63 inches, for example? From the second line of Table 6-1, we find the probability is 6 in 100, or .06. Similarly, the probabilities for all the other possible outcomes can be found in the relative frequency column. Therefore, we label this column $p(x)$ to show that it can be viewed as the probability distribution not only of the population, but also of a single observation taken at random. This is an important insight:

> **Each individual observation in a random sample has the population probability distribution $p(x)$.** (6-1)

From $p(x)$, we calculate the population mean μ and standard deviation σ, which we emphasize are the mean and standard deviation of an individual observation. Then in Figure 6-1*a* we graph this distribution $p(x)$, and sketch it as a smooth curve.

B—THE RANDOM SAMPLE

Now let us draw a sample from this population, a sample of $n = 5$ students, for example. As noted in Chapter 1, a sample is called a *simple random sample* (SRS) if each individual in the population is equally likely to be chosen every time we draw an observation. For example, as suggested earlier, two ways we could take a random sample of 5 students in the physical education class of 100 men are:

1. *Draw chips from a bowl.* As illustrated in Figure 6-1*b*, the most graphic method is to record each student's height on a chip, mix all

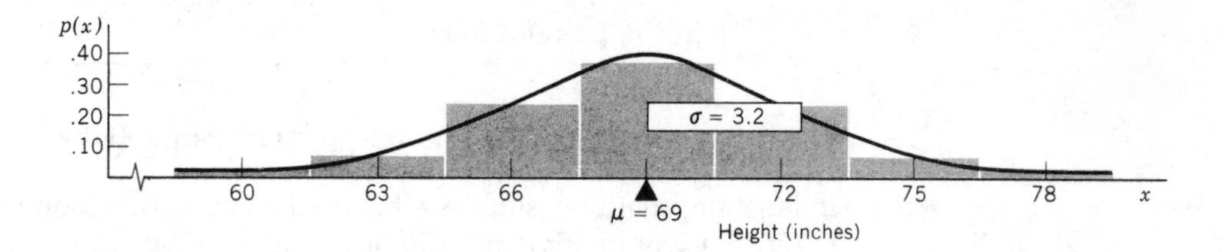

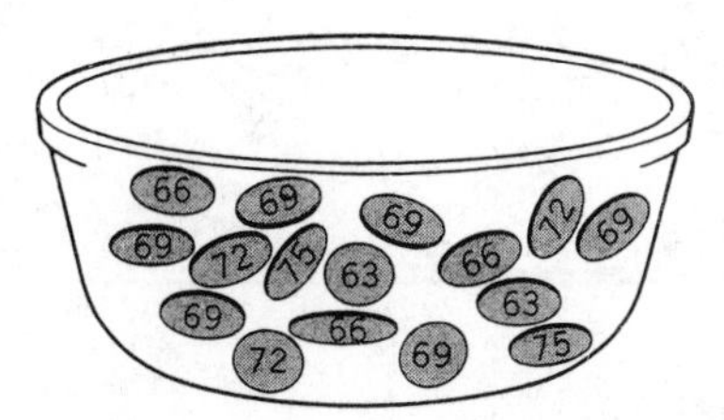

FIGURE 6-1
Population of 100 students' heights. (a) Bar graph of distribution in Table 6-1. (b) Bowl-of-chips equivalent.

these 100 chips in a large bowl, and then draw the sample of $n = 5$ chips.

2. *Assign each student a serial number, and then select serial numbers at random.* For example, let the class assign itself numbers by counting off from 00 to 99. Then we could get our sample from the random digits in Appendix Table I. For example, if we start at the third line, we would select the 5 students with numbers 72, 20, 47, 33, and 84.

These two sampling methods are mathematically equivalent. Since the second is simpler to employ, it is commonly used in practical sampling. However, the bowlful of chips is conceptually easier; consequently, in our theoretical development of random sampling, we will often visualize drawing chips from a bowl.

Randomness makes it likely that a sample is representative of the underlying population from which it is drawn. Figure 6-2 illustrates this, with the gray dots as usual representing all of the actual individuals in the population, ordered according to their height. The 5 blue dots then show the sample of individuals that we might happen to draw. The *average* of these 5 observations (the sample mean $\overline{X}$) is also shown in blue. Note that it is not as extreme; that is, it is closer to the population mean μ than most of the individual observations in the sample. This is because in calculating the sample mean, an extreme individual observation such as $X = 74$ tends to be diluted by more typical observations like $X = 70$, or even tends to be offset by an observation at the other end like $X = 68$. We therefore conclude:

Because of averaging, the sample mean $\overline{X}$ is not as extreme (doesn't vary so widely) as the individuals in the population.	(6-2)

C—SAMPLING WITH OR WITHOUT REPLACEMENT

In large populations, such as all American men, the "population bowl" in Figure 6-1 would contain millions of chips, and it would make practically no difference whether or not we replace each chip before drawing the

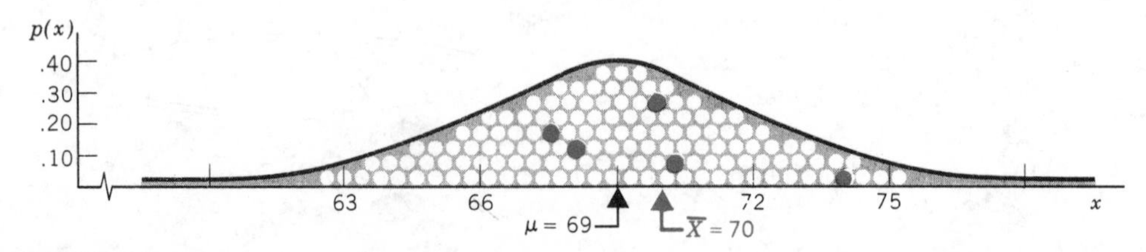

FIGURE 6-2
A typical random sample (blue) drawn from a population (gray), showing how the sample mean tends to "average out" any extreme observations.

next. After all, what is one chip in millions? It cannot substantially change the relative frequencies, $p(x)$.

However, in small populations such as the 100 heights in Figure 6-1, replacement of each sampled chip becomes an important issue. If each chip drawn is recorded and then replaced, it restores the population to exactly its original state. Thus, later chips are completely independent of each chip drawn earlier. On the other hand, if each chip is *not* replaced, the probabilities involved in the draw of later chips *will* change. (For example, if the first chip drawn happens to be the only 78″ chip in the bowl, then the probability of getting that chip in succeeding draws becomes zero; it's no longer in the bowl.) In this case, later chips *are* dependent on each chip drawn earlier.

D—CONCLUDING DEFINITION

If we sample with replacement, the n observations in a sample are independent. And in large populations, even if we sample without replacement, it is practically the same as with replacement, so that we still essentially have independence. All these cases where the observations are independent are easy to analyze, and lead to very simple formulas. We therefore call them *very simple random samples:*

A *very simple random sample* (VSRS) is a sample whose n observations $X_1, X_2, \ldots, X_n$ are independent. The distribution of each X is the population distribution $p(x)$; that is,[1]

$$\begin{aligned} p(x_1) = p(x_2) = \cdots &= p(x_n) \\ &= \text{population distribution, } p(x) \end{aligned} \qquad (6\text{-}3)$$

Then each observation has the mean μ and standard deviation σ of the population.

The exception to this independence occurs when the chips are drawn from a small population, *and* are not replaced. This procedure of course is more efficient: Because it ensures that no chip can be repeated, each observation brings fresh information. However, the gains in efficiency from keeping out the chips require a complicated formula, and are substantial only when the population is small. We therefore defer this type of

[1] Strictly speaking, (6-3) is not precise enough. It would be more accurate to let p_1 denote the probability function of X_1, etc., and then write:

$$p_1(x) \equiv p_2(x) \equiv p_3(x) \equiv \cdots \equiv p_n(x) \equiv p(x)$$

where $\equiv$ means "identically equal for all x." This is the same mathematical subtlety we first encountered in footnote 1 on p. 157.

sampling to Section 6-5. Everywhere else, we will assume a VSRS, and often refer to it simply as a *random sample*.

E—HOW RELIABLE IS THE SAMPLE?

The purpose of random sampling, of course, is to make an inference about the underlying population. As a familiar example, we hope the sample mean $\overline{X}$ is a close estimate of the population mean μ. There are two ways we can study just how close $\overline{X}$ comes to μ:

1. Recall how we sampled the blue dots from the gray population in Figure 6-2, and then calculated the sample mean $\overline{X}$. We could repeat this and get a new $\overline{X}$, over and over. By recording how $\overline{X}$ varies from sample to sample, we would build up the *sampling distribution of* $\overline{X}$, denoted $p(\overline{x})$.

   Rather than *actually* sampling a physical population, we can *simulate* this sampling (just as we simulated the roll of a die earlier). This is normally done on a computer, where even complicated sampling can be repeated hundreds of times every second. Since this process—described in detail in Section 6-6—may be viewed as something like "rolling dice," it is called *Monte Carlo* sampling. (The relationship between gambling games and statistics has a long history; in fact, it was gamblers who provided the impetus for probability theory about 300 years ago.)
2. A more precise and useful (but often more difficult) alternative is to derive mathematical formulas for the sampling distribution of $\overline{X}$. Once we have derived such formulas (as we do in the next section) they can be applied broadly to a whole multitude of sampling problems.

PROBLEMS

6-1 A firm selling stationery in California found it could get a tax-exemption on past orders that were for resale (rather than personal use). Since its records did not state which orders were for resale, however, the firm had to estimate this from a survey.

From the 552,000 customers who purchased from it in the past, the firm randomly sampled 5000 by mail questionnaire. Of the 5000, there were 2970 replies, broken down as follows (simplified version of Freedman, 1986):

Sample Replies	*Total Dollar Value*
280 for resale	\$ 8,030
2690 for personal use	\$30,130
2970 total	\$38,160

a. The value of all 552,000 orders was \$7,010,000. Estimate the value of just the *resale* orders.

b. What assumptions did you make? Why might they be questionable? Do you think the true figure would therefore be higher or lower than your answer in **a**?

c. If the tax rate was $6\frac{1}{2}\%$, use your answer in **a** to estimate the size of the tax refund.

6-2 Because of possible product liability suits, suppose that the hundreds of small U.S. toy manufacturers require varying amounts of legal advice, as follows:

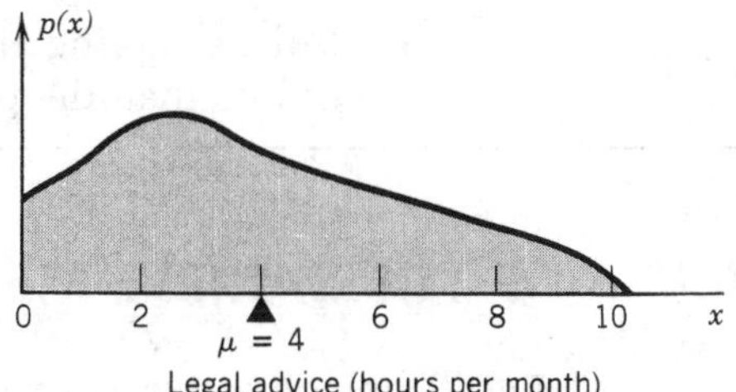

a. Suppose a questionnaire is sent to a random sample of 15 firms. It is returned, however, by only those 5 that have been sued in the past and are therefore most concerned with this issue. Sketch on the graph where the sample of 15 might typically be located, and the 5 replies. Where would the average reply be? How close to the target μ?

b. Repeat part **a** for a random sample of just 5 questionnaires, carefully followed up to obtain a 100% response rate. Is $\overline{X}$ likely to be closer or further from μ?

6-3 In a small and hypothetical midwestern city, the 10,000 adults watch football on TV in widely varying amounts. The weekly amount X varies from 0, 1, 2, . . . , 9 hours, and for each of these levels of X, there are 1000 adults.

a. Graph the population distribution $p(x)$.

b. To simulate drawing one adult (a value of X) at random, take the first digit from Table I. Similarly, to simulate a small sample survey of 5 adults, take the first 5 digits from Table I. Mark these 5 observations in the graph in part **a**.

c. Calculate the population mean μ. (Or, by symmetry, what must it be?)

d. Calculate the sample mean $\overline{X}$. Is it closer to μ than most of the individual observations? Does this illustrate equation (6-2)?

***6-4** **a.** Repeat the simulation of Problem 6-3, a dozen times in all (each time starting at a different place in Table I, of course).

b. Pool your data with a few other students, and tabulate the few dozen values of $\bar{X}$. (We suggest grouping the values of $\bar{X}$ in cells of width .6, taking the cell midpoints to be 0.3, 0.9, 1.5, . . .)

c. Graph the distribution of $\bar{X}$ tabulated in part **b**.

d. If millions of values of $\bar{X}$ had been graphed, instead of just a few dozen, the distribution of $\bar{X}$ would be complete and accurate, with the irregularities smoothed out. Over the graph in part **b**, roughly sketch what this smooth distribution would be. It is called the *sampling distribution of* $\bar{X}$.

e. About where is this sampling distribution of $\bar{X}$ centered? How does that compare to μ calculated in Problem 6-3?

f. Is the sampling distribution of $\bar{X}$ spread out more than, equally, or less than the population distribution p(x)?

6-2 MOMENTS OF THE SAMPLE MEAN

Recall our objective is to estimate a population mean μ. If we take a random sample of observations from this population and calculate the sample mean $\bar{X}$, how good will $\bar{X}$ be as an estimator of its target μ?

To answer this, we can use the theory developed in earlier chapters. The sample mean $\bar{X}$ was defined as:

$$\bar{X} \equiv \frac{1}{n}[X_1 + X_2 + \cdots + X_n] \qquad \text{(6-4) (2-3) repeated}$$

Being a linear combination of random variables, $\bar{X}$ itself will also be a random variable. How does it fluctuate? In particular, what is its expectation and variance?

By applying (5-17) we can easily calculate the expectation:

$$E(\bar{X}) = \frac{1}{n}[E(X_1) + E(X_2) + \cdots + E(X_n)]$$

Recall from (6-3) that each observation X has the population distribution p(x) with mean μ. Thus, $E(X_1) = E(X_2) = \cdots = \mu$, and therefore:

$$E(\bar{X}) = \frac{1}{n}[\mu + \mu + \cdots + \mu]$$

$$= \frac{1}{n}[n\mu] = \mu$$

$$\boxed{E(\bar{X}) = \mu} \qquad \text{(6-5)}$$

This is indeed encouraging. It tells us that *on average*, the sample mean $\overline{X}$ will be "on target," that is, equal to μ.

Of course, an *individual* sample mean is likely to be a little above or below its target μ because of sampling fluctuation (the luck of the draw). The key question is: How much above or below? To answer this, we need to find the variance of $\overline{X}$. According to (6-3) again, all the observations X_1, $X_2, \ldots$ are independent, and so the simple formula (5-22) can be applied to (6-4):

$$\text{var}\ \overline{X} = \frac{1}{n^2}[\text{var}(X_1) + \text{var}(X_2) + \cdots + \text{var}(X_n)]$$

Again, we note that each observation X has the population distribution $p(x)$, with variance σ^2, so that:

$$\text{var}\ \overline{X} = \frac{1}{n^2}[\sigma^2 + \sigma^2 + \cdots + \sigma^2]$$

$$= \frac{1}{n^2}[n\sigma^2] = \frac{\sigma^2}{n} \tag{6-6}$$

$$\text{Standard deviation of } \overline{X} = \frac{\sigma}{\sqrt{n}}$$

This typical deviation of $\overline{X}$ from its target μ represents the estimation error, and so it is commonly called the *standard error*, or SE:

Standard error of $\overline{X}$

$$\text{SE} = \frac{\sigma}{\sqrt{n}} \tag{6-7}$$

This formula shows explicitly that the larger the value of n, the smaller SE becomes; that is, the standard error shrinks as the sample size n increases. This then adds precision to the simple idea that the larger the sample, the more accurately $\overline{X}$ estimates the population mean μ.

An example will illustrate how useful these two formulas are.

EXAMPLE 6-1

The population of men's heights shown in Figure 6-1 had $\mu = 69$ inches and $\sigma = 3.2$ inches.

a. If many random samples of size $n = 4$ were collected, and in each case the sample mean $\overline{X}$ was calculated, how would these sample means $\overline{X}$ fluctuate?

b. In Figure 6-2, the one sample shown in color had $\overline{X} = 70$. Is this a fairly typical sample, or was it a lucky one, particularly close to μ?

c. Suppose the sample size quadrupled to $n = 16$. Repeat part **a** above.

d. Answer True or False. If False, correct it: A doubling of sample size quadruples the accuracy of $\overline{X}$ in estimating μ. The reason is the square root divisor in (6-7).

SOLUTION

a.

$$E(\overline{X}) = \mu = 69 \qquad \text{(6-5) repeated}$$

$$SE = \frac{\sigma}{\sqrt{n}} = \frac{3.2}{\sqrt{4}} = 1.6 \qquad \text{(6-7) repeated}$$

Thus, the many possible values of the sample mean $\overline{X}$ would fluctuate around the target of 69 inches, with a standard error of 1.6 inches.

b. This particular sample mean $\overline{X} = 70$ deviates from its target $\mu = 69$ by 1 inch. Since 1 inch is not far from the standard error of 1.6 inches, this sample is fairly typical.

c. For a larger sample size $n = 16$, $\overline{X}$ would still fluctuate around its target $\mu = 69$, but with a reduced standard error:

$$SE = \frac{\sigma}{\sqrt{n}} = \frac{3.2}{\sqrt{16}} = 0.8$$

d. False. A *quadrupling* of sample size *doubles* the accuracy . . .

PROBLEMS

6-5 Suppose that 10 men were sampled randomly (from the population such as Table 6-1) and their average height $\overline{X}$ was calculated. Then imagine the experiment repeated many times to build up the sampling distribution of $\overline{X}$. Answer True or False; if False, correct it.

a. The tall and short men in the sample tend to average out, making $\overline{X}$ fluctuate less than a single observation.

b. To be specific, the sample mean $\overline{X}$ fluctuates around its target μ with a standard error of only σ/n.

6-6 **a.** The population of American men in 1975 had incomes that averaged $\mu = 10$ thousand, with a standard deviation of 8 thousand, approximately. If a random sample of $n = 100$ men was drawn to estimate μ, what would be the standard error of $\overline{X}$?

b. The population of men in California is about 1/10 as large, but suppose it had the same mean and standard deviation. If a random sample of $n = 100$ was drawn, what would be the standard error of $\overline{X}$ now?

6-7 **a.** Continuing Problem 6-6, the population size was 78 million. If a 1% sample was taken (i.e., n = 1% of 78 million = 780 thousand), what would be the standard error of $\overline{X}$?

b. If a 1% sample of men in California was drawn, what would be the standard error of $\overline{X}$?

*6-8 In 1985, U.S. household income had the following distribution, crudely grouped:

Income x	Proportion $p(x)$
$10,000	.40
$30,000	.40
$50,000	.20

(*Stat. Abst. of the U.S.*, 1987, p. 431.)

a. Calculate the mean μ and standard deviation σ, and show them on a graph of the population distribution.

b. Now suppose a random sample of $n = 2$ incomes is drawn, X_1 and X_2, say. Since each observation has the population distribution, it is easy to tabulate the joint distribution of X_1 and X_2. Then calculate the sampling distribution of $\overline{X}$.

c. From the distribution of $\overline{X}$, calculate the expected value and standard error, and show them on a graph of the sampling distribution of $\overline{X}$.

d. From formulas (6-5) and (6-7), calculate the expected value and standard error of the sampling distribution:

i. When $n = 2$. Does this agree with part **c**?

ii. When $n = 5$.

iii. When $n = 20$.

6-3 THE SHAPE OF THE SAMPLING DISTRIBUTION

In Section 6-2 we found the expected value and standard error of $\overline{X}$. The remaining issue is the *shape* of the sampling distribution.

Across the top of Figure 6-3, we show three different populations. In the column below each, successive graphs show how the sampling distribu-

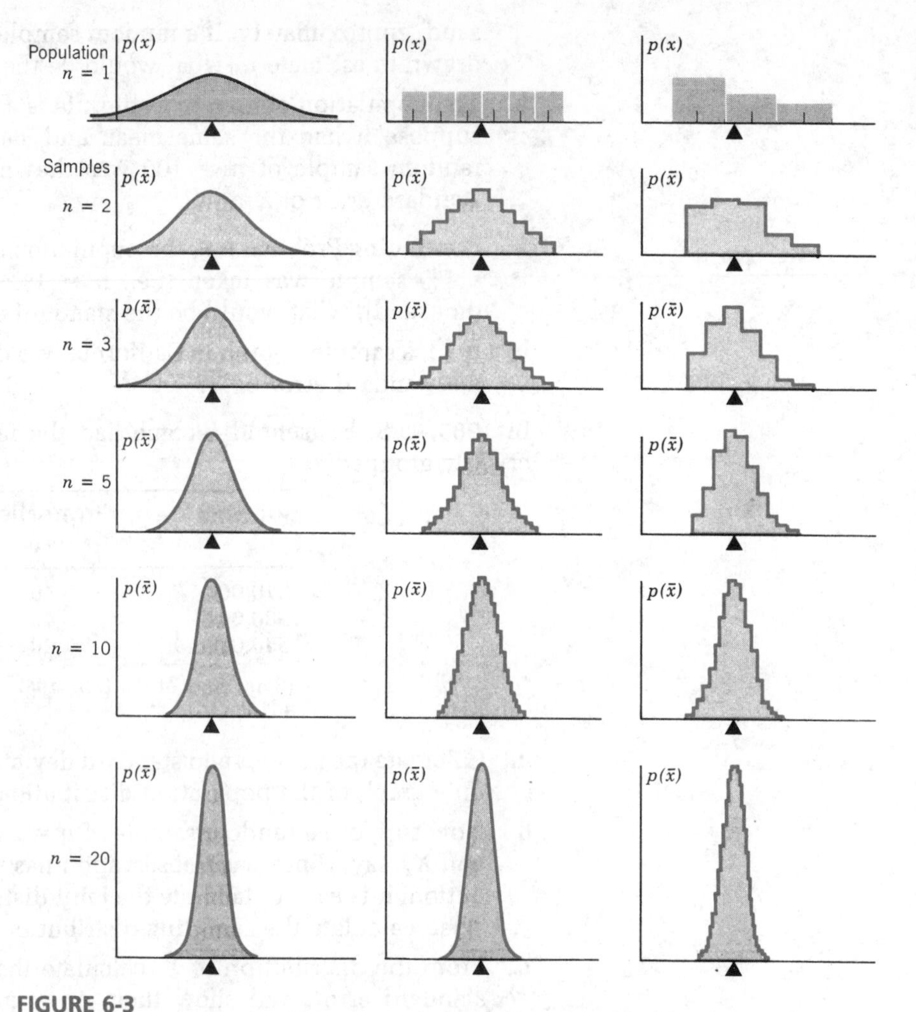

FIGURE 6-3
The sampling distribution of $\overline{X}$ (in color) contrasted with the parent population distribution (in gray). The left column shows sampling from a normal population. As sample size n increases, the standard error of $\overline{X}$ decreases. The next two columns show that even when the population is not normal, the sampling distribution still becomes approximately normal.

tion of $\overline{X}$ changes shape as sample size n increases. Thus, the first column shows how $\overline{X}$ behaves when sampling from a normal population. The sampling distribution of $\overline{X}$ is normal too (fluctuating around μ with less and less error as n increases, as noted already in Section 6-2).

In the second column, the population distribution is rectangular. Despite this, the sampling distribution of $\overline{X}$ becomes normal as n increases; indeed it becomes practically normal when n is only 5 or 10.

The third column is astounding: Even though the population distribution is skewed, the sampling distribution of $\overline{X}$ still becomes normal—although it takes a larger sample size this time. (Notice that it becomes practically normal by the time n = 10 or 20.) This remarkable phenomenon can be proved to be generally true:

If the parent population is normal, *or* the sample size is large (often $n = 10$ or 20 will be large enough), then *in either case* the sampling distribution of $\bar{X}$ has an approximately normal shape. (6-8)

Our conclusions so far on random sampling may be summarized into one statement:

The Normal Approximation Rule. **In random samples (VSRS) of size n, the sample mean $\bar{X}$ fluctuates around the population mean μ with a standard error of $\sigma/\sqrt{n}$ (where σ is the population standard deviation).** (6-9)

Therefore, as n increases, the sampling distribution of $\bar{X}$ concentrates more and more around its target μ. It also gets closer and closer to normal (bell-shaped).

This rule is customarily called the *Central Limit Theorem*, and is of such fundamental importance that it is illustrated in Figure 6-4 (and discussed

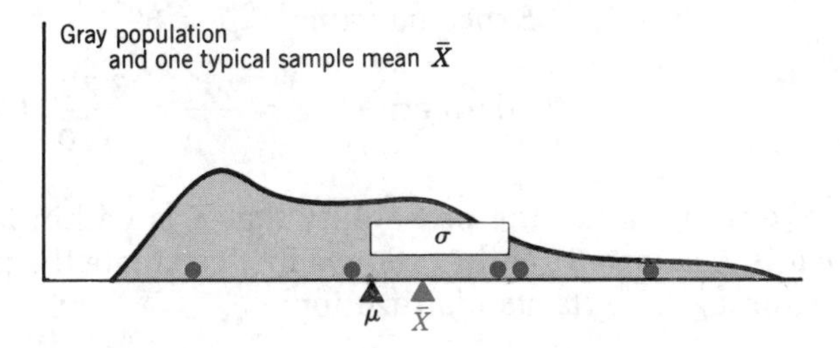

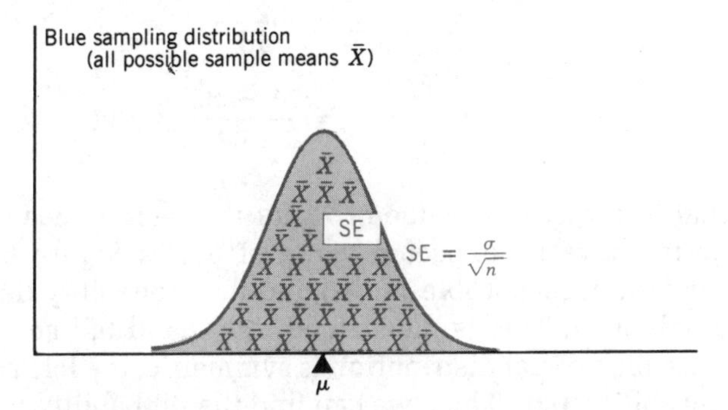

FIGURE 6-4
The sampling distribution of $\bar{X}$ is approximately normal, and more concentrated around μ than is the population. It is colored blue to distinguish it from the population in gray.

further in Appendix 6-3). In Figure 6-4 we continue a convention that distinguishes the sampling distribution from the population distribution:

Populations are gray. **Samples and sampling distributions are blue.**	(6-10)

The Normal Approximation Rule allows us to use the familiar normal tables to determine how closely a sample mean $\bar{X}$ will estimate a population mean μ, as the following example illustrates:

EXAMPLE 6-2

A population of men on a large midwestern campus has a mean height $\mu = 69$ inches, and a standard deviation $\sigma = 3.22$ inches. If a random sample of $n = 10$ men is drawn, what is the chance the sample mean $\bar{X}$ will be within 2 inches of the population mean μ?

SOLUTION

According to the Normal Approximation Rule (6-9), $\bar{X}$ is normally distributed, with

$$\text{Expected value} = \mu = 69$$

$$\text{Standard error, SE} = \frac{\sigma}{\sqrt{n}} = \frac{3.22}{\sqrt{10}} = 1.02$$

We want to find the probability that $\bar{X}$ is within 2 inches of $\mu = 69$—that is, between 67 and 71. So we first calculate the probability above 71, beginning with its standardization:

$$Z = \frac{\bar{X} - \mu}{SE} \qquad \text{like (4-23)}$$

$$= \frac{71 - 69}{1.02} = 1.96$$

That is, the critical value of 71 for the sample mean is nearly 2 standard errors above its expected value of 69, as Figure 6-5 shows. From the standard normal Table IV, we find the probability that Z will exceed 1.96 is only .025. This is the shaded right-hand tail shown in the figure. Because the normal distribution is symmetric, the left-hand tail has the same probability .025. Thus, we can find the probability we want in the central chunk:

$$\text{Probability} = 1.000 - .025 - .025$$
$$= .950$$

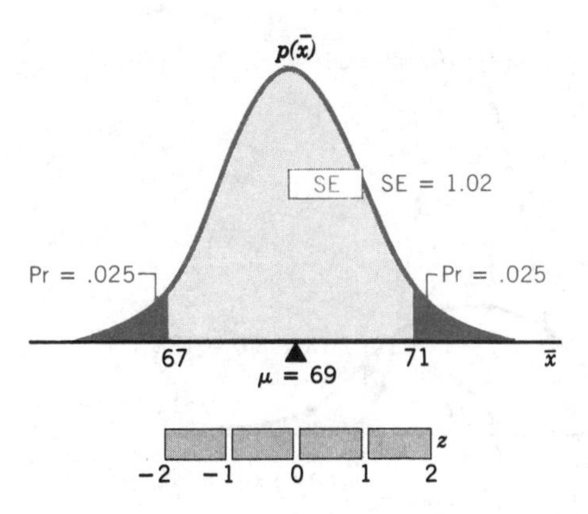

FIGURE 6-5
Standardization of $\overline{X}$.

We therefore conclude that there is a 95% chance that the sample mean will be within 2 inches of the population mean.

Notice that the key to such questions is to standardize the critical $\overline{X}$ value into a Z value:

$$Z = \frac{\overline{X} - \mu}{\text{SE}} \tag{6-11}$$

like (4-23)

Then, for this Z value, we look up the probability in the normal Table IV.

We have often remarked that "averaging out" reduces the chance of an extreme value of $\overline{X}$. Another example will make this clear.

EXAMPLE 6-3

a. Suppose a large class in statistics has marks normally distributed around a mean of 72 with a standard deviation of 9. Find the probability that an individual student drawn at random will have a mark over 80.

b. Find the probability that a random sample of 10 students will have an average mark over 80.

c. If the population were not normal, what would be your answer to part **b**?

SOLUTION

a. The distribution for an individual student (i.e., the population distribution) is shown as the flat gray distribution $p(x)$ in Figure 6-6. The score $X = 80$ is first standardized with its mean $\mu = 72$ and standard deviation $\sigma = 9$:

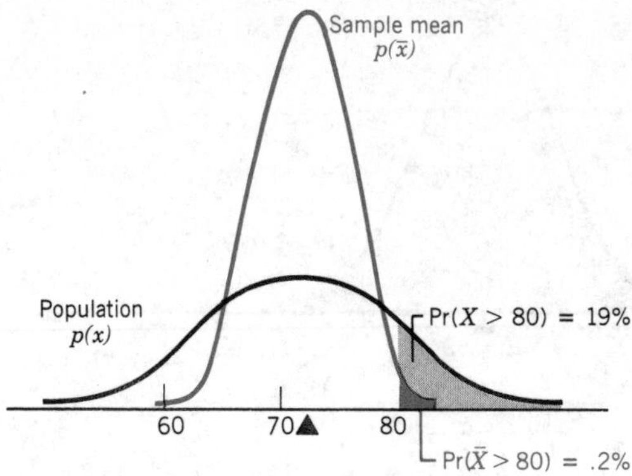

FIGURE 6-6
The sample mean mark is less variable than the individual mark.

$$Z = \frac{X - \mu}{\sigma} = \frac{80 - 72}{9} = .89 \qquad \text{(4-23) repeated}$$

Thus,
$$\Pr(X > 80) = \Pr(Z > .89)$$
$$= .187 \simeq 19\%$$

b. The Normal Approximation Rule (6-9) assures us that $\bar{X}$ has an approximately normal distribution shown by the blue curve, with expected value $= \mu = 72$ and standard error $SE = \sigma/\sqrt{n} = 9/\sqrt{10} = 2.85$. We use these to standardize the critical score $\bar{X} = 80$:

$$Z = \frac{\bar{X} - \mu}{SE} \qquad \text{(6-11) repeated}$$

$$= \frac{80 - 72}{2.85} = 2.81$$

Thus,
$$\Pr(\bar{X} > 80) = \Pr(Z > 2.81)$$
$$= .002$$

These two probability calculations may be easily compared in Figure 6-6. Although there is a reasonable chance (about 19%) that a single student will get over 80, there is very little chance (only about .2%) that a sample average of 10 students will perform this well. Once again we see how "averaging out" tends to reduce the extremes.

c. The Normal Approximation Rule (6-9) tells us that, when n is large, $\bar{X}$ has an approximately normal shape, no matter what the shape of the parent population. We would therefore get approximately the same answer.

The next example will show how a problem involving a *total* can be solved by simply rephrasing it in terms of a mean.

EXAMPLE 6-4

A ski lift is designed with a total load limit of 10,000 pounds. It claims a capacity of 50 persons. Suppose the weights of all the people using the lift have a mean of 190 pounds and a standard deviation of 25 pounds. What is the probability that a random group of 50 persons will total more than the load limit of 10,000 pounds?

SOLUTION

First, we rephrase the question: "A random sample of 50 persons will total more than 10,000 pounds" is exactly the same as "A random sample of 50 persons will *average* more than 10,000/50 = 200 pounds each."

From the Normal Approximation Rule, the sample average $\overline{X}$ has an approximately normal distribution with expected value = μ = 190, and a standard error = $\sigma/\sqrt{n} = 25/\sqrt{50} = 3.54$. We use these to standardize the critical average of 200 pounds:

$$Z = \frac{\overline{X} - \mu}{SE} = \frac{200 - 190}{3.54} = 2.83$$

Thus,

$$\Pr(\overline{X} > 200) = \Pr(Z > 2.83)$$
$$= .002$$

Thus the chance of an overload is only .2%.

The knowledge that the sample mean is normally distributed is very important—not only in making statements about a sample *mean*, but also in making statements about a sample *total* (such as the load limit in the last example).

PROBLEMS

6-9 **a.** The workers in a large meat packing plant earn annual incomes with mean μ = \$30,000 and standard deviation σ = \$9000. A labor lawyer plans to randomly sample 25 incomes from this population. Her sample mean $\overline{X}$ will be a random variable that will only imperfectly reflect the population mean μ. In fact, the possible values of $\overline{X}$ will fluctuate around an expected value of ____ with a standard error of ____, and with a distribution shape that is ____.

b. The lawyer is worried that her sample mean will be misleadingly high. A statistician assures her that it is unlikely that $\overline{X}$

will exceed μ by more than 10%. Calculate just how unlikely this is.

6-10 The millions of SAT math scores of the population of U.S. college-bound seniors in 1978 were approximately normally distributed—around a mean of 470, with a standard deviation of 120.

a. For a student drawn at random, what is the chance of a score above 500? Show this on a graph of the distribution.

b. The registrar of Elora College does not know the mean score of the population, so she estimates it with the mean $\overline{X}$ of a random sample of 250 scores. She hopes $\overline{X}$ will be no more than 10 points off. What are the chances of this?

Show this on a graph of the distribution that shows how $\overline{X}$ fluctuates from sample to sample.

6-11 "One pound" packages filled by a well-worn machine have weights that vary normally around a mean of 16.2 oz, with a standard deviation of .12 oz. An inspector randomly samples a few packages from the production line to see whether their average weight is at least 16 oz. If not, the firm faces a $500 fine. What is the chance of such a fine if the sample size is:

a. $n = 1$?

b. $n = 4$?

c. $n = 16$?

6-12 Suppose that the population of weights of passengers on Flyways Airline has a mean of 150 pounds and standard deviation of 25 pounds. Flyways' commuter plane has a capacity of 7800 pounds, and Flyways is considering equipping it with a configuration of 50 passenger seats.

a. If it does so, what are the chances the aircraft would be overloaded on a fully booked flight?

b. What other information would you want to know before advising Flyways on whether or not it should use this seat configuration?

6-13 The managers of Mercury Mufflers find that the time t (in minutes) required for a worker to replace a muffler varies. Over a period of a year, they collected the following data:

t	*Relative Frequency*
20	10%
30	50%
40	30%
50	10%

a. Calculate the mean and standard deviation of the replacement time t.

b. They plan to do 50 mufflers with 4 men in a day and hope to finish them all between 9 a.m. and 5 p.m. What proportion of the days will they fail to finish on time?

c. What crucial assumption did you implicitly make? Suggest some circumstances where it would be seriously violated. Then how would the correct answer be different?

6-14 A bicycle manufacturer requires chains that are within 1/4 inch of 54 inches. Because of slight variations in the manufacturing process, the individual links are not exactly uniform. They fluctuate slightly around a mean length of 1/2 inch, with a standard deviation of 1/100 inch.

a. How many links should be strung together to form a chain?

b. What proportion of the chains would then meet the given standard?

6-4 PROPORTIONS (PERCENTAGES)

A—PROPORTIONS ARE NORMAL, LIKE MEANS

As we first mentioned in Chapter 1, the sample proportion P is an estimate of the population proportion π. Like $\overline{X}$, P also fluctuates from sample to sample in a pattern (sampling distribution) that is easily summarized:

> ***The Normal Approximation Rule for Proportions.*** **In random samples (VSRS) of size n, the sample proportion P fluctuates around the population proportion π with a standard error of $\sqrt{\pi(1-\pi)/n}$.**
>
> **Therefore, as n increases, the sampling distribution of P concentrates more and more around its target π. It also gets closer and closer to normal (bell-shaped)**

(6-12)
like (6-9)

(Notice how this Normal Approximation Rule for proportions is very similar to the rule for means. This is no accident: A proportion in fact is just a disguised mean, as we will show in part C later.)

To illustrate the Normal Approximation Rule, in Figure 6-7 we show a population of voters—60% Republican (dark) and 40% Democratic (light). Several random samples (polls) of size $n = 100$ are indicated schematically as subsets, each with its different sample proportion P. All possible values of P form the sampling distribution—normally distributed around the target $\pi = .60$, with a standard error $SE = \sqrt{\pi(1-\pi)/n} = \sqrt{.60(.40)/100} = .05$. From this, we can calculate any desired probability, as the next two examples illustrate.

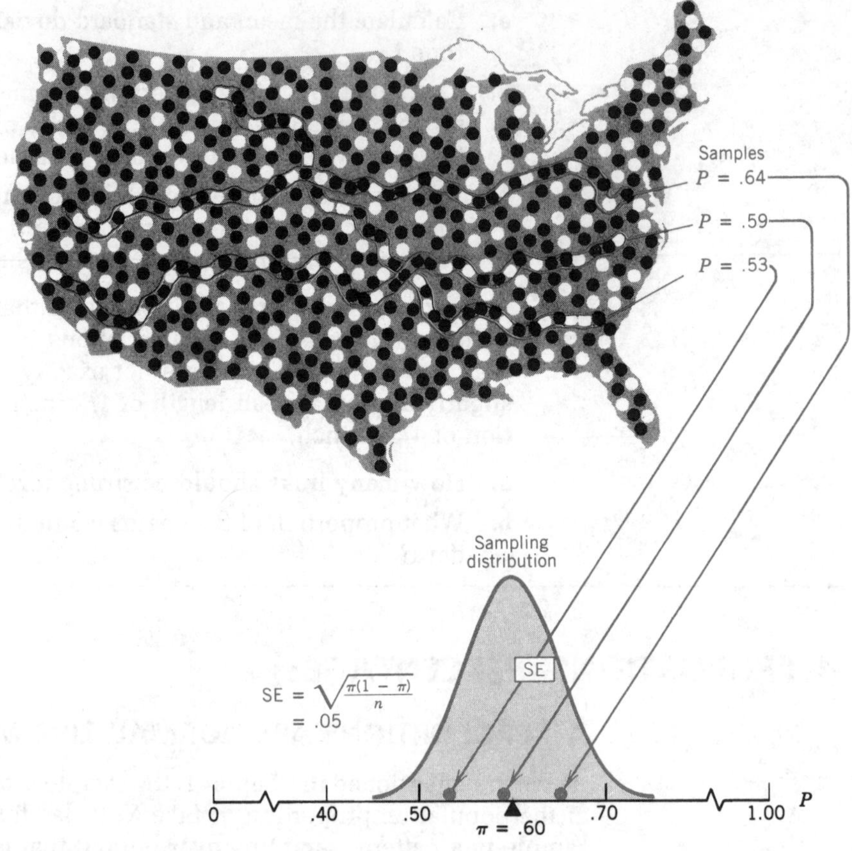

FIGURE 6-7
Various possible samples give different proportions of Republicans, P. All possible values of P form the sampling distribution.

EXAMPLE 6-5

How likely is it that the poll above would contain a minority of Republicans?

SOLUTION

A minority means the proportion of Republicans P is less than 50%. To calculate this probability under the normal curve, we first standardize the critical value $P = .50$:

$$Z = \frac{P - \pi}{SE} \qquad \text{like (6-11)}$$

$$= \frac{.50 - .60}{.05} = -2.00$$

Thus, $$\Pr(P < .50) = \Pr(Z < -2.00)$$
$$= .023 \simeq 2\%$$

Thus the chance of an erroneous conclusion from the poll is only 2%.

EXAMPLE 6-6

Of your first 15 grandchildren, what is the chance there will be more than 10 boys?

SOLUTION

First we rephrase the question: "More than 10 boys" is exactly the same as "The *proportion* of boys is more than 10/15." In this form, we can use the Normal Approximation Rule (6-12): P fluctuates normally around $\pi = .50$ with a standard error $= \sqrt{\pi(1 - \pi)/n} = \sqrt{.50(.50)/15} = .129$. We use these to standardize the critical proportion $P = 10/15$,

$$Z = \frac{P - \pi}{SE}$$

$$= \frac{\frac{10}{15} - .50}{.129} = 1.29 \tag{6-13}$$

Thus, $$\Pr\left(P > \frac{10}{15}\right) = \Pr(Z > 1.29)$$

$$= .099 \simeq 10\% \tag{6-14}$$

The chance of more than 10 boys is about 10%.

Example 6-6 is recognized as a binomial problem. It could have been answered more precisely, but with a lot more work, by adding up the probability of getting 11 boys, plus the probability of getting 12 boys, and so on—with each of these probabilities calculated from the binomial formula (4-8). Since the normal approximation is so much easier to evaluate we shall use it henceforth, and refer to it as the *normal approximation to the binomial.*

*B—CONTINUITY CORRECTION

The Normal Approximation Rule (6-12) is only an approximation, and therefore does involve some error. To illustrate this error, note that we could have answered the question in Example 6-6 *equally well* by rephrasing it differently at the beginning: "More than 10 boys" is exactly the same as "11 or more boys." If we had begun in this way, in (6-13) we would have been evaluating a critical proportion of 11/15 rather than 10/15. Then we would, of course, arrive at an answer different from (6-14), but nevertheless an equally good approximation. Rather than having to choose between these two approximations, we would get an even better approximation by striking a compromise right at the beginning: Instead of 10 boys or 11 boys, use $10\frac{1}{2}$ boys. When this is used in (6-13), we obtain

$$Z = \frac{\frac{10\frac{1}{2}}{15} - .50}{.129} = 1.55$$

Thus,

$$\Pr\left(P > \frac{10\frac{1}{2}}{15}\right) = \Pr(Z > 1.55) = .061 \qquad (6\text{-}15)$$

This compromise agrees very well with the correct answer of .059, which we would have obtained if we had gone back and answered the question the absolutely correct (but tedious) way of fighting our way through the binomial distribution.

Why is this compromise so good? We arrived at the crude answer of .098 in (6-14) by approximating a discrete distribution (the binomial) with a continuous distribution (the normal). This involves a slight mismatch, and the compromise (6-15) allowed us to correct for this. Thus the compromise is customarily called the *continuity correction* (and is further explained in Appendix 6-4). It is so helpful that it is worth stating carefully.

> ***The continuity correction*** **(c.c) to the binomial is obtained by first phrasing the question in the two possible ways (for example, "more than 10" or "11 or more.") Then the halfway value ($10\frac{1}{2}$) is used in the subsequent normal approximation.** (6-16)

*C—PROPORTIONS AS SAMPLE MEANS

We can show that the sample proportion is just a disguised sample mean, and this has two benefits: (1) It provides a simple introduction to dummy variables, an indispensable concept in applied statistics. (2) It gives us "two concepts for the price of one," and so halves the new material we have to learn. In particular, we will show how the normal approximation rules are related—that is, how proportions in (6-12) follow from means in (6-9).

Once more we think of the population as a bowl of chips. Sometimes, as in our example of men's heights, the chips have many possible numbers written on them. At other times, in simple quality control, for example, there may be only two kinds of items—acceptable or not acceptable. Earlier, in the binomial distribution, we called the two alternatives "success" and "failure." As another example, let us next look at a poll where there are only two parties.

EXAMPLE 6-7

An election may be interpreted as asking every voter in the population, "How many votes do you cast for the Republican candidate?" If this is an honest election, the voter has to reply either 0 or 1. In the 1984 Presidential election, 60% voted Republican ($X = 1$), while 40% voted Democratic ($X = 0$). The population distribution was therefore as follows:

x = Number of Republican Votes by an Individual	$p(x)$ = Relative Frequency
0	.40
1	.60

a. What is the population mean? The population variance? The population proportion of Republicans?

b. When 10 voters were randomly polled, they gave the following answers:

1, 0, 1, 1, 1, 0, 1, 0, 1, 1

What is the sample mean? The sample proportion of Republicans?

SOLUTION

a. We calculate the population mean and variance in Table 6-2—a short and peculiar table. In fact, it's as short as a table can possibly be. This makes the arithmetic very simple, however, and we easily find the mean is .60—which exactly equals the proportion of Republicans.

We also find the variance is .24—which equals .60 × .40 (the proportion of Republicans and Democrats, respectively). It is remarkable that a table can be so simple to calculate, and at the same time yield such interesting answers.

b. The sample mean is $\overline{X} = \Sigma X/n = 7/10 = .70$. The sample proportion is $P = 7/10$, which exactly equals the sample mean. Once again, just as in part a, we have found *the proportion coincides with the mean.*

TABLE 6-2 Population Mean and Variance for a 0-1 Variable
(a) When the Proportion of Republicans is 60%, as in Example 6-7
(b) In General, When the Proportion is π

(a) x = Number of Republican votes an Individual Casts	$p(x)$ = Relative Frequency = Population Proportion	$xp(x)$	$x^2p(x)$
0	.40	0	0
1	.60	.60	.60
		$\mu = .60$	$E(X^2) = .60$

Therefore, from (4-35),

$$\sigma^2 = E(X^2) - \mu^2 = .60 - .60^2 = .24$$

(b) x	$p(x)$	$xp(x)$	$x^2p(x)$
0	$(1 - \pi)$	0	0
1	π	π	π
		$\mu = \pi$	$E(X^2) = \pi$

$$\text{Therefore } \sigma^2 = E(X^2) - \mu^2 = \pi - \pi^2 = \pi(1 - \pi)$$

$$\sigma = \sqrt{\pi(1 - \pi)}$$

REMARKS

Baseball fans have long recognized that a proportion is just a mean (average). For example, if a player makes 62 hits out of 200, his *proportion* of hits is 62/200 = .310. More commonly, however, we say his batting *average* is .310.

From this example, we can easily generalize. To set things up, for a single voter drawn at random, let

$$X = \text{the number of Republican votes this individual casts} \quad (6\text{-}17)$$

If this seems a strange way to define such a simple random variable, we could explicitly define it as a 0-1 variable:

$$\begin{aligned} X &= 1 \quad \text{if the individual votes Republican} \\ &= 0 \quad \text{otherwise} \end{aligned} \quad (6\text{-}18)$$

Thus the population of voters may be thought of as the bowl of chips, marked 0 or 1, shown in Figure 6-8. As usual, we shall let π denote the population proportion that is Republican (proportion of chips marked 1).

FIGURE 6-8
A 0-1 population (population of voters).

Then, as shown in Table 6-2, the moments of the population can be expressed in terms of this proportion,

$$\text{Population mean } \mu = \text{population proportion } \pi \qquad (6\text{-}19)$$

$$\text{Population standard deviation } \sigma = \sqrt{\pi(1-\pi)} \qquad (6\text{-}20)$$

What is true for the population (6-19) is also true for the sample:

$$\boxed{\text{Sample mean } \overline{X} = \text{sample proportion } P} \qquad \begin{matrix}(6\text{-}21)\\ \text{like } (6\text{-}19)\end{matrix}$$

To confirm (6-21), note that when we take a sample, its mean is calculated by adding up the 1's (counting up the Republicans), and dividing by n. But, of course, this is just the sample proportion of Republicans.

Thus we have found an ingenious way to handle a proportion: It is simply a disguised mean—the mean of a 0-1 variable. (Since it provided such a simple way of counting the number of Republicans, the 0-1 variable is also called a *counting variable*. Other names are *on-off variable, indicator variable, binary variable*, or, most commonly, *dummy variable*.)

Since P is just the sample mean $\overline{X}$ in disguise, we can find its expected value by recalling the general theory of sampling already developed:

$$\text{Expected value of } \overline{X} = \text{population mean } \mu \qquad \text{like } (6\text{-}5)$$

Therefore, substituting (6-21) and (6-19):

$$\boxed{\text{Expected value of } P = \text{population proportion } \pi} \qquad (6\text{-}22)$$

The standard error of P is similarly obtained by recalling (6-7), and then substituting into it (6-21) and (6-20):

$$\text{Standard error of } P = \sqrt{\frac{\pi(1-\pi)}{n}} \tag{6-23}$$

With these moments of the sample proportion P in hand, what is the *shape* of its distribution? Recall that the Normal Approximation Rule (6-9) tells us that, if a large sample is taken from essentially *any* population (even the 0-1 population we are now considering), the sample mean will be approximately normal. In this case the sample mean is the sample proportion; thus the normal approximation rule is true for proportions too.

PROBLEMS

If you want high accuracy in your answers (optional), you should do them with continuity correction (wcc) as given in (6-16), especially if the sample size n is small.

6-15 Los Angeles has about four times as many voters as San Diego. To estimate the proportion who will vote for a bond to finance bicycle paths, a random sample of 1000 in Los Angeles will be about ____ as accurate as a random sample of 250 in San Diego.

6-16 In a large production run of millions of electronic chips, only 2% are defective. What is the chance that of 1000 chips pulled off the assembly line, 40 or more would be defective?

6-17 The 1982 model Q-cars had to be recalled because of a slight defect in the suspension. Of those recalled, 20% required repairs. A small dealer with an overworked service department hopes that no more than 5 of his 50 recalled cars will require repairs. What is the chance of his being so lucky?

6-18 In Problems 6-16 and 6-17, what assumption did you make to get your answer? Suggest some circumstances when it would be seriously violated. Then how would the correct answer be different?

6-19 In the 1988 U.S. Presidential election, 53.9% of the voters were for Bush. If a Gallup poll of 1000 voters had been randomly sampled from this population, what is the chance it would have erroneously predicted Bush to have a minority?

6-20 When a fair coin is flipped 10 times, what is the chance of getting 7 or more heads? Answer in three ways:

a. Exactly, using the binomial distribution.

b. Approximately, using the normal distribution.

***c.** Approximately, using the normal approximation with continuity correction.

Note that the normal approximation with continuity correction can be an excellent approximation, even for n as small as 10.

6-21 When a fair coin is flipped, what is the chance of getting about 50% heads—specifically, between 40% and 60% (inclusive)?

a. for $n = 10$ flips

b. for $n = 100$ flips

c. for $n = 1000$ flips.

Note how the chance of getting about 50% heads approaches certainty, as n increases. This is an example of the "law of large numbers."

6-22 In 1980, approximately 50% of Americans felt that inflation was the country's most important problem. If a random poll of 1500 Americans was taken (about the size of the Gallup poll), what is the chance that its proportion would accurately reflect the population proportion within 3 percentage points?

***6-23** In sampling from a 0-1 population, the *proportion* of successes P is related to the *total number* of successes S. For example, when the total number of Republicans was $S = 7$ in a sample of $n = 10$, we calculated $P = 7/10$, and, in general:

$$P = \frac{S}{n}$$

$$\text{or } S = nP$$

Using the moments of P and the theory of linear transformations, prove that the moments of S are those given in (4-13).

*6-5 SMALL-POPULATION SAMPLING

When the population size N is small and the observations (or chips from the bowl) are kept out as they are drawn, the sampling is no longer strictly random [as we showed following equation (6-3)]. Keeping out the chips is more efficient because we do not risk "drawing the same chip" over again and repeating information already known.

For example, suppose we sample the heights of ten men on a small college campus; suppose further that the first student we sample happens to be the 7-foot star of the basketball team. Clearly, we now face the problem of a sample average that is too high. If we replace, then in the next nine men who are chosen, the star *could* turn up again, thus distorting our sample mean for the second time. But if we don't replace, then we don't have to worry about this tall individual again. In summary, sampling without replacement yields a less variable sample mean because extreme values, once sampled, cannot return to haunt us again.

The reduction in variability depends in general on the relative size of the population and sample (N and n):

> **If observations are kept out as they are drawn (sampling without replacement), the standard error of $\bar{X}$ or P is reduced by the factor:**
>
> $$\textbf{SE reduction factor} = \sqrt{\frac{N-n}{N-1}} \tag{6-24}$$

In other words, the standard error of $\bar{X}$ changes from $\sigma/\sqrt{n}$ to

$$\text{SE of } \bar{X} = \frac{\sigma}{\sqrt{n}}\sqrt{\frac{N-n}{N-1}} \tag{6-25}$$

Similarly,

$$\text{SE of } P = \frac{\sqrt{\pi(1-\pi)}}{\sqrt{n}}\sqrt{\frac{N-n}{N-1}} \tag{6-26}$$

Certain special sample sizes shed further light on the reduction factor (6-24):

1. When there is only $n = 1$ chip sampled, it does not matter whether or not it is replaced (because we never take another chip out of the bowl). This is reflected in the reduction factor becoming 1.00. [If you have wondered where the 1 came from in the denominator of (6-24), you can see that it is needed to logically make (6-25) and (6-7) equivalent—as they must be—for a sample size of one.]
2. When $n = N$, the entire population is sampled. Since every sample coincides with the whole population, every sample mean must be the same—the population mean. The variance of the sample mean, being a measure of its fluctuation, must be zero. This is reflected in the reduction factor becoming 0.
3. On the other hand, in a large population where the population size N is far greater than the sample size n, then the reduction factor is practically 1, and therefore can be ignored. For example, in the typical poll where $N \simeq 100{,}000{,}000$ and $n \simeq 1{,}000$,

$$\text{Reduction factor} = \sqrt{\frac{N-n}{N-1}}$$

$$= \sqrt{\frac{100{,}000{,}000 - 1{,}000}{100{,}000{,}000 - 1}} = .999995 \simeq 1.00$$

We conclude that (6-25) and (6-26) apply to a population of *any* size. But in the large populations we consider hereafter in this book, the reduction factor becomes approximately 1, and can therefore be dropped.

*PROBLEMS

6-24 Rework each of the following problems, assuming a finite population size N (and sampling is without replacement):

a. Problem 6-9, assuming $N = 80$.

b. Problem 6-16, assuming $N = 10{,}000$.

c. Problem 6-17, assuming $N = 50{,}000$.

6-25 We can easily obtain a simpler view of (6-24). Its denominator $N - 1$ is practically the same as N whenever N is large, and so we get approximately:

$$\text{SE reduction factor} \approx \sqrt{\frac{N-n}{N}} = \sqrt{1 - \frac{n}{N}} \qquad (6\text{-}27)$$

Now n/N is the fraction of the population that is sampled. Once these n items appear in the sample, there is no longer any uncertainty about them. To reflect this reduced uncertainty, the "sampling fraction" n/N is subtracted in (6-27).

a. What is the approximate reduction in the SE, if the sampling fraction is 10%? 5%? 1%?

b. Earlier we stated that if "the population size N is far greater than the sample size n, then the reduction factor is practically 1." To be specific, if we want the reduction factor to be within 1% of 1, how much greater must N be than n?

6-26 **a.** In a bridge hand (13 out of 52 cards), what is the probability that there will be at least 7 spades? At least 7 of one suit?

b. In a poker hand (5 out of 52 cards), what is the probability that there will be at least 2 aces?

6-27 In the game of bridge, a simple scoring system allots points to each card as follows:

Card	*Points*
Each card below Jack	0
Jack	1
Queen	2
King	3
Ace	4

a. For the population of 52 cards, find the mean number of points, and the standard deviation.

b. In a randomly dealt hand of 13 cards, what is the probability that there will be at least 13 points? (Bridge players beware: no points counted for distribution.)

*6-6 MONTE CARLO

Although the star on this section indicates it may be skipped, the Monte Carlo method nonetheless provides some very useful insights into sampling. In particular, it confirms clearly why $\overline{X}$ is a reliable estimate of μ. (Monte Carlo does far more than confirm, however. In situations that are mathematically intractable, Monte Carlo often provides the only practical way to determine sampling distributions.)

A—SAMPLING OF A SMALL POPULATION USING RANDOM DIGITS

Suppose the 100 employees of a small furniture firm have their absenteeism recorded in Table 6-3 (X = number of days absent during the first quarter of 1990, excluding major medical). In the last column we assign each individual in this population a serial number—a "tag" to draw them out for a random sample.

In Figure 6-9 we graph this population, and show its mean as the customary center of gravity ($\mu = 1.5$ was computed from Table 6-3, along with $\sigma = 1.4$).

Now let us see what happens in the usual situation when we come to this population "blind"—without any knowledge of it—and try to estimate μ by taking a small random sample (VSRS) of $n = 5$ observations. We draw 5 pairs of random digits in Appendix Table I. We can start anywhere, since all numbers in this table are purely random. If we start at line

TABLE 6-3 Absenteeism in a Population of 100 Employees, Set Up for Random Sampling

Population Distribution			Associated Serial Numbers
Days Absent, x	Frequency	Relative Freq. $p(x)$	
0	30	.30	01–30
1	26	.26	31–56
2	22	.22	57–78
3	12	.12	79–90
4	7	.07	91–97
5	2	.02	98–99
6	1	.01	00
	$N = 100$	1.00✓	

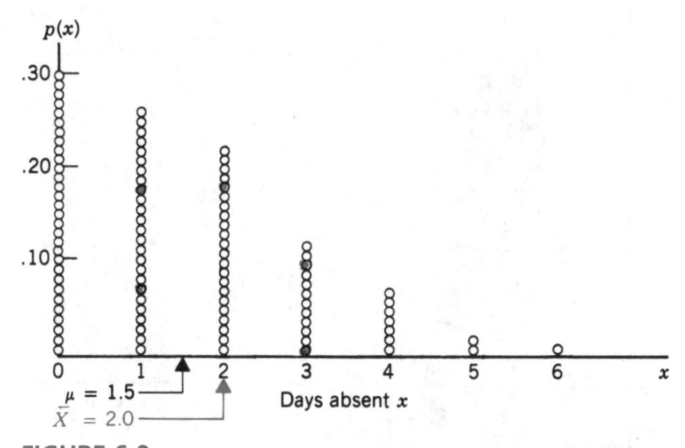

FIGURE 6-9
Absenteeism in a population of 100 employees shown as dots, from Table 6-3. Random sample of $n = 5$ shown as colored dots.

five, for example, the first pair of random digits is 37, which is found in Table 6-3 to be the serial number of an employee who was absent $X = 1$ day. Continuing to draw the remaining observations in the same way, we obtain the sample of $n = 5$ observations in Table 6-4. [Because we are sampling with replacement (VSRS), the luck of the draw might give us the same serial number twice, in which case that individual would be included both times in our sample.]

To summarize this sample, the sample mean $\overline{X} = 2.0$ is calculated in Table 6-4. Then $\overline{X}$, along with the whole sample of 5 colored dots, is graphed in Figure 6-9. Just as in Figure 6-2, we note that the random sample is quite representative of the population, and so the sample mean $\overline{X} = 2.0$ is quite a good estimate of the population mean $\mu = 1.5$.

Now we can repeat the sampling over and over. Each time we draw a sample of 5 observations, we can calculate the mean $\overline{X}$, and then place it on Figure 6-10. (The circled $\overline{X}$ in Figure 6-10 is our first sample mean from Figure 6-9.) Thus we build up the sampling distribution, which shows how $\overline{X}$ fluctuates around its target μ. An example will provide the details.

TABLE 6-4 A Random Sample Drawn From Table 6-3

Serial Number	*Days Absent X*
37	1
48	1
79	3
88	3
74	2
$\overline{X} = 10/5 = 2.0$	

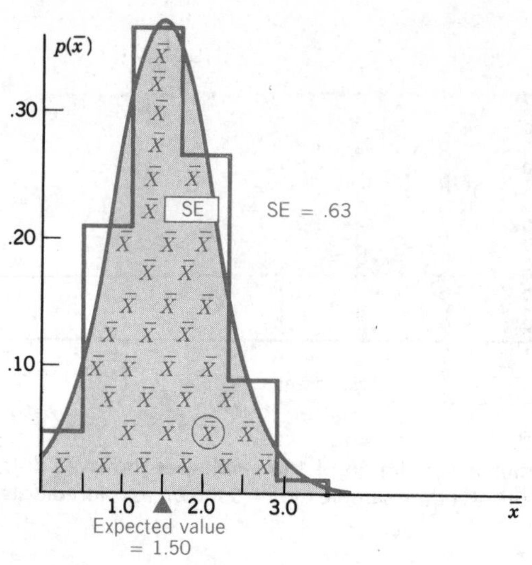

FIGURE 6-10
Sampling distribution of $\bar{X}$, for $n = 5$.

EXAMPLE 6-8

a. Consider again the population in Table 6-3. Let each student in your class draw a sample of $n = 5$ observations (starting at a different place in Appendix Table I, of course), and then calculate the sample mean $\bar{X}$.

If your class is small, each student can repeat the experiment several times, so that the class obtains at least 50 values of $\bar{X}$. Then let the instructor tabulate and graph the frequency distribution of $\bar{X}$. (We recommend grouping the values of $\bar{X}$ into cells of width .6, taking the cell midpoints to be .2, .8, 1.4, ...)

b. Calculate the mean and standard error of the distribution of $\bar{X}$. How are they approximately related to $\mu = 1.50$ and $\sigma = 1.4$ for the parent population?

SOLUTION

a. By repeating the sampling experiment over and over like this, we begin to understand the luck of the draw, just as in repeated spinning of a roulette wheel. That is why it is called Monte Carlo, after the European gambling center.

If this Monte Carlo experiment were carried out for millions of values of $\bar{X}$ (rather than just 50 or so), then the relative frequencies would settle down to the probabilities calculated in the table below and shown as the bars or steps in Figure 6-10. (Your relative frequencies, based on 50 or so values of $\bar{X}$, will roughly resemble these probabilities.) Also shown is the approximate normal curve we would get if we used more finely divided cells.

Sampling Distribution		*Calculation of the Expected Value*	*Calculation of the Standard Error*	
$\bar{x}$ *(Midpoint)*	$p(\bar{x})$ *(Rel Freq)*	$\bar{x}p(\bar{x})$	$(\bar{x}-1.50)^2$	$(\bar{x}-1.50)^2p(\bar{x})$
.2	.05	.010	1.69	.085
.8	.21	.168	.49	.103
1.4	.37	.518	.01	.004
2.0	.27	.540	.25	.068
2.6	.09	.234	1.21	.109
3.2	.01	.032	2.89	.029
		Expected Value = 1.50		Variance = .398 SE = $\sqrt{.398}$ = .63

b. The expected value of $\bar{X}$ is calculated from the sampling distribution in the table above, and turns out to be 1.50, the same as the population mean ($\mu = 1.50$). The standard error of $\bar{X}$ is also calculated, and turns out to be .63, which is $1/\sqrt{5}$ times the standard deviation of the population ($\sigma = 1.4$). Your classroom calculations (based on 50 or so values of $\bar{X}$) will be fairly close to this.

Example 6-8 has nicely demonstrated the Normal Approximation Rule: Even though the population is quite skewed, nevertheless the sample mean $\bar{X}$ fluctuates approximately normally around the target μ, with standard error $\sigma/\sqrt{n}$.

B—SAMPLING A POPULATION OF ANY SIZE

Now let us consider a much larger population. For example, suppose absenteeism among the 30,000 employees of a large corporation takes on the same pattern of *relative* frequencies as absenteeism in the small firm given earlier in Table 6-3. Specifically, this larger population is shown in Table 6-5.

When we sample our first observation from the population of 30,000, what is the chance it will be $X = 1$, for example? The relative frequency, of course, which is 7800/30,000 = .26. This is the same chance as before. So the same simulation will work: You can visualize the same serial numbers in Table 6-5 as in Table 6-3. Thus the sampling simulation will be exactly the same, and this is a point worth emphasizing in general.

In sampling with replacement, only the *relative* frequencies matter. The size of the population *N* is irrelevant.	(6-28)

TABLE 6-5 Absenteeism in a Large Population. 30,000 Employees With the Same Pattern as Table 6-3.

Days Absent, x	*Frequency*	*Relative Freq. p(x)*
0	9000	.30
1	7800	.26
2	6600	.22
3	3600	.12
4	2100	.07
5	600	.02
6	300	.01
	N = 30,000	1.00✓

C—MONTE CARLO BY COMPUTER

The sampling by hand calculation that we have done so far has provided a lot of insight. In practice, however, a computer is much better at such repetitive calculations. A computer can easily draw a sample and calculate its mean $\overline{X}$, then repeat this procedure hundreds of times a second to build up the sampling distribution of $\overline{X}$.

As an example, suppose we are to simulate a random sample (of $n = 10$ observations) from a normal population of men's heights with $\mu = 69$ and $\sigma = 3.2$. The computer uses four steps that initially differ from the hand calculation earlier:

1. The "Monte Carlo wheel is spun" in the computer to pick a standard normal value at random, such as $Z = 1.5$ (just as we might select a random Z value from Table II).
2. We don't want to stop there, with a *standard* normal value Z; instead we want a normally distributed *height* X. We can easily convert Z into X by recalling the equation relating the two:

$$Z = \frac{X - \mu}{\sigma} \qquad \text{(4-23) repeated}$$

   Rearranging this yields

$$X = \mu + Z\sigma \qquad \text{(6-29)}$$

   Thus the standard value $Z = 1.5$ translates into a height of:

$$X = 69 + 3.2(1.5) = 73.8 \text{ inches}$$

   This is our first sample observation.

3. This process is repeated 10 times altogether, to get a random sample of $n = 10$ men's heights. Then their mean $\overline{X}$ is computed.

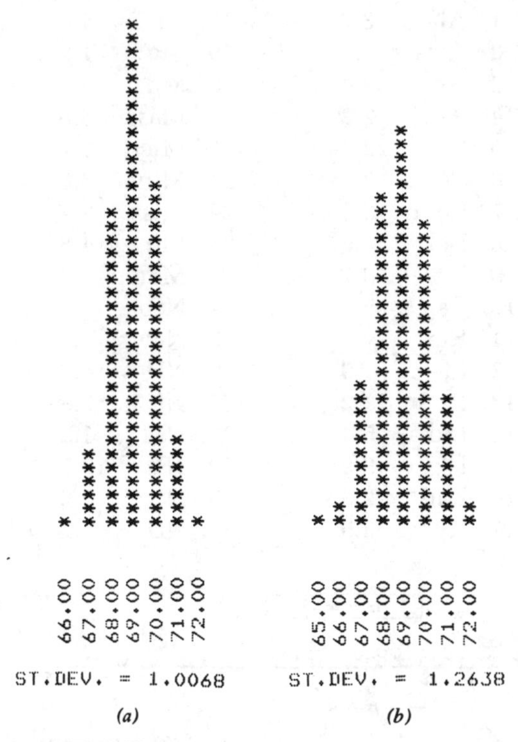

FIGURE 6-11
Sampling distributions computed by Monte Carlo, for sample size $n = 10$ from a normal population. (a) the sample mean $\overline{X}$. (b) The sample median $\check{X}$ (more unreliable, since its standard deviation or standard error is larger.)

4. In the same way a lot more sample means $\overline{X}$ are computed and arrayed in a graph—the sampling distribution of $\overline{X}$, as shown in Figure 6-11*a*.

Of course, the computer could just as easily calculate the sampling distribution of some other statistic, such as the median $\check{X}$—as shown in Figure 6-11*b*. This shows us that for estimating the center of a normal population, $\check{X}$ is less reliable than $\overline{X}$. The computer could simulate sampling from non-normal populations as well.

To sum up: Monte Carlo studies are useful not only as a check on theoretical results such as the normal approximation rule (6-9). They are particularly valuable in providing sampling distributions that cannot be easily derived theoretically.

*PROBLEMS

6-28 The 1978 populations of the 50 states were as follows, numbered in alphabetical order (DC included in Maryland).

1. Ala	3.7	18. La	4.0	35. Oh	10.7
2. Alas	.4	19. Me	1.1	26. Okla	2.8
3. Ariz	2.4	20. Md	4.8	37. Ore	2.5
4. Ark	2.2	21. Mass	5.8	38. Pa	11.8
5. Cal	22.3	22. Mich	9.2	39. RI	.9
6. Col	2.7	23. Minn	4.0	40. SC	2.9
7. Conn	3.1	24. Miss	2.4	41. SD	.7
8. Del	.6	25. Mo	4.8	42. Tenn	4.3
9. Fla	8.7	26. Mon	.8	43. Tex	13.0
10. Ga	5.1	27. Neb	1.6	44. Ut	1.3
11. Ha	.9	28. Nev	.7	45. Vt	.5
12. Ida	.9	29. NH	.9	46. Va	5.2
13. Ill	11.2	30. NJ	7.3	47. Wash	3.8
14. Ind	5.4	31. NM	1.2	48. W.Va	1.9
15. Ia	2.9	32. NY	17.7	49. Wis	4.7
16. Kan	2.3	33. NC	5.6	50. Wy	.4
17. Ky	3.5	34. ND	.7		

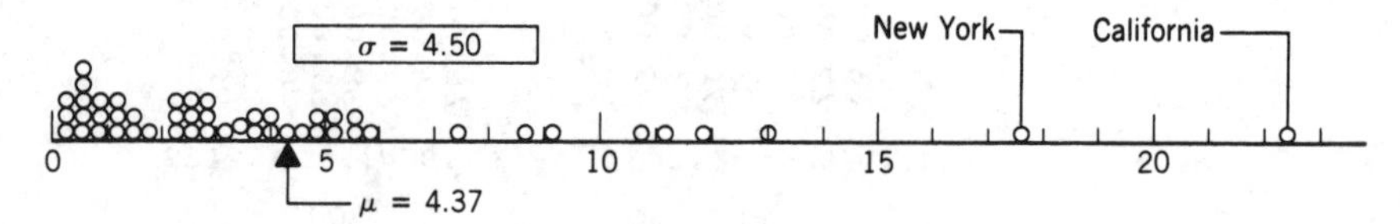

a. Using the random digits from Appendix Table I, draw a random sample of $n = 5$ states. Calculate $\overline{X}$ to estimate μ.

b. On the graph above, mark the 5 observations and their mean $\overline{X}$. Is $\overline{X}$ closer to the target μ than the typical individual observation?

c. Estimate the total population of the country, and compare to the actual population (218 million).

6-29 **a.** Repeat the sampling experiment in Problem 6-28**a** several more times. Then graph the different values of $\overline{X}$ in order to see roughly how $\overline{X}$ varies from sample to sample.

b. If this sampling experiment was repeated *millions* of times, would the millions of values of $\overline{X}$ fall in any sort of pattern? If so, sketch it in the graph in part **a**.

6-30 The owner of a ski resort has just installed a small gondola that routinely waits until it is filled before going up. The owner is worried that the time required to fill it will exceed the patience of the skiers, in particular, will exceed 10 minutes.

Suppose the gondola holds 8 skiers and they arrive at random to board it. To be precise, denote the waiting time for the first skier by T_1, then the additional time for the second skier by T_2, and so on

Suppose that these successive waiting times $T_1, T_2, \ldots, T_8$ are independent, with the same distribution (in minutes):

Waiting Time t	0	1	2	3	4	5	6	7	8	9
p(t)	.33	.22	.14	.09	.07	.05	.04	.03	.02	.01

a. Simulate one loading of the gondola. What is the waiting time required? Did it happen to exceed ten minutes?

b. Using the theory of Section 6-3, calculate the probability that the total waiting time will exceed 10 minutes.

6-31 **a.** Simulate drawing a random sample of five observations from a normal population of women's heights, with $\mu = 65''$, $\sigma = 3''$. Calculate the sample mean and median.

***b.** By pooling the answers from all the students in the class, have the instructor graph the sampling distribution of the sample mean and median. Which seems to be more accurate? Are the results similar to Figure 6-11?

***c.** As an alternative to part **b**, carry out the simulation by computer. (We suggest somewhere between 10 and 1000 samples be simulated.)

CHAPTER 6 SUMMARY

6-1 A *random* sample is one where all individuals in the population are equally likely to be sampled. Its great advantage is its fairness, which ensures *unbiased* estimation of the underlying population. Another important advantage is that sampling uncertainty can be evaluated.

In calculating the sample mean, an extreme observation tends to be diluted by more typical observations. Because of this averaging out, the sample mean doesn't vary as widely as the individual observations in the population.

6-2 To be specific, the sample mean $\overline{X}$ fluctuates around its target μ (the population mean) with a standard error of only $\sigma/\sqrt{n}$ (where σ is the standard deviation of the population, and n is the number of observations in the sample).

6-3 As sample size n increases, the sampling distribution of $\overline{X}$ concentrates more and more around its target μ. It also gets closer and closer to the normal shape. This normal approximation rule makes probability calculations very easy: We just standardize with $Z = (\overline{X} - \mu)/SE$, and refer to the standard normal table.

6-4 Proportions are very similar to means. The sample proportion P fluctuates normally about its target π, with a standard error of $\sqrt{\pi(1-\pi)/n}$. This similarity of P to $\bar{X}$ is no accident. If the two categories such as Democrat-Republican are handled with a 0-1 variable, then it turns out that P is just a special case of $\bar{X}$.

***6-5** Keeping out the chips as they are drawn (sampling without replacement) is more efficient than sampling with replacement. Specifically, it reduces the standard error of $\bar{X}$ (or P) by the factor $\sqrt{(N-n)/(N-1)}$, where N is the population size. (In large populations this "reduction factor" approaches 1, so it doesn't matter whether or not sampling is with replacement.)

***6-6** Monte Carlo (sampling simulation) confirms theoretical results like the normal approximation rule. Done quickly and cheaply on a computer, Monte Carlo is even more valuable in providing sampling distributions that are too difficult to derive theoretically.

REVIEW PROBLEMS

6-32 Match the symbol on the left with the phrase on the right:

μ sample mean
$\bar{X}$ sample variance
σ^2 population proportion
s^2 population variance
π sample proportion
P population mean

6-33 Fill in the blank:

In the 1984 Presidential election the United States and California were alike in their proportion of Republican voters ($\pi = 58\%$), the only difference being that the United States is about ten times as large a population. In order to get an equally reliable sampling estimate of π, the U.S. sample should be ____ as large as the California sample.

6-34 A manufacturer of diesel engines found that the diameters of the cylinders drilled into an engine block vary slightly. They are normaly distributed around the "target value" of 12.500 cm, with a standard deviation of .002 cm. If the diameter is within .003 cm of its target, it is acceptable.

a. What proportion of the cylinders are acceptable?

b. The production manager specifies that an engine block is acceptable if all four of its cylinders are acceptable. What is the probability that a block will be acceptable?

c. The assistant feels that an engine block should be regarded as acceptable if the *average* diameter of its four cylinders is within .003 cm of its target. What proportion of the blocks satisfy this criterion?

d. Who is right, the production manager or the assistant?

e. What important assumption did you make in calculating the answers in **b** and **c**?

6-35 To get a cross section of public opinion, the Gallup poll typically interviews 1500 Americans. This poll in some ways is more reliable than simple random sampling. For example, it deliberately selects an equal number of men and women, rather than leaving the split to chance. (This is called *stratified sampling.*)

In other ways, the Gallup poll is less expensive and a little less reliable than simple random sampling. For example, once a location has been randomly chosen, several people can be selected at random from it almost as easily as one person. Such *multistage sampling* makes it relatively easy to fill up the sample with 1500 people. Yet to the extent that people sampled later in a given location tend to think like those who were sampled first, they do not provide as much independent information as in a simple random sample, where each person is chosen entirely independently of the others.

These two features—the increased reliablity of stratified sampling and the decreased reliability of multistage sampling—tend to offset each other, so that the reliability of the sample is about the same as the reliability of a very simple random sample (VSRS).

a. The Gallup poll interviews a fresh sample of 1500 adults several times a year—say 20 times. Roughly, what are the chances they will interview *you* sometime in the next 10 years? (Use the 1980 U.S. population of 230 million, with 160 million being adults over 18)

b. As part **a** shows, the Gallup poll has a very small chance of ever picking any given voter. In view of this, can they make any legitimate claims to be representative, and provide a reliable picture of the *whole country*?

6-36 In the 1980 presidential election, 34.9 million voted Democratic and 43.2 million voted Republican (Carter versus Reagan, ignoring third parties as usual). The typical political poll randomly samples 1500 voters. What is the probability that such a poll would correctly forecast the election winner—that is, that a majority of the sample would be Republican?

6-37 American women have heights that are approximately normally distributed around a mean of 64 inches, with a standard deviation of 3 inches. Calculate and illustrate graphically each of the following:

a. If an American woman is drawn at random, what is the chance her height will exceed 66 inches (5 ft, 6 in.)?

b. If a sample of 25 women is randomly drawn, what is the chance that the sample average will exceed 66 inches?

6-38 The 1200 tenants of a large apartment building have weights distributed as follows:

Weight (Pounds)	*Proportion of Tenants*
50	.20
100	.30
150	.40
200	.10

Each elevator in the building has a load limit of 2800 pounds. If 20 tenants crowd into one elevator, what is the probability it will be overloaded?

6-39 A population of potential jurors is 60% women. If a group of 30 potential jurors (called a "venire") is chosen at random, what is the probability that 10 or fewer would be women?

6-40 Suppose the annual incomes (in $000) of an MBA class of 80 students ten years later had the distribution shown in the illustration.

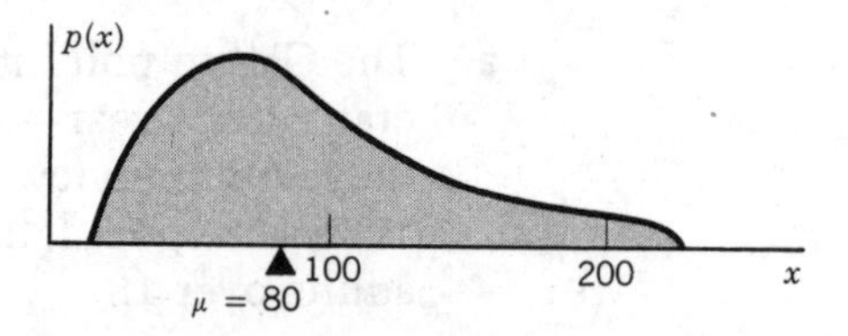

a. Suppose the 12 alumni who returned to their tenth reunion tended to be those who were more prosperous. (The least prosperous couldn't afford it; indeed, a few didn't have a mailing address and therefore didn't hear about the reunion.) Sketch on the graph where this "convenience" sample of a dozen incomes might be. Then where would their average be? How close to the target μ?

b. Repeat part **a**, if instead a *random* sample of 12 alumni had been chosen, and then carefully followed up to obtain a 100% response rate.

6-41 Hourly wages for construction workers in America in 1985 were higher than in any other sector (*Stat. Abst. of U.S.*, 1987, p. 394), averaging $12.30 with a standard deviation of $2.80. In a random survey that included 110 construction workers, what is the chance that their average would be at least $12.00?

6-42 On March 1, a large greenhouse installs 1000 ultraviolet lamps. The manufacturer specifies that the length of life is normally distributed around a mean of 100 days, with a standard deviation of 25 days.

a. What is the expected number that will have to be replaced by June 1 (92 days later)?

b. What is the chance that more than 400 will have to be replaced by June 1?

6-43 At Las Vegas, roulette is played with a wheel that has 38 slots—20 losing slots and 18 winning slots. Your chances of losing your dollar are therefore 20/38, and of winning a dollar are 18/38.

a. In the very long run, what is the average loss per play?

b. What are your chances of ending up a net loser, if you play a dollar:

i. 5 times? **ii.** 25 times? **iii.** 125 times?

6-44 ***A Final Challenge: Is Overbooking Worth It?***

Transamerican Airlines has a daily flight from Chicago to Boise, Idaho, and 8% of the passengers are "no-shows." Consequently, even when 75 seats are fully booked, the plane often leaves with empty seats and lost revenue (as in Problem 4-46).

a. Transamerican therefore planned to "overbook," making reservations for $n = 78$ passengers. Assuming they form a random sample from the whole population of passengers, what is the chance of an overload crisis, that is, more than 75 actually showing up for the flight?

b. Transamerican also considered the riskier plan of making reservations for $n = 80$ passengers. Using the binomial formula, a computer printed out the following schedule of how many passengers would show up (y):

y	$p(y)$	y	$p(y)$
80	.00	73	.15
79	.01	72	.12
78	.03	71	.08
77	.07	70	.05
76	.11	69	.03
capacity 75	.15	68	.02
74	.17	67	.01

Now what is the chance of an overload crisis?

c. To determine whether the overbooking in **b** was worth it, various costs have to be considered. The simplest costs to quote are the conceptual losses in revenue, incurred by failing to achieve the opportunity of a plane ideally loaded with exactly $y = 75$ passengers showing up. Called "Opportunity Losses" in management science, they are the same idea as "Opportunity Costs" in economics.

Opportunity Losses:

i. If $y < 75$, each empty seat costs $200 in lost revenue.

ii. If $y > 75$, each extra passenger who gets turned away costs $400, because of a "double your money back" guarantee.

What is the expected opportunity loss (EOL) for booking $n = 80$?

d. What is the EOL for the conservative booking $n = 75$? (Hint: What is the expected number who don't show? How much does each cost?)

e. Which is the better policy, booking $n = 75$ or $n = 80$? Over the 365 flights in a year, about how much would they gain from using the better policy (instead of the other)?

***f.** Using Minitab or similar softwear, verify that the better policy in **e** is the very best of all. (Hint: For $n = 80$, use the BINOMIAL or PDF command to generate the table given in **b.** Also tabulate the opportunity losses, so you can finally compute the EOL for $n = 80$, and so verify your answer to **c.** Now it is easy to repeat this, for $n = 79$, then $n = 78$, etc, to verify there is no better n.)

CHAPTER 7

Point Estimation

Education is man's going forward from cocksure ignorance to thoughtful uncertainty.

DON CLARKS' SCRAPBOOK

7-1 POPULATIONS AND SAMPLES

In Table 7-1, we review the concepts of population and sample. It is essential to remember that the population mean μ and variance σ^2 are constants (though generally unknown). These are called population *parameters*.

By contrast, the sample mean $\overline{X}$ and sample variance s^2 are random variables. Each varies from sample to sample, according to its sampling distribution. For example, the distribution of $\overline{X}$ was found to be approximately normal in (6-9). A random variable such as $\overline{X}$ or s^2, which is calculated from the observations in a sample, is given the technical name *sample statistic*. In Table 7-1 and throughout the rest of the text, we shall leave the *population gray* and make the *sample colored* in order to keep the distinction clear, just as we did in Chapter 6.

Now we can address the problem of statistical inference that we posed in Chapter 1: How can the population be estimated by the sample? Suppose, for example, that to estimate the nation's mean household income μ, we take a random sample of 100 incomes. Then the sample mean $\overline{X}$ surely is a reasonable estimator of μ. By the normal approximation rule (6-9), we know that $\overline{X}$ fluctuates about μ; sometimes it will be above μ, sometimes below. Even better than estimating μ with the single *point* estimate $\overline{X}$ would be to construct an *interval* estimate about $\overline{X}$ that is likely to bracket μ—a task we shall leave to Chapter 8.

For now, this chapter will concentrate on point estimates. How good is the sample mean $\overline{X}$ as an estimator of μ? Would the sample median be better? To answer such questions, we now develop criteria for judging a good estimator.

7-2 EFFICIENCY OF UNBIASED ESTIMATORS

A—UNBIASED ESTIMATORS

We already have noted that the sample mean $\overline{X}$ is, on average, exactly on its target μ. We therefore call $\overline{X}$ an *unbiased* estimator of μ.

To generalize, we consider any population parameter θ (Greek theta) and denote its estimator by U. If, on average, U is exactly on target as

TABLE 7-1 Review of Population versus Sample

A Random Sample is a Random Subset of the Population	
Relative frequencies f/n are used to compute	Probabilities $p(x)$ are used to compute
$\overline{X}$ and s^2	μ and σ^2
These random variables are examples of statistics or estimators.	These fixed constants are examples of parameters or targets.

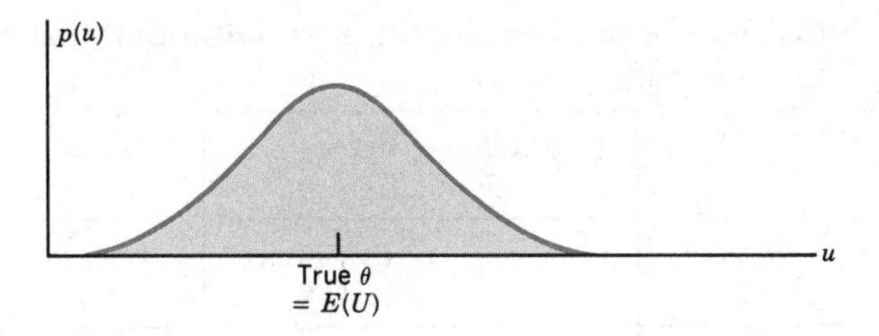

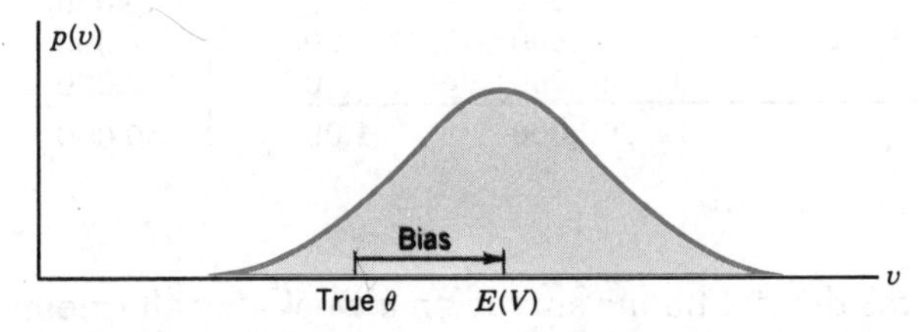

FIGURE 7-1
Comparison of (a) unbiased estimator, and (b) biased estimator.

shown in Figure 7-1*a*, it is called an unbiased estimator. More formally, we define:

$$U \text{ is an unbiased estimator of } \theta \text{ if } \quad E(U) = \theta \tag{7-1}$$

like (6-5)

Of course, an estimator V is called biased if $E(V)$ is different from θ. In fact, bias is defined as this difference:

$$\text{Bias} \equiv E(V) - \theta \tag{7-2}$$

Bias is illustrated in Figure 7-1*b*, where the distribution of V is off-target. Since $E(V)$ is greater than θ, the bias given by (7-2) is positive—reflecting the tendency of V to be too high.

As we stressed already, to avoid bias we have to randomly sample from the whole population. To show the difficulty we can encounter if we fail to follow this fundamental principle, consider an example of nonresponse bias.

EXAMPLE 7-1

Let us give a concrete example of the sample survey mentioned at the beginning of Chapter 6. Suppose each of the 200,000 adults in a city under study has eaten a number X of fast-food meals in the past week. However,

TABLE 7-2 Target Population, and Subpopulation Who Would Respond

	Whole Target Population		Subpopulation Responding	
X = Number of Meals	Freq. f	Rel. Freq. f/N	Freq. f	Rel. Freq. f/N
0	100,000	.50	38,000	.76
1	40,000	.20	6,000	.12
2	40,000	.20	4,000	.08
3	20,000	.10	2,000	.04
	200,000	1.00	50,000	1.00

a residential phone survey on a week-day afternoon misses those who are working—the very people most likely to eat fast foods. As shown in Table 7-2 below, this leaves a small subpopulation who would respond, especially small for higher values of X.

a. What is the mean μ of the whole target population, and the mean μ_R of the subpopulation who would respond?

b. A random sample of 200 phone calls will bring a response of about 50, whose average $\bar{R}$ will be used to estimate μ. What is its bias?

SOLUTION

a. Using the probabilities (rel. freq.) for the whole target population, we obtain $\mu = 0(.50) + 1(.20) + \ldots = .90$.
Similarly, using the probabilities for the responding subpopulation, we obtain $\mu_R = 0(.76) + 1(.12) + \ldots = .40$.

b. The sample mean $\bar{R}$ has an obvious nonresponse bias. Since heavy buyers of fast foods are far less likely to respond, $\bar{R}$ will tend to be much too small. To calculate just how serious the bias is, note that $\bar{R}$ is the average of a random sample drawn from the subpopulation with mean μ_R. Therefore, $E(\bar{R}) = \mu_R$ according to (6-5), and consequently,

$$\text{Bias} = E(\bar{R}) - \mu \qquad \text{like (7-2)}$$

$$= \mu_R - \mu$$

$$= .40 - .90 = -.50 \qquad (7\text{-}3)$$

Thus the bias is indeed very large—an underestimate of .50 meals per week.

B—EFFICIENT ESTIMATORS (MINIMUM VARIANCE)

As well as being on target on the average, we also would like the distribution of an estimator to be highly concentrated—that is, to have a small variance. This is the notion of *efficiency*, shown in Figure 7-2. We describe the estimator V in panel (a) as more efficient than the estimator W in panel (b) because it has smaller variance. More formally, we define the relative efficiency of two unbiased estimators:

$$\textbf{Efficiency of } V \textbf{ compared to } W \equiv \frac{\text{var } W}{\text{var } V} \tag{7-4}$$

For example, in the rare case when the population being sampled is exactly symmetric, its center can be estimated without bias by either the sample mean $\overline{X}$ or median $\check{X}$. For some populations, $\overline{X}$ is more efficient; for others, $\check{X}$ is more efficient. In sampling from a normal population for instance, we show in Appendix 7-2 that for large samples:

$$\text{var } \check{X} \simeq 1.57\ \sigma^2/n \tag{7-5}$$

Since $\overline{X}$ has variance σ^2/n, as given in (6-6), this smaller variance makes it

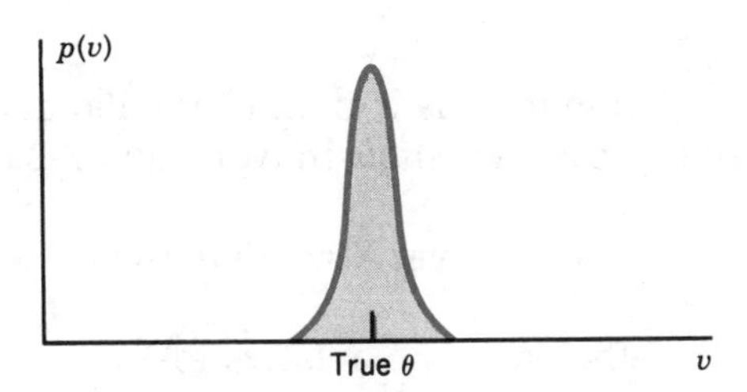

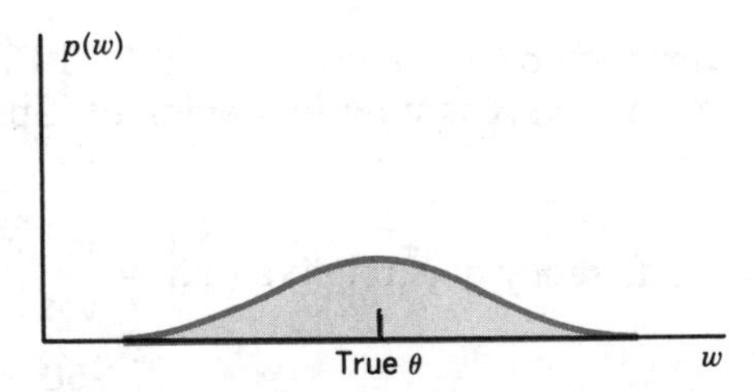

FIGURE 7-2
A comparison of (a) efficient estimator, and (b) inefficient estimator.

more efficient. Specifically, for normal populations,

$$\text{Efficiency of } \overline{X} \text{ relative to } \overset{\downarrow}{X} \equiv \frac{\text{var } \overset{\downarrow}{X}}{\text{var } \overline{X}} \qquad \text{like (7-4)}$$

$$\simeq \frac{1.57\sigma^2/n}{\sigma^2/n}$$

$$= 1.57 = 157\% \qquad (7\text{-}6)$$

The greater efficiency of the sample mean is nicely confirmed by the Monte Carlo study in Figure 6-11—where the ratio of variances was also 1.57 ($\simeq 1.26^2/1.01^2$). We conclude that, in estimating the center of a *normal* population, the sample mean $\overline{X}$ is about 57% more efficient than the sample median $\overset{\downarrow}{X}$. (In fact, it could be proved that the sample mean is more efficient than *every* other estimator of the center of a normal population.)

Of course, by increasing sample size n, we can reduce the variance of either the sample mean or median. This provides an alternative way of looking at the greater efficiency of the sample mean (in sampling from normal populations). The sample median will yield as accurate an estimate only if we take a 57% larger sample. Hence the sample mean is more efficient because it costs less to sample. Note how the economic and statistical definitions of efficiency coincide in this case.

Is the sample mean always more efficient than the median? An example will give the answer.

EXAMPLE 7-2

One of the population models with thicker tails than the normal is called the Laplace. In this case, we show in Appendix 7-2 that for large samples:

$$\text{var } \overset{\downarrow}{X} \simeq .50\, \sigma^2/n \qquad (7\text{-}7)$$

Now what is the efficiency of $\overline{X}$ relative to $\overset{\downarrow}{X}$?

SOLUTION

Again, $\overline{X}$ has variance σ^2/n, as given in (6-6). In this case it has larger variance than $\overset{\downarrow}{X}$, and so $\overline{X}$ is now less efficient. Specifically, for Laplace populations,

$$\text{Efficiency of } \overline{X} \text{ relative to } \overset{\downarrow}{X} \equiv \frac{\text{var } \overset{\downarrow}{X}}{\text{var } \overline{X}} \qquad \text{like (7-4)}$$

$$\simeq \frac{.50\, \sigma^2/n}{\sigma^2/n} \qquad (7\text{-}8)$$

$$= .50 = 50\% \qquad (7\text{-}9)$$

Although the Laplace distribution is a mathematical rarity, it nicely illustrates a very practical point: If a population has thick tails, so that outlying observations are likely to occur, then the sample mean has larger variance—because it takes into account all the observations, even the distant outliers that the sample median ignores. In Chapter 16 we will pursue this issue further.

PROBLEMS

7-1 Assuming as usual that samples are random, answer True or False; if False, correct it.

a. Samples are used for making inferences about the population from which they are drawn.

b. μ is a random variable (varying from sample to sample), and is an unbiased estimator of the parameter $\overline{X}$.

c. If we double the sample size, we halve the standard error of $\overline{X}$, and consequently double its accuracy in estimating the population mean.

d. The sample proportion P is an unbiased estimator of the population proportion π.

7-2 Based on a random sample of 2 observations, consider two competing estimators of the population mean μ:

$$\overline{X} \equiv \frac{1}{2}X_1 + \frac{1}{2}X_2$$

$$\text{and } U \equiv \frac{1}{3}X_1 + \frac{2}{3}X_2$$

a. Are they unbiased?

b. Which estimator is more efficient? How much more efficient?

7-3 An economist gathers a random sample of 500 observations, and loses the records of the last 180. This leaves only 320 observations from which to calculate the sample mean. What is the efficiency of this, relative to what could have been obtained from the whole sample?

7-4 What is the efficiency of the sample median relative to the sample mean in estimating the center of a normal population? [Hint: Recall from (7-6) that the efficiency of the mean relative to the median was 157%.]

7-5 **a.** Answer True or False; if False, correct it.

In both Problems 7-3 and 7-4 we have examples of estimates that are only 64% efficient. In Problem 7-3, this inefficiency was obvious, because 36% of the observations were lost in calculating $\overline{X}$. In Problem 7-4, the inefficiency was more subtle, because it was caused merely by using the sample median instead of the sample mean. However, in terms of results—producing an estimate with more variance than necessary—both inefficiencies are equally damaging.

b. In view of part **a**, what advice would you give to a researcher who spends $100,000 collecting data, and $100 analyzing it?

7-6 Suppose that a surveyor is trying to determine the area of a rectangular field, in which the measured length X and the measured width Y are independent random variables that fluctuate widely about the true values, according to the following probability distributions:

x	$p(x)$	y	$p(y)$
8	1/4	4	1/2
10	1/4	6	1/2
11	1/2		

The calculated area $A = XY$ of course is a random variable, and is used to estimate the true area. If the true length and width are 10 and 5, respectively,

a. Is X an unbiased estimator of the true length?

b. Is Y an unbiased estimator of the true width?

c. Is A an unbiased estimator of the true area? (Hint: see Problem 5-38)

7-7 **a.** To guide long-term planning, an automobile executive commissioned two independent sample surveys to estimate the proportion π of car owners who intend to buy a smaller car next time. The first survey showed a proportion $P_1 = 60/200 = 30\%$. The second and larger survey showed a proportion $P_2 = 240/1000 = 24\%$. To get an overall estimate, the simple average $P^* = 27\%$ was taken. What is the variance of this estimate? [Hint: You may assume simple random sampling, so that var $P \simeq P(1 - P)/n$]

b. The first poll is clearly less reliable than the second. So it was proposed to just throw the first away, and use the estimate $P_2 = 24\%$. What is the variance of this estimate? What then is its efficiency relative to P^*?

c. The best estimate of all, of course, would count each *observation* equally (not each *sample* equally). That is, take the overall proportion in favor, $P = (60 + 240)/(200 + 1000) = 25\%$. What is the variance of this estimate? Then what is its efficiency relative to P^*?

d. True or False? If False, correct it:
It is important to know the reliability of your sources. For exam-

ple, if an unreliable source is not discounted appropriately, using it can be worse than simply throwing it away.

7-3 EFFICIENCY OF BIASED AND UNBIASED ESTIMATORS

In comparing unbiased estimators, we chose the one with minimum variance. Now suppose we are comparing both biased and unbiased estimators, as in Figure 7-3. It may no longer be appropriate to select the estimator with least variance: W qualifies on that score, but is unsatisfactory because it is so badly biased. Nor do we necessarily pick the estimator with least bias: U has zero bias, but seems unsatisfactory because of its high variance. Instead, the estimator that seems to be closest to the target overall is V, because it has the best *combination* of small bias and small variance.

How can we make precise the notion of being "closest to the target overall"? We are interested in how an estimator, V let us say, is spread around its *true target* θ:

$$\textbf{Mean squared error (MSE)} \equiv E(V - \theta)^2 \tag{7-10}$$

like (4-34)

This is similar to the variance, except that it is measured around the true target θ rather than around the (possibly biased) mean of the estimator. Then, as Appendix 7-4 proves, MSE does indeed turn out to be a combination of variance and bias:

$$\textbf{MSE = (variance of estimator) + (its bias)}^2 \tag{7-11}$$

We choose the estimator that minimizes this MSE.

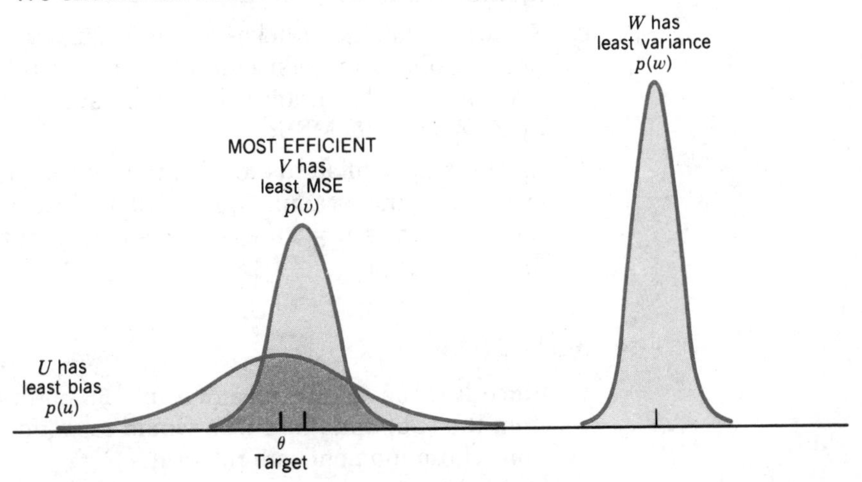

FIGURE 7-3
V is the estimator with the best combination of small bias and variance.

This confirms two earlier conclusions: if two estimators with equal variance are compared (as in Figure 7-1), the one with less bias is preferred; and if two unbiased estimators are compared (as in Figure 7-2), the one with smaller variance is preferred. In fact, if two estimators are unbiased, it is evident from (7-11) that the MSE reduces to the variance. Thus, MSE may be regarded as a general kind of variance, applying to either unbiased or biased estimators. This leads to a general definition of the relative efficiency of two estimators:

For any two estimators—whether biased or unbiased—

$$\text{Efficiency of } V \text{ compared to } W \equiv \frac{\text{MSE}(W)}{\text{MSE}(V)} \qquad \text{(7-12) like (7-4)}$$

To sum up, because it combines the two attractive properties of small bias and small variance, the concept of minimum MSE (or maximum efficiency) becomes the single most important criterion for judging between estimators. An example will illustrate.

EXAMPLE 7-3

In Example 7-1, recall the phone survey of 50 responses from 200 calls, that had a serious nonresponse bias. In addition, the average response $\overline{R}$ has variability too.

a. To measure how much $\overline{R}$ fluctuates around its target μ overall, calculate its MSE.

b. If the sample size was increased fivefold, how much would the MSE be reduced?

c. A second statistician takes a sample survey of only $n = 20$ phone calls, with persistent follow-up until he gets a response. Let this small but unbiased sample have a sample mean denoted by $\overline{X}$. What is its MSE?

d. In trying to publish his results, the second statistician was criticized for using a sample only 1/10 as large as the first. In fact, his sample size $n = 20$ was labeled "ridiculous." What defense might he offer?

SOLUTION

a. Since $\overline{R}$ is the sample mean for $n = 50$ observations drawn only from the subpopulation who would respond, this is the population whose moments are relevant:

Subpopulation Who Would Respond (from Table 7-2)

r	$p(r)$	$rp(r)$	$(r - \mu_R)$	$(r - \mu_R)^2$	$(r - \mu_R)^2 p(r)$
0	.76	0	−.4	.16	.1216
1	.12	.12	.6	.36	.0432
2	.08	.16	1.6	2.56	.2048
3	.04	.12	2.6	6.76	.2704
	confirmed: $\mu_R = .40$				$\sigma_R^2 = .64$

Thus we can confirm that the bias in $\bar{R}$ was:

$$\text{Bias} = .40 - .90 = -.50 \qquad \text{(7-3) repeated}$$

Also, from the subpopulation variance $\sigma_R^2 = .64$ in the table, we can deduce the variance of $\bar{R}$:

$$\text{var}(\bar{R}) = \frac{\sigma_R^2}{n} = \frac{.64}{50} = .013 \qquad \text{like (6-6)}$$

Now we can put the bias and variance together to get the MSE:

$$\begin{aligned} \text{MSE} &= \text{var} + \text{bias}^2 \qquad \text{(7-11) repeated} \\ &= .013 + .25 = .263 \end{aligned}$$

b. A sample five times as large would reduce the variance:

$$\text{var}(\bar{R}) = \frac{\sigma_R^2}{n} = \frac{.64}{5 \times 50} = .003$$

Unfortunately it would not reduce the bias—the same nonresponse would merely be repeated more often. Thus,

$$\begin{aligned} \text{MSE} &= \text{var} + \text{bias}^2 \\ &= .003 + .25 = .253 \end{aligned} \qquad \text{(7-13)}$$

Since the predominant term is the bias, which is unaffected by sample size, the MSE was reduced hardly at all (from .263 to .253).

c. By persistent follow up, the statistician gets everybody to reply. He is therefor sampling from the whole target population, whose distribution now becomes the relevant one:

Total Target Population (from Table 7-2)

x	$p(x)$	$xp(x)$	$(x-\mu)$	$(x-\mu)^2$	$(x-\mu)^2p(x)$
0	.50	0	−.90	.81	.405
1	.20	.20	.10	.01	.002
2	.20	.40	1.10	1.21	.242
3	.10	.30	2.10	4.41	.441
	confirmed: μ = .90				$\sigma^2 = 1.09$

Since this sample is drawn from the whole population, $\overline{X}$ is now unbiased, with

$$\text{var}(\overline{X}) = \frac{\sigma^2}{n} = \frac{1.09}{20} = .055$$

Thus we can calculate the MSE:

$$\text{MSE} = \text{var} + \text{bias}^2 \qquad \text{(7-11) repeated}$$
$$= .055 + 0 = .055 \qquad \text{(7-14)}$$

d. His defense would simply be that his estimator is far better because it has a far smaller MSE—four times smaller! Or, in less mathematical terms, "it's the quality of the sample that counts, not mere quantity." He might even point out the lesson of part **b:** Increasing the sample size (even by 5 times) without dealing with its bias would provide little practical improvement.

PROBLEMS

7-8 Each of three guns is being tested by firing 12 shots at a target from a clamped position. Gun A was not clamped down hard enough, and wobbled. Gun B was clamped down in a position that pointed slightly to the left, due to a misaligned sight. Gun C was clamped down correctly.

a. Which of the following patterns of shots belongs to gun A? gun B? gun C?

b. Which guns are biased? Which gun has minimum variance? Which has the largest MSE? Which is most efficient? Which is least efficient?

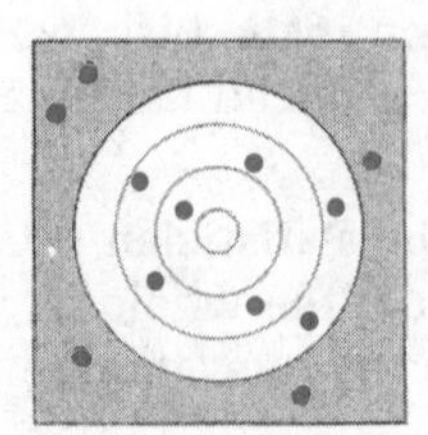

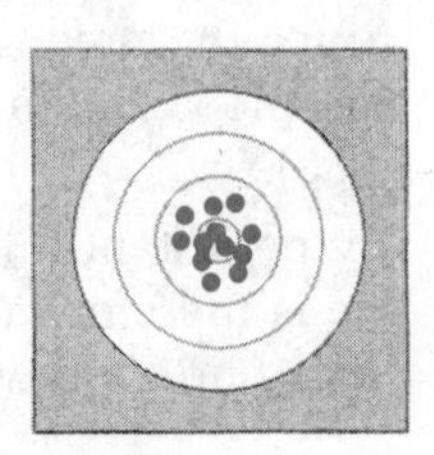

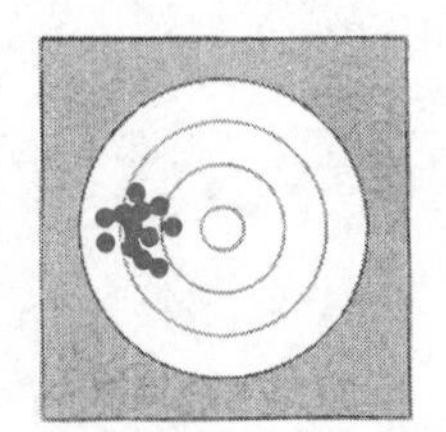

7-9 A large chain of shops specializing in tuneups has to choose one of four gauges to measure the gap in a spark plug. When tested, each gauge showed a slight error (in hundredths of mm.):

Gauge	A	B	C	D
bias	none	−10	5	2
standard dev.	10	none	5	8

Which gauge has the smallest MSE (greatest accuracy)?

7-10 A market survey of young business executives was undertaken to determine what sort of computer would suit a combination of their professional and personal needs. Since those with more children were thought to be more likely to buy a home computer, one of the questions each executive was asked was, "How many children do you have?"

Unfortunately, those with more children tend to have less time and inclination to reply to the survey, as the following table shows:

	Total Population (Target)		*Subpopulation Who Would Respond*	
x = *Number of Children Over 5 Years Old*	*Frequency f*	*Rel. Frequency f/N*	*Frequency f*	*Rel. Frequency f/N*
0	20,000	.40	6,200	.62
1	12,000	.24	2,100	.21
2	10,000	.20	1,200	.12
3	6,000	.12	400	.04
4	2,000	.04	100	.01
	N = 50,000	1.00	N = 10,000	1.00

Two types of sample survey were proposed:

i. *High volume*, with 1000 executives sampled, and with no follow up. Their overall response rate would be 10,000/50,000 = 20% as given by the table, yielding 200 replies.

ii. *High quality*, with 25 executives sampled, and enough follow-up to get a 100% response rate.

a. Calculate the mean number of children in the population μ.

b. In estimating μ, does either survey have a sample mean $\overline{X}$ that is unbiased?

c. Which survey has the smallest MSE (greatest accuracy)?

***7-11** In Problem 7-10, note how the response rate of executives drops as the number of children X increases. For example, when $X = 0$, the response rate is 6200/20,000 = 31%, while for $X = 4$, the response rate drops to 100/2000 = 5%. This is what causes the nonresponse bias, of course.

Now suppose a sample survey with enough follow-up to guarantee 100% response was prohibitively expensive. So a compromise was suggested: Sample 100 executives, with enough follow-up to get a response rate of 12,000/20,000 = 60% when $X = 0$; and then, for $X = 1, 2, 3, 4$, response rates of 40%, 30%, 30%, and 30%, respectively.

How would the MSE of this compromise survey compare to the other two surveys in Problem 7-10?

*7-4 CONSISTENT ESTIMATORS

A—CONSISTENCY: EVENTUALLY ON TARGET

Like efficiency, consistency is one of the desirable properties of estimators. But consistency is more abstract, because it is defined as a limit: A consistent estimator is one that concentrates in a narrower and narrower band around its target as sample size n increases indefinitely. This is sketched in Figure 7-4, and made more precise in Appendix 7-4.

One of the conditions that makes an estimator consistent is if its MSE approaches zero in the limit. In view of (7-11), this may be reexpressed as follows.

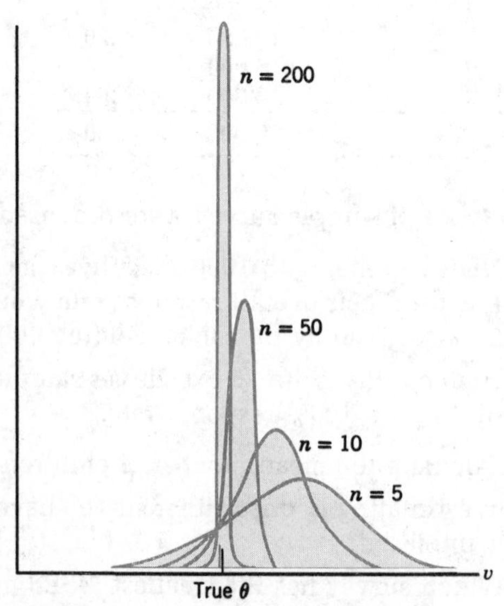

FIGURE 7-4

A consistent estimator, showing how the distribution of V concentrates on its target θ as sample size n increases.

One of the conditions that makes an estimator consistent is:

if its bias and variance *both* approach zero. (7-15)

EXAMPLE 7-4

a. Is $\overline{X}$ a consistent estimator of μ?
b. Is P a consistent estimator of π?
c. Is the average response $\overline{R}$ in Example 7-1 (based on a 25% response rate) a consistent estimator of μ?

SOLUTION

a. From the normal approximation rule (6-9), we know that $\overline{X}$ has:

$$\text{Bias} = 0 \quad \text{for all } n$$

$$\text{var} = \frac{\sigma^2}{n}, \text{ which approaches zero}$$

Thus (7-15) assures us that $\overline{X}$ is a consistent estimator of μ.

b. From the normal approximation rule for P given in (6-12), we similarly see that P is a consistent estimator of π.

c. Recall the nonresponse bias: The estimator $\overline{R}$ concentrated around the value $\mu_R = .40$, which is far below the target $\mu = .90$. So $\overline{R}$ is inconsistent.

B—ASYMPTOTICALLY UNBIASED ESTIMATORS

Sometimes an estimator has a bias that fortunately tends to zero as sample size n increases. Then it is called *asymptotically unbiased*. If its variance also tends to zero, (7-15) then assures us it will be consistent. An example will illustrate.

EXAMPLE 7-5

Consider the mean squared deviation:

$$\text{MSD} = \frac{1}{n}\Sigma(X - \overline{X})^2 \qquad \text{(7-16)} \quad \text{(2-10) repeated}$$

This is a biased estimator of the population variance σ^2. Specifically, on the average it will underestimate, as can be seen very easily in the case of

$n = 1$. Then $\overline{X}$ coincides with the single observed X, so that (7-16) gives MSD = 0, no matter how large the population variance σ^2 may be.

However, if we inflate MSD by dividing by $n - 1$ instead of n, we obtain the sample variance:

$$s^2 \equiv \frac{1}{n-1} \Sigma(X - \overline{X})^2 \qquad \text{(7-17)} \quad \text{(2-11) repeated}$$

It can be proved (Lindgren, 1976) that this slight adjustment inflates s^2 just enough to make it perfectly unbiased. [And in the extreme case above, where $n = 1$, the zero divisor in (7-17) makes s^2 undefined. This provides a simple warning that σ^2 cannot be estimated with a single X, since a single isolated observation gives us no idea whatsoever how spread out the underlying population may be.]

If you were puzzled earlier by the divisor $n - 1$ used in defining s^2, you now can see why. It is to ensure that s^2 will be an *unbiased* estimator of the population variance.

a. Although we have seen that MSD is biased, is it nevertheless asymptotically unbiased?

b. Suppose we used an even larger divisor, $n + 1$, to obtain the following estimator:

$$s_*^2 \equiv \frac{1}{n+1} \Sigma(X - \overline{X})^2 \qquad \text{(7-18)}$$

Is s_*^2 asymptotically unbiased?

SOLUTION

a. Let us write MSD in terms of the unbiased s^2:

$$\text{MSD} = \left(\frac{n-1}{n}\right) s^2 = \left(1 - \frac{1}{n}\right) s^2 \qquad \text{like (2-22)}$$

$$E(\text{MSD}) = \left(1 - \frac{1}{n}\right) E(s^2)$$

Finally, since s^2 is an unbiased estimator of σ^2,

$$E(\text{MSD}) = \left(1 - \frac{1}{n}\right) \sigma^2 = \sigma^2 - \left(\frac{1}{n}\right) \sigma^2$$

Since $1/n$ tends to zero, the last term—the bias—also tends to zero. So the MSD is indeed asymptotically unbiased.

b. Similarly, we may write:

$$s_*^2 = \left(\frac{n-1}{n+1}\right) s^2 = \left(1 - \frac{2}{n+1}\right) s^2$$

And since $2/(n+1)$ tends to zero, this is also asymptotically unbiased.

REMARKS

We have shown that both MSD and s_*^2 are asymptotically unbiased. And s^2 itself is unbiased for *any* sample size n. It could further be shown that all three estimators have variance that approaches zero, so that they are all consistent.

Which of the three estimators should we use? Since all three are consistent, we need a stronger criterion to make a final choice, such as efficiency. For many populations, including the normal, it turns out that s_*^2 is most efficient.

C—CONCLUSIONS

Although consistency has an abstract definition, it often provides a useful preliminary criterion for sorting out estimators.

Nevertheless, to finally sort out the best estimator, a stronger criterion such as efficiency is required—as we saw in Example 7-5. Another familiar example will illustrate: In estimating the center of a normal population, both the sample mean and median satisfy the consistency criterion. To choose between them, efficiency is the criterion that will finally select the winner (the sample mean).

*PROBLEMS

7-12 The population of American personal incomes is skewed to the right (as we saw in Figure 2-5, for men in 1975, for example). Which of the following will be consistent estimators of the population mean μ?

- **a.** From a random sample of incomes, the sample mean? The sample median? The sample mode?
- **b.** Repeat part **a**, for a sample of incomes drawn at random from the cities over one million.

7-13 When S successes occur in n trials, the sample proportion $P = S/n$ customarily is used as an estimator of the probability of success π. However, sometimes there are good reasons to use the estimator

$P^* \equiv (S + 1)/(n + 2)$. Alternatively, P^* can be written as a linear combination of the familiar estimator P:

$$P^* = \frac{nP + 1}{n + 2} = \left(\frac{n}{n + 2}\right) P + \left(\frac{1}{n + 2}\right)$$

a. What is the MSE of P? Is it consistent?

b. What is the MSE of P^*? Is it consistent? (Hint: Calculate the mean and variance of P^*, in terms of the familiar mean and variance of P.)

c. To decide which estimator is better, P or P^*, does consistency help? What criterion *would* help?

d. Tabulate the efficiency of P^* relative to P, for example when $n = 10$ and $\pi = 0, .1, .2, \ldots, .9, 1.0$.

e. State some possible circumstances when you might prefer to use P^* instead of P to estimate π.

CHAPTER 7 SUMMARY

7-1 Statistics such as $\overline{X}$ from random samples (colored blue) are used to estimate parameters such as μ from populations (gray).

7-2 An estimator is called unbiased if, on average, it is exactly on target. An unbiased estimator is called efficient if it has the smallest variance.

7-3 For estimators with bias as well as variance, minimum MSE (mean squared error) is the appropriate measure of efficiency. MSE remains disappointingly high for estimators with persistent bias, such as nonresponse bias.

*7-4 A consistent estimator is one that eventually is on target. (Not only on target on average, but the whole sampling distribution gets squeezed onto the target, as the sample size n increases infinitely.)

REVIEW PROBLEMS

7-14 An estimator that has small variance (but may be biased) is called *precise*. An estimator that has small MSE is called *accurate*. To illustrate: A standard 100-gm mass was weighed many many times on a scale A, and the distribution of measurements is graphed below. A similar distribution was obtained for scale B, and finally for scale C.

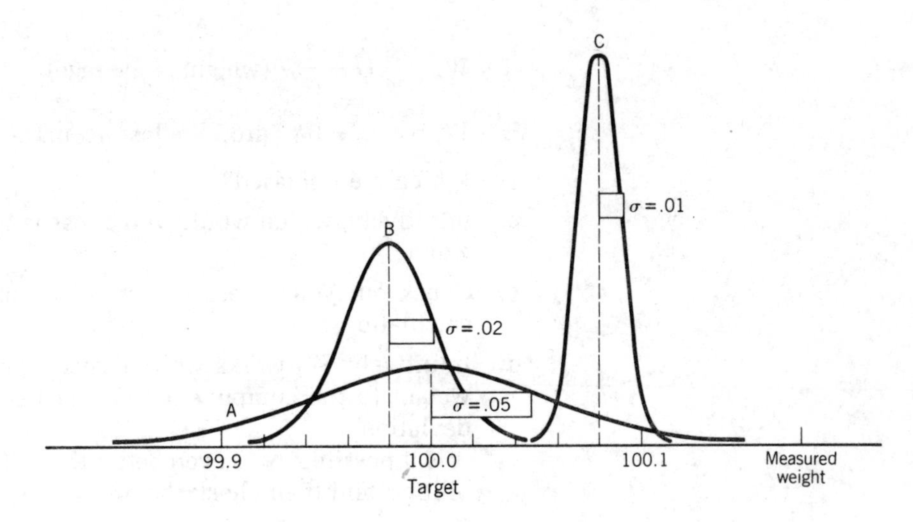

Scale A: $\mu = 100.00, \sigma = .05$
Scale B: $\mu = 99.98, \sigma = .02$
Scale C: $\mu = 100.08, \sigma = .01$

a. Which scale is most precise? Most accurate?

b. What is the relative efficiency of scale A relative to B? Of scale C relative to B? Do these answers agree with part **a**?

c. Which is more important: for an estimator to be precise or accurate?

7-15 **a.** Continuing Problem 7-14, since the scales were not perfect, it was decided in each case to weigh an object 25 times and take the average as the best estimate of the true weight. When used this way, which scale gives the most accurate $\bar{X}$?

b. Answer True or False; if False, correct it:

If a single measurement is taken, the random part (σ) and the systematic part (bias) are equally important.

When several measurements are averaged, the random part of the error gets averaged out, while the systematic part persists. Then it is particularly important to have little bias.

7-16 Suppose that two economists estimate μ (the average expenditure of American families on food), with two unbiased (and statistically independent) estimates U and V. The second economist is less careful than the first—the standard deviation of V is 3 times as large as the standard deviation of U. When asked how to combine U and V to get a publishable overall estimate, three proposals are made:

i. $W_1 = \frac{1}{2}U + \frac{1}{2}V$ (simple average)

ii. $W_2 = \frac{3}{4}U + \frac{1}{4}V$ (weighted average)

iii. $W_3 = 1U + 0V$ (drop the less accurate estimate)

a. Which are unbiased?

b. Intuitively, which would you guess is the best estimator? The worst?

c. Check out your guess in part **b** by making the appropriate calculations.

*d. Intuitively, W_2 works well because it gives only ⅓ as much weight to the component (V) that has 3 times the standard deviation.

Is it possible to do even better than W_2? Suggest some possibilities, and then check them out.

7-17 A processor of sheet metal produces a large number of square plates, whose size must be cut within a specified tolerance. To measure the final product, a slightly worn gauge is used: Its measurement error is normally distributed with a mean $\mu = 0$ and standard deviation $\sigma = .10$ inch. To improve the accuracy, and to protect against blunders, two independent measurements of a plate's length are taken with this gauge, say X_1 and X_2. To find the area of a plate, the quality control manager is in a dilemma:

i. Should he square first, and then average:

$$\frac{X_1^2 + X_2^2}{2}$$

ii. Should he average first, and then square:

$$\left(\frac{X_1 + X_2}{2}\right)^2$$

a. Are methods **i** and **ii** really different, or are they just two different ways of saying the same thing? (Hint: Try a simulation. Suppose, for example, the two measured lengths are $X_1 = 5.9$ and $X_2 = 6.1$.)

b. Which has less bias? [Hint: See equation (4-36).]

c. As an alternative estimator of the area, what is the bias of X_1X_2? (Hint: See Problem 5-38.)

***7-18** A free-trade agreement has opened up a new market of 50 million potential customers for personal computers, and a market survey of these customers is being planned. People with higher incomes are more likely to buy a computer within the next 6 months, and also more likely to respond to a phone survey, as the following table shows:

Income Level	Proportion Who Will Buy	Total Population (Target) Frequency f (millions)	Subpopulation Who Would Respond Frequency f (millions)
$0–20,000	2%	40	7
20–40,000	4%	5	1
40–80,000	10%	3	1
over 80,000	20%	2	1
		N = 50	N = 10

a. In the 50 million population, how many will buy a computer? Answer as a total figure, and then as a percentage.

b. A market survey of 1000 random phone calls would bring about how many replies? Among these replies, the percentage P who will buy is a natural estimator of the population percentage in **a**. What is the bias and MSE of P?

c. A smaller survey was also considered, with just 100 calls but enough follow-up to get a 100% response. What is the bias and MSE of the resulting estimator P^*?

7-19 To interpret MSE concretely, we could take its square root to get the "typical" error (more precisely, the Root-Mean-Square or RMS error—just like we took the square root of the variance to get the standard deviation).

In Problem 7-18, calculate this RMS error:

a. For P and P^*, the two competing estimators of the percentage of the population who will buy.

b. For the two corresponding estimators of the *total* number in the population who will buy (the "market size").

7-20 ***A Final Challenge: How Much Follow-Up Should a Survey Use?***

A market survey was being planned to estimate the number of drug circulars physicians have read in the past seven days. Physicians who read more were also more likely to respond to the survey, as the following table shows:

X = Number of Circulars Read	Whole Target Population Frequency f	Subpopulation Responding to First Contact Frequency f	Subpopulation Responding to First or Second Contact Frequency f
0	40,000	2,000	14,000
1	5,000	1,000	2,000
2	5,000	2,000	4,000
	N = 50,000	N = 5,000	N = 20,000

To get an accurate estimate of the total number of circulars read, determine which of the following surveys would be better.

i. A large survey of 1000 physicians contacted just once.

ii. A small survey of only 25 physicians, with relentless follow-up to get a 100% response rate.

iii. A compromise survey of 100 physicians contacted a second time if necessary, that would obtain the response rate given in the final column.

CHAPTER 8

Confidence Intervals

I went to a watchmaker again. He took the watch all to pieces while I waited, and then said the barrel was "swelled." He said he could reduce it in three days. After this the watch *averaged* well, but nothing more. For half a day it would go like the very mischief, and keep up such a barking and wheezing and whooping and sneezing and snorting, that I could not hear myself think for the disturbance; and so long as it held out there was not a watch in the land that stood any chance against it. But the rest of the day it would keep on slowing down and fooling along until all the clocks it had left behind caught up again. So at last, at the end of twenty-four hours, it would trot up to the judges' stand all right and just in time. It would show a fair and square average, and no man could say it had done more or less than its duty. But a correct average is only a mild virtue in a watch, and I took this instrument to another watchmaker.

—MARK TWAIN, SKETCHES OLD AND NEW

8-1 A SINGLE MEAN

A—THEORY

In Chapter 7, we considered various *point estimators*. For example, we concluded that $\overline{X}$ was a good estimator of μ for populations that are approximately normal. Although *on average* $\overline{X}$ is on target, the specific sample mean $\overline{X}$ that we happen to observe is almost certain to be a bit high or a bit low. Accordingly, if we want to be reasonably confident that our inference is correct, we cannot claim that μ is precisely equal to the observed $\overline{X}$. Instead, we must construct an *interval estimate* or *confidence interval* of the form:

$$\mu = \overline{X} \pm \text{sampling error} \tag{8-1}$$

The crucial question is: How wide must this allowance for sampling error be? The answer, of course, will depend on how much $\overline{X}$ fluctuates, which we review in Figure 8-1.

First we must decide how confident we wish to be that our interval estimate is right—that it does indeed bracket μ. It is common to choose 95% confidence; in other words, we will use a technique that will give us, in the long run, a correct interval 19 times out of 20.

To get a confidence level of 95%, we select the smallest range under the normal distribution of $\overline{X}$ that will just enclose a 95% probability. Obviously, this is the middle chunk, leaving $2\frac{1}{2}\%$ probability excluded in each tail. From Table IV, we find that this requires a z value of 1.96. That is, we must go above and below the mean by 1.96 standard errors (SE), as shown in Figure 8-1. In symbols:

$$\Pr(\mu - 1.96\ \text{SE} < \overline{X} < \mu + 1.96\ \text{SE}) = 95\% \tag{8-2}$$

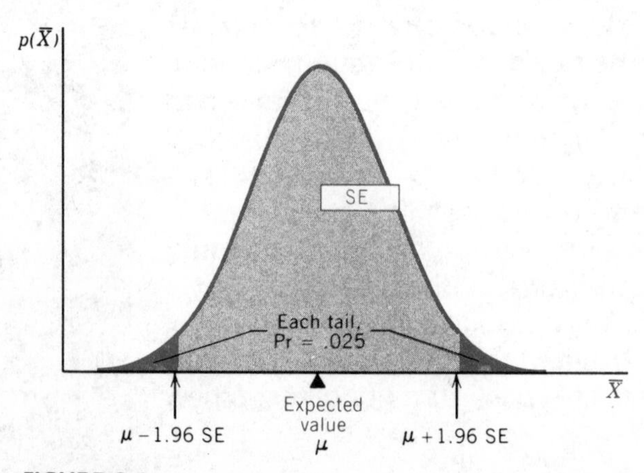

FIGURE 8-1
Normal distribution of the sample mean around the fixed but unknown parameter μ. 95% of the probability is contained within $\pm$ 1.96 standard errors.

which is just the algebraic way of saying, "There is a 95% chance that the random variable $\overline{X}$ will fall between $\mu - 1.96$ SE and $\mu + 1.96$ SE."

The inequalities within the brackets may now be solved for μ—turned around—to obtain the equivalent statement:

$$\Pr(\overline{X} - 1.96\ \text{SE} < \mu < \overline{X} + 1.96\ \text{SE}) = 95\% \tag{8-3}$$

We must be exceedingly careful not to misinterpret (8-3). μ has not changed its character in the course of this algebraic manipulation. It has not become a variable but has remained a population constant. Equation (8-3), like (8-2), is a probability statement about the random variable $\overline{X}$, or, more precisely, the *random interval* $\overline{X} - 1.96$ SE to $\overline{X} + 1.96$ SE. *It is this interval that varies, not* μ.

B—ILLUSTRATION

To appreciate the fundamental point that the confidence interval fluctuates while μ remains constant, consider an example. Suppose we wish to construct an interval estimate for μ, the mean height of the population of men on a large midwestern campus, on the basis of a random sample of $n = 10$ men. Moreover, to clearly illustrate what is going on, suppose that we have some supernatural knowledge of the population μ and σ. Suppose that we know, for example, that:

$$\mu = 69$$

$$\sigma = 3.22$$

Then the standard error of $\overline{X}$ is:

$$\text{SE} = \frac{\sigma}{\sqrt{n}} \qquad \text{(8-4)} \quad \text{(6-7) repeated}$$

$$= \frac{3.22}{\sqrt{10}} = 1.02$$

Now let us observe what happens when the statistician (who does not have our supernatural knowledge of course) tries to estimate μ using (8-3). To appreciate the random nature of his task, suppose he makes 50 such interval estimates, each time from a different random sample of 10 men. Figure 8-2 shows his typical experience (compare to Figure 6-5).

First, in the normal distribution at the top we illustrate equation (8-2): $\overline{X}$ is distributed around $\mu = 69$, with a 95% probability that it lies as close as:

$$\pm 1.96\text{SE} = \pm 1.96(1.02) = \pm 2.0 \tag{8-5}$$

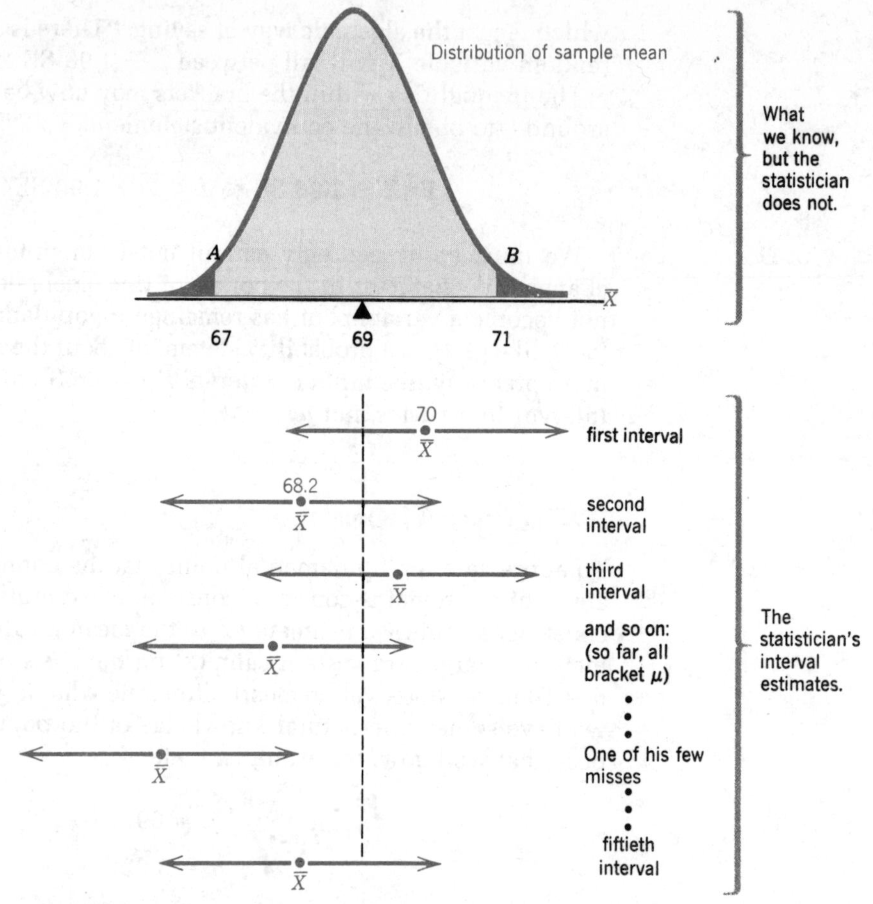

FIGURE 8-2
Constructing 50 interval estimates: About 95% correctly bracket the target μ.

That is, there is a 95% probability that any $\bar{X}$ will fall in the range 67 to 71 inches.

But the statistician does not know this; he blindly takes his random sample, from which he computes the sample mean—let us say[1] $\bar{X} = 70$. From (8-3), he calculates the interval for μ:

$$\bar{X} \pm 1.96\text{SE} \tag{8-6}$$
$$= 70 \pm 1.96\,(1.02)$$
$$= 70 \pm 2$$
$$= 68 \text{ to } 72 \tag{8-7}$$

[1] Strictly speaking, a specific realized value such as this should be denoted by the lower-case letter $\bar{x}$ to distinguish it from the potential value (random variable) denoted by $\bar{X}$. From now on, however, we will not bother to distinguish the realized value from the potential value, and will use $\bar{X}$ to refer to either. And for certain other variables, such as s, in order to conform to common usage we will always use a lower-case letter.

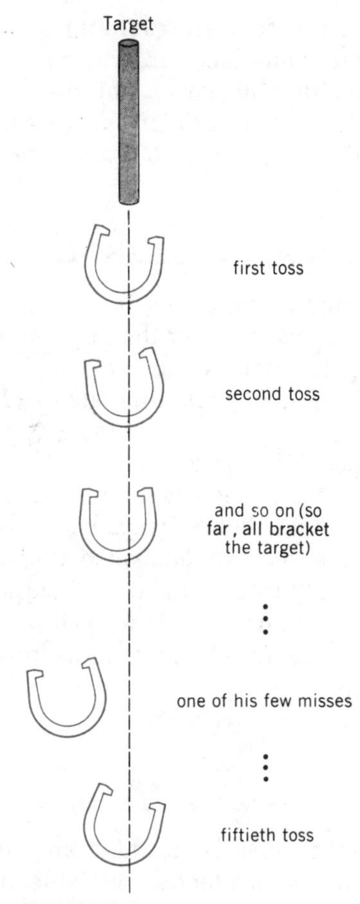

FIGURE 8-3

How an expert pitching 50 horseshoes is like the statistician in Figure 8-2: About 95% of his attempts correctly bracket the target.

This interval estimate for μ is the first one shown in Figure 8-2. In his first effort, the statistician is right; μ is enclosed in this interval.

In his second sample, suppose he happens to draw a shorter group of individuals, and duly computes $\overline{X}$ to be 68.2 inches. From a similar evaluation of (8-6), he comes up with his second interval estimate shown in the diagram, and so on. If he continues in this way to construct 50 interval estimates, about 95% of them will bracket the target μ. Only about 2 or 3 will miss the mark.

We can easily see why the statistician is correct so often. For each interval estimate, he is simply adding and subtracting 2 inches from the sample mean; and this is the same ± 2 inches that was calculated in (8-5) and defines the 95% range AB around μ. Thus, if and only if he observes a sample mean within this range AB, will his interval estimate bracket μ. And this happens 95% of the time, in the long run.

In practice, of course, a statistician would not take many samples—but only one. When the one confidence interval is then constructed, it is either right or wrong; it either brackets μ or it does not. But the important point to recognize is that the statistician is using a method with a 95% chance of success; in the long run, 95% of the intervals constructed this way will bracket μ.

C—ANALOGY: PITCHING HORSE SHOES

Constructing 95% confidence intervals is like pitching horseshoes. In each case there is a fixed target, either the population μ or the stake. We are trying to bracket it with some chancy device, either the random interval or the horseshoe. This analogy is illustrated in Figure 8-3.

There are two important ways, however, that confidence intervals differ from pitching horseshoes. First, only *one* confidence interval is customarily constructed. Second, the target μ is not visible like a horseshoe stake. Thus, whereas the horseshoe player always knows the score (and specifically, whether or not the last toss bracketed the stake), the statistician does not. He continues to "throw in the dark," without knowing whether or not a specific interval estimate has bracketed μ. All he has to go on is the statistical theory that assures him that, in the long run, he will succeed 95% of the time.

D—REVIEW

To review, we briefly emphasize the main points:

1. The population parameter μ is constant, and remains constant. It is the interval estimate that is a random variable, because its center $\overline{X}$ is a random variable.
2. To appreciate where it came from, the confidence interval (8-6) may be written as

$$\boxed{\mu = \overline{X} \pm z_{.025}\,\text{SE}} \tag{8-8}$$

where $z_{.025}$ is the value 1.96 obtained from Appendix Table IV—that is, the z value that cuts off $2\frac{1}{2}$% in the upper tail (and by symmetry, also $2\frac{1}{2}$% in the lower tail). Equation (8-8) is extremely useful as the prototype for all confidence intervals that we will study. When we substitute (8-4) into (8-8), we obtain another very useful form:

95% confidence interval

$$\mu = \overline{X} \pm z_{.025}\frac{\sigma}{\sqrt{n}} \tag{8-9}$$

3. As sample size n is increased, $\overline{X}$ has a smaller standard error $\sigma/\sqrt{n}$, and the confidence interval becomes narrower. This increased accuracy is the value of increased sample size.
4. Suppose we wish to be more confident, for example, 99% confident. Then the range must be large enough to encompass 99% of the probability. Since this leaves .005 in each tail, the formula (8-9) would use $z_{.005} = 2.58$ (found in Table IV). Thus the confidence interval becomes wider—that is, vaguer. This is exactly what we would expect. The more certain we want to be about a statement, the more vague we must make it.

An example will illustrate how easily confidence intervals can be calculated.

EXAMPLE 8-1

A sample survey to estimate the fast-food market in a large city was kept small enough to allow repeated follow-up. The high response rate meant that the sample was essentially random. The survey recorded the number of fast-food meals eaten by each person in the previous 7 days, and to summarize: $\overline{X} = .82$, $s = .48$, and $n = 180$. Calculate a 95% confidence interval for the mean of the whole population of this city.

SOLUTION

Formula (8-9) requires the population standard deviation σ, which of course we do not know. But it seems reasonable to use the sample standard deviation s as a good approximation. (The next section shows this is legitimate if $n \geq 100$.) We therefore substitute $\overline{X} = .82$, $\sigma \approx s = .48$, and $n = 180$ into (8-9):

$$\mu = .82 \pm 1.96 \frac{(.48)}{\sqrt{180}}$$

$$= .82 \pm .07$$

That is, the 95% confidence interval for μ is

$$.75 < \mu < .89$$

Since confidence intervals are an ideal way to allow for sampling fluctuation, we will develop many other confidence intervals in this chapter and indeed throughout the whole book. To make it easy to refer to them, we have listed them all inside the back cover in a guide called WHERE TO FIND IT. Here we list the commonest statistical problems that occur in practice, and how to deal with each, including the appropriate confidence interval and examples of how problems can be solved.

E—WHEN SHOULD WE USE THE MEAN?

Throughout this chapter and continuing on to Chapter 15, we will build many other confidence intervals like the prototype (8-9) around the sample mean $\overline{X}$.

Occasionally we may want to build a confidence interval around the sample median, or some other central measure (to be studied in Chapter 16). But we must always remember that in the many cases where a total is required, explicitly or implicitly, the mean is the only central measure that will retrieve it. For example, if a real estate board reports that their 2000 residential sales during March had a mean of \$52,000, a median of \$46,000, and a mode of \$45,000, it is the *mean* that gives the total value ($2000 \times \$52{,}000 = \$104{,}000{,}000$).

PROBLEMS

8-1 Make the correct choice in each square bracket:

a. The sample mean [$\overline{X}$, μ] is an unbiased estimate of the population mean [$\overline{X}$, μ]—assuming the sample is [random, very large].

b. $\overline{X}$ fluctuates from sample to sample with a standard deviation equal to [σ/n, $\sigma/\sqrt{n}$], which is also called the [standard error SE, population standard deviation].

c. If we make an allowance of about [$\sqrt{n}$, 2] standard errors on either side of $\overline{X}$, we obtain an interval wide enough that it has a 95% chance of covering the target μ. This is called the 95% confidence interval for [$\overline{X}$, μ].

d. A statistician who constructed a thousand of these 95% confidence intervals over his lifetime would miss the target [practically never, about 50 times, about 950 times]. Of course, he [would, would not] know just which times these were.

e. For greater confidence such as 99%, the confidence interval must be made [narrower, wider].

8-2 **a.** Suppose that you took a random sample of 100 accounts in a large department-store chain, and found that the mean balance due was \$74, and the standard deviation was \$86. Find the 95% confidence interval for the mean balance due. (Since the sample is so large, the population standard deviation σ can be safely approximated with the sample standard deviation $s = \$86$.)

b. If there were 243,000 accounts altogether, find a 95% confidence interval for the total balance due. Briefly explain to the vice president the meaning of your answer.

c. Suppose that the skeptical vice president undertook a complete accounting of the whole population of balances due, and found a total of \$19,714,000. What would you say?

8-3 A random survey of 225 of the 2700 institutions of higher learning in the United States was conducted in 1976 by the Carnegie Commission. The survey showed a mean enrolment of 3700 students per institution, with a standard deviation of 6000 students. Construct a 95% confidence interval for the total student enrolment in all 2700 institutions.

8-4 To determine the average age of its customers, a large manufacturer of men's clothing took a random sample of 50 customers and found $\overline{X} = 36$. If you knew $\sigma = 12$:

a. Find a 95% confidence interval for the mean age μ of all the customers.

b. Suppose you need to make the 95% confidence interval narrower—to be specific, ± 2 years. How large a sample is now required?

c. In part (b) we found out what sample size n was required to achieve a specified sampling error allowance $e = 2$. Show that the general formula for n in terms of *any* specified e and σ is:

$$n = \left(1.96 \frac{\sigma}{e}\right)^2 \tag{8-10}$$

d. How large should n be if you need to reduce the sampling allowance to ± 1?

e. To achieve 16 times the accuracy (i.e., to reduce e to one-sixteenth of its former value) how much larger must the sample be?

8-2 SMALL SAMPLE *t*

In the previous section it was assumed, quite unrealistically, that a statistician knows the true population standard deviation σ. In this section, we consider the practical case where σ is unknown.

With σ unknown, the statistician wishing to evaluate the confidence interval (8-9) must use some estimate of σ—with the most obvious candidate being the *sample* standard deviation s. (Note that s, along with $\overline{X}$, can always be calculated from the sample data.) But the use of s introduces an additional source of unreliability, especially if the sample is small. To retain 95% confidence, we must therefore widen the interval. We do so by replacing the $z_{.025}$ value taken from the standard normal distribution with a larger $t_{.025}$ value taken from a similar distribution called *Student's t distribution*. (The close relationship between the standard normal and the t distribution is described in detail in Figure 9-2.)

When we substitute s and the compensating $t_{.025}$ into (8-9), we obtain:

95% confidence interval for the population mean (8-11)

$$\mu = \bar{X} \pm t_{.025}\frac{s}{\sqrt{n}}$$

The value $t_{.025}$ is listed in the shaded column of Appendix Table V, and is tabulated according to the degrees of freedom (d.f.):

$$\text{d.f.} \equiv \text{amount of information used in calculating } s^2 \equiv \text{divisor in } s^2$$ (8-12) like (2-16)

To explain this, recall from Section 2-3 that we can calculate the variance s^2 only if our sample size n exceeds 1. That is, in calculating s^2, there are essentially only $(n - 1)$ pieces of information (degrees of freedom):

$$\text{d.f.} = n - 1$$ (8-13)

And this was the divisor in calculating s^2, you recall.

For example, if the sample size is $n = 4$, we read down Table V to d.f. = 3 (in the left-hand column), which gives $t_{.025} = 3.18$ to use in (8-11). (Note that this is indeed larger than $z_{.025} = 1.96$.)

In practice, when do we use the normal z table, and when the t table? (Incidentally, these are the two most useful tables in statistics. So useful, in fact, that we repeat them inside the front cover, for easy reference.) In the rare case when σ is known, the normal z value in (8-9) is appropriate. In the usual case when σ is estimated with s, the t value in (8-11) is appropriate—regardless of sample size. However, as the sample size grows larger than 100, say, the normal z becomes a good approximation to the t. (For example, as we read down Table V, for d.f. = 120 we should use $t_{.025} = 1.98$; but using $z_{.025} = 1.96$ is an excellent approximation.)

So in practice when σ is unknown, t needs to be used *only for small samples*[2] $(n < 100)$. An example will illustrate.

[2] A word of caution is in order. When R. A. Fisher mathematically derived the confidence interval (8-11) about 1920, he used the simplifying assumption that the parent population was normal. It therefore is strictly correct only for normal populations.

However, even when the population is quite non-normal, this confidence interval still has approximately a 95% chance of covering the true mean, and is therefore called *robust* in coverage. The one exception to this robustness is the rare combination of a *small* sample drawn from a very *skewed* population using a *one*-sided confidence interval to be discussed later (Pearson and Please, 1975). Then an even more robust alternative to the confidence interval (8-11) may be appropriate, as given in Chapter 16.

TABLE 8-1 Analysis of One Sample

Observed Grade X	$(X - \overline{X})$	$(X - \overline{X})^2$
64	−10	100
66	−8	64
89	15	225
77	3	9
$\overline{X} = \frac{296}{4} = 74$	0	$s^2 = \frac{398}{3} = 132.7$

EXAMPLE 8-2

From a large class, a random sample of 4 grades were drawn: 64, 66, 89, and 77. Calculate a 95% confidence interval for the whole class mean μ.

SOLUTION

Since $n = 4$, d.f. $= 3$. Then from Table V inside the front cover, $t_{.025} = 3.18$. In Table 8-1, we calculate $\overline{X} = 74$ and $s^2 = 132.7$. When all these are substituted into (8-11), we obtain:

$$\mu = 74 \pm 3.18 \frac{\sqrt{132.7}}{\sqrt{4}}$$

$$= 74 \pm 18 \qquad (8\text{-}14)$$

That is, with 95% confidence we conclude that the mean grade of the whole class is between 56 and 92. This is a pretty vague interval because the sample is so small.

To sum up, we note that (8-11) is of the following form:

$$\boxed{\mu = \overline{X} \pm t_{.025} \text{ (estimated standard error)}} \qquad (8\text{-}15)$$

This equation is just like (8-8), the only difference being that the *estimated* standard error in (8-15) requires using the larger t value instead of the z value.

PROBLEMS

8-5 Answer True or False; if False, correct it:
If σ is unknown, then we must use (8-11) instead of (8-9). This involves replacing σ with its estimator s, an additional source of

unreliability; and to allow for this, $z_{.025}$ is replaced by the larger $t_{.025}$ value in order to keep the confidence level at 95%.

8-6 A real estate agency wants to estimate the average selling price of houses in a suburb of Atlanta. It randomly samples 25 recent sales and calculates the average price $\overline{X} = \$148,000$ and the standard deviation $s = \$62,000$.

a. Calculate a 95% confidence interval for the mean of all recent selling prices.

b. We recently heard that a friend paid $206,000 for a house in this suburb. Is that plausible, or is there some reporting error?

8-7 A random sample of 5 states gave the following areas (in 1000 square miles; same data as Problem 2-38, incidentally):

147, 84, 24, 85, 159

a. Find the 95% confidence interval for the mean area for all 50 states in the United States.

b. Find the 95% confidence interval for the total area of the United States.

c. The total area in fact is 3620 thousand square miles. Does the confidence interval bracket it?

8-8 Repeat 8-7 **a**, **b**, and **c**, for a different sample that might have been drawn:

11, 41, 77, 84, 8

d. Instead of just these two, suppose a thousand random samples were drawn and a thousand 95% confidence intervals calculated. Would any of them be wrong? Why?

8-9 A random sample of 40 cars were clocked as they passed by a checkpoint, and their speeds were as follows (km per hour):

49	83	58	65	68	60	76	86	74	53
71	74	65	72	64	42	62	62	58	82
78	64	55	87	56	50	71	58	57	75
58	86	64	56	45	73	54	86	70	73

Construct a 95% confidence interval for the average speed of all cars passing by that checkpoint. (*Hint:* If your calculator doesn't have the $\overline{X}$ and s functions, you may find it reduces your work to group the observations into cells of width 5.)

8-3 DIFFERENCE IN TWO MEANS, INDEPENDENT SAMPLES

A—IF POPULATION VARIANCES ARE KNOWN (IN THEORY)

Two population means are commonly compared by forming their difference:

$$(\mu_1 - \mu_2) \tag{8-16}$$

This difference is the population target to be estimated. A reasonable estimate of this is the corresponding difference in *sample* means:

$$(\overline{X}_1 - \overline{X}_2)$$

Using a familiar argument, we could develop the appropriate confidence interval around the estimate:

$$(\mu_1 - \mu_2) = (\overline{X}_1 - \overline{X}_2) \pm z_{.025}\ \text{SE} \tag{8-17}$$

like (8-8)

In Appendix 8-3 we derive the formula for the SE; substituting it into (8-17) yields:

95% confidence interval, using independent samples

$$(\mu_1 - \mu_2) = (\overline{X}_1 - \overline{X}_2) \pm z_{.025} \sqrt{\frac{\sigma_1^2}{n_1} + \frac{\sigma_2^2}{n_2}} \tag{8-18}$$

When σ_1 and σ_2 are known to have a common value, say σ, this 95% confidence interval reduces to:

$$(\mu_1 - \mu_2) = (\overline{X}_1 - \overline{X}_2) \pm z_{.025}\, \sigma \sqrt{\frac{1}{n_1} + \frac{1}{n_2}} \tag{8-19}$$

B—IF POPULATION VARIANCE IS UNKNOWN (IN PRACTICE)

In practice, the population σ is not known, and has to be replaced with an estimate, customarily denoted by s_p. Then $z_{.025}$ has to be replaced with the broader value $t_{.025}$, and so (8-19) becomes:

95% confidence interval, using independent samples, when both populations have the same underlying variance:

$$(\mu_1 - \mu_2) = (\overline{X}_1 - \overline{X}_2) \pm t_{.025}\, s_p \sqrt{\frac{1}{n_1} + \frac{1}{n_2}} \tag{8-20}$$

How do we derive the estimate s_p? Since both populations have the same variance σ^2, it is appropriate to pool the information from both samples to estimate it. So our estimate is called the *pooled* variance s_p^2. We add up all the squared deviations from both samples, and then divide by the total d.f. in both samples, $(n_1 - 1) + (n_2 - 1)$. That is:

$$s_p^2 = \frac{\Sigma(X_1 - \bar{X}_1)^2 + \Sigma(X_2 - \bar{X}_2)^2}{(n_1 - 1) + (n_2 - 1)} \tag{8-21}$$

where X_1 (or X_2) represents the typical observation in the first (or second) sample. To complete (8-20), we need the d.f. for t. As suggested by (8-12), this is just the divisor used in calculating s_p^2.

$$\text{d.f.} = (n_1 - 1) + (n_2 - 1) \tag{8-22}$$

We will assume for the rest of this book that population variances are about equal, so that the pooling in (8-21) is appropriate. An example will illustrate.

EXAMPLE 8-3

From a large class, a sample of 4 grades were drawn: 64, 66, 89, and 77. From a second large class, an independent sample of 3 grades were drawn: 56, 71, and 53. Calculate the 95% confidence interval for the difference between the two class means, $\mu_1 - \mu_2$.

SOLUTION

In Table 8-2 we calculate the sample means and the squared deviations. Thus:

TABLE 8-2 Analysis of Two Independent Samples

Class 1			*Class 2*		
X_1	$(X_1 - \bar{X}_1)$	$(X_1 - \bar{X}_1)^2$	X_2	$(X_2 - \bar{X}_2)$	$(X_2 - \bar{X}_2)^2$
64	−10	100	56	− 4	16
66	− 8	64	71	11	121
89	15	225	53	− 7	49
77	3	9			
$\bar{X}_1 = \frac{296}{4} = 74.0$	0✓	398	$\bar{X}_2 = \frac{180}{3} = 60.0$	0✓	186

$$s_p^2 = \frac{398 + 186}{3 + 2} = \frac{584}{5} = 117 \qquad \text{like (8-21)}$$

In the divisor we see d.f. = 5, so that from Table V, $t_{.025} = 2.57$. Substituting into (8-20), we obtain:

$$\begin{aligned}(\mu_1 - \mu_2) &= (74.0 - 60.0) \pm 2.57\sqrt{117}\sqrt{\frac{1}{4} + \frac{1}{3}} \\ &= 14 \pm 21 \qquad (8\text{-}23) \\ &= -7 \text{ to } +35\end{aligned}$$

Thus with 95% confidence we conclude that the average of the first class (μ_1) may be 7 marks below the average of the second class (μ_2). Or μ_1 may be 35 marks above μ_2—or anywhere in between. There is a very large sampling allowance in this example because the samples were so small.

We emphasize that the confidence intervals in this section require the two samples to be *independent* as in Example 8-3. As another example, consider just one class of students, examined at two different times—say fall and spring terms. The fall population and spring population of grades could then be sampled and compared using (8-20)—provided, of course, that the two samples are independently drawn. (They would not be independently drawn, for example, if we made a point of canvassing the same students twice.)

PROBLEMS

8-10 To determine the effectiveness of a feed supplement for cattle, High-Grade Feeds conducts a pilot study. Eight steers are randomly divided into a group of 4 steers to be fed the supplement, and another group of 4 steers to be fed exactly the same diet except for the supplement. The weight gains (lbs) over a period of 6 months were as follows:

Supplement Group	*Control Group*
330	290
360	320
400	340
350	370

a. Construct a 95% confidence interval for the effect of the supplement.

b. Suppose steers wholesale for 90¢ per pound. If the supplement costs $80 per steer for the whole 6-month period, is it profitable to use it?

8-11 In a large American university in 1969, the men and women professors were sampled independently, yielding the annual salaries given below (in thousands of dollars. From Katz, 1973):

Women	*Men*
9	16
12	19
8	12
10	11
16	22

a. Calculate a 95% confidence interval for the mean salary difference between men and women.

b. How well does this show the university's discrimination against women?

8-12 Repeat Problem 8-11 using the complete data given in Problem 2-2—independent random samples with the following characteristics:

Women	*Men*
$n = 5$	$n = 25$
$\bar{X} = 11.0$	$\bar{X} = 16.0$
$\Sigma(X - \bar{X})^2 = 40$	$\Sigma(X - \bar{X})^2 = 786$

8-13 How seriously does alcohol affect prenatal brain development? To study this issue (Jones and others, 1974), six women were found who had been chronic alcoholics during pregnancy. The resulting children were tested at age 7, producing a sample of six IQ scores with a mean of 78, and $\Sigma(X - \bar{X})^2 = 1805$.

A control group of 46 women were found who on the whole were similar in many respects (same average age, education, marital status, etc.)—but without alcoholism in their pregnancy. Their 46 children had IQ scores that averaged 99, and $\Sigma(X - \bar{X})^2 = 11{,}520$.

a. If this had been a randomized controlled study, what would be the 95% confidence interval for the difference in IQ that prenatal alcoholism makes?

b. Since this in fact was an observational study, how should you modify your claim in part **a**?

8-4 DIFFERENCE IN TWO MEANS, MATCHED SAMPLES

In the previous section we were using *independent* samples, for instance, a sample of students' grades in the fall was compared to a fresh sample of students' grades in the spring. In this section we will consider *dependent* samples, called *matched* or *paired* samples.

A—ANALYSIS BASED ON INDIVIDUAL DIFFERENCES

Suppose a comparison of fall and spring grades is done using the *same* students both times. Then the paired grades (spring X_1 and fall X_2) for each of the students can be set out, as in Table 8-3.

The natural first step is to see how each student changed; that is, calculate the difference $D = X_1 - X_2$, for each student. Once these differences are calculated, then the original data, having served its purpose, can be discarded.

We proceed to treat the four differences D now as a *single sample*, and analyze them just as we analyze any other single sample (e.g., the sample in Table 8-1). First, we calculate the average difference $\bar{D}$. Then we use this *sample* $\bar{D}$ appropriately to construct a confidence interval for the average *population* difference Δ, obtaining:

95% confidence interval, using matched samples

$$\Delta = \bar{D} \pm t_{.025} \frac{s_D}{\sqrt{n}} \tag{8-24}$$

like (8-11)

For our example in Table 8-3, we calculate $\bar{D} = 11$ and $s_D = \sqrt{15.3}$. In the divisor of s_D we saw d.f. $= n - 1 = 3$, so that $t_{.025} = 3.18$. Substituting into (8-24), we obtain

$$\begin{aligned} \Delta &= 11 \pm 3.18 \frac{\sqrt{15.3}}{\sqrt{4}} \\ &= 11 \pm 6 \\ &= 5 \text{ to } 17 \end{aligned} \tag{8-25}$$

TABLE 8-3 Analysis of Two Paired Samples

	Observed Grades		Difference		
Student	X_1 (*Spring*)	X_2 (*Fall*)	$D = X_1 - X_2$	$(D - \bar{D})$	$(D - \bar{D})^2$
Trimble	64	57	7	−4	16
Wilde	66	57	9	−2	4
Giannos	89	73	16	5	25
Ames	77	65	12	1	1
			$\bar{D} = \frac{44}{4} = 11$	0✓	$s_D^2 = \frac{46}{3} = 15.3$

Since the mean of the differences (Δ) exactly equals[3] the difference of the means ($\mu_1 - \mu_2$), we can re-express (8-24) as:

$$(\mu_1 - \mu_2) = (\bar{X}_1 - \bar{X}_2) \pm t_{.025} \frac{s_D}{\sqrt{n}} \tag{8-26}$$

In this form, it is clear that in (8-26) we are estimating the same parameter (the difference in two population means) as we did in the earlier formula (8-20). But the matched-pair approach (8-26) is better, because it has a smaller sampling allowance.

B—THE ADVANTAGE OF PAIRED SAMPLES

We have just seen how pairing samples reduces the sampling allowance (specifically, ± 6 in (8-25) compared to the ± 21 in (8-23) when the samples were independently drawn). The reason for this is intuitively clear. Pairing achieves a match that keeps many of the extraneous variables constant. In using the same four students, we kept sex, IQ, and many other factors exactly the same in both samples. We therefore had more leverage on the problem at hand—the difference in fall versus spring grades.

To summarize the chapter so far, we finish with an example that illustrates the important formulas for means.

EXAMPLE 8-4

To measure the effect of a fitness campaign, a ski club randomly sampled 5 members before the campaign, and another 5 after. The weights were as follows (along with the person's initials):

Before: J.H. 168, K.L. 195, M.M. 155, T.R. 183, M.T. 169
After: L.W. 183, V.G. 177, E.P. 148, J.C. 162, M.W. 180

a. Calculate a 95% confidence interval for:

i. The mean weight before the campaign.
ii. The mean weight after the campaign.
iii. The mean weight loss during the campaign.

b. It was decided that a better sampling design would be to measure the same people after, as before. In scrambled order, their figures were:

After: K.L. 194, M.T. 160, T.R. 177, M.M. 147, J.H. 157

---

[3] This is also true for samples:

$$\bar{D} = \bar{X}_1 - \bar{X}_2$$

For example, for the data in Table 8-3, $\bar{D} = 11$, while $\bar{X}_1 - \bar{X}_2 = 74 - 63 = 11$, too.

On the basis of these people, calculate a 95% confidence interval for the mean weight loss during the campaign.

SOLUTION

a.

Before			After		
X_1	$(X_1 - \bar{X}_1)$	$(X_1 - \bar{X}_1)^2$	X_2	$(X_2 - \bar{X}_2)$	$(X_2 - \bar{X}_2)^2$
168	−6	36	183	13	169
195	21	441	177	7	49
155	−19	361	148	−22	484
183	9	81	162	−8	64
169	−5	25	180	+10	100
$\bar{X}_1 = \frac{870}{5} = 174$	0√	944	$\bar{X}_2 = \frac{850}{5} = 170$	0√	866

i. $\mu_1 = 174 \pm 2.78\frac{\sqrt{944/4}}{\sqrt{5}}$ like (8-11)

$= 174 \pm 19$

ii. $\mu_2 = 170 \pm 2.78\frac{\sqrt{866/4}}{\sqrt{5}}$ like (8-11)

$= 170 \pm 18$

iii. $\mu_1 - \mu_2 = (174 - 170) \pm 2.31\sqrt{\frac{944 + 866}{4 + 4}}\sqrt{\frac{1}{5} + \frac{1}{5}}$ like (8-20)

$= 4 \pm 22$

b. **We must be sure to list the people in the same matched order so that it is meaningful to calculate the individual weight losses:**

Person	X_1	X_2	$D = X_1 - X_2$	$(D - \bar{D})$	$(D - \bar{D})^2$
J.H.	168	157	11	4	16
K.L.	195	194	1	−6	36
M.M.	155	147	8	1	1
T.R.	183	177	6	−1	1
M.T.	169	160	9	2	4
			$\bar{D} = \frac{35}{5}$, $\bar{D} = 7$	0√	$s_D^2 = \frac{58}{4} = 14.5$

$\Delta = 7 \pm 2.78\frac{\sqrt{14.5}}{\sqrt{5}}$ like (8-24)

$= 7 \pm 5$

Thus the paired samples give a much more precise interval estimate for the weight loss (± 5 vs. ± 22).

Pairing is obviously a desirable feature to design into any experiment, where feasible. If pairing cannot be achieved by using the same individual twice, we should look for other ways. For example, we might use pairs of twins—ideally identical twins. This would keep genetic and environmental factors constant. Of course, to decide which person within the pair is to be given the treatment, and which is to be left as the control, we would have to be fair and unbiased—that is, do it at random (with the flip of a coin, for example).

A further subtlety involved in pairing may be illustrated by the agricultural experiments that have historically played such an important role in statistics. If a plot of land is used in two successive years, many conditions in the second year will be different—rainfall, temperature, and so on. Therefore, it is much more effective to take two adjacent plots in the *same* year (the *split-plot* design).

PROBLEMS

8-14 A petrochemical R&D lab has developed a new extrusion process that it hopes will increase the strength of nylon rope. On six randomly selected batches it tries the new process for half the batch, and the old process for the other half. The breaking strength of a rope from each half-batch is then recorded:

batch	*old process*	*new process*
1	620	660
2	600	620
3	640	670
4	630	620
5	570	580
6	600	630

Construct a 95% confidence interval for the improvement the new process makes.

8-15 How much does an interesting environment affect the actual physical development of the brain? To answer this, for rats at least, Rosenzweig and others (1964) took 10 litters of purebred rats. From each litter, one rat was selected at random for the treatment group, and one for the control group. The two groups were treated the same, except that the treated rats lived altogether in a cage with interesting playthings, while the control rats lived in bare isolation. After a month, every rat was killed and its cortex (highly developed part of the brain) was weighed, with the following results (in centigrams) for the 10 pairs of littermates:

Litter:	1	2	3	4	5	6	7	8	9	10
Treatment:	68	65	66	66	67	66	66	64	69	63
Control:	65	62	64	65	65	64	59	63	65	58

a. Construct an appropriate 95% confidence interval.

b. State your answer to part **a** in a sentence or two that would be intelligible to a layperson.

8-16 Small white worms that reduce strawberry yield can be treated with fumigation. A new additive was developed to make the fumigation persist longer, but with unknown side effects on the strawberry plants themselves.
To test its overall effect, 5 plots were randomly selected in a large experimental farm, planted with strawberries, then split in half, with one-half randomly selected for treatment with the standard fumigation, and the other half with the new additive (a "split-plot" design). The strawberry yields were as follows (in quarts).

plot	*standard*	*additive*
1	109	107
2	68	72
3	82	88
4	104	101
5	93	97

a. Construct a 95% confidence interval for the difference the additive makes.

b. Suppose each plot was 1/20 acre. Re-express your answer to **a** in terms of the average yield per acre (rather than per plot).

8-5 PROPORTIONS

A—LARGE SAMPLE FORMULA

Confidence intervals for proportions (percentages) are very similar to means. We simply use the appropriate form of the normal approximation rule (6-12), and so obtain the 95% confidence interval for π:

$$\pi = P \pm 1.96\sqrt{\frac{\pi(1-\pi)}{n}}$$

For the unknown π that appears under the square root, we can substitute the sample P. (This is a strategy we have used before, when we substituted s for σ in the confidence interval for μ. This approximation introduces another source of error, which fortunately tends to zero as sample size n increases.) Thus:

95% confidence interval for the proportion, for large n

$$\pi = P \pm 1.96\sqrt{\frac{P(1-P)}{n}} \qquad (8\text{-}27)$$

For this to be a good approximation, the sample size n ought to be large enough so that at least 5 successes and 5 failures turn up. As an example, the voter poll in Chapter 1 used this formula.

B—GRAPHICAL METHOD, LARGE OR SMALL SAMPLES

There is a graphical way to find an interval estimate for π, and it is very easy to see how it works for both large and small sample sizes. (The more complicated question—*why* it works—is covered in Appendix 8-5.) For example, suppose we observe 16 Republicans in a sample of 20 voters in a Kansas City suburb.

We first calculate $P = 16/20 = .80$. Then in Figure 8-4 we read up the vertical line passing through $P = .80$, noting where it cuts the curves labelled $n = 20$ (highlighted in white). These two points of intersection define the confidence interval for π, shown in color:

$$.55 < \pi < .95 \tag{8-28}$$

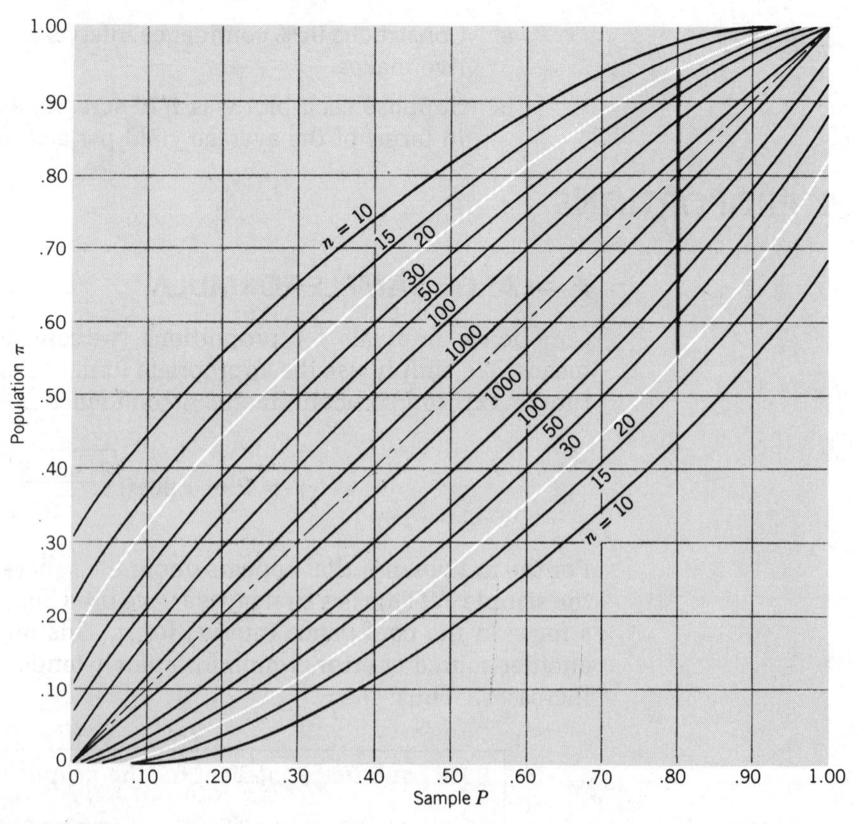

FIGURE 8-4
95% confidence intervals for the population proportion π. (Clopper and Pearson, 1934.)

This confidence interval is not symmetric about the estimate $P = .80$; the sampling allowance below is $.80 - .55 = .25$, while the allowance above is only $.95 - .80 = .15$. Why is it longer below? The answer may be seen by examining a more extreme case, where $P = 1.00$. Then the sampling allowance would have to be *entirely* below P, since π cannot exceed 1.00. (From Figure 8-4, we find $.83 < \pi < 1.00$.)

Although specifically designed for proportions, Figure 8-4 has illustrated two interesting features about confidence intervals that apply in wider contexts too: Confidence intervals are not always given by a formula, nor are they always defined symmetrically around the point estimate.

C—DIFFERENCE IN TWO PROPORTIONS, LARGE SAMPLES

Just as we derived the confidence interval to compare two means, we could similarly derive the confidence interval to compare two population proportions:

95% confidence interval for the difference in proportions, for large n_1 and n_2, and independent samples

$$(\pi_1 - \pi_2) = (P_1 - P_2) \pm 1.96\sqrt{\frac{P_1(1 - P_1)}{n_1} + \frac{P_2(1 - P_2)}{n_2}} \qquad (8\text{-}29) \text{ like } (8\text{-}18)$$

PROBLEMS

8-17 In a random sample of tires produced by a large European multinational firm, 10% did not meet proposed new standards of blowout resistance. Construct a 95% confidence interval for the proportion π (in the whole population of tires) that would not meet the standards, if the sample size is:

a. n = 10

b. n = 25

c. n = 50

d. n = 200

8-18 *The declining acceptance of marijuana.* The Gallup poll periodically takes a random sample (or its equivalent) of about 1500 Americans. The percentage who favor the acceptance (decriminalization) of marijuana possession declined from 52% in 1980 to 46% in 1985.

a. Construct a 95% confidence interval for the population percentage in favor, in each year.

b. Find a 95% confidence interval for the change in this percentage from 1980 to 1985.

8-19 Economists have long realized that GNP alone does not measure total welfare of a country. Less tangible factors are important too, such as leisure and freedom from pollution and crime. To get some idea of how these other factors vary among countries, in the 1970s a worldwide poll was undertaken (Gallup, 1976). To throw light on the issue of crime, the question was asked: "Are you afraid to walk the neighboring streets at night?" The replies were as follows:

	United States	*Japan*	*Latin America*
Yes	40%	33%	57%
No	56%	63%	42%
No opinion	4%	4%	1%

Assuming each country's poll was equivalent in accuracy to a simple random sample of $n = 300$ people, find a 95% confidence interval for the difference in the percentage answering "yes":

a. between the United States and Japan

b. between the United States and Latin America

8-20 Repeat Problem 8-19 assuming that "No Opinion" replies were discarded, and thus not included in the samples.

8-21 In 1954 a large-scale experiment was carried out to test the effectiveness of a new polio vaccine. Among 740,000 children selected from grade 2 classes throughout the United States, 400,000 volunteered. Half of the volunteers were randomly selected for the vaccine shot; the remaining half were given a placebo shot of salt water. The results were as follows (taken, with rounding, from Meier, 1978):

Group	*Number of Children*	*Number of Cases of Polio*
Vaccinated	200,000	57
Placebo (control)	200,000	142
Refused to volunteer	340,000	157

a. For each of the three groups, calculate the polio rate (cases per 100,000).

b. Estimate the reduction in the polio rate that vaccination produces, including a 95% confidence interval.

c. Suppose *all* the volunteers had been vaccinated, leaving the refusals as the control group:
   i. Before analyzing the data, criticize this procedure.
   ii. What kind of data would you have obtained? Would it have given the correct answer to question **b**?

*8-6 THE BOOTSTRAP

So far, we have found standard confidence intervals for population means and proportions. But how do we construct confidence intervals in situations too complex for standard theory to handle? An ingenious answer has been recently developed—the bootstrap. Instead of using theory, it uses extensive computing to lift the sample "by its own bootstraps" to construct a confidence interval.

To show how it works, recall that samples are *randomly* drawn in order to be fair or *representative* of the population. This was illustrated in Figure 6-2, and is even more obvious for larger random samples: the n observations are scattered throughout the population in an unbiased and representative way.

The bootstrap simply exploits this similarity of the sample to the population. In fact, it just reconstructs an approximate or "bootstrap" population by replicating the sample a millionfold. Then it does a Monte-Carlo study to estimate, say, the mean of this bootstrap population. That is, it draws many samples from the bootstrap population to get many values of $\bar{X}$, which are displayed as the "bootstrap" sampling distribution. The central 95% of this distribution then provides the desired confidence interval for μ. An example will illustrate.

EXAMPLE 8-5

A random sample of $n = 10$ observations turned out as follows:

$$X = 16, 12, 14, 6, 43, 7, 0, 54, 25, 13$$

To mimic the true population, we imagine these few representative numbers repeated a million times each, to give the bootstrap population.

a. From it, draw a random sample of 10 observations (using the random digits in Appendix Table I). Calculate the sample mean $\bar{X}$.

b. Repeat for a second random sample, to get a second $\bar{X}$. Then repeat many times—either by computer, or by pooling results for your class—to get many values of $\bar{X}$.

c. Arrange all these $\bar{X}$ values into a histogram—the "bootstrap" sampling distribution." Take the middle 95% of it to get the desired "bootstrap confidence interval."

SOLUTION

a. Each of the 10 different X values has the same chance (1/10) to be drawn,[4] which can be simulated with 1 random digit out of 10. We therefore associate X values with random digits as follows:

random digit	*associated X observation*	*random digit*	*associated X observation*
1	16	6	7
2	12	7	0
3	14	8	54
4	6	9	25
5	43	0	13

So that our work is easy to follow, we start at the beginning of Table I, reading the 10 random digits 3, 9, 6, 5, 7, 6, 4, 5, 4, 5. These give the associated observations:

$$X = 14, 25, 7, 43, 0, 7, 6, 43, 6, 43$$

$$\text{hence } \overline{X} = \frac{194}{10} = 19.4$$

b. The next 10 random digits from Table I are 1, 9, 9, 0, 6, 9, 6, 4, 6, 1, which give the random sample: 16, 25, 25, 13, 7, 25, 7, 6, 7, 16. The mean of this sample is $\overline{X} = 14.7$.

c. We continue to take many samples like this, in each case getting another $\overline{X}$. An example of 1000 such values of $\overline{X}$, computed from MINITAB, is displayed as a histogram in Figure 8-5. Selecting the middle 95% of these values finally gives the bootstrap 95% confidence interval for the population mean:

$$9 < \mu < 26 \tag{8-30}$$

This was an unrealistically simple example, designed primarily to show how easy the bootstrap is in principle. It also shows how well the bootstrap works, because standard methods give us a basis for compari-

[4] Instead of replicating the 10 X-values a million times each, we equivalently could have used just the 10 X-values (unreplicated) as our population, but sampled *with* replacement. This would give us the same 1/10 chance on every draw, and so be equivalent. In fact, in the literature this is how the bootstrap is commonly presented.

It is interesting, by contrast, to see what would happen if we sampled just the 10 X-values *without* replacement. We would get back exactly these 10 X-values, of course—every time, without variability—an absolutely useless result. So what makes the bootstrap work is simply the difference between sampling with replacement and without.

```
HISTOGRAM OF MEAN    N = 1000
EACH * REPRESENTS 5 OBS.

MIDPOINT   COUNT
     6        4  *
     8       20  ****
    10       55  ***********
    12      117  ************************
    14      125  *************************
    16      158  ********************************
    18      190  **************************************
    20      117  ************************
    22      116  ************************
    24       53  ***********
    26       32  *******
    28        8  **
    30        3  *
    32        2  *
```

FIGURE 8-5
The bootstrap sampling distribution of $\overline{X}$. The central 95% chunk marks off the 95% confidence interval for μ.

son. Since the sample in Example 8-5 has $\overline{X} = 19.0$ and $s = 17.1$, we can calculate the standard 95% confidence interval:

$$\mu = \overline{X} \pm t_{.025} \frac{s}{\sqrt{n}} \qquad \text{like (8-11)}$$

$$= 19.0 \pm 2.26 \frac{(17.1)}{\sqrt{10}} = 19 \pm 12 \qquad (8\text{-}31)$$

$$7 < \mu < 31 \qquad (8\text{-}32)$$

To see how well the bootstrap works, note that the bootstrap 95% confidence interval (8-30) agrees pretty well with this standard confidence interval.[5]

In practice, bootstrapping is used in more complex cases where nothing else works, as we already noted. For example, it may be used to replace a standard confidence interval that doesn't work well in a non-normal population, or to estimate very complicated parameters. Many similar techniques have been developed recently, with names like "jackknife," "cross-validation," "balanced repeated replication," or "random subsampling." Like bootstrapping, they all achieve great generality and power. Their disadvantage is that they require a lot of computing, but this is getting more affordable every year.

---

[5] Although the bootstrap sampling distribution wasn't *centered* at the same place as the true sampling distribution (it was centered near $\overline{X} = 19$, not μ), nevertheless it displayed about the same *variability* as the true sampling distribution. It is this remarkable property that permits the bootstrap to make confidence intervals of about the correct width.

The agreement could have been made even better if we had made some simple adjustments to the bootstrap. For example, to allow for the given sample being small, we could use a *t*-like adjustment that widens the bootstrap confidence interval (8-30) so it agrees even more closely with the standard confidence interval (8-32).

*PROBLEMS

8-22 To estimate the standard deviation σ of a skewed population, a random sample of 10 observations was drawn:

16, 43, 13, 7, 12, 14, 6, 25, 0, 54

a. Calculate s, to estimate σ.

b. To get some idea of the reliability of your estimate in **a**, calculate a bootstrap value of s in the usual way: Imagine the 10 given X values replicated a million times each. From this "bootstrap population," draw a random sample of 10 observations, and calculate its standard deviation s.

c. Using the procedure in **b** over and over, MINITAB quickly computed a thousand bootstrap values of s, as follows:

```
HISTOGRAM OF STDEV      N = 1000
EACH * REFRESENTS 5 OBS.

MIDPOINT    COUNT
       0        1  *
       2        6  **
       4       27  ******
       6       54  ***********
       8       34  *******
      10       73  ***************
      12      159  ********************************
      14      241  *************************************************
      16      245  *************************************************
      18      135  ***************************
      20       25  *****
```

What is the bootstrap 95% CI (confidence interval) for σ?

d. Now let's compare this with the classical CI (based on "chi-square") for the standard deviation σ of a normal population:

$$\frac{s}{\sqrt{2.11}} < \sigma < \frac{s}{\sqrt{.300}} \tag{8-33}$$

Using s found in **a**, calculate this classical 95% confidence interval.

e. The actual population (from which we secretly drew the sample in **a** by simulation) had the value $\sigma = 10$. Using this benchmark, which confidence interval for σ is better—the bootstrap CI in **c** or the classical CI in **d**?

f. What happened in **e** wasn't just the luck of the draw. To see why, suppose we gathered 100 different random samples, and each time constructed a bootstrap 95% CI for σ. We would find about 95 of the 100 bootstrap CI would correctly cover the true value $\sigma = 10$. This shows how well the bootstrap works.

But we would find far fewer than 95 of the 100 classical CI would cover $\sigma = 10$. This poor performance[6] shows why an alternative like the bootstrap is necessary. Now, by reading (8-33) carefully, can you see why the classical CI should never have been used?

g. Underline the correct choice: To summarize f, we say that the bootstrap CI for σ is [robust, always correct], and the classical CI is [nearly always correct, too sensitive to non-normality].

CHAPTER 8 SUMMARY

8-1 From the normal tables, we find that 95% of the time, $\bar{X}$ will be within 1.96 standard errors of μ. This yields the 95% confidence interval (8-9):

$$\mu = \bar{X} \pm 1.96 \frac{\sigma}{\sqrt{n}}$$

8-2 In practice, σ is unknown in the formula above, and has to be estimated with s. To allow for the additional uncertainty, we replace the value $z_{.025} = 1.96$ with the wider value $t_{.025}$.

8-3 To compare two population means, for independent samples we take the difference of the two sample means, $\bar{X}_1 - \bar{X}_2$. To construct the confidence interval, we pool all the squared deviations in both samples to calculate the pooled variance s_p^2.

8-4 To compare two population means, for *dependent* (paired) samples we start by calculating the *individual* differences D. Their average $\bar{D}$ is then calculated, and the confidence interval built around it.

Paired samples are more efficient than independent samples, since pairing keeps many of the extraneous variables constant. Pairing should therefore be used whenever feasible.

8-5 Confidence intervals for proportions are like means, for large samples at least. For a small sample, a graphical alternative is best, reading the confidence interval off a 95% confidence band.

***8-6** In situations where the sampling distribution of an estimator is not known—and this occurs very often in practice—robust confidence intervals can often be constructed with the "bootstrap." Instead of theory, the bootstrap uses intensive computing to "lift the sample by its own bootstraps." Specifically, by replicating the given sam-

[6] Just how poor is the performance? For the highly skewed exponential population such as we drew from, the classical CI for σ is about half as wide as it should be (Mosteller and Tukey 1977, p. 142). Thus the classical 95% CI is correct only about 68% of the time. (Instead of the purported range of ±2 SE, it really covers only a range of ±1 SE.)

ple a millionfold, we construct a "bootstrap" population. From this we draw many samples, and the many values of $\overline{X}$ (or other estimator) form the "bootstrap" sampling distribution. This distribution displays the variability of the estimator, and its middle 95% provides the desired confidence interval.

REVIEW PROBLEMS

8-23 *The decline of cigarettes:* Over the years, the Gallup poll has asked random samples of 1500 Americans: "Have you, yourself, smoked any cigarettes in the past week?" The percentage answering "yes" fluctuated as follows:

1972	43%
1977	38%
1981	35%
1983	38%
1985	35%

a. Sketch a graph showing how this percentage fluctuates.

b. Calculate a 95% confidence interval for the population proportion who smoked in 1972. Also for 1985.

c. Calculate a 95% confidence interval for the change in the population proportion who smoked between 1972 and 1985. Also the change from 1981 to 1983.

d. Underline the correct choice:

The change in the sample proportion P between 1981 and 1983 was relatively [large, small] and consequently [stood out, did not stand out] above the sampling allowance, that is, the ± figure.

By contrast, the change from 1972 to 1985 was [large, small] enough that it [did, did not] stand out above the sampling allowance. This illustrates the great [value, drawback] of confidence intervals: They [confuse, distinguish between] real and illusory changes. Looking back on the graphs in **a**, the fluctuations between 1972 and 1985 can now be interpreted as [fascinating detail, mostly sampling "noise".]

8-24 A firm producing plate glass has developed a less expensive tempering process to allow glass for fireplaces to rise to a higher temperature without breaking. To test it, five different plates of glass were drawn randomly from a production run, then cut in half, with one-half tempered by the new process, and the other half by the old. The two halves then were heated until they broke, yielding the following data:

breaking temperature	
new	*old*
475	485
436	438
495	493
483	486
426	433

Construct a 95% confidence interval for the mean improvement in breaking temperature.

8-25 To see what difference class attendance made, a professor sampled grades from his large statistics class of 530 students. From the 220 students who attended class less than half the time (the "irregulars"), he took a random sample of 5 grades. From the remaining 310 students who attended at least half the time (the "regulars"), he took an independent random sample of 5 other grades:

irregulars	*regulars*
41	69
81	56
52	83
69	70
62	92

a. Construct a 95% confidence interval for the mean difference between the two groups of students.

b. To what extent does this support the contention that "it is worth 18 marks to come to class regularly"?

8-26 Soon after he took office in 1963, President Johnson was approved by 160 out of a sample of 200 Americans. With growing disillusionment over his Vietnam policy, by 1968 he was approved by only 70 out of a sample of 200 Americans.

a. What is the 95% confidence interval for the percentage of all Americans who approved of Johnson in 1963? In 1968?

b. What is the 95% confidence interval for the change?

8-27 A "Union Shop" clause in a contract requires every worker to join the union soon after starting to work for the company. In 1973 there were 31 states that permitted the Union Shop, and 19 states (mostly southern) that had earlier passed "Right-to-Work" laws that outlawed the Union Shop and certain other practices. A random sample of 5 states from each group showed the following average hourly wage within the state:

States With Union Shop, etc.	*States With Right-to-Work*
$4.00	$3.50
3.10	3.60
3.60	3.20
4.20	3.90
$4.60	$2.80

On the basis of these figures, a friend claims that the Right-to-Work laws are costing the average worker 50¢ per hour. Do you think this claim should be modified? If so, how?

8-28 Lack of experimental control (e.g., failure to randomly assign the treatment and control) may affect the degree of enthusiasm with which a new medical treatment is reported. To test this hypothesis, 38 studies of a certain operation were classified as follows (Gilbert and others, 1977):

	Reported Effectiveness of Operation	
Degree of Control	*Moderate or Marked*	*None*
Well Controlled	3	3
Uncontrolled	31	1

a. Assuming these 38 studies constitute a random sample, construct an appropriate 95% confidence interval. [Although (8-29) is only a rough approximation for small samples, it's the best you have, so use it.]

b. Do you agree with the following interpretations reported by the authors?

"... Nothing improves the performance of an innovation as much as the lack of controls."

"... weakly controlled trials ... may make proper studies more difficult to mount, as physicians become less and less inclined, for ethical reasons, to subject the issue to a carefully controlled trial lest the 'benefits' of a seemingly proven useful therapy be withheld from some patients in the study."

8-29 Suppose a 10% random sample from a stand of 380 trees gave the following distribution of volumes:

Volume	*Frequency*
20	8
40	16
60	12
80	2
Total	38

Calculate a 95% confidence interval for:

a. The mean volume.

b. The total volume.

8-30 Texoil has asked you to roughly estimate which of its gasolines, A or B, gives the better mileage. So you take a random sample of 4 cars, and drive each over the same route twice, once with gasoline A and once with gasoline B. Calculate a 95% confidence interval for the mean difference, based on the mileages of the four cars:

Gas A	*Gas B*
23	20
17	16
16	14
20	18

8-31 A random sample of 3864 first marriages showed the following 5-year survival characteristics, by wife's church attendance (simplified version of Balakrishnan and others, 1987):

	Church Attendance			
	Weekly or More	*Sometimes*	*Rarely or Never*	*Totals*
Still married	1071	1339	1082	3492
Divorced or separated	42	128	202	372
totals	1113	1467	1284	3864

a. Calculate a 95% confidence interval for the 5- year survival rate of all marriages. Then repeat three times, for the three subpopulations defined by the three levels of church attendance.

b. Calculate a 95% confidence interval for the difference in survival rates—for marriages where the wife attends church "weekly or more" vs. "rarely or never."

c. How well does the data support the conclusion that regular church attendance helps marriages survive?

8-32 *A Final Challenge: Does a New Hospital Routine Really Help?*

In the hospital-birth example in Section 1-2, recall that a sample of 14 mothers were initially kept from their infants (the control procedure), while a sample of 14 others were given extensive early contact with their infants (the treatment).

At the end of the experiment, each mother was evaluated (blind, of course) in several ways, such as how often she reported picking up her crying infant, and how much interest she showed during the monthly physical exam of her infant. The component scores were added up to give a total score, ranging from 0 to 12, that turned out to be quite different for the treatment and control groups (Klaus and others, 1972):

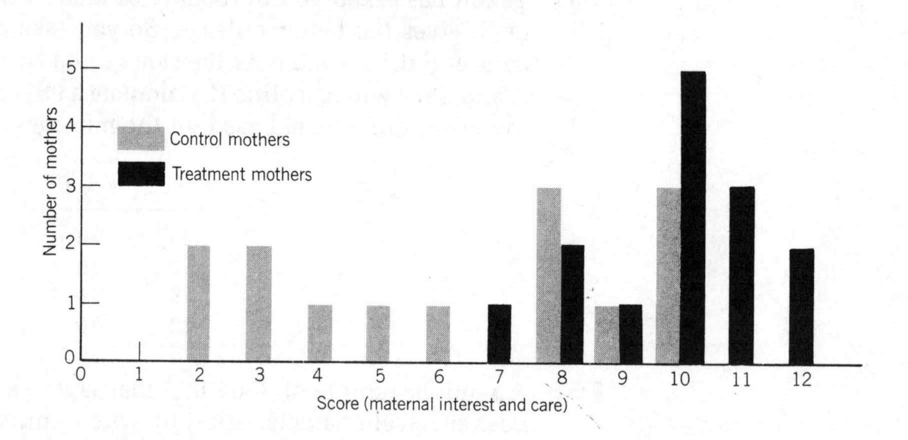

a. At a glance, do you think that the difference can be explained by chance sampling fluctuation? Or does it indicate that the population means are really different? Just guess intuitively, for now.

b. To back up your guess in **a**, construct a 95% confidence interval for the difference. Define your terms, as well. (*Hint:* Convert the graph of the frequency distributions to a table, where the appropriate calculations can be carried out.)

c. To what extent does this prove the value of the new treatment? (*Hint:* Reread Section 1-2 to see how carefully the experiment was carried out.)

CHAPTER 9

Hypothesis Testing

Say not "I have found the truth," but rather, "I have found a truth."

KAHLIL GIBRAN, *THE PROPHET*

9-1 HYPOTHESIS TESTING USING CONFIDENCE INTERVALS[1]

A—A MODERN APPROACH

A statistical *hypothesis* is simply a *claim about a population* that can be put to a test by drawing a random sample. A typical hypothesis, for example, is that the Democrats have a majority in a population of voters, such as the Kansas City suburb analyzed in (8-28). In fact, this hypothesis can be rejected, because the sample of 20 voters showed (at a 95% level of confidence) that between 55% and 95% of the population were Republicans; the Republicans, rather than the Democrats, had the majority.

This voter example illustrates how we can use a confidence interval to test an hypothesis. Another example will show this in more detail. (Recall that in the format of this book, a numbered Example is a problem for you to work on first; the solution in the text should only be consulted later as a check.)

EXAMPLE 9-1

SEX DIFFERENCE IN SALARIES

In a large American university, 10 men and 5 women professors were independently sampled in 1969, yielding the annual salaries given below (in thousands of dollars. Same source as Problem 2-1):

Men (X_1)		Women (X_2)
13	20	9
11	14	12
19	17	8
15	14	10
22	15	16
$\overline{X}_1 = 16$		$\overline{X}_2 = 11$

These sample means give a rough estimate of the underlying population means μ_1 and μ_2. Perhaps they can be used to settle an argument: A husband claims that there is no difference between men's salaries (μ_1) and women's salaries (μ_2). In other words, if we denote the difference as $\Delta = \mu_1 - \mu_2$, he claims that

$$\Delta = 0 \tag{9-1}$$

---

[1] *Reminder to instructors:* This chapter is designed so that you may spend as much or as little time on hypothesis testing as you judge appropriate. At the end of any section you may skip ahead to the next chapters and thus have more time to cover ANOVA and regression.

His wife, however, claims that the difference is as large as 7 thousand dollars:

$$\Delta = 7 \tag{9-2}$$

Settle this argument by constructing a 95% confidence interval.

SOLUTION

The 95% confidence interval is, from (8-20),

$$\Delta = (\overline{X}_1 - \overline{X}_2) \pm t_{.025}\, s_p \sqrt{\frac{1}{n_1} + \frac{1}{n_2}}$$

$$= (16 - 11) \pm 2.16 \sqrt{\frac{146}{13}} \sqrt{\frac{1}{10} + \frac{1}{5}}$$

$$= 5.0 \pm 2.16(1.84) \tag{9-3}$$

$$= 5.0 \pm 4.0 \tag{9-4}$$

Thus, with 95% confidence, Δ is estimated to be between 1.0 and 9.0. Thus the claim $\Delta = 0$ (the husband's hypothesis) seems implausible, because it falls outside the confidence interval. On the other hand the claim $\Delta = 7$ (the wife's hypothesis) seems more plausible, because it falls within the confidence interval.

In general, any hypothesis that lies outside the confidence interval may be judged implausible—that is, can be *rejected*. On the other hand, any hypothesis that lies within the confidence interval may be judged plausible or *acceptable*.[2] Thus:

> **A confidence interval may be regarded as just the set of acceptable hypotheses.** (9-5)

If a 95% confidence interval is being used, it would be natural to speak of the hypothesis as being tested at a 95% *confidence level*. In conforming to tradition, however, we usually speak of testing at an *error level* of 5%.

Thus, to return to our example, we formally conclude from (9-4) that, with a 5% chance of error (a "5% error level"), we can reject the hypothesis of no difference ($\Delta = 0$). In other words, we have collected enough evidence (and, consequently, have a small enough sampling allowance) so that we can discern a difference between men's and women's salaries.

[2] We use *acceptable* simply as a convenient shorthand that avoids the potentially confusing double negative in the more precise term *not rejected*.

We therefore call the difference *statistically discernible* at the 5% error level.

Our formal statistical language must not obscure the important commonsense aspects of this problem, of course. Although we have shown (at the 5% error level) that men's and women's salaries are different, we have *not* shown that discrimination necessarily exists. There are many alternative explanations. For example, men may have more education than women, on average. What we really should do then is compare men and women of the *same qualifications*. (This will in fact be done later, using *multiple regression*, in Problem 14-27.)

EXAMPLE 9-2

SEX DIFFERENCE IN SALARIES, BUT WEAKER DATA

Suppose the confidence interval (9-4) had been based on a smaller sample and, consequently, had been vaguer. (Note how smaller sample sizes n_1 and n_2 increase the size of the sampling allowance.) Specifically, suppose we calculated the 95% confidence interval to be:

$$\Delta = 5 \pm 8 \tag{9-6}$$

$$-3 < \Delta < 13 \tag{9-7}$$

Are the following interpretations (at the 5% error level) true or false? If false, correct them:

a. Since the hypothesis $\Delta = 0$ falls within the interval (9-7), it cannot be rejected.

b. The true (population) difference may well be 0. That is, the population of men's salaries may be the same as the women's on average. The difference in *sample* means ($\overline{X}_1 - \overline{X}_2 = 5$) may represent only random fluctuation, and therefore cannot be used to show that a real difference exists in the population means.

c. The plausible population differences within the interval (9-7) include both negative and positive values; that is, we cannot even decide whether men's salaries on the whole are better or worse than women's.

d. In (9-6), we see that the sampling allowance (± 8) overwhelms the estimated difference (5). Whenever there is this much sampling "fog," we call the difference *statistically indiscernible*.

SOLUTION

Each of these statements is correct, and illustrates that *samples that are too small produce statistical indiscernibility* (that is, keep us from a statistically discernible conclusion).

In summary, once a confidence interval has been calculated, it can be used immediately to test any hypothesis. For example, to use our Kansas City suburb example again, the claims that 60%, 70%, or 80% of the voters are Republican are acceptable hypotheses, because they fall within the confidence interval (8-28). But the hypotheses that only 30%, 40%, or 50% are Republican can be rejected because these hypotheses fall outside the confidence interval.

B—THE TRADITIONAL APPROACH

The hypothesis $\Delta = 0$ in (9-1) is of particular interest. Since it represents no difference whatsoever, it is called the *null hypothesis* H_0. In rejecting it because it lies outside the confidence interval (9-4), we established the important claim that there was indeed a difference between men's and women's income. Such a result is traditionally called *statistically significant* at the *5% significance level*.

There is a problem with the term "statistically significant." It is a technical phrase that simply means enough data has been collected to establish that a difference does exist. It does *not* mean the difference is necessarily important. For example, if we had taken huge samples from nearly identical populations, the 95% confidence interval, instead of (9-4), might have been:

$$\Delta = .0005 \pm .0004$$

This difference is so miniscule that we could dismiss it as being of no human or scientific significance, even though it is just as statistically significant as (9-4). In other words, *statistical* significance is a technical term, with a far different meaning than *ordinary* significance.

There is also a problem with the term "5% significance level." It sounds like the higher this value (say 10% rather than 5%) the better the test. But precisely the reverse is true. (Our level of confidence would only be 90%, rather than 95%.)

Unfortunately, but understandably, many people tend to confuse statistical significance with ordinary significance.[3] To reduce the confusion, we prefer the word discernible instead of significant. In conclusion, therefore:

---

[3] To make matters worse, some writers simply use the single word "significant." While they may mean "statistically significant," their readers often interpret this to mean "ordinarily significant" or "important."

As an example of this, an article in a highly respected journal used the words "highly significant" to refer to relatively minor findings uncovered in a huge sample of 400,000 people. (For example, one such finding was that the youngest child in a family had an IQ that was 1 or 2 points lower on average than the second youngest child.)

From this example, it may be concluded that a large sample is like a large magnifying glass that allows us to discern the smallest molehill (smallest difference between two populations). It is unwise to use a phrase (such as "significant" or "highly significant") that makes this molehill sound like a mountain.

> **"Statistically *significant* at the 5% *significance* level" is the traditional phrase typically encountered in the scientific literature. It means exactly the same thing as our "statistically *discernible* at the 5% *error* level."** (9-8)

PROBLEMS

9-1 For each of Problems 8-24 to 8-26, state whether the differences are statistically discernible at the 5% level.

9-2 A real estate broker employs two appraisers to estimate the value of houses for sale, and wonders whether the less experienced appraiser (A) is as good as the other (B). As a test, he has each of them appraise the same 5 randomly selected houses.

	Appraised Value ($000)	
House	*by A*	*by B*
1	94	81
2	60	55
3	39	32
4	116	106
5	136	121

a. Calculate a 95% confidence interval to estimate the difference in the average appraisals of A and B. Then you can answer the following questions, at level $\alpha = 5\%$:

b. Does the point estimate exceed the sampling allowance?

c. Was there enough data to discern a real difference?

d. Is the confidence interval—the range of plausible values for this difference—entirely positive, so that A is unambiguously higher than B?

e. What is the null hypothesis? Can it be rejected?

9-3 In Problem 9-2, the actual selling prices (in order) turned out to be:

86, 50, 30, 119, 126.

Now calculate the "appraisal errors" of A (absolute difference between appraised price and selling price) and also of B. On average, how much higher is As "appraisal error" than Bs?

Answer with a 95% confidence interval, and continue with the same questions as in Problem 9-2.

9-2 p-VALUE (ONE-SIDED)

A—WHAT IS A *p*-VALUE?

In Section 9-1 we developed a simple way to test *any* hypothesis, by examining whether or not it falls within the confidence interval. Now we take a new perspective by concentrating on just one hypothesis, the null hypothesis H_0. We will calculate just how little it is supported by the data.

EXAMPLE 9-3

TV TUBE PRODUCTION IMPROVED?

A standard manufacturing process has produced millions of TV tubes, with a mean life $\mu = 1200$ hours and a standard deviation $\sigma = 300$ hours. A new process, recommended by the engineering department as better, produces a sample of 100 tubes, with an average $\overline{X} = 1265$. Although this sample makes the new process look better, is this just a sampling fluke? Is it possible that the new process is really no better than the old, and we have just turned up a misleading sample?

To give this problem more structure, we state the null hypothesis: the new process would produce a population that is no different from the old—that is, H_0: $\mu = 1200$, which is sometimes abbreviated:

$$\mu_0 = 1200 \tag{9-9}$$

The claim of the engineering department that the new process is better is called the *alternative hypothesis*,[4] H_A: $\mu > 1200$, which is also abbreviated:

$$\mu_A > 1200 \tag{9-10}$$

How consistent is the sample $\overline{X} = 1265$ with the null hypothesis $\mu_0 = 1200$? Specifically, if the null hypothesis were true, what is the probability that $\overline{X}$ would be as high as 1265?

SOLUTION

In Figure 9-1 we show the hypothetical distribution of $\overline{X}$, if H_0 is true. (Here, for the first time, we show the convention of drawing hypothetical distributions in ghostly white.) By the Normal Approximation Rule, this

---

[4] In practice, the null and alternative hypotheses often are determined as follows: H_A is the claim that we want to prove (9-10). Then H_0 is really everything else, $\mu \leq 1200$. But we need not use all of this; instead, in (9-9) we use just the boundary point, $\mu = 1200$. Any other μ below 1200 would be easier to distinguish from H_A since it is "further away," and so we do not bother with it.

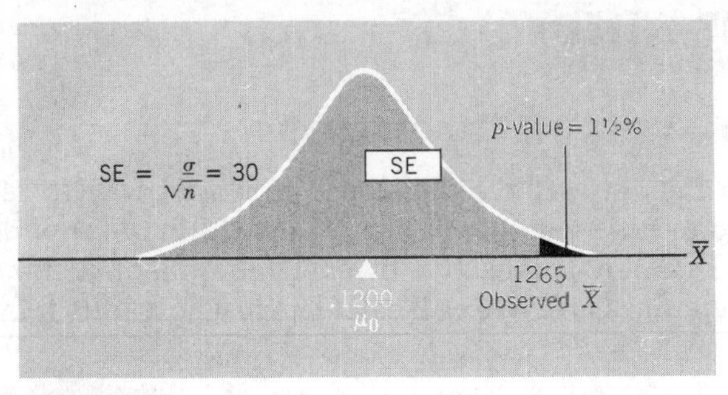

FIGURE 9-1
p-value ≡ Pr($\overline{X}$ would be as large as the value actually observed, if H_0 is true).

distribution is normal, with mean $\mu_0 = 1200$, and standard error $= \sigma/\sqrt{n} = 300/\sqrt{100} = 30$. We use these to standardize the observed value $\overline{X} = 1265$:

$$Z = \frac{\overline{X} - \mu_0}{\sigma/\sqrt{n}}$$

$$= \frac{1265 - 1200}{30} = 2.17 \tag{9-11}$$

Thus
$$\Pr(\overline{X} \geq 1265) = \Pr(Z \geq 2.17) = .015 \tag{9-12}$$

What does this mean in plain English? If the new process were no better (that is, if H_0 were true), there would be only 1½% probability of observing $\overline{X}$ as large as 1265. This 1½% is therefore called the p-value for H_0 (or more specifically, the *one-sided* p-value, matching the one-sided alternative hypothesis in (9-10)).

The p-value summarizes very clearly how much agreement there is between the data and H_0. In this example the data provided very little support for H_0; but if $\overline{X}$ had been observed closer to H_0 in Figure 9-1, the p-value in the tail would have been larger.

In general, for any hypothesis being tested, we define the p-value as.[5]

$$\textbf{p-value} \equiv \Pr\begin{pmatrix}\text{The sample value would be as large} \\ \text{as the value actually observed,} \\ \text{if } H_0 \text{ is true}\end{pmatrix} \tag{9-13}$$

---

[5] For brevity, we use the term "as large as" to mean "*at least* as large as."

The p-value in Figure 9-1 is calculated in the right-hand tail, because the alternative hypothesis is on the right side ($\mu > 1200$). On the other hand, if the alternative hypothesis were on the left side ($\mu < 1200$), then the p-value would be calculated in the left-hand tail:

$$\text{p-value} = \Pr\begin{pmatrix}\text{the sample value would be } \textit{as small} \\ \text{as the value actually observed,} \\ \text{if } H_0 \text{ is true}\end{pmatrix}$$

The p-value is an excellent way to *summarize what the data says*[6] *about the credibility of* H_0.

B—USING STUDENT'S *t* AND CONFIDENCE INTERVALS

We have seen how $\bar{X}$ was standardized so that the standard normal table could be used. The key statistic we evaluated was

$$Z = \frac{\bar{X} - \mu_0}{\sigma/\sqrt{n}} = \frac{\bar{X} - \mu_0}{\text{exact SE}} \qquad \text{(9-14) like (9-11)}$$

Usually σ is unknown, and has to be estimated with the *sample* standard deviation s. Then the statistic is called t instead of Z:

$$t = \frac{\bar{X} - \mu_0}{s/\sqrt{n}} = \frac{\bar{X} - \mu_0}{\text{estimated SE}} \qquad \text{(9-15)}$$

Since $\bar{X}$ fluctuates around μ_0, Z fluctuates around 0. Similarly t fluctuates around 0—but with wider variability, as already noted in Chapter 8. (We no longer know the exact value σ, but instead have to use an estimate s, with its inevitable uncertainty.) The resulting wider distribution of t is shown in Figure 9-2.

There are many t distributions, one for each sample size; hence, one for each d.f. (degrees of freedom). In Figure 9-2 we see that the larger the sample size, the less spread out is the t distribution. (The larger the sample, the more reliable is the estimate s, and consequently the less variable is t). Eventually, as sample size approaches infinity, s^2 estimates σ^2 dead on, and then the t distribution coincides with the normal z. This is reflected in the t table. Each of the distributions in Figure 9-2 corresponds to a row in Table V. In the last row, where d.f. = ∞, the t and z values become identical. And in the two rows above, where d.f. = 60 and 120, the t and z values are very close.

It is therefore worthwhile repeating the advice given earlier in Chapter 8: In practice, when σ is unknown, t in Table V needs to be used only for small samples. For large samples of 50, 100, or more, t is typically not required; z can be used instead, as a reasonable approximation.

Of course, (9-15) can be easily generalized to cover any of the other situations encountered in Chapter 8:

---

[6] Of course, the data is not the only thing to be considered if we want to make a final judgment on the credibility of H_0; common sense, or what sometimes is more formally called "personal prior probability," must be considered, too, especially when the sample is small and hence unreliable.

For example, if you picked a coin up off the street, flipped it 10 times, and found that it showed 9 heads, the p-value for H_0 (fair coin) would be a mere .01 (from the binomial Table IIIc). But obviously it would be inappropriate to conclude from this that the coin was unfair. We know that practically all coins are fair; thus our common sense tells us that our sample result of 9 heads was likely "the luck of the draw," and we should discount it accordingly.

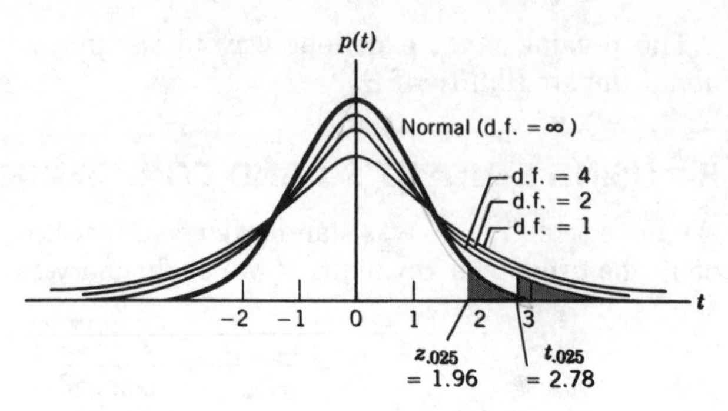

FIGURE 9-2
The standard normal distribution and the t distributions compared.

$$t = \frac{\text{estimate} - \text{null hypothesis}}{\text{SE}} \tag{9-16}$$

where SE is the brief notation we will henceforth reserve for just the *estimated* standard error. Often the null hypothesis is 0, in which case (9-16) takes on a very simple form.

If the null hypothesis is zero, then

$$t = \frac{\text{estimate}}{\text{SE}} \tag{9-17}$$

This makes good intuitive sense—in this case, the t ratio simply measures the size of the estimate relative to its SE. Furthermore, suppose we have already calculated a confidence interval (as in Chapter 8) of the form:

$$\text{parameter} = \text{estimate} \pm t_{.025}(\text{SE})$$ (9-18) like (8-15)

Then the estimate and its SE can be easily extracted to calculate t in (9-17).

An example will show how easy it is to use such a confidence interval to find the p-value for H_0.

EXAMPLE 9-4

SEX DIFFERENCE IN SALARIES ONCE AGAIN

For the mean difference in men's and women's salaries (in thousands of dollars, annually), we calculated the following 95% confidence interval:

$$\Delta = (\bar{X}_1 - \bar{X}_2) \pm t_{.025}\,\text{SE}$$
$$= 5.0 \pm 2.16(1.84) \qquad (9\text{-}19)$$
(9-3) repeated

where there were 13 d.f. in calculating SE, and therefore 13 d.f. for the t distribution.

Calculate the p-value for the null hypothesis (no difference in mean salaries).

SOLUTION

Since the null hypothesis is $\Delta = 0$, we can use the short form (9-17). And (9-19) gives us the estimate (5.0) and standard error (1.84) we need:

$$t = \frac{\text{estimate}}{\text{SE}} = \frac{5.0}{1.84} = 2.72$$

Since d.f. = 13, we scan along the thirteenth row of Table V, and find that the observed t value of 2.72 lies beyond $t_{.01} = 2.65$. As Figure 9-3 shows, this means that the tail probability is smaller than .01, that is,

$$\text{p-value} < .01$$

Since the p-value is a measure of the credibility of H_0, such a low value leads us to conclude that H_0 is implausible.

C—PROPORTIONS

As another example of how a confidence interval gives us what we need for calculating a p-value, consider a problem involving a proportion. (For proportions, Appendix 9-2 shows how to refine p-values.)

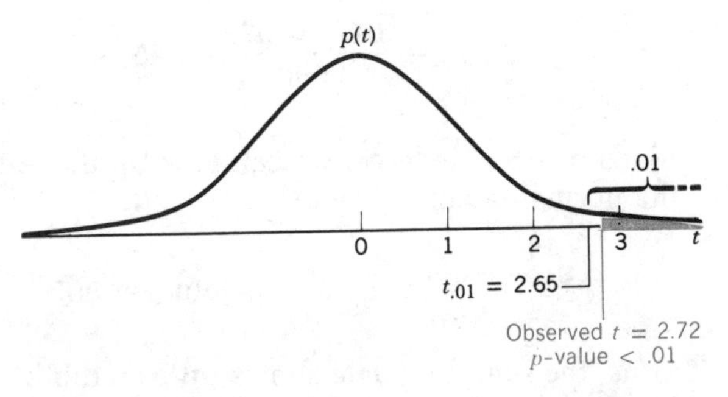

FIGURE 9-3
p-value found using t in Table V.

EXAMPLE 9-5

HAS QUALITY DETERIORATED?

Suppose General Electric regularly receives shipments of cooling units to install in its refrigerators and over the past 18 months, only 2% of these units have been substandard. When the supplier switches production to a new plant however, General Electric is concerned that quality may have deteriorated. Therefore they randomly sample 500 units of the next shipment, and find that 21 are substandard.

a. **Calculate the 95% confidence interval for the proportion of substandard units in the whole shipment.**

b. **Calculate the p-value for the null hypothesis that quality remains unchanged ($\pi_0 = .02$).**

SOLUTION

a. **The sample proportion of substandards is $P = 21/500 = .042$. Around it we construct the familiar 95% confidence interval for π, the population proportion:**

$$\pi = P \pm 1.96 \sqrt{\frac{P(1-P)}{n}} \qquad \text{(9-20)} \quad \text{(8-27) repeated}$$

$$= .042 \pm 1.96 \sqrt{\frac{.042(.958)}{500}}$$

$$= .042 \pm 1.96(.0090) \qquad \text{(9-21)}$$

$$= 4.2\% \pm 1.8\%$$

b. **The estimate and its SE are given in the confidence interval (9-21), and are substituted into the *t* ratio:**

$$t = \frac{\text{estimate} - \text{null hypothesis}}{\text{SE}} \qquad \text{like (9-16)}$$

$$= \frac{.042 - .02}{.0090} = 2.45 \qquad \text{(9-22)}$$

Since $n = 500$ is large, we can look up the tail area above 2.45 in the *normal* table:

$$\text{p-value} = .007 \qquad \text{(9-23)}$$

That is, the sampling data shows little credibility for the null hypothesis that the new shipment has maintained the same quality.

PROBLEMS

9-4 A company assembling watches in Hong Kong wants to test the relative effectiveness of two new training programs for its employees. They assigned 15 workers drawn at random from their work force to the first program, and 15 to the second. Then the two samples gave a 95% confidence interval for the mean difference in productivity:

$$2.8 \pm 1.8 \text{ watches per week.}$$

Answer True or False; if False, correct it:

a. The null hypothesis H_0 is that the two new training programs give equally high productivity on average; that is, $\overline{X}_1 = \overline{X}_2$.

b. In the confidence interval, ± 1.8 represents $\pm t_{.025}$SE. Since $t_{.025} = 2.05$ (with 28 d.f.), we can solve for the unknown SE $= 1.8/2.05 = 0.88$.

c. Thus $t = 2.8/.88 = 3.18$, and consequently the p-value for H_0 is less than .0025. That is, H_0 has very great credibility.

d. If we repeated the experiment, and if H_0 were true, the chance of drawing samples that produce a t value as large as the one observed (3.18) is very small ($<.0025$).

e. To eliminate bias, the *best* 30 workers should have been chosen for the test, and then *allowed to choose* which new training program they preferred.

9-5 For each of Problems 8-24 to 8-26, calculate the p-value for H_0.

9-6 How much do seat belts help? To answer this, a study was undertaken of cars that had been equipped with seat belts (lap-and-shoulder belts) and that had subsequently been involved in accidents. A random sample of 10,000 occupants showed the following injury rates (reconstructed from U.S. Department of Transportation, 1981):

Severe or Fatal Injury	*Seat Belt Worn* Yes	No	*Totals*
Yes	3	119	122
No	829	9049	9878
Totals	832	9168	10,000

a. State H_0 in words and symbols.

b. To what extent does the data prove that seat belts help?

c. Would the study have been more effective if it had included not only cars with seat belts, but also those without? Why?

9-3 CLASSICAL HYPOTHESIS TESTS

A—WHAT IS A CLASSICAL TEST?

Suppose we have the same data as in Example 9-3. Recall that the traditional manufacturing process had produced a population of millions of TV tubes, with a mean life $\mu = 1200$ hours and a standard deviation $\sigma =$ 300 hours. To apply a classical hypothesis test of whether a new process is better, we will proceed in three steps—the first two before any data is collected:

1. The null hypothesis (H_0: $\mu = 1200$) is formally stated. At the same time, we set the sample size (such as $n = 100$), and the error level of the test (such as 5%) hereafter referred to as α.
2. We now assume temporarily that the null hypothesis is true—just as we did in calculating the p-value. And we ask, what can we expect of a sample mean drawn from this sort of world? Its specific distribution is again shown in Figure 9-4, just as it was in Figure 9-1. But there is one important difference in these two diagrams: Whereas in Figure 9-1 the shaded p-value was calculated from the observed $\overline{X}$, in Figure 9-4 the shaded area is arbitrarily set at $\alpha = 5\%$. This defines the critical range for rejecting the null hypothesis (shown as the big arrow). All this is done before any data is observed.
3. The sample is now taken. If the observed $\overline{X}$ falls in the rejection region in Figure 9-4, then it is judged sufficiently in conflict with the null hypothesis to reject H_0. Otherwise H_0 is not rejected.

The critical value $\overline{X}_c = 1249$ for this test was calculated by noting from Appendix Table IV that a 5% tail is cut off the normal distribution by a critical Z value of $z_{.05} = 1.64$; that is:

$$\text{Critical } Z = \frac{\overline{X}_c - \mu_0}{\sigma/\sqrt{n}} = 1.64 \tag{9-24}$$

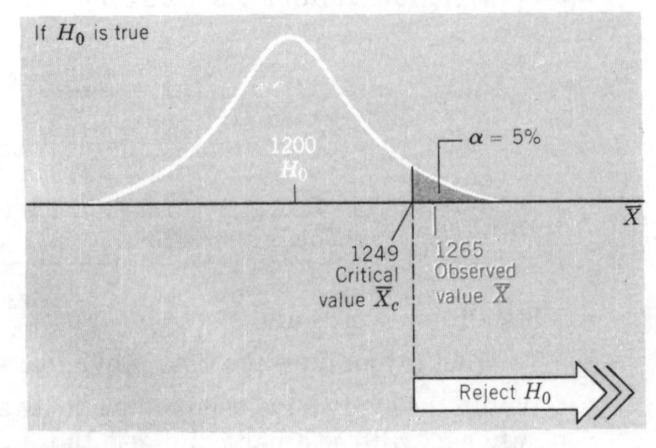

FIGURE 9-4
A classical test at level α = 5%.

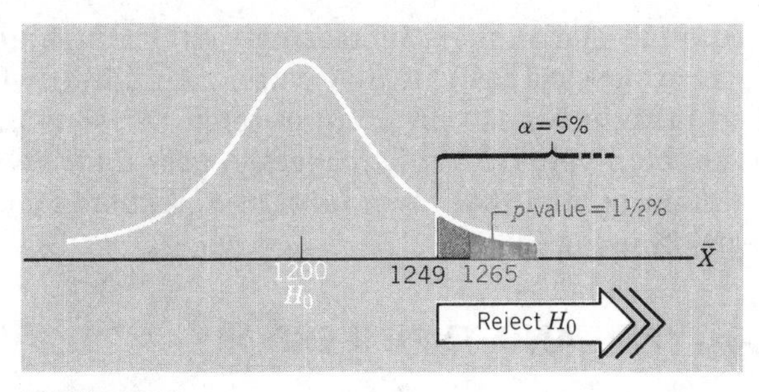

FIGURE 9-5
Classical hypothesis testing and p-value.

$$\frac{\overline{X}_c - 1200}{300/\sqrt{100}} = 1.64 \qquad \text{(9-25) like (9-14)}$$

$$\overline{X}_c = 1249 \qquad \text{(9-26)}$$

In our example, the observed $\overline{X} = 1265$ is beyond this critical value, thus leading us to reject H_0 at the 5% error level.

There is another way of looking at this testing procedure. If we get an observed $\overline{X}$ exceeding 1249, there are two explanations:

1. H_0 is true, but we have been exceedingly unlucky and got a very improbable sample $\overline{X}$. (We're born to be losers; even when we bet with odds of 19 to 1 in our favor, we still lose.)
2. H_0 is not true after all. Thus it is no surprise that the observed $\overline{X}$ was so high.

We opt for the more plausible second explanation. But we are left in some doubt; it is just possible that the first explanation is the correct one. For this reason we qualify our conclusion to be "at the 5% error level."

B—CLASSICAL HYPOTHESIS TESTING AND p-VALUE

For the example above, a comparison of classical testing and p-value is set out in Figure 9-5. Since the p-value [1½% from (9-12)] is less than $\alpha = 5\%$, the observed $\overline{X}$ is correspondingly in the rejection region; that is:

$$\boxed{\text{Reject } H_0 \text{ if its p-value} \leq \alpha} \qquad \text{(9-27)}$$

To restate this, we recall that the p-value is a measure of the credibility of H_0. If this credibility falls below α, then H_0 is rejected.[7]

[7] Figure 9-5 provides another useful interpretation of p-value. Note that if we had happened to set the level of the test at the p-value of 1½% (rather than 5%), it would have been just barely possible to reject H_0. Accordingly:

p-value is the lowest that we could push the level α and still be able (barely) to reject H_0. (9-28)

Applied statisticians increasingly prefer p-values to classical testing, because classical tests involve setting α arbitrarily (usually at 5%). Rather than introduce such an arbitrary element, it is often preferable just to quote the p-value, leaving readers to pass their own judgment on H_0. [By determining first their own level of α, readers may then reach their own decision using (9-27).]

C—TYPE I AND TYPE II ERRORS

In the decision-making process we run the risk of committing two distinct kinds of error. The first is shown in panel (a) of Figure 9-6 (a reproduction of Figure 9-4), which shows what the world looks like if H_0 is true. In this event, there is a 5% chance that we will observe $\overline{X}$ in the shaded region, and thus erroneously reject the true H_0. Rejecting H_0 when it is true is called a *type I error*, with its probability of course being α, the error level of the test. (Now we see that when we use the term "error level of a test" we could say more precisely, "the type I error level of a test.")

But suppose the claim of the engineering department is true, and the mean lifetime μ is indeed greater than 1200. This is customarily called the *alternative hypothesis* H_A: $\mu > 1200$. This is a real possibility, and we had

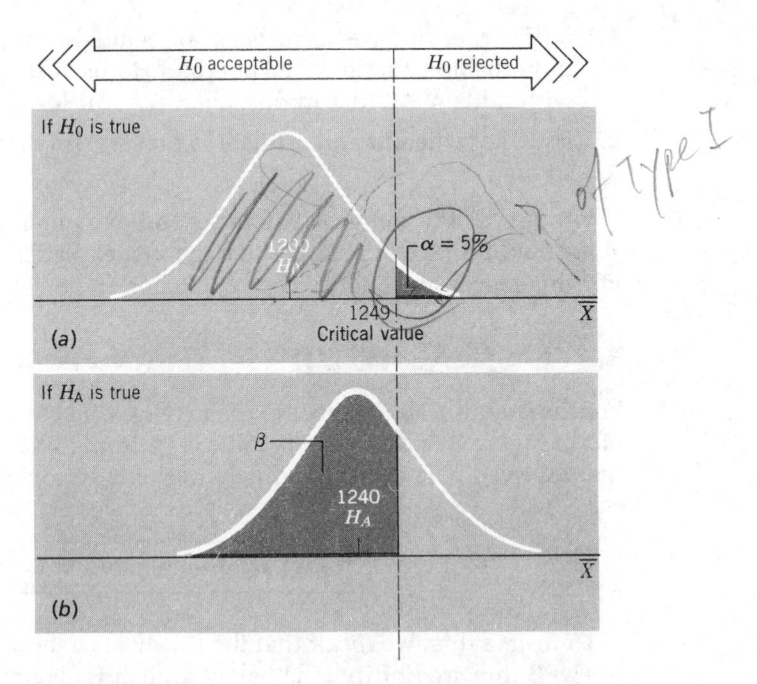

FIGURE 9-6
The two kinds of error that can occur in a classical test. (a) If H_0 is true, then α = probability of erring (by rejecting the true hypothesis H_0). (b) If H_A is true, then β = probability of erring (by judging that the false hypothesis H_0 is acceptable).

TABLE 9-1 Four Possible Results of an Hypothesis Test (Based on Figure 9-6)

	Decision	
State of the World	*H_0 Acceptable*	*H_0 Rejected*
If H_0 is true	Correct decision. Probability = $1 - \alpha$ = confidence level	Type I error. Probability = α = level of the test
If H_0 is false (H_A true)	Type II error. Probability = β	Correct decision. Probability = $1 - \beta$ = power of the test

better investigate it as thoroughly as we did the null hypothesis. To be specific, suppose $\mu = 1240$, so that $\overline{X}$ fluctuates around 1240, as shown in panel (b). The correct decision in this case would be to reject the false null hypothesis H_0. An error would occur if $\overline{X}$ were to fall in the H_0 acceptance region. Such acceptance of H_0 when it is false is called a *type II error*. Its probability is called β, and is shown as the shaded area in panel (b).

Table 9-1 summarizes the dilemma of hypothesis testing: The state of the real world is unknown. We don't know whether H_0 is true or false. If a decision to reject or not reject must be made[8] in the face of this uncertainty, we have to take the risk of one error or another.

A legal analogy may help. In a murder trial, the jury is being asked to decide between H_0, the hypothesis that the accused is innocent, and the alternative H_A, that he is guilty. A type I error is committed if an innocent man is condemned, while a type II error occurs if a guilty man is set free. The judge's admonition to the jury that "guilt must be proved beyond a reasonable doubt" just means that α should be kept very small.

PROBLEMS

9-7 Consider the problem facing an air traffic controller at Chicago's O'Hare Airport. If a small irregular dot appears on the screen, approaching the flight path of a large jet, she must decide between:

H_0: All is well. It's only a bit of interference on the screen.
H_A: A collision with a small private plane is imminent.

[8] Of course, other more complicated decision rules may be used. For example, the statistician may decide to suspend judgment if the observed $\overline{X}$ is in the region around 1250 (say $1240 < \overline{X} < 1260$). If he observes an ambiguous $\overline{X}$ in this range, he then would undertake a second stage of sampling—which might yield a clear-cut decision, or might lead to further stages (i.e., "sequential sampling").

Fill in the blanks:

a. If H_0 is true, a "false alarm" could occur, called a type ____ error, with probability denoted by ____.

b. If H_A is true, a "missed alarm" could occur, called a type ____ error, with probability denoted by ____.

c. By making the equipment more sensitive and reliable, it is possible to reduce both ____ and ____.

9-8 An anecdote by Crichton (1968) goes like this: There's this desert prison, see, with an old prisoner, resigned to his life, and a young one just arrived. The young one talks constantly of escape, and, after a few months, he makes a break. He's gone a week, and then he's brought back by the guards. He's half dead, crazy with hunger and thirst. He describes how awful it was to the old prisoner. The endless stretches of sand, no oasis, no signs of life anywhere. The old prisoner listens for a while, then says, "Yep, I know, I tried to escape myself, twenty years ago." The young prisoner says, "You did? Why didn't you tell me, all these months I was planning my escape? Why didn't you let me know it was impossible?" And the older prisoner shrugs, and says, "So who publishes negative results?"

This simple story reflects a serious concern by social scientists about classical 5% testing (Light and Pillemer, 1984). To elaborate, suppose a revolutionary hypothesis has been proposed by the famous Professor Brainstorm, and yet if the truth were known, it really wouldn't fit the facts. In formal language, it is the *null* hypothesis that is true, not Brainstorm's hypothesis.

a. If 100 researchers investigated this phenomenon, about how many would obtain "statistically significant" results so that they could claim the Brainstorm hypothesis was true after all (at the 5% level)?

b. Now suppose the *Journal of Statistically Significant Results* used "statistical significance at the 5% level" as its sole criterion for publishing. (An exaggeration, of course, but we will use it to illustrate some real problems.) If all 100 researchers submitted their papers to this journal, which ones would get published?

For anyone who looks at the published evidence, what would he conclude about the Brainstorm hypothesis?

9-9 (Acceptance Sampling) The prospective purchaser of several new shipments of waterproof gloves hopes they are as good as the old shipments, which had a 10% rate of defective pairs. But he fears that they may be worse. So for each shipment, he takes a random sample of 100 pairs and counts the proportion P of defective pairs so that he can run a classical test. The level of this test was determined by such relevant factors as the cost of a bad shipment, the cost of an alternative supplier, and the new shipper's reputation. When all these factors were taken into account, suppose the appropriate level of this test was $\alpha = .09$.

a. State the null and alternative hypotheses, in words and symbols.

b. What is the critical value of P? That is, how large must P be in order to reject the null hypothesis (i.e., reject the shipment)?

c. Suppose that for 6 shipments, the values of P turned out to be 12%, 25%, 8%, 16%, 24%, and 21%. Which of these shipments should be rejected?

9-10 In Problem 9-9, suppose that the purchaser tries to get away with a small sample of only 10 pairs. Suppose that instead of setting $\alpha = .09$, he sets the rejection region to be $P \geq 20\%$ (i.e., he will reject the shipment if there are 2 or more defective pairs among the 10 pairs in the sample).

For this test, what is α? (*Hint:* Rather than using the normal approximation, the binomial distribution is easier and more accurate.)

9-11 In manufacturing machine bolts, the quality control engineer finds that it takes a sample of $n = 100$ to detect an accidental change of .5 millimeter in the mean length of the manufactured bolt. Suppose he wants more precision, to detect a change of only .1 millimeter, with the same α and β. How much larger must his sample be? (*Hint:* Rephrase the problem in terms of confidence intervals. To make a confidence interval 5 times as precise, how much larger must the sample be?)

9-12 In 1980, the Gallup poll asked Americans whether current safety regulations made nuclear power plants safe enough. Of the 420 respondents aged 18 to 30, 24% answered "yes." Of the 510 respondents aged 30 to 50, 34% answered "yes."

a. Calculate the p-value for H_0 (age makes no difference).

b. At level $\alpha = 5\%$, can H_0 be rejected? Is the difference statistically discernible?

***9-13** Consider the classical test shown in Figure 9-6.

a. If the observed $\overline{X}$ is 1245, do you reject H_0?

b. Suppose that you had designed this new process, and you were convinced that it was better than the old; specifically, on the basis of sound engineering principles, you really believed H_A: $\mu = 1240$. Common sense suggests that H_0 should be rejected in favor of H_A. In this conflict of common sense with classical testing, which path would you follow? Why?

c. Suppose that sample size is doubled to 200, while you keep $\alpha = 5\%$ and you continue to observe $\bar{X}$ to be 1245. What would be the classical test decision now? Would it, therefore, be true to say that your problem in part **a** may have been inadequate sample size?

d. Suppose now that your sample size n was increased to a million, and in that huge sample you observed $\bar{X} = 1201$. An improvement of only one unit over the old process is of no economic significance (i.e., does not justify retooling, etc.); but is it statistically significant (discernible)? Is it therefore true to say that a sufficiently large sample size may provide the grounds for rejecting any specific H_0—no matter how nearly true it may be—simply because it is not *exactly* true?

*9-4 CLASSICAL TESTS RECONSIDERED

A—REDUCING α AND β

In panel (*a*) of Figure 9-7 we show again the two error probabilities of Figure 9-6: α, if H_0 is true; and β, if H_A is true. In panel (*b*), we illustrate how decreasing α (by moving the critical point to the right to, say, 1270) will at the same time increase β. That is, pushing down α will raise β. Figure 9-8 emphasizes this trade-off between conflicting objectives.

Consider again the analogy with a murder trial. Many legal reforms, such as limiting the power of the police to obtain a confession, have been introduced in order to reduce α, the probability that an innocent person will be condemned. At the same time, they inadvertently increase β, the probability that a guilty person will evade punishment. There is no way of pushing α down to 0 (ensuring absolutely against convicting an innocent person) without letting β rise to 1 (letting every defendant go free and making the trial meaningless).

The only way that one error can be reduced without increasing the other is by gathering better evidence. For example, Figure 9-7*c* shows how increasing the sample size n makes the sampling distributions more accurate. Hence β can be made smaller without increasing α.

B—SOME PITFALLS IN CLASSICAL TESTING

Figure 9-7 can be used to illustrate some of the difficulties that may be encountered in applying a classical reject-or-accept hypothesis test at an arbitrary level α. In panel (*a*), suppose we have observed a sample $\bar{X} = 1245$. This is not quite extreme enough to allow rejection of H_0 at level $\alpha = 5\%$, so $\mu_0 = 1200$ is accepted. But if we had set $\alpha = 10\%$, then H_0 would have been rejected. This illustrates once again how an arbitrary specification of α leads to an arbitrary decision.

There is an even deeper problem. Accepting $\mu_0 = 1200$ (at level $\alpha = 5\%$)

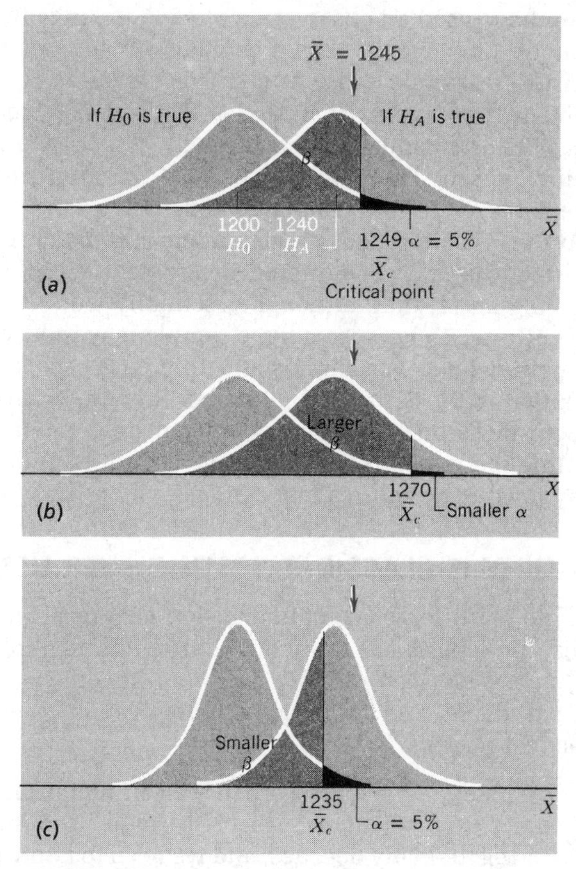

FIGURE 9-7
(a) Hypothesis test of Figure 9-6 showing α and β. (b) How a reduction in α increases β, other things being equal. (c) How an increase in sample size allows one error probability (β) to be reduced, without increasing the other (α).

is a disaster, if we had prior grounds for believing H_A is true—that is, for expecting that the new process would yield a mean $\mu_A = 1240$. In this case, our prior belief in the new process is strongly supported by the sample observation of 1245. Yet we have used this *confirming* sample result (in this classical hypothesis test) to *reverse* our original view. That

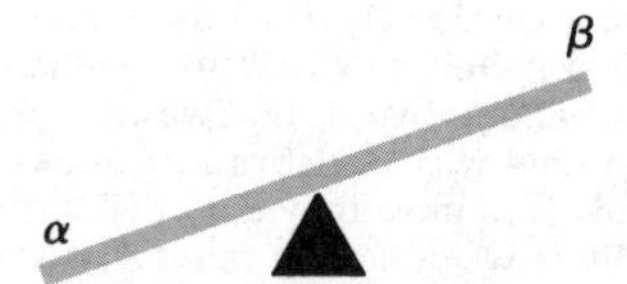

FIGURE 9-8
The Trade-off between α and β: If α is pushed down, then β is raised.

is, we have used an observation of 1245 to judge in favor of a population value of 1200, and against a population value of 1240. In this case our decision makes no sense at all. This serves as a warning of the serious problem that may exist in a classical test if a small sample is used to accept a null hypothesis.[9] Accordingly, it is wise to stop short of explicitly saying "accept H_0." Instead, we use the more reserved phrase "H_0 is acceptable,"[10] or "H_0 is not rejected."[11]

At the other extreme, a huge sample size may lead us into another kind of error [the one encountered in Problem 9-13(d)]. This is the error of rejecting an H_0 that, although essentially true, is not exactly true. This difficulty arises because a huge sample may reduce the standard error to the point where even a miniscule difference becomes statistically discernible; that is, H_0 is rejected, although it is practically true.

Both these pitfalls of classical testing can often be avoided by simply quoting the *p*-value for H_0 instead. Then it is unnecessary to set an arbitrary level of α, and readers can make their own judgment.

C—WHY IS CLASSICAL TESTING EVER USED?

In light of all these accumulated reservations about a classical accept-or-reject hypothesis test, why do we take the time to study it?

As we have seen, it clarifies certain theoretical issues like type I and type II errors, and their probabilities α and β. As well, there are two practical reasons:

1. We study classical testing so we can understand the scientific literature. Social scientists, especially, have used the language of classical testing for many decades, and we need to know this language even if it isn't ideal.
2. A classical hypothesis test may be preferred to calculating the *p*-value if the test level α can be determined rationally, and if many many samples are to be classified. [In industrial quality control, for example, samples of output are periodically taken to see whether production is still properly in control—i.e., to see whether H_0 ("no problems") is still acceptable, or whether it should be rejected.]

---

[9] In Figure 9-7, it was the small sample in panel (*a*) that misled us into judging H_0 acceptable. By contrast, the large sample shown in panel (*c*) would allow us to reject H_0.

[10] That is, we conclude that H_0 is one of many acceptable hypotheses (without passing judgment on which of these, if any, should actually be accepted).

[11] Thus we see that, although classical testing provides a rationale for rejecting H_0, it provides no formal rationale for accepting H_0. The null hypothesis may sometimes be uninteresting, and one that we neither believe nor wish to establish; it is selected because of its simplicity. In such cases, it is the alternative H_A that we are trying to establish, and we prove H_A by rejecting H_0. We can see now why statistics sometimes is called *the science of disproof.* H_0 cannot be proved, and H_A is proved by disproving (rejecting) H_0. It follows that if we wish to prove some proposition, we often will call it H_A and set up the contrary hypothesis H_0 as the "straw man" we hope to destroy. And, of course, if H_0 is only such a straw man, then it becomes absurd to accept it in the face of a small sample result that really supports H_A.

To illustrate this second point, consider again the familiar Example 9-3; but now suppose we are considering five new production processes, rather than just one. If a sample of 100 tubes is taken in each case, suppose the results are as shown below.

New Process	$\overline{X}$	*Is Process Really Better Than the Old Process (Where μ = 1200)?*
1	1265	?
2	1240	?
3	1280	?
4	1150	?
5	1210	?

We now have two options. We can calculate five *p*-values for these five processes, just as we calculated the *p*-value for the first process in Example 9-3. But this will involve a lot more work than using a classical test, which requires only that we specify α (at say 5%) and then calculate one single figure, the critical value $\overline{X}_c = 1249$ derived in (9-26). Then all five of the sample values can be evaluated routinely without any further calculation. (Note that H_0 is rejected only for processes 1 and 3; in other words, these are the only two that may be judged superior to the old method.)

But if a classical hypothesis test is to be used for such routine work, the level of α should not be arbitrarily set. Instead, α should be determined rationally, on the basis of two considerations:

Prior belief. To again use our example, the less confidence we have in the engineering department that assured us these new processes are better, the smaller we will set α (i.e., the stronger the evidence we will require to judge in their favor). So we need to answer questions such as: Are the engineers' votes divided? How often have they been wrong before?

Losses involved in making a wrong decision. The greater the costs of a type I error (i.e., needlessly retooling for a new process that is actually no better), the smaller we will set α, the probability of making that sort of error. Similarly, the greater the cost of a type II error (i.e., failing to switch to a new process that is actually better), the smaller we will set β.

Such prior beliefs and losses can be included in a more complete analysis called *Bayesian decision theory*, developed in Chapter 20.

*PROBLEMS

9-14 Answer True or False. If False, correct it.

a. Comparing hypothesis testing to a jury trial, we may say that the type I error is like the error of condemning a guilty person.

b. Suppose, in a certain test, that the p-value turns out to be .013. Then H_0 would be acceptable at the 5% level and also at the 1% level.

c. There are two disadvantages in arbitrarily specifying α at 5%, in a classical accept-or-reject test:

If the sample is very small, we may find H_0 acceptable even when H_0 is quite false.

If the sample is very large, we may reject H_0 even when H_0 is approximately correct and hence a good working hypothesis.

9-15 In the jury trial analogy, what would be the effect on α and β of reintroducing capital punishment on a large scale?

9-16 Consider a very simple example in order to keep the philosophical issues clear. Suppose that you are gambling with a single die, and lose whenever the die shows 1 dot (ace). After 100 throws, you notice that you have suffered a few too many losses—20 aces. This makes you suspect that your opponent is using a loaded die; specifically, you begin to wonder whether this is one of the crooked dice recently advertised as giving aces one-quarter of the time.

a. Find the critical proportion of aces beyond which you would reject H_0 at the 5% level.

b. Illustrate this test with a diagram similar to Figure 9-6. From this diagram, roughly estimate α and β.

c. With your observation of 20 aces, what is your decision? Suppose that you are playing against a strange character you have just met on a Mississippi steamboat. A friend passes you a note indicating that this stranger cheated him at poker last night; and you are playing for a great deal of money. Are you happy with your decision?

d. If you double α, use the diagram in part **b** to roughly estimate what happens to β.

***9-17** In Problem 9-10, suppose the alternative hypothesis is that the shipment is 30% defective.

a. State this in symbols.

b. Calculate β.

***9-18** Repeat the problem above, for Problem 9-9 in place of 9-10. Then, is it fair to say that an increased sample size reduced both α and β?

*9-5 OPERATING CHARACTERISTICS CURVE (OCC)

Now that we have defined and discussed the type II error probability β at some length, it is time to actually calculate it.

EXAMPLE 9-6
CALCULATING β FOR TV TUBE PRODUCTION

Consider the test shown in Figure 9-6, where the cutoff value $\overline{X}_c$ is 1249, and the alternative hypothesis is $\mu_A = 1240$.

Calculate β (the probability that when H_A is true, we will make the error of finding H_0 acceptable). For your solution, recall that $\overline{X}$ was based on a sample of $n = 100$ observations, and the population standard deviation was $\sigma = 300$.

SOLUTION

According to Figure 9-6*b* (where H_1 is true), the error of accepting H_0 occurs when $\overline{X}$ falls below the cutoff value $\overline{X}_c = 1249$. To find the probability of this, we standardize the critical value $\overline{X}_c = 1249$, seeing how far it deviates from the mean $\mu_A = 1240$:

$$Z = \frac{\overline{X}_c - \mu_A}{SE}$$

$$= \frac{1249 - 1240}{300/\sqrt{100}} = .30$$

Thus,

$$\Pr(\overline{X} < 1249) = \Pr(Z < .30)$$

$$= 1 - .382 = .618$$

$$\beta = 62\% \tag{9-29}$$

In many situations, it is unrealistic to pin down the alternative hypothesis to one specific value. For example, a more realistic version of Example 9-6 would include several possible alternative hypotheses, as follows.

EXAMPLE 9-7
CALCULATING THE OCC FOR TV TUBE PRODUCTION

Continuing Example 9-6, calculate the type II error probability β for several more alternative hypotheses:

a. $\mu_A = 1280$

b. $\mu_A = 1320$

SOLUTION

We use exactly the same method as in Example 9-6

a.

$$Z = \frac{1249 - 1280}{300/\sqrt{100}} = -1.03$$

Thus

$$\Pr(\overline{X} < 1249) = \Pr(Z < -1.03) = .152$$

$$\beta = 15\%$$

b. $$Z = \frac{1249 - 1320}{300/\sqrt{100}} = -2.37$$

Thus $$\Pr(\bar{X} < 1249) = \Pr(Z < -2.37) = .009$$
$$\beta = 1\%$$

The values of β in Examples 9-6 and 9-7 (corresponding to $\mu_A = 1240$, 1280, and 1320) are shown in Figure 9-9 as the three shaded areas (to the left of the cutoff point, where we accept H_0). Of course, an even more realistic alternative hypothesis would include *any* number larger than $\mu_0 = 1200$; that is,

$$\mu_A > 1200 \qquad \text{(9-10) repeated}$$

In other words,

$$\mu_A = 1201$$
$$\text{or } \mu_A = 1202$$
$$\text{or } \mu_A = 1203$$

An hypothesis like this, composed of many possibilties, is called a *composite* hypothesis. For each possible μ_A, we can calculate the corresponding β—as we already have for $\mu_A = 1240$, 1280, and 1320. When all the values of β are graphed, we obtain the *β function* in Figure 9-10—more commonly called the *operating characteristics curve* (*OCC*).

Figure 9-10 shows very graphically that as the alternative hypothesis μ_A gets further away from $\mu_0 = 1200$, the probability of error β drops. That is,

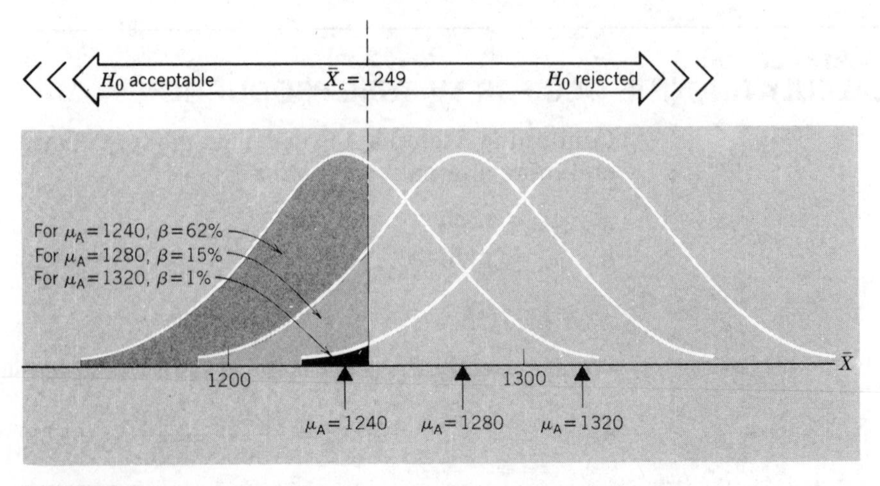

FIGURE 9-9
Calculation of β, the probability of type II error, for a composite H_A.

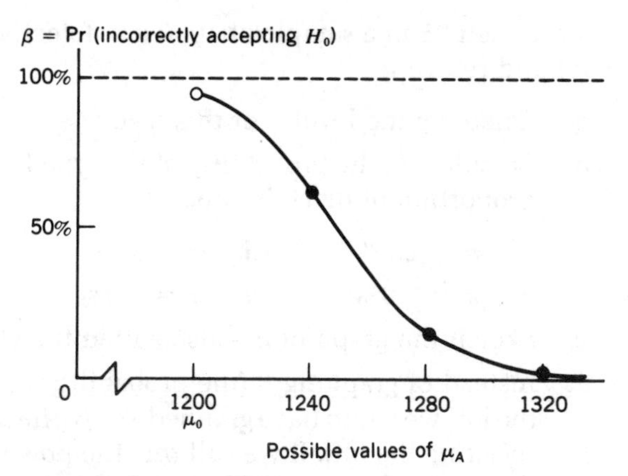

FIGURE 9-10
The β function, or Operating Characteristics Curve (OCC).

the bigger the difference between μ_0 and μ_A, the less chance of confusing the two.

*PROBLEMS

9-19 A certain type of seed has always grown to a mean height of 8.5 inches, with a standard deviation of 1 inch. A sample of 100 seeds is grown under new enriched conditions to see whether the mean height might be improved.

a. At the 5% level, calculate the cutoff value $\overline{X}_c$ above which H_0 should be rejected.

b. If the sample of 100 seeds actually turns out to have a mean height $\overline{X} = 8.8$ inches, do you reject H_0?

c. Roughly graph the OCC for this test. (*Hint:* Calculate β for a rough grid of values, say $\mu_A = 8.6, 8.8, 9.0$. Then sketch the curve joining these values.)

d. What would be the approximate chance of failing to detect a mean height improvement, if the sample of 100 seeds were to come from a population whose mean was 8.9 inches?

9-20 **a.** For the acceptance sampling in Problem 9-9, sketch the OCC.

b. Repeat part **a,** for Problem 9-10.

c. By comparing part **a** with part **b,** note how a larger sample gives a better OCC.

9-21 A large electronics firm buys printed circuits in lots of 50,000 each, and in the past has found the proportion that are substandard is $\pi = 2\%$ (the null hypothesis). To protect themselves against a possible deterioration of quality, they decide to sample each lot: If more than 25 in a sample of 1000 are defective, they will reject the lot and return it.

a. Calculate the level α of this test.

b. Calculate β, the probability of the type II error of this test, if the proportion of defectives is:

i. $\pi = 2.5\%$ iii. $\pi = 3.5\%$

ii. $\pi = 3.0\%$ iv. $\pi = 4.0\%$

c. Sketch the graph of β—also called the OCC.

d. Instead of graphing β (the probability of mistakenly accepting the lot) we could have graphed $1 - \beta$ (the probability of correctly *rejecting* the lot). If we call this the *power* curve, what relation does it have to the OCC? Graph this power curve.

e. Suppose 50 shoddy lots were shipped, each having 3% defective. About how many would be detected as shoddy, and rejected?

---

*9-6 TWO-SIDED TESTS

So far we have concentrated on the one-sided test, in which the alternative hypothesis, and consequently the rejection region and p-value, are just on one side. The one-sided test is appropriate when there is a one-sided claim to be made, such as, "more than," "less than," "better than," "worse than," "at least," and so on.

However, there are occasions when it is more appropriate to use a two-sided test. They often may be recognized by symmetrical claims such as, "different from," "changed for better or worse," "unequal," and so on. This section discusses the minor modifications required.

A—TWO-SIDED *p*-VALUE[12]

An example will show how easy it is to accommodate a two-sided hypothesis.

EXAMPLE 9-8
TV TUBE PRODUCTION AGAIN: TWO-SIDED *p*-VALUE

Consider again the testing of TV tubes in Example 9-3. Suppose that the null hypothesis remains as

$$H_0: \mu_0 = 1200$$

[12] Since the one-sided p-value is fundamental, it is often called simply the p-value (as in Section 9-2). To avoid confusion, therefore, whenever we mean a two-sided p-value, we specifically refer to it as "two-sided."

But now change the alternative hypothesis by supposing that our engineers cannot advocate the new process as better but must concede that it may be worse. Then the alternative hypothesis would be:

$$H_A: \mu > 1200 \quad \text{or} \quad \mu < 1200$$

That is:

$$\mu \neq 1200 \tag{9-30}$$

In other words, we now are testing whether the new process is *different* (whereas in Example 9-3, we were testing whether it was better). Thus, even before we collect any data, we can agree that a value of $\overline{X}$ well below 1200 would be just as strong evidence against H_0 as a value of $\overline{X}$ well above 1200; that is, what counts is how far away $\overline{X}$ is, on *either side*.

If the sample mean $\overline{X} = 1265$, what is the two-sided p-value? That is, what is the probability that $\overline{X}$ would be this distant (in either direction) from the null hypothesis $\mu_0 = 1200$? (For your solution, recall that $\overline{X}$ was based on a sample of $n = 100$ observations, and the population standard deviation was $\sigma = 300$.)

SOLUTION

As usual, we measure how far away $\overline{X}$ is from the null hypothesis μ_0 by standardizing:

$$Z = \frac{\overline{X} - \mu_0}{SE}$$

$$= \frac{1265 - 1200}{300/\sqrt{100}} = 2.17 \qquad \text{like (9-11)}$$

Thus, $\qquad \Pr(\overline{X} > 1265) = \Pr(Z > 2.17) = .015$

This is the chance that we would observe $\overline{X}$ this far above μ_0, as shown in the right-hand tail of Figure 9-11. But there is the same probability

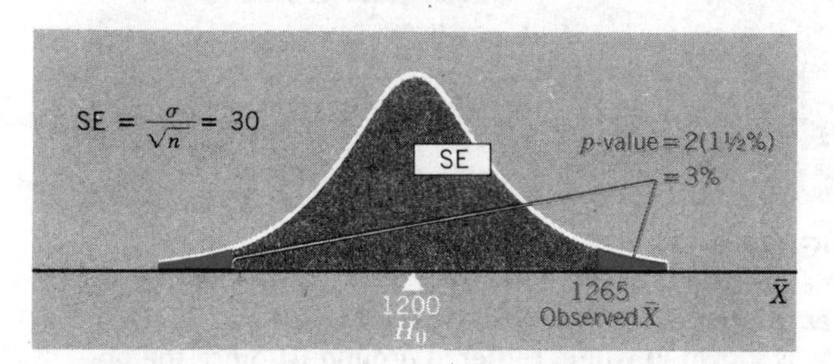

FIGURE 9-11
Two-sided *p*-value ≡ Pr($\overline{X}$ would be as extreme as the value actually observed, if H_0 is true). Compare with Figure 9-1.

(.015) that we would observe $\overline{X}$ this far below μ_0, as shown in the left-hand tail. Therefore,

$$\text{two-sided p-value} = 2(.015) = .030.$$

In general, whenever the alternative hypothesis is two-sided, it is appropriate to calculate the two-sided p-value for H_0. As we have just seen in Figure 9-11, whenever the sampling distribution is symmetric, the two-sided p-value is just twice the one-sided p-value.

B—TWO-SIDED TESTS AND CONFIDENCE INTERVALS

It is easy to modify a one-sided classical test to a two-sided classical test; we merely reject H_0 if the *two*-sided p-value falls below the specified level α. For instance, in Example 9-8 where the two-sided p-value was only 3%, H_0 could be rejected at the 5% level.

In a repetitive situation where we need to test many samples, instead of calculating the many p-values we could calculate once and for all a classi-

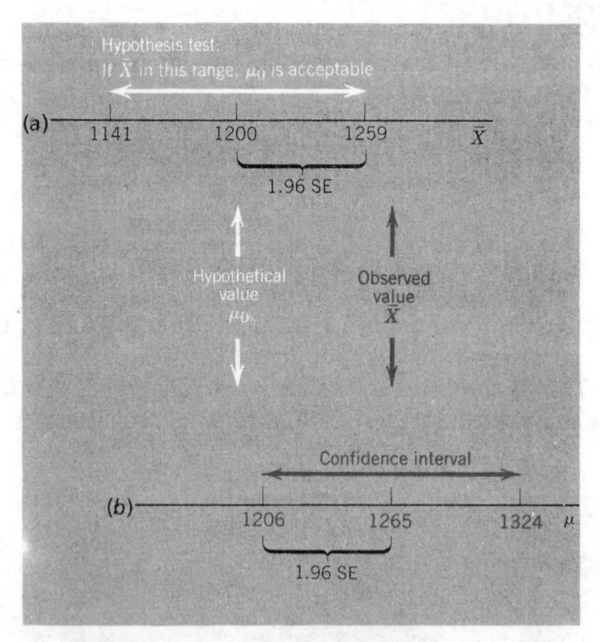

FIGURE 9-12
The equivalence of a two-sided classical test and confidence interval. (a) The classical hypothesis test at level α = 5% is shown in white, centered around μ_0. Since the observed $\overline{X}$ falls beyond the cutoff points, we can reject H_0. (b) The 95% confidence interval is shown in blue, centered around $\overline{X}$. Since μ_0 falls beyond the confidence limits we can reject H_0.

cal rejection region—a two-sided region that cuts off $2\frac{1}{2}\%$ in each tail, for a total of $\alpha = 5\%$. Figure 9-12*a* illustrates this for the TV-tube data of Example 9-8. We note that an observed $\overline{X} = 1265$ would mean H_0 is rejected.

Whenever a two-sided test is appropriate, an ordinary two-sided confidence interval also is appropriate, as shown in Figure 9-12*b*. Since the null hypothesis $\mu_0 = 1200$ lies outside this confidence interval, it can be rejected. It is clear why the confidence interval and the test are exactly equivalent. In both cases, we simply check whether the magnitude of the difference $|\overline{X} - \mu_0|$ exceeds 1.96 standard errors. These two approaches differ only because the classical test uses the null hypothesis μ_0 as its reference point, whereas the confidence interval uses the observed $\overline{X}$ as its reference point. Thus, (9-5) finally is confirmed.

C—ONE-SIDED TESTS AND CONFIDENCE INTERVALS

Just as a two-sided confidence interval is equivalent to a two-sided test, so we can now develop a one-sided confidence interval that will be equivalent to a one-sided test.

Like the one-sided test, the one-sided confidence interval puts all the 5% error allowance in just one tail. This means there is a cutoff point only in that one tail, and not in the other. For instance, for a single mean,

95% confidence interval (one-sided)

$$\mu > \overline{X} - z_{.05}\frac{\sigma}{\sqrt{n}} \qquad \begin{array}{r}(9\text{-}31)\\ \text{like (8-9)}\end{array}$$

An example will show how easily this can be calculated.

EXAMPLE 9-9
HOW MUCH IMPROVED IS TV TUBE PRODUCTION?

In producing the new TV tube in Example 9-3, we asked whether the new tube was a discernible improvement over the old. The key question now becomes: At a 95% level of confidence, *how good* is the new tube? That is, the average lifetime of the new tube will be *at least* how many hours?

To answer this, construct a one-sided confidence interval for μ, the mean of the new tube. (Recall that $\overline{X} = 1265$, $n = 100$, and σ was assumed known to be 300.)

SOLUTION

From the normal table (or the bottom line of the *t* table) we find the critical value that leaves all 5% error in one tail is $z_{.05} = 1.64$. We substitute this, along with the given $\overline{X}$, n, and σ, into the 95% confidence interval:

$$\mu > \overline{X} - z_{.05}\frac{\sigma}{\sqrt{n}} \qquad \text{like (9-31)}$$

$$\mu > 1265 - 1.64\left(\frac{300}{\sqrt{100}}\right)$$

$$\mu > 1216$$

That is, the new mean is at least 1216. This makes possible a stronger claim for the new tube than the lower bound of 1206 given by the two-sided confidence interval in Figure 9-12. We must pay a price, however: The one-sided confidence interval has no upper bound at all.

If we had wanted to state that a population mean is *below* a certain figure, we would use the alternative one-sided confidence interval:

$$\mu < \overline{X} + z_{.05}\frac{\sigma}{\sqrt{n}} \qquad \text{(9-32) like (9-31)}$$

Finally, we note that *any* two-sided confidence interval can be made one-sided. For example, for two samples,

$$(\mu_1 - \mu_2) < (\overline{X}_1 - \overline{X}_2) + t_{.05}s_p\sqrt{\frac{1}{n_1} + \frac{1}{n_2}} \qquad \text{(9-33) like (8-20)}$$

D—SOME PARTING ADVICE

We have discussed one-sided and two-sided forms for both confidence intervals and classical hypothesis tests. In practice, which of these 4 approaches is preferred? The two-sided confidence interval is often the standard form, for several reasons:

- **i.** It is easiest to understand.
- **ii.** It usually gives the crucial point estimate too—which may be even more useful than the sampling allowance that surrounds it.
- **iii.** It is the form most naturally related to some of the more advanced techniques that we will discuss later.

A very useful complement to the 95% confidence interval is the *p*-value, which avoids the arbitrary 95% or 5% level, and states instead just how little credibility H_0 has. The *p*-value should usually be one-sided, especially if there are key words such as, "at least, better than, more than, less than," etc. On the other hand, the *p*-value should occasionally be two-sided, if there is an explicitly two-sided alternative hypothesis such as "different from."

*PROBLEMS

9-22 Answer True or False; if False, correct it.

a. If the alternative hypothesis is two-sided, then the p-value, classical test, and confidence interval should be two-sided too.

b. To decide whether the probability π of a die coming up ace is fair, suppose we are testing the hypothesis

$$H_0: \pi = 1/6 \quad \text{against} \quad H_A: \pi < 1/6$$

Then we should use a two-sided test, rejecting H_0 when π turns out to be large.

9-23 In a Gallup poll of 1500 Americans in 1975, 45% answered "yes" to the question, "Is there any area right around here—that is, within a mile—where you would be afraid to walk alone at night?" In an earlier poll of 1500 Americans in 1972, only 42% had answered "yes."

a. Construct a two-sided 95% confidence interval for the change in proportion who are afraid.

b. Calculate the two-sided p-value for the null hypothesis of no change.

c. At the error level $\alpha = 5\%$, is the increase from 42% to 45% statistically discernible? That is, can H_0 be rejected? Answer in two ways, making sure that both answers agree:

i. Is H_0 excluded from the 95% confidence interval?

ii. Does the p-value for H_0 fall below 5%?

9-24 Repeat Problem 9-23, with the appropriate changes in wording, for the following income data sampled from U.S. physicians in 1979 (net income after expenses, but before taxes):

	General Practitioners	*Psychiatrists*
Sample size n	200	100
Mean income $\overline{X}$	\$62,000	\$62,600
Standard deviation s	\$32,000	\$35,000
Pooled standard deviation s_p = \$33,000		

Stat. Abst. of U.S., 1981, p. 108

9-25 A manufacturing process has produced millions of lightbulbs with a mean life $\mu = 14{,}000$ hours, and $\sigma = 2000$ hours. A new process produced a sample of 25 bulbs with $\overline{X} = 14{,}740$ (but assume σ remains unchanged at 2000).

a. Construct a one-sided 95% confidence interval to show how good the new process is.

b. Calculate the one-sided p-value for the null hypothesis of no improvement (over the old value of 14,000 hours).

c. At the one-sided 5% error level, is the new process discernibly better? That is, can H_0 be rejected? Answer in two ways, making sure that both answers agree:

i. Is H_0 excluded from the 95% confidence interval?

ii. Does the p-value for H_0 fall below 5%?

9-26 Repeat Problem 9-25, with the appropriate changes in wording, for the following data (from Katz, 1973):

The mean of a random sample of ten men professors' salaries was 16 (thousand dollars, annually); the mean of a random sample of five women professors' salaries was only 11. The pooled variance s_p^2 was 11.7.

CHAPTER 9 SUMMARY

9-1 The values inside a 95% confidence interval are called acceptable hypotheses (at the 5% error level), while the values outside are called rejected hypotheses. The no-difference hypothesis is called the null hypothesis H_0; when it is rejected, a difference is established and so the result is called statistically discernible (significant).

9-2 The p-value is defined as the chance of getting a value of $\overline{X}$ as large as the one actually observed, if H_0 were true. That is, it is the tail area (of the distribution centered on μ_0) beyond the observed value of $\overline{X}$. The p-value therefore summarizes how much credibility the data attributes to H_0.

9-3 For a classical test, we reject H_0 if its p-value (credibility) falls below a specified error level α (usually 5%). Alternatively, a classical test can be set up with extreme values of $\overline{X}$ forming a "rejection region," which is particularly useful for repetitive situations such as industrial quality control. Whenever $\overline{X}$ falls into this extreme region, H_0 is rejected.

***9-4** Classical tests may be misleading—especially if H_0 is acceptable on the basis of a small sample, or H_0 is rejected on the basis of a very large sample.

***9-5** When the alternative hypothesis H_A is true, the luck of the draw may erroneously lead us to conclude that H_0 is acceptable. The chance of this "type II error" is called β, and the graph of β is called the OCC (operating characteristics curve).

***9-6** The two-sided p-value is double the one-sided p-value, and is appropriate whenever the alternative hypothesis is two-sided. An hypothesis test using the two-sided p-value is equivalent to a test using a two-sided confidence interval.

REVIEW PROBLEMS

9-27 Walking along a railroad track in a daydream, suppose you are suddenly aware of a loud noise right behind you. What would be the type I error? Type II error? Which is more serious? So what would you do?

9-28 Suppose an economist concludes that a difference in sample means is "statistically significant (discernible) at the 1% level." Answer True or False; if False, correct it.

a. The p-value for H_0 (population means are exactly equal) is more than 1%.

b. The difference would also be statistically significant at the 5% level.

c. If there were no difference in the population means, the chance of getting such a difference (or more) in the sample means is 1% or less.

d. The economist's conclusion is sound evidence that a difference in population means does exist. Yet it doesn't indicate whether or not this difference is large enough to be of practical importance. This illustrates that statistical significance and practical significance are two entirely different concepts.

9-29 In Boston in 1968, Dr. Benjamin Spock, a famous pediatrician and activist against the Vietnamese war, was tried for conspiracy to violate the Selective Service Act (Military Draft). The judge who tried Dr. Spock had the following interesting record (a simplified version of Zeisel and Kalven, 1978).

Of the 700 people the judge had selected for jury duty in his previous trials, only 15% were women. Yet in the city as a whole, about 29% of the eligible jurors were women.

a. Let π denote the probability that a juror drawn by the judge is a woman. Then to test the judge's fairness in selecting women, what should H_0 be?

b. Calculate the p-value (one-sided) for the null hypothesis.

c. At the level $\alpha = 5\%$, can H_0 be rejected?

9-30 ***A Final Challenge: Can Quality Control Cut Costs?***

A firm manufacturing a small but intricate switch found that even when everything was going right, 20% of them were defective.

And when trouble developed somewhere in the production process, 60% were defective. It was therefore important to detect trouble without delay.

Ted Knudsen, production vice president, proposed the following quality control test: A sample of 10 switches would be randomly drawn from the first hour's production each day. If 3 or more of the 10 switches were defective, production would be shut down to look for the trouble.

a. His most experienced supervisor argued that even when production was "in control" (everything going right), the sample would sometimes, just by the luck of the draw, include enough defectives to sound a false alarm and shut down the process unnecessarily. What is the probability of this? And what is this probability called, in the language of hypothesis testing?

b. After talking to the marketing vice president, who has been getting a lot of flack for an unreliable product, Ted recognizes he has another headache. If production does go "out of control" with about 60% defective, then by chance the sample may not include enough defectives to shut down the process. What is the probability of this missed alarm? And what is this probability called?

c. Can Ted reduce costs by selecting a different sample size rather than the arbitrary $n = 10$ set in the test above? And a different critical number of defectives, instead of the arbitrary $k = 3$? To answer these questions, he first tracks down the following cost information:

1. Past records indicate that production goes "out of control" about 5% of the days. Then if there is a missed alarm, it costs about $18,000 to replace the additional defectives produced unnecessarily.
2. On the other hand, if production is in control and is erroneously stopped by a false alarm, the estimated cost is $3000.
3. The final cost to consider is the cost of each sample. There is a $100 fixed cost, plus $10 for each item sampled and tested.

Calculate the total cost (daily average) associated with faulty production and its detection under the proposed sampling plan (to ring the alarm if there are $k = 3$ or more defectives in a sample of 10).

Further Analysis to Optimize Sampling

In the same way as part **c**, let us calculate the total cost under some more sampling alternatives.

d. As a basis for comparison, what is the total cost under the old system, which used no sampling at all?

e. Would the total cost calculated in part **c** be reduced if k were increased from 3 defectives, to 4? Then 5? Then 6?

f. Would it be better to sample more than 10 switches? Try sampling 12 switches and find the best critical number k.

g. Advanced "Bayesian" techniques prove that the optimal sampling scheme is: $n = 18$ and $k = 8$. How low does this make the total cost?

h. Briefly summarize your analysis for Ted Knudsen.

CHAPTER 10

Analysis of Variance (ANOVA)

Models are to be used, not believed.

HENRI THEIL

10-1 ONE-WAY ANOVA

In Chapters 8 and 9, we made inferences about one population mean, and then compared two means. Now we will compare several means.

As an illustration, suppose that three machines are to be compared. Because these machines are operated by people, and because of other, inexplicable reasons, output per hour is subject to chance fluctuation. In the hope of "averaging out" and thus reducing the effect of chance fluctuation, a random sample of 5 different hours is obtained from each machine and set out in Table 10-1, where each sample mean is then calculated. (The part of the table below this can be ignored for now.)

A—VARIANCE BETWEEN SAMPLES

The first question is "Are the machines really different?" That is, are the sample means $\bar{X}_1$, $\bar{X}_2$, and $\bar{X}_3$ in Table 10-1 different because of differences in the underlying population means μ_1, μ_2, and μ_3 (where μ_1 represents the life-time performance of the first machine, etc.)? Or may these differences in the $\bar{X}$'s be reasonably attributed to chance fluctuations alone?

To illustrate, suppose that we collect three samples from just *one* machine, as shown in Table 10-2. As expected, sampling fluctuations cause

TABLE 10-1 Sample Outputs of Three Machines

	Machine 1	*Machine 2*	*Machine 3*	
	47	55	54	
	53	54	50	
	49	58	51	
	50	61	51	
	46	52	49	
$\bar{X}_i$	$\bar{X}_1 = 49$	$\bar{X}_2 = 56$	$\bar{X}_3 = 51$	$\bar{\bar{X}} = 52$
$(\bar{X}_i - \bar{\bar{X}})$	−3	4	−1	$\Sigma(\bar{X}_i - \bar{\bar{X}}) = 0$
$(\bar{X}_i - \bar{\bar{X}})^2$	9	16	1	$\Sigma(\bar{X}_i - \bar{\bar{X}})^2 = 26$

TABLE 10-2 Three Sample Outputs of the Same Machine

Sample 1	*Sample 2*	*Sample 3*
49	52	55
55	51	51
51	55	52
52	58	52
48	49	50
$\bar{X}_1 = 51$	$\bar{X}_2 = 53$	$\bar{X}_3 = 52$

small differences in the $\bar{X}$'s in the bottom row even though the μ's in this case are identical. So the question may be rephrased, "Are the differences in the $\bar{X}$'s of Table 10-1 of the same order as those of Table 10-2 (and thus attributable to chance fluctuation), or are they large enough to indicate a difference in the underlying μ's?" The latter explanation seems more plausible; but how do we develop a formal test?

As usual, the hypothesis of "no difference" in the population means is called the null hypothesis:[1]

$$H_0: \mu_1 = \mu_2 = \mu_3 \tag{10-1}$$

A test of this hypothesis first requires a numerical measure of how much the sample means $\bar{X}_i$ differ. We therefore calculate their variance at the bottom of Table 10-1. (This first required a calculation of $\bar{\bar{X}}$, the *grand mean* of the $\bar{X}_i$). Thus we obtain:

$$s_{\bar{X}}^2 = \frac{26}{2} = 13 \tag{10-2}$$

The variance formula we used here, of course, is (2-11)—where $\bar{X}_i$ is substituted for X, and a (the number of sample means or columns) is substituted for n, so that:

$$s_{\bar{X}}^2 = \frac{1}{a-1} \Sigma(\bar{X}_i - \bar{\bar{X}})^2 \tag{10-3}$$

B—VARIANCE WITHIN SAMPLES

The variance between machines that we have just calculated does not tell the whole story. For example, consider the data of Table 10-3, which has the same $s_{\bar{X}}^2$ as Table 10-1, yet more erratic machines that produce large

TABLE 10-3 Sample Outputs of Three Erratic Machines

Machine 1	*Machine 2*	*Machine 3*
50	48	57
42	57	59
53	65	48
45	59	46
55	51	45
$\bar{X}_1 = 49$	$\bar{X}_2 = 56$	$\bar{X}_3 = 51$

[1] All three populations are assumed to be normal, with a common variance σ^2. But the conclusions in this chapter are approximately true for non-normal populations too. And even if variances are unequal among the populations, the conclusions are still approximately true so long as the sample sizes are about equal (the usual case).

Thus ANOVA is called *robust*—just like the two-sample t in Chapter 8.

chance fluctuations within each column. The implications of this are shown in Figure 10-1. In panel (*b*), the machines are so erratic that all samples could be drawn from the same population. That is, the differences in sample means may be explained by chance. On the other hand, the same differences in sample means can hardly be explained by chance in panel (*a*), because the machines in this case are *not* so erratic.

We now have our standard of comparison. In panel (*a*) we conclude that the μ's are different—reject H_0—because the variance in sample means ($s_{\bar{X}}^2$) is large *relative* to the chance fluctuation.

How can we measure this chance fluctuation? Intuitively, it seems to be the spread (or variance) of observed values *within* each sample. Thus we compute the squared deviations within the first sample in Table 10-1:

$$\sum_{t=1}^{n} (X_{1t} - \bar{X}_1)^2 = (47 - 49)^2 + (53 - 49)^2 + \cdots = 30$$

where X_{1t} is the typical observation in the first sample.

Similarly, we compute the squared deviations within the second and third samples, and add them all up. Then we divide by the total d.f. in all three samples ($n - 1 = 4$ in each). We thus obtain the pooled variance s_p^2 (just as we did for the two-sample case in Chapter 8):

$$s_p^2 = \frac{30 + 50 + 14}{4 + 4 + 4} = \frac{94}{12} = 7.83 \tag{10-4}$$

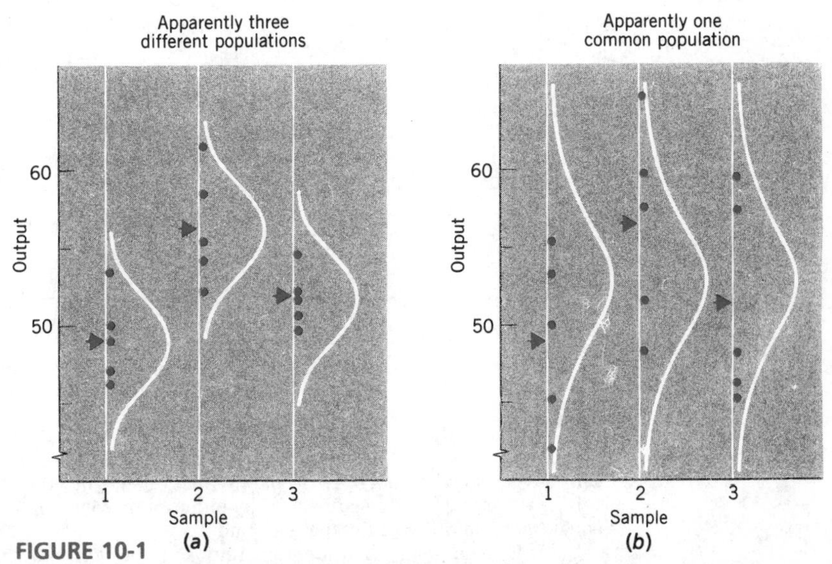

FIGURE 10-1
(a) Outputs of 3 relatively predictable machines (data from Table 10-1) (b) Outputs of 3 erratic machines (data from Table 10-3). They have the same sample means $\bar{X}$, hence the same $s_{\bar{X}}^2$, as the machines in (a).

The generalization is easy to see. If the number of samples is a, with n observations in each sample, then:

$$s_p^2 = \frac{\Sigma(X_{1t} - \bar{X}_1)^2 + \Sigma(X_{2t} - \bar{X}_2)^2 + \cdots}{a(n-1)} \tag{10-5}$$

like (8-21)

C—THE *F* TEST

The key question now can be stated. Is $s_{\bar{X}}^2$ large relative to s_p^2? That is, is the ratio $s_{\bar{X}}^2/s_p^2$ large? It is customary to examine a slightly modified ratio, called F in honor of the renowned English statistician Sir Ronald Fisher (1890–1962):

$$\boxed{F = \frac{ns_{\bar{X}}^2}{s_p^2}} \tag{10-6}$$

Here n has been introduced into the numerator to make it equal on average to the denominator (when H_0 is true)—that is, to make the F ratio fluctuate[2] around 1.

If H_0 is not true (and the μ's are not the same), then $ns_{\bar{X}}^2$ will be relatively large compared to s_p^2, and the F ratio in (10-6) will tend to be much greater than 1. The larger is F, therefore, the less credible is the null hypothesis.

---

[2] Why does F fluctuate around 1? The three samples are drawn from three populations, and when H_0 is true, these populations are identical. We could then regard the three samples as all coming from this one common population. And so there would be two alternative ways of estimating its variance σ^2:

1. Average the variance within each of the three samples. This is s_p^2 in the denominator of (10-6).
2. Or, infer σ^2 from $s_{\bar{X}}^2$, the observed variance between the sample means. Recall how the variance of the sample means ($\sigma_{\bar{X}}^2$, which we have so far been referring to as SE²) is related to the variance of the population (σ^2) as follows:

$$\sigma_{\bar{X}}^2 = \frac{\sigma^2}{n}$$

like (6-6)

Thus:

$$\sigma^2 = n\sigma_{\bar{X}}^2$$

This suggests estimating σ^2 with $ns_{\bar{X}}^2$, which is recognized as the numerator of (10-6).

If H_0 is true, we could estimate σ^2 by either of these methods; since the two will be about equal, their ratio F will fluctuate around 1.

But if H_0 is not true, then the numerator in (10-6) will blow up because the difference in population means will result in a large spread in the sample means (large $s_{\bar{X}}^2$). At the same time, the denominator s_p^2 will still estimate σ^2. Then the F ratio will be large.

To measure the credibility of H_0 numerically, we find its p-value—in this case, the probability in the tail of the F distribution beyond the observed value. We get this p-value from Appendix Table VI, which lists the critical values of the F distribution when H_0 is true (just like Table V lists the critical values of t). In Table VI, the F distribution depends on the degrees of freedom in the numerator variance $(a - 1)$, and in the denominator variance $[a(n - 1)]$. This is written briefly as:

$$\text{d.f.} = (a - 1) \text{ and } a(n - 1) \qquad (10\text{-}7)$$

An example is the easiest way to demonstrate the actual calculation of the p-value.

EXAMPLE 10-1
ARE THE MACHINES REALLY DIFFERENT?

For the data in Table 10-1, we have already calculated how much variance there is *between* the 3 sample means:

$$s_{\bar{X}}^2 = 13 \qquad (10\text{-}2) \text{ repeated}$$

and how much residual variance there is *within* the 3 samples (of 5 observations each):

$$s_p^2 = 7.83 \qquad (10\text{-}4) \text{ repeated}$$

a. Calculate the F ratio.

b. Calculate the degrees of freedom for F.

c. Find the p-value for H_0 (no difference in population means).

SOLUTION

a.

$$F = \frac{ns_{\bar{X}}^2}{s_p^2} \qquad (10\text{-}6) \text{ repeated}$$

$$= \frac{5(13)}{7.83} = 8.3$$

b.

$$\text{d.f.} = (a - 1) \text{ and } a(n - 1) \qquad (10\text{-}7) \text{ repeated}$$

$$= (3 - 1) \text{ and } 3(5 - 1)$$

$$= 2 \text{ and } 12 \qquad (10\text{-}8)$$

c. We look up Table VI where d.f. = 2 and 12, and find five critical values listed in a column that we scan down—till we find that the observed F-value of 8.3 lies beyond $F_{.01} = 6.93$. As Figure 10-2 shows, we conclude that:

$$\text{p-value} < .01 \qquad (10\text{-}9)$$

This means that if H_0 were true, there is less than a 1% chance of getting sample means that differ so much. Accordingly we reject H_0 and conclude that the 3 machines in Table 10-1 are different.

EXAMPLE 10-2
SAMPLES THAT SHOW NO DIFFERENCE

a. Calculate the p-value for H_0 using the data in Table 10-2, which showed 3 samples from the same machine. In that case $s_{\bar{X}}^2$ was only 1.0, while s_p^2 was 7.83.

b. Calculate the p-value for H_0, using the data in Table 10-3, which showed 3 erratic machines. Thus s_p^2 took on the large value 39.0, while $s_{\bar{X}}^2$ was 13.0.

SOLUTION

a.

$$F = \frac{5(1)}{7.83} = .64 \qquad (10\text{-}10)$$

Using d.f. = 2 and 12 again, we find the observed F value of .64 falls far short of the first critical value $F_{.25} = 1.56$. Therefore,

$$\text{p-value} >> .25$$

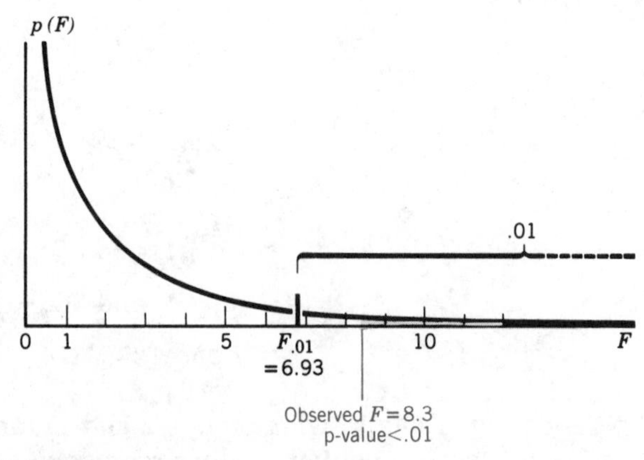

FIGURE 10-2
The *p*-value found using *F* in Table VI (compare to Figure 9-3).

Since the p-value is much greater than .25, H_0 is very credible. This is the correct conclusion, of course, since we generated these 3 samples in Table 10-2 from the same machine.

b.

$$F = \frac{5(13)}{39} = 1.67 \tag{10-11}$$

Using d.f. = 2 and 12 still, we find the observed F value of 1.67 lies just beyond $F_{.25} = 1.56$. Therefore:

$$p\text{-value is just less than } .25$$

This credibility level for H_0 is sufficiently high that we do not reject H_0. The large difference in sample means may well have occurred because each machine is erratic, not because of a difference in machines.

Of course, the F distribution shown in Figure 10-2 is only one of many. As Figure 10-3 illustrates, there is a different F distribution for every combination of d.f. in the numerator and denominator (like the different t distributions in Figure 9-2).

D—THE ANOVA TABLE

The calculations we have done so far can be followed more easily if we summarize them in a table of standard form, called the ANOVA table. As

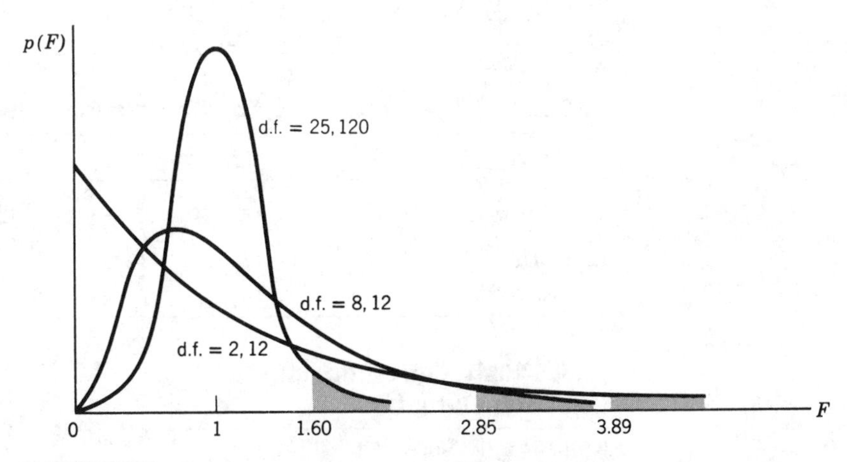

FIGURE 10-3
Some typical F distributions, with various d.f. in the numerator and denominator. Note how the 5% critical point (beyond which H_0 is customarily rejected) moves left toward 1 as d.f. increase.

Table 10-4 shows, it is mostly a bookkeeping arrangement, with the first row showing calculations for the numerator of the F ratio, and the second row for the denominator. Panel (a) gives the ANOVA table in general symbols, while panel (b) gives the numerical results for the data in Table 10-1. Finally, panel (c) gives the same numerical results computed on MINITAB.

In addition, the ANOVA table provides a handy check on our calculations. For example, in Table 10-4b consider each Sum of Squares of deviations (SS, informally called *variation*) in the second column. At the bottom we list the total SS, which is obtained by ignoring the column-by-column structure of the data. That is, we just take all 15 numbers within Table 10-1 and calculate how much each deviates from the overall mean $\bar{\bar{X}}$. All the resulting deviations $(X - \bar{\bar{X}})$ are then squared and summed, to produce the total SS. To indicate that we must sum over the whole table, both rows and columns, we write the Σ sign twice:

TABLE 10-4a ANOVA Table, General

Source of Variation	*Sum of Squares, SS*	*d.f.*	*Mean Square, MS*	*F Ratio*
FACTOR A: differences between machine means $\bar{X}_i$	$SS_A = n \sum_{i=1}^{a} (\bar{X}_i - \bar{\bar{X}})^2$	$(a - 1)$	$MS_A = SS_A/(a-1)$ $= ns_{\bar{X}}^2$	$F = \frac{MS_A}{MS_E}$ $= \frac{ns_{\bar{X}}^2}{s_p^2}$
RESIDUAL (ERROR): differences between observations X_{it} and means $\bar{X}_i$	$SS_E = \sum_{i=1}^{a} \sum_{t=1}^{n} (X_{it} - \bar{X}_i)^2$	$a(n - 1)$	$MS_E = SS_E/a(n-1)$ $= s_p^2$	
TOTAL	$SS = \sum_{i=1}^{a} \sum_{t=1}^{n} (X_{it} - \bar{\bar{X}})^2$	$na - 1$		

TABLE 10-4b ANOVA Table, for Observations Given in Table 10-1

Source	*SS*	*d.f.*	*MS*	*F Ratio*	*p-Value*
MACHINES	130	2	65	$\frac{65}{7.83} = 8.3$	$p < .01$
RESIDUAL	94	12	7.83		
TOTAL	224√	14√			

TABLE 10-4c Corresponding Computer Output

```
ANALYSIS OF VARIANCE
SOURCE      DF        SS         MS         F
FACTOR       2    130.00      65.00      8.30
ERROR       12     94.00       7.83
TOTAL       14    224.00
```

$$\text{total SS} = \Sigma\Sigma(X - \overline{\overline{X}})^2 \tag{10-12}$$

$$= (47 - 52)^2 + (53 - 52)^2 + \cdots + (49 - 52)^2$$

$$= 25 + 1 + \cdots + 9 = 224 \tag{10-13}$$

Then we note that the first two SS in Table 10-4*b* add up to this total—a remarkable result proved generally true in Appendix 10-1:

$$\boxed{\textbf{total SS} = \textbf{SS}_A + \textbf{SS}_E} \tag{10-14}$$

Just as the SS in the second column of Table 10-4*b* add up, so do the d.f. in the next column, which we indicate with a check(√).

When each SS is divided by its appropriate d.f., we obtain the Mean Square (MS, informally called *variance*) in Table 10-4. The variance between columns (machines) is *explained* by the fact that the columns in Table 10-1 may come from different parent populations (machines that perform differently). The residual variance within columns is *unexplained* because it is the random or chance variance that cannot be systematically explained (by differences in machines). Thus F is sometimes referred to as the variance ratio:

$$\boxed{F = \frac{\textbf{explained variance}}{\textbf{unexplained variance}}} \tag{10-15}$$

This suggests a possible means of strengthening the F test. Suppose, for example, that much of the unexplained variance was due to differences in the operators. If we could eliminate operator differences, the denominator of (10-15) would be reduced. With the larger F value that would result, we would have a more powerful test of the machines (i.e., we would be in a stronger position to reject H_0). Thus, our ability to detect whether one factor (machine) is important would be strengthened by introducing another factor (operator) to help explain variance. In fact, we shall carry out precisely this calculation in the next section, two-way ANOVA.

*E—UNEQUAL SAMPLE SIZES

The most efficient design is to make all samples the same size n. However, when this is not feasible, it still is possible to modify the ANOVA calculations. Table 10-5 provides the necessary modifications of Table 10-4 to take into account different sample sizes n_1, n_2, and so on. Note especially that the definition of $\overline{\overline{X}}$ is no longer the simple average of $\overline{X}_i$, but rather a *weighted* average with weights n_i.

TABLE 10-5 Modification of ANOVA Table 10-4 for Unequal Sample Sizes $n_1, n_2, \ldots, n_i, \ldots$

Source	Sum of Squares, SS	d.f.	Mean Square, MS	F Ratio
FACTOR A: differences between machine means $\bar{X}_i$	$SS_A = \sum_{i=1}^{a} n_i(\bar{X}_i - \bar{\bar{X}})^2$	$(a-1)$	$MS_A = SS_A/(a-1)$	$F = \frac{MS_A}{MS_E}$
RESIDUAL (ERROR): differences between observations X_{it} and means $\bar{X}_i$	$SS_E = \sum_{i=1}^{a}\sum_{t=1}^{n_i}(X_{it} - \bar{X}_i)^2$	$\sum_{i=1}^{a}(n_i - 1)$	$MS_E = SS_E/\Sigma(n_i - 1)$	
TOTAL	$SS = \sum_{i=1}^{a}\sum_{t=1}^{n_i}(X_{it} - \bar{\bar{X}})^2$	$\sum_{i=1}^{a} n_i - 1$		

Where $\bar{\bar{X}} \equiv$ the grand average of all the X_{it}:

$$\bar{\bar{X}} \equiv \frac{\Sigma\Sigma X_{it}}{\Sigma n_i} = \frac{\Sigma n_i \bar{X}_i}{\Sigma n_i}$$

PROBLEMS

For Problems 10-1 to 10-3, calculate the ANOVA table, including the p-value for the null hypothesis.

10-1 Twelve plots of land are divided randomly into 3 groups. Fertilizers A and B are applied to the first two groups, while the third group is a control C with no fertilizer. The yields were as follows:

A	B	C
75	74	60
70	78	64
66	72	65
69	68	55

10-2 In a large American university in 1969, the male and female professors were sampled independently, yielding the following annual salaries (in thousands of dollars, rounded. From Katz, 1973):

Men	Women
12	9
11	12
19	8
16	10
22	16

10-3 Suppose a random sample of 5 sales of single-family homes in several cities in 1985 yielded the following prices ($000):

City	*Population*	*Sample of Home Prices*	$\bar{X}$	$\Sigma(X - \bar{X})^2$
Boston	2,800,000	110, 160, 93, 206, 171	148	8,510
Indianapolis	1,200,000	72, 38, 45, 108, 42	61	3,480
Rochester	1,000,000	88, 66, 112, 47, 52	73	2,910
San Diego	2,100,000	57, 81, 181, 165, 106	118	11,410

Reconstructed from *Stat. Abst. of U.S.*, 1987, p. 708.

10-4 How much does household income vary with the education of the householder? Suppose a random sample of 50 households from each of three educational levels in 1985 yielded the following annual incomes (in $000):

School Completed	$\bar{X}$	$\Sigma(X - \bar{X})^2$
Elementary school	17	6,000
High school	26	13,000
4-year college	44	28,000

Reconstructed from *Stat. Abst. of U.S.*, 1987, p. 432.

a. Calculate the ANOVA Table.

b. Is it fair to say that high school education increased household income by almost 50%? And college by about another 50%? Why?

10-5 To reduce costs, a large fast-food chain is thinking of replacing its present cooking oil A with a cheaper oil B. They are concerned, however, that oil B may turn rancid sooner, and so be a short-sighted economy. This logic led them to also consider a more expensive oil C. All three oils were then tried out, 10 times each, in a completely randomized design:

Number of cooking hours oil remains usable

	oil A	*oil B*	*oil C*
	30	32	28
	36	26	40
	⋮	⋮	⋮
$\bar{X}$	33.0	29.0	40.0
$\Sigma(X - \bar{X})^2$	240	363	315
s_x^2	26.7	40.3	35.0

Calculate the ANOVA table to determine whether the differences between oils are discernible.

***10-6** In Problem 10-3, suppose the last three prices were missing from Boston and from Indianapolis (and $\overline{X}$ and $\Sigma(X - \overline{X})^2$ were correspondingly changed). Now calculate the appropriate ANOVA Table.

***10-7** When all n_i are equal to a common value n, verify that the ANOVA Table 10-5 reduces to the ANOVA Table 10-4. Specifically, show that $\overline{\overline{X}}$, SS_A, residual d.f., and total d.f. all reduce to the simpler form of Table 10-4.

10-2 TWO-WAY ANOVA

A—INTRODUCTION

To compare machines in one-way ANOVA in Table 10-1, we took independent random samples of 5 outputs for each of the 3 machines, thus using 15 different operators. We could eliminate a lot of "extraneous noise" by using just 5 operators, and letting each one use all 3 machines. The result is 3 *matched* samples from the 3 machines—where the differences between these samples fortunately reflect just the differences between machines, and *not* differences in operators.

The data we would get would be roughly similar to what we got in Table 10-1. For convenience, let's suppose the numbers just happened to be exactly the same, but in a different order, as shown in Table 10-6. Because of this 2-way classification of the data (by machine and operator) our notation must be complicated somewhat. We now are interested in the average of each operator (each row average $\overline{X}_{\cdot j}$) as well as the average of each machine (each column average $\overline{X}_{i\cdot}$).[3]

Now the picture is clarified; some operators are highly productive (the first and fourth), and some are not. The machines are not that erratic, after all; there is just a wide difference in the productivity of the operators. We will show that an explicit adjustment for this will, just as we hoped, reduce the unexplained variance in the denominator of F in (10-15). Since the numerator will remain unchanged, we will have a larger F ratio, and smaller *p*-value, and consequently stronger grounds for rejecting H_0.

To sum up, it appears that another factor (difference in operators) was indeed responsible for a lot of extraneous noise in our simple one-way

[3] The dot indicates the subscript over which summation occurs. For example:

$$\overline{X}_{i\cdot} = \frac{\sum_{j=1}^{b} X_{ij}}{b}$$

TABLE 10-6 Sample of Production X_{ij} of Three Machines and Five Operators

Given Data, With Averages Calculated					*Operator SS*	
	Machine					
Operator	*i* = 1	2	3	*Operator Means* $\bar{X}_{.j}$	$(\bar{X}_{.j} - \bar{\bar{X}})$	$(\bar{X}_{.j} - \bar{\bar{X}})^2$
j = 1	53	61	51	55	3	9
2	47	55	51	51	−1	1
3	46	52	49	49	−3	9
4	50	58	54	54	2	4
5	49	54	50	51	−1	1
Machine Means $\bar{X}_{i.}$	49	56	51	$\bar{\bar{X}} = 52$	0√	24 × ③ = 72 ← Number of machines, *a*

	Machine SS			
$(\bar{X}_{.j} - \bar{\bar{X}})$	−3	4	−1	0√
$(\bar{X}_{.j} - \bar{\bar{X}})^2$	9	16	1	26 × ⑤ = 130 ← Number of operators, *b*

analysis in the previous section. By removing this noise, we will get a more powerful test of the machines.

B—THE ANOVA TABLE

The formal analysis begins with calculating the familiar machine SS in Table 10-6. Then we similarly calculate the operator SS.

The residual calculation is the trickiest feature. In one-way ANOVA we calculated the residual SS by seeing how far each observation strayed from its fitted value, the machine mean. Now in two-way ANOVA the fitted or predicted values involves the operator mean as well as the machine mean.

For example, how would we predict the output on machine 2 by operator 1? The second machine is relatively good (from the next-to-lowest margin in Table 10-6, we see it is 4 units above average). And the first operator is also relatively good (from the second-last margin on the right, we see she is 3 units above average). Adding these two components to the overall grand mean $\bar{\bar{X}} = 52$ provides the following predicted value $\hat{X}$ of her output on this machine.

$$\text{Predicted } \hat{X}_{21} = 52 + 4 + 3 = 59 \tag{10-16}$$

Comparing this to the observed $X_{21} = 61$, we calculate the residual to be $61 - 59 = 2$.

In general, the predicted value $\hat{X}_{ij}$ is similarly:

$$\hat{X}_{ij} = \underset{\substack{\text{overall}\\ \text{mean}}}{\overline{\overline{X}}} + \underset{\substack{\text{machine}\\ \text{adjustment}}}{(\overline{X}_{i\cdot} - \overline{\overline{X}})} + \underset{\substack{\text{operator}\\ \text{adjustment}}}{(\overline{X}_{\cdot j} - \overline{\overline{X}})} \tag{10-17}$$

And the residual is calculated by comparing this predicted or fitted value with the observed value X_{ij}:

$$\text{Residual} = X_{ij} - \hat{X}_{ij}$$

In Table 10-7 the residual is calculated for all cells; then it is squared and summed as usual, to find the residual SS of 22.

The three SS—machine, operator, and residual—are then summarized in Table 10-8. Panel (*a*) is general, and panel (*b*) is specific to the data of Table 10-6.

Note that the residual SS (94) earlier in Table 10-4*b* has been broken down in Table 10-8*b* into a major component that is explained by operators (72) and a minor remaining residual SS (22). Thus all the component SS still must sum to the total SS in the last line, just as they did earlier in one-way ANOVA. (Appendix 10-2 gives the formal proof):

$$\boxed{\text{total SS} = \text{SS}_A + \text{SS}_B + \text{SS}_E} \qquad \text{(10-18) like (10-14)}$$

C—THE F TEST

Now that we have broken the total SS down into its components, we can test whether there is a discernible difference in machines. We also can test whether there is a discernible difference in operators. In either test, the extraneous influence of the other factor will be taken into account.

TABLE 10-7 Calculation of Residuals from Table 10-6

Fitted Values $\hat{X}_{ij} = \overline{\overline{X}} + (\overline{X}_{i\cdot} - \overline{\overline{X}}) + (\overline{X}_{\cdot j} - \overline{\overline{X}})$			*Residuals* $X_{ij} - \hat{X}_{ij}$		
52	59	54	1	2	−3
48	55	50	−1	0	1
46	53	48	0	−1	1
51	58	53	−1	0	1
48	55	50	1	−1	0

Residual Sum of Squares, $\text{SS}_E = 1^2 + 2^2 + \ldots + 0^2 = 22$

TABLE 10-8a Two-Way ANOVA, General

Source	Sum of Squares, SS	d.f.	Mean Square, MS	F
FACTOR A: differences between the a machine means $\overline{X}_{i\cdot}$	$SS_A = b\sum_{i=1}^{a}(\overline{X}_{i\cdot} - \overline{\overline{X}})^2$	$a - 1$	$MS_A = \frac{SS_A}{a-1}$	$\frac{MS_A}{MS_E}$
FACTOR B: differences between the b operator means $\overline{X}_{\cdot j}$	$SS_B = a\sum_{j=1}^{b}(\overline{X}_{\cdot j} - \overline{\overline{X}})^2$	$b - 1$	$MS_B = \frac{SS_B}{b-1}$	$\frac{MS_B}{MS_E}$
RESIDUAL (ERROR): differences between actual observations X_{ij} and fitted values $\hat{X}_{ij} = \overline{X}_{i\cdot} + \overline{X}_{\cdot j} - \overline{\overline{X}}$	$SS_E = \sum_{i=1}^{a}\sum_{j=1}^{b}(X_{ij} - \overline{X}_{i\cdot} - \overline{X}_{\cdot j} + \overline{\overline{X}})^2$	$(a-1) \times (b-1)$	$MS_E = \frac{SS_E}{(a-1)(b-1)}$	
TOTAL	$SS = \sum_{i=1}^{a}\sum_{j=1}^{b}(X_{ij} - \overline{\overline{X}})^2$	$ab - 1$		

TABLE 10-8b Two-Way ANOVA, for Observations Given in Table 10-6

Source	SS	d.f.	MS	F	p-Value
Machines	130	2	65	23.6	$p < .001$
Operators	72	4	18	6.5	$p < .05$
Residual	22	8	2.75		
Total	224√	14√			

On the one hand, we test for differences in machines by constructing the F ratio:

$$F = \frac{\text{variance explained by machines}}{\text{unexplained variance}} \quad (10\text{-}19) \text{ like } (10\text{-}15)$$

Specifically, from Table 10-8b, we have:

$$F = \frac{65}{2.75} = 23.6$$

If H_0 is true, this has an F distribution. We therefore look up Table VI, with d.f. = 2 and 8, and find the observed F value of 23.6 lies beyond $F_{.001} = 18.5$. Therefore:

$$\text{p-value} < .001$$

This is stronger evidence against H_0 than we got from one-factor ANOVA in (10-9). The denominator is much smaller, since the effect of the operators' differences has been netted out.[4] Thus, our statistical leverage on H_0 has been increased.

Similarly, we can get a powerful test of the null hypothesis that the operators perform equally well. Once again, F is the ratio of explained to unexplained variance, but this time, of course, the numerator is the variance between operators. Thus:

$$F = \frac{\text{variance explained by operators}}{\text{unexplained variance}} = \frac{18}{2.75} = 6.5 \qquad (10\text{-}20)$$

We look up Table VI, with d.f. = 4 and 8, and find the observed F value of 6.5 lies beyond $F_{.05} = 3.84$. Therefore:

$$p\text{-value} < .05$$

Accordingly, we could conclude that at the 5% level, there is a discernible (significant) difference in operators.

D—THE IMPORTANCE OF EXPERIMENTAL DESIGN

Recall that in one-way ANOVA (Table 10-1) we took *independent* random samples of 5 outputs from each of the 3 machines, thus using 15 randomly chosen operators altogether (the "Completely Randomized Design," CRD).

On the other hand, in two-way ANOVA, we just use 5 randomly chosen operators. Then the first operator runs all three machines, to give the first line of Table 10-6—a matched block of data. Then the second operator runs all three machines, to give the second matched block, and so on (the "Randomized Blocks Design," RBD).

These matched blocks provide precisely the same advantage as the matched pairs in Chapter 8. Recall that to compare the fall and spring grades of a class (in Table 8-3), the best approach was not two independent random samples. Instead, we took the *same* students' grades in the spring as in the fall, to get *matched pairs* of grades. Similarly in this chapter, by taking the *same* operators on all three machines, we get *matched blocks* of outputs.

E—FURTHER COMPLICATIONS

1. Just as we took into account 2 variables—machines and operators—in the 2-way ANOVA developed above, in more complex studies we

[4] Specifically, note that in one-factor ANOVA, differences in operators are not taken into account, so they contribute to the relatively large residual variance of 7.83 in Table 10-4*b*.
On the other hand, in two-factor ANOVA, differences in operators *are* taken into account. The residual variance left over after netting out these differences in operators is consequently the much smaller value of 2.75 in Table 10-8*b*.

may wish to take 3 or 4 variables into account, using 3- or 4-way ANOVA. As we add more variables, we sharpen our tests by further reducing the residual variance.

2. In our treatment of two-way ANOVA, we have assumed a simple "additive model," where the effects of the two factors are simply added together as in (10-16). That is, we have assumed there is no interaction between the two factors—as would occur, for example, if certain operators did unusually well on certain machines. Such interaction would require several observations per cell, and a more complex ANOVA table.

3. There may also be a problem of missing data. Suppose, for example, that the first cell in Table 10-6 is blank. In calculating the machine means, is it fair simply to ignore it? The answer is no, because the first cell corresponds to one of the better operators, and ignoring it would unfairly depress the average of the first machine. So something more subtle must be done, as we will see in Section 14-2.

PROBLEMS

10-8 To refine the experimental design of Problem 10-1, suppose that the 12 plots of land are on 4 blocks (3 plots on each). Since you suspect that there may be a difference in fertility between blocks, you retabulate the data in Problem 10-1, according to fertilizer *and* block, as follows:

	Fertilizer		
Block	A	B	C
1	69	72	60
2	75	74	64
3	70	78	65
4	66	68	55

For this *randomized blocks design*, calculate the ANOVA table, including the *p*-value for the two null hypotheses.

10-9 Three men work on an identical task of packing boxes. The number of boxes packed by each in three selected hours is shown in the table below.

	Man		
Hour	A	B	C
11–12 A.M.	24	19	20
1–2 P.M.	23	17	14
4–5 P.M.	25	21	17

Calculate the ANOVA table, including the p-value for the two null hypotheses.

10-10 Three methods of estimating inventory value were used at the end of each month, for a six-month period, thus producing the following 18 estimates:

	Month						
Method	*J*	*F*	*M*	*A*	*M*	*J*	*Averages*
Method 1	14	12	16	15	10	11	13
Method 2	18	16	17	19	13	13	16
Method 3	16	14	12	14	13	9	13
Averages	16	14	15	16	12	11	14

Part of the ANOVA table is given below. Finish it.

Source	SS
Between months	66
Between methods	36
Residual	
Total	124

***10-11** Any number of factors can be studied by ANOVA, not just one or two. For example, suppose that Problem 10-8 was extended to also investigate two different seed varieties—X and Y. The data would then start out like this:

		Fertilizer		
Block 1	*Seed*	*A*	*B*	*C*
	X	69	72	60
	Y	73	78	65

		Fertilizer		
Block 2	*Seed*	*A*	*B*	*C*
	X	75	74	64
	Y	80	77	68

·
·
·

Block 4

If we assume as usual the simple additive model, the ANOVA table would then start out like this:

Source	*SS*	*d.f.*	*MS*	*F*	*p-Value*
Fertilizers	608	2			
Seeds	183	1			
Blocks	261	3			
Residual	___	___	___	_	___
Total	1152				

Complete the ANOVA table.

10-3 CONFIDENCE INTERVALS

A—A SINGLE CONFIDENCE INTERVAL

So far we have concentrated on testing the null hypothesis of no difference between means. But it is often more useful to find *confidence intervals* for the differences (as we noted already on page 318, and again in Appendix 10-3). To compare two means, we can use the familiar formula:

$$(\mu_1 - \mu_2) = (\bar{X}_1 - \bar{X}_2) \pm t_{.025}\, s \sqrt{\frac{1}{n_1} + \frac{1}{n_2}} \qquad \text{(10-21) like (8-20)}$$

where

μ_1, μ_2 = the two population means to be compared;
$\bar{X}_1, \bar{X}_2$ = the two corresponding sample means (for example, the first two column means);
n_1, n_2 = the number of observations that we average to get $\bar{X}_1$ and $\bar{X}_2$;
s^2 = the residual variance in the ANOVA table (also called MS_E);
$t_{.025}$ = the t value with d.f. associated with s^2 in the ANOVA table.

This is just like the original formula (8-20), except for the more reliable value of s that contains as much information as possible about the unknown σ.

We could equally well have used subscripts 2 and 3 if we had wanted to compare the second and third means; or we could similarly compare *any* pair of means. An example will illustrate.

EXAMPLE 10-3
HOW MUCH BETTER IS THE SECOND MACHINE?

Construct a 95% confidence interval for the difference between the second and third machines in Table 10-1 (whose ANOVA calculations were given in Table 10-4*b*).

SOLUTION

We substitute the appropriate quantities into (10-21). We are careful to use $s^2 = 7.83$ from the ANOVA Table 10-4*b*, and its corresponding d.f. = 12 for the $t_{.025}$ value. Thus:

$$(\mu_2 - \mu_3) = (56 - 51) \pm 2.18\sqrt{7.83}\sqrt{\frac{1}{5} + \frac{1}{5}}$$

$$= 5.0 \pm 3.9 \simeq 5 \pm 4 \tag{10-22}$$

At the 95% level of confidence, we can therefore conclude that the second machine is from 1 to 9 units more productive than the third machine.

B—A FAMILY OF CONFIDENCE INTERVALS

In Example 10-3 there are two other differences we could find—between μ_1 and μ_2, and between μ_1 and μ_3. Then all three related confidence intervals could be called a "family":

$$\left.\begin{aligned} \mu_1 - \mu_2 &= -7.0 \pm 3.9 \\ \mu_1 - \mu_3 &= -2.0 \pm 3.9 \\ \mu_2 - \mu_3 &= +5.0 \pm 3.9 \end{aligned}\right\} \tag{10-23}$$

Since *each* of these statements has a 5% chance of being wrong, however, the chance that the whole *family* will somewhere be wrong is nearly 15%. If we want full 95% confidence that *all* the statements are simultaneously correct, we need to increase our confidence in each statement by using a broader confidence allowance. Therefore we replace $t_{.025}$ in (10-21) with the larger allowance:

$$\boxed{\sqrt{(k-1)F_{.05}}} \tag{10-24}$$

When we substitute (10-24) into (10-21), we get the desired family of confidence intervals:

With 95% confidence, all the following intervals are simultaneously true:

$$(\mu_1 - \mu_2) = (\bar{X}_1 - \bar{X}_2) \pm \sqrt{(k-1)F_{.05}}\, s\sqrt{\frac{1}{n_1} + \frac{1}{n_2}}$$

$$(\mu_1 - \mu_3) = (\bar{X}_1 - \bar{X}_3) \pm \sqrt{(k-1)F_{.05}}\, s\sqrt{\frac{1}{n_1} + \frac{1}{n_3}} \tag{10-25}$$

$$\vdots$$

$$(\mu_{k-1} - \mu_k) = (\bar{X}_{k-1} - \bar{X}_k) \pm \sqrt{(k-1)F_{.05}}\, s\sqrt{\frac{1}{n_{k-1}} + \frac{1}{n_k}}$$

where

n_1 = the number of observations on which the average $\overline{X}_1$ is based. Similarly, $n_2, n_3 \ldots$ are defined.

s^2 = the residual variance in the ANOVA table (also called MS_E).

$F_{.05}$ = the critical value of F that leaves 5% in the upper tail. Its d.f. are given in the ANOVA table—the same d.f. we used in looking up F to find the p-value.

k = the number of means to be compared. For example, in one-way ANOVA (Table 10-1) it would be the number of columns (3 machines). In two-way ANOVA (Table 10-6) it could be the number of columns (3 machines), or the number of rows (5 operators).

EXAMPLE 10-4
WHAT DIFFERENCES ARE THERE AMONG *ALL* MACHINES?

Construct a family of simultaneous 95% confidence intervals for *all* the differences between machines in Table 10-1 (whose ANOVA calculations were given in Table 10-4*b*).

SOLUTION

The $t_{.025}$ value used in Example 10-3 is now replaced with $\sqrt{(k-1)F_{.05}}$. Here k = the number of machines to be compared (3), and the d.f. for $F_{.05}$ are 2 and 12 as already calculated in the ANOVA Table 10-4*b*. Thus from Table VI, $F_{.05} = 3.89$, and so (10-25) becomes:

$$\mu_1 - \mu_2 = (49 - 56) \pm \sqrt{(3-1)3.89}\,\sqrt{7.83}\,\sqrt{\frac{1}{5} + \frac{1}{5}}$$

That is,

Similarly,

$$\left.\begin{aligned} \mu_1 - \mu_2 &= -7.0 \pm 4.9 \\ \mu_1 - \mu_3 &= -2.0 \pm 4.9 \\ \mu_2 - \mu_3 &= +5.0 \pm 4.9 \end{aligned}\right\} \tag{10-26}$$

These allowances in (10-26) are vaguer than they were in (10-23)—the price we pay for *simultaneous* confidence in the whole family of statements.

PROBLEMS

10-12 **a.** Construct a family of 95% simultaneous confidence intervals for Problems 10-1 and 10-2.

b. Do the same for Problems 10-8 and 10-9.

10-13 An executive moving from Rochester to San Diego in 1985 was interested in comparing average house prices in the two cities. Using the data in Problem 10-3, construct the appropriate confidence interval:

a. That has 95% confidence, by itself.

b. That can be included with all other comparisons, at the 95% simultaneous confidence level.

10-14 A sociologist sampled 25 incomes from each of 8 groups, and then tested H_0 with a one-factor ANOVA F test. He then proposed to compare every possible pair using the 95% confidence interval (10-21) based on t. (The value of s_p^2 was obtained by pooling all 8 groups.)

a. How many such pairs are there to be compared?

b. Then what is the expected number that will be wrong?

c. If he wanted 95% certainty that *all* these confidence intervals will be right, by how much should he increase their width?

CHAPTER 10 SUMMARY

10-1 When more than two population means are to be compared, we need an extension of the two-sample t test. This is provided by the F test, which compares the variance explained by differences *between* the sample means, with the unexplained variance *within* the samples. The ANOVA table provides an orderly way to calculate F, step by step, to test whether the factor is statistically discernible.

10-2 A second factor can be introduced—not only for its own intrinsic interest, but also to sharpen the analysis of the first factor. For this two-factor ANOVA, we have shown just the simplest additive model, without interaction.

10-3 ANOVA can be used to construct confidence intervals as well as test hypotheses. To compare all possible differences among a set of means, we simply broaden the ordinary confidence interval by replacing $t_{.025}$ with $\sqrt{(k-1)F_{.05}}$.

This gives us 95% simultaneous confidence that the whole family of comparisons are true.

REVIEW PROBLEMS

10-15 To compare 3 varieties of potatoes, an experiment was conducted by assigning each variety at random to 3 equal-size plots at each of 3 different soil types. The following yields, in bushels per plot, were recorded:

	Variety of Potato		
Soil	A	B	C
Sand	21	20	16
Clay	16	18	11
Loam	23	31	24

a. Construct the ANOVA table.

b. Calculate the family of 95% simultaneous confidence intervals for the differences in the 3 varieties.

***c.** The botanist who developed variety B remarked that he had worked 10 years to find something that grew well in a loam soil. As you glance at the data, do you think he succeeded? In the light of this information, what would you say about your analysis in parts **a** and **b**?

10-16 ***A Final Challenge: What Does Crowding Do To People?***

To study the effect of high population density on human behavior, Freedman (1975, p. 150) did a revealing experiment with about 160 student volunteers. Each student delivered a prepared speech to a small group of about 8 other people, listened to their criticisms, and then reported the extent to which he or she found it to be a good learning experience—the "response variable" X.

The conditions under which each student spoke varied in two ways:

1. The room was either large or small (low or high density).
2. The group of listeners, under instruction from the social scientists conducting the experiment, made comments that were either entirely positive or entirely negative.

Thus each student faced one of the 4 different experimental treatments shown in the 4 cells in the table below.

Since each of the 160 students was assigned at random to one of the 4 treatments, there were about 40 responses X reported in each cell of the table. For simplicity, only the averages are given below. For example, the first entry 2.1 is the average of 40 individual scores:

$$\overline{X} = (2 + 3 + 1 + 3 + \ldots)/40 = 2.1.$$

Average Value of the Learning Experience as a Function of Density and Criticism

	+ criticism	−criticism	average
low density	2.1	1.7	1.9
high density	2.3	1.5	1.9
average	2.2	1.6	1.9

a. From the given averages, estimate the overall or average effect of positive criticism (compared to negative). Similarly, estimate the overall effect of high density (compared to low).

b. Although high density had no *overall* effect in **a**, it did have a statistically discernible effect on learning *when criticism was positive*. How much, would you estimate? Similarly, estimate how much effect high density had *when criticism was negative*?

When the effect of density depends on the level of criticism like this, we say there is *interaction* of density with criticism.

c. Underline the correct choice in each bracket:

i. When the effect of one factor depends on the level of the other factor, we call it (additivity, interaction). By contrast, the simpler model discussed in Section 10-2 assumed each factor had the same effect, regardless of the level of the other factor, and was therefore called (additive, simplex).

ii. What happens if we inadvertently overlook interaction, as we did in part **a**, and just look at the overall effects—called the *main* effects? Then our answer—in this case, "density has no effect"—may be too (simplistic, complex).

iii. We have illustrated this general lesson: Like any other tool, a statistical model needs to be carefully selected to match the problem at hand. Just as we should not use a tack hammer to drive a spike, so we should not use an (additive, interactive) model to analyze an experiment in which one factor may have quite different effects at different levels of the other factor.

iv. Now let's draw some lessons from this interaction. Positive criticism (improves, weakens) learning—and this effect is made (more, less) intense by high density. Negative criticism (improves, weakens) learning—and this effect is made (more, less) intense by high density.

In conclusion, high density (intensifies, reduces) the effect of criticism on learning.

Epilogue

If high population density is an intensifier in general, some important conclusions for our large cities can be drawn: To the extent they are made positive environments, their high population density will make them even more attractive.

The author himself nicely summarizes this issue (Freedman 1975, p. 112): "It would be a great misfortune for the cities to decline in population, for any government agency to encourage a decrease in the concentration of people in the cities, or for anyone to think that the solution to society's problems lies even in part in depopulating the urban centers."

It is satisfying to find randomized controlled experiments like this consistent with the best of the observational studies on population density, such as Problem 1-11 for example.

REVIEW PROBLEMS, CHAPTERS 6 TO 10

10-17 When a new coating was tried out on a random sample of ball bearings, the improvement in wear was estimated (with a 95% confidence interval) to be $\mu = 170 \pm 20$ hours. Answer True or False; if False correct it.

a. Any hypothesis in the interval $150 < \mu < 190$ is called the null hypothesis, while any hypothesis outside this interval is called the alternate hypothesis.

b. The population mean is a random variable with expectation 170 and standard deviation 20.

c. If this sampling experiment were repeated many times, and if each time a confidence interval were similarly constructed, 95% of these confidence intervals would cover $\mu = 170$.

10-18 Hoping to improve the performance of his 88 sales representatives, a sales manager decided to send a random sample of 5 to a highly recommended workshop on selling. Their sales before and after the workshop were:

Sales Rep.	*Sales in the year before ($000)*	*Sales in the year after ($000)*
J.M.	530	660
K.W.	820	880
R.N.	380	470
S.C.	420	740
R.S.	650	600

a. Calculate a 95% confidence interval for the average improvement in sales.

b. On rereading Chapter 1 of his statistics text, he realized that he should be very careful in attributing this improvement to the workshop. He had not used controls!

What confounding factors might be present? Could he make allowance for them, in order to get an unbiased estimate of the effect of the workshop?

10-19 The admissions record for a large Graduate School in 1973 was as follows (same data as Problem 1-18):

	Men		*Women*	
Faculty	*Number of Applicants*	*Number Admitted*	*Number of Applicants*	*Number Admitted*
Arts	2300	700	3200	900
Science	6000	3000	1100	600
Total	8300	3700	4300	1500

a. Construct a 95% confidence interval for the difference in admission rates between men and women for:

i. Arts

ii. Science

iii. The whole school

b. What is the underlying population being discussed in part **a**?

c. In words, summarize the evidence of sex discrimination.

10-20 Answer True or False; if False, correct it:

a. Problems 10-18 and 19 illustrate a crucial principle: Confidence intervals are a useful way to express the uncertainty of an estimate. Yet in observational studies, getting an *unbiased estimate* in the first place is even more important.

b. For randomized controlled experiments that are free of bias, confidence intervals deliver what they promise. That is, intervals of this form cover the true parameter 95% of the time:

$$\text{Parameter} = \text{estimate} \pm \text{SE}$$

10-21 The relationship between oxygen therapy and infant mortality was investigated in a randomized controlled experiment by Schunk and Lehman (1954). All infants who had birth weights between 1000 and 1850 grams and were less than 12 hours old on admission to the nursery were assigned at random either to high oxygen concentration or to low oxygen concentration treatments. The results were as follows:

Concentration of Oxygen	*Three-Month Survival*		
	Died	*Survived*	*Totals*
High	9	36	45
Low	12	28	40
Totals	21	64	85

a. Calculate the appropriate confidence interval to estimate the effect of oxygen concentration on infant mortality.

b. Calculate the p-value for H_0 (no effect).

c. Give a simple verbal interpretation of your answers in **a** and **b**.

10-22 To reduce conflicts among its junior executives, a large corporation tried out two programs (A and B) that taught personal skills. From among their 50 newly hired MBAs, they randomly selected 4 for Program A, and 4 for program B. One year later, each person was ranked by superiors and peers according to openness, cooperation, integrity, and so on, to obtain an overall score. Ranked from best to worst, the scores turned out as follows:

Scores, Program A	Scores, Program B
60	72
50	66
46	52
44	50

At first glance, Program B seems to be better. But is the evidence strong enough to back this up?

a. Calculate the appropriate 95% confidence interval, and state in simple language what it means.

b. Calculate the two-sided p-value for H_0, and state what it means.

c. Are the two programs discernably different, at level $\alpha = 5\%$?

10-23 To help decide whether or not to buy a prime corner lot for a service station, an oil company wanted to estimate the traffic intensity. The number of cars passing by was counted during each of 12 randomly selected hours (from 7 a.m. to 7 p.m., weekdays). The average turned out to be 186 cars per hour and the standard deviation was 84.

Calculate a 95% confidence interval for the mean traffic intensity.

10-24 Each week a hospital administrator monitors the number of deaths in the intensive care unit in order to be warned if anything starts to go wrong. Over the past year when everything was working well, records showed that 7% of the admitted patients died.

At present, approximately 90 patients are admitted each week. The administrator decides that if the number of deaths ever exceed 10 in a given week, an investigation should be automatically initiated.

a. In a year when everything is working well, about how many needless investigations (false alarms) will result from this rule?

b. Suppose a serious uncorrected mistake causes 6 needless deaths in a certain week. What is the chance that this will fail to trigger an investigation (i.e., what is the chance of a missed alarm?)

10-25 In the language of hypothesis testing, what do we customarily call the two errors in Problem 10-24? And their probabilities?

10-26 For each of two education levels, a random sample of 3 American household incomes was drawn in thousands of dollars, 1978):

Education of Householder

8 Years or Less	*9 to 12 Years*
10	18
12	11
8	19

Simulated from *Stat. Abst. of U.S.*, 1980.

Calculate a 95% confidence interval for the mean difference in income:

a. With the ordinary confidence interval (from Chapter 8, using the t table).

b. With the simultaneous confidence interval (from Chapter 10, using the F table).

c. In parts **a** and **b**, did you get the same answer? Did you make the same assumptions? What were these assumptions?

10-27 Repeat Problem 10-26, calculating p-values for H_0 instead of confidence intervals.

10-28

Education of Householder

8 Years or Less (Elementary)	*9 to 12 Years (High School)*	*13 to 15 (College)*	*16 or More (College Completed)*
10	18	15	40
12	11	32	25
8	19	10	16

Simulated from the *Stat. Abst. of U.S.*, 1980.

a. The data above is just an extension of the earlier data in Problems 10-26 and 10-27. Would you guess the p-value for H_0 will be the same as earlier? Why?

Calculate the ANOVA table and p-value to verify your guess.

b. Would you guess the 95% simultaneous confidence intervals for all comparisons will be the same width as earlier? Why?

Calculate them to verify your guess.

10-29 Based on your experience in Problems 10-26 and 10-28, answer True or False; if False, correct it:

a. The traditional comparison of 2 independent samples (using the t table) can be extended to several independent samples (using the F table); this extension is called one-factor ANOVA.

b. In other words, F in ANOVA gives exactly the same answer as t for 2 samples, and then goes on to give answers for any number of samples.

10-30 A household income was randomly drawn from each of 4 U.S. regions and 2 races (in thousands of dollars, 1978):

	Race	
Region	*White*	*Black*
Northeast	18.7	11.7
Northcentral	19.0	13.6
South	17.1	9.9
West	18.8	10.8

Simulated from the *Stat. Abst. of U.S.*, 1980.

Repeat the same questions as in Problems 10-26, 10-27, and 10-29, for the mean difference in household income between races.

10-31 Referring to Problem 10-28, what can we say is the effect on household income of the 8 or more years of education separating the last group from the first?

P A R T 

Regression: Relating Two or More Variables

CHAPTER 11

Fitting a Line

But of all these principles, least squares is the most simple: by the others we would be led into the most complicated calculations.

K. F. GAUSS, 1809

11-1 INTRODUCTION

In practice, we often want to study more than an isolated single variable (by examining, say, its mean). We usually want to look at how one variable is related to other variables—what statisticians call *regression*.

To illustrate, consider how wheat yield depends on the amount of fertilizer applied. If we graph the yield Y that follows from various amounts of fertilizer X, a scatter similar to Figure 11-1 might be observed. From this scatter it seems clear that the amount of fertilizer does affect yield. In addition, it should be possible to describe *how*, by fitting a curve through this scatter. In Chapters 11 and 12, we will stick to the simplest case, where Y is related by a straight line to just one variable X. This is called the *simple regression* of Y against X.

Since yield depends on fertilizer, it is called the *dependent variable* or *response* Y. Since fertilizer application is not dependent on yield, but is determined independently by the experimenter, it is referred to as the *independent variable* or *factor* or *regressor* X.

EXAMPLE 11-1

In a study of how wheat yield depends on fertilizer, suppose that funds are available for only seven experimental observations. So X is set at seven different levels, with one observation Y in each case, as shown in Table 11-1.

a. Graph these points, and roughly fit a line by eye.

b. Use this line to predict yield Y, if fertilizer application X is 400 pounds.

TABLE 11-1 Fertilizer and Yield Observations

X Fertilizer (lb/acre)	Y Yield (bu/acre)
100	40
200	50
300	50
400	70
500	65
600	65
700	80

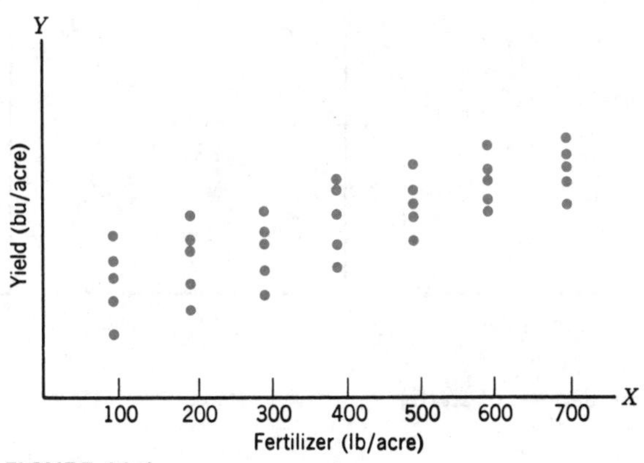

FIGURE 11-1

Observed relation of wheat yield to fertilizer application on 35 experimental plots.

SOLUTION

a. In Figure 11-2 we fit a line by eye to the scatter of observations.

b. With a fertilizer application of $X = 400$ pounds, the predicted yield (denoted with a hat) is the height $\hat{Y} \simeq 60$ bushels. This is the point on the fitted line in Figure 11-2 above the X value of 400. The deviation d of the actual value Y from its predicted value $\hat{Y}$ is of particular interest. Roughly speaking, in fitting the line by eye we have tried to keep this pattern of vertical deviations as small as possible.

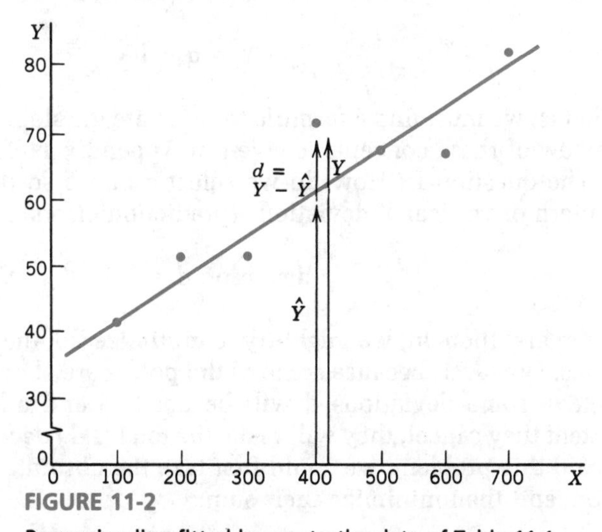

FIGURE 11-2

Regression line fitted by eye to the data of Table 11-1.

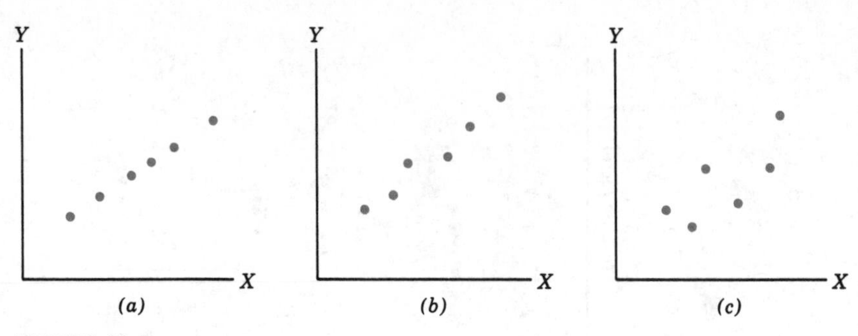

FIGURE 11-3
Various degrees of scatter.

How good is a rough fit by eye, such as we used in Example 11-1? In Figure 11-3, we note in panel (*a*) that if all the points were exactly in a line, then the line could be fitted by eye perfectly accurately. (Since all the points would be on this line, every one of the deviations would be zero.) But as we progress to the highly scattered case in panel (*c*), we need to find another method—a method that is more objective, and is easily computerized. The following section, therefore, sets forth algebraic formulas for fitting a line.

11-2 ORDINARY LEAST SQUARES (OLS)

A—THE LEAST SQUARES CRITERION

Our objective is to fit a line whose equation is of the form

$$\hat{Y} = a + bX \tag{11-1}$$

That is, we must find a formula to calculate the slope b and intercept a. (A review of these concepts is given in Appendix 11-1.)

The question is: How do we select a and b so that we minimize the pattern of vertical Y deviations (prediction errors) in Figure 11-2, where

$$\text{deviation } d = Y - \hat{Y}$$

On first thought, we might try to minimize Σd, the sum of all the deviations. However, because some of the points are above the line and others below, some deviations d will be positive and others negative; to the extent they cancel, they will make the total (Σd) deceptively near zero. To avoid this problem, we could first take the *absolute value* of each deviation, and then minimize their sum:

$$\text{minimize } \Sigma|d| = \Sigma|Y - \hat{Y}|$$

A familiar alternative is to *square* each deviation, and then minimize the sum of all of these:

$$\boxed{\text{minimize } \Sigma d^2 = \Sigma(Y - \hat{Y})^2} \tag{11-2}$$

like (2-10)

This is called the criterion of *Ordinary Least Squares* (OLS), and it selects a unique line called the OLS line.

B—THE LEAST SQUARES FORMULAS

Recall the line to be fitted is

$$\hat{Y} = a + bX \quad \text{(11-1) repeated}$$

The OLS slope b is calculated from the following formula (derived in Appendix 11-2):

$$b = \frac{\Sigma(X - \overline{X})(Y - \overline{Y})}{\Sigma(X - \overline{X})^2} \tag{11-3}$$

The deviations $(X - \overline{X})$ and $(Y - \overline{Y})$ will appear so often that it is worthwhile abbreviating them. Let

$$\left.\begin{aligned} x &\equiv X - \overline{X} \\ y &\equiv Y - \overline{Y} \end{aligned}\right\} \tag{11-4}$$

The small x (or y) notation provides a reminder that the deviations x are typically smaller numbers than the original values X. (This is apparent in the first four columns of Table 11-2). With this notation, the formula for b can now be simplified:

TABLE 11-2 Fitting the OLS Line to the Data of Example 11-1

Data		*Deviation Form*		*Products*	
X	Y	$x = X - \overline{X}$ $= X - 400$	$y = Y - \overline{Y}$ $= Y - 60$	xy	x^2
100	40	−300	−20	6000	90,000
200	50	−200	−10	2000	40,000
300	50	−100	−10	1000	10,000
400	70	0	10	0	0
500	65	100	5	500	10,000
600	65	200	5	1000	40,000
700	80	300	20	6000	90,000
$\overline{X} = 400$	$\overline{Y} = 60$	$\Sigma x = 0\surd$	$\Sigma y = 0\surd$	$\Sigma xy = 16{,}500$	$\Sigma x^2 = 280{,}000$

$$b = \frac{\Sigma xy}{\Sigma x^2} \tag{11-5}$$

Once b is calculated, the intercept a can then be found from another simple formula (also derived in Appendix 11-2):

$$a = \overline{Y} - b\overline{X} \tag{11-6}$$

For the data in Example 11-1, the calculations for a and b are laid out in Table 11-2. We calculate Σxy and Σx^2, and substitute them into (11-5):

$$b = \frac{\Sigma xy}{\Sigma x^2} = \frac{16{,}500}{280{,}000} = .059$$

Then we use this slope b (along with $\overline{X}$ and $\overline{Y}$ calculated in the first two columns of Table 11-2) to calculate the intercept a from (11-6):

$$a = \overline{Y} - b\overline{X} = 60 - .059(400) = 36.4$$

Plugging these estimated values a and b into (11-1) yields the equation of the OLS line:

$$\hat{Y} = 36.4 + .059X \tag{11-7}$$

From its graph in Figure 11-4, we can see how closely this OLS line resembles the fit by eye in Figure 11-2. And it easily gives an estimate of yield for any desired fertilizer application. For example, if $X = 400$ lbs. of fertilizer,

$$\hat{Y} = 36.4 + .059(400) = 60 \text{ bushels} \qquad \text{like (11-7)}$$

C—MEANING OF THE SLOPE b

By definition, the slope of a line is the change in height Y, when we move to the right by one unit in the X direction. That is,

$$\text{Slope } b = \text{change in } Y \text{ that accompanies a unit change in } X \tag{11-8}$$

This is illustrated geometrically in Appendix 11-1. It is so important that we give an alternative algebraic derivation here. Suppose in (11-7), for example, that fertilizer X was increased by 1 unit, from 75 to 76

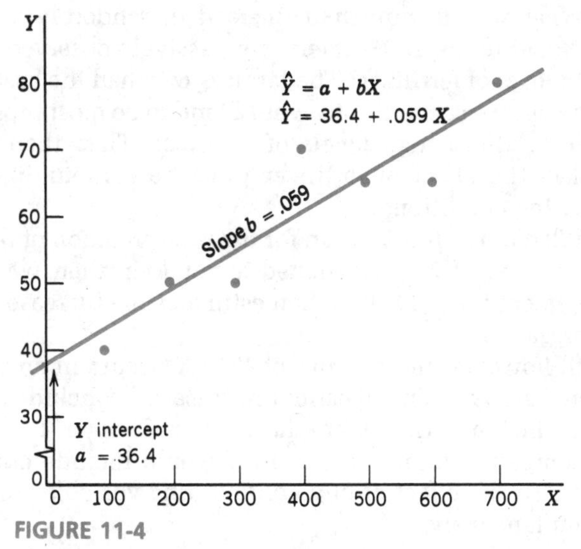

FIGURE 11-4
The least squares line fitted to the data of Example 11-1.

pounds, say. Then to calculate the increase in yield Y:

$$
\begin{aligned}
\text{Initial } Y &= 36.4 + .059(75) \\
\text{New } Y &= 36.4 + .059(75 + 1) \\
&= 36.4 + .059(75) + .059 \\
&= \text{initial } Y + .059
\end{aligned}
$$

That is, Y has increased by .059 as X has increased by 1—which is the slope b. And so (11-8) is established.

D—RANDOMIZED EXPERIMENTS VS. OBSERVATIONAL STUDIES

In Chapter 1 we emphasized the importance of making experiments fair, by randomly assigning treatment and control.

In regression we can similarly eliminate bias by randomly assigning the various levels of X. For example, to study the effect of a new fertilizer on wheat yield, suppose we had to rely on a sample of 100 farmers from across the state.[1] We should assign the highest and lowest level of fertilizer just like we assigned treatment and control in Chapter 1—at random, to be fair. Then the plots with the highest level of fertilizer would on average start out equal to the plots with the lowest level. If we randomly assigned all other levels of fertilizer too, the subsequent regression slope would then reflect the effect of the fertilizer alone.

---

[1] Real agricultural experiments are commonly done all in one experimental station of course, where tight control and matching is possible. We sketch this hypothetical scenario because many social scien experiments have to be done on a scattered volunteer basis like this.

What would happen if, instead of randomly assigning the levels of fertilizer to the 100 farmers, we passively observed how they chose their own level of fertilizer? The farmers who had the best levels of rainfall and other growing conditions would tend to be most prosperous, and the most able to afford high levels of fertilizer. Then their higher yields would reflect the effect of fertilizer plus the confounding effect of the better growing conditions.

What does all this mean for the interpretation of the slope b in (11-8)? If the values of X are assigned at random, then we can make a stronger statement than (11-8): b then estimates the increase in Y *caused* by a unit increase in X.

If, however, the relation of Y to X occurs in an uncontrolled observational study, then we cannot necessarily conclude anything about causation. In that case, as emphasized in Chapter 1, the increase in Y that accompanies a unit change in X would include not only the effect of X, but also *the effect of any confounding variables* that might be changing simultaneously.

PROBLEMS

11-1 In a pilot study of a new fertilizer, 4 levels were randomly assigned to 4 standard plots, resulting in the following yields of corn:

Fertilizer X (pounds)	*Yield Y* (pounds)
1	70
2	70
4	80
5	100

a. Calculate the regression line of yield against fertilizer.

b. Graph the 4 points and the regression line. Check that the line fits the data reasonably well.

c. Use the regression equation to predict:

i. The yield from 3 pounds of fertilizer.

ii. The yield from 4 pounds of fertilizer.

iii. The increase in yield for every additional pound of fertilizer.

Show these on the graph.

11-2 To see how productivity was related to level of maintenance, a firm randomly selected 5 of its high speed machines for an experiment. Each machine was randomly assigned a different level of maintenance X, and then had its average number of stoppages Y recorded:

Machine	Hours of Maintenance per Week, X	Average Stoppages per Week, Y
A	4	1.6
B	6	1.2
C	8	1.1
D	10	0.5
E	12	0.6

Repeat the same questions as in 11-1, appropriately rephrased.

11-3 During the 1950s, radioactive waste leaked from a storage area near Hanford, Washington, into the Columbia River nearby. For nine counties downstream in Oregon, an index of exposure X was calculated (based on distance from Hanford, and distance of the average citizen from the river, etc.). The cancer mortality Y was also calculated (deaths per 100,000 person-years, 1959–64), giving the following data (Fadeley 1965, via Anderson and Sclove, 1978):

County	Radioactive Exposure X	Cancer Mortality Y
Clatsop	8.3	210
Columbia	6.4	180
Gilliam	3.4	130
Hood River	3.8	170
Morrow	2.6	130
Portland	11.6	210
Sherman	1.2	120
Umatilla	2.5	150
Wasco	1.6	140

From this data, summary statistics were computed:

$$\overline{X} = 4.6 \qquad \overline{Y} = 160$$

$$\Sigma x^2 = 97.0 \qquad \Sigma y^2 = 9400 \qquad \Sigma xy = 876$$

a. Calculate the regression line for predicting Y from X.

b. Estimate the cancer mortality if X were 5.0. And if X were 0.

c. Graph the nine counties, and your answers in parts **a** and **b**.

d. To what extent does this data prove the harmfulness of radioactive exposure?

11-4 Suppose the data in Figure 11-1 was collected by an agricultural research station in Kansas, in order to make recommendations for fertilizer application within the state. Consider two ways the data might have been obtained:

i. Thirty-five farmers are chosen at random from the state, and each one reports his average yield Y and fertilizer application X for the current crop of wheat.

ii. Thirty-five one-acre plots of land are chosen at random from the state; the seven levels of fertilizer are assigned at random to these plots, and applied by the agricultural station. Although each farmer's permission must be obtained, of course, he is not told what level of fertilizer was assigned, and is instructed to care for his plot in the usual fashion.

a. Which method is likely to give the better estimate of the value of fertilizer?

b. Can you suggest an easier and perhaps more effective way to collect the data?

11-3 ADVANTAGES OF OLS AND WLS

Ordinary least squares (OLS) is the basis for developing many of the other formulas that appear in Chapters 11 through 15. Since it is used so extensively, we should ask just why it is chosen as the criterion for fitting a line (that is, selecting a and b). For example, why didn't we instead minimize the *absolute* deviations? There are several good reasons:

1. OLS leads to relatively simple formulas for calculating a and b, as we have just seen in Section 11-2.
2. OLS is closely related to ANOVA, as we will see in Chapter 14.
3. The squaring that occurs in (11-2) is like the squaring that occurred in defining the variance s^2 in Chapter 2. The analogy goes further: In the special case where Y has no relation to X (i.e., the slope b is zero), then the OLS fit (11-1) becomes simply

$$\hat{Y} = a$$

But noting (11-6) and the zero value of b in this special case, a becomes $\overline{Y}$; thus,

$$\hat{Y} = \overline{Y} \qquad (11\text{-}9)$$

That is, the best prediction we can make of Y is just the sample mean $\overline{Y}$. The sample mean is therefore a special case of OLS. In other words, OLS can be viewed as an extension of the sample mean.

4. Since OLS is an extension of the sample mean, it has many of the same attractive properties. For example, OLS is often efficient and unbiased.

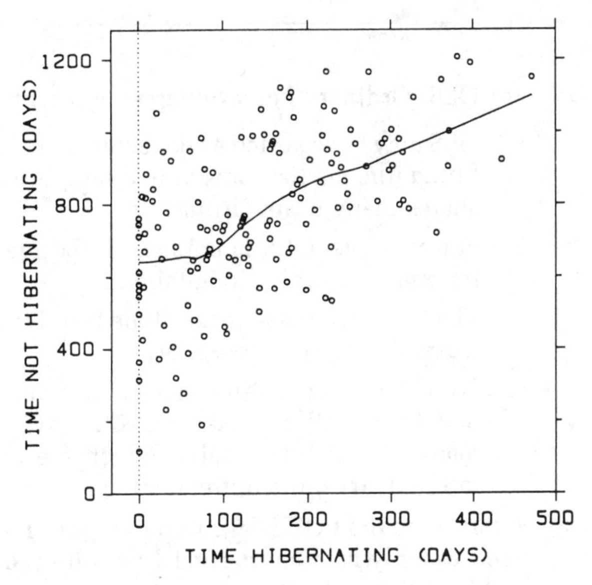

FIGURE 11-5
LOWESS curve showing the average relation of time awake to time hibernating in the lifetime of 144 hamsters (Cleveland 1985, p. 170).

5. The OLS criterion involves summing up all the squared deviations, giving equal weight to each. But if some observations are less reliable than others, we could easily give them less weight. The resulting weighted regression (Weighted Least Squares, WLS) can be very flexible and robust.

This flexibility of weighted regressions is so important it deserves more comment. Suppose, for example, in Figure 11-4 the second observation had a Y value of 80 rather than 50. Such an outlier would have a great influence, and produce a regression line dramatically different from the one shown. To reduce the effect of this outlier, we could give it a smaller weight—that is, use weighted regression.

One of the most ingenious forms of weighted regression is called LOWESS (Locally Weighted Scatterplot Smoother, Cleveland 1985). It is appropriate for a "scatterplot"—a large number of points broadly spread out, such as Figure 11-5. Note how hard it is for the eye to discern the pattern: Is it linear or not? Roughly speaking, LOWESS uses weighted regression to fit the first few points with a little piece of line, then moves on to the next few points with another little piece of fitted line, and so on. These little pieces are then strung together and smoothed, to trace out a curve relating Y to X. This procedure is effortlessly done on a computer, and is less influenced by outliers than is OLS.

PROBLEMS

11-5 For OLS (Ordinary Least Squares), underline the correct choice:

a. OLS may be regarded as the extension of a familiar technique—fitting [the median, mean] to a sample as in Chapter 2—and so shares many of its virtues.

b. For example, OLS is efficient if the underlying population is [normal, extremely long-tailed].

c. The OLS formulas for the slope b and intercept a are relatively [easy, difficult] to compute.

d. Weighted least squares or WLS is a very flexible modification of [OLS, MAD]. For example [BLUE, LOWESS] uses WLS to fit many bits of line locally, which are then strung together to form a [curve, the optimal straight line].

11-6 Referring to the LOWESS curve in Figure 11-5, it could be summarized roughly as a short level line followed by a long rising line with a slope of about ____.

CHAPTER 11 SUMMARY

11-1 To show how a response Y is related to a factor (regressor) X, a line can be fitted called the regression line, $\hat{Y} = a + bX$.

11-2 Using the criterion of ordinary least squares (OLS), the slope b and intercept a can be calculated from simple formulas. The slope b gives the change in Y that accompanies a unit change in X.

11-3 OLS has many advantages: It is simple; like ANOVA, it is an extension of the sample mean, and therefore is often efficient and unbiased; and it is easily modified to give unreliable observations less weight.

REVIEW PROBLEMS

11-7 Suppose a random sample of 4 pharmaceutical firms had the following profits and research expenditures:

Profit, P (Thousands of Dollars)	*Research Expenditure, R (Thousands of Dollars)*
50	40
60	40
40	30
50	50

a. Fit a regression line of P against R.

b. Graph the data and the fitted line.

c. How well does this regression line show how research generates profits for pharmaceutical firms?

11-8 ***A Final Challenge: The Origin of the Term "Regression" Line.***

Each of the 300 dots in this figure represents a pair of heights: a son's height Y plotted against his father's height X. Note that very few sons are exactly the same height as their father (i.e., very few dots are on the 45° line where $Y = X$). Instead, the dots are scattered quite widely around the 45° line, in a pattern very similar to a classic study carried out about 1900 by a geneticist (Galton and Lee, 1903).

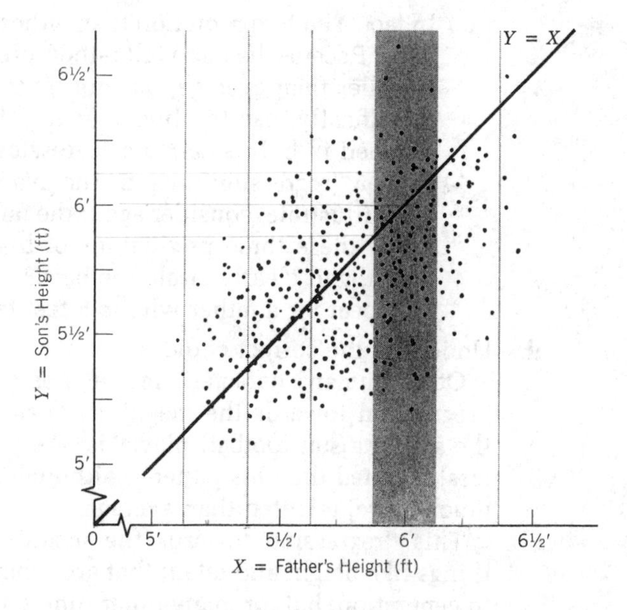

a. Suppose we had to predict the height of the son, if we know the father is 6 feet. The relevant father-son pairs are those in the shaded vertical strip above 6 feet.

Roughly guessing by eye, mark the average son's height Y in this strip with a small horizontal bar. This average height of course represents the best prediction. Repeat for all the other fathers' heights (from $5\frac{1}{4}$, $5\frac{2}{4}$, up to $6\frac{1}{4}$ ft).

These predicting bars lie roughly on a line. Sketch it in, by eye.

b. Calculate the OLS line of Y against X from the following summary statistics (in feet):

$$\overline{X} = 5.8 \qquad \overline{Y} = 5.8$$

$$\Sigma x^2 = 18.3 \qquad \Sigma y^2 = 19.0$$

$$\Sigma xy = 9.1$$

Graph this line, marking it $\hat{Y} = a + bX$. How does it compare to the line in (**a**)?

c. There are several ways to predict a son's height:

i. Put complete faith in the father's height, and predict that the son's height will be the same, that is, use the line $Y = X$.

ii. Pay no attention at all to the father's height, and predict that the son's height will be the same as the average $\overline{Y}$ given in **b**. In other words, to predict the son's height use the horizontal line $Y = 5.8$ feet. Graph this line.

iii. In fact, a better prediction than either of these is a compromise: Because he has a tall father, predict that the son will be taller than average, but not quite so tall as his father. Specifically, use the line $\hat{Y} = a + bX$ you have already graphed in **b**. It is called a regression line, since it represents a "regression towards the average".

To illustrate, consider again the father who is 6 feet tall. Show these three predictions of his son's height on the graph, and clearly circle the best.

Repeat for a father who is 5 feet tall.

d. Underline the correct choice:

Other human characteristics such as talent follow the same "regression towards the mean" as does height. For example, the son of a star football player is likely to be [more, equally, less] talented than his father—[although still more, and much much more] talented than average.

This "regression towards the mean" occurs not only for things like height and talent that are inherited from generation to generation, but for many other time series too. For example, if we look at relative corporate performance from year to year, we often find that the star performers last year tend to perform [even better, equally, not so well] this year—[although still better, and much much better] than average.

A common explanation for this regression toward the mean is that a very high performance often represents luck as well as skill. After the luck disappears, only the skill remains. While this skill will keep performance better than average, without luck performance [will not, still will] attain its original very high level.

CHAPTER 12

Simple Regression

To err is human, to forgive divine—but to include errors in your design is statistical.

LESLIE KISH

So far, our treatment of a sample scatter of observations has been descriptive: We have just summarized it with a fitted line. Now we wish to make inferences about the parent population from which this sample was drawn. To do so, we must build a statistical model that allows us to construct confidence intervals and test hypotheses.

12-1 THE REGRESSION MODEL

A—SIMPLIFYING ASSUMPTIONS

Suppose in Figure 12-1*a* that we set fertilizer at level X_1 for many, many plots. The resulting yields will not all be the same, of course; the weather might be better for some plots, the soil might be better for others, and so on. Thus we would get a distribution (or population) of Y values, appropriately called the probability distribution of Y_1 given X_1, or $p(Y_1|X_1)$. There will similarly be a distribution of Y_2 at X_2, and so forth. We can therefore visualize a whole set of Y populations such as those shown in Figure 12-1*a*. There would obviously be great problems in analyzing populations as peculiar as these. To keep the problem manageable, therefore, we make three assumptions about the regularity of these Y distributions—as shown in Figure 12-1*b*:

1. *Homogeneous Variance:* All the Y distributions have the same spread. Formally, this means that the probability distribution $p(Y_1|X_1)$ has the same variance σ^2 as $p(Y_2|X_2)$ and so on.

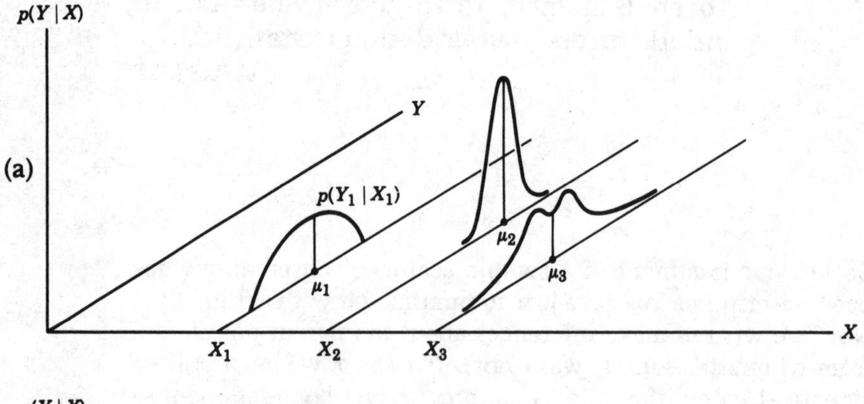

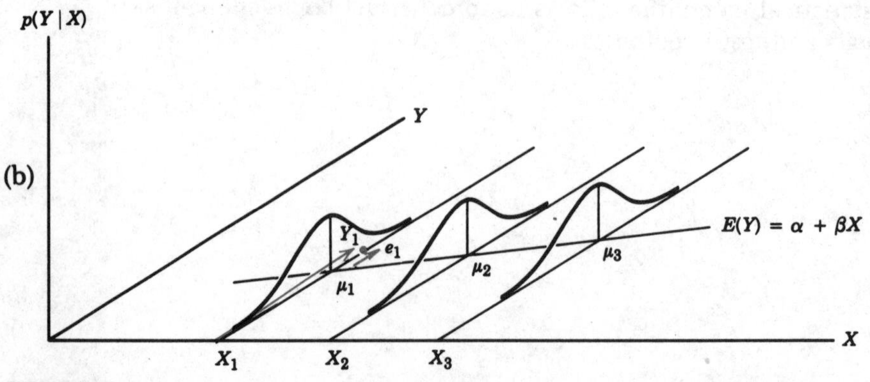

FIGURE 12-1
(a) General populations of Y, given X. (b) The special form of the populations of Y assumed in simple linear regression.

2. *Linearity:* For each Y distribution, the mean $E(Y_i|X_i)$—or more briefly $E(Y_i)$ or just μ_i—lies on a straight line, known as the true (population) regression line:

$$E(Y_i) = \mu_i = \alpha + \beta X_i \quad (12\text{-}1)$$

The population parameters α and β (alpha and beta) specify the line, and are to be estimated from sample information.
3. *Independence:* The random variables $Y_1, Y_2, \ldots$ are statistically independent. For example, if Y_1 happens to be large, there is no reason to expect Y_2 to be large (or small); that is, Y_2 is statistically unrelated to Y_1.

These three assumptions may be written more concisely as:

> The random variables $Y_1, Y_2, \ldots Y_i \ldots$ are independent, with
>
> $$\text{Mean} = \alpha + \beta X_i$$
> $$\text{Variance} = \sigma^2$$

(12-2)

On occasion, it is useful to describe the deviation of Y from its expected value as the disturbance or error e, so the model may alternatively be written as:

> $$Y_i = \alpha + \beta X_i + e_i$$
>
> where $e_1, e_2, \ldots e_i \ldots$ are independent errors, with
>
> $$\text{Mean} = 0$$
> $$\text{Variance} = \sigma^2$$

(12-3)

For example, in Figure 12-1*b* the first observed value Y_1 is shown in color, along with the corresponding error term e_1.

B—THE NATURE OF THE ERROR TERM

Now let us consider in more detail the purely random part of Y, the error[1] term e. Why does it exist? Why doesn't a precise and exact value of Y follow, once the value of X is given? The error may be regarded as the sum of two components:

[1] We use "error" in the original sense of "wandering"—as in "knight errant"—rather than "incorrect." It is these error terms that distinguish statistical models from other models.

1. *Measurement error.* There are various reasons why Y may be measured incorrectly. In measuring crop yield, there may be an error resulting from sloppy harvesting or inaccurate weighing. If the example is a study of the consumption of families at various income levels, the measurement error in consumption might consist of budget and reporting inaccuracies.
2. *Inherent variability* occurs inevitably in biological and social phenomena. Even if there were no measurement error, repetition of an experiment using exactly the same amount of fertilizer would result in somewhat different yields. The differences could be reduced by tighter experimental control—for example, by holding constant soil conditions, amount of water, and so on. But complete control is impossible—for example, seeds cannot be exactly duplicated.

C—ESTIMATING α and β

Suppose the true (population) regression, $Y = \alpha + \beta X$, is the black line shown in Figure 12-2. This is unknown to the statistician, who must estimate it as best he can by observing X and Y. If at the first level X_1, the random error e_1 happens to take on a negative value as shown in the diagram, he will observe Y_1 below the true line. Similarly, if the random errors e_2 and e_3 happen to take on positive values, he will observe Y_2 and Y_3 above the true line.

Now the statistician applies the least squares formulas to the only information he has—the sample points Y_1, Y_2, and Y_3. This produces an estimated line $\hat{Y} = a + bX$, which we color blue in Figure 12-2.

Figure 12-2 is a crucial diagram. Before proceeding, you should be sure that you can clearly distinguish between: (1) the true regression and its surrounding e distribution; since these are population values and cannot be observed they are shown in black. (2) the Y observations and the

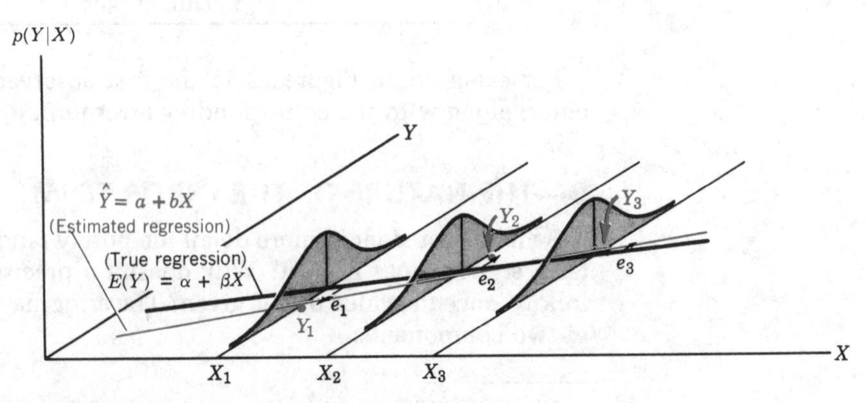

FIGURE 12-2
True (population) regression and estimated (sample) regression.

resulting fitted regression line; since these are sample values, they are known to the statistician and colored blue.

Unless the statistician is very lucky indeed, it is obvious that his estimated line will not exactly coincide with the true population line. The best he can hope for is that it will be reasonably close to the target. In the next section we develop this idea of "closeness" in more detail.

PROBLEMS

12-1 (Monte Carlo). Suppose the true (long-run average) relation of corn yield Y to fertilizer X is given by the line

$$Y = 2.40 + .30X$$

where Y is measured in tons of corn per acre, and X is measured in hundreds of pounds of fertilizer per acre. In other words, the population parameters are $\alpha = 2.40$ and $\beta = .30$.

a. First, play the role of nature. Graph the line for $0 \leq X \leq 12$. Suppose the yield varies about its expected value on this line, with a standard deviation $\sigma = 1$, and a distribution that is normal. Simulate a sample of five such yields, one each for $X = 2, 4, 6, 8, 10$. (*Hint:* First calculate the five mean values from the given line. Then add to each a random normal error e from Appendix Table II.)

b. Now play the role of the statistician. Calculate the least squares line that best fits the sample. Graph the sample and the fitted line.

c. Finally, let the instructor be the evaluator. Have him graph several of the lines found in part **b**. Then have him tabulate all the values of b, and graph their relative frequency distribution. How good are the estimates b? Specifically, find the expected value and standard error of b, approximately.

d. Why are the expected value and standard error in part **c** only approximate? Suggest how you could get better answers.

12-2 SAMPLING VARIABILITY

A—SAMPLING DISTRIBUTION OF *b*

How close does the estimated line come to the true population line? Specifically, how is the slope estimate b distributed around its target β? (Because of its greater importance, we shall concentrate for the rest of this chapter on the slope b, rather than the intercept a.)

While the sampling distribution of b can be approximately derived using Monte Carlo methods, statisticians have been able to do even better. They have theoretically derived its distribution, just as they derived the distribution of the sample mean $\bar{X}$. The moments of b, for example, are derived in Appendix 12-2.

Once again they found a sampling distribution that is approximately normal, regardless of whether or not the shape of the parent population—shaded in gray in Figure 12-2—is normal. (As one might expect, if the parent population is highly skewed, or otherwise non-normal, then it will take a larger sample size for b to reach approximate normality.) Specifically:

> ***Normal Approximation Rule for Regression***
> **The slope estimate b is approximately normally distributed, with**
>
> $$\text{Expected value of } b = \beta \qquad (12\text{-}4)$$
>
> like (6-9)
>
> $$\text{Standard error of } b = \frac{\sigma}{\sqrt{\Sigma x^2}}$$

Here σ represents the standard deviation of the Y observations about the population line, and each small x as usual represents the deviation of X from the mean $\bar{X}$. The normal distribution of b is shown in Figure 12-3.

B—THE STANDARD ERROR OF *b*

Although (12-4) may be the easiest formula to calculate the standard error of b, the easiest formula for *understanding* the standard error is obtained by re-expressing it:

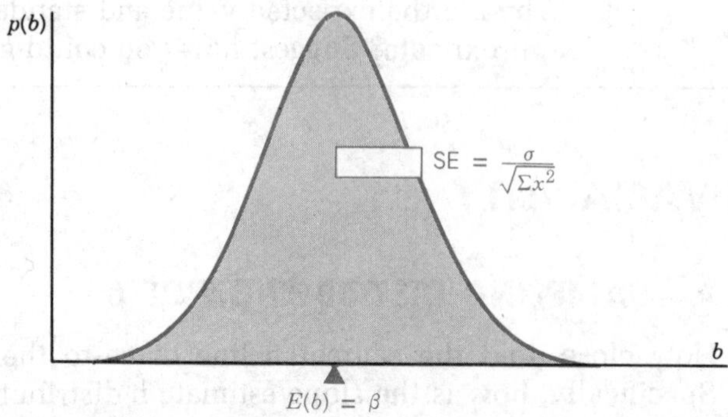

FIGURE 12-3
The sampling distribution of the estimate *b*.

$$\text{standard error} = \frac{\sigma}{\sqrt{n\left(\frac{\Sigma x^2}{n}\right)}} \tag{12-5}$$

Now recall that $\Sigma x^2/n$ is just the MSD, which is approximately the variance s_X^2. Thus (12-5) can be written as

$$\boxed{\text{standard error} \simeq \frac{\sigma}{\sqrt{n}} \cdot \frac{1}{s_X}} \tag{12-6}$$

like (6-7)

In this form, we can see there are three ways the standard error can be reduced to produce a more accurate estimate b:

1. By reducing σ, the inherent variability of the Y observations.
2. By increasing n, the sample size.
3. By increasing s_X, the spread of the X values, which are determined by the experimenter. (Recall in our example how the experimenter fixed the fertilizer levels.)

This third point is particularly interesting: Because increasing s_X improves b, s_X is called the *leverage* of the X values on b.

To illustrate, Figure 12-4 shows why increasing the leverage s_X in-

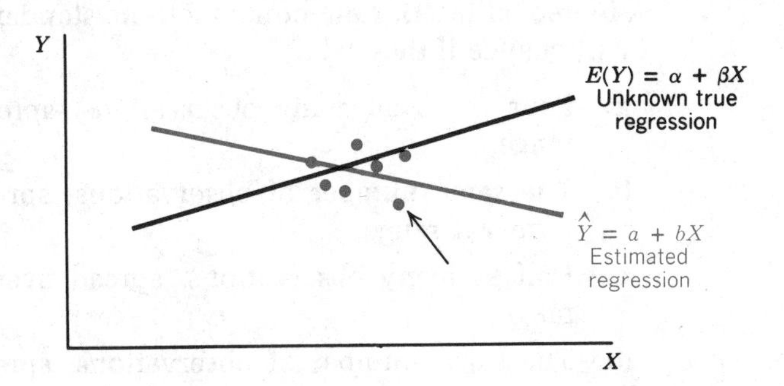

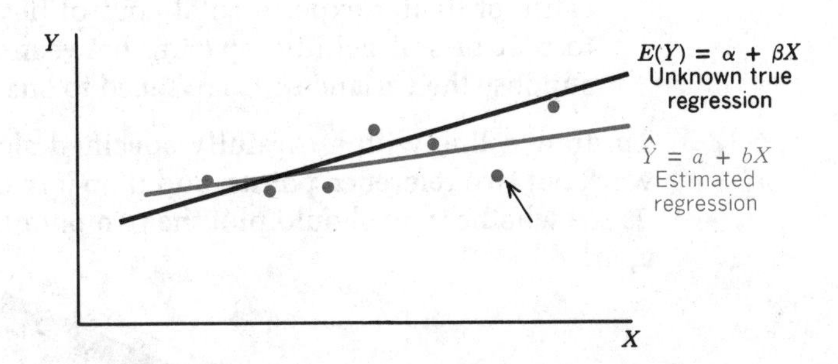

FIGURE 12-4
(a) Unreliable b when the X values are very close (leverage s_X is small). (b) More reliable b when the X values are spread out (leverage s_X is larger).

creases the reliability of the slope b. In panel (a), the X values are bunched together with very little spread (s_X is small). This means that the small part of the line being investigated is obscured by the error e, making the slope estimate b very unreliable. In this specific instance, our estimate has been pulled badly out of line by the errors—in particular by the one indicated by the arrow.

By contrast, in panel (b) we show how the X values have more leverage when they are more spread out (that is, when s_X is larger). Even though the errors e remain the same, the estimate b is much more reliable.

As a concrete example, suppose we wish to examine how sensitive U.S. imports Y are to the international value of the dollar X. A much more reliable estimate should be possible using the recent periods when the dollar has been floating (and taking on a range of values) than in earlier periods when currencies were fixed and only allowed to fluctuate within very narrow limits.

PROBLEMS

12-2 At an agricultural research station investigating the effect of fertilizer on soybean yield, several proposals were made to change the experimental design. If we can assume that yield Y increases linearly with fertilizer application X (over the range of X values considered, at least), state how much the standard error of the slope b will change if they take:

a. Four times as many observations, spread over the same X range.

b. The same number of observations, spread over 4 times the former X range.

c. Half as many observations, spread over twice the former X range.

d. The same number of observations, spread over 5 times the former X range, and with each observation more accurate because of tighter experimental control (less variation from plot to plot of soil acidity, spacing between plants, etc.). In fact, suppose the variance σ^2 is reduced to one-half its former value.

12-3 To draw a line with a carefully specified slope, you plan to first work out two reference points, and then join them with a ruler. Let us see whether you should plot the two points close together, or far apart:

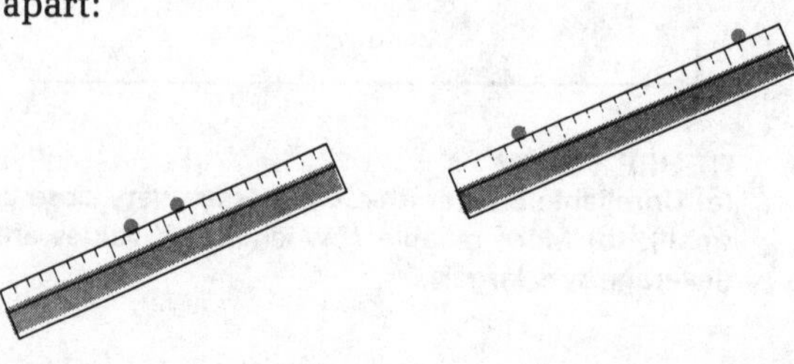

a. Intuitively, would it give a more accurate slope to choose the two points 1 inch apart, or 4 inches? *How much* more accurate? (That is, how much smaller would the error in the slope be? To work this out, for simplicity assume that only the right-hand point is in error—by .01 inch vertically.)

b. Answer **a** using an appropriate formula in the text.

12-3 CONFIDENCE INTERVALS AND TESTS FOR β

A—ESTIMATING THE STANDARD ERROR OF b

With the expected value, standard error, and normality of b established, statistical inferences about β are now in order. But first there is one remaining problem: From (12-4), the standard error of b is $\sqrt{\sigma^2/\Sigma x^2}$, where σ^2 is the variance of the Y observations about the population line. But σ^2 is generally unknown, and must be estimated. A natural way to estimate σ^2 is to use the deviations of Y about the fitted line. Specifically, consider the mean squared deviations about the fitted line:

$$\frac{1}{n}\Sigma d^2 = \frac{1}{n}\Sigma(Y - \hat{Y})^2 \qquad \text{like (11-2)}$$

We make one small modification: Instead of n we use the divisor $n - 2$. [The reason is familiar: Two degrees of freedom (d.f.) have already been used up in calculating a and b in order to get the fitted line. This then leaves $(n - 2)$ d.f. to estimate the variance.][2] We therefore estimate σ^2 with the *residual variance* s^2, defined as

$$\boxed{s^2 \equiv \frac{1}{n-2}\Sigma(Y - \hat{Y})^2} \qquad \text{(12-7) like (2-11)}$$

When s is substituted for σ in (12-5), we obtain the *estimated* standard error, which we denote from now on simply as SE:

$$SE = \frac{s}{\sqrt{\Sigma x^2}} \qquad \text{(12-8)}$$

With this in hand, statistical inferences can now be made.

[2] A more detailed view may be helpful. If there were only $n = 2$ observed points, a least-squares line could be fitted—indeed it would turn out to provide a perfect fit. (Through *any* two points, a line can always be drawn that goes through them exactly.) Thus, although a and b would be determined easily enough, there would be no "information left over" to tell us anything about σ^2, the variance of the observations about the regression line. Only to the extent that n exceeds 2 can we get information about σ^2. That is, $n - 2$ d.f. remain when we use s^2 to estimate σ^2.

B—CONFIDENCE INTERVALS

Using the same argument as in Chapter 8 earlier, we could easily show that the 95% confidence interval for β is

$$\beta = b \pm t_{.025}\, \text{SE} \qquad (12\text{-}9) \text{ like } (8\text{-}15)$$

Substituting SE from (12-8) yields

95% confidence interval for the slope[3]

$$\beta = b \pm t_{.025} \frac{s}{\sqrt{\Sigma x^2}} \qquad (12\text{-}10)$$

where the degrees of freedom for t are the same as the divisor used in calculating s^2:

$$\text{d.f.} = n - 2 \qquad (12\text{-}11)$$

EXAMPLE 12-1

The slope relating wheat yield to fertilizer was found to be .059 bu/lb. Of course, this was based on a mere sample of $n = 7$ observations. If millions of observations had been collected, what would the resulting population slope be? Calculate a 95% confidence interval. (Use the statistics calculated in Table 11-2.)

SOLUTION

We first use (12-7) to calculate s^2 in Table 12-1. The critical t value then has d.f. $= n - 2 = 7 - 2 = 5$ (the same as the divisor in s^2). From Appendix Table V, this $t_{.025}$ is found to be 2.57. Finally, note that Σx^2 was

---

[3] Regression coefficients share many of the properties of sample means, as first noted in Section 11-3. As another example, even if the underlying populations in Figure 12-1 are quite non-normal, the confidence interval (12-10) still has approximately a 95% chance of covering the true β, and is therefore called *robust* in coverage.

A similar robust 95% confidence interval can be derived for the Y-intercept (see Problem 12-17)

$$\alpha = (\overline{Y} - b\overline{X}) \pm t_{.025}\, s \sqrt{\frac{1}{n} + \frac{\overline{X}^2}{\Sigma x^2}} \qquad (12\text{-}12)$$

TABLE 12-1 Calculations for the Residual Variance s^2

X	Y	$\hat{Y} = 36.4 + .059X$	$Y - \hat{Y}$	$(Y - \hat{Y})^2$
100	40	42.3	−2.3	5.29
200	50	48.2	1.8	3.24
300	50	54.1	−4.1	16.81
400	70	60.0	10.0	100.00
500	65	65.9	−0.9	.81
600	65	71.8	−6.8	46.24
700	80	77.7	2.3	5.29
				$s^2 = \frac{177.68}{7-2}$
				$= 35.5$

already calculated in Table 11-2. When these values are substituted into (12-10),

$$\beta = .059 \pm 2.57 \frac{\sqrt{35.5}}{\sqrt{280{,}000}}$$

$$= .059 \pm 2.57(.0113) \tag{12-13}$$

$$= .059 \pm .029 \tag{12-14}$$

$$.030 < \beta < .088 \tag{12-15}$$

C—TESTING HYPOTHESES

The hypothesis that X and Y are unrelated may be stated mathematically as H_0: $\beta = 0$. To test this hypothesis at the 5% error level, we merely note whether the value 0 is contained in the 95% confidence interval.

EXAMPLE 12-2

In Example 12-1, test at the 5% level the null hypothesis that yield is unrelated to fertilizer.

SOLUTION

Since $\beta = 0$ is excluded from the confidence interval (12-15), we reject this null hypothesis, and conclude that yield is indeed related to fertilizer.

Equivalently, we note that the estimate of .059 in (12-14) stands out beyond its sampling allowance, so we can conclude that it is statistically discernible.

D—*p*-VALUE

Rather than simply accept or reject, a more appropriate form for a test is the calculation of the p-value. We first calculate the t statistic:

$$\boxed{t = \frac{b}{SE}} \qquad \text{(12-16) like (9-17)}$$

Then we look up the probability in the tail beyond this observed value of t; this is the p-value.

EXAMPLE 12-3

In Example 12-1, what is the p-value for the null hypothesis that yield does not increase with fertilizer?

SOLUTION

In the confidence interval (12-13) we have already calculated b and its standard error, which we can now substitute into (12-16):

$$t = \frac{.059}{.0113} = 5.2$$

In Appendix Table V, we scan the row where d.f. = 5, and find the observed t value of 5.2 lies beyond $t_{.0025} = 4.77$. Thus

$$\text{p-value} < .0025 \qquad \text{(12-17)}$$

This provides so little credibility for H_0 that we could reject it, and conclude once again that yield does indeed increase with fertilizer.

In this example, we calculated the one-sided p-value (that is, the p-value in only one tail). But in other cases, it may be appropriate to calculate a two-sided p-value—as detailed in Appendix 12-3.

PROBLEMS

12-4 For Problems 11-1 and 11-2, construct a 95% confidence interval for the population slope β.

12-5 Suppose that a random sample of 4 families had the following annual incomes and savings:

Family	*Income X (Thousands of $)*	*Saving S (Thousands of $)*
A	22	2.0
B	18	2.0
C	17	1.6
D	27	3.2

a. Estimate the population regression line $S = \alpha + \beta X$.

b. Construct a 95% confidence interval for the slope β.

c. Graph the 4 points and the fitted line, and then graph as well as you can the acceptable slopes given by the confidence interval in **b.**

d. Which of the following hypotheses is rejected by the data at the 5% level?

$$\beta = 0? \qquad \beta = .05? \qquad \beta = .10? \qquad \beta = .50?$$

***12-6** In Problem 12-5, suppose the population marginal propensity to save (β) is known to be positive, if it is not 0. Accordingly, you decide on a one-sided test.

a. State the null and alternative hypotheses in symbols.

b. Calculate the p-value for H_0.

c. Construct a one-sided 95% confidence interval of the form, "β is at least as large as such and such."

d. At the one-sided 5% level, can we reject the null hypothesis $\beta = 0$? Test in two ways:
i. Is the p-value less than 5%?
ii. Is $\beta = 0$ excluded from the confidence interval?

12-7 Repeat Problems 12-5 and 12-6 for the following data:

Income X	*Saving S*
30	3
70	6
20	2
30	1
50	3

12-4 PREDICTING Y AT A GIVEN LEVEL OF X

So far we have considered broad aspects such as the position of the whole line (determined by α and β). In this section, we will consider the narrower, but often very practical, problem of predicting what Y will be, for a given level of X.

A—CONFIDENCE INTERVAL FOR μ_0, THE MEAN OF Y AT X_0

For a given value X_0 (say 550 lbs. of fertilizer), what is the confidence interval for μ_0, the corresponding mean value of Y_0 (wheat yield)? This is the interval that the chemical company may want to know, to describe the long-run (mean) performance of its fertilizer.

As we can see in panel (*a*) of Figure 12-5, the point μ_0 that we are trying

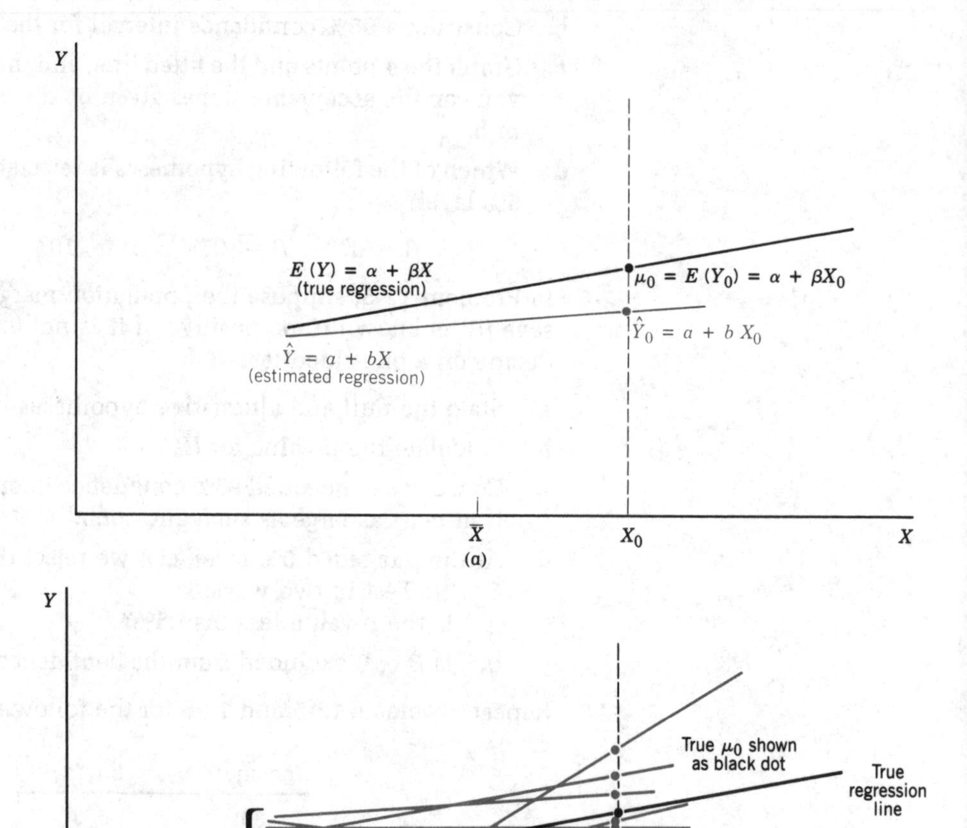

FIGURE 12-5
How the estimator $\hat{Y}_0$ is related to its target. (a) One single $\hat{Y}_0$ (b) A whole series of possible $\hat{Y}_0$ illustrates the sampling distribution of $\hat{Y}_0$

to estimate is the point on the true regression line above X_0. The best point estimate is, of course, the point on the *estimated* regression line:

$$\hat{Y}_0 = a + bX_0 \tag{12-18}$$

As a point estimate, this involves some error because of the sampling error in a and b. For example, panel (a) shows the estimate $\hat{Y}_0$ (on the blue sample line) lying below the target μ_0 (on the population line). In this case $\hat{Y}_0$ underestimates μ_0 because b underestimated β.

Panel (b) shows what happens if sampling is repeated. Each sample would give a different regression line, and hence a different estimate $\hat{Y}_0$. All these $\hat{Y}_0$ values would be scattered around the target μ_0, illustrating the sampling distribution of $\hat{Y}_0$. The standard error of $\hat{Y}_0$ is derived in Appendix 12-4; using this, we construct the confidence interval:

95% confidence interval for the mean (of Y_0) at level X_0

$$\mu_0 = (a + bX_0) \pm t_{.025}\, s \sqrt{\frac{1}{n} + \frac{(X_0 - \overline{X})^2}{\Sigma x^2}} \tag{12-19}$$

The two terms under the square root reflect the uncertainty in estimating the height of the line α and the uncertainty in estimating the slope of the line β. This second source of uncertainty is seen in Figure 12-5 to be particularly serious if X_0 is far removed from the center of the data $\overline{X}$. Then the $(X_0 - \overline{X})^2$ appearing at the end of (12-19) becomes large, and the estimate of μ_0 becomes very unreliable.

B—PREDICTION INTERVAL FOR A SINGLE OBSERVATION Y_0

Now consider a different question: How widely would we hedge our estimate if we are making a single application of $X_0 = 550$ lbs. of fertilizer and wish to predict the one yield Y_0 that will result? This is the sort of interval that an individual farmer might want to know, in order to plan his budget for the coming year.

In predicting this single Y_0, we will face all the problems involved in estimating the mean μ_0; namely, we will have to recognize the sampling error involved in the estimates a and b. But now we have an additional problem because we are trying to estimate only one observed Y (with its inherent fluctuation) rather than the stable average of all the possible Y's. It is no surprise that this produces an interval similar to (12-19) except for an additional large term at the end:

95% Prediction Interval[4] for an *individual* Y_0 at level X_0

$$Y_0 = (a + bX_0) \pm t_{.025}\, s \sqrt{\frac{1}{n} + \frac{(X_0 - \overline{X})^2}{\Sigma x^2} + 1} \qquad (12\text{-}20)$$

We call (12-20) a *prediction interval* (for a single observation Y_0) to contrast it with the earlier *confidence interval* (for the parameter μ_0).

C—COMPARISON OF THE TWO INTERVALS

An example will illustrate the confidence interval for μ_0 and the wider prediction interval for the individual Y_0.

EXAMPLE 12-4

In the fertilizer-yield example, we earlier calculated the following statistics:

$$n = 7 \qquad \overline{X} = 400$$
$$a = 36.4 \qquad \Sigma x^2 = 280{,}000$$
$$b = .059 \qquad s = \sqrt{35.5} = 5.96$$

a. If 550 pounds of fertilizer is to be applied over and over, find a 95% confidence interval for the long-run (mean) yield.

b. If the 550 pounds of fertilizer is to be applied to just one plot, find a 95% prediction interval for the one resulting yield.

SOLUTION

a.

$$\mu_0 = (a + bX_0) \pm t_{.025}\, s \sqrt{\frac{1}{n} + \frac{(X_0 - \overline{X})^2}{\Sigma x^2}} \qquad (12\text{-}19) \text{ repeated}$$

$$= (36.4 + .059 \times 550) \pm 2.57\,(5.96) \sqrt{\frac{1}{7} + \frac{(550 - 400)^2}{280{,}000}}$$

$$= 69 \pm 2.57\,(5.96)\sqrt{.223} \qquad (12\text{-}22)$$

$$= 69 \pm 7 \qquad (12\text{-}23)$$

[4] As n gets very large, the first two terms under the square root approach zero, leaving just the 1. Then the 95% prediction interval is approximately:

$$Y_0 \simeq (a + bX_0) \pm t_{.025}\, s \qquad (12\text{-}21)$$

In view of this, s (which we have so far called the "residual standard deviation") is sometimes also called the *standard error of the estimate.*

b. For the prediction interval, we add 1 under the square root of (12-22):

$$Y_0 = 69 \pm 2.57\,(5.96)\,\sqrt{.223 + 1}$$
$$= 69 \pm 17 \qquad (12\text{-}24)$$

This interval is more than twice as wide as (12-23), which shows how much more difficult it is to predict an *individual* Y observation than the *mean of Y*.

Figure 12-6 illustrates the two intervals calculated in this example. As well as at $X_0 = 550$, it gives the intervals at all possible values of X_0; the result is two colored bands. The dark inner band shows the relatively precise confidence interval for μ_0, while the light outer band shows the vaguer prediction interval for an individual Y_0. Note that both bands become more vague as X_0 moves away from the center of the data $\bar{X}$—a feature we first saw in Figure 12-5.

We also note that only the outer band captures all 7 original observations. It is this band that is wide enough to be 95% certain of capturing yet another observation Y_0.

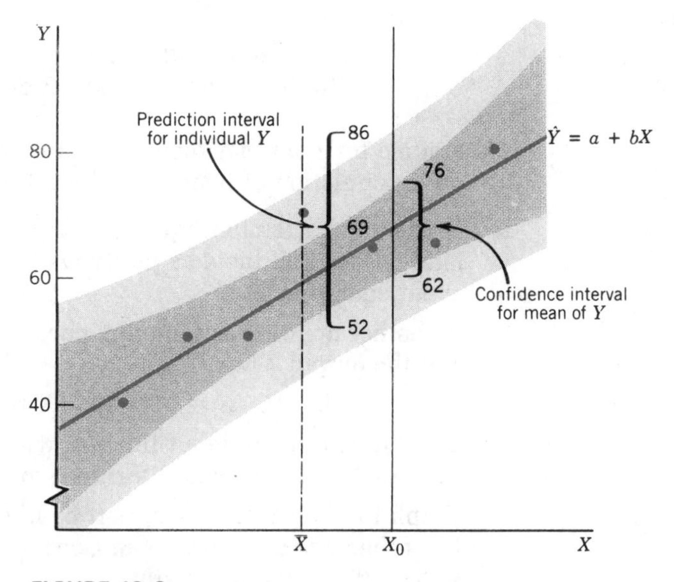

FIGURE 12-6
95% confidence interval for the mean μ_0 (dark blue), and wider 95% **prediction** interval for an individual Y_0 (light blue).

PROBLEMS

12-8 For 48 successive months, the output of a hosiery mill X and the corresponding total cost of production Y was plotted below (Dean, 1941).

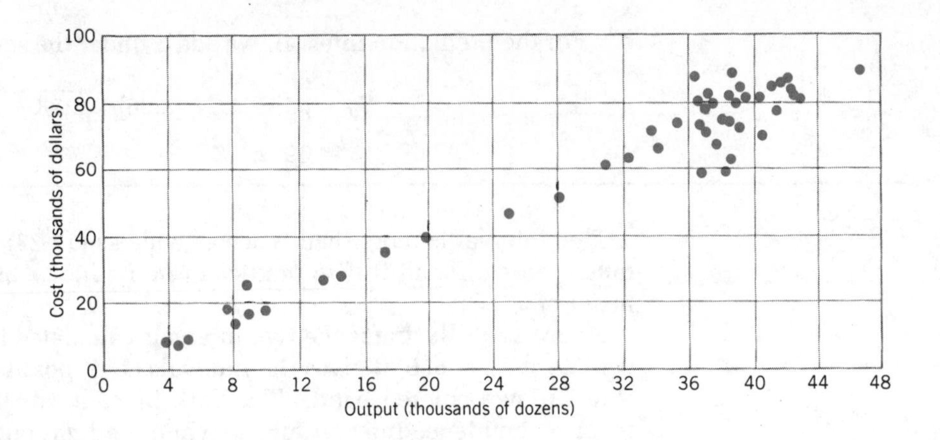

$\bar{X} = 30$ $\Sigma x^2 = 6900$ $\Sigma xy = 13{,}800$

$\bar{Y} = 63$ $\Sigma y^2 = 29{,}000$ $n = 48$

Regression equation $\hat{Y} = 3.0 + 2.0X$
Residual standard deviation, $s = 6$

We assume for now that these 48 points are a random sample from the population of many years' production.

a. Verify the regression equation, and graph it on the given figure. Does it fit the data pretty well? Is the typical residual about equal to $s = 6$?

b. If another month was sampled, guess the cost of production Y if the output X was:

i. $X = 6$, **ii.** $X = 18$, **iii.** $X = 30$, **iv.** $X = 42$.

In each case, include an interval wide enough so that you can be 95% sure it would turn out to be correct.

c. Graph the four intervals in part **b,** and sketch the band that joins them, as in Figure 12-6. Does this band contain about 95% of the individual points?

d. Graph the approximate band (12-21) given in footnote 4.

12-9 Repeat Problem 12-8 parts **b** and **c,** if we are now interested in predicting the long-run *average* of Y at each given level of X.

***12-10** Circle the correct choice in each pair of brackets:

a. Suppose n is at least 25, and X_0 is no more than 2 standard deviations s_X away from the central value $\bar{X}$. Then the exact 95% prediction interval (12-20) for Y_0 would be at most [4%,

10%] [wider, narrower] than the approximation (12-21)—as we saw in Problem 12-8.

b. The intuitive reason this approximation works so well is that we can safely ignore the minor source of uncertainty, which is [the position of the population line, the inherent variability of the observations].

c. This approximation is not only adequate for many purposes, but it is also easy to graph—because it is just a band of two [divergent curves, parallel straight lines] on either side of the regression line.

12-5 EXTENDING THE MODEL

A—EXTRAPOLATION

In predicting Y_0, the given level X_0 may be *any* value. If X_0 lies *among* the observed values $X_1, \ldots, X_n$, the process is called *interpolation*. If X_0 lies *beyond* the observed values $X_1, \ldots, X_n$—either to the left or right—then the process is called *extrapolation*. The further we extrapolate beyond the observed X values, the greater the risk we run—for two reasons:

1. We emphasized in the previous section that both intervals (12-19) and (12-20) get wider as X_0 moves further from the center $\bar{X}$. This is true, even if all the assumptions underlying our model hold exactly.
2. In practice, we must recognize that a mathematical model is never absolutely correct. Rather, it is a useful approximation. In particular, we cannot take seriously the assumption that the population means are strung out *exactly* in a straight line. If we consider the fertilizer example, it is likely that the true relation increases initially, but then bends down eventually as a "burning point" is approached, and the crop is overdosed. This is illustrated in Figure 12-7, which is an extension of Figure 11-2 with the scale appropriately changed. In the

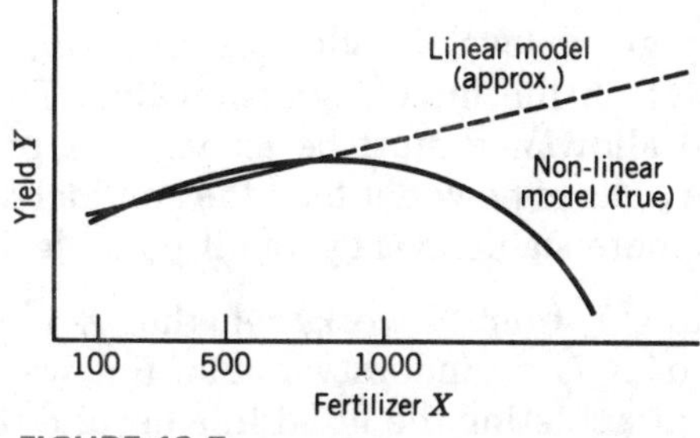

FIGURE 12-7

Comparison of linear and nonlinear models.

region of interest, from 0 to 700 pounds, the relation is *practically* a straight line, and no great harm is done in assuming the linear model. However, if the linear model is extrapolated far beyond this region of experimentation, the result becomes meaningless. In such cases, a nonlinear model should be considered (as in Chapter 14).

B—EXTENSION TO UNCONTROLLED OR RANDOM *X*

So far we have thought of the independent variable X as set at successive fixed levels (for example, fertilizer application was set at 100, 200, . . .). But in many cases—for example, in predicting a student's verbal aptitude *Y* from his math aptitude *X*—we must recognize that *X* is a random variable just like Y. Fortunately, this chapter remains valid for predictions even when X is a random variable, provided the model (12-3) is appropriately interpreted, as follows:

For every X, we can calculate the conditional distribution of Y, and hence the conditional expected value and variance. Then we require these expected values to lie on a straight line, and the conditional variances to be a constant value σ^2. In Chapter 15 we will say more about this.

CHAPTER 12 SUMMARY

12-1 The actual observations must be recognized as just a sample from an underlying population. As usual in describing a population, we use a Greek letter for the slope β. This is the target being estimated by the sample slope b.

12-2 If sampling is random, then from sample to sample *b* fluctuates around β with a specified standard error—just as $\bar{X}$ fluctuated around μ earlier.

12-3 We can therefore construct a confidence interval for β, or calculate the p-value for $H_0: \beta = 0$. In doing so, we estimate the variance σ^2 around the population line with the residual variance s^2 around the sample line.

12-4 For any given level X_0, the corresponding predicted value $\hat{Y}_0$ is the point on the fitted regression line. To be 95% confident, an interval allowance must be made. This *prediction* interval for a single Y_0 has to be wider than the *confidence* interval for the mean μ_0 (the more stable average of all possible Y_0's).

12-5 Predicting *Y* from *X* works whether *X* is set at successive fixed levels, or *X* is a random variable. But we must be very cautious about extrapolating the fitted line beyond the given data.

REVIEW PROBLEMS

12-11 In 1970, a random sample of 50 American men aged 35 to 54 showed the following relation between annual income Y (in dollars) and education X (in years). (Reconstructed from the 1970 U.S. Census sample of 1 in 10,000 Americans):

$$\hat{Y} = 1200 + 800X$$

Average income was $\overline{Y} = \$10,000$ and average education was $\overline{X} = 11.0$ years, with $\Sigma x^2 = 900$. The residual standard deviation about the fitted line was $s = \$7300$.

a. Calculate a 95% confidence interval for the population slope.

b. Is the relation of income to education statistically discernible at the 5% level?

c. Predict the income of a man who completed 2 years of high school ($X = 10$). Include an interval wide enough that you would bet on it at odds of 95 to 5.

d. Would it be fair to say that each year's education is worth \$800. Why?

12-12 **a.** In Problem 5-14, part **a**, we calculated $E(Y|X)$, for four values of X. Graph these 4 points. Is the linearity assumption in (12-2) satisfied?

b. Continue Problem 5-14: calculate $\text{var}(Y|X)$ for each value of X. Is the assumption of constant variance in (12-2) satisfied?

12-13 A 95% confidence interval for a regression slope was calculated on the basis of 1000 observations: $\beta = .38 \pm .27$. Calculate the p-value for the null hypothesis that Y does not increase with X.

12-14 A class of 150 registered students wrote two tests, for which the grades were denoted X_1 and X_2. The instructor calculated the following summary statistics:

$$\overline{X}_1 = 60 \qquad \overline{X}_2 = 70$$

$$\Sigma(X_1 - \overline{X}_1)^2 = 36{,}000 \qquad \Sigma(X_2 - \overline{X}_2)^2 = 24{,}000$$

$$\Sigma(X_1 - \overline{X}_1)(X_2 - \overline{X}_2) = 15{,}000$$

Residual variance of regression of X_1 against X_2, $s^2 = 180$

Residual variance of regression of X_2 against X_1, $s^2 = 120$

The instructor then discovered that there was one more student, who was unregistered; worse yet, one of this student's grades (X_1)

was lost, although the other grade was discovered ($X_2 = 55$). The dean told the instructor to estimate the missing grade X_1 as closely as possible.

a. Calculate the best estimate you can, including an interval that you have 95% confidence will contain the true grade.

b. What assumptions did you make implicitly?

12-15 In order to estimate this year's inventory (excess inventory), a tire company sampled 6 dealers, in each case getting inventory figures for both this year and last:

X = *Inventory Last Year*	Y = *Inventory This Year*
70	60
260	320
150	230
100	120
20	50
60	60

Summary statistics are $\overline{X} = 110$, $\overline{Y} = 140$.

$$\Sigma x^2 = 36{,}400 \qquad \Sigma y^2 = 61{,}800 \qquad \Sigma xy = 46{,}100.$$

a. Calculate the least squares line showing how this year's inventory Y is related to last year's X.

b. Suppose that a complete inventory of all dealers is available for last year (but not for this year). Suppose also that the mean inventory for last year was found to be $\mu_X = 180$ tires per dealer. On the graph below, we show this population mean μ_X

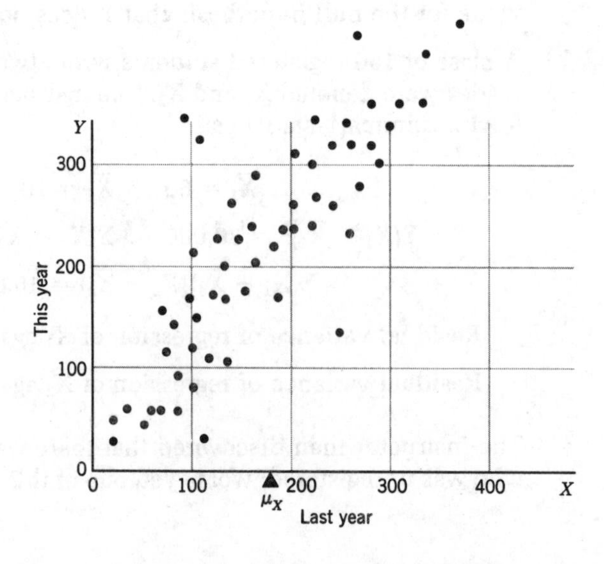

and sketch the population scatter (although this scatter remains unknown to the company, because Y values are not available yet). On this graph, plot the six observed points, along with $\overline{X}$, $\overline{Y}$, and the estimated regression line.

c. Indicate on the graph how μ_Y should be estimated. Construct a 95% confidence interval for μ_Y.

d. Construct a 95% confidence interval for μ_Y, if last year's data X had been unavailable or ignored (i.e., using only Y values).

e. Comparing part **c** to **d**, state in words the value of exploiting prior knowledge about last year's inventory.

12-16 **a.** In Problem 12-15, for the fitted regression line $\hat{Y} = a + bX$, what was $\Sigma(Y - \hat{Y})^2$ (the prediction errors, squared and summed)?

b. Suppose a vice president of the tire company suggests using the following prediction: $\hat{Y} = 10 + X$ (that is, this year is predicted to be just 10 more than last year). Can you say what $\Sigma(Y - \hat{Y})^2$ will now be, compared to (a)? Why? Then calculate $\Sigma(Y - \hat{Y})^2$.

12-17 **a.** Prove (12-12). [*Hint:* (12-19)]

b. For the data in Problem 12-15, calculate a 95% confidence interval for α.

12-18 *A Final Challenge: Predicting Old Faithful*

So that visitors to Yellowstone National Park can be told when to expect Old Faithful to erupt again, an attempt was made to

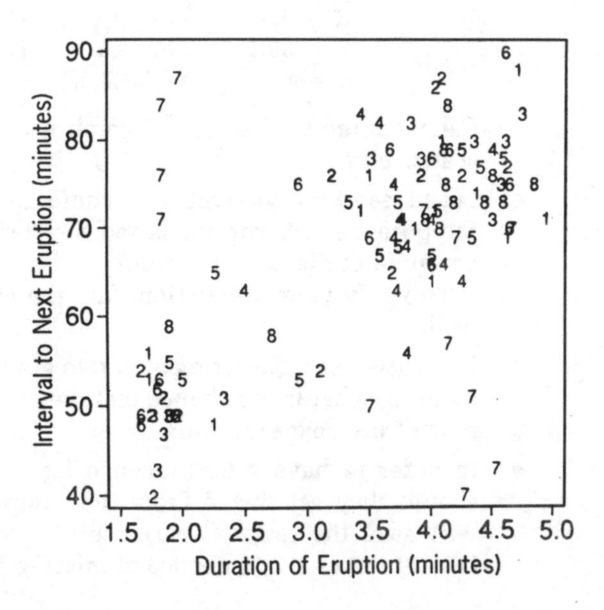

predict the interval till the next eruption (Y) on the basis of the *duration* of the last eruption (X).

Data for 8 days was plotted above (Denby and Pregibon 1987), with each observation plotted by day number (from 1 to 8) instead of just a blank dot.

a. Is there anything suspicious about the data?

b. When the data was corrected, the scatter plot changed (Weisberg 1985):

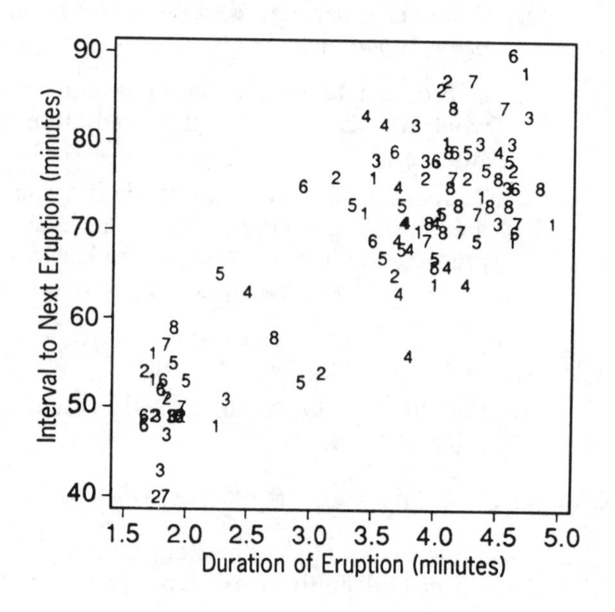

$$\bar{X} = 3.46 \qquad \Sigma(X - \bar{X})^2 = 113.8$$
$$\bar{Y} = 68.2 \qquad \Sigma(Y - \bar{Y})^2 = 17{,}820$$
$$n = 107 \qquad \Sigma(X - \bar{X})(Y - \bar{Y}) = 1{,}222$$

Calculate the OLS line, and graph it to show how it fits the scatter plot.

c. Let us see how the OLS line could be used for prediction. Suppose the last eruption lasted $X = 2$ minutes. When would you predict the next eruption?

To verify your calculation, find the answer graphically as well.

d. If tourists used the estimate in **c** to guide their arrival at Old Faithful, what is the chance that they would catch the beginning of the next eruption?

e. In order to have a 90% chance for catching it, how soon should they get there? From the computed regression, you will need the residual variance $s^2 = 44.7$. (*Hint:* Whereas (12-20) leaves a $2\frac{1}{2}$% chance of missing Y_0 on each side, now use a one-sided version that leaves a 10% chance of missing Y_0 on the low side.)

f. In **e**, calculate the approximation like (12-21) in footnote 4. Do you think it is adequate, when $X = 2$ minutes? When $X = 5$ minutes?

g. Graph this approximation over the range it is adequate. Mark it heavily, as the final graph you would hang in the rangers' cabin in Yellowstone Park.

CHAPTER 13

Multiple Regression

Truth is rarely pure, and never simple.
OSCAR WILDE

13-1 WHY MULTIPLE REGRESSION?

Multiple regression is the extension of simple regression, to take account of more than one independent variable X. It is obviously the appropriate technique when we want to investigate the effect on Y of several X variables simultaneously. Yet, even if we are interested in the effect of only one variable, it usually is wise to include the other variables in a multiple regression analysis, for two reasons:

a. In observational studies, it is essential to eliminate the bias of some of the confounding variables by including them as regressors—a point first emphasized in Chapter 1.

b. In both observational studies and randomized experiments, including additional variables as regressors can reduce the residual variance s^2, and hence improve confidence intervals and tests—just as including a second factor strengthened ANOVA tests.

To illustrate the first and most important point of eliminating bias, let us reconsider the agricultural example of Chapter 11. Suppose the fertilizer and yield observations in Example 11-1 were taken at seven different plots across the state, in an observational study. That is, each plot was not randomly assigned its dose of fertilizer. Instead it was observed with the dose of fertilizer that the farmer had already selected. But the farmers on land that was highly productive because it received more rainfall could likely afford more fertilizer. Thus their land got more fertilizer *and* more rainfall, and their high yields were due to both.

Can we remove the bias of this confounding variable rainfall—sometimes called a "lurking," or "masquerading" variable—to find the effect of fertilizer alone?

EXAMPLE 13–1

Table 13-1 records the levels of rainfall (X_2), along with the levels of fertilizer (X_1) and yield (Y) recorded earlier in Table 11-1. In Figure 13-1 we also update the graphical representation of Figure 11-1, by tagging each point with its rainfall level X_2. Finally, we lightly shade in the simple regression line (11-7) calculated earlier.

Figure 13-1 clearly exposes the bias of the simple regression line. As the levels of fertilizer X_1 increase from 100 to 700, the levels of rainfall X_2 also tend to increase, too, from 10 to 30. This clearly shows how the higher yields are caused not only by fertilizer, but by the confounding effect of rainfall too. Thus the simple regression line is too steep; it is biased because it attributes all the increase in yield to fertilizer, and ignores the fact that part of that increase is due to rainfall.

a. To eliminate the bias, we need to know how yield Y increases with fertilizer X_1 *while rainfall* X_2 *remains constant.* So pick out

TABLE 13-1 Observations of Yield, Fertilizer, and Rainfall

Y Wheat Field (bu/acre)	X_1 Fertilizer (lb/acre)	X_2 Rainfall (inches)
40	100	10
50	200	20
50	300	10
70	400	30
65	500	20
65	600	20
80	700	30

the points where X_2 stays at one level—for example, the lowest level of 10 inches—and fit a line to these points alone.

Repeat, for the other levels of X_2.

b. If rainfall is kept constant, estimate overall the slope of yield against fertilizer, that is, the increase in yield per pound of additional fertilizer.

SOLUTION

a. As shown in Figure 13-2, when rainfall stays constant at $X_2 = 10$ there are just two points, through which we easily fit a line.

Similarly, we fit a second line for $X_2 = 20$, and a third for $X_2 = 20$.

b. The slope of the first line is $10/200 = .05$; the slope of the third line is $10/300 = .03$; and the slope of the middle line is somewhere in between. So overall, the slope is about .04. That is, the

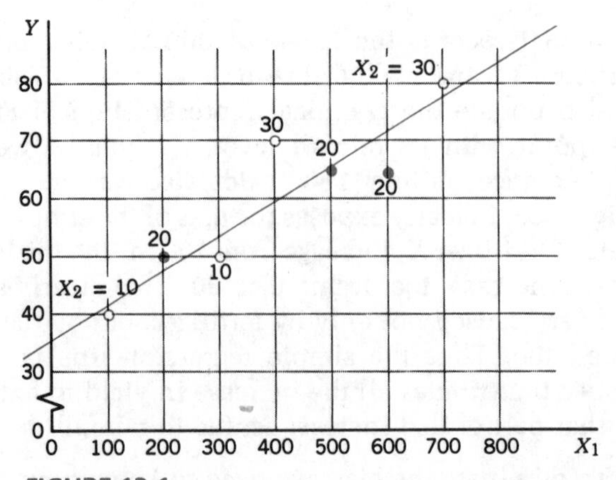

FIGURE 13-1
Yield Y plotted against fertilizer X_1 and rainfall X_2 (as tags).

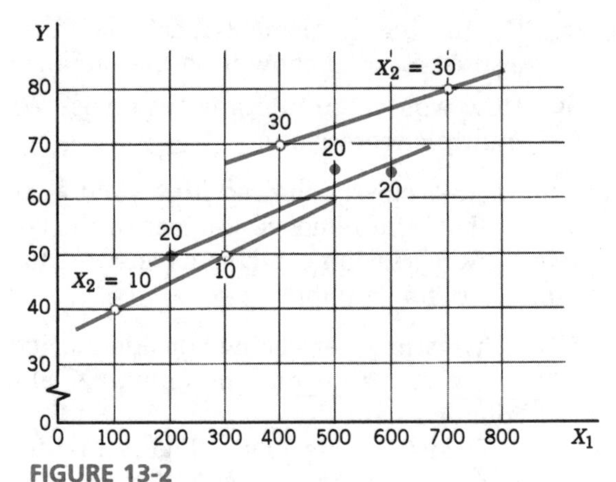

FIGURE 13-2
How yield depends on fertilizer X_1 with rainfall X_2 kept constant.

yield increases about .04 bushels for each pound of additional fertilizer, *while rainfall is constant.*

Figure 13-2 has demonstrated clearly how to obtain an unbiased slope of about .04. It shows the effect of fertilizer alone on yield, by very carefully holding constant the confounding factor rainfall. As we will see in the next section, multiple regression is just a formal way of doing this. Contrast this with the biased and steeper slope of about .06 obtained by simple regression that ignored rainfall, as sketched in Figure 13-1.

PROBLEMS

13-1 Suppose that a random sample of 5 families yielded the following data (Y and X_1 are measured in thousands of dollars annually):

Family	*Saving Y*	*Income X_1*	*Children X_2*
A	2.1	15	2
B	3.0	28	4
C	1.6	20	4
D	2.1	22	3
E	1.2	10	2

a. On the (X_1Y) plane, graph the 5 points (and tag each point with its value of X_2). Then fit a line by eye to just those points tagged with the lowest value of X_2. Repeat, for those points tagged with the highest value of X_2.

b. If X_2 is kept constant, estimate the change in Y for a unit increase in X_1.

13-2 a. Continuing Problem 13-1, calculate the simple regression of Y against X_1, and show it on the same graph.

b. How would you interpret the slope? Why is it less than in the multiple regression?

13-3 Figure 13-2 clearly showed how yield Y depends on fertilizer X_1 alone, that is, it removed the bias of the confounding variable X_2. Multiple regression can give us answers to other interesting questions, too, for example:

a. If irrigation were being considered, it would be important to know how Y depends on rainfall X_2 alone (without being confounded with X_1).

To answer this, look at Figure 13-2 where *fertilizer* X_1 is now constant, say at $X_1 = 400$. If X_2 were to change from 10 to 30 inches, how much would yield increase? For *each* inch of rainfall, what is the estimated increase in yield?

b. Forecasting is another important function of multiple regression. For example, use Figure 13-2 to predict the yield from a plot getting 300 pounds of fertilizer and 30 inches of rainfall.

13-2 THE REGRESSION MODEL AND ITS OLS FIT

We have shown graphically how to eliminate the confounding effect of one variable, rainfall. What about the others—temperature, soil fertility, cultivation, and so on? This confounding of many variables that occurs in practice requires an algebraic approach that can be easily computerized—called multiple regression.

A—THE GENERAL LINEAR MODEL (GLM)

In regressing yield Y on two factors such as fertilizer X_1 and rainfall X_2, we typically suppose that the relationship is of the form:

$$E(Y) = \beta_0 + \beta_1 X_1 + \beta_2 X_2 \qquad \text{(13-1) like (12-1)}$$

For simplicity we are developing multiple regression initially with just two regressors, so that geometric interpretations are easy. Equation (13-1) can be graphed as a plane in the three-dimensional space shown in Figure 13-3. (The geometry of lines and planes is reviewed in Appendix 11-1 at the back of the book.) For any given combination of factors (X_1, X_2), the expected Y is the point on the plane directly above, shown as a hollow dot. The observed yield Y, shown as usual as a colored dot, will be somewhat different of course, and the difference is the random error. Thus any

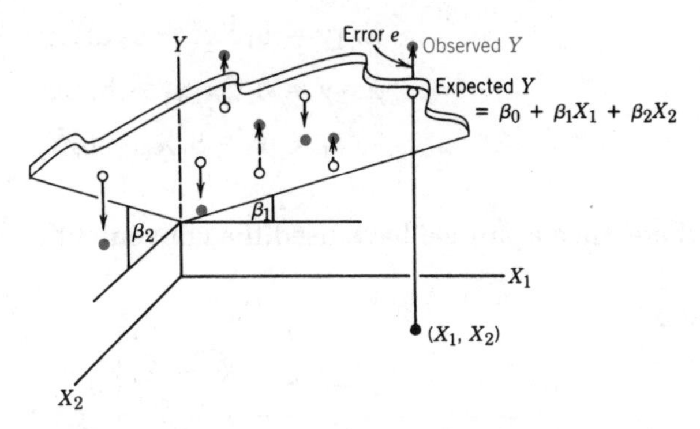

FIGURE 13-3
Scatter of observed points about the true regression plane
(like Figure 12-1*b*)

observed Y may be expressed as its expected value plus the random error e:

$$Y = \underbrace{\beta_0 + \beta_1X_1 + \beta_2X_2}_{E(Y)} + e \qquad \text{(13-2) like (12-3)}$$

And we make the same assumptions about e as in Chapter 12.

β_1 is geometrically interpreted as the slope of the plane as we move in the X_1 direction keeping X_2 constant, sometimes called the marginal effect of fertilizer X_1 on yield Y, or just "the marginal productivity of fertilizer". Similarly β_2 is the slope of the plane as we move in the X_2 direction keeping X_1 constant, called the marginal effect of X_2 on Y.

If equation (13-2) is extended to more than two regressors, then:

$$Y = \beta_0 + \beta_1X_1 + \beta_2X_2 + \beta_3X_3 + \cdots + e \qquad \text{(13-3)}$$

We will see (in Chapter 14) how ingenious choices of the regressors can make this model very useful indeed—of such general applicability that it is often called the *General Linear Model* (GLM).

B—THE LEAST SQUARES FIT

As in simple regression, the problem is that the statistician does not know the true equation (13-2). Instead, he must fit an *estimated* equation of the form

$$\hat{Y} = b_0 + b_1X_1 + b_2X_2 \qquad \text{(13-4) like (11-1)}$$

When we apply the usual least squares criterion for a good fit in multiple regression, we unfortunately do not get easy formulas for b_0, b_1, and b_2. Instead, we get 3 equations to solve, sometimes called *estimating equations* or *normal equations*:

$$\Sigma x_1 y = b_1 \Sigma x_1^2 + b_2 \Sigma x_1 x_2 \tag{13-5}$$

$$\Sigma x_2 y = b_1 \Sigma x_1 x_2 + b_2 \Sigma x_2^2 \tag{13-6}$$

$$b_0 = \bar{Y} - b_1 \bar{X}_1 - b_2 \bar{X}_2 \tag{13-7}$$

where once again we have used the convenient deviations:

$$\left.\begin{aligned} x_1 &\equiv X_1 - \bar{X}_1 \\ x_2 &\equiv X_2 - \bar{X}_2 \\ y &\equiv Y - \bar{Y} \end{aligned}\right\} \tag{13-8}$$

Equations (13-5) and (13-6) may be simultaneously solved for b_1 and b_2. (The algebraic solution of a set of simultaneous linear equations is reviewed in Appendix 13-2.) Then equation (13-7) may be solved for b_0. For the data of Table 13-1, these calculations are shown in Table 13-2, and yield the fitted multiple regression equation

$$\boxed{\hat{Y} = 28 + .038X_1 + .83X_2} \tag{13-9}$$

TABLE 13-2 Calculations for the Multiple Regression of Y Against X_1 and X_2

Data (From Table 13-1)			*Deviation Form*			*Products*				
Y	X_1	X_2	$y = Y - \bar{Y}$	$x_1 = X_1 - \bar{X}_1$	$x_2 = X_2 - \bar{X}_2$	x_1y	x_2y	x_1^2	x_2^2	x_1x_2
40	100	10	−20	−300	−10	6000	200	90,000	100	3000
50	200	20	−10	−200	0	2000	0	40,000	0	0
50	300	10	−10	−100	−10	1000	100	10,000	100	1000
70	400	30	10	0	10	0	100	0	100	0
65	500	20	5	100	0	500	0	10,000	0	0
65	600	20	5	200	0	1000	0	40,000	0	0
80	700	30	20	300	10	6000	200	90,000	100	3000
$\bar{Y} =$ 60	$\bar{X}_1 =$ 400	$\bar{X}_2 =$ 20	0✓	0✓	0✓	$\Sigma x_1y =$ 16,500	$\Sigma x_2y =$ 600	$\Sigma x_1^2 =$ 280,000	$\Sigma x_2^2 =$ 400	$\Sigma x_1x_2 =$ 7000

Estimating equations (13-5) and (13-6)
$$\begin{cases} 16{,}500 = 280{,}000b_1 + 7000b_2 \\ 600 = 7000b_1 + 400b_2 \end{cases}$$

$$\text{Solution} \begin{cases} b_1 = .0381 \\ b_2 = .833 \end{cases}$$

From (13-7), $b_0 = 60 - .0381(400) - .833(20)$
$b_0 = 28.1$

TABLE 13-3 Computer Solution for Wheat Yield Multiple Regression (Data in Table 13-1)

```
      > READ'Y','X1','X2'
DATA>          40 100  10
DATA>          50 200  20
DATA>          50 300  10
DATA>          70 400  30
DATA>          65 500  20
DATA>          65 600  20
DATA>          80 700  30

      > REGRESS'Y' ON 2 REGRESSORS'X1','X2'

THE REGRESSION EQUATION IS
Y = 28.1 + 0.0381 X1 + 0.833 X2
```

As we mentioned in the preface, statistical calculations are usually done on a computer package. This is particularly true of multiple regression, where the calculations generally become much too complicated to do by hand. (Imagine what Table 13-2 would look like with 100 rows of data and 5 regressors—a fairly typical situation.) For example, in Table 13-3 we show the MINITAB computation of the regression equation (13-9).

We recommend that you use a computer yourself for some of the homework problems. It is a good opportunity to meet the machine, since a good multiple regression package is available in practically every computer center (or even in some sophisticated pocket calculators).

If a computer is not available, you can still calculate the regression in a tableau like Table 13-2. Or you can skip the calculation entirely, and go on to the rest of the problem where the interpretation of the regression is discussed—this is the part that requires the human touch. For instance, the next example will show how the multiple regression equation (13-9) provides essentially the same estimates we derived informally in Example 13-1.

EXAMPLE 13-2

a. Graph the relation of yield Y to fertilizer X_1 given by (13-9), when rainfall has the constant value:

(i) $X_2 = 10$, **(ii)** $X_2 = 20$, **(iii)** $X_2 = 30$

b. Compare to the earlier Figure 13-2.

SOLUTION

a. Substitute $X_2 = 10$ into (13-9):

$$\hat{Y} = 28 + .038X_1 + .83X_2 \qquad \text{(13-9) repeated}$$

$$\hat{Y} = 28 + .038X_1 + .83(10)$$
$$= 36.3 + .038X_1 \qquad (13\text{-}10)$$

This is a line with slope .038 and Y intercept 36.3. Similarly, when we substitute $X_2 = 20$ and then $X_2 = 30$ we obtain the lines

$$\hat{Y} = 44.6 + .038X_1 \quad (13\text{-}11)$$

$$\hat{Y} = 52.9 + .038X_1 \quad (13\text{-}12)$$

These are lines with the same slope .038, but higher and higher intercepts, as shown in Figure 13-4.

b. These three lines given by the multiple regression model are not only parallel, they are also evenly spaced because the values of X_2 were evenly spaced.

The three lines fitted earlier in Figure 13-2 were only approximately equal in slope and spacing. But they told essentially the same story.

The computed multiple regression (13-9) yields answers more easily than the primitive graphical analysis in Figure 13-2. For example, consider the primary question of how much a pound of fertilizer will increase yield. In Figure 13-2, the graphical analysis required averaging three lines to get an overall slope of about .04, whereas the multiple regression equation (13-9) immediately and more accurately gives a slope of .038.

Similarly, in Figure 13-2 the graphical analysis required some effort (in Problem 13-3) to estimate that an inch of rainfall will increase yield by about .8, whereas the multiple regression equation (13-9) immediately gives the estimate of .83.

The greatest advantage of computing a multiple regression, however, is that it gives answers in complex situations—with more than two X vari-

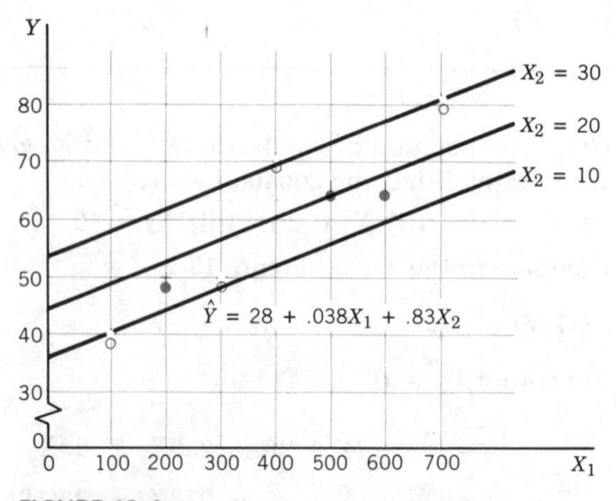

FIGURE 13-4
The graph of the computed multiple regression (13-9).

ables, and vast amounts of data—where a primitive graphical analysis like Figure 13-2 simply won't work at all.

PROBLEMS

13-4 Using the data in Problem 13-1, the multiple regression of Y against X_1 and X_2 was computed to be

$$\hat{Y} = .77 + .148X_1 - .52X_2$$

a. Graph the relation of Y to X_1 when X_2 has the constant value:
(i) $X_2 = 2$, **(ii)** $X_2 = 3$, **(iii)** $X_2 = 4$.
Compare to the graph in Problem 13-1.

b. If X_2 is kept constant, estimate the change in Y for a unit increase in X_1.

***c.** Using a computer, or a tableau like Table 13-2, calculate the multiple regression coefficients and verify that they agree with the given equation.

13-5 In the midterm U.S. congressional elections (between Presidential elections), the party of the President usually loses seats in the House of Representatives. To measure this loss concretely, we take as our base the average congressional vote for the President's party over the previous 8 elections; the amount that the congressional vote drops in a given midterm election, relative to this base, will be our *standardized vote loss Y*.

Y depends on several factors, two of which seem important and easily measurable: X_1 = Gallup poll rating of the President at the time of the midterm election (percent who approved of the way the President is handling his job) and X_2 = change over the previous year in the real disposable annual income per capita.

Year	*Y = Standardized Vote Loss*	*X_1 = President's Gallup Rating*	*X_2 = Change in Real Income Over Previous Year*
1946	7.3%	32%	−$40
1950	2.0	43	100
1954	2.3	65	− 10
1958	5.9	56	− 10
1962	−.8	67	60
1966	1.7	48	100

From the above data (Tufte, 1974), the following multiple regression equation was computed:

$$\hat{Y} = 10.9 - .13X_1 - .034X_2$$

a. On the (X_1Y) plane, graph the 6 points (and tag each point with its X_2 value). Then graph the grid of 4 lines you get from the regression equation by setting $X_2 = 100, 50, 0$, and -50.

b. If X_2 is kept constant, estimate the change in Y for a unit change in X_1.

c. If X_1 is kept constant, estimate the change in Y for a unit change in X_2.

d. Estimate the vote loss Y for a midterm election when $X_1 =$ 60% approval, and $X_2 =$ \$50 increase in real income.

***e.** Using a computer or a tableau like Table 13-2, calculate the multiple regression coefficients, and verify that they agree with the given equation.

13-6 (Continuing Problem 13-5)

a. From the graph, find the fitted 1946 vote loss Y, given that $X_1 =$ 32% and $X_2 =$ \$$-$40. Confirm it exactly from the regression equation. Compared to the actual vote loss $Y =$ 7.3%, what is the error?

b. Now consider a real prediction. Put yourself back in time, just before the 1970 midterm election, when President Nixon's rating was $X_1 =$ 56%, and the change in real income was $X_2 =$ \$70. From the graph, predict the 1970 vote loss. Confirm it exactly from the regression equation. It turns out that the actual vote loss Y was 1.0%; what therefore is the prediction error?

13-7 In the estimating equation (13-5), suppose it is known a priori that Y has no relation whatever to X_2; in other words, $b_2 = 0$. When you solve for b_1, what do you get?

13-3 CONFIDENCE INTERVALS AND STATISTICAL TESTS

A—STANDARD ERROR

As in simple regression, the true relation of Y to any X is measured by the unknown population slope β; we estimate it with the sample slope b. Whereas the true β is fixed, the estimate b varies randomly from sample to sample, fluctuating around its target β with an approximately normal distribution. The estimated standard error (SE) of b is customarily computed at the same time as b itself, as shown in Table 13-4. The meaning and use of SE are quite analogous to the simple regression case. For example, SE forms the basis for confidence intervals and tests.

TABLE 13-4 Computed Standard Deviation or SE, and *t* Ratio, for each Coefficient

COLUMN	COEFFICIENT	ST. DEV. OF COEF.	T-RATIO = COEF/S.D.
	28.095	2.491	11.28
X1	0.038095	0.005832	6.53
X2	0.8333	0.1543	5.40

B—CONFIDENCE INTERVALS AND *p*-VALUES

For each β coefficient, the formula for estimating it with a 95% confidence interval is of the standard form:

$$\beta = b \pm t_{.025}\ \text{SE} \qquad \text{(13-13) like (12-9)}$$

When there are k regressors as well as the constant term, there are $(k + 1)$ coefficients to estimate, which leaves $n - (k + 1)$ d.f. That is,

$$\text{d.f.} = n - k - 1 \qquad \text{(13-14) like (12-11)}$$

As usual, the observed t ratio to test $\beta = 0$ is

$$t = \frac{b}{\text{SE}} \qquad \text{(13-15) like (12-16)}$$

The p-value is then the tail area read from Appendix Table V. An example will illustrate.

EXAMPLE 13-3

From the computer output in Table 13-4:

a. Calculate a 95% confidence interval for the coefficient β_1.

b. Calculate the p-value for the null hypothesis $\beta_1 = 0$ (fertilizer doesn't increase yield).

SOLUTION

a. From (13-14), d.f. $= 7 - 2 - 1 = 4$, so that Appendix Table V gives $t_{.025} = 2.78$. Also substitute b_1 and its SE from Table 13-4; then (13-13) gives, for the fertilizer coefficient,

$$\beta_1 = .03810 \pm 2.78(.00583) \quad (13\text{-}16)$$
$$= .038 \pm .016 \quad (13\text{-}17)$$

b. In (13-16), b and its SE are given, so that we can easily form their ratio:

$$t = \frac{.03810}{.00583} = 6.53 \quad (13\text{-}18)$$

Or, equivalently, this same t ratio can be read from the last column of Table 13-4. In any case, we again refer to Appendix Table V, scanning the row where d.f. = 4. We find that the observed t value of 6.53 lies beyond $t_{.0025} = 5.60$. Thus

$$\text{p-value} < .0025 \quad (13\text{-}19)$$

With such little credibility, the null hypothesis can be rejected; we conclude that yield is indeed increased by fertilizer.

It is possible to summarize Example 13-3 (and similar calculations for the other regression coefficients) by arranging them in equation form as follows:

	YIELD = 28 + .038 FERTILIZER	+ .83 RAINFALL	
SE	.0058	.154	(13-20)
95% CI	± .016	± .43	
t ratio	6.5	5.4	
p-value	< .0025	< .005	

C—A WARNING ABOUT DROPPING A REGRESSOR

In equation (13-20), both fertilizer and rainfall are kept in the model as statistically discernible (significant) regressors because their t values are large enough to allow H_0 to be easily rejected in each case.

But now suppose we had a smaller sample and therefore weaker data; specifically, suppose that SE for rainfall was much larger—say .55 instead of .15. Then the t ratio would be $t = .83/.55 = 1.51$, so we could *not* reject H_0 at the 5% level. If we use this evidence to actually accept H_0 (no effect of rainfall) and thus drop rainfall as a regressor, *we may seriously bias the remaining coefficients*—as we emphasized in Section 13-1. A decision to accept H_0 would also suffer from the problem discussed earlier in Section 9-4. Since this argument is so important in regression analysis, let us briefly review it.

Although it is true that a t ratio of 1.51 for rainfall would be statistically indiscernible, this *would not prove* there is no relationship between rainfall and yield. It is easy to see why. We have strong biological grounds for believing that yield is positively related to rainfall. This belief would be confirmed by the positive coefficient $b = .83$. Thus our statistical evidence would be consistent with our prior belief, even though it would be weaker confirmation than we would like. To actually accept the null hypothesis $\beta = 0$, and conclude there is no relation, would be to contradict directly both the (strong) prior belief and the (weak) statistical evidence. We would be reversing a prior belief, even though the statistical evidence weakly confirmed it. And this would remain true for any positive t ratio—although, as t became smaller, our statistical confirmation would become weaker. Only if the coefficient were zero or negative would the statistical results contradict our prior belief.

To summarize: If we have strong prior grounds for believing that X is related positively to Y, X generally should not be dropped from the regression equation if it has the right sign. Instead, it should be retained along with the information in its confidence interval and p-value.

D—WHEN CAN A REGRESSOR BE DROPPED?

Continuing our example, suppose now our prior belief is that H_0 is approximately true. Then our decision on whether or not to drop a variable would be quite different. For example, a weak observed relationship (such as $t = 1.51$) would be in some conflict with our prior expectation of no relationship. But it is a minor enough conflict that is easily explained by chance (p-value $\simeq .10$. Hence, resolving it in favor of our prior expectation and continuing to use H_0 as a working hypothesis might be a reasonable judgment. In this case, the regressor could be dropped from the equation.

We conclude once again that classical statistical theory alone does not provide firm guidelines for accepting H_0; acceptance must be based also on extrastatistical judgment. Such prior belief plays a key role, not only in the initial specification of which regressors should be in the equation, but also in the decision about which ones should be dropped in light of the statistical evidence.

PROBLEMS

13-8 The following regression was calculated for a class of 66 students of nursing (Snedecor and Cochran, 1967):

$$\hat{Y} = 3.1 + .021X_1 + .075X_2 + .043X_3$$

	X_1	X_2	X_3
SE	(.019)	(.034)	(.018)
95% CI	( )	( )	( )
t ratio	( )	( )	( )
p-value	( )	( )	( )

where Y = student's score on a theory examination
X_1 = student's rank (from the bottom) in high school
X_2 = student's verbal aptitude score
X_3 = a measure of the student's character

a. Fill in the blanks.

b. What assumptions were you making in part **a**? How reasonable are they?

c. Which regressor gives the strongest evidence of being statistically discernible? (This also tends to be the regressor producing the largest change in student's score Y.)

***d.** In writing up a final report, would you keep the first regressor in the equation, or drop it? Why?

13-9 In Problem 13-5, the congressional vote loss of the President's party in midterm elections (Y) was related to the President's Gallup rating (X_1) and change in real income over the previous year (X_2). Specifically, the following regression was computed from $n = 6$ points:

$$\hat{Y} = 10.9 - .13X_1 - .034X_2$$
$$\text{SE} \quad (.046) \qquad (.010)$$

Answer the same questions as in Problem 13-8.

13-10 Suppose that your roommate is a bright student, but that he has studied no economics, and little statistics. (Specifically, he understands only simple—but not multiple—regression.) In trying to explain what influences the U.S. price level, he has regressed U.S. prices on 100 different economic variables one at a time (i.e., in 100 simple regressions). Moreover, he apparently selected these variables in a completely haphazard way without any idea of potential cause-and-effect relations. He discovered 5 variables that were statistically discernible at the level $\alpha = 5\%$, and concluded that each of these has an influence of U.S. prices.

a. Explain to him what reservations you have about his conclusion.

b. If he had uncovered 20 statistically discernible variables, what reservations would you now have? How could he improve his analysis?

13-4 REGRESSION COEFFICIENTS AS MULTIPLICATION FACTORS

A—SIMPLE REGRESSION

The coefficient in a linear regression model has a very simple but important interpretation. Recall the simple regression model,

$$Y = a + bX \tag{13-21}$$
like (11-1)

The coefficient b is the slope:

$$\frac{\Delta Y}{\Delta X} = b \tag{13-22}$$

where ΔX is any change in X, and ΔY is the corresponding change in Y. We can rewrite (13-22) in another form:

$$\Delta Y = b\,\Delta X \tag{13-23}$$

Since this is so important, we write it verbally:

$$\boxed{\text{Change in } Y = b \text{ (change in } X)} \tag{13-24}$$

For example, consider the fertilizer-yield example,

$$Y = 36 + .06X$$
(like (11-7)

How much higher would yield Y be, if fertilizer X were 5 pounds higher? From (13-24) we find,

$$\text{Change in yield} = .06(5) = .30 \text{ bushel} \tag{13-25}$$

Since any change that occurs in X is multiplied by b in order to find the corresponding change in Y, we can call b the *multiplication* factor.

Of course, when the change is $\Delta X = 1$, then (13-24) becomes: Change in $Y = b$; that is,

$$\boxed{b = \text{change in } Y \text{ that accompanies a unit change in } X} \tag{13-26}$$
like (11-8)

Thus, for example, the coefficient $b = .06$ means that a change of .06 bushel in yield Y accompanies a 1-pound change in fertilizer X, as illustrated in Figure 13-5.

B—MULTIPLE REGRESSION: "OTHER THINGS BEING EQUAL"

Consider now the multiple regression model

$$Y = b_0 + b_1X_1 + b_2X_2 \tag{13-27}$$
like (13-4)

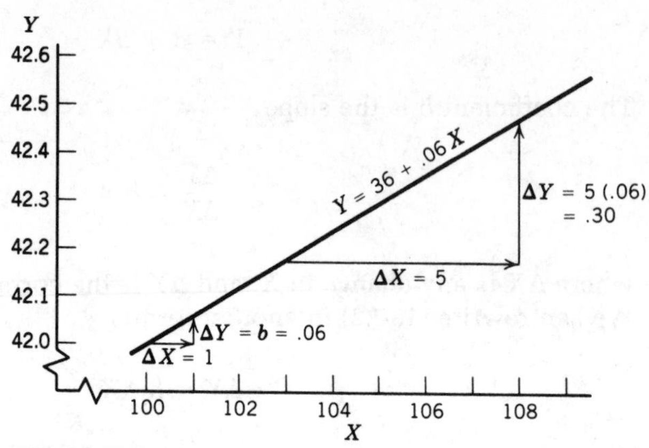

FIGURE 13-5
Interpretation of slope: b = change in Y that accompanies a unit change in X.

If X_2 *remains constant*, it is still true that:

$$\Delta Y = b_1 \Delta X_1 \tag{13-28}$$

like (13-23)

Equation (13-28) is so important that it is worthwhile giving a simple proof: If we keep X_2 constant, while we increase X_1 to $(X_1 + \Delta X_1)$, then from (13-27),

$$\begin{aligned} \text{initial } Y &= b_0 + b_1 X_1 + b_2 X_2 \\ \text{new } Y &= b_0 + b_1(X_1 + \Delta X_1) + b_2 X_2 \\ \hline \text{difference: } \Delta Y &= b_1 \Delta X_1 \end{aligned}$$

(13-28) proved

Of course, we can easily generalize to the case of several regressors: (13-28) still describes how Y will be related to any one of the X regressors, *provided all the others remain constant*—that is, that "other things remain equal."

> **If one regressor, say X_1, changes while all the others remain constant, then change in $Y = b_1$ (change in X_1)** (13-29)

For example, suppose wheat yield Y is related to fertilizer X_1, rainfall X_2, and temperature X_3, as follows:

$$Y = 30 + .036X_1 + .81X_2 + .02X_3$$

How much would yield Y increase if fertilizer X_1 were increased 5 pounds, while X_2 and X_3 did not change? From (13-29),

$$\text{Change in yield} = .036(5) = .18 \text{ bushel} \tag{13-30}$$

Thus the coefficient $b_1 = .036$ is a multiplication factor in multiple regression.

Again, when the change is $\Delta X_1 = 1$, then (13-29) becomes:

b_1 = change in Y that accompanies a unit change in the regressor X_1, if all the other regressors remain constant. (13-31)

So far we have only seen what happens when one regressor changes. But what happens if all the regressors change simultaneously? Just as we proved (13-28), we could now show that the change in Y is just the sum of the individual changes:

$$\text{If } Y = b_0 + b_1X_1 + b_2X_2 + \cdots, \quad \text{then } \Delta Y = b_1\Delta X_1 + b_2\Delta X_2 + \cdots. \tag{13-32}$$

To contrast the different uses of multiple and simple regression, we end with an example.

EXAMPLE 13-4

The simple and multiple regressions of yield against fertilizer and rainfall (obtainable from Table 13-2) are as follows:

$$\text{YIELD} = 36 + .059 \text{ FERT} \tag{13-33}$$

$$\text{YIELD} = 30 + 1.50 \text{ RAIN} \tag{13-34}$$

$$\text{YIELD} = 28 + .038 \text{ FERT} + .83 \text{ RAIN} \tag{13-35}$$

a. If a farmer adds 100 more pounds of fertilizer per acre, how much can he expect his yield to increase?

b. If he irrigates with 3 inches of water, how much can he expect his yield to increase? (Assume that water from irrigation and rainfall have the same effect.)

c. If he simultaneously adds 100 more pounds of fertilizer per acre, and irrigates with 3 inches of water, how much can he expect his yield to increase?

d. We have already remarked that high fertilizer application tends to be associated with high rainfall, in the data on which these three regression equations were calculated. If this same tendency persisted, how much more yield would you expect on an acre that has been getting 3 more inches of rainfall than another acre?

SOLUTION

a. The question is: What happens if he adds 100 pounds of fertilizer, with rainfall unchanged? The answer therefore is provided by the multiple regression equation. We multiply the 100 pounds by the multiple regression coefficient .038 (i.e., the magnification factor for fertilizer):

$$.038(100) = 3.8 \text{ bushels} \qquad \text{like (13-28)}$$

b. The question is: What happens if he adds 3 inches of water, with fertilizer held constant? Again, the answer lies in the multiple regression equation. We multiply the 3 inches by the multiple regression coefficient .83 (i.e., the magnification factor for water):

$$.83(3) = 2.5 \text{ bushels}$$

c. From (13-32),

$$\begin{aligned} \Delta Y &= .038(100) + .83(3) \\ &= 3.8 + 2.5 \\ &= 6.3 \text{ bushels} \end{aligned} \qquad (13\text{-}36)$$

d. Now we are not holding fertilizer constant, but letting it vary as rainfall varies, in the same pattern that produced (13-34) (i.e., a pattern where, for example, farmers that get more rainfall are more prosperous and can afford more fertilizer). So we do *not* want to use the coefficient of .83 in (13-35), because this shows how yield rises with rainfall alone (with fertilizer constant). Instead, we go back to (13-34), whose coefficient of 1.50 shows how yield rises with rainfall when fertilizer is changing too:

$$1.50(3) = 4.5 \text{ bushels}$$

To sum up: This is larger than our answer in part **b**—because the simple regression coefficient of 1.50 shows how yield is affected by rainfall *and* the associated fertilizer increase.

PROBLEMS

13-11 To determine the effect of various influences on land value in Florida, the sale price of residential lots in the Kissimmee River

Basin was regressed on several factors. With a data base of n = 316 lots, the following multiple regression was calculated (Conner and others, 1973; via Anderson and Sclove, 1978):

$$\hat{Y} = 10.3 + 1.5X_1 - 1.1X_2 - 1.34X_3 + \cdots$$

where

Y = price per front foot

X_1 = year of sale ($X_1 = 1, \ldots, 5$ for $1966, \ldots, 1970$)

X_2 = lot size (acres)

X_3 = distance from the nearest paved road (miles)

a. Other things being equal, such as year of sale and distance from the nearest paved road, was the price (per front foot) of a 5 acre lot more or less than a 2 acre lot? How much?

b. Other things being equal, how much higher was the price (per front foot) if the lot was $\frac{1}{2}$ mile closer to the nearest paved road?

c. Was the average selling price of a lot (per front foot) higher in 1970 than in 1966? How much?

13-12 A study of several hundred professors' salaries in a large American university in 1969 yielded the following multiple regression. (From Katz, 1973. These same professors were discussed in Problems 2-2 and 8-11. But now we are using more factors than just sex. In order to be brief, however, we do not write down all the factors that Katz included.)

$$\hat{S} = 230B + 18A + 100E + 490D + 190Y + 50T + \cdots$$

	B	A	E	D	Y	T
SE	(86)	(8)	(28)	(60)	(17)	(370)
95% CI	( )	( )	( )	( )	( )	( )
t ratio	( )	( )	( )	( )	( )	( )
p-value	( )	( )	( )	( )	( )	( )

where, for each professor,

S = the annual salary (dollars)

B = number of books written

A = number of ordinary articles written

E = number of excellent articles written

D = number of Ph.D's supervised

Y = number of years' experience

T = teaching score as measured by student evaluations, severely rounded: the best half of the teachers were rounded up to 100% (i.e., 1); the worst half were rounded down to 0.

a. Fill in the blanks below the equation.
b. For someone who knows no statistics, briefly summarize the influences on professors' incomes, by indicating where strong evidence exists and where it does not.
c. Answer True or False; if False, correct it.
  i. The coefficient of B is estimated to be 230. Other social scientists might collect other samples from the same population and calculate other estimates. The distribution of these estimates would be centered around the true population value of 230.
  ii. Other things being equal, we estimate that a professor who has written one or more books earns \$230 more annually. Or, we might say that \$230 estimates the value (in terms of a professor's salary) of writing one or more books.
  iii. Other things being equal, we estimate that a professor who is 1 year older earns \$190 more annually. In other words, the annual salary increase averages \$190.
d. Similarly, interpret all the other coefficients for someone who knows no statistics.

13-13 In a classic example, the average annual values of hay yield Y, temperature T, and rainfall R were recorded in England over a 20 year period (Hooker, 1907; via Anderson, 1958), so that the following regressions could be calculated:

$$\hat{Y} = 40.4 - .208T$$
$$\text{SE} \qquad (.112)$$

$$\hat{Y} = 12.2 + 3.22R$$
$$\text{SE} \qquad (.57)$$

$$\hat{Y} = 9.14 + .0364T + 3.38R$$
$$\text{SE} \qquad (.090) \qquad (.70)$$

When these regressions were calculated, estimate how much the yield would increase from one year to the next:

a. If rainfall increases 3, and temperature remains the same.
b. If temperature increases 10, and rainfall remains the same.
c. If rainfall increases 3, and temperature increases 10.
d. If rainfall increases 3, and we don't know how much temperature changes (although we know it likely will drop, since wet seasons tend to be cold).

e. If rainfall increases 3, and temperature decreases 13.

f. If temperature increases 10, and we don't know how much rainfall changes (although we know it will likely fall, since hot seasons tend to be dry).

13-14 In Problem 13-13:

a. What yield would you predict if $T = 50$ and $R = 5$?

b. What yield would you predict if $T = 65$ and $R = 7$?

c. By how much has yield increased in part **b** over part **a**? Confirm this answer using (13-32).

d. Is (13-31) a special case of (13-32)? Explain briefly.

13-15 Answer True or False; if False, correct it:

a. The simple regression equations in Problem 13-13 occasionally can be useful. For example, in the absence of any information on temperature, the second equation would correctly predict that a year with below-average rainfall would produce above-average yield.

b. In view of the positive multiple regression coefficient, however, it would improve the crop to irrigate.

***13-16** In Problem 13-13, parts **a** and **b**, put 95% confidence intervals on your answers, assuming the 20 years formed a random sample. What is the population being sampled?

---

*13-5 SIMPLE AND MULTIPLE REGRESSION COMPARED

A—DIRECT AND INDIRECT EFFECTS

The idea of regression coefficients being multiplication factors or multipliers is so useful that we will illustrate it with another example—an observational study in demography:

EXAMPLE 13-5

In a fertility survey of 4700 Fiji women (Kendall and O'Muircheartaigh, 1977), the following variables were observed for each woman:

$$\text{AGE} = \text{woman's present age, at time of the study}$$

$$\text{EDUC} = \text{woman's education, in years}$$

$$\text{CHILDN} = \text{number of children the woman has borne}$$

From this data, two regression equations were calculated:

$$\text{CHILDN} = 3.4 + .059\ \text{AGE} - .16\ \text{EDUC} \qquad (13\text{-}37)$$

$$\text{EDUC} = 7.6 - .032\ \text{AGE} \qquad (13\text{-}38)$$

a. For a woman who is 1 year older than another, calculate:
   i. The expected change in CHILDN, if EDUC is constant.
   ii. The expected change in EDUC.
   iii. The expected change in CHILDN, if EDUC is changing too.

b. What is the simple regression coefficient of CHILDN against AGE?

SOLUTION

a. A diagram will help to keep all these equations and questions straight. In Figure 13-6, *regression coefficients are shown as thin black arrows*, with the dependent Y variable on the right. Thus, the two arrows b_1 and b_2 leading to CHILDN are the multiple regression coefficients in (13-37), while the single downward arrow b is the simple regression coefficient in (13-38).

Noting that the change in age is ΔAGE $= 1$, we can now answer the questions:

   i. Since EDUC is constant, the expected change for CHILDN is given by the multiple regression coefficient b_1 (i.e., the arrow pointing from AGE to CHILDN): There is an expected increase of .059 children.

   ii. The expected change in EDUC is given by the regression coefficient b (i.e., the arrow pointing down from AGE to EDUC): There is an expected increase of $-.032$ years of education, that is, .032 *fewer* years of education.

   iii. Since EDUC is changing simultaneously, the expected change in CHILDN is found from the *simple* regression of CHILDN against AGE, which is unfortunately not given. Let us see if we can calculate it from the regressions that *are*

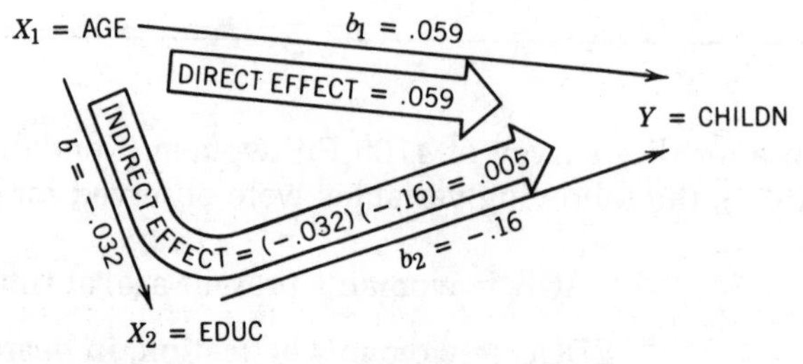

FIGURE 13-6
The direct and indirect effects of age on children.

given. If we consider women 1 year older (ΔAGE = 1), two effects must be considered:

1. *The direct effect:* By itself, we have already seen in **i** that AGE produces an increase of .059 in CHILDN (black arrow b_1).
2. *The indirect effect:* AGE affects CHILDN indirectly because, following the lower two black arrows, AGE affects EDUC, which in turn affects CHILDN. Specifically, in part **ii** we saw that the 1-year change in AGE produced a change of $-.032$ in EDUC, which in turn produces a change in CHILDN of:

$$\Delta\text{CHILDN} = b_2\, \Delta\text{EDUC}$$
$$= -.16(-.032) = +.005 \qquad (13\text{-}39)$$

The broad white arrows in the diagram sum up these two effects:

Direct effect of AGE on CHILDN	$b_1 = .059$
Indirect effect, via EDUC	$bb_2 = (-.032)(-.16) = .005$
Total effect	$b_1 + bb_2 = .064$

Notice that to calculate the indirect effect, we simply *follow the arrows*, multiplying the coefficients as we go along.

b. If we were to calculate the simple regression coefficient of CHILDN against AGE, we would *not* be holding EDUC constant; so we would be capturing both the direct and indirect effects estimated above. We would therefore expect:

$$\text{Simple regression coefficient} = \text{Total effect} = .064 \qquad (13\text{-}40)$$

This is indeed what happens. When we computed the simple regression coefficient from the data, it turned out to be .064, just as expected.

We can generally prove (in Appendix 13-5) our discovery in Example 13-5 that the simple regression coefficient gives the total effect[2]:

[2] Equation (13-41) over the page—and equation (13-44) later on—have been easier to state and understand in terms of cause-and-effect relationships. But remarkably this analysis still holds even if there is no such cause and effect. (For example, X_1 need not influence X_2 as black arrow b in Figure 13-5 suggests. It might be that X_2 influences X_1, or that some other factor influences both.) Whatever the relation, the regression coefficients still satisfy equation (13-41). This is a remarkably general result, and as Appendix 13-5 proves, is a consequence of the way that regression coefficients are calculated—algebraically, without any reference whatsoever to cause and effect.

$$\boxed{\begin{aligned}&\textbf{Simple regression coefficient}\\&\quad= \textbf{total effect}\\&\quad= \textbf{direct + indirect effect}\\&\quad= b_1 + bb_2\end{aligned}} \tag{13-41}$$

The advantage of this decomposition into direct and indirect effects is that we can immediately see their relative importance. We can also identify the bias that will occur if we erroneously used the simple regression coefficient (the total effect) when we should be using the multiple regression coefficient (the direct effect), as we will next examine in detail.

B—BIAS FROM OMITTING CONFOUNDING REGRESSORS

Recall that in Example 13-5a we want to know how AGE affects CHILDN, other things (i.e., EDUC) being constant; in other words, we want to estimate how many more children a woman will have if she is 1 year older than another woman with exactly the same education. Specifically, this estimate is given by the *multiple* regression coefficient $b_1 = .059$ that results from a regression of CHILDN on both AGE and EDUC.

Now suppose EDUC was not included in this study. Perhaps it was too hard to measure, or perhaps it was not even thought of. Then the simple regression of CHILDN against AGE alone would be calculated, and as we show in (13-41), it would pick up both the direct effect we want ($b_1 = .059$) and the indirect effect we don't want ($bb_2 = .005$). This indirect effect that throws us off target is the *bias* or *confounding* and the EDUC variable responsible for it is the *confounding* variable, or what we more colorfully called the *lurking* or *masquerading* variable.

To sum up: If we want to know how AGE affects CHILDN, *other things being constant*, we should include these other things (like EDUC) in a *multiple* regression. If we ignore them, they won't quietly go away; they will confound or bias the simple regression. The bias is shown graphically in Figure 13-6 as the indirect effect in the lower white arrow.

Observational studies generally have more than one confounding variable that should be included in a multiple regression, of course. A mark of good research is to identify the most important of these confounding variables, measure them as well as possible, and then include them in the regression. In other words:

The more confounding variables we omit from an observational study (even unintentionally), the more bias we risk—with the riskiest case being simple regression, which omits them all. (13-42)

C—RANDOMIZATION REMOVES *ALL* BIAS

Equation (13-42) points out a real difficulty with observational studies: In many cases it is impossible to measure—or even think of—all the confounding variables that we should be including.

For example, suppose that we carried out an observational study of how fertilizer affects yield, collecting data from various farmers across the state who chose to apply various amounts of fertilizer. In any simple regression of yield against fertilizer, we face the problem encountered before. Farmers who are more prosperous because they get more rainfall, for instance, are the very ones who can afford the most fertilizer. Thus their increased yield reflects not only more fertilizer, but also more rainfall. If such a confounding variable isn't included in the regression, it will introduce bias. Worse yet, there are many other confounding variables lurking in this study—the quality of the soil, infestation by insects and fungus, the timing of planting and harvesting, and the dozens of other factors that effect crop yields. To avoid bias, all of these confounding variables should be included in a multiple regression, and it may be difficult or impossible to do so.

Fortunately, there is another way of removing bias—by randomization: Let the level of fertilizer be assigned to farmers at random, rather than through their own choice. Thus high levels of fertilizer would be assigned equally often, on average, to farmers with small and large amounts of rainfall. This would break the tendency of the land with more rainfall to get the most fertilizer, and thus would cut out its bias. Similarly, randomization cuts out the bias of every other possible confounding variable, including the lurking variables we cannot measure, or don't even know exist. Then a simple regression would provide an unbiased estimate of the effect of fertilizer on yield. Thus we confirm an important conclusion in Chapter 1:

Random assignment of treatment cuts out the bias of *all* the potentially confounding variables. (13-43) like (1-5)

D—MULTIPLE REGRESSION REDUCES RESIDUAL VARIANCE

It is possible for high rainfall and high fertilizer to occur together in a small sample even if the assignment of fertilizer levels is randomized in a well controlled experiment. (Such an imbalance would be a fluke, like 8 or 9 heads in 10 tosses of a coin.) In this case the error in the simple regression slope in Figure 13-1 would be a random error rather than bias, and would average out if the sample size increased indefinitely. In a finite and realistic sample, however, this random error would not quite average out, and it may still be helpful to use multiple regression to remove it.

In removing this random error, multiple regression estimates the slope with greater accuracy. As Figure 13-4 shows, the better fit of multiple regression would give a smaller residual variance s^2, and consequently a more accurate confidence interval.

In other words, to measure the effect of one variable more accurately, multiple regression includes other variables—just as two-way ANOVA did in Chapter 10.

*PROBLEMS

13-17

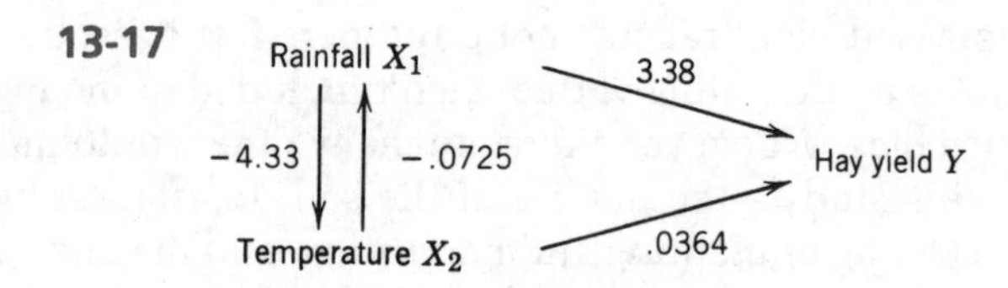

The diagonal arrows above show the multiple regression of Y against X_1 and X_2, and the vertical arrows show the simple regression of X_2 against X_1 and vice versa (same data as Problem 13-13).

a. What is the direct relation of rainfall to yield?

b. What is the total relation of rainfall to yield?

c. If an inch of irrigation was added every year, what effect do you estimate it would have?

d. What is the simple regression coefficient of yield against rainfall? And yield against temperature?

13-18 In the first figure, we repeat the data of Figure 13-4, which we suppose was gathered from an observational study. In the second figure, we show explicitly the positive relation of fertilizer X_1 and rainfall X_2, including the fitted regression line.

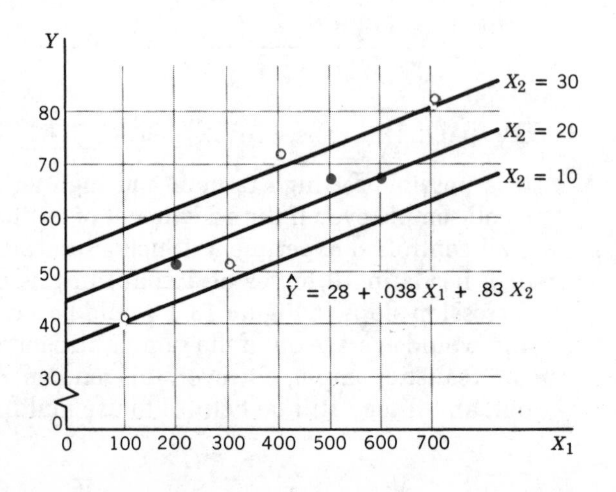

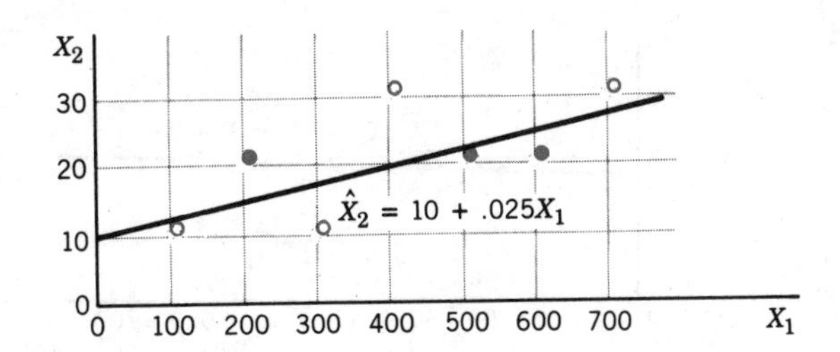

a. Fill in the numerical regression coefficients in this figure (like Figure 13-6):

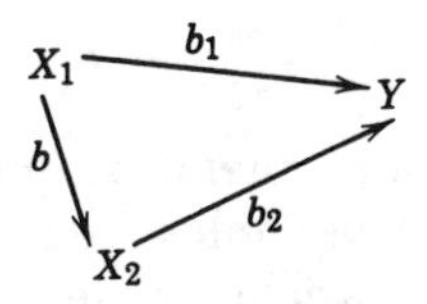

b. Calculate the indirect relation bb_2 and hence the total relation (simple regression of Y on X_1).

c. Graph the simple regression in the top figure, using the slope found in part **b**. (The Y-intercept is $a = 36$.) Does this simple regression fit the data well?

d. As the sample gets larger, would you expect the relation of fertilizer X_1 to rainfall X_2 to disappear? Would you therefore expect the indirect effect to disappear?

13-19 Repeat Problem 13-18 when fertilizer is assigned at *random* to 20 fields, producing the results below. (To draw the graph in part **c**, the Y-intercept is $a = 44$.)

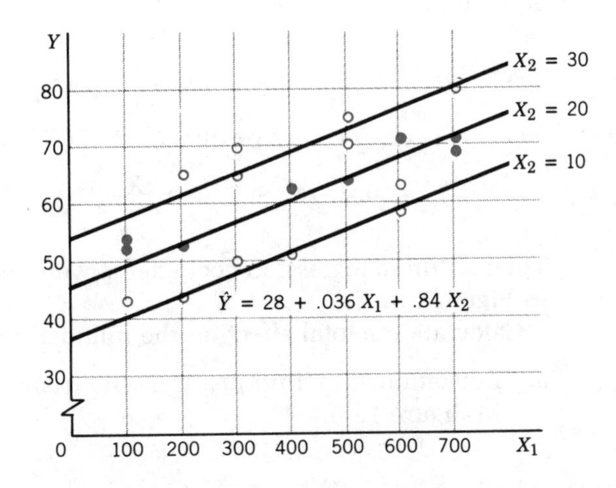

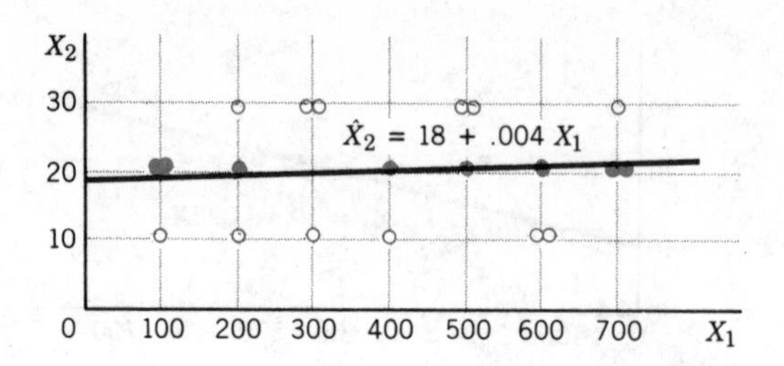

*13-6 PATH ANALYSIS

A *path analysis* is just a generalization of Figure 13-6: The first step is to lay out a sequence of variables from left to right, typically in order of cause and effect. Each variable is then regressed against all the "previous" variables to its left that influence it. Using this information, we can then show how the total effect of one variable on another is the sum of its direct and indirect effects, just as we did in Figure 13-6. An example will show how easily this earlier procedure can be generalized.

EXAMPLE 13-6

A more extensive study of the fertility (number of children, CHILDN) of the 4700 Fiji women in Example 13-5 included another influence: the regressor X_3 = AGEMAR = the woman's age at marriage. Then the new, appropriately ordered set of variables became the ones shown in Figure 13-7. Each variable was regressed against all the previous variables to its left, with the following results (ignoring constants in each regression equation):

$$Y = .062X_1 - .05X_2 - .28X_3$$

$$X_3 = .012X_1 + .38X_2$$

$$X_2 = -.032X_1$$

Then all these regression coefficients were recorded on the path diagram in Figure 13-7.

Calculate the total effect on the number of children Y of:

a. Education X_2. (*Hint:* Just treat the triangle X_2X_3Y like the triangle in Figure 13-6.)

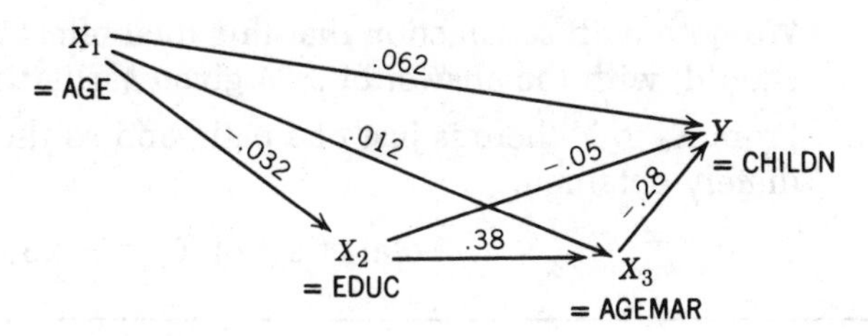

FIGURE 13-7
Path diagram of Fiji fertility.

b. Present age X_1. (*Hint:* Extending the approach in part **a**, calculate *all* the paths between X_1 and Y, and sum them.)

c. Marriage age X_3.

SOLUTION

a. From X_2 to Y there are two paths—the direct path from X_2 to Y and the indirect path via X_3. Thus, the triangle X_2X_3Y has exactly the same structure as the triangle in Figure 13-6, and the calculations are similar.

Direct effect of X_2 *on* Y		$= -.05$
Indirect effect via X_3	$(.38)(-.28)$	$= -.11$
	Total effect	$= -.16$

That is, a better educated woman has fewer children on average (.16 fewer children for each year of education she has received). Partly this is because more education *directly* reduces childbearing, and partly because of an *indirect effect:* More education tends to produce a later marriage age, which in turn results in fewer children.

b. From X_1 to Y there are so many paths that it is helpful to work them out systematically so that nothing is missed. As well as the direct path, there are now several indirect paths through the intervening variables X_3 and X_2; we consider each in turn:

Direct effect of X_1 *on* Y		$= .062$
Indirect effect via X_3		$(.012)(-.28) = -.003$
Indirect effect via X_2:	via X_2 alone	$(-.032)(-.05) = +.002$
	via X_2 and X_3	$(-.032)(.38)(-.28) = +.003$
		Total effect $= .064$

We note with satisfaction that this total effect agrees, as it should, with the answer of .064 given earlier in Example 13-5.

c. From X_3 to Y there is just one path, and so the answer is immediately obtained:

$$\text{Total effect of } X_3 = -.28$$

To sum up: The total effect of one variable (say X_1) on a later variable (say Y) is defined as the change occurring in Y when X_1 changes one unit—taking into account all the changes in the intervening variables between X_1 and Y. The total effect can be calculated from the network of direct effects using a natural extension of (13-41): As we follow each path from X_1 to Y, we multiply together all the coefficients we encounter. Then

Total effect of X_1 on Y = the sum of all paths (following the arrows from X_1 to Y)	(13-44) like (13-41)

---

*PROBLEMS

13-20 In the following path diagram, the variables are defined as in Figure 13-7. (The sample, however, is taken from the Indian subpopulation of Fiji, so the path coefficients are slightly different.)

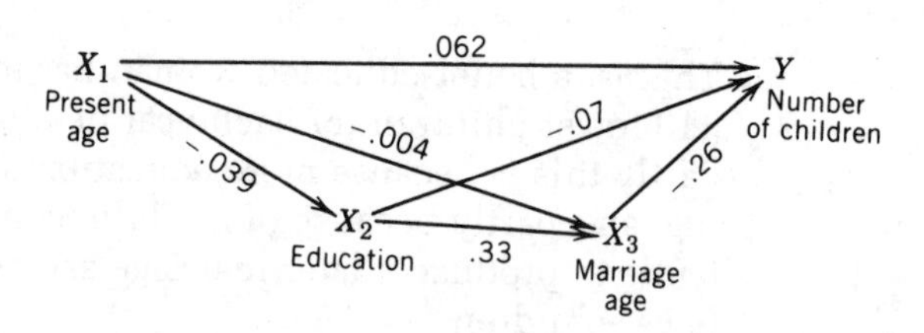

Calculate the total effect on Y (number of children) of each of the following:

a. The total effect of X_3.

b. The total effect of X_2.

c. The total effect of X_1.

13-21 In Problem 13-20, how many children would you expect of:

a. A woman whose marriage was 1 year later than the marriage of a woman of the same age and education?

b. A woman having 1 year more education than a woman of the same age, and the same age at marriage?

c. A woman having 1 year more education than a woman of the same age? (Age at marriage not known, but probably different, of course.)

d. A woman who is 1 year older than another woman? (Education and age at marriage not known, but probably different, of course.)

13-22 Suppose the demographer who did the Fiji study in Problem 13-20 had not measured X_3 (marriage age). Then his path diagram would look like this:

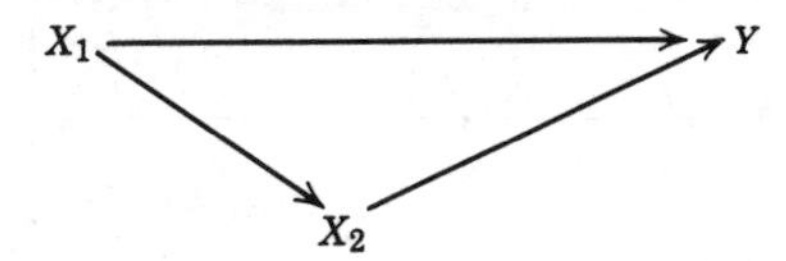

Suppose that otherwise his data were exactly the same, based on the same women. When he calculates the multiple regression coefficients (path coefficients), what will they be? [*Hint:* The path from X_1 to Y, for example, will be the sum of two former paths: the direct path, and the indirect path via X_3, which is now omitted.]

13-23 How can one explain the choice of occupation? A study of Blau and Duncan (1967, via Van de Geer, 1971) measured the following variables:

X_1 = father's education level

X_2 = father's occupational status

X_3 = son's educational level

X_4 = occupational level of son's first job

Y = occupational level of son's second job

Then the multiple regression of each variable on the previous ones was calculated as follows:

$$X_2 = .52X_1$$

$$X_3 = .31X_1 + .28X_2$$

$$X_4 = .02X_1 + .22X_2 + .43X_3$$

$$Y = -.01X_1 + .12X_2 + .40X_3 + .21X_4$$

a. Draw the path diagram that illustrates these equations.

b. Find the total effect on Y of:

(i) X_3 **(ii)** X_2 **(iii)** X_1

c. If father's education level X_1 increased 3 units, what change would you expect in the occupational level of the son's second job Y if:

i. The other variables were constant?

ii. If nothing was known about the other variables (except that they probably changed in response to the change in X_1)?

CHAPTER 13 SUMMARY

13-1 Multiple regression reduces the bias of confounding variables in an observational study. It also reduces residual variance and narrows confidence intervals, in observational studies and randomized experiments alike.

13-2 The underlying population regression as usual is denoted by Greek letters: $E(Y) = \beta_0 + \beta_1 X_1 + \beta_2 X_2 + \cdots$. The sample regression $\hat{Y} = b_0 + b_1 X_1 + b_2 X_2 + \cdots$ is typically computed with a standard regression package, using the same OLS criterion (ordinary least squares) as in simple regression.

13-3 The regression package also computes the estimated standard error (SE) of each b, from which confidence intervals and p-values are easily calculated.

13-4 In the model $Y = b_0 + b_1 X_1 + b_2 X_2 + \cdots$, the change in Y is given by $\Delta Y = b_1 \Delta X_1 + b_2 \Delta X_2 + \cdots$. That is, each change ΔX is multiplied by its coefficient b to give its effect on Y.

In particular, if only one regressor is changing, say X_1, then $\Delta Y = b_1 \Delta X_1$. That is, b_1 shows how X_1 is related to Y, if all the other regressors are constant.

***13-5** The total effect of a regressor on Y (the simple regression coefficient) can be expressed as the sum of the direct effect (the multiple regression coefficient) and the indirect effects. The indirect effects represent the bias in an observational study that omits important confounding variables.

***13-6** A path diagram typically involves many variables listed in order of cause and effect, each variable being related to the previous ones by a multiple regression. The total effect of one variable on another can be obtained by summing along all the paths from one to the other.

REVIEW PROBLEMS

13-24 A multiple regression was computed for a sample of 50 men randomly sampled from a large population of workers (Lefcoe and Wonnacott, 1974). Lung capacity Y (in milliliters), was regressed against age (in years), height (in inches), amount of smoking (in packs per day), and several other possible confounding factors:

Variable	*Coefficient*	*SE*	*95% CI*	*p-Value*
AGE	−39.0	9.1		
HEIGHT	+98.4	32.0		
SMOKING	−180.0	206.4		
.				
.				
.				

a. Fill in the last two columns.

b. If the whole population were run through the computer, rather than a mere sample of 50, in what range would you expect to find each of the computed coefficients?

c. Other things being equal, what would you estimate is the effect of:

i. Smoking 1 pack per day?

ii. Being 5 years older?

iii. Smoking 2 packs per day and being 10 years older?

d. As far as lung capacity is concerned, the effect of smoking 1 pack per day is equivalent to aging how many years?

e. Your answer to part **d** is only approximate. What are the sources of error?

13-25 A simple regression of life expectancy Y (in years) on smoking X (in packs per day) for U.S. males (age 21) would yield the following approximate regression equation (U.S. Surgeon-General, 1979):

$$\hat{Y} = 70 - 5X$$

Is it fair to say that smoking cuts 5 years off the end of your life, for each pack smoked? If so, why? If not, how *would* you estimate the effect of smoking 1 pack per day?

13-26 The cost of air pollution (in terms of higher disease and mortality rates) was studied by two economists (Lave and Seskin, 1977). They introduced the problem as follows:

> "The cause of a disease is often difficult to establish. For chronic diseases, establishing a cause-and-effect relationship is especially difficult. Many studies show that populations exposed to urban air pollution have a shorter life expectancy and higher incidence of lung cancer, emphysema, and other chronic respiratory diseases. Yet it is a long step to assert that this observed association between air pollution and ill health is proof that air pollution causes ill health . . .
>
> "The situation is similar to the controversy as to whether cigarette smoking causes lung cancer. Both the cigarette smoking and air pollution controversies stem from the fact that many other possible causal factors are present. Urban dwellers live in more crowded conditions, get less exercise, and tend to live more tense lives. Since each of these factors is known to increase the morbidity and mortality rates, care must be taken to control or account for each factor before drawing inferences . . ."

a. Before drawing inferences about causation, the authors suggest three factors that should be controlled or accounted for: crowding, lack of exercise, and tenseness. What other confounding (lurking) variables might be important?

b. Suggest how they might control or account for these confounding factors.

13-27 The authors in Problem 13-26 continued:

> . . . the basic problem is one of allowing for all causal variables. Accounting for confounding factors in observed data is one of the purposes of multivariate statistical analysis. Since we have some notion of the model and desire estimates of the direct contribution of each factor, an appropriate technique is multiple regression."

To carry out this multiple regression, they collected measurements on the following variables, in each of 117 SMSA's (Standard Metropolitan Statistical Areas) in 1960:

M = mortality rate (deaths per 10,000 people annually)

P = pollution (mean of the biweekly suspended particulate readings, in $\mu g/m^3$)

SP = sulphate pollution (the smallest of the biweekly sulphate readings, in $\mu g/m^3$)

D = density of population (people per square mile)

B = percentage of population that is nonwhite

E = percentage of population that is elderly (over 65)

The regression equation of mortality against pollution and the confounding factors was:

$$\begin{array}{lllllll} M = & 19.6 + & .041P + & .71SP + & .001D + & .41B + & 6.87E \\ \text{(SE)} & & (.016) & (.22) & (.0006) & (.07) & (.36) \end{array}$$

a. For Pittsburgh, a typical SMSA, the levels of the various factors were: $P = 170$, $SP = 6.0$, $D = 790$, $B = 6.8$ and $E = 9.5$. What is Pittsburgh's predicted mortality rate? Pittsburgh's actual mortality rate was 103 (deaths per 10,000 annually). How accurate was the prediction?

b. For all 117 SMSAs, the average levels of the various factors were $\overline{P} = 120$, $\overline{SP} = 4.7$, $\overline{D} = 760$, $\overline{B} = 12.5$, and $\overline{E} = 8.4$. What was the average mortality rate?

c. Other things being equal, estimate how much the average mortality rate would change:

i. If the proportion of elderly people was halved (from an average of 8.4 percent given in **b** down to 4.2 percent).

ii. If the population density was halved.

iii. If both forms of pollution (both P and SP) were halved.

d. Suppose the 117 SMSAs are regarded as a sample from a large conceptual population. Then for the population coefficient of pollution P:

i. What would be the 95% confidence interval?

ii. What would be the p-value for H_0?

iii. At the 5% level, would pollution be a statistically discernible factor?

13-28 **a.** In Problem 13-27, part **c**, we measured the effects of three factors in terms of relative changes. In this sense, which of the three factors is most important? Least important?

b. Since the percentage of elderly people E was found to be very important, what might have happened if it had been omitted from the study?

c. Note that variables such as occupational exposure, personal habits and smoking were omitted from the study. Would you agree with the authors that if these variables "are related to the level of air pollution, then our pollution estimates will be biased as indicators of causality." Then why do you suppose they were omitted?

***13-29** Suppose that $Y = a + b_1X_1 + b_2X_2 + b_3X_3$. Prove that, if X_3 remains constant while X_1 and X_2 change:

$$\Delta Y = b_1\Delta X_1 + b_2\Delta X_2$$

13-30 ***A Final Challenge: What Is Crime Related To?***

In a study of 230 blocks randomly sampled in Peoria, Illinois, Choldin and Roncek (1976) calculated the simple regression of the crime rate Y (violent crime) against population density. They also calculated the simple regression of Y against some other interesting factors listed in the table below.

By contrast, the last column gives the *multiple* regression coefficient, when Y was regressed against all the X factors together.

Regressions of Crime Rate *Y* Against Various Factors *X*

Factor[a]	*Simple Regression Coefficient, Y against each X*	*Multiple Regression Coefficient, Y against all X's*
X_1 = population density	.17	.00 (insig[b])
X_2 = percent of households with intact husband-wife families	−.32	−.34
X_3 = index of housing value	−.37	−.25
X_4, X_5 . . . other relevant variables such as age, etc.		

[a] All factors, as well as Y, are in the standardized form $(X - \bar{X})/s$. This makes each regression coefficient independent of the arbitrary scale used, and hence makes the comparison of several coefficients more meaningful.
[b] All coefficients except this one are statistically discernible at the 5% level.

a. Suppose a rezoning proposal for a block would increase density by 0.40 units, with no measurable change in the kinds of people or in housing values, however. Estimate what this would do to the crime rate.

b. Suppose, a little more realistically, that the rezoning proposal would also result in new and better housing, so that the index of housing X_3 was raised by 1.20 units. Estimate what both these changes together would do to the crime rate.

c. I am planning to move from a block where population density is $X_1 = 0.87$, to a new block where $X_1 = 1.07$. What changes in the crime rate can I expect:

i. If nothing is known about the other variables $X_2, X_3, \ldots$?

ii. If it is known that the other variables will be the same, except for an increase in the intact families from X_2 = 0.50 to 0.70?

d. Suppose as the city manager, you are petitioned to keep down the crime rate (among other things), by keeping population density low. Write a brief reply.

CHAPTER 14

Regression Extensions

Any astronomer can predict just where every star will be at half past eleven tonight. He can make no such prediction about his daughter.

JAMES TRUSLOW ADAMS

In this chapter we will see how versatile a tool multiple regression can be, when it is given a few clever twists. It can be used on categorical data (such as yes-no responses) as well as the numerical data we have dealt with so far. And it can be used to fit curves as well as linear relations.

14-1 DUMMY (0-1) VARIABLES

A—PARALLEL LINES FOR TWO CATEGORIES

In Chapter 6 we introduced dummy variables for handling data that came in two categories (such as Democrat versus Republican, or treatment versus control). By associating numbers (0 and 1) with the two categories, a dummy variable ingeniously transformed the problem into a numerical one, and so made it amenable to all the standard statistical tools. (For example, standard errors and confidence intervals could be constructed.) Now we shall see how a dummy variable can be equally useful in regression analysis.

EXAMPLE 14-1

A certain drug (drug A) is suspected of having the unfortunate side effect of raising blood pressure. To test this suspicion, 10 women were randomly sampled, 6 of whom took the drug once a day, and 4 of whom took no drug, and hence served as the control group. To transform "drug use" into a numerical variable, for each patient let:

$$D = \text{number of doses of this drug she takes daily} \qquad \begin{array}{r}(14\text{-}1)\\ \text{like } (6\text{-}17)\end{array}$$

that is,

$$\left.\begin{aligned} D &= 1 \text{ if she took the drug} \\ &= 0 \text{ if she did not (i.e., was a control)} \end{aligned}\right\} \qquad \begin{array}{r}(14\text{-}2)\\ \text{like } (6\text{-}18)\end{array}$$

In the form (14-1), it is clear that D is a variable that can be run through a regression computer program like any other variable. Moreover, in the form (14-2) it is clear that D is a 0-1 variable that clearly distinguishes between the two groups of women; and this is the form most commonly used.

We want to investigate how this drug affects blood pressure Y, keeping constant confounding factors such as age X. Following blood pressure Y in column 1 of Table 14-1, therefore, we type in as regressors both age X (rounded to the nearest decade in column 2) and drug use D (in column 3). The computer calculates the equation (rounded and rearranged):

$$\hat{Y} = 70 + 5D + .44X \qquad (14\text{-}3)$$

a. Graph the relation of Y to X given by (14-3), when

i. $D = 0$

ii. $D = 1$

TABLE 14-1 Drug Trials Using a Dummy Variable *D*.

```
  > READ'Y','X', 'D'
DATA>      85  30   0
DATA>      95  40   1
DATA>      90  40   1
DATA>      75  20   0
DATA>     100  60   1
DATA>      90  40   0
DATA>      90  50   0
DATA>      90  30   1
DATA>     100  60   1
DATA>      85  30   1

  > REGRESS'Y' ON 2 REGRESSORS'X','D'

THE REGRESSION EQUATION IS
Y = 69.5 + 0.442 X + 4.65 D

                                  ST. DEV.      T-RATIO =
COLUMN        COEFFICIENT         OF COEF.      COEF/S.D.
                  69.535           2.905          23.93
X                 0.44186          0.07301         6.05
D                  4.651           1.885           2.47
```

b. What is the meaning of the coefficient of D? Answer using the graph in **a**. Also answer using the fundamental interpretation (13-31).

c. Construct a 95% confidence interval for the (true) population coefficient of D. Is it discernible at the 5% level?

SOLUTION

a. Equation (14-3) takes on two forms, depending on whether D is zero or one.

For the control group, set $D = 0$: $$\hat{Y} = 70 + .44X \quad (14\text{-}4)$$

For the treatment group, set $D = 1$: $$\hat{Y} = 70 + 5 + .44X \quad (14\text{-}5)$$ $$\hat{Y} = 75 + .44X \quad (14\text{-}6)$$

When these two parallel lines are graphed in Figure 14-1, we see that the treatment group (where $D = 1$) exceeds the control group by 5 units—the coefficient of D.

b. On the graph, suppose we keep age constant, at $X = 55$ for example. The difference the drug makes is 5 units, the vertical distance between the lines.

Alternatively, we could use the fundamental interpretation for any regression coefficient: The coefficient of D is the change in Y that accompanies a unit change in D (while X remains constant). This unit change in D can only be from 0 to 1—that is, from no drug to drug. Thus there is an increase in blood pressure Y of 5 as we go from a woman without the drug ($D = 0$) to a woman of

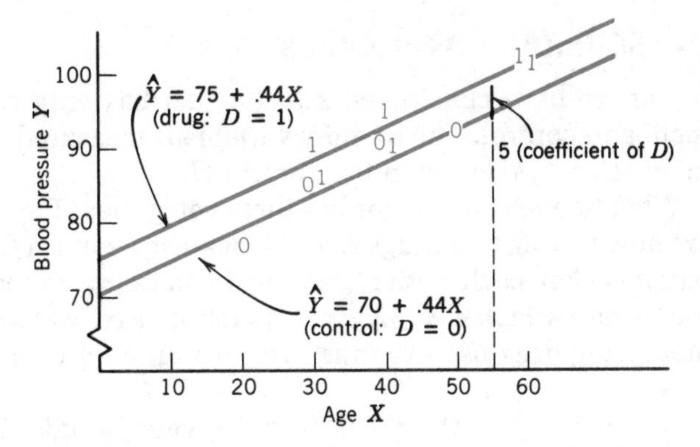

FIGURE 14-1
Graph of equation (14-3) relating blood pressure to age and treatment. (1 represents a patient who was given the drug, while 0 represents a patient who was not.)

the same age with the drug ($D = 1$). This agrees with the interpretation in the previous paragraph.

c. The 95% confidence interval can be found as usual from the coefficient and its estimated standard error (SE) or standard deviation, given in the very last line of Table 14-1. For $t_{.025}$, we use d.f. $= n - k - 1 = 10 - 2 - 1 = 7$. Thus

$$\begin{aligned} \text{Population coefficient} &= \text{estimate} \pm t_{.025}\,\text{SE} && \text{like (13-13)} \\ &= 4.65 \pm 2.36(1.88) \\ &\simeq 4.7 \pm 4.4 && \text{(14-7)} \end{aligned}$$

Since the estimate 4.7 exceeds the sampling allowance 4.4, the relationship between D and Y is discernible at the 5% level. (But we should be careful about concluding that D *causes* an increase in blood pressure Y, because the drug was not assigned at random to the women. Thus our multiple regression kept constant only one of the possible confounding factors—age X).

In conclusion, this example shows how a two-category factor can be nicely handled with a 0-1 regressor, and in general:

> **Suppose D is a 0-1 variable in the regression model**
>
> $$\hat{Y} = b_0 + b_1 D + b_2 X$$
>
> **Relative to the reference line where $D = 0$, the line where $D = 1$ is parallel and b_1 units higher. And the standard confidence intervals and tests can be computed using b_1 and b_2 along with their standard errors.** (14-8)

B—SEVERAL CATEGORIES

So far we have considered a factor that has only two categories—treatment and control. The dummy variable D measured the effect of the treatment ($D = 1$) relative to the control ($D = 0$).

What happens if a factor has three categories? For example, suppose we are now testing two drugs A and B against a control C, with a sample of 30 patients. For each patient, we again measure the response Y and confounding variables $X_1, X_2 \ldots$ (such as age, weight, etc.). But now, in measuring drug use, we must use two dummy variables:

$$D_A = 1 \text{ if drug } A \text{ given; 0 otherwise} \tag{14-9}$$

$$D_B = 1 \text{ if drug } B \text{ given; 0 otherwise} \tag{14-10}$$

Thus, typical data would start out as follows (illustrating the three different ways drug could be assigned):

Comments		*Data*				
Person	*Drug*	Y	D_A	D_B	X_1	$X_2 \cdots$
Koval	On drug *A*	.	1	0	. . .	. . .
Bellhouse	On drug *B*	.	0	1	. . .	. . .
Haq	Control *C*	.	0	0	. . .	. . .
.	.	.	.	.	. . .	. . .
.	.	.	.	.	. . .	. . .
.	.	.	.	.	. . .	. . .

Suppose the regression computed from this data turned out to be

$$\hat{Y} = 70 + 5D_A + 8D_B + .44X_1 + \cdots \tag{14-11}$$

From this regression, we can easily write down the three separate equations for the three groups:

$$\begin{aligned}
&\text{For the control group,} \\
&\text{set } D_A = 0,\ D_B = 0: && \hat{Y} = 70 + .44X_1 + \cdots \\
&\text{For the group on drug A,} \\
&\text{set } D_A = 1,\ D_B = 0: && \hat{Y} = 75 + .44X_1 + \cdots \\
&\text{For the group on drug B,} \\
&\text{set } D_A = 0,\ D_B = 1: && \hat{Y} = 78 + .44X_1 + \cdots
\end{aligned} \tag{14-12}$$

When these three parallel lines are graphed in panel (*a*) of Figure 14-2, we see again that the group on drug A exceeds the controls by 5 units—the coefficient of D_A. Similarly, the group on drug B exceeds the controls by 8 units—the coefficient of D_B.

If desired, comparison of drug B with drug A is easily obtained by subtraction. Looking again at panel (*a*) of Figure 14-2, we see that the group on drug B exceeds the group on drug A by $8 - 5 = 3$ units.

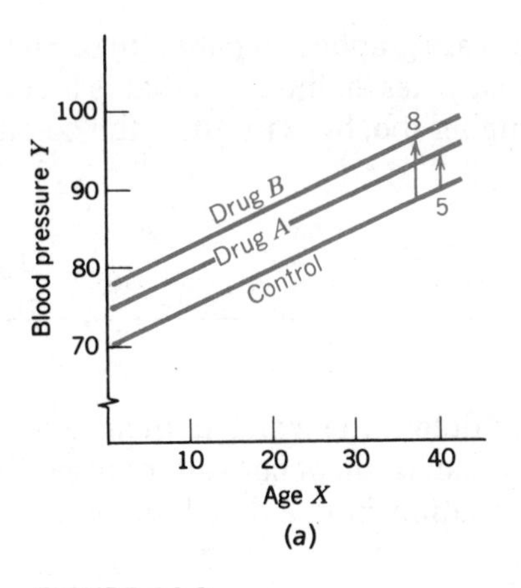

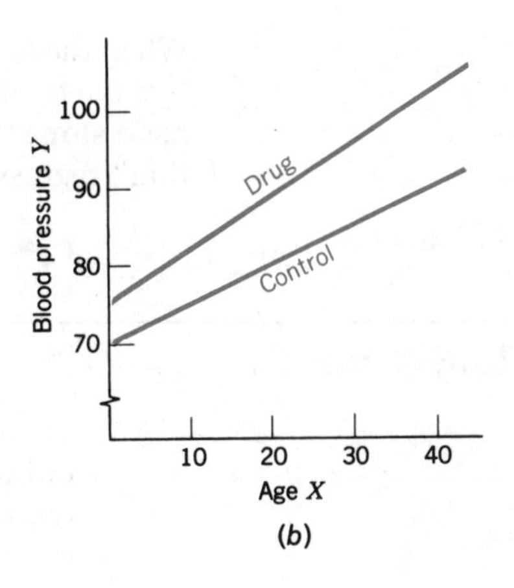

FIGURE 14-2
Two ingenious uses of dummy variables (a) Comparing several categories (b) different slopes as well as intercepts.

In general, what do we do for any number of categories? For example, suppose in a study of multinational corporation profits, 6 different countries are to be compared. As a reference or control group, it is natural to choose the largest or most visible country (for example, the United States). Then for each of the other 5 countries, we would define a dummy variable (for example, $D_J = 1$ for Japanese data, 0 otherwise). The general lesson is clear: We need one less dummy than there are categories, since one category has to be left as a reference.

C—DIFFERENT SLOPES AS WELL AS INTERCEPTS

The regression model (14-3) compared treatment and control groups by a set of parallel lines. It is easy to extend the model to have different slopes as well as different intercepts.

We simply introduce one more regressor, DX. (After the variables Y, X, and D are entered into the data file, the variable D times X is computed. In Table 14-1, for example, this would produce a final column, that reads 0, 40, 40, 0, 60, ...) Suppose the regression then turns out to be:

$$\hat{Y} = 70 + 5D + .44X + .21DX \tag{14-13}$$

From this regression, we easily obtain the two separate equations for the two groups:

For the control group, set $D = 0$: $\hat{Y} = 70 + .44X$

For the treatment group, set $D = 1$: $\hat{Y} = 70 + 5 + .44X + .21X = 75 + .65X$

When these two lines are graphed in panel (*b*) of Figure 14-2, we see again that the treatment group has an intercept that is 5 units higher. And now it has a slope that is higher too, by .21 units—the coefficient of the "interaction" regressor *DX*.

PROBLEMS

14-1 To help firms determine which of their executive salaries might be out of line, a management consultant fitted the following multiple regression equation from a data base of 270 executives under the age of 40:

$$\begin{array}{llll} \text{SAL} = 43.4 + 1.24\ \text{EXP} & + 3.60\ \text{EDUC} & + 0.74\ \text{MALE} \\ \text{(SE)} \qquad\qquad (.30) & (1.20) & (1.10) \end{array}$$

$$\text{residual standard deviation } s = 16.4$$

where SAL = the executive's annual salary ($000)
EDUC = number of years of post-secondary education
EXP = number of years of experience
MALE = dummy variable, coded 1 for male, 0 for female

a. From this regression, a firm can calculate the fitted salary of each of its executives. If the actual salary is much lower or higher, it can be reviewed to see whether it is appropriate.

Fred Kopp, for example, is a 32-year old vice president of a large restaurant chain. He has been with the firm since he obtained a 2-year MBA at age 25, following a 4-year degree in economics. He now earns $126,000 annually.

i. What is Fred's fitted salary?

ii. How many standard deviations is his actual salary away from his fitted salary? Would you therefore call his salary exceptional?

iii. Closer inspection of Fred's record showed that he had spent two years studying at Oxford as a Rhodes Scholar before obtaining his MBA. In light of this information, recalculate your answers to **i** and **ii**.

b. In addition to identifying unusual salaries in specific firms, this regression can be used to answer questions about the economy-wide structure of executive salaries in *all* firms. For example,

i. Is there evidence of sex discrimination?

ii. Is it fair to say that each year's education (beyond high school) increases the income of the average executive by $3600 a year?

14-2 A regression equation related personal income Y (annual, in \$1000) to education E (in years) and geographical location, measured with dummies as follows:

$$D_S = 1 \text{ if in the South; 0 otherwise}$$
$$D_W = 1 \text{ if in the West; 0 otherwise}$$

The remaining region (Northeast) is left as the reference region.

a. Suppose the regression fitted from $n = 32$ people was

$$\hat{Y} = 4.5 + 0.5E - 1.0D_S + 1.5D_W$$

Graph the estimated income $\hat{Y}$ as a function of E, for each of the 3 regions, with E running from 8 to 16.

b. Redraw the graph in part **a**, according to the following interactive model:

$$\begin{aligned} \hat{Y} &= 4.5 + \underset{(0.2)}{0.5E} + \underset{(0.4)}{1.4D_S} + \underset{(0.3)}{0.3D_W} - \underset{(0.3)}{0.2D_SE} + \underset{(0.2)}{0.1D_WE} \end{aligned}$$

(SE)

c. Estimate the difference in slopes between two underlying population lines—for the South and for the Northeast. Use a 95% confidence interval. Is the difference in slopes statistically discernible at level $\alpha = 5\%$?

14-3 In an environmental study of 1072 men, a multiple regression was calculated to show how lung function was related to several factors, including some hazardous occupations (Lefcoe and Wonnacott, 1974):

$$\begin{aligned} \text{AIRCAP} = 4500 &- \underset{(1.8)}{39\ \text{AGE}} - \underset{(2.2)}{9.0\ \text{SMOK}} \\ &- \underset{(46)}{350\ \text{CHEMW}} - \underset{(53)}{380\ \text{FARMW}} - \underset{(54)}{180\ \text{FIREW}} \end{aligned}$$

(SE)

where

AIRCAP = air capacity (milliliters) that the worker can expire in one second
AGE = age (years)
SMOK = amount of current smoking (cigarettes per day)
CHEMW = 1 if subject is a chemical worker, 0 if not
FARMW = 1 if subject is a farm worker, 0 if not
FIREW = 1 if subject is a firefighter, 0 if not

A fourth occupation, physician, served as the reference group, and so did not need a dummy. Assuming these 1072 people were a random sample,

a. Calculate the 95% confidence interval for each coefficient.

Fill in the blanks, and choose the correct word in square brackets:

b. Other things being equal (things such as ____), chemical workers on average have AIRCAP values that are ____ milliliters [higher, lower] than physicians.

c. Other things being equal, chemical workers on average have AIRCAP values that are ____ milliliters [higher, lower] than farmworkers.

d. Other things being equal, on average a man who is 1 year older has an AIRCAP value that is ____ milliliters [higher, lower].

e. Other things being equal, on average a man who smokes one pack (20 cigarettes) a day has an AIRCAP value that is ____ milliliters [higher, lower].

f. As far as AIRCAP is concerned, we estimate that smoking one pack a day is roughly equivalent to aging ____ years. But this estimate may be biased because of ____.

14-4 In the same study as Problem 14-3, each worker's lungs were alternatively evaluated by whether or not he had bronchitis—using a dummy variable:

$$\text{BRONC} = 1 \text{ if worker has bronchitis, 0 otherwise}$$

Then BRONC was regressed on the same factors:

$$\begin{aligned}\text{BRONC} = -.04 &+ \underset{(.0009)}{.0021}\ \text{AGE} + \underset{(.0011)}{.0047}\ \text{SMOK} \\ &+ \underset{(.024)}{.065}\ \text{CHEMW} + \underset{(.027)}{.002}\ \text{FARMW} - \underset{(.027)}{.032}\ \text{FIREW}\end{aligned}$$

This represents something new: a dummy variable for the response, as well as dummy variables as regressors. Nevertheless, the interpretation is still the same. For example, other things being equal, an increase of 10 years in age means an increase in BRONC of $10 \times .0021 = .021$—that is, an increase of 2.1 percentage points in the bronchitis rate (or in the *probability* of an individual having bronchitis).

Answer the same questions as in Problem 14-3, substituting BRONC for AIRCAP (and for the units, substitute percentage points for milliliters).

14-5 In an observational study to determine the effect of a drug on blood pressure it was noticed that the treated group (taking the drug) tended to weigh more than the control group. Thus, when the treated group had higher blood pressure on average, was it because of the treatment or their weight? To untangle this knot, some regressions were computed, using the following variables:

$$\begin{aligned} BP &= \text{blood pressure} \\ WEIGHT &= \text{weight} \\ D &= 1 \text{ if taking the drug, 0 otherwise} \end{aligned}$$

When the 15 patients' records were run through the computer, the following outputs were obtained:

D	WEIGHT	BP
0	180	81
0	150	75
0	210	83
0	140	74
0	160	72
0	160	80
0	150	78
0	200	80
0	160	74
1	190	85
1	240	102
1	200	95
1	180	86
1	190	100
1	220	90

THE REGRESSION EQUATION IS
BP = 54.0 + 10.6 D + 0.139 WEIGHT

COLUMN	COEFFICIENT	ST. DEV. OF COEF.	T-RATIO = COEF/S.D.
	54.040	8.927	6.05
D	10.596	2.984	3.55
WEIGHT	0.13950	0.05248	2.66

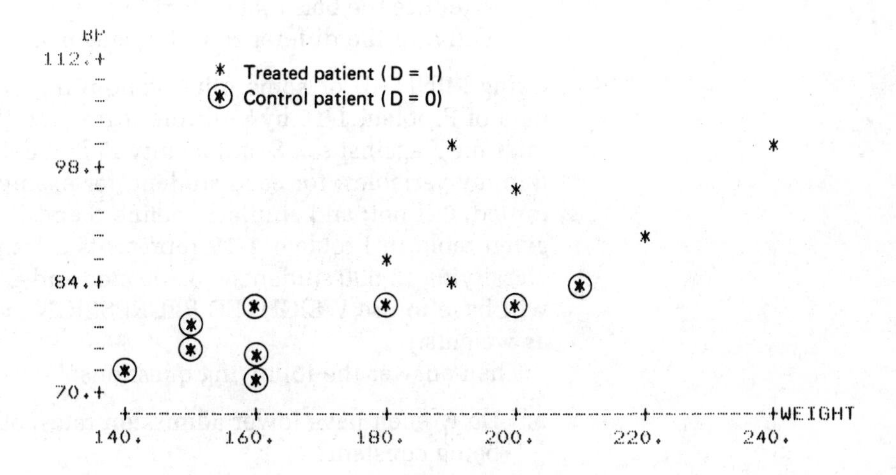

a. Verify that the computer has correctly graphed the first two patients. Then graph the regression equation.

b. How much higher on average would the blood pressure be:

i. For someone of the same weight who is on the drug?

ii. For someone on the same treatment who is 10 lbs. heavier?

c. On the computer graph, show your answers to part **b.**

d. How would the simple regression coefficient compare to the multiple regression coefficient for weight? Why?

14-6 a. Continuing Problem 14-5, sort out the values of *BP* into two groups according to whether they had taken the drug or not (treatment and control groups). Then calculate the confidence interval for the difference in two means, using (8-20).

b. Calculate the confidence interval for the simple regression coefficient of *BP* against *D*, using the following computer output:

```
THE REGRESSION EQUATION IS
BP = 77.4 + 15.6 D

                                  ST. DEV.      T-RATIO =
COLUMN        COEFFICIENT         OF COEF.      COEF/S.D.
                   77.444            1.784          43.42
D                  15.556            2.820           5.52
```

c. Which of the two confidence intervals above is a better measure of the effect of the drug? Is there an even better measure?

d. To generalize, answer True or False; if False, correct it. The confidence interval comparing means for two independent samples is equivalent to using simple regression on a 0-1 regressor. However, it is much better to use *multiple* regression to reduce the bias that occurs in simple regression (or equivalently, in the difference in two means).

*14-7 Using MINITAB or some other computing package, analyze the data of Problem 1-18 by multiple regression (Hint: to regress admission *Y* against sex *S* and faculty *F*, first define the appropriate dummy variables: for each student, for example, let $Y = 1$ if admitted, 0 if not; and similarly define *S* and *F*. Then note that the given table in Problem 1-18 represents a frequency distribution classifying 12,600 students—8,300 men and 4,300 women. So you will have to use WEIGHTED REGRESSION, with the frequencies as weights.)

Then answer the following questions:

a. Do women have lower admission rates, other things (faculty) being constant?

b. Reread the last paragraph of Problem 1-18. Could your multiple regression accommodate other confounding factors such as graduate record exam scores?

*14-8 Using MINITAB or some other computing package, analyze the data of Problem 5-24. (Hint: As in Problem 14-7, define appropriate dummy variables, and use the frequencies for weighted regression.)

14-2 ANALYSIS OF VARIANCE (ANOVA) BY REGRESSION

A—ONE-FACTOR ANOVA

In Example 14-1, we were mainly concerned with the effect on blood pressure of the dummy regressor (drug), and introduced the numerical regressor (age) primarily to keep this extraneous variable from biasing the estimate of the drug effect. Used in this way, multiple regression is sometimes called *analysis of covariance* (ANOCOVA, with a table similar to the ANOVA Table 10-4).

If the numerical regressors are omitted entirely so that dummy regressors alone are used, then the multiple regression reduces to a form such as:

$$\hat{Y} = 5 + 30D_A + 20D_B \qquad (14\text{-}14)$$

where D_A and D_B are dummy regressors to distinguish patients on drug A and B from the control group.

A regression of this form is equivalent to the traditional one-factor ANOVA in Chapter 10. (There the single factor was machines; here it is drugs.)

B—TWO-FACTOR ANOVA

It is possible to use dummy variables to introduce a second factor, or more. For example, in the drug study, suppose we want to see the effect of another factor, sex. We can take care of it with one dummy variable:

$$M = 1 \text{ if male; 0 if female} \qquad (14\text{-}15)$$

Then the fitted regression equation, instead of (14-14), would be something like

$$\hat{Y} = 5 + 30D_A + 20D_B + 15M \qquad (14\text{-}16)$$

One convenient way to graph (14-16) is like Figure 14-1—with M playing the former role of age X, and D_A and D_B playing the former role of the dummy D. This graph is shown in Figure 14-3*a*.

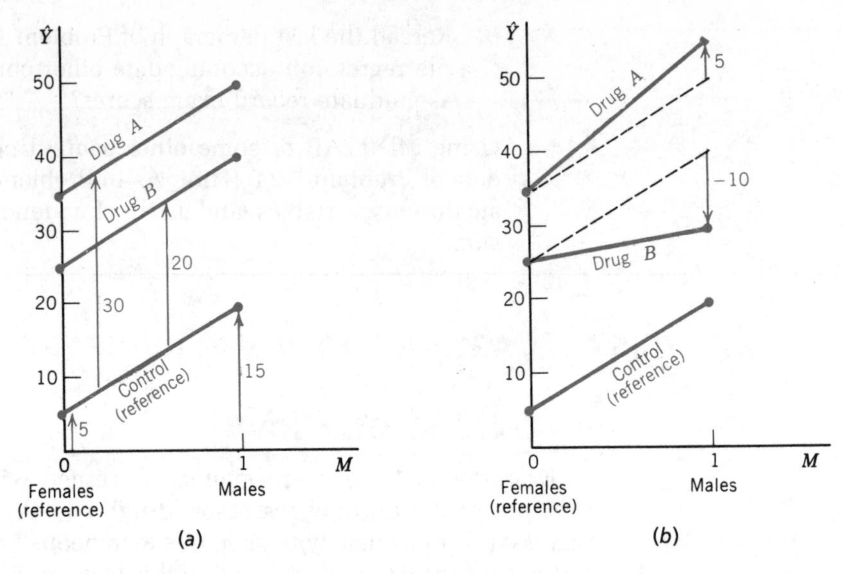

FIGURE 14-3
Graph of two-factor ANOVA. (a) Additive model. (b) Interactive model.

This multiple regression with dummies is equivalent to traditional two-factor ANOVA in Chapter 10. (There the two factors were machines and operators; here they are drugs and sex.) Multiple regression is more flexible, however, for two reasons:

i. It easily handles "imbalanced" data, where there are fewer observations in some cells (drug-sex combinations).

ii. It can easily include numerical factors too ("covariates"), such as age and other confounding variables that should be taken into account.

C—TWO-FACTOR ANOVA, INTERACTIVE MODEL

To extend (14-16) to a model with different slopes as well as different intercepts, we again introduce interaction terms. Then the estimated regression would be something like:

$$\hat{Y} = 5 + 30D_A + 20D_B + 15M + 5MD_A - 10MD_B \qquad \text{(14-17) like (14-13)}$$

This relationship is graphed in panel (b) of Figure 14-3. In this interactive model, it is clear that drug A has a greater effect than B, especially for males. [Contrast this with the simple additive model in panel (a), where the effect of drug A was the same for males as females.] We therefore say that there is *positive interaction* or *synergism* between drug A and being male.

PROBLEMS

14-9 Twelve plots of land are divided randomly into three groups. The first is held as a control group C, while fertilizers A and B are applied to the other two groups. Yield is observed to be:

C	A	B
60	75	74
64	70	78
65	66	72
55	69	68

The regression of yield Y was computed to be:

$$\hat{Y} = 61 + 9D_A + 12D_B$$

where the dummies are defined as

$$D_A = 1 \text{ if fertilizer } A \text{ used, 0 otherwise}$$

$$D_B = 1 \text{ if fertilizer } B \text{ used, 0 otherwise}$$

a. What is the estimated yield $\hat{Y}$ for 3 different plots:
   i. Left as the control C?
   ii. With fertilizer A?
   iii. With fertilizer B?

b. Looking back to the original data matrix, we see it is natural to calculate the mean yield for each fertilizer (column). This in fact is the first step in a traditional ANOVA.
   When you calculate these three means, how do they compare with your answer in part **a**?

c. Is this called one-factor or two-factor ANOVA? What is the "response"? What are the "factor(s)"?

***d.** Using a computer, verify the given multiple regression.

14-10 Two new drugs, A and B, along with a control C, were tried out on men and women to estimate their effect on blood pressure Y. Since the numbers of men and women were unequal, it was decided that a multiple regression would be easier than traditional ANOVA. The following dummies were defined:

$$D_A = 1 \text{ if patient on drug } A, \text{ 0 otherwise}$$

$$D_B = 1 \text{ if patient on drug } B, \text{ 0 otherwise}$$

$$M = 1 \text{ if male, 0 otherwise.}$$

Two regression models were fitted:

a. Additive $\hat{Y} = 65 + 5D_A - 10D_B + 10M$

b. Interactive $\hat{Y} = 68 + 6D_A - 15D_B + 5M - 2D_AM + 9D_BM$

Graph each, as in Figure 14-3.

14-11 **Fitted Response $\hat{Y}$**

	Sex	
Drug	*Female*	*Male*
A		
B		
Control C		

a. Fill in the table above for each of the two models in Problem 14-10, and check that your answers agree with the graphs there.

b. Make the correct choice in each bracket: In the [additive, interactive] model, the improvement of males over females is the same for all drugs. Then it is equally true that the improvement of drug *A*—or drug *B*—over the control C is the same for [both sexes, all treatments].

14-12 The strength of yarn produced by 4 machines varied according to the type of raw material used. In fact, a sample of several hundred pieces of yarn gave the following fitted responses:

Yarn Strengths

	Machine			
Material	*I*	*II*	*III*	*IV*
A	14	12	15	12
B	18			
C	19			

a. Fill in the blank cells, assuming the model is additive.

b. Make the correct choice in each bracket: Consider now a general 2-way table, with $a \times b$ cells. Suppose the fitted response has been filled in, across the top row and down the left-hand column. To fill in the remaining [ab, $(a-1)(b-1)$] cells of the table, it is enough to additionally know either (1) the values of all the interaction coefficients; or (2) that all the interaction coefficients are zero—that is, the model is [additive, interactive].

14-3 SIMPLEST NONLINEAR REGRESSION

Straight lines and planes are called *linear* functions. They are characterized by a simple equation (such as $Y = a + bX$) where the independent variable appears just as X, rather than in some more complicated nonlinear way such as X^2, $\sqrt{X}$, or $1/X$. In this section we will look at some nonlinear functions.

A—EXAMPLE

Let us reconsider how wheat yield Y depends on fertilizer X. When very large amounts of fertilizer are applied to some of the test plots, suppose the crop is burnt so that yield falls. An appropriate model might therefore be a second-degree equation (parabola) as shown in Figure 14-4 of the form:

$$\hat{Y} = b_0 + b_1X + b_2X^2 \tag{14-18}$$

To find the equation that best fits the data, we simply define new variables X_1 and X_2 as:

$$\left.\begin{aligned} X_1 &\equiv X \\ X_2 &\equiv X^2 \end{aligned}\right\} \tag{14-19}$$

Then (14-18) becomes the ordinary multiple regression:

$$\hat{Y} = b_0 + b_1X_1 + b_2X_2 \tag{14-20}$$

This is of the standard form that can be run through a computer, as Table 14-2 shows. The given data Y and X—the dots in Figure 14-4—were read into the computer, and the values of X were then squared to give a new variable, "X SQ." The computed regression was then:

$$\hat{Y} = 36 + 24X - 3.9X^2 \tag{14-21}$$

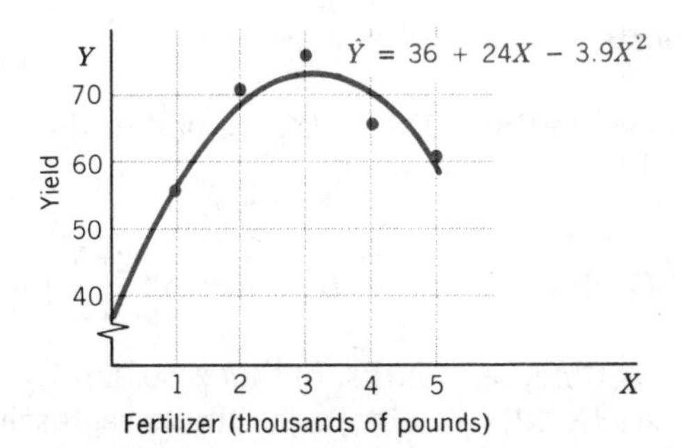

FIGURE 14-4
How yield depends on fertilizer—a parabolic relation.

TABLE 14-2 Parabolic Fit Using Multiple Regressi((See Figure 14-4).

Y	X	X SQ
55	1	1
70	2	4
75	3	9
65	4	16
60	5	25

```
> REGRESS'Y' ON 2 REGRESSORS'X','X SQ'

THE REGRESSION EQUATION IS
Y = 36.0 + 24.1 X - 3.93 X SQ
```

COLUMN	COEFFICIENT	ST. DEV. OF COEF.	T-RATIO = COEF/S.D.
	36.000	8.502	4.23
X	24.071	6.479	3.72
X SQ	-3.929	1.059	-3.71

This is the least squares regression graphed in Figure 14-4. It shows a nice fit to the data. (It is the best fit, of course, in the sense of least squared error.)

Of course, the computer output can be used for standard statistical tests too. For example, suppose we wish to test whether the parabolic model is really necessary—that is, whether it is necessary to have X^2 appear in this equation. The answer lies in prior knowledge and the statistical discernibility (significance) of the regressor X^2. Our prior expectation that this was a downward bending parabola is confirmed with the very negative t value of -3.71 in Table 14-2; so we retain X^2.

*B—GENERALIZATION

As well as parabolas, there are many other nonlinear functions that can be fitted using multiple regression on redefined variables. For example:

1. General Polynomials: $\hat{Y} = b_0 + b_1X + b_2X^2 + b_3X^3 + \cdots$

2. Reciprocals: $\hat{Y} = b_0 + \dfrac{b_1}{X}$

   In this case, letting $X_1 = 1/X$, we obtain the linear regression,

   $$\hat{Y} = b_0 + b_1X_1$$

3. Annual Cycles: $\hat{Y} = b_0 + b_1 \sin\left(\dfrac{2\pi X}{12}\right) + b_2 \cos\left(\dfrac{2\pi X}{12}\right)$

   where X is time, in months. In this case, letting $X_1 = \sin(2\pi X/12)$ and $X_2 = \cos(2\pi X/12)$, we obtain the linear regression,

   $$\hat{Y} = b_0 + b_1X_1 + b_2X_2$$

This method—simply redefining variables so that the regression becomes a linear one—works in all the equations above because the only nonlinearity is in the X variables. The coefficients b_0, b_1, and b_2 still appear in the same linear way as they did in Chapter 13. In other words, in each of these models, Y is a linear combination of the b coefficients. (Nowhere do terms like $\sqrt{b}$ or e^{3b} or b_1b_2 appear.)

PROBLEMS

14-13 To see how tomato yield depends on irrigation, various amounts of irrigation (I) were assigned at random to 24 experimental plots, with the resulting 24 yields Y used to fit the following least squares regression:

$$\begin{array}{lccc} Y = & 42 & + \; 12\,I & - \; 1.5\,I^2 \\ \text{(SE)} & & (.8) & (.4) \end{array}$$

a. Consider the null hypothesis H_0: Expected yield Y increases *linearly* with irrigation I. Before you had a look at the data, how credible would you find H_0?

b. To find out how much credibility the data gives to H_0, calculate its p-value. Does this answer confirm **a**, or not?

c. Graph the fitted parabola. Where does the maximum yield occur? Is this the appropriate level to irrigate?

d. What is the estimated increase in Y if I is increased one unit, from $I = 2$ to $I = 3$?

14-14 In testing the efficiency of a chemical plant producing nitric acid from ammonia, the stack losses and several related variables were measured for $n = 17$ different days. Then the following regression equation was fitted by least squares (Daniel and Wood, 1971):

$$Y = 1.4 + .07X_1 + .05X_2 + .0025X_1X_2$$

where Y = stack loss (% of ammonia lost)
X_1 = air flow (deviation from average flow)
X_2 = temperature of cooling water (deviation from average temperature)

a. Graph the relation of Y to X_1 when:
i. $X_2 = -4$ **ii.** $X_2 = 0$ **iii.** $X_2 = 4$ **iv.** $X_2 = 8$

b. When air flow is 4 units above average, and the temperature is 6 units above average, what would you predict the stack loss to be? Show this on the graph too.

c. Choose the correct alternative: This model is called [additive, interactive] because the effect of X_1 [depends, does not depend] on the level of X_2.

It was [easy, difficult] to estimate the coefficients from the 17 data points, because [nonlinearity requires a special program to minimize the sum of squared deviations $\Sigma(Y - \hat{Y})^2$, we could use multiple regression of Y on the three regressors X_1 and X_2 and X_1X_2].

*14-4 NONLINEARITY REMOVED BY LOGS

In Section 14-3 we saw how equations that were nonlinear in the X variables could still be handled with multiple regression, as long as they were linear in the b coefficients. Now we will look at some multiplicative models where the nonlinearity involves the b coefficients too. For example,

$$Y = b_0 X_1^{b_1} X_2^{b_2} \tag{14-22}$$

To find the least squares estimates, we simply transform the equation so that it becomes linear in the b coefficients. An extended example will illustrate.

A—A SIMPLE GROWTH MODEL

Panel (a) of Figure 14-5 shows the U.S. population during a period of sustained growth (1850–1900). It curves up in a way that suggests *exponential* growth (*constant percentage* growth, like compound interest or unrestrained biological growth). To verify this, in panel (b) we plot the same values of P on a *log scale*,[1] which is explicitly designed to transform exponential curves into straight lines. Since the points in panel (b) lie very close to a straight line, we conclude that the appropriate model is indeed an exponential one:

$$P = Ae^{bX} \tag{14-23}$$

where P is the population (in millions), X is time (in years, since 1850), A and b are coefficients to be estimated, and $e \simeq 2.718$ is the base for natural logarithms.

---

[1] It is also called a ratio scale, since a fixed chunk along the Y-axis represents a fixed increase in the ratio of P itself (for example, each half-inch along the Y axis represents a doubling of P itself—from 10 to 20 to 40 to 80, etc.).

Incidentally, a ratio scale was first encountered in plotting the Dow Jones Average in Figure 2-18, where the doubling was again clearly shown.

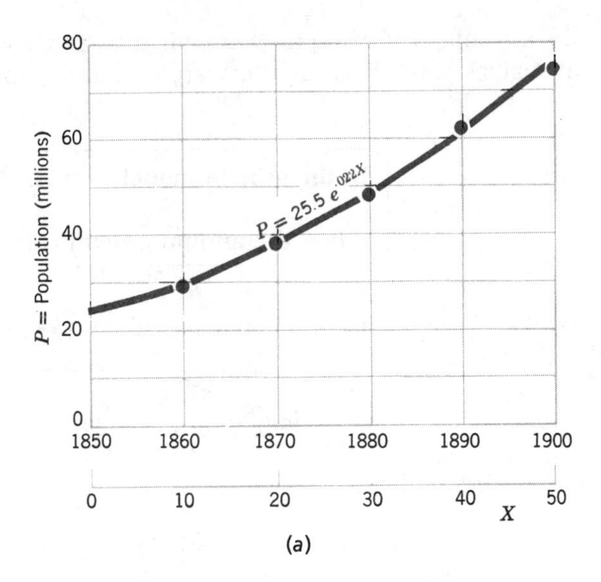

(a)

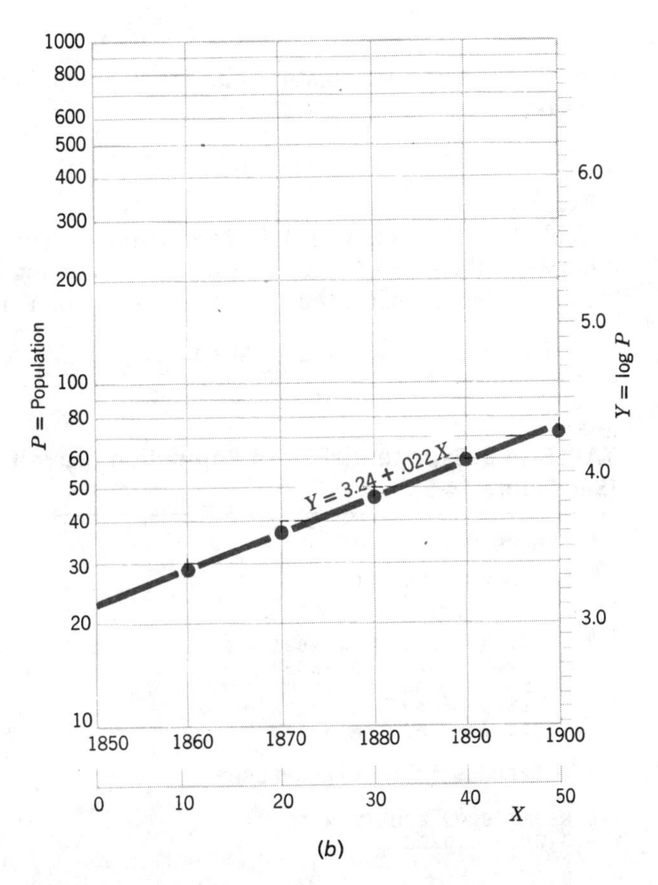

(b)

FIGURE 14-5
(a) U.S. population growth, and its exponential fit. (b) Same curve plotted on a log or ratio scale.

One advantage of using the base e is that, as we will show in Example 14-3, it gives b a very straightforward and useful interpretation:

$$\boxed{\begin{array}{c}\textbf{In the growth model } P = Ae^{bX},\\ b \approx \textbf{the annual growth rate}\end{array}} \tag{14-24}$$

If we take logs of the multiplicative model (14-23), we transform it into the additive form:

$$\log P = \log A + bX \tag{14-25}$$

Then we simply define:

$$Y \equiv \log P \tag{14-26}$$

$$a \equiv \log A \tag{14-27}$$

Substituting this new notation into (14-25) yields the standard linear regression:

$$Y = a + bX \tag{14-28}$$

Table 14-3 shows how a and b are computed. The given data P and X—the dots in Figure 14-5—were read in, and $Y = \log P$ is computed. Then the computer estimates the simple regression of Y against X:

$$Y = \log P = 3.24 + .022X \tag{14-29}$$

TABLE 14-3 Exponential Fit of Population growth (See Figure 14-5).

```
> LOGE OF 'P' INTO 'Y'

> PRINT'P','X','Y'
      P        X          Y

    31.4      10     3.44681
    39.8      20     3.68387
    50.2      30     3.91601
    63.0      40     4.14313
    76.0      50     4.33073

> REGRESS'Y' ON 1 REGRESSOR'X'

THE REGRESSION EQUATION IS
Y = 3.24 + 0.0223 X

                                      ST. DEV.      T-RATIO =
COLUMN          COEFFICIENT           OF COEF.      COEF/S.D.
                    3.23598            0.01825        177.30
X                 0.0222712          0.0005503         40.47
```

Taking exponentials (reversing our original log transformation):

$$P = e^{3.24}e^{.022X}$$

That is,

$$P = 25.5e^{.022X} \tag{14-30}$$

The graph of (14-29) is the straight line in panel (b) of Figure 14-5, which becomes the curved exponential growth (14-30) in panel (a). The coefficient 25.5 (millions) is the P intercept—the fitted population in 1850 (when $X = 0$). The coefficient $b = .022 = 2.2\%$ is the fitted annual growth.

Although a fit like (14-30) may adequately summarize past growth, there are important "time series" complications described in Figure 14-11 that prevent it from being used naively to forecast.

B—LOGS AS RELATIVE CHANGES

In general, there are many models consisting of factors multiplied together, which can be simplified into a standard additive regression by taking logs. After the regression has been estimated, it is often preferable to leave it in its log form such as (14-29) instead of transforming it back, because logs have a very useful interpretation: For small changes in any variable X,

Change in log $X \simeq$ *relative* change in X itself. (14-31)

We can illustrate this equation[2] for the variable P by using Figure 14-5b. Values of P are on the left axis, while corresponding values of log P are on the right axis. As P changes from 50 to 60, note that log P correspondingly changes from 3.9 to 4.1. Thus:

$$\text{Change in log } P = 4.1 - 3.9 = .20$$

$$\text{Relative change in } P \text{ itself} = \frac{60 - 50}{50} = .20\surd \quad \text{(14-31) confirmed}$$

To further illustrate how useful (14-31) is, we will give two more examples.

---

[2] This equation requires that the base for the log continue to be $e \simeq 2.718$. In fact, this peculiar number e was developed by mathematicians precisely for this reason, to keep equation (14-31) along with (14-24) as simple as possible. That is why they are called "natural" logs (which is abbreviated to ln on most calculators. So press the button marked ln, not log.)

To appreciate this point, if any other base is used, such as 10—the base for "common" logs—then equation (14-31) takes a more complicated form:

$$\text{Change in } \log_{10}X \simeq \log_{10}e \text{ (relative change in } X \text{ itself)}$$

EXAMPLE 14-2

In economics, a common model for the quantity supplied Q as a function of price P is

$$Q = AP^b \tag{14-32}$$

When we take logs, we obtain a more convenient sum:

$$\log Q = \log A + b \log P \tag{14-33}$$

Letting $\log Q \equiv Y$, $\log A \equiv a$, and $\log P \equiv X$, this equation takes the standard form

$$Y = a + bX$$

The coefficients a and b can now be computed with a standard regression program. Suppose, for example, they turned out to be $a = 5.1$ and $b = 2.0$. In terms of (14-33), this means:

$$\log Q = 5.1 + 2.0 \log P \tag{14-34}$$

If price P increases by 1%, how much change is there in Q, the quantity supplied?

SOLUTION

The *relative* change in P is given as 1% = .01. By (14-31), this is the change in $\log P$, the regressor. Because the regression coefficient is 2,

$$\begin{aligned} &\text{Change in response (i.e., change in } \log Q) \\ &= 2(.01) = .02 \qquad \text{like (13-24)} \end{aligned}$$

Since $\log Q$ thus increases by .02, (14-31) assures us that Q itself has a relative increase of .02. That is, quantity supplied increases by 2%.

In Example 14-2, a 1% increase in price resulted in a 2% increase in the quantity supplied. This value 2 is called the *elasticity* of supply (formally defined as the relative change in quantity ÷ relative change in price). In general:

$$\boxed{\begin{array}{c}\textbf{If } \log Q = a + b \log P, \\ \textbf{then } b = \textbf{elasticity.}\end{array}} \tag{14-35}$$

The higher the elasticity, the greater the quantity supplied as price increases.

EXAMPLE 14-3

Mexico's population P (in millions) has grown over time X (in years, since 1975) approximately according to

$$P = 60e^{.03X} \tag{14-36}$$

like (14-23)

Taking logs, $\log P = 4.1 + .03X$

How much did the population grow in 1 year?

SOLUTION

The given change in the regressor X is 1 year. From (13-24), the change in the response (i.e., the change in $\log P$) is therefore .03. Accordingly, (14-31) assures us that the relative change in P is also .03 = 3%. That is, the annual *growth rate* in P is 3%.

In (14-36) the annual growth rate was just the coefficient of X. In general, this coefficient is called b, and so (14-24) is established.

To sum up: Log transformations are so useful that researchers often apply them routinely, unless they have good reason not to. Two important advantages of logs are:

1. Logs transform a multiplicative model into an additive model that can be estimated with a standard regression program.
2. Logs have a useful interpretation as relative changes. Further detail on logs is given in Appendix 14-4.

C—BEYOND TRANSFORMATIONS

Certain models are intractably nonlinear. For example, suppose a country consists of two subgroups growing at two different rates, so that the total population is the sum of exponentials:

$$Y = A_1e^{b_1X} + A_2e^{b_2X}$$

Since there is addition as well as multiplication, logs cannot be taken. In fact there is no transformation at all that will make this equation linear in the parameters.

Fortunately, high-speed computers can still provide least-squares estimates and confidence intervals. A huge amount of calculation replaces the relatively simple formulas of linear models, but this is becoming less and less of a burden as computers become more powerful.

*PROBLEMS

14-15

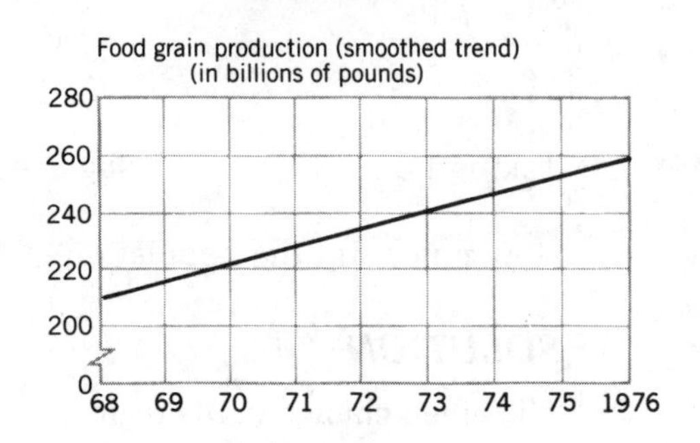

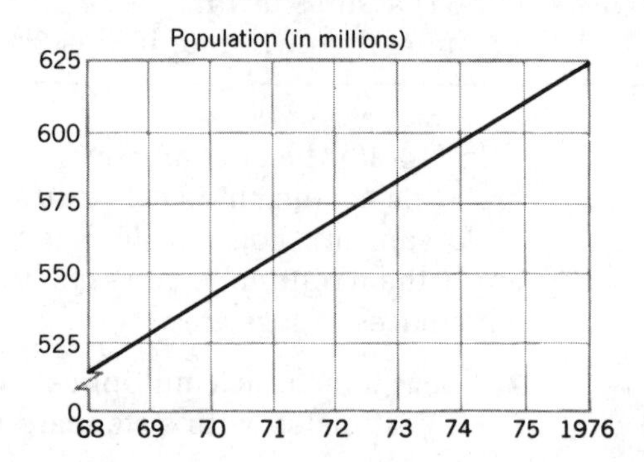

This is a simplified version of a "gee whiz" graph that appeared in Time in 1977 (reprinted in Problem 2-28). To emphasize its point, Time showed a crowd of hungry people in the background of the second graph.

a. Judging from a glance (as most readers do), would you say that India's food grain production was keeping ahead or falling behind population increase?

b. To actually check your answer in part **a,** calculate the percentage change from 1969 to 1976 in food grain production, and then in population. Which has increased more?

c. The graphs as they appear were obviously misleading. We can avoid this kind of deception by using an appropriate scale—the log or ratio scale that is specifically designed to show percentage or ratio changes.

Therefore on the ratio scale below (which is similar to Figure 14-5*b*), plot both food grain production and population. Then at a glance, see which increased at the faster rate.

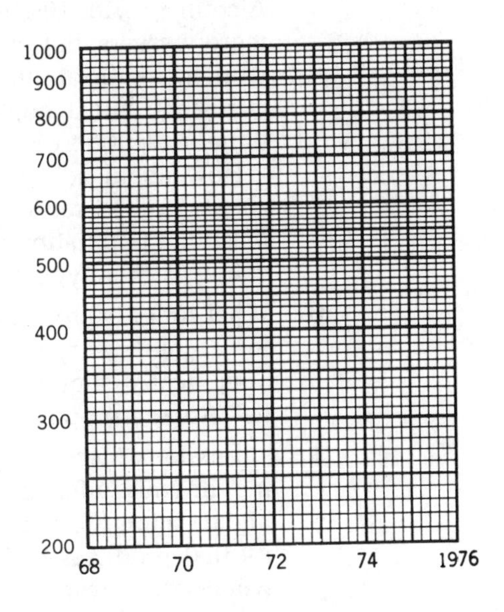

14-16 To see whether the population size and standard of living of a country affect its scientific productivity, a log regression was computed (Simon 1986, p 78) for a sample of over 75 countries:

$$\log \text{AUTHORS} = -2.77 + \underset{(.079)}{1.110} \log \text{POP} + \underset{(.15)}{1.90} \log \text{GNP/POP} + \ldots$$

(SE)

where, for each country,

AUTHORS = its number of scientific authors

POP = its population size

GNP/POP = its GNP per capita, or "standard of living" roughly

. . . = potentially confounding variables included in the regression to keep them from biasing the result.

a. On average, how many scientific authors would one country have more than another country, if the only measurable difference was that it had:

i. a 10% higher standard of living?

ii. a 10% higher population?

iii. both of the above?

b. Calculate a 95% confidence interval for:

i. the coefficient of log POP.

ii. your answer to **a(ii)** above.

c. A country with 10% more population would have about 10% more workers, but not necessarily 10% more of each *kind* of worker. For example, it might not have 10% more cabinet ministers, but it might have more than 10% more multinational executives.

How about scientific authors? It is plausible to suppose about 10% more. This "proportionality" hypothesis would mean the population regression coefficient of log POP is what value? Is this hypothesis acceptable at level $\alpha = 5\%$?

d. What roughly are the policy implications from this equation, for a country trying to increase its scientific productivity? Specifically, should they try to achieve a higher GNP per capita? And zero population growth?

e. Let us look more carefully into what causes what. For example, in your judgment is it higher GNP per capita that causes higher scientific productivity, or higher scientific productivity that produces higher GNP per capita—or does causation work both ways?

In view of this complexity, do you think a technique more sophisticated than multiple regression is needed to carefully answer policy questions such as **d**?

14-17 Would it ever make sense to take logs of the response before applying ANOVA? Why, or why not?

14-18 Suppose a study of quantity supplied as a function of price gave the following regression:

$$\log Q = 5.2 + 1.3 \log P$$

a. What is the elasticity of supply?

b. If price increased by 3%, how much would the quantity supplied increase?

c. What price increase would be required to increase the quantity supplied by 10%?

14-19 In explaining how a nation's output Q is related to its input of capital K and labor L, the following *Cobb-Douglas* model is sometimes used:

$$Q = \beta_0 K^{\beta_1} L^{\beta_2}$$

If we take log Q, what does the model become? How can it be estimated?

14-20 Continuing Problem 14-19, suppose 25 observations gave the regression:

$$\log Q = 1.40 + .70 \log K + .50 \log L$$

a. Estimate how much output increases if K increases by 10%, while L remains unchanged.

b. As wage rates have increased, capital has been substituted for labor. Specifically, suppose it has been found that a 12% increase in capital has been associated with a 3% reduction in labor. Would output increase or decrease as a consequence? By how much?

c. Suppose both capital and labor increase by 20%. Would output increase 20% too?

14-21 For each of the following models, outline the method you would use to estimate the parameters β_i:

a. $Y = \beta_0 + \beta_1 X + \beta_2 X^2 + \beta_3 X^3$

b. $Y = \beta_0 + \beta_1 T + \beta_2 \sin\left(\frac{2\pi T}{12}\right)$

(linear growth over time T, plus a 12-month cycle)

c. $Y = \beta_0(1 + \beta_1)^T$

d. $Y = \beta_0 \beta_1^T \beta_2^X$

e. $Y = \beta_0 + \beta_1 X + \beta_2 T + \beta_3 X^2 + \beta_4 T^2 + \beta_5 XT$

(fully quadratic model in 2 variables)

f. $Y = \beta_0 + \beta_1 e^{\beta_2 X}$

*14-5 DIAGNOSIS BY RESIDUAL PLOTS

Once a computer has calculated and plotted the regression equation, it can routinely plot the residuals $Y - \hat{Y}$ too. Such a residual plot lets us pick out which individuals are unusually high or low—as we have already seen in Problem 14-1, for example, where the residuals represented discrepancies in executive salaries.

Now let us investigate how residual plots can be used to diagnose whether the regression model itself is inadequate. In this chapter so far, we have looked at a bewildering variety of models besides ordinary multiple regression: dummy variables, polynomials, log transformations. How is one to decide which to use?

In the physical sciences, theory is often adequate to specify the appropriate model. For example, bacteria that are unrestricted by food or space limitations often grow exponentially (i.e., at a constant growth rate).

Social scientists can sometimes do the same. For example, money left to accumulate at a fixed interest rate will, like bacteria, grow exponentially.

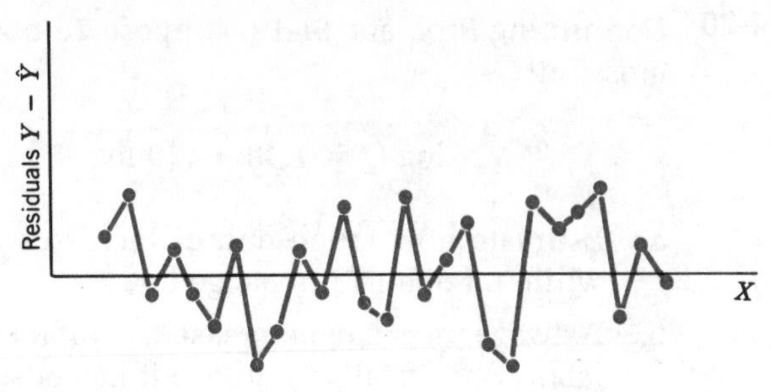

FIGURE 14-6
The residuals from a correctly specified model are statistically independent—pure white noise.

But this is the exception. Usually, social scientists have to rely heavily on statistical analysis to choose an adequate model. For example, we have already discussed how the regressor X^2 in (14-21) can be tested to see whether it should be included, or dropped to simplify the equation. Now let's look at the other side of the coin: What are the warning signs that a model is *too* simple, and needs to be made more complex by including *more* regressors?

One way of diagnosing this kind of trouble is to examine the residuals $Y - \hat{Y}$. First, as a basis of comparison we show in Figure 14-6 what the residuals $Y - \hat{Y}$ ought to look like in a correctly specified model. All the assumptions of (12-3) are satisfied: The residuals are of constant variance, and independent. Because they contain no message or information, they are sometimes called *pure noise* or *white noise*. This means that the model has been correctly specified; that is, it has squeezed all the information from the data. The residuals that are left over reveal nothing.

On the other hand, Figures 14-7 to 14-10 show a few examples where the model has *not* squeezed out all the available information; some useful

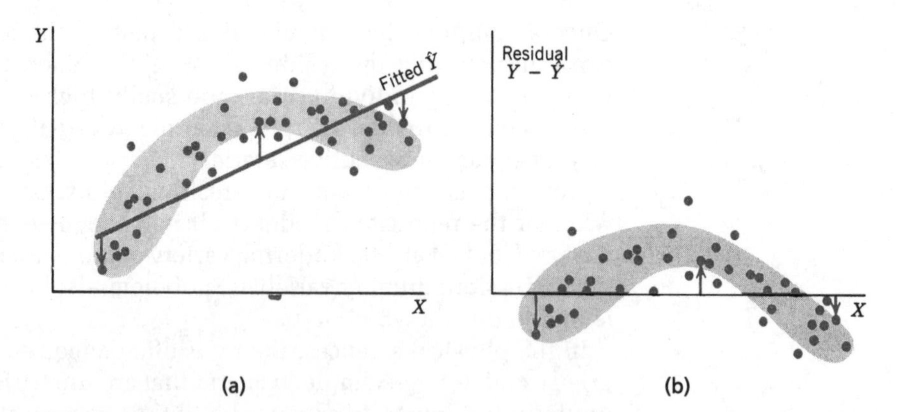

FIGURE 14-7
When residuals are bow-shaped, the model may require a term in X^2 to make it a parabola. (a) Original data, Y vs. X. (b) Corresponding residual plot ($Y - \hat{Y}$) plotted against X—with 3 typical residuals indicated by arrows.

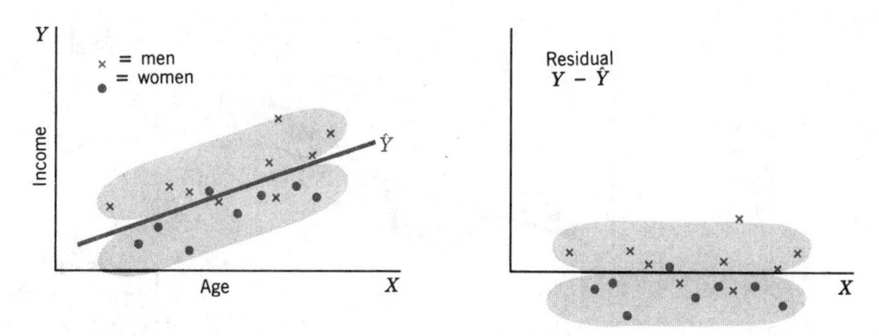

FIGURE 14-8
Residuals show that Y is related to sex. (At any age level X, men tend to have higher income; i.e., they tend to have positive residuals, and women negative residuals.) This indicates that a dummy sex variable should be included as another regressor.

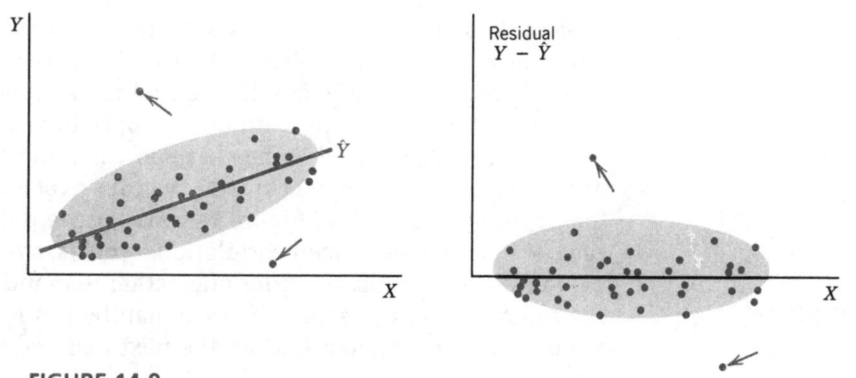

FIGURE 14-9
Outliers indicate data should be checked to ensure they were recorded correctly. Instead of ordinary least squares, perhaps a method of estimation less sensitive to outliers should be used, such as the "robust" regression described in Chapter 16.

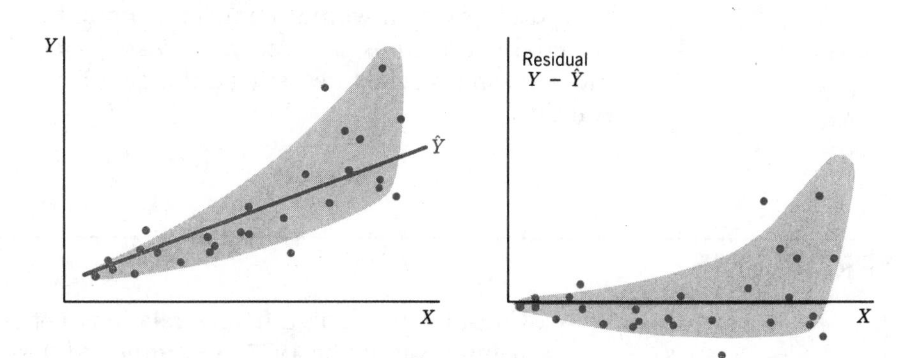

FIGURE 14-10
Residuals with a bow shape and increasing variability (i.e., the error increases as Y increases), indicate that a log transformation of Y is required; that is, instead of regressing Y on X, regress log Y on X.

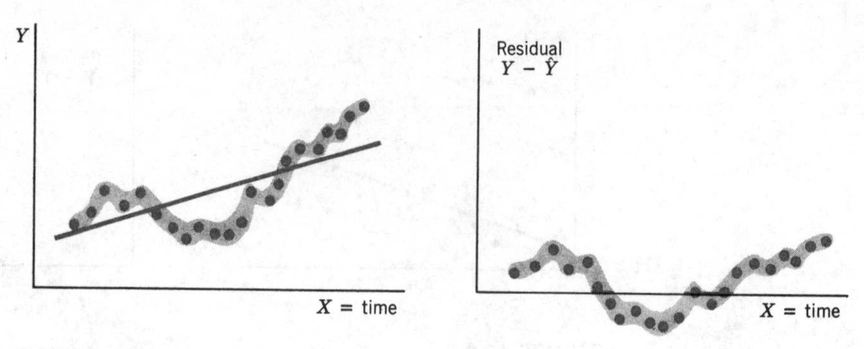

FIGURE 14-11
Serial correlation in the residuals. (When one residual is high, the next tends to be high.) This requires the special tools of time series analysis.

message remains in the residuals. In the cases illustrated, the residuals tell us how the model is misspecified, and how it should be corrected. For multiple regression, it is possible to plot the residuals against each of the regressors X in turn to pick up an appropriate message.

Figure 14-11 shows what may happen when the data comes in the form of a *time series*—a sequence of observations over a period of time, such as the population growth of Figure 14-5. When we plot the residuals against time, we often detect *serial correlation*—that is, a tendency for each residual to be similar to the previous one, rather than independent white noise. For example, in Figure 14-11 we see that the last residual is positive, like the ones that preceeded it. And the next residual will likely be positive also.

When serial correlation like this is diagnosed, special techniques of time series analysis are required—especially if forecasts are to be made. For example, in panel *a* of Figure 14-11 we see how mistaken it would be to make a naive forecast using the fitted equation—that is, to forecast that the next observation would plummet down to the fitted line. Because of the serial correlation, the observations are much more likely to change gradually, and special forecasting techniques have been developed to deal with this.

*PROBLEMS

14-22 Consider the four different relations between Y and X plotted below (Anscombe 1973)—a simplified version of some common phenomena.

a. In each case, roughly fit a line by eye.

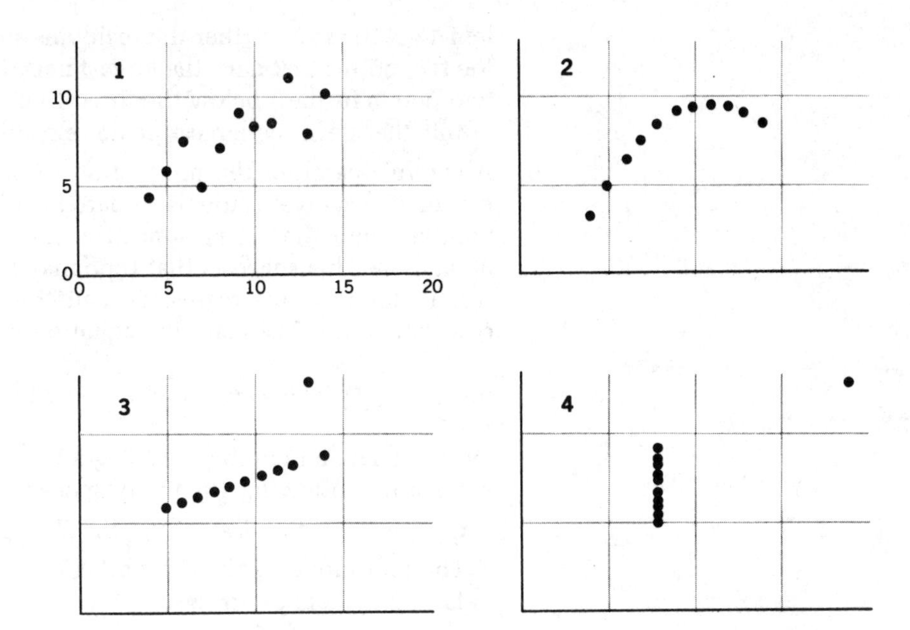

b. In fitting a straight line by OLS, the summary statistics for all four cases are exactly the same:

$$\overline{X} = 9.0 \qquad \Sigma x^2 = 110$$
$$\overline{Y} = 7.5 \qquad \Sigma y^2 = 41.25$$
$$\Sigma xy = 55.0$$

Calculate the regression line, and graph it in panel *1*. Then repeat it for the other panels.

c. The summary statistics and lines in **b** completely failed to distinguish the vital differences—differences easily picked up from the graphs of the data. For example, state which graph above corresponds to this situation:

i. The relation is really curved, rather than linear.

ii. The positive relation is entirely the result of just one data point.

iii. The residual variance is entirely the result of just one data point—which may very well be recorded in error.

iv. It makes good sense to use the regression line for prediction.

d. Briefly, what lesson does this show?

14-23 **a.** Let us reconsider the factory cost of producing hosiery, and the fitted regression $\hat{Y} = 3.0 + 2.0X$ that you graphed in Problem 12-8. To see whether the residuals show a pattern, circle the two points that have the largest negative residual (i.e., the two points furthest below the fitted line). Also circle the two points that have the largest positive residual.

b. A careful search of the production records showed that the two most negative residuals in part **a** occurred at $T = 1$ and 3 months, while the two most positive residuals occurred at $T =$ 33 and 34. This suggests that time may be an influence, so it was included in the regression equation, in both linear and quadratic form. The resulting equation was:

$$\hat{Y} = -13.6 + 2.07X + 1.3T - .022T^2$$

On the diagram in Problem 12-8, graph $\hat{Y}$ as a function of X for each of the following 4 (equally spaced) time periods:

i. $T = 1$ **ii.** $T = 17$ **ii.** $T = 33$ **iv.** $T = 49$

The four circled points in part **a** now have reduced residuals. Show them as arrows.

14-24 Continuing Problem 14-23, circle the correct choice in each pair of brackets: The p-value for H_0—that the population coefficients of T and T^2 are both zero—turned out to be less than .0001. This shows that there [is, is not] a discernible time dependence, and, consequently, it is [almost certain, hardly possible] that the sample is a random sample as first assumed in Problem 12-8.

CHAPTER 14 SUMMARY

14-1 To handle a factor with two categories (such as male-female, or treatment-control), we define a dummy variable. Similarly, to handle a factor with several categories such as regions, we keep one region as a reference and define a dummy for each of the other regions.

14-2 When every factor is categorical and handled with dummy regressors, then regression gives essentially the same results as ANOVA in Chapter 10. But regression is more flexible: it easily handles imbalanced data, and numerical factors—especially confounding variables (covariates).

14-3 Standard computer programs can also handle regression models that are nonlinear in the variables if they are still linear in the coefficients b. For example, if $Y = b_0 + b_1X + b_2X^2$, the program can read the column of X^2 values just like any other column of numbers, and then use those values in calculating a standard regression.

***14-4** Exponential and multiplicative models can be transformed by logarithms into standard linear form. Logs also have a very useful interpretation: The change in log Y approximately equals the *relative* change in Y itself. Thus logs are particularly useful in estimating growth rates, and elasticities of supply or demand.

***14-5** An examination of residuals provides a diagnostic check on the model. When the model is inadequately specified, the residuals are not just pure noise; instead, they contain a message that can help us to specify a better model.

REVIEW PROBLEMS

14-25 Multiple regression (or GLM, the General Linear Model) is very versatile and powerful. Choose the correct alternative in each pair of brackets:

a. It can handle categorical factors such as [income, race], by using [nonnegative variables, dummy variables].

b. It can handle ANOVA, which deals with [just categorical factors, just numerical factors]. In fact, it is particularly [suitable, unsuitable] to handle ANOVA when the number of observations in each cell varies.

c. It can handle polynomials, by using [dummy variables, X and X^2 and X^3 . . . as the regressors].

d. It [can, cannot] help to remove the bias of confounding factors in observational studies, because each confounding factor that can be [measured, conceived of] can be entered into the regression equation.

Then the coefficient of interest is interpreted as the change in Y that accompanies a [unit, significant] change in the regressor, if these confounding factors were [insignificant, constant].

e. In observational studies, multiple regression [can, cannot] always tell us exactly how X causes Y, because [some omitted confounding factors may be causing some of the change in Y, the sign and size of the coefficient of X tells us the direction and size of the change that X produces in Y].

14-26

Output X (Thousands)	*Marginal Cost Y*
1	32
2	20
3	20
4	28
5	50

From the above data, the following quadratic polynomial was fitted:

$$\hat{Y} = 55 - 28.2X + 5.4X^2$$
$$\text{SE} \qquad (1.56) \qquad (.26)$$

a. Graph the 5 points.

b. Calculate and graph Y for $X = 1, 2, 3, 4, 5$. Then sketch the fitted parabola that passes through these 5 points.

c. From (b), what is the estimated increase in Y when X increased 1 unit, from 4 to 5? Is this the same as the coefficient of X? Is this consistent with the fundamental interpretation (13-26)?

d. How credible is the hypothesis that marginal cost increases *linearly*?

***e.** Using a computer, verify the given regression coefficients.

14-27 A random sample of men and women in a large American university in 1969 gave the following annual salaries ($000):

Men	12, 11, 19, 16, 22
Women	9, 12, 8, 10, 16

Denote income by Y and denote sex by a dummy $X = 1$ for women, 0 for men.

a. Graph Y against X.

b. Estimate by eye the regression line of Y against X. (*Hint:* Where will the line pass through the men's salaries? through the women's salaries?)

c. Estimate by least squares the regression line of Y against X. How well does your eyeball estimate in part **b** compare?

d. Construct a 95% confidence interval for the coefficient of X. Explain what it means in simple language.

e. In Problem 8-11 the data was analyzed as two independent samples, and gave the 95% confidence interval: $\mu_W - \mu_M = -5.0 \pm 5.8$ ($000). How does this compare to your answer in **d**?

f. How well does the answer in **d** show the university's discrimination against women?

14-28 Now we can consider more precisely the regression equation for several hundred professors' salaries in Problem 13-12 by including some additional regressors (Katz, 1973):

$\hat{S} = 230B + \cdots$	$+ 50T$	$- 2400X$	$+ 1900P$	$+ \cdots$
SE	(370)	(530)	(610)	
95% CI	( )	( )	( )	
t ratio	( )	( )	( )	
p-value	( )	( )	( )	

where S = the professor's annual salary (dollars)
T = 1 if the professor received a student evaluation score above the median; 0 otherwise
X = 1 if the professor is female; 0 otherwise
P = 1 if the professor has a Ph.D.; 0 otherwise

a. Fill in the blanks below the equation.

b. Answer True or False; if False, correct it.

i. A professor with a Ph.D. earns annually \$1900 more than one without a Ph.D.

ii. Or, we might say that \$1900 estimates the value (in terms of a professor's salary) of one more unit (in this case, a Ph.D.).

iii. The average woman earns \$2400 more than the average man.

iv. To be 95% confident of bracketing the true coefficient for the whole population, the estimate in **iii** should be hedged: \$2400 ± \$270.

c. Give an interpretation of the coefficient of T.

14-29 For the raw data of Problem 14-28, the mean salaries for male and female professors were \$16,100 and \$11,200, respectively. By referring to the coefficient of X there, answer True or False; if False, correct it:

After holding constant all other variables, women made \$2400 less than men. Therefore, \$2400 is a measure of the extent of sex discrimination, and \$2500 (16,100 − 11,200 − 2400) is a measure of the salary differential due to other factors, for example, productivity and experience.

14-30 In Problem 14-28, the following additional independent variables were proposed:

a. Professor's faculty (arts, science, social science, business, or engineering).

b. Professor's rank (instructor, assistant professor, associate professor, or full professor).

c. Professor's marital status.

d. Professor's height.

In each case, state why or why not the variable would be a wise addition to the multiple regression, and if so, how it would be handled computationally (with dummy variables, or . . . ?).

***14-31** In Problem 14-28, teaching evaluation T appeared in a severely rounded form (which was explicitly stated earlier in Problem 13-12). What are the advantages and disadvantages of such rounding?

14-32 *A Final Challenge: Does Compulsory Auto Inspection Help to Reduce the Accident Mortality Rate?*

Carefully answer each part in this question before reading on to the next.

In 1960, 15 states had inspection (compulsory auto inspection), compared to the other 33 states in the continental U.S. with no inspection. Mortality rates varied with sex and race, so to keep the problem simple, we will use only the following information on white males aged 15–64 (Colton and Buxbaum 1977); conclusions for other groups were similar.

Selected Number of Automobile Deaths During 1960

15 Inspection States	*# Deaths*	*33 Noninspection States*	*# Deaths*
Colorado	247	Alabama	389
⋮	⋮	⋮	⋮
West Virginia	212	Wyoming	93
total =	5,144	total =	13,380

a. What is the average number of deaths per state, in the inspection states? In the noninspection states? What then is the difference? Express it as a percentage.

How well does this estimate the effectiveness of inspection? In particular, suggest how a better estimate could be obtained.

b. The estimate in **a** is hopelessly crude. For example, if the inspection states tended to be smaller states, their average number of deaths would tend to be small, making inspection look a lot better than it really was.

In fact, the 15 inspection states had a total population of 16.7 million white males aged 15–64, while the 33 noninspection states had 30.0 million. Use these figures to get a better estimate than in **a**.

Is this data obtained from a randomized controlled experiment, or an observational study? Then how could this answer be improved?

c. Two of the confounding factors that might bias the answer in **b** are **(i)** age distribution, and **(ii)** population density. In simple language, suggest how each of these two factors might cause bias.

d. To control for these two confounding factors, the following multiple regression was computed for the 48 states (Langbein 1980, p. 154):

$$\text{MR60} = 847 - 90.8\ \text{LOGPD} - 63.4\ \text{INSP}$$
$$\text{(SE)} \qquad\qquad (10.3) \qquad\qquad (30.6)$$

where

MR60 = 1960 mortality rate per million white males aged 15–64 in the state, adjusted for age differences in a way that prevents age from being a confounding factor. (This age-adjustment is achieved by using the mortality rate that would occur if each state had the same age distribution—the "standard" distribution of the U.S. as a whole.)

LOGPD = natural log of the population density in persons/square mile. (Including this regressor controls for the other confounding factor of population density.)

INSP = dummy variable, with a value of 1 if the state had compulsory auto inspection by 1960, 0 otherwise. This is the factor of interest.

Other things being equal, what difference does inspection make? Is it statistically discernible at level $\alpha = 5\%$?

Further Light on Compulsory Auto Inspection

To give a glimpse into how complex good research can become, we will continue the Final Challenge with an improved multiple regression.

e. Let's look at an even more important confounding factor—the crucial "which-causes-which" issue, which was first explained in Problem 1-9. States with the highest mortality rates in the past might be the very ones most anxious to reduce them by legislation such as compulsory auto inspection. So we ought to control for past mortality rates by including them as another regressor:

Let MR50 = the corresponding 1950 mortality rate (per million white males aged 15–64 in the state, again adjusted for age).

Regressing present mortality rates against past rates will introduce very tight control, similar to the before-and-after matching in Section 8-4.

Also, to appropriately pick up the effect of *introducing* inspection between 1950 and 1960, we drop from the database the few states that had inspection even before 1950. The multiple regression then becomes (Langbein 1980, p. 156):

$$\begin{array}{lllll} \text{MR60} = 483 & - \ 62.5 \text{ LOGPD} & + \ .52 \text{ MR50} & - \ 8.1 \text{ INSP} \\ \text{(SE)} & (14.0) & (.13) & (39.8) \end{array}$$

Other things being equal, now what difference does inspection make? Is it statistically discernible at level $\alpha = 5\%$?

f. Using the last and best regression equation above, some other interesting questions can be answered:

i. Does greater population density decrease or increase the mortality rate? Does this square with your intuitive answer in part **c(ii)** above?

ii. Which makes a greater difference in a state's mortality rate—introducing auto inspection or having double the population density? (*Hint:* from Figure 14-5b we see that doubling a variable on the left axis, say from P = 100 to 200, increases its log on the right axis by about 0.7. So we are comparing a change of 0.7 in LOGPD with a change of 1 in INSP.)

g. Let us review what we have learned about estimating the effect of compulsory auto inspection on mortality rates (for white males 15–64 years old). We purposely started in part **a** with an estimated decrease so naive that no one could fail to notice its bias. It is listed first in this summary table.

	Estimated Decrease in Mortality Rate	*Improvement Over Previous Line*
Part a	63 per state = 15% decrease	
Part b	138 per million = 31% decrease	uses annual mortality rates per million people
Part d	____ per million = ___% decrease	
Part e	____ per million = ___% decrease	

Continue to fill out this table, showing how the estimate improves line by line.

How would you express the final estimate, in words simple enough for the average citizen to understand?

h. Can you suggest some other important confounding variables that should be controlled for?

Epilogue

This data has been studied many different ways by researchers who thought of many different answers to **h**, and who had different levels of persistence. (Colton and Buxbaum 1977, pp. 140–142, or Tufte 1974, pp. 5–29). Nearly all of them reached roughly the same conclusion as given in part **e**: compulsory inspection seems to give a small benefit, often indiscernibly small.

In spite of this consensus, there remains the nagging fear that an observational study like this, which tries to pick up a small effect, may be overwhelmed by the bias of confounding factors not measured or even measurable. A possible cure for this might be a randomized controlled experiment. In the words of Colton and Buxbaum (1977, p. 142):

> an analogue of the controlled clinical trial as used for evaluating new drugs, medical and surgical procedures could be adopted for evaluating effects on traffic safety.

CHAPTER 15

Correlation

Q. What is the difference between capitalism and socialism?

A. Under capitalism, man exploits man. Under socialism, it's just the opposite.

ANONYMOUS

15-1 SIMPLE CORRELATION

Simple regression analysis showed us *how* variables are linearly related; correlation analysis will show us the *degree* to which variables are linearly related. In regression analysis, a whole function is estimated (the regression equation); but correlation analysis yields a single number—an index designed to give an immediate picture of how closely two variables move together. Although correlation is a less powerful technique than regression, the two are so closely related that correlation often becomes a useful aid in interpreting regression. In fact, this is the major reason for studying it.

A—SAMPLE CORRELATION r

Recall how the regression coefficient of Y against X was calculated: We first expressed X and Y in deviation form (x and y), and then calculated

$$b = \frac{\Sigma xy}{\Sigma x^2} \qquad (15\text{-}1)$$

(11-5) repeated

The correlation coefficient r uses the same quantities Σxy and Σx^2, and uses Σy^2 as well:

Correlation of X and Y

$$r \equiv \frac{\Sigma xy}{\sqrt{\Sigma x^2}\sqrt{\Sigma y^2}} \qquad (15\text{-}2)$$

Note that in this formula, y appears symmetrically in exactly the same way as x. Thus the correlation r does not make a distinction between the response y and the regressor x, the way the regression coefficient b does. [In the denominator of the regression formula (15-1), the regressor x appears, but the response y does not.]

To illustrate, how are math and verbal scores related? A sample of the scores of 8 college students is given in the first two columns of Table 15-1. In the next two columns we calculate the deviations, and then the sums Σxy, Σx^2, and Σy^2. If we wanted to see how Y can be predicted from X, we would calculate the regression coefficient:

$$b = \frac{\Sigma xy}{\Sigma x^2} = \frac{654}{1304} = .50 \qquad (15\text{-}3)$$

TABLE 15-1 Math Score (X) and Corresponding Verbal Score (Y) of a Sample of Eight Students Entering College

Data		*Deviation Form*		*Products*		
X	Y	$x = X - \bar{X}$	$y = Y - \bar{Y}$	xy	x^2	y^2
80	65	20	15	300	400	225
50	60	−10	10	−100	100	100
36	35	−24	−15	360	576	225
58	39	−2	−11	22	4	121
72	48	12	−2	−24	144	4
60	44	0	−6	0	0	36
56	48	−4	−2	8	16	4
68	61	8	11	88	64	121
$\bar{X} = 60$	$\bar{Y} = 50$	0✓	0✓	$\Sigma xy = 654$	$\Sigma x^2 = 1304$	$\Sigma y^2 = 836$

On the other hand, if we wanted to measure *how much* X and Y are related, we would calculate the correlation coefficient:

$$r = \frac{\Sigma xy}{\sqrt{\Sigma x^2}\sqrt{\Sigma y^2}} = \frac{654}{\sqrt{1304}\sqrt{836}} = .63 \tag{15-4}$$

B—HOW r MEASURES THE DEGREE OF RELATION

We have claimed that the correlation r measures how much X and Y are related. Now let's support that claim by analyzing what formula (15-2) really means. First, recall how we interpret a deviation from the mean:

$$x \equiv X - \bar{X} \qquad \text{(11-4) repeated}$$

The deviation x tells us how far an X value is from its mean $\bar{X}$. Similarly, the deviation y tells us how far a Y value is from its mean $\bar{Y}$. Therefore, when we plot an observed pair (x, y) in two dimensions, we see how far this observation is from the center of the data $(\bar{X}, \bar{Y})$—as Figure 15-1 illustrates.

Suppose we multiply the x and y values for each student, and sum them to get Σxy. This gives us a good measure of how math and verbal scores tend to move together, as we can see in Figure 15-1: For any observation such as P_1 in the first or third quadrant, x and y agree in sign, so their product xy is positive.[1] Conversely, for any observation such as P_2 in the second or fourth quadrant, x and y disagree in sign, so their product xy is negative. If X and Y move together, most observations will fall in the first

[1] The point P_1 is given in the first line of Table 15-1. It represents a student with excellent scores, $X = 80$ and $Y = 65$—or in deviation form, $x = 20$ and $y = 15$. Note that the product xy is indeed positive (+300).

For the point P_2, $x = -10$ and $y = +10$. So now the product xy is negative (−100).

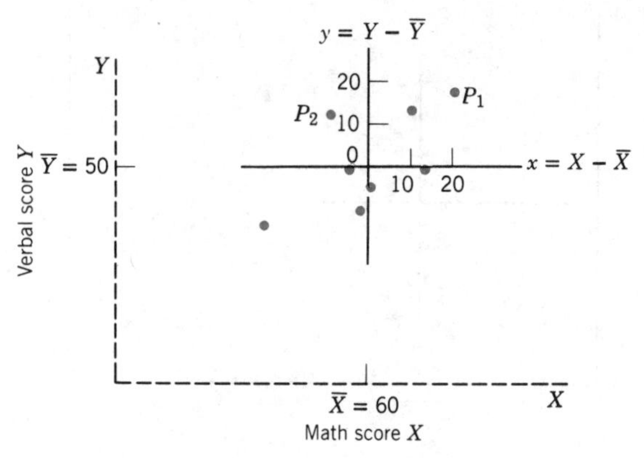

FIGURE 15-1
Scatter of math and verbal scores, from Table 15-1.

and third quadrants; consequently most products xy will be positive, as will their sum—a reflection of the positive relationship between X and Y. But if X and Y are negatively related (i.e., when one rises, the other falls), most observations will fall in the second and fourth quadrants, yielding a negative value for our Σxy index. We conclude that as an index of correlation, Σxy at least carries the right sign. Moreover, when there is no relationship between X and Y, with the observations distributed evenly over the four quadrants, positive and negative xy values will cancel, and Σxy will be 0.

To measure how X and Y vary together, Σxy suffers from just one defect: It depends on the units that X and Y are measured in. For example, suppose in Table 15-1 that X were marked on a different scale—specifically, a scale that is 10 times larger. (In other words, suppose the math score X is marked out of 1000 instead of 100.) Then every deviation x would be 10 times larger and so, therefore, would the whole sum Σxy.

We would like a measure of relation that is not so fickle—that is, one that remains "invariant to scale" even if we decide to use an X scale that is 10 times larger. How can we adjust Σxy to obtain such a measure? First, note that the quantity $\sqrt{\Sigma x^2}$ would also change by the same[2] factor 10. So if we divide Σxy by $\sqrt{\Sigma x^2}$, the factor of 10 cancels out, and we are left with an invariant measure. Of course, to protect against changes in the Y scale, we should divide by $\sqrt{\Sigma y^2}$ too. The result is

$$\frac{\Sigma xy}{\sqrt{\Sigma x^2}\sqrt{\Sigma y^2}}$$

Thus our search for an appropriate measure of how closely two variables are related has indeed led us to the correlation coefficient (15-2).

[2] This is because each x^2 and consequently the whole sum Σx^2 would be 100 times larger. But when we take the square root, $\sqrt{\Sigma x^2}$ is reduced to being 10 times larger.

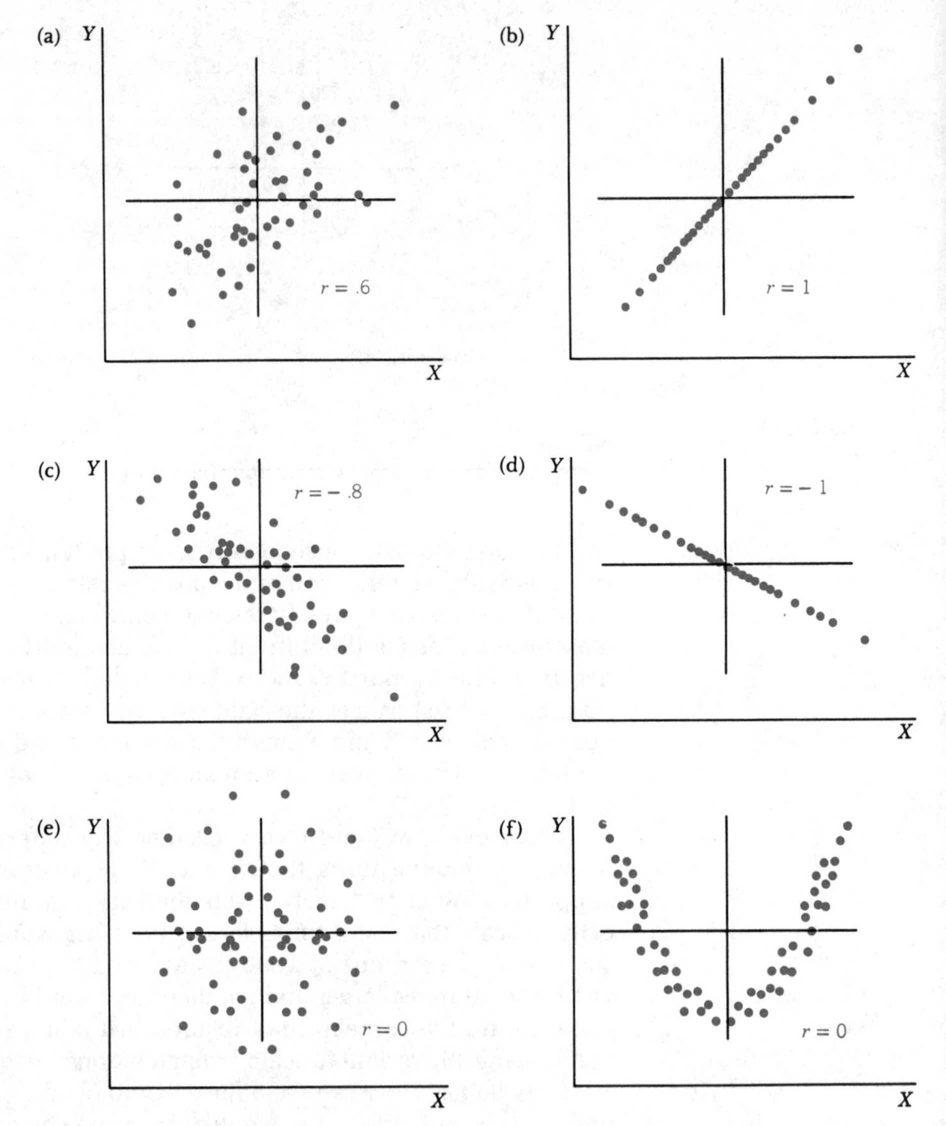

FIGURE 15-2
Various correlations illustrated.

To get a further idea of the meaning of r, in Figure 15-2 we have plotted various scatters and their correlation coefficients. In panel (a), for example, we show a larger sample than the 8 points in Figure 15-1. Nevertheless, the outline of the scatter displays about the same degree of relation, so it is no surprise that r is about the same value .60.

In panel (b) of Figure 15-2 there is a perfect positive association, so that the product xy is always positive. Accordingly, r takes on its largest possible value, which turns out to be $+1$. Similarly, in panel (d), where there is a perfectly negative association, r takes on its most negative possible value, which turns out to be -1. We therefore conclude:

$$\boxed{-1 \le r \le 1} \tag{15-5}$$

Finally consider the symmetric scatters shown in panels (*e*) and (*f*) of Figure 15-2. The calculation of r in either case yields 0, because every positive product *xy* is offset by a corresponding negative product *xy* in the opposite quadrant. Yet these two scatters show quite different patterns: In (*e*) there is no relation between X and Y; in (*f*), however, there is a strong relation (knowledge of X will tell us a great deal about Y). A zero value for r therefore does not necessarily mean "no relation." Instead, it means "no *linear* relation" (no straight-line relation). Thus:

$$\boxed{r \text{ is a measure of linear relation only}} \tag{15-6}$$

C—POPULATION CORRELATION ρ

Once we have calculated the sample r, how can it be used to make inferences about the underlying population? For instance, in our example the population might be the math and verbal marks scored by *all* college entrants. This population might appear as in Figure 15-3, with millions of dots in the scatter, each representing another student. Let us assume the population is *bivariate normal*, which means, among other things, that the X scores are normally distributed, and so are the Y scores. Then this scatter can be nicely represented by an ellipse that encloses most of the points (about 85%), called the *ellipse of concentration*.

If we were to calculate (15-2) using all the observations in the population, the result would be the *population correlation* coefficient ρ that we first encountered in Chapter 5. (This is proved in Appendix 15-1. Notice

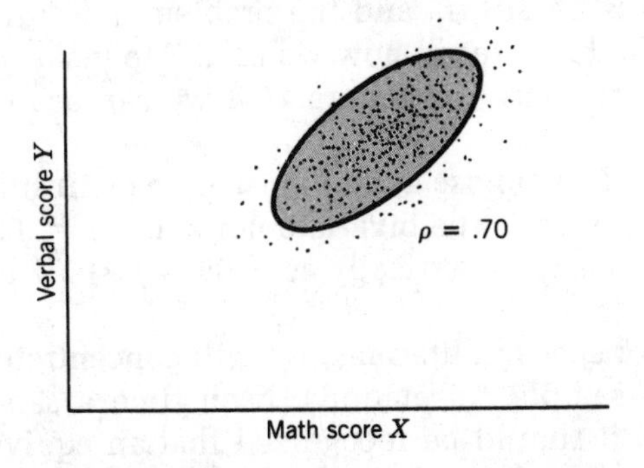

FIGURE 15-3
Bivariate population scatter, with its ellipse of concentration.

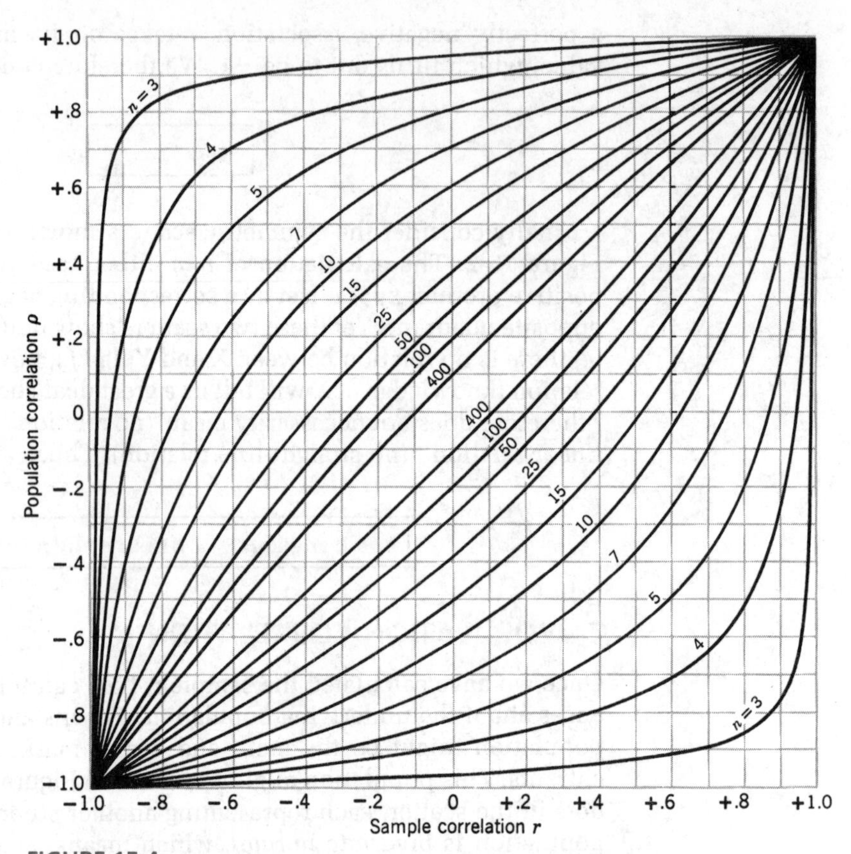

FIGURE 15-4
95% confidence bands for correlation ρ in a bivariate normal population, for various sample sizes *n*.

that, as always, we use the Greek letter ρ—rho, the equivalent of r—to denote a population parameter.) Of course, as always in statistics, the population is unknown, and the problem is to infer ρ from an observed sample r. To do so, recall how we used P to make an inference about π in Figure 8-4. Similarly, in Figure 15-4 we can use r to make an inference about ρ.

For example, suppose a random sample of 10 students is drawn from a population known to be bivariate normal. If $r = .60$, the 95% confidence interval for ρ is read vertically as $-.05 < \rho < .87$ as shown by the heavy blue line.

Because of space limitations, we will concentrate in the balance of this chapter on sample correlations. Each time a sample concept like r is introduced, it should be recognized that an equivalent population concept is similarly defined, and inferences may be made about it, as in Figure 15-4 (assuming the population is bivariate normal).

When the population is not bivariate normal, however, such inferences may be invalid. (We therefore say they are "not robust." For a more robust alternative to Figure 15-4, see the "bootstrap" in Section 8-7.) To take an extreme but common example, in Figure 11-2 the fertilizer levels X were not normally distributed. In fact, it is not proper to speak of them as having a probability distribution at all. Instead, the X values were selected at specified levels by the experimenter. In this case, it is not meaningful to even talk about a population correlation.

PROBLEMS

15-1 A random sample of 6 states gave the following figures for X = annual per capita cigarette consumption and Y = annual death rate per 100,000, from lung cancer (Fraumini, 1968):

State	X	Y
Delaware	3400	24
Indiana	2600	20
Iowa	2200	17
Montana	2400	19
New Jersey	2900	26
Washington	2100	20
Averages	2600	21

a. Calculate the sample correlation r. A correlation calculated from aggregated data such as this is called an *ecological* correlation.

b. Find a 95% confidence interval for the population correlation ρ, assuming a bivariate normal population.

c. At the 5% error level, test whether cigarette consumption and lung cancer are unrelated.

15-2 In Problem 15-1, suppose Y had been measured in annual deaths per *million*, from lung cancer. What difference would that make to:

a. r?

b. b?

c. $t = b/SE$?

d. p-value for H_o?

15-3 A random sample of baseball players was drawn, out of all the National League baseball players who came to bat at least 100 times in both the 1979 and 1980 seasons. Their batting averages were approximately as follows:

Player and Team	1979	1980
Boroughs (Atlanta)	.220	.260
Cedeno (Houston)	.260	.310
Foote (Chicago)	.250	.240
Henderson (NY)	.310	.290
Scott (St. Louis)	.260	.250
Average	.260	.270

a. Calculate r.

b. Find the 95% confidence interval for ρ. What major assumption are you making? Do you think it is approximately true?

c. Calculate the regression line you would use to predict the batting average in 1980 from 1979, and find a 95% confidence interval for β.

d. Graph the estimated regression line and the scatter of 5 observations.

e. At the 5% error level, can you reject:

i. The null hypothesis $\beta = 0$?

ii. The null hypothesis $\rho = 0$?

15-2 CORRELATION AND REGRESSION

A—REGRESSION SLOPE *b* AND CORRELATION *r*

As noted when we set out their formulas (15-1) and (15-2), b and r are very similar. In fact, it can easily be shown (in Appendix 15-2) that we can write b explicitly in terms of r as

$$\boxed{b = r\frac{s_Y}{s_X}} \tag{15-7}$$

Thus, for example, if either b or r is 0, the other will also be 0. Similarly, if either of the population parameters β or ρ is 0, the other will also be 0. Thus it is no surprise that the tests for $\beta = 0$ and for $\rho = 0$ are equivalent ways of examining "no linear relation between X and Y" (as Problem 15-3**e** illustrated).

B—EXPLAINED AND UNEXPLAINED SUM OF SQUARES

The sample of math (X) and verbal (Y) scores are reproduced in Figure 15-5, along with the line regressing Y against X. Suppose we want to predict the verbal Y score of a given student—to be concrete, the student farthest to the right in Figure 15-5.

If the math score X were not known, the only available prediction would be to use the sample average $\overline{Y}$. Then the prediction error would be $Y - \overline{Y}$. In Figure 15-5, this appears as the large error (deviation) shown by the longest blue arrow.

However, if X is known we can do better: We predict Y to be $\hat{Y}$ on the regression line. Note how this reduces our error, since a large part of our deviation $(\hat{Y} - \overline{Y})$ is now explained. This leaves only a relatively small unexplained deviation $(Y - \hat{Y})$. The total deviation of Y is the sum:

$$\begin{array}{lcl} (Y - \overline{Y}) & = (\hat{Y} - \overline{Y}) & + (Y - \hat{Y}) \\ \text{total} & = \text{explained} & + \text{unexplained} \\ \text{deviation} & \text{deviation} & \text{deviation} \end{array} \tag{15-8}$$

Surprisingly, it can be proved that this same equality holds true for the sum of squares (SS) of these deviations:

$$\begin{array}{lcl} \Sigma(Y - \overline{Y})^2 & = \Sigma(\hat{Y} - \overline{Y})^2 & + \Sigma(Y - \hat{Y})^2 \\ \text{total } SS & \text{explained } SS & + \text{unexplained } SS \end{array} \tag{15-9}$$

The explained SS is explained by the regressor; it is therefore no surprise that, as Appendix 15-2 shows, we can reexpress the middle term in (15-9) using b and x:

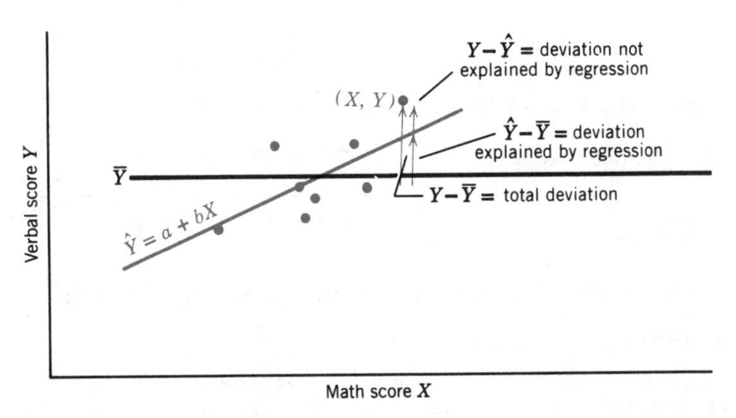

FIGURE 15-5
The value of regression in reducing the deviation of Y.

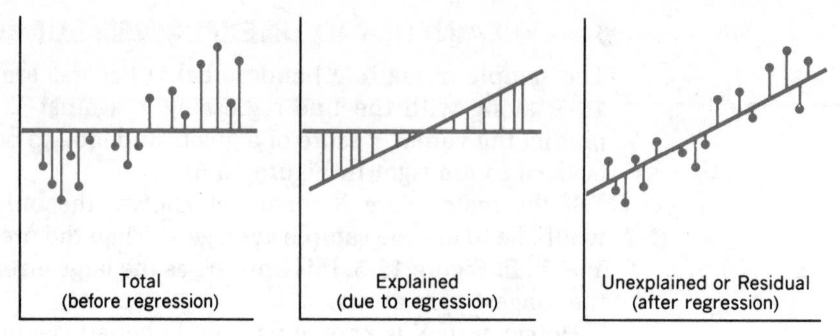

FIGURE 15-6
How regression reduces deviations as a whole (and *SS*).

$$\begin{array}{llll} \Sigma(Y - \bar{Y})^2 & = b^2\Sigma x^2 & + \Sigma(Y - \hat{Y})^2 \\ \text{total } SS & = SS \text{ explained by } X & + \text{ unexplained } SS \text{ (residual)} \end{array} \qquad (15\text{-}10) \text{ like } (10\text{-}14)$$

This breakdown or analysis of the total SS into its component parts is so important that it is illustrated in Figure 15-6. Again it is called *analysis of variance* (ANOVA), and displayed in an ANOVA table such as Table 15-2. In the last column, we test the null hypothesis $\beta = 0$ (i.e., Y has no linear relation to X). Just as in the standard ANOVA test in Chapter 10, the question is whether the ratio of explained to unexplained *MS* (variance) is large enough to reject H_o. Specifically, we form the variance ratio

TABLE 15-2 ANOVA Table for Linear Regression (*a*) General

Source of Variation	*Sum of Squares, SS*	*d.f.*	*Mean Square, MS*	*F Ratio*
Explained (by regression)	$\Sigma(\hat{Y} - \bar{Y})^2$ or $b^2\Sigma x^2$	1	$\frac{b^2\Sigma x^2}{1}$	$\frac{b^2\Sigma x^2}{s^2}$
Unexplained (residual)	$\Sigma(Y - \hat{Y})^2$	$n - 2$	$s^2 = \frac{\Sigma(Y - \hat{Y})^2}{n - 2}$	
Total	$\Sigma(Y - \bar{Y})^2$	$n - 1$		

(*b*) Computed for Math and Verbal Scores (in Table 15-1)

```
ANALYSIS OF VARIANCE

 DUE TO       DF          SS       MS=SS/DF
REGRESSION     1      328.00         328.00
RESIDUAL       6      508.00          84.67
TOTAL          7      836.00
```

$$F = \frac{\text{variance explained by regression}}{\text{unexplained variance}} \qquad \text{like (10-15)}$$

$$= \frac{b^2\Sigma x^2}{s^2} \qquad (15\text{-}11)$$

In panel (*b*) of Table 15-2 we give the computer printout for the math and verbal score example, which gives an F ratio of 328/84.67 = 3.87. Scanning Table VI where d.f. = 1 and 6, we find this observed F value of 3.87 falls beyond $F_{.10} = 3.78$. Therefore,

$$\text{p-value} < .10 \qquad (15\text{-}12)$$

Thus the F test (based on an ANOVA table) is just an alternative way of testing the null hypothesis that $\beta = 0$. The other method is to use $t = b/SE$ in (12-16)—which is equivalent,[3] and preferable if a confidence interval is also desired.

To sum up, there are three equivalent ways of testing the null hypothesis that X has no relation to Y: the ANOVA F test, the regression t test of $\beta = 0$, and the correlation test of $\rho = 0$. All three will now be illustrated in an example.

EXAMPLE 15-1

Using the level $\alpha = 5\%$, test for a relationship between the math and verbal scores of Table 15-1 in the following 3 ways:

a. Using the calculations in the ANOVA Table 15-2, calculate the F test of the null hypothesis that $\beta = 0$.

b. Test the same null hypothesis by alternatively using the t confidence interval.

c. Test the equivalent null hypothesis $\rho = 0$ using the confidence interval for ρ (based on our observed r = .63).

[3] To show that the F and t tests are equivalent, we re-express (15-11) as

$$F = \frac{b^2}{s^2/\Sigma x^2} \qquad (15\text{-}13)$$

According to (12-8), the denominator is just SE^2, so that

$$F = \left(\frac{b}{SE}\right)^2 = t^2 \qquad (15\text{-}14)$$

H_o is rejected whenever F is large, or equivalently, whenever t is very positive or negative—the appropriate test against a two-sided alternative hypothesis $\beta \neq 0$.

SOLUTION

a. From the F-value calculated in Table 15-2, we have already concluded that

$$.05 < p\text{-value} < .10 \qquad \text{like (15-12)}$$

Since the p-value for H_o is more than 5%, H_o is too credible to be rejected.

b. We use the confidence interval

$$\beta = b \pm t_{.025} \frac{s}{\sqrt{\Sigma x^2}} \qquad \text{(12-10) repeated}$$

where $b = .50$ from (15-3)

$t_{.025} = 2.45$ from Appendix Table V

$s^2 = 84.7$ from Table 15-2b

$\Sigma x^2 = 1304$ from Table 15-1

$$\text{Thus } \beta = .50 \pm 2.45 \frac{\sqrt{84.7}}{\sqrt{1304}}$$

$$= .50 \pm 2.45\ (.255)$$

$$= .50 \pm .62 \qquad (15\text{-}15)$$

Since $\beta = 0$ is included in the confidence interval, we cannot reject the null hypothesis at the 5% level.

c. In Figure 15-4, we must interpolate to find $n = 8$ and $r = .63$. This yields the approximate 95% confidence interval:

$$-.15 < \rho < +.90$$

Since $\rho = 0$ is included in the confidence interval, we cannot reject the null hypothesis at the 5% level. This agrees with the conclusions in **a** and **b**.

C—COEFFICIENT OF DETERMINATION, r^2

As proved in Appendix 15-2, the SS in the ANOVA table can be related to r:

$$\boxed{r^2 = \frac{\text{explained } SS}{\text{total } SS}} \qquad (15\text{-}16)$$

This equation provides a clear intuitive interpretation of r^2. Note that this is the *square* of the correlation coefficient r, and is often called the *coefficient of determination. It is the proportion of the total SS in Y explained by fitting the regression.* Since the numerator cannot exceed the denominator, the maximum value of the right-hand side of (15-16) is 1; hence the limits on r are ± 1. These two limits were illustrated in Figure 15-2: in panel (b), $r = +1$ and all observations lie on a positively sloped straight line; in panel (d), $r = -1$ and all observations lie on a negatively sloped straight line. In either case, regression explains 100%.

At the other extreme, when $r = 0$, then the proportion of the SS that is explained is $r^2 = 0$, and a regression line explains nothing. That is, when $r = 0$, then $b = 0$; again note that these are just two equivalent ways of formally stating "no observed linear relation between X and Y."

In Appendix 15-2, we finally show that the MS (variance) can also be related to r:

$$\boxed{s^2 \simeq (1 - r^2)s_Y^2} \tag{15-17}$$

That is, the residual unexplained variance s^2 is just a fraction of the total variance s_Y^2 before regression—with this fraction being the *coefficient of indetermination* $(1 - r^2)$. For example, if $r^2 = .40$,

$$s^2 \simeq .60 s_Y^2 \tag{15-18}$$

In other words, 60% of the total variance of Y before regression remains unexplained.

D—ASSUMPTIONS

Both the regression and correlation models require that Y be a random variable. But the two models differ in the assumptions made about X. The regression model makes few assumptions about X, but the more restrictive correlation model of this chapter requires that X be a random variable, as well as Y. We therefore conclude that regression has wider application. It may be used for example to describe the fertilizer-yield problem in Chapter 11 where X was fixed at prespecified levels, or the verbal/math score problem in this chapter where math score X was a variable; however, correlation describes only the latter.

E—SPURIOUS CORRELATION

Even though simple correlation (or simple regression) may have established that two variables move together, no claim can be made that this necessarily indicates cause and effect. For example, the correlation of teachers' salaries and the consumption of liquor over a period of years turned out to be .90. This does not prove that teachers drink, nor does it prove that liquor sales increase teachers' salaries. Instead, both variables moved together, because both are influenced by a confounding variable—long-run growth in national income and population. (To establish whether or not there is a cause-and-effect relationship, confounding factors like this would have to be neutralized, as in a randomized controlled study—or their effects allowed for, as in multiple regression.)

Such a correlation (or regression) that is attributable entirely to a confounding variable is often called a *spurious* or *nonsense* correlation. It might be more accurate to say that the correlation is real enough, but any naive inference of cause and effect is nonsense.

PROBLEMS

15-4 A random sample of 15 less-developed countries showed the following relation between population density X and economic growth rate Y (Simon, 1981):

Country	*Population Density Per KM² (X)*	*Percent Annual Change in Per Capita Income (Y)*
A	27	3.3
B	32	0.8
C	118	1.4
D	270	5.4
E	10	1.4
.	.	.
.	.	.
.	.	.
Average	54	2.4
Total SS	80,920	46.9
MS (variance)	5780	3.35
St. dev.	76.0	1.83
Correlation, r	.54	

a. Calculate the regression line of Y on X. Graph the regression line, along with the first 5 points.

b. To start the ANOVA table for the regression of Y on X, use the following steps to get the column of SS:

i. Calculate the explained SS, using b found in part **a**, and $\Sigma x^2 = 80{,}920$ given in the table above.

ii. Copy down the total SS $= \Sigma(Y - \overline{Y})^2 = 46.9$ given in the table above.

iii. Find the residual SS by subtraction.

Carry through the ANOVA table as far as the p-value for H_0. Can you reject H_0 at the 5% error level?

c. Using the slope in part **a** and the residual variance in part **b**, calculate the 95% confidence interval for β. Can you reject H_0 at the 5% error level?

d. Find the 95% confidence interval for ρ. Can you reject H_0 at the 5% error level?

e. Do you get consistent answers in parts **b, c,** and **d** for the question "Are X and Y linearly related?"

f. From the ANOVA table in **b**, find the proportion of the SS that is explained by the regression. Does it agree with r^2?
Also find the proportion left unexplained. Does it agree with $(1 - r^2)$?

15-5 A random sample of 50 U.S. women gave the following data on X = age (years) and Y = concentration of cholesterol in the blood (grams/liter):

	X	Y
	30	1.6
	60	2.5
	40	2.2
	20	1.4
	50	2.7
	.	.
	.	.
Average	41	2.1
Total SS	10,600	11.9
MS (variance)	216	.243
St. dev.	14.7	.493
Correlation, r	.693	

Repeat the same questions as in Problem 15-4.

15-3 THE TWO REGRESSION LINES

A—REGRESSION OF *Y* AGAINST *X*

In Figure 15-7 we show a bivariate normal population of math and verbal scores, represented by the ellipse of concentration that outlines most of the possible observations. If we know a student's math score, say X_1, what is the best prediction of her verbal score Y? If we consider just the students who scored X_1 in math, they are represented by the vertical slice of dots above X_1. The question is: Among these likely dots (Y values), which is the best guess? The central one, of course, indicated by P_1.

Similarly, for any other given math score X, we could find the central Y value that is the best prediction. These best predictions, marked by the heavy dots, form the *population regression line* of Y against X (an exactly straight line, given that the distribution of X and Y is bivariate normal). The equation of this line is, of course:

$$Y = \alpha + \beta X \tag{15-19}$$

This is the line that is estimated by the *sample* regression:

$$\hat{Y} = a + bX \tag{15-20}$$

where, you recall,

$$\left.\begin{aligned} b &= \frac{\Sigma xy}{\Sigma x^2} = r\,\frac{s_Y}{s_X} \\ a &= \overline{Y} - b\overline{X} \end{aligned}\right\} \qquad \text{(15-21) like (11-5)}$$

B—"REGRESSION TOWARDS THE MEAN"

If we are given X_1 in Figure 15-7 and are asked to predict Y, it is important to fully understand why we would not select the point Q_1 on the major axis of the ellipse, even though Q_1 represents equivalent performance on the two tests. Since the math score X_1 is far above average, an equivalent verbal score Q_1 seems too optimistic a prediction. Recall that there is a large random element involved in performance. There are a lot of students

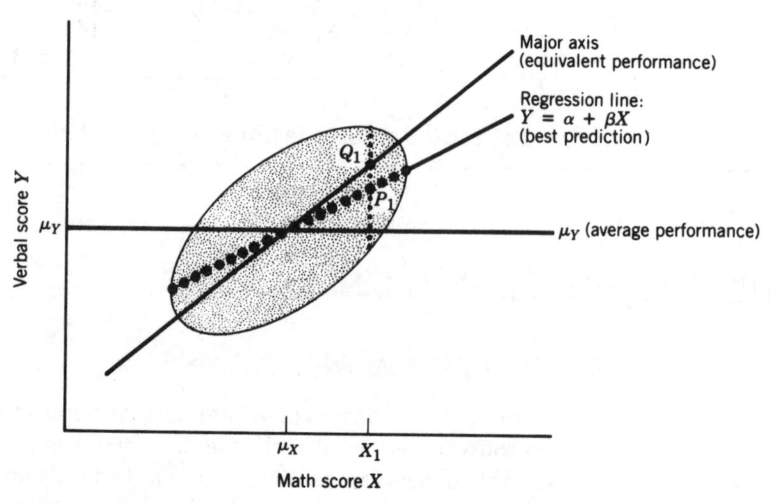

FIGURE 15-7
The population regression line of Y against X.

who will do well in one exam, but not so well in the other; in other words, the correlation is less than 1 for this population. Therefore, instead of predicting at Q_1, we are more moderate and predict at P_1—a compromise between equivalent performance at Q_1 and average performance at μ_Y.

Hence we have the origin of the word "regression." Whatever a student's score in math, there will be a tendency for the verbal score to regress toward the population average. It is evident from Figure 15-7 that this is equally true for a student with a very low math score; in this case, the predicted verbal score regresses upward toward the average.

(We met this same kind of regression toward the mean earlier in Problem 11-8, you may recall, in the context of a sample rather than a population.)

C—THE REGRESSION OF X AGAINST Y

The bivariate distribution of Figure 15-7 is repeated in Figure 15-8, along with the regression line of Y on X.

Now let us turn around our question: If we know a student's *verbal* score Y_1, what is the likeliest prediction of his *math* score X? Can we still use the regression line $Y = \alpha + \beta X$? If we do, we obtain the estimate P_2, which is absurdly large—it even lies outside the scatter of likely values. Instead, we recognize that, with Y_1 given, the range of likely X values is the *horizontal* slice of dots, with the best prediction again being the midpoint P_1. As before, this is a compromise between equivalent performance Q_1 and average performance μ_X.

Similarly, for any other given verbal score Y, we could find the central X value that is the best prediction. These best predictions, marked by

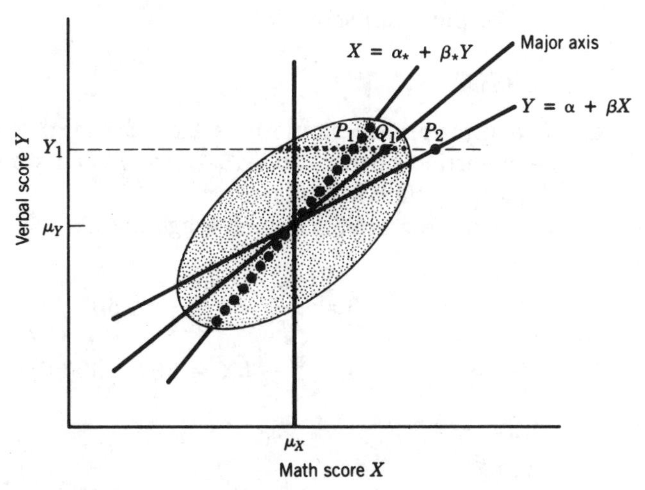

FIGURE 15-8
The two population regression lines.

heavy dots, again form a straight line, called the *population regression line* of X against Y:

$$X = \alpha_* + \beta_* Y \tag{15-22}$$

This population line again may be estimated by the *sample* regression line:

$$\hat{X} = a_* + b_* Y \tag{15-23}$$

where the estimates b_* and a_* are obtained from the usual regression formulas—interchanging X and Y, of course:

$$\left.\begin{aligned} b_* &= \frac{\Sigma yx}{\Sigma y^2} = r\frac{s_X}{s_Y} \\ a_* &= \overline{X} - b_*\overline{Y} \end{aligned}\right\} \qquad \text{(15-24) like (15-21)}$$

EXAMPLE 15-2

Using the sample of math and verbal scores in Table 15-1 and their summary statistics:

a. Calculate the regression of Y against X, and the regression of X against Y. Graph these two lines.

b. For a student with a math score $X = 90$, what is the best prediction of the verbal score Y?

c. For a student with a verbal score $Y = 10$, what is the best prediction of the math score X?

SOLUTION

a. The appropriate calculations Σxy, Σx^2, and so on, have already been carried out in Table 15-1. So we can simply substitute into the appropriate formula:

For the regression line of Y against X,

$$b = \frac{\Sigma xy}{\Sigma x^2} = \frac{654}{1304} = .50 \qquad \text{(15-21) repeated}$$

$$a = \overline{Y} - b\overline{X} = 50 - .50(60) = 20$$

Thus

$$\hat{Y} = 20 + .50X \tag{15-25}$$

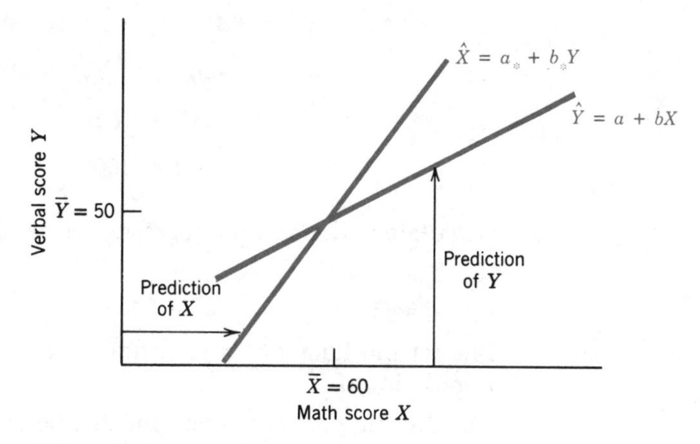

FIGURE 15-9
The two estimated regression lines for the verbal and math scores in Table 15-1.

For the regression line of X against Y,

$$b_* = \frac{\Sigma xy}{\Sigma y^2} = \frac{654}{836} = .78 \qquad \text{(15-24) repeated}$$

$$a_* = \overline{X} - b_*\overline{Y} = 60 - .78(50) = 21$$

Thus

$$\hat{X} = 21 + .78Y \qquad (15\text{-}26)$$

These two estimated regressions are graphed in Figure 15-9.

b. We substitute $X = 90$ into (15-25):

$$\hat{Y} = 20 + .50(90) = 65$$

c. We substitute $Y = 10$ into (15-26):

$$\hat{X} = 21 + .78(10) = 29$$

In both **b** and **c** note how the predicted grade regresses toward the average.

PROBLEMS

15-6 In a random sample of 200 pairs of father-son heights (X, Y), the summary statistics were computed as follows (in inches):

$$\bar{X} = 68 \qquad \bar{Y} = 69$$
$$\Sigma x^2 = 1920 \qquad \Sigma y^2 = 2040$$
$$\Sigma xy = 1010$$
$$n = 200$$

a. Calculate and graph the regression line of:
  i. Y against X.
  ii. X against Y.

b. Predict the height of a man drawn at random from the same population if:
  i. Nothing is known, except that he is a father.
  ii. His son's height is 73 inches.
  iii. He is one of the sons, and his father's height is 64 inches.

c. How much is:
  i. Y correlated to X?
  ii. X correlated to Y?

15-7

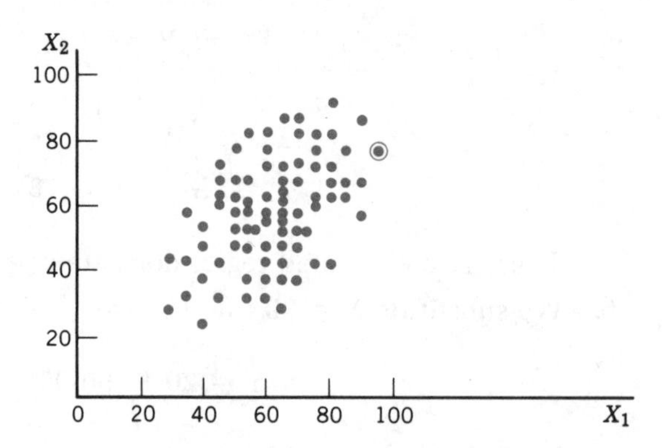

In an experimental program, 80 pilot trainees were drawn at random, and each given 2 trial landings. Their scores X_1 and X_2 were recorded in the above graph, and the following summary statistics were calculated:

$$\bar{X}_1 = 62, \qquad \bar{X}_2 = 62$$
$$\Sigma(X_1 - \bar{X}_1)^2 = 18{,}000 \qquad \Sigma(X_2 - \bar{X}_2)^2 = 21{,}000$$
$$\Sigma(X_1 - \bar{X}_1)(X_2 - \bar{X}_2) = 11{,}000$$

a. By comparison with Figure 15-2, guess the approximate correlation of X_1 and X_2. Then calculate it.

b. Draw in the line of equivalent performance, the line $X_2 = X_1$. For comparison, calculate and then graph the regression line of X_2 on X_1.

c. What would you predict would be a pilot's second score X_2, if his first score was $X_1 = 90$? Or $X_1 = 40$?

d. On the figure below we graph the marginal distributions of X_1 and of X_2. The arrow indicates that the pilot who scored $X_1 = 95$ later scored $X_2 = 80$. (This is the pilot in the original graph who is circled on the extreme right.) Draw in similar arrows for all three pilots who scored $X_1 = 90$. What is the mean of their three X_2 scores? How does it compare to the answer in **c**?

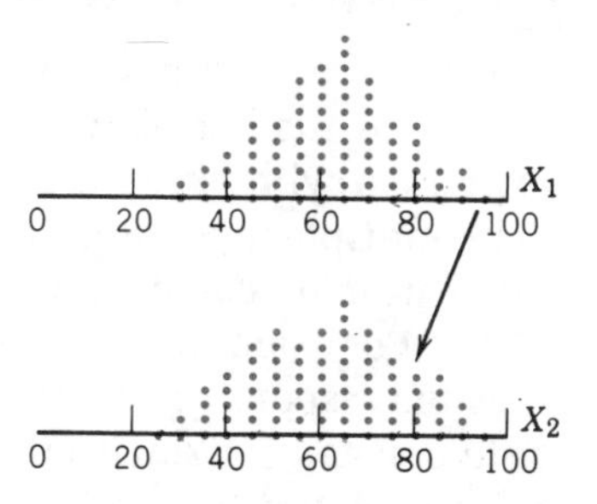

e. Repeat part **d** for all the pilots who scored $X_1 = 40$.

f. Answer True or False; if False, correct it.

The pilots who scored very well or very badly on the first test X_1 were closer to the average on the second test X_2.

One possible reason for this "regression toward the mean" is that a very high score probably represents some good luck as well as good skill. On another test, the good luck may not persist. So the second score will generally be not so good as the first, although still better than average.

15-8 Repeat Problem 15-7, interchanging X_1 and X_2 everywhere.

15-9 **a.** When the flight instructors in problem 15-7 graded the pilots, they praised them if they did well, or criticized them if they did poorly. They noticed that the pilots who had been praised did worse the next time, while the pilots who had been criticized did better; so they concluded that criticism works better than praise. Comment.

b. This example was a loose reconstruction of Tversky and Kahneman, 1973, who go on to conclude:

"This true story illustrates a saddening aspect of the human condition. We normally reinforce others when their behavior is good and punish them when their behavior is bad. By regression alone, therefore, they are most likely to improve after being punished and most likely to deteriorate after being rewarded. Consequently, we are exposed to a lifetime schedule in which we are most often rewarded for punishing others, and punished for rewarding."

Suggest how the flight instructors could have found unbiased estimates of the effects of praise and criticism. (Incidentally, when psychologists calculated unbiased estimates, they generally found that praise works better than criticism.)

15-4 CORRELATION IN MULTIPLE REGRESSION

A—PARTIAL CORRELATION

In simple regression we have already seen that the coefficient b is closely related to the correlation r. Accordingly, the relation of Y to X can be expressed with either b or r.

In multiple regression the same general idea holds true: For each *multiple regression* coefficient there is an equivalent *partial correlation* coefficient.[4] For example, just as the multiple regression coefficient b_1 measures how the response Y is related to the regressor X_1 (with the other regressors held constant), likewise the partial correlation coefficient r_1 is defined as the correlation between Y and X_1 (with the other regressors held constant). Thus the relation of Y to X_1 can be expressed with either b_1 or r_1, as we will illustrate in Example 15-3 below.

B—MULTIPLE CORRELATION *R*

Whereas the partial correlations measure how Y is related to each of the regressors one by one, the multiple correlation R measures how Y is related to *all* the regressors at once. To calculate R, we first use the multiple regression equation to calculate the fitted value $\hat{Y}$:

$$\hat{Y} = b_0 + b_1X_1 + b_2X_2 + \cdots$$

Then the multiple correlation R is defined as the ordinary, simple correlation between these fitted $\hat{Y}$ values and the observed Y values. That is,

$$\boxed{R \equiv r_{\hat{Y}Y}} \tag{15-27}$$

As a kind of simple correlation coefficient, this has the familiar algebraic properties already noted in describing simple correlation in Section 15-1

[4] Because of this equivalence, the multiple regression coefficient is sometimes called the *partial regression* coefficient. It also corresponds to the *partial* derivative in calculus (where all other variables are held constant).

earlier. In particular, we note that when we square R, we get the *multiple coefficient of determination:*

$$R^2 = \frac{SS \text{ explained by all the regressors}}{\text{total } SS} \tag{15-28}$$

like (15-16)

Since R^2 gives the proportion of the total SS (Sum of Squares of deviations) that is explained by all the regressors, it measures how well the multiple regression fits the data. As we add additional regressors to our model, we can see how much they add in explaining Y by noting how much they increase R^2.

C—CORRECTED R^2

Since the inclusion of even an irrelevant regressor will increase R^2 a little,[5] it usually is desirable to correct for this by reducing R^2 appropriately. If there are k regressors, we define the *corrected* coefficient of determination as:

$$\bar{R}^2 \equiv \frac{(n-1)R^2 - k}{n-k-1} \tag{15-29}$$

Then $1 - \bar{R}^2$ is the corrected coefficient of *indetermination*, and gives the proportion of the total *MS* (variance s_Y^2) that is left unexplained as the residual *MS* (variance s^2), that is,

$$s^2 = (1 - \bar{R}^2)s_Y^2 \tag{15-30}$$

like (15-17)

An example will illustrate these concepts.

EXAMPLE 15-3

In a chemical plant (Brownlee, 1965), the percent of ammonia that was lost (Y) depended on the following factors:

---

[5] By an irrelevant regressor (say X_4) we mean a regressor whose population regression coefficient β_4 is 0. Nevertheless, in a *sample* the estimated coefficient b_4 will be slightly nonzero—as some small part of the fluctuation in Y, but sheer chance happens to coincide with the fluctuation in X_4. Then X_4 will appear to be explaining Y, and R^2 will accordingly increase a little.

X_1 = rate of operation

X_2 = temperature of the cooling water

X_3 = concentration of nitric acid

Based on $n = 21$ runs, the fitted regression equation was

$$\hat{Y} = -40.0 + .72X_1 + 1.29X_2 - .15X_3$$

Standard error (SE) (.13) (.37) (.16)

$$R = .956$$

a. For each regressor:

i. Calculate t and the p-value for H_o.

ii. Is the regressor discernibly related to Y, at the level α = 5%?

iii. Calculate the partial correlation with Y, from the formula:

$$\text{partial } r = \frac{b/SE}{\sqrt{(b/SE)^2 + (n - k - 1)}} \tag{15-31}$$

b. Calculate $\overline{R}^2$.

c. If the variance of Y before regression was $s_Y^2 = 18.0$, what is the residual variance s^2?

SOLUTION

a. We show in detail the calculations for the first regressor X_1.

i.

$$t = \frac{b}{SE} = \frac{.72}{.13} = 5.54 \qquad \text{like (13-15)}$$

To find the p-value, we use Table V with d.f. $= n - k - 1 = 21 - 3 - 1 = 17$. The observed $t = 5.54$ far exceeds the last tabled value of $t_{.0005} = 3.97$. Thus

$$\text{p-value} \ll .0005$$

ii. Since the p-value < 5%, H_0 is easily rejected. Thus we conclude that ammonia loss Y is positively related to the rate of operation X_1 (discernible at the 5% level).

iii.

$$\text{partial } r = \frac{.72/.13}{\sqrt{(.72/.13)^2 + (21 - 3 - 1)}} = .80 \qquad \text{like (15-31)}$$

When similar calculations for all three regressors are done, they are customarily recorded on the regression equation:

$$\hat{Y} = -40.0 + .72X_1 + 1.29X_2 - .15X_3$$

(SE)	(.13)	(.37)	(.16)
t	5.54	3.49	−.94
p-value	≪.0005	<.0025	<.25
Partial r	.80	.65	−.22
Discernible at 5%?	Yes	Yes	No

b. $$\bar{R}^2 = \frac{(n-1)R^2 - k}{(n-k-1)}$$ like (15-29)

$$= \frac{(21-1)(.956)^2 - 3}{21 - 3 - 1} = .90$$

c. Since $\bar{R}^2 = .90$, therefore 90% of the variance in Y is explained by the three regressors, leaving 10% as the residual variance:

$$s^2 = (1 - \bar{R}^2)s_Y^2$$ like (15-30)

$$= (1 - .90)18.0 = 1.80$$

In the rest of this chapter, we will have a chance to see how the multiple coefficient of determination illuminates further important issues in regression.

D—USING $\bar{R}^2$ IN STEPWISE REGRESSION

When there are a large number of regressors, a computer is sometimes programmed to introduce them one at a time, in a so-called *stepwise regression*. The order in which the regressors are introduced may be determined in several ways, two of the commonest being:

1. The statistician may specify a priori the order in which the regressors are to be introduced. For example, among many other regressors suppose there were 3 dummy variables to take care of 4 different geographical regions; then it would make sense to introduce these 3 dummy variables together in succession, without interruption from other regressors.
2. The statistician may want to let the data determine the order, using one of the many available computer programs (with names such as "backward elimination," "forward selection," "all possible subsets," etc.).

One of the commonest programs, called *forward selection*, introduces the statistically most important regressors first. It achieves this by having the computer choose the sequence that will make $\bar{R}^2$ climb as quickly as possible. Suppose, for example, that two regressors have already been introduced. In deciding which of the remaining regressors should be added in the next step, the computer tries each of them in turn, and selects the one that increases $\bar{R}^2$ the most.

TABLE 15-3 Stepwise Regression of Lung Capacity for n = 309 Physicians

Step	*New Regressor Added*	*Coeff. of Det.* ($\bar{R}^2$)
1	age	.367
2	height	.459
3	cigarette smoking	.474
4	pipe and cigar smoking	.476
5	past cigarette smoking	.477

The computer customarily prints the regression equation after each step (after each new regressor is introduced). Then at the end, the computer prints a summary consisting of the list of regressors in the order they were introduced and the corresponding value of $\bar{R}^2$ at each step. This is illustrated in Table 15-3, for some data relating lung capacity to many possible factors (Lefcoe and Wonnacott, 1974). Since this table was produced by forward selection, it has included the regressors in the rough order of their statistical importance—easily and automatically. Notice how the first regressors included make a big contribution in raising $\bar{R}^2$, while the later, less important regressors make less contribution.

To judge how far down the list of regressors we ought to go to finally make up the "best" regression equation, there are as many answers as there are ways to interpret "best": Do we want brevity, accuracy of prediction, coefficients unbiased by confounding factors, or some combination of all three?

Having obtained the "best" equation, how do we judge its reliability? Many of the classical statistical tests or confidence intervals discussed in Section 13-3 are of limited use in this freewheeling model-building. Instead, more modern methods such as the bootstrap (in Section 8-6) or Bayesian methods (in Section 19-5) can be adapted to regression.

PROBLEMS

15-10 The regression of hay yield Y on rainfall X_1 and temperature X_2 was calculated in Problem 13-13 to be

$$
\begin{array}{rccc}
 & \hat{Y} = 9.14 + & 3.38X_1 + & .0364X_2 \\
\text{SE} & & (.70) & (.090) \\
t\text{ ratio} & & (\quad) & (\quad) \\
\text{Partial } r & & (\quad) & (\quad) \\
p\text{-value} & & (\quad) & (\quad) \\
 & & R = .803, & n = 20
\end{array}
$$

a. Fill in the blanks.

b. If the variance of Y is $s_Y^2 = 87$, what is the residual variance s^2 after regression?

15-11 **a.** In Table 12-1, values of $\hat{Y}$ and Y are given. Use them to calculate R from the definition (15-27).

b. Calculate r for the same yield-fertilizer example, using the definition (15-2). (In Table 11-2, calculate Σy^2. Then combine it with Σx^2 and Σxy already calculated there.) Does your answer agree with R in part **a**?

15-12 **a.** In the case of simple regression (with $k = 1$), show that the formula (15-31) reduces to

$$\text{Simple r} = \frac{t}{\sqrt{t^2 + (n - 2)}} \tag{15-32}$$

b. For the 7 observations of yield and fertilizer in Problem 15-11, we found earlier that the regression coefficient had a t ratio of 5.2. Substitute this into the formula in **a** to calculate r. Does your answer agree with Problem 15-11?

c. Choose the correct term in the brackets:

When there is just one regressor, both the multiple correlation R and the partial correlation r_p [coincide with, are less than, are greater than] the simple correlation r.

In general, when there are several regressors, [R,r_p] measures how much all of them together are related to Y, whereas [R,r_p] measures how much each individual regressor is related to Y while all the other regressors are [ignored, held constant].

15-5 MULTICOLLINEARITY

When two regressors are very closely related, it is hard to "untangle" their separate effects on Y. When one increases, the other increases *at the same time*. To which increase do we then attribute the increase in Y? It's very hard to say—and that is the problem of multicollinearity in a nutshell.

Since multicollinearity is such a common problem, however, it warrants a more detailed discussion, starting with an analogy in simple regression.

A—IN SIMPLE REGRESSION

In Figure 12-4, we showed how the slope b became unreliable if the X values were closely bunched—that is, if the regressor X had little variation. It will be instructive to consider the limiting case, where the X values are completely bunched at one single value $\overline{X}$, as in Figure 15-10. Then the slope b is not determined at all. There are any number of differently sloped lines passing through $(\overline{X},\overline{Y})$ that fit equally well: For each line in Figure 15-10, the sum of squared deviations is the same, since the

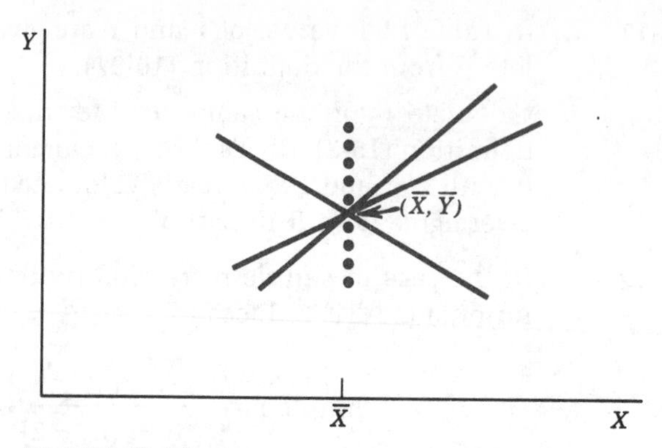

FIGURE 15-10
Degenerate regression: Because the X values are completely bunched at a point $\overline{X}$, the regression slope b is not determined.

deviations are measured vertically from $(\overline{X},\overline{Y})$. [This geometric fact has an algebraic counterpart. When all observed X values are the same—that is, when all deviations x are zero—then Σx^2 in the denominator of (11-15) is zero, and b is not defined.]

In conclusion, when the values of X show no variation, then the *relation* of Y to X can no longer be sensibly investigated. But if the issue is just *predicting* Y, this bunching of the X values does not matter *provided that* we confine our prediction to this same value $\overline{X}$—where we can predict that Y will be $\overline{Y}$.

B—IN MULTIPLE REGRESSION

Again consider the limiting case where the values of the regressors X_1 and X_2 are completely bunched up—on a line L in the three-dimensional Figure 15-11. Since L represents a linear relationship between X_1 and X_2, the regressors are said to suffer from *collinearity*. Since similar bunching can occur in higher dimensions when there are more than two regressors, it is more often called the problem of *multicollinearity*.

In Figure 15-11, multicollinearity means that all the observed points in our scatter lie in the vertical plane running up through L. You can think of the three-dimensional space shown here as a room in a house: The observations are not scattered throughout this room, but instead lie embedded in the pane of glass shown standing vertically on the floor.

In explaining Y, multicollinearity makes us lose one dimension. In the earlier case of simple regression, our best fit for Y degenerated from a line to the point $(\overline{X},\overline{Y})$. In this multiple regression case, our best fit for Y degenerates from a plane to the line F—the least squares fit through the points on the vertical pane of glass. In *predicting* Y no special problems will arise, *provided that* we confine our predictions to this same pane of glass—where we can predict Y from the regression line F on the glass.

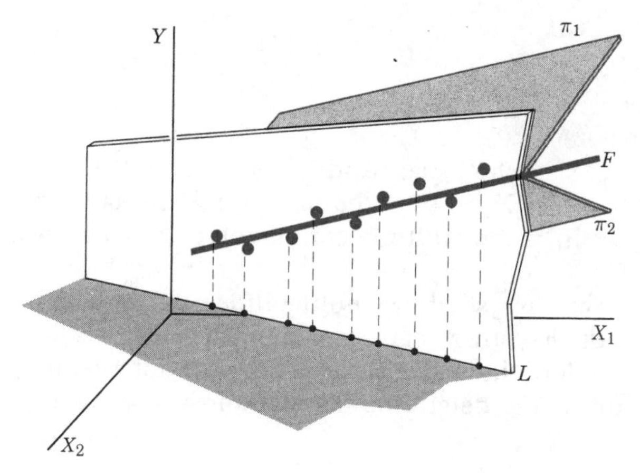

FIGURE 15-11
Multicollinearity: Because the X_1 and X_2 values are completely bunched on a line L, the regression slopes b_1 and b_2 are not determined.

But there is no way to determine the *relation of* Y to X_1 and X_2 separately. For example, any attempt to define the slope b_1 in the X_1 direction involves moving off that pane of glass; and we have no sample information whatsoever on what the world out there looks like. Or, to put it differently, if we try to explain Y with a plane—rather than a line F—we find that there are any number of planes running through F (e.g., π_1 and π_2) that fit our observations equally well: Since each passes through F, each yields an identical sum of squared deviations. [This is confirmed algebraically in the estimating equations (13-5) and (13-6): When X_1 is a linear function of X_2, it can be shown that these two equations cannot be solved uniquely for b_1 and b_2.]

Now let us be less extreme in our assumptions and consider the more realistic case where X_1 and X_2 are *almost* on a line (i.e., where all the observations in the room lie very close to a vertical pane of glass). In this case, a plane can be fitted to the observations, but the estimating procedure is very unstable; it becomes very sensitive to random errors, reflected in very large standard errors of the estimators b_1 and b_2. This is analogous to the argument in the simple regression case in Figure 12-4.

C—IN TERMS OF CORRELATION

The scatter of black points (X_1, X_2) in Figure 15-11 that lie flat on the line L have a perfect correlation of 1.00. (Note how that pattern of black points is similar to Figure 15-2*b*, for example.) In general, the higher the correlation of the regressors, the worse the problem of multicollinearity—and the formulas for the standard errors reflect this. For example, b_1—the coefficient of X_1—has a standard error given by:

$$SE_1 = \frac{s}{\sqrt{\Sigma x_1^2}\sqrt{1 - R_1^2}} \qquad \text{(15-33) like (12-8)}$$

where

s^2 = the usual residual variance = $\Sigma(Y - \hat{Y})^2/(n - k - 1)$
$x_1 = X_1 - \overline{X}_1$ = the regressor X_1 in its usual deviation form
R_1 = the multiple correlation of X_1 with all the other regressors

Thus we see how multicollinearity hurts. The more X_1 is correlated with the other regressors (i.e., the larger is R_1), the larger is SE_1 and therefore the wider is the confidence interval for β_1—and the more difficult it is to determine the relationship between Y and X_1.

D—IN DESIGNED EXPERIMENTS, MAKE THE REGRESSORS UNCORRELATED

In (15-33), note that SE_1 is at a minimum—as we would like it to be—when $R_1 = 0$—that is, when X_1 is completely uncorrelated with the other regressors. One of the first principles of experimental design, therefore, is to choose the levels of the X regressors to make them uncorrelated. One of the simplest ways to achieve this is with a square or rectangular array like the one on the "floor" of Figure 15-12. This design is a perfectly natural one: Each variable takes on a range of values independent of the other. Then there is no tendency for them to move together, and hence no problem of multicollinearity.

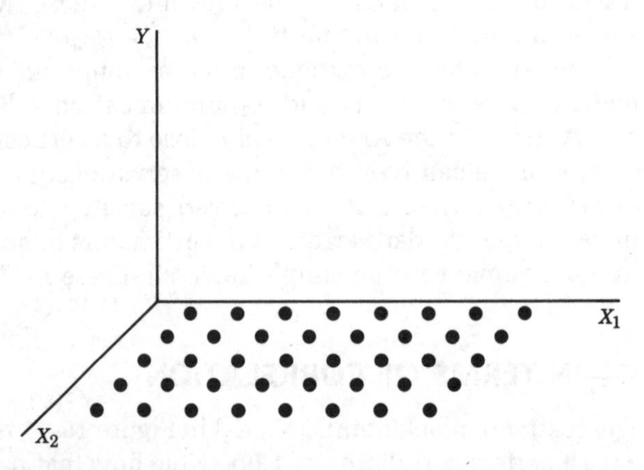

FIGURE 15-12
In a designed experiment, select an uncorrelated grid of X_1 and X_2 values to eliminate any problem of multicollinearity.

E—IN OBSERVATIONAL STUDIES, CHOOSE THE REGRESSORS WISELY

In observational studies, we usually have to take the values of the regressors as they come, and so the problem of multicollinearity seems incurable. There is a partial remedy, however: Choose the *form* of the regressors wisely.

For example, suppose that demand for a group of goods is being related to (1) prices and (2) income, with the overall price index being the first regressor. Suppose the second regressor is income measured in money terms. Since this is real income multiplied by the same price index, the problem of multicollinearity may become a serious one. The solution is to use real income, rather than money income, as the second regressor. And in general, try to choose regressors that have as little intercorrelation as possible.

PROBLEMS

15-13 In the regression of Y on X_1 and X_2, match up the equivalent statements:

a. There is multicollinearity in the regressors.

b. Y has a nearly perfect linear relation to X_1 and X_2.

c. The multiple correlation of Y on X_1 and X_2 is nearly one.

d. The residual variance after regression is very small compared to the variance of Y without regression.

e. X_1 and X_2 have high correlation.

15-14 In Figure 14-4 and equation (14-21), the two regressors used were

$$X_1 = X \qquad \text{and} \qquad X_2 = X^2$$

a. Tabulate X_1 and X_2 for $X = 1, 2, 3, 4, 5$, and then calculate their correlation r.

b. Is multicollinearity therefore any problem?

c. The residual variance after regression was $s^2 = 15.7$. Using (15-33), calculate the standard error of b_1 and of b_2.

***d.** Suppose the regressor X_2 had turned out to be statistically indiscernible, and it was decided to drop it.

To predict Y, can you in fact just "drop off" the X_2 term from the multiple regression, or do you need to calculate the regression equation afresh, using just the regressor X_1?

15-15 Repeat Problem 15-14, if another statistician chose an alternative pair of regressors (called *orthogonal polynomials*):

$$X_1 = X - 3$$
$$X_2 = X^2 - 6X + 7$$

Assume the same values of X—that is, $X = 1, 2, 3, 4, 5$.

***15-16** In Problem 15-15, the two orthogonal polynomials were deliberately chosen (defined) to have zero correlation, and so are completely free of multicollinearity. They have a further advantage: the multiple regression equation is easy to compute—so easy, in fact, that it is feasible to do it by hand.

Carry out this hand calculation on the data in Table 14-2 on page 450, using (13-5) and (13-6). Do you get the same answer as in (14-21)?

CHAPTER 15 SUMMARY

15-1 The correlation coefficient r measures how closely two variables are linearly related; its value is 0 if there is no relation, and +1 or −1 for a perfectly positive or negative relation.

15-2 Correspondingly, the coefficient of determination r^2 lies between 0 and 1 (0% and 100%). And r^2 gives the percent of the variation in one variable that is explained by regressing it on the other variable. There are other close connections between correlation and regression: The null hypothesis (that Y is unrelated to X), can equivalenty be tested by using r or the regression slope b (or even the F test in the ANOVA table).

15-3 The regression line for predicting X from Y is quite different from the regression line for predicting Y from X. And each regression line is a compromise or "regression" from equivalent performance back towards the mean.

15-4 In multiple regression, to measure how closely Y is related to any particular regressor (while the other regressors are constant), we use the partial correlation. To measure how closely Y is related to the *whole set* of regressors, we use the multiple correlation R.

15-5 The problem of multicollinearity occurs when two (or more) regressors are highly correlated; that is, when one changes, there is a strong tendency for the other to change as well. Then the separate effects of the two regressors are difficult to sort out, and the two regressors coefficients consequently have large standard errors.

REVIEW PROBLEMS

15-17 Suppose men always married women who were 4 inches shorter than themselves. What would be the correlation between husbands' and wives' heights?

15-18 **a.** Referring to the math and verbal scores of Table 15-1, suppose that only the students with math scores exceeding 65 were admitted to college. For this subsample of 3 students, calculate the correlation of X and Y.

b. For the other subsample of the 5 remaining students, calculate the correlation of X and Y.

c. Are these 2 correlations in the subsamples greater or less than the correlation in the whole sample? Do you think this will be generally true? Why?

15-19 Suppose that a bivariate normal distribution of scores is perfectly symmetric in X and Y, with $\rho = .50$ and with an ellipse of concentration as follows:

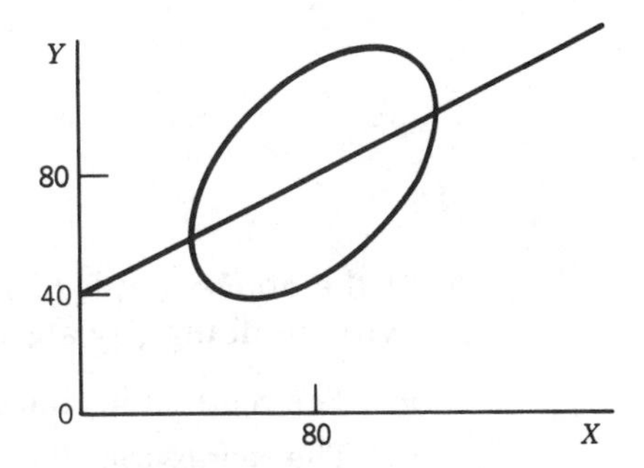

Answer true or false; if false, correct it.

a. The regression of Y on X is the line shown, with equation

$$Y = 40 + .5X$$

b. The variance of Y is 1/4 the variance of X.

c. The proportion of the Y variation explained by X is only $\frac{1}{4}$.

d. Thus, the residual Y values (after fitting X) would have $\frac{3}{4}$ the variation of the original Y values.

e. For a student with a Y score of 70, the predicted X score is 60.

15-20 Let b and b_* be the sample regression slopes of Y against X, and X against Y for any given scatter of points. Answer True or False; if False, correct it:

a. $b = r\dfrac{s_Y}{s_X}$

b. $b_* = r\dfrac{s_X}{s_Y}$

c. $bb_* = r^2$

d. $b_* = \dfrac{1}{b}$

15-21

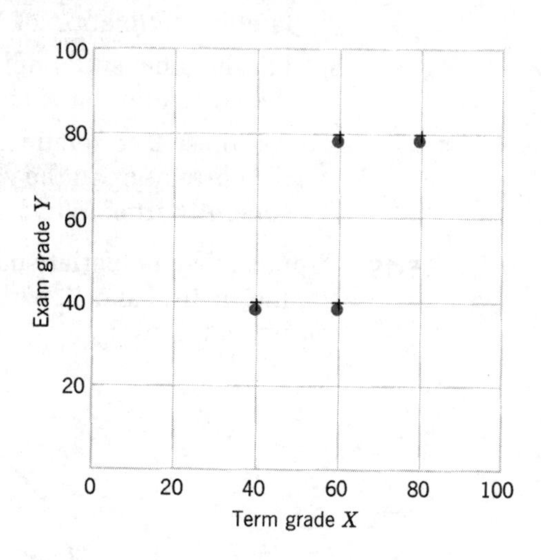

In the above graph of four students' marks, find geometrically (without doing any algebraic calculations):

a. The regression line of Y against X.

b. The regression line of X against Y.

c. The correlation r (*Hint:* Problem 15-20**c**).

d. The predicted Y for a student with $X = 70$.

e. The predicted X for a student with $Y = 70$.

15-22 Answer True or False; if False, correct it:

a. $$R^2 = \frac{\text{SS explained by all the regressors}}{\text{residual SS}}$$

b. Multicollinearity occurs when the response is highly correlated with the regressors.

c. Multicollinearity implies that the regression coefficients have large standard errors.

Some regressors therefore may be statistically indiscernible; they may be dropped from the model if the purpose is to predict Y for a combination of $(X_1, X_2, \ldots)$ that is similar to the given data (extrapolation instead of interpolation).

d. Suppose a regressor is dropped in part **c**. To obtain the appropriate prediction equation it is necessary to recalculate the regression equation with that regressor omitted.

e. Multicollinearity often is a problem in the social sciences, when the regressors have high correlation. On the other hand, in the experimental sciences, the values of the regressors often can be designed to avoid multicollinearity.

15-23 Suppose that all the firms in a certain industry recorded their profits P (after tax) in 1984 and again in 1985, as follows (hypothetical and simplified data):

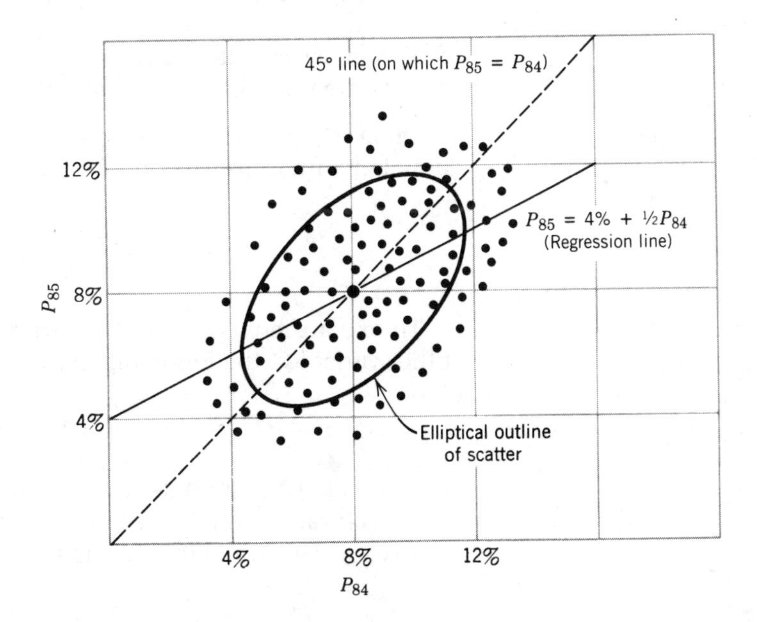

Answer True or False; if False, correct it:

a. Both the firms with extremely high profits and extremely low profits in 1984 tended to have less extreme profits in 1985.

b. This indicates, but does not prove, that some factor (perhaps a too progressive taxation policy, or a more conservative outlook by business executives, etc.) caused profits to be much less extreme in 1985 than in 1984.

c. This shows, among other things, how difficult it is to stay near the top.

d. The scatter is pretty well symmetrical about the 45° line where $P_{85} = P_{84}$. Therefore, for a firm with a 1984 profit of 11%, the best single prediction of its 1985 profit would be 11% too.

15-24 *A Final Challenge: What Determines the Size of the Police Force?*

The costs and control of crime have now become important questions addressed by statisticians. In each of the 121 Standard Metropolitan Statistical Areas (SMSA) of more than 250,000 inhabitants in the United States in 1970, the following variables were measured (Jacobs, 1979):

P = number of policemen per 100,000 inhabitants
D = disparity or inequality of income
I = mean family income annually (dollars)
S = number of small drug and liquor stores per 100,000 inhabitants
R = number of riots between 1960 and 1970
C = crime rate as measured by FBI crimes known to the police

Often a regression is carried out with *standardized* variables, denoted with a prime symbol (′) and defined as

$$X' \equiv \frac{X - \overline{X}}{s_X} \qquad \text{like (4-23)}$$

To explain how the number of policemen P depended on the other variables, the following multiple regression was calculated:

$$P' = .34D' + .15I' + .44S' - .004R' + .27C' + \cdots$$

As indicated by the dots, the multiple regression also included other relevant variables (such as % unemployment, population size, etc.). The following simple regressions were also calculated:

$$P' = .63D', \qquad P' = .47R', \qquad P' = .41C'$$

a. Suppose we compared an SMSA that had 2 standard deviations more income disparity than another SMSA; that is, $\Delta D' = 2$. How many more police do you estimate it would have if the two SMSA's were:

i. Alike in all other respects?

ii. Alike in all other respects except that the one with the greater income disparity also had a crime rate that was 1 standard deviation lower?

iii. Just drawn at random from the 121 available?

b. Sue and Laurie are having an argument. Sue thinks the evidence shows that the number of police by 1970 was increased substantially in reaction to the riots in the 1960s. Do you agree or disagree? Why?

c. Income I had a mean of \$10,000 and standard deviation of \$1200 approximately. If the original variable I had been used instead of the standardized I' in the multiple regression, what would be its coefficient b?

d. Choose the correct alternative in each bracket: One of the advantages of standardizing is that the regression coefficient is [independent of, closely related to] the units in which the variable is measured. Then a large coefficient, for example, assures us that the impact of the variable itself is [small, large]—a property not found in the unstandardized form. Thus we can conclude that the variable with the largest impact on number of police is [number of riots R, number of small stores S].

In standardizing *simple* regression, there is a further advantage: the regression coefficient equals the [correlation coefficient, coefficient of determination].

REVIEW PROBLEMS, CHAPTERS 11–15

15-25 Answer True or False; if False, correct it:

a. In observational studies, simple regression can be very misleading about how X causes Y, because the simple regression coefficient picks up the effect of not only X, but all the confounding variables too.

b. Nevertheless, for *predicting* Y, simple regression can be very effective—especially if the correlation of X and Y is near 0.

c. In observational studies, multiple regression can allow for all the confounding factors by including them as regressors.

d. In both observational studies and randomized experiments, multiple regression reduces s^2, and hence reduces the uncertainty in the regression coefficients and in predicting Y.

e. One severe limitation of multiple regression is that it cannot include (1) factors that are categorical, or (2) nonlinearities such as polynomials and exponentials.

15-26 A group of 4 physicians hired a management consultant to see whether he could reduce the long waiting times of their patients. He randomly sampled 200 patients, and found their waiting times had an average of 32 minutes, and a standard deviation of 15 minutes. To determine the factors that influence waiting time, he ran a multiple regression:

$$\begin{array}{llll} \text{WAIT} = 22 + .09\ \text{DRLATE} & -\ .24\ \text{PALATE} & +\ 2.61\ \text{SHORT} & \\ \text{(SE)} \qquad\quad (.01) & \qquad (.05) & \qquad (.82) & R^2 = .72 \end{array}$$

where WAIT = waiting time, in minutes

DRLATE = the lateness of the doctors in arriving that morning (sum of their times, in minutes)

PALATE = the lateness of the patient in arriving for his appointment (in minutes)

SHORT = 1 if the clinic was short staffed, and some of the appointments had to be rebooked; 0 if fully staffed with all 4 physicians

Answer True or False; if False, correct it:

a. Since the coefficient of SHORT is biggest, it is the most important factor in accounting for the variation in WAIT.

b. If two of the doctors were late that morning (by 20 minutes and 40 minutes), the expected increase in waiting time for a patient that day would be 2.7 minutes.

c. If the consultant had studied *all* the patients, he would have found, with 95% confidence, that:

i. Their average waiting time would be somewhere between 2 and 62 minutes.

ii. The regression coefficient of PALATE would be somewhere between −.12 and −.36.

d. Since patients who are late are likely to wait longer, the office staff is providing a strong incentive for patients to arrive on time.

e. If he included another factor in the multiple regression, R^2 would necessarily be larger, as would the corrected $\overline{R}^2$.

15-27 Continuing Problem 15-26:

a. For each of the three coefficients, calculate the 95% confidence interval, t ratio, and p-value. Also calculate the partial correlation of each regressor with the waiting time.

b. If a patient is drawn at random, predict how long he has to wait:

i. If nothing else is known.

ii. If he turns out to be 15 minutes late, on a day when the clinic was fully staffed but the four physicians were late by 10, 30, 0, and 60 minutes.

c. The patient in part **b** actually had to wait 22 minutes. Which of the predictions in **b** was closer, and by how much?

***d.** Is the answer to part **c** typical of all 200 patients?

15-28 A certain drug (e.g., tobacco, alcohol, marijuana) is taken by a proportion of the American population. To investigate its effect on health (for example, mortality rate), suppose that certain people are to be studied for a five-year period, at the end of which each person's mortality will be recorded as follows:

$$\begin{aligned} M &= 0 \text{ if he lives} \\ &= 1 \text{ if he dies} \end{aligned}$$

For each person, also let D represent his average monthly dose of the drug.

Criticize the scientific merit of the following four proposals. (If you like, criticize their ethical and political aspects too.) Which proposal do you think is scientifically soundest? Can you think of a better proposal of your own?

a. Draw a random sample of n persons. For each person, record the drug dose D that he chooses to take, and his mortality M after five years. From these n points, calculate the regression line of M against D, interpreting the coefficient of D as the effect of the drug.

b. Again, draw a random sample of n persons. For each person, record such characteristics as age, sex, grandparents' longevity, and so on, as well as drug dose D and mortality M after five years. Then calculate the multiple regression of M on all the other variables, interpreting the coefficient of D as the effect of the drug.

c. Once again, draw a random sample of n persons. Then construct a 95% confidence interval for the difference in mortality rates between drug users and nonusers, using (8-20):

$$\text{drug effect, } (\mu_1 - \mu_2) = (\overline{M}_1 - \overline{M}_2) \pm t_{.025}\, s_p \sqrt{(1/n_1) + (1/n_2)}$$

where n_1 and n_2 are the numbers of drug users and nonusers, respectively (so that $n_1 + n_2 = n$, the size of the random sample), and s_p^2 is the pooled sample variance.

d. Ask for volunteers who would be willing to use or not use the drug, as determined by the flip of a coin. The control group of volunteers is allowed no drug, while the treatment group is given a standard dose, over the 5-year period. Then a 95% confidence interval for the difference between drug users and nonusers would be the formula above.

PART IV

Topics in Classical and Bayesian Inference

CHAPTER 16

Nonparametric and Robust Statistics

(Requires Chapter 9)

Public agencies are very keen on amassing statistics—they collect them, add them, raise them to the *n*th power, take the cube root and prepare wonderful diagrams. But what you must never forget is that every one of those figures comes in the first instance from the village watchman, who just puts down what he damn pleases.

SIR JOSIAH STAMP

16-1 INTRODUCTION: MEAN OR MEDIAN?

So far we have estimated the population mean rather than, say, the median or mode. This has been appropriate because often the population target that we want to estimate is the total, which is related to the mean. For example, in testing a new sales program, a firm will be interested in its total sales. This total can be estimated simply by taking the mean sales per agent, and multiplying it by the total number of agents.

It is not possible to estimate total sales using the median, however, because it uses only the middle observation, and disregards all the others—such as the spectacular sales of that one agent who just couldn't seem to miss a sale during the test period. But in business, a dollar is a dollar, no matter what its source. A very large sale should not be disregarded, since it has the same effect on the bottom line as many small sales.

It is not just business problems that require averages and totals: Economists are interested in wheat production per acre and the nation's total wheat production; demographers are interested in total population; and medical researchers are interested in total mortality. In such cases we use the mean because it alone captures the relevant information about all the observations.

However, it should be recognized that there are some circumstances in which outlying observations should be discounted. For example, if it seems likely that spectacular outliers are simply errors in data collection, to include them in calculating the mean would simply be adding irrelevant "noise." In situations like this, it is more appropriate to discount outliers by using the median instead of the mean.

One of the curious advantages of medians is that inferences about them are entirely free of the assumption of normality; they are therefore called *distribution free*, or more commonly, *nonparametric* statistics.

16-2 SIGN TEST FOR THE MEDIAN

Just as the sample mean $\overline{X}$ estimates the population mean μ, so the sample median $\breve{X}$ estimates the population median ν (nu, pronounced "new," which follows μ in the Greek alphabet). In the next two sections, we will develop a nonparametric test and confidence interval for ν—analogous to the t test for μ developed in Chapter 8 and 9.

A—SINGLE SAMPLE

Suppose the median (ν) of family income in the U.S. South in 1971 was claimed to be only \$5000. The sign test examines each observation to see whether it is above (+) or below (−) this claimed value. For example, in the random sample of nine families shown as the dots in Figure 16-1, seven have an income above \$5000, while only two have an income be-

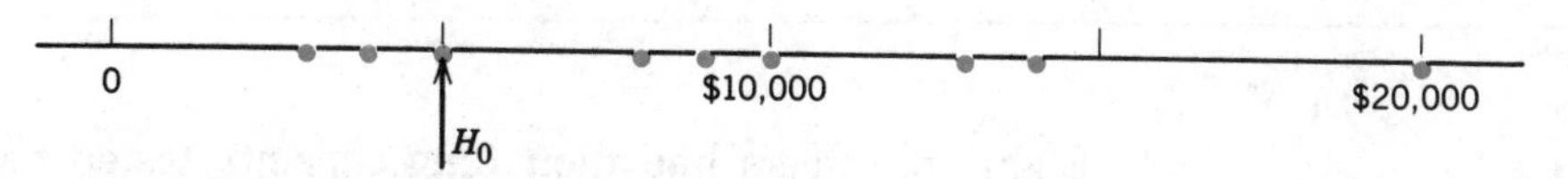

FIGURE 16-1
A sample of 9 incomes.

low. Does this evidence allow us to reject the claim (the null hypothesis) that

$$H_0: \quad \nu = \$5000?$$

If H_0 is true, half the population incomes lie above \$5000. This does not mean that half the incomes in *a sample* will necessarily be above \$5000; but it does mean that if each observation is randomly drawn, the probability π that it lies above \$5000 is:

$$H_0: \quad \pi = 1/2 \tag{16-1}$$

We recognize this as being just like the hypothesis that a coin is fair. To state it more explicitly, we have two events that are mathematically equivalent:

A "random observation will fall above the median" is equivalent to "A coin will turn up heads"	(16-2)

If H_0 is true, the sample of $n = 9$ observations is just like tossing a fair coin 9 times. The total number of successes S (families above \$5000) will have the binomial distribution.

So it is easy to calculate the p-value for H_0—that is, the probability that we would again observe S equal to 7 or more, in 9 trials. This is found in Appendix Table IIIc, under $n = 9$ and $\pi = .50$:

$$\text{p-value} = \Pr(S \geq 7)$$
$$= .090 = 9\% \tag{16-3}$$

This means that if the population median really is \$5000 (i.e., H_0 is true) there is only a 9% chance that the sample would be so lopsided. H_0 has little credibility.

B—TWO PAIRED SAMPLES

With a little imagination, we can use the sign test for the difference in two paired samples [just as we used the earlier t test (8-24)].

EXAMPLE 16-1

Eight volunteers had their lung capacity tested before and after a new treatment for asthma, with the data given in Table 16-1. Use the binomial distribution to calculate the p-value for the null hypothesis that the treatment has no effect.

SOLUTION

In Table 16-1, the original matched pairs in the first two columns can be forgotten, once the differences (improvements) have been found in the last column. These differences D form a single sample to which we can apply the sign test. The null hypothesis (that the treatment provides no improvement) can be rephrased: In the population, the median difference is zero—that is,

$$H_0: \quad \nu = 0$$

or

$$\pi = \Pr\text{ (observing a positive } D) = 1/2$$

The question is: Are the 6 positive D's (6 "heads") observed in a sample of 8 observations (8 "tosses") consistent with H_0? The probability of this is found in Appendix Table IIIc:

$$\begin{aligned} p\text{-value} &= \Pr(S \geq 6) \\ &= .145 = 14\% \end{aligned} \tag{16-4}$$

This p-value is high enough that we cannot reject H_0 (that the treatment is ineffective) at the 5% level, or even the 10% level.

TABLE 16-1 Lung Capacity of 8 Patients

X (Before)	Y (After)	D = Y − X
750	850	+100
860	880	+ 20
950	930	− 20
830	860	+ 30
750	800	+ 50
680	740	+ 60
720	760	+ 40
810	800	− 10

In applying the sign test, the occasional observation may yield $D = 0$ exactly, so it has no sign. This result is like a coin falling on its edge, and it is simplest just to discard the observation.

*C—EXTENSIONS

This analysis of medians may be extended in many ways. Whereas in Table 16-1 we were using paired samples (each before-and-after measurement was on the same individual), there is a similar test (Lindgren, 1976) called the *median test,* that can be applied if the two samples are independent. Moreover, for more than two samples, there is an analysis (Mosteller and Tukey, 1977) called *median polish,* which is like ANOVA using medians instead of means.

Even for regression there is a kind of median analysis. The "weighted least squares" described in Section 11-3 can have weights appropriately chosen to discount outliers in a way that will provide a median-type fit (Mosteller and Tukey 1977, p. 365).

PROBLEMS

16-1 When polarized light is passed through α-lactose sugar, its angle of rotation is 90°. An industrial chemist made the following 6 independent measurements of the angle of rotation of an unknown sugar:

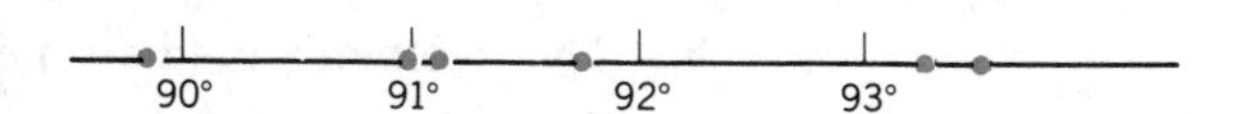

a. What is the p-value for the hypothesis that the sugar is α-lactose? (As usual, use the one-sided p-value in these problems.)

b. What is the p-value for the hypothesis that the sugar is D-xylose (whose true angle of rotation is 92°)?

16-2 A random sample of annual incomes (thousands of dollars) of 10 brother-sister pairs was ordered according to the man's income as follows:

Brother's Income (M)	Sister's Income (W)
18	28
28	20
32	16
32	28
36	26
38	32
44	24
46	80
50	26
156	48

Calculate the p-value for the following null hypotheses:

a. That men's median income is 30 thousand

b. That women's median income is 30 thousand

c. That women's incomes equal men's.

16-3 A random sample of 8 brother-sister pairs gave the following heights (in inches):

Brother's Height (M)	*Sister's Height (W)*
65	63
67	62
69	64
70	65
71	68
73	66
76	71
77	69

Calculate the p-value for the following null hypotheses:

a. That men's median height is 66 inches.

b. That women's median height is 63 inches.

c. That women's heights equal men's.

16-4 A random sample of 20 bolts produced by a new process showed the following shearing strengths:

10.4	9.6	10.6	11.0	9.9	10.1	10.5	8.7	11.1	11.1
10.6	10.7	8.9	8.6	9.5	8.4	11.5	11.3	10.7	9.1

a. Graph the data as 20 points on the x-axis.

b. The old process produced bolts with a median strength of 9.75. Calculate the p-value for the null hypothesis that the new process is no better.

***c.** Calculate the p-value for the hypothesis that the lower quartile is 8.50.

16-3 CONFIDENCE INTERVAL FOR THE MEDIAN

Recall the sample of 9 incomes from the U.S. South, shown again in Figure 16-2. When the X's are listed in order of size, they are called *order statistics* and given a *bracketed* subscript. Thus in Figure 16-2, $X_{(1)}$ is the smallest observation, $X_{(2)}$ the next, and so on. Then the median will be

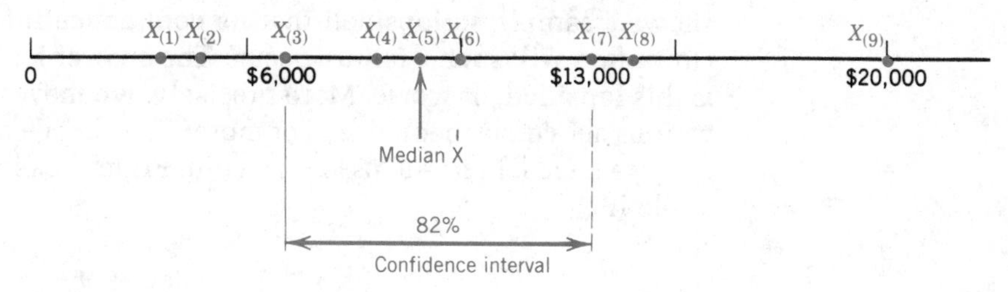

FIGURE 16-2
Nine ordered observations of income, showing an 82% confidence interval for the population median ν.

$X_{(5)}$, which leaves 4 below and 4 above. This sample median $\check{X} = X_{(5)} =$ \$9000 is a good point estimate of the unknown population median ν.

But how do we construct a confidence interval? That is, how far do we go above and below this point estimate? One possible answer is to go two observations on either side of the median, from $X_{(3)}$ to $X_{(7)}$:

$$X_{(3)} \leq \nu \leq X_{(7)}$$

$$6000 \leq \nu \leq 13{,}000 \qquad (16\text{-}5)$$

But that leaves the question: How much confidence do we have that this interval will cover the target ν? To answer this, panel (*a*) of Figure 16-3 illustrates the underlying population, from which the observations are drawn. Note how half of this population is above ν, and half below. (Also note that the population is not normal—nonparametric statistics in this chapter are perfectly valid for *any* population shape.) Panel (*b*) shows a typical sample that yields a confidence interval covering ν. Panel (*c*)

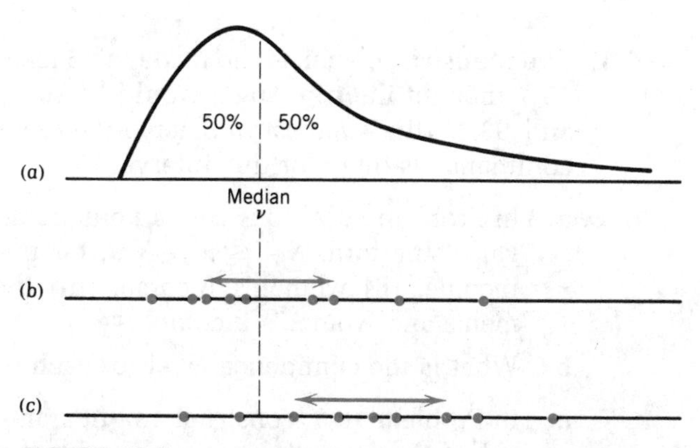

FIGURE 16-3
Confidence intervals are usually right, but occasionally wrong. (a) Underlying population, showing the target ν. (b) Typical sample, where the interval covers ν. (c) Unusually lopsided sample, where the interval fails to cover ν.

shows a sample so lopsided that its confidence interval fails to cover ν. How often will such a failure occur? The answer is: Whenever the sample is this lopsided, or worse. More precisely, whenever the number of observations above the median is 7, or more. The chance of this is the same as 7 or more heads, in $n = 9$ tosses of a coin. From the binomial distribution in Table IIIc,

$$\Pr(S \geq 7) = .090 \simeq 9\% \qquad \text{like (16-3)}$$

Of course, the confidence interval could go wrong equally often by being lopsided in the other direction, with 7 or more observations to the left of the median (like 7 or more tails). Thus the chance of going wrong one way or another is 2(9%), and the confidence level is therefore:

$$100\% - 2(9\%) = 82\% \qquad (16\text{-}6)$$

Thus, as Figure 16-2 illustrates, our 82% confidence interval for the median is

$$\$6000 < \nu < \$13{,}000$$

Of course, if we have a large sample size n, then we use the normal approximation to the binomial. This is illustrated in Problem 16-11, part **c**.

As always, a confidence interval like (16-5) can be used to test a null hypothesis. We simply reject the null hypothesis if it falls outside the confidence interval.

PROBLEMS

16-5 The industrial chemist who made the 6 measurements in Problem 16-1 thought the true angle would be somewhere between 89.9° and 93.4° (the smallest and largest measurements). How much confidence is there for this interval?

16-6 **a.** In Problem 16-2, construct a nonparametric confidence interval of the form $X_{(2)} \leq \nu \leq X_{(9)}$, for the median of (i) men's income, (ii) women's income, (iii) the difference between men's and women's income.

b. What is the confidence level for each of these intervals?

16-7 **a.** In Problem 16-3, construct a nonparametric confidence interval of the form $X_{(2)} \leq \nu \leq X_{(7)}$, for the median of (i) men's height, (ii) women's height, (iii) the difference between men's and women's height.

b. What is the confidence level for each of these intervals?

16-8 **a.** Referring to Problem 16-6, do you think that the population of men's incomes is distributed normally?

b. Do you think the nonparametric confidence interval would be narrower than the classical confidence interval?

c. To check your conjecture in **b**, go ahead and calculate the 98% confidence interval of the form (8-11).

16-9 **a.** Referring to Problem 16-7, do you think that the population of men's heights is distributed normally?

b. Do you think that the nonparametric confidence interval would be narrower than the classical confidence interval?

c. To check your conjecture in **b**, go ahead and calculate the 93% confidence interval of the form (8-11). [*Hint:* If you interpolate Table V, you will find $t_{.035} = 2.14$.]

16-10 Write a summary of what you learned from Problems 16-8 and 16-9.

16-11 A random sample of 25 working students yielded the following summer incomes (in \$100s, arranged in order):

4,5,5,5,6 7,9,10,12,13 14,14,15,17,18

18,19,23,25,27 30,32,39,40,52

a. Estimate the population median income ν.

b. One possible confidence interval for the median is $7 \leq \nu \leq 27$. How much confidence would we have in an interval this wide? [*Hint:* Use the binomial approximation.]

c. Calculate the 95% confidence interval for ν. [*Hint:* Since you are now starting with the confidence *level* and working towards the confidence *interval* (rather than vice versa), you will have to reverse the steps in **b**.]

16-12 Using the data in Problem 16-4, calculate a 95% confidence interval for the median shearing strength in the whole population.

16-4 WILCOXON RANK TEST

A—WHY USE RANKS?

The sign test for the median was extremely simple: It merely recorded whether or not each observation was above or below the hypothetical median (+ or −). On the other hand, the classical t test used much more information: In calculating the sample mean $\overline{X}$ it took into account the actual size of each observation. The *rank tests* we now consider are a compromise: In ranking numbers, we see which observation is first (or second, etc.), but we ignore *by how much* it is first.

Rank tests are very efficient, and therefore very popular. To see how they work, we shall study a typical and popular form, the Wilcoxon test[1] for two independent samples.

B—ILLUSTRATION

Suppose that independent random samples of annual income were taken from two different regions of the United States in 1980, and then ordered as in Table 16-2.

Let us test the null hypothesis that the two underlying populations are identical. Suppose that the alternative hypothesis is that the South is poorer than the Pacific, so that a one-sided test is appropriate.

We first rank the combined X_1 and X_2 observations, as shown in Table 16-3. The actual income levels now are discarded in favor of this ranking. (Consequently, the test is not affected by skewness, or any other distributional peculiarity—in other words, it is a distribution-free test.) Then *Wilcoxon's Rank Sum W* is defined as the sum of all the ranks in the smaller sample; in this case:

$$W = 1 + 2 + 6 + 9 = 18 \tag{16-7}$$

Then the p-value for H_0 can be found by looking up $W = 18$ in Appendix Table VIII:

$$p\text{-value} = .238 \simeq 24\% \tag{16-8}$$

TABLE 16-2 Two Independent Samples of Income

South X_1	Pacific X_2
6,000	11,000
10,000	13,000
15,000	14,000
29,000	17,000
	20,000
	31,000
Size $n_1 = 4$	$n_2 = 6$

[1] The Wilcoxon test was discovered by Mann and Whitney in an equivalent form that is more complicated to understand and calculate; so we will stick with the Wilcoxon form.

TABLE 16-3 Combined Ranking Yields the W Statistic

Combined Ordered Observations		Combined Ranks	
X_1	X_2	R_1	R_2
6,000		1	
10,000		2	
	11,000		3
	13,000		4
	14,000		5
15,000		6	
	17,000		7
	20,000		8
29,000		9	
	31,000		10

$$W = 18$$

This value is large, so the null hypothesis (of equal incomes) cannot be rejected.

C—GENERALIZATION

To keep the calculation of W as simple as possible, we arrange it so that we add up just a relatively few small numbers by following two conventions:

> **The W statistic is the rank sum of the *smaller* sample; and we start ranking at the end where this smaller sample is concentrated.** (16-9)

For example, in Table 16-3, the South (X_1) was the smaller sample; and it was concentrated at the low-income end, so that is where we started ranking. (Note that adding up the ranks in the other sample would mean more work: more numbers, and bigger numbers).

Appendix Table VIII gives the corresponding one-sided p-value, for $n_1 \leq 5$ and $n_2 \leq 10$. For larger sample sizes, an approximation is given in the next section. (See especially Problem 16-17.)

PROBLEMS

16-13 Independent random samples of men and women gave the following incomes, in order:

Men's incomes ($000)	*Women's income ($000)*
38	14
46	18
52	25
77	36
	45
	48

Calculate the p-value for H_0 (equal incomes).

16-14 Two makes of cars were randomly sampled, to determine the mileage (in thousands) until the brakes required relining. Calculate the p-value for the null hypothesis that make A is no better than B.

MAKE A: 61, 30, 49, 48, 41
MAKE B: 26, 32, 22, 39

16-15 (TIES) Observations that are tied with one another should be given the same rank—their average rank. For example, if the 6th and 7th ranked observations are tied, they should each be assigned the rank 6 1/2.

This assignment may produce a fractional value of W, in which case the p-value can be appropriately interpolated. Use this procedure to find the p-value for H_0, for the following more extensive samples than in Problem 16-14:

MAKE A: 61, 30, 49, 48, 41
MAKE B: 26, 32, 22, 39, 41, 30, 41, 36

16-16 Sometimes data is not collected in numerical form; instead, it is only ordered from best to worst, or highest to lowest. For example, to compare the wine from vineyards C and M, several bottles were selected at random from each, and labeled $C_1 \ldots C_5$ and $M_1 \ldots M_{10}$. Then in a blind test a wine-taster listed them in order of preference. The results were as follows (listed from highest to lowest preference):

M_7 M_5 M_3 M_{10} M_2 M_6 C_3 M_1 C_5 M_4 M_9 C_4 M_8 C_1 C_2

A rank test is ideally suited to test the null hypothesis that the two vineyards produce wine of equal quality. What is the p-value for this hypothesis?

16-5 RANK TESTS IN GENERAL

We have seen that rank tests are very easy to understand and calculate. Like many other nonparametric statistics, they are so easy that they are sometimes called "quick and dirty" statistics. As well, rank tests have a crucial advantage for data that comes originally in ranked rather than numerical form (such as the wine rankings in Problem 16-16), where numerical operations such as calculating an average are just not possible.

In fact, rank tests are so useful and efficient that it is worthwhile extending them to cover other cases besides the Wilcoxon test. We can develop *many rank tests at once* from the following general strategy:

> ***Rank Transformation Test:***
> **If outliers (or some other form of non-normality) seem to be a problem, rank the data. Then just perform the usual test (such as t or F) on the *ranks*, instead of the original data.** (16-10)

One of the most straightforward examples of this strategy is to extend the Wilcoxon test to a *rank test for k independent samples.* An example will illustrate:

EXAMPLE 16-2

Suppose we have three regions to compare, instead of just the two given earlier. Table 16-4 gives independent random samples (of annual income in the United States in 1980) from the three different regions.

Carry out the rank test in two steps:

a. Rank the 12 observations

b. Do the usual one-way ANOVA F test on the ranks to get the p-value for H_0.

TABLE 16-4 Three Independent Samples of Income (compare to Table 16-2)

South X_1	Pacific X_2	Northeast X_3
6,000	11,000	7,000
10,000	13,000	14,000
15,000	17,000	18,000
29,000	131,000	25,000

SOLUTION

a. The ranks are found just as in the Wilcoxon test of Table 16-3:

Table of ranks

R_1	R_2	R_3
1	4	2
3	5	6
7	8	9
11	12	10
$\bar{R}$ = 5.50	7.25	6.75

b. Using the average ranks calculated above, we obtain the following ANOVA table:

Source	SS	df	MS	F
Between regions	6.5	2	3.25	.21
Within regions	136.5	9	15.2	($p > .25$)
Total	143.0√	11√		

Since $p > .25$, H_0 is not rejected.

Using the same two steps—transform the data into ranks, and then apply a standard test—we can similarly carry out a nonparametric test in a wide variety of situations. Such an approach is much easier than working through one rank test after another in exacting detail. And there are only two costs:

1. Using (16-10) gives only an approximate p-value. Although this is usually smaller than the exact p-value, it is often good enough in practice. If not, a more exact p-value is readily available in Conover 1980, or in many computer packages (such as MINITAB).
2. Although (16-10) is often perfectly straightforward, it sometimes has to be given a slight twist. For example, see Problems 16-19 and 16-20.

PROBLEMS

In each of the following problems, carry out the two steps of (16-10):

a. Transform to ranks.

b. Carry out the classical test.

16-17 Wilcoxon rank test for two independent samples

a. For the data in Table 16-2, verify that the ranks are as follows:

Original Data, Ordered		*Ranks*	
6,000	11,000	1	3
10,000	13,000	2	4
15,000	14,000	6	5
29,000	17,000	9	7
	20,000		8
	31,000		10
		$\overline{R} = 4.5$	6.2

b. Do the usual two-sample *t* test (8-20) on the ranks (i.e., test the difference between the two means 4.5 and 6.2) to get the p-value for H_0.

16-18 Kruskal-Wallis rank test for *k* independent samples, or one-factor ANOVA

a. For the data in Table 10-1, verify that the ranks are as follows:

Original Data, Ordered			*Ranks*		
46	52	49	1	9	3.5
47	54	50	2	11.5	5.5
49	55	51	3.5	13	7.5
50	58	51	5.5	14	7.5
53	61	54	10	15	11.5

b. Do the usual one-factor ANOVA on the ranks to get the p-value for H_0.

16-19 Wilcoxon rank test for two paired samples

a. For the data in Table 16-1, let us temporarily ignore the + and − signs of the differences, and rank them from smallest to largest. Then let us put back the + and − signs on the ranks. Thus verify that we obtain the following "signed ranks":

Original Data, Ordered by Size of Differences			
X	Y	D	*Signed Ranks of Differences*
810	800	− 10	−1
950	930	− 20	−2.5
860	880	+ 20	+2.5
830	860	+ 30	+4
720	760	+ 40	+5
750	800	+ 50	+6
680	740	+ 60	+7
750	850	+100	+8

b. Treating the final column like the differences calculated in the usual paired t test (8-24), calculate the p-value for H_0.

c. Is your answer in part **b** the same as the p-value found earlier in equation (16-4)? Why?

16-20 Friedman rank test for k matched samples, or two-factor ANOVA

a. Consider again the data in Table 10-6. For each operator, let us rank the 3 machines. (This is *not* the usual combined ranking that we did in Problem 16-18, for example. Instead, we begin by ranking the 3 machines for the first operator, temporarily ignoring the others. Then we start afresh, ranking the 3 machines for the second operator. And so on.) Verify that we obtain the following ranks:

Original Data (Unordered)			*Ranked in Each Row*		
53	61	51	2	3	1
47	55	51	1	3	2
46	52	49	1	3	2
50	58	54	1	3	2
49	54	50	1	3	2

b. Carry out the usual two-factor ANOVA on these ranks. There will be absolutely no differences in rows (since all row averages will be 2.0). But the differences in columns (machines) will be interesting, and the F ratio will give the desired p-value for H_0.

16-21 In the preceding four problems, we have illustrated a good variety of rank tests, one for each cell of the following table:

	2 Samples	*k Samples*
Independent		
Matched		

In each cell, write in the name of the nonparametric rank test (e.g., Friedman two-factor ANOVA).

16-22 In Problem 16-20, use the Friedman test to find the p-value for the null hypothesis of no differences between *operators* (rows).

16-23 Spearman rank correlation.

a. In Problem 15-1, verify that the ranks within the X and Y columns separately are as follows:

Original Data		Ranked in Each Column	
X	Y	R_X	R_Y
3400	24	6	5
2600	20	4	3.5
2200	17	2	1
2400	19	3	2
2900	26	5	6
2100	20	1	3.5

b. Calculate the rank correlation coefficient, and from Figure 15-4 determine whether it is discernibly different from 0 at the 5% level (2-sided).

16-6 RUNS TEST FOR INDEPENDENCE

One of the crucial assumptions we have used throughout this text (much more important than the normality assumption) is the assumption that our sampling is random. Now we shall develop a test of whether or not this assumption is justified.

By definition, a random sample consists of observations that are drawn *independently* from a *common* population. Thus, if the observations are graphed in the time order in which they were sampled, the graph should look somewhat like panel (*a*) in Figure 16-4. On the other hand, if the observations are correlated, they will display some "tracking," as in panel (*b*). Or, if the last seven observations come from a different population than the first seven, they will appear to be displaced, as in panel (*c*).

How can we quantify these differences that are obvious to the eye, and find some numerical measure to test H_0, the null hypothesis of randomness? We note that when H_0 is true in panel (*a*), the path of the observations crosses the median line quite frequently; but when H_0 is not true, this happens much less frequently. This is the basis for the runs test.

For example, in panel (*b*), we mark observations *H* (for high) or *L* (for low), depending on whether they fall above or below the sample median. With slashes indicating the crossovers, this sequence is

$$LLL/HHHHH/LLLL/HH \tag{16-11}$$

A run is defined as an unbroken sequence of *H* or *L* values. In this case the number of runs $R = 4$.

Let us suppose in general that there are *n* observations. (If the sample size is odd, the median line will pass through the median observation, which should be counted neither *L* nor *H*. With this observation discarded, *n* then refers to the even number of observations remaining.)

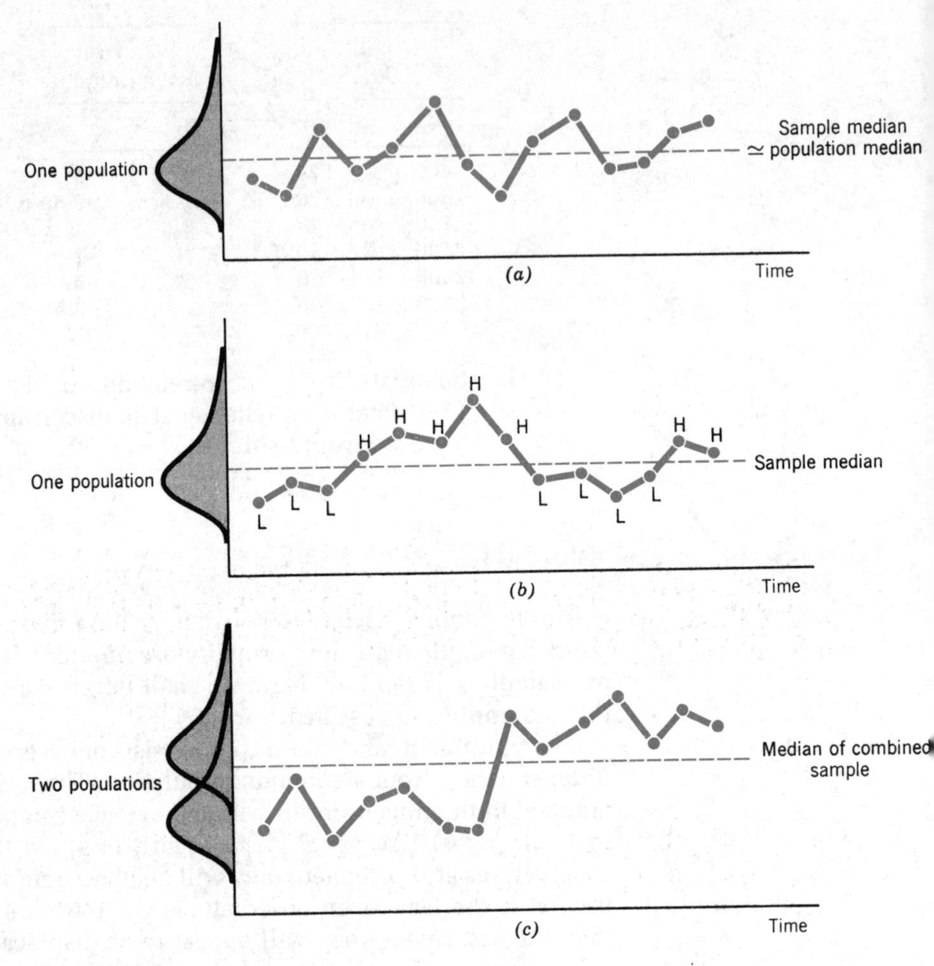

FIGURE 16-4
(a) Independent observations from one population. (b) Serially correlated observations from one population. (c) Observations from two populations.

When H_0 is true, the number of runs R has a sampling distribution that is approximately normal, with:

$$E(R) \simeq \frac{n}{2} + 1$$
$$\text{SE} \simeq \frac{\sqrt{n-1}}{2} \tag{16-12}$$

For example, in Figure 16-4b, n = 14, so that (16-12) yields:

$$E(R) \simeq \frac{14}{2} + 1 = 8$$

$$SE \simeq \frac{\sqrt{14 - 1}}{2} = 1.80$$

In Figure 16-4*b*, the observed number of runs is $R = 4$. What *p*-value for H_0 does this give? Since *p*-value is the probability of getting a value as extreme as the one we've observed, the *p*-value is therefore $\Pr(R \leq 4)$. To calculate this, we first must standardize the critical value $R = 4$, using the mean and standard error:

$$Z = \frac{R - E(R)}{SE}$$

$$= \frac{4 - 8}{1.80} = -2.22$$

$$\Pr(R \leq 4) = \Pr(Z \leq -2.22)$$

$$= .013$$

$$p\text{-value} = 1\%$$

This provides strong evidence that the sample is not random.

PROBLEMS

16-24

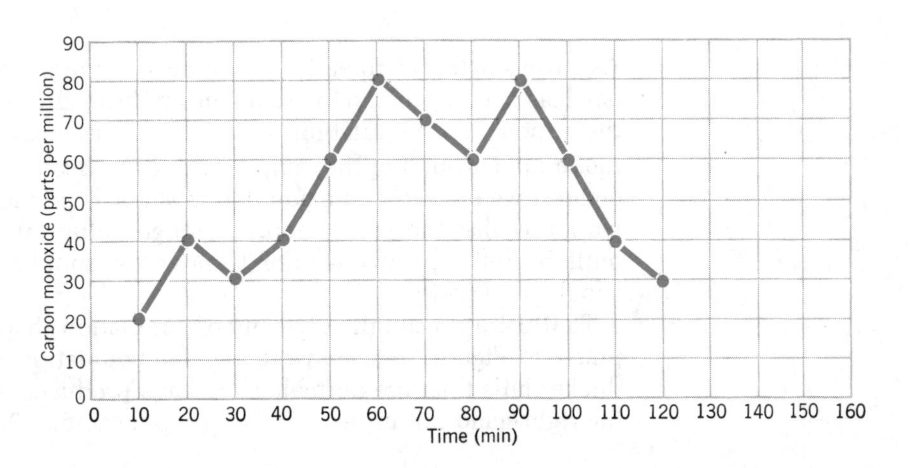

The above graph shows a sample of 12 air pollution readings, taken every 10 minutes over a period of 2 hours. To what extent can we claim that these are statistically independent observations from a fixed (rather than a drifting) population? Answer by calculating the p-value for the null hypothesis.

16-25 Repeat Problem 16-24 for the following sample of 25 observations (read across):

67, 63, 58, 79, 62, 55, 56, 50, 57, 55, 43, 47, 23, 31, 38, 49, 33, 43, 34, 42, 51, 66, 54, 46, 55

16-7 ROBUST STATISTICS: TRIMMING AND WEIGHTING

A—ROBUST AND NONPARAMETRIC STATISTICS COMPARED

Like the nonparametric statistics we have studied so far, robust statistics were developed to handle a wide variety of population shapes other than the normal. But there are important differences:

i. Under a wide variety of population shapes, nonparametric (distribution free) statistics exactly achieve the 95% confidence claimed. While robust statistics maintain approximate 95% confidence, their main virtue is providing estimates that are relatively stable (of low variance). Consequently, their confidence intervals are relatively narrow and precise.[2]

ii. Whereas nonparametric statistics usually can be figured out on the back of an envelope, robust statistics often are so complicated they require a computer.

B—THE SAMPLE MEAN VS. MEDIAN AGAIN

As always in this chapter, let us assume that there is no compelling reason (such as needing *totals*) to use the mean. Instead, we just want to estimate the center of a population, as efficiently as possible. Should we use the sample mean $\overline{X}$ or the sample median $\overset{|}{X}$? Section 7-2 showed that $\overline{X}$ is better if we know that the population shape is normal, while $\overset{|}{X}$ is better if we know that the population has longer fatter tails that produce more outliers. But typically we don't know the population shape, so which should we choose?

To illustrate again the diversity of population shapes that may occur in practice, Figure 16-5 shows a typical population that has longer and thicker tails than the normal. They have produced the outlier shown by the right-hand dot in the colored random sample. Such outliers have far

[2] In the language of testing in Chapter 9: Nonparametric statistics make α exactly the 5% claimed. Robust statistics keep α approximately 5%, and more important, keep β low too. Unfortunately, we don't have space to give the complex formulas for these robust confidence intervals. But they can be painlessly included in computer packages.

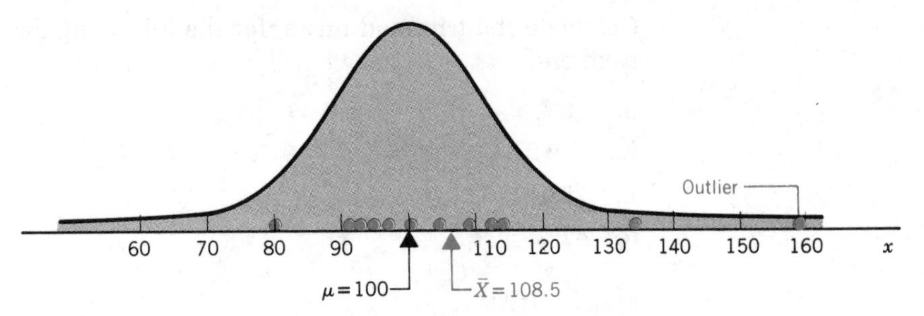

FIGURE 16-5
A long-tailed distribution produces outliers that throw off the sample mean.

too great a leverage on $\overline{X}$, the center of gravity of the sample, and make it an unreliable estimator of the population center: As Figure 16-5 shows, $\overline{X}$ is pretty far off target.

While $\overline{X}$ uses too *many* observations (all of them, including the problem outliers), the sample median $\tilde{X}$ would use too *few* (only the middle one). A compromise between $\overline{X}$ and $\tilde{X}$, such as the rank tests discussed in Section 16-4, might work better. Let's look at some more ingenious compromises—robust statistics—that work well under a wide variety of population shapes.

C—THE TRIMMED MEAN

One compromise between the median and the mean is to average just the *middle half* of the observations. By trimming 25% of the observations from each end, the outliers are removed: accordingly it is called the *trimmed mean*, or more precisely, the 25% trimmed mean. (In trimming 25% from each end, we use round numbers. For example, in a sample of $n = 45$ observations, we would trim 1/4 of $45 \simeq 11$ observations from each end.)

Of course, other degrees of trimming are possible, too. The percentage trimmed from each end can be written as a subscript; for example, $\overline{X}_{.10}$ is the 10% trimmed mean. An example will illustrate.

EXAMPLE 16-3

A random sample of $n = 12$ observations was drawn and ordered as follows:

81	106
94	110
95	113
95	114
97	135
102	160

Calculate the trimmed mean, for the following degrees of trimming from each end:

a. 0%
b. 8%
c. 25%
d. 42%

SOLUTION

a. Zero trim gives us just the ordinary mean $\overline{X}$:

$$\overline{X}_0 = \overline{X} = \frac{81 + 94 + \cdot \cdot \cdot + 135 + 160}{12} = \frac{1302}{12} = 108.5$$

b. For 8% trim, we take 8% of 12 = 1 observation from each end. Thus:

$$\overline{X}_{.08} = \frac{94 + \cdot \cdot \cdot + 135}{10} = \frac{1061}{10} = 106.1$$

c. For 25% trim, we take 25% of 12 = 3 observations from each end. Thus:

$$\overline{X}_{.25} = \frac{95 + 97 + 102 + 106 + 110 + 113}{6} = \frac{623}{6} = 103.8$$

d. For 42% trim, we take 42% of 12 = 5 observations from each end. That leaves just the middle two observations, whose midpoint of course is the median $\overset{\downarrow}{X}$:

$$\overline{X}_{.42} = \overset{\downarrow}{X} = \frac{102 + 106}{2} = 104.0$$

REMARKS

This sample, in fact, is the one shown in Figure 16-5, where the center (target) is known to be 100. We note that the large outlier $X = 160$ does indeed exert so much leverage that it makes the sample mean unduly large ($\overline{X}_0 = 108.5$). Trimming off this outlier gives a better estimate ($\overline{X}_{.08} = 106.1$), closer to the target of 100. Further trimming cuts off the next outlier, and improves the estimate further ($\overline{X}_{.25} = 103.8$). But if we trim as much as possible, we go a little too far: We get right down to the sample median, which is not quite as accurate ($\overline{X}_{.42} = 104.0$).

Of course, the one random sample in Example 16-3, like one play at Las Vegas, does not prove much. Repeated sampling (Monte Carlo) is necessary. Such sampling experiments have confirmed that for populations with the sort of long tails shown in Figure 16-5, the mean involves too little trimming, and the median too much. 25% trimming provides about the best estimate, and works well in a wide variety of populations. The 25% trimmed mean thus provides a good robust estimate of the population center.

*D—THE BIWEIGHTED MEAN ($\bar{X}_b$)

A closer look at the 25% trimmed mean in Example 16-3(c) shows an interesting feature: The observations in the outside quarters don't count at all, while the observations in the middle half all count equally. When we graph these weights in panel (*a*) of Figure 16-6, we note the sudden drop at the upper and lower quartiles. This "black and white" weighting makes the computation simple, but lacks subtlety. Why not *gradually* weight the observations as in panel (*b*), with the least weight on the problem outliers (as suggested by Mosteller and Tukey, 1977)? Specifically, the weighting formula for any observation X is:

$$w = (1 - Z^2)^2 \quad \text{if } |Z| \leq 1 \tag{16-13}$$

$$= 0 \quad \text{if } |Z| > 1 \tag{16-14}$$

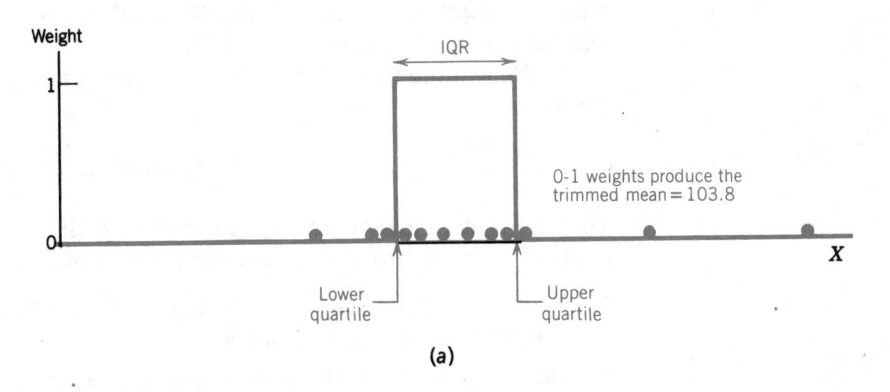

(*a*)

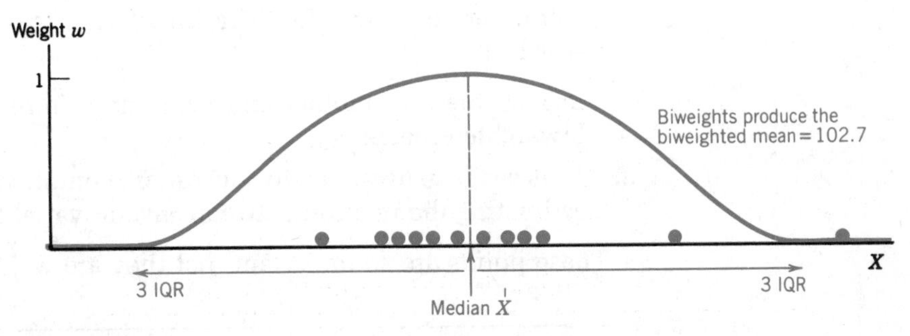

(*b*)

FIGURE 16-6
Two weighting functions that reduce the influence of the outliers, for the sample of Figure 16-5. (a) Weights for the 25% trimmed mean. (b) More gradual biweights.

where Z is a kind of standardized X value—standardized with the median $\check{X}$ and the interquartile range IQR:

$$Z = \frac{X - \check{X}}{3(\text{IQR})} \tag{16-15}$$

like (4-23)

To see how this formula works, suppose X deviates from the median $\check{X}$ by more than 3 times the IQR; then (16-15) gives $|Z| > 1$, and so from (16-14), $w = 0$. (Any observation that is so far out is given a zero weight.) On the other hand, if X is within this broad range, then $|Z| \leq 1$ and X is given a positive weight according to (16-13). And the closer X is to the median $\check{X}$, the larger this weight will be. (In other words, w peaks at the median $\check{X}$.)

Because w in (16-13) has Z squared twice, it is called the *bisquare weight*, or more briefly, the *biweight*. To make the formula complete, we finally use the biweights to calculate the mean:

$$\textbf{Biweighted mean } \overline{X}_b \equiv \frac{\Sigma wX}{\Sigma w} \tag{16-16}$$

This weight formula is familiar. For example, if the weights were frequency weights f, instead of biweights w, then (16-16) would reduce to the ordinary mean $\overline{X} = \Sigma Xf/\Sigma f = \Sigma Xf/n$.

For the sample in Figure 16-5, the computer calculated the biweighted mean:

$$\overline{X}_b = 102.7$$

This is slightly closer than any of the other estimates to the target $\mu = 100$. And so we have illustrated two important points that are generally true:

1. In many populations, the biweighted mean $\overline{X}_b$ is slightly better than the other proposed estimates.
2. But $\overline{X}_b$ involves a lot more calculation. By hand, it is not worth it. By computer, however, the extra calculation is so trivial that $\overline{X}_b$ is well worth it.

   In fact, there is another and *even more important* advantage to the biweighted mean:
3. $\overline{X}_b$ is easily generalized to cover more complicated situations, such as estimating the relation between several variables in part **F** below.

These points are so important that they are well worth emphasizing:

The computer has made feasible many robust estimates like the biweighted mean $\overline{X}_b$ that provide insurance against possible outliers, even in complicated situations. (16-17)

*E—THE BIWEIGHTED ITERATED MEAN ($\overline{X}_{bi}$)

One of the great advantages of computers is that they can rapidly make the same calculations over and over. We can thus calculate and recalculate an estimate, improving it slightly each time—a technique called *iteration*. Let's see how it works for the biweighted mean $\overline{X}_b$.

How could $\overline{X}_b$ possibly be improved? The weighting function is centered at the median $\overset{|}{X}$—roughly, the observed center of the data. But once $\overline{X}_b$ has been calculated, then it becomes a better estimate of the center. So we send the computer through all the calculations again. Here are the details:

We start now with $\overline{X}_b$ instead of $\overset{|}{X}$ in defining weights:

$$Z = \frac{X - \overline{X}_b}{3(\text{IQR})} \qquad (16\text{-}18)$$

like (16-15)

The improved weights then give in (16-16) an improved value of $\overline{X}_b$. And so we keep repeating: Each time we get an improved value of $\overline{X}_b$, we plug it into (16-18) and get an even better value of $\overline{X}_b$ out of (16-16).

When no further real improvement occurs, the computer prints the final answer, and calls it the *biweighted iterated mean*, $\overline{X}_{bi}$. Not only is it a bit better than the original $\overline{X}_b$; even more important, it is particularly adaptable to more general statistical techniques like regression, as we will see next.

*F—BIWEIGHTED LEAST SQUARES

In Section 11-3, we suggested reducing the influence of outliers by giving them less weight in least squares regression, thus converting ordinary least squares (OLS) to weighted least squares (WLS). Now we will outline how biweights can achieve this routinely on a computer.

First, to determine whether or not an observation Y is an outlier, we measure its distance from the OLS fitted value $\hat{Y}$; that is, we measure each deviation as we did in Figure 11-2:

$$d = Y - \hat{Y} \qquad (16\text{-}19)$$

To see how *relatively* large this is, we convert it into a kind of standardized deviation:

$$Z = \frac{Y - \hat{Y}}{3S} \qquad (16\text{-}20)$$

like (16-15)

where S is some overall measure of deviation or spread. (For example, S could be the interquartile range of all the deviations *d*.) Then we compute the *biweights:*

$$w = (1 - Z^2)^2 \quad \text{if } |Z| \leq 1 \qquad (16\text{-}21)$$
$$= 0 \quad \text{if } |Z| > 1 \qquad \text{like } (16\text{-}13)$$

Notice how the second equation is simply stating that an observation will be given zero weight if it is an outlier—that is, if its deviation d in (16-19) is so large that it makes the Z value in (16-20) greater than 1. Moreover, the first equation above describes how we weight all other observations: An observation will be given less weight the further it is from the regression line—that is, the greater is its deviation d and hence its Z value.

The weights determined in (16-21) are now used in all the regression formulas:

$$\boxed{b = \frac{\Sigma wxy}{\Sigma wx^2}} \qquad \begin{array}{r}(16\text{-}22)\\ \text{like } (11\text{-}5)\end{array}$$

$$\boxed{a = \overline{Y} - b\overline{X}} \qquad \begin{array}{r}(16\text{-}23)\\ \text{like } (11\text{-}6)\end{array}$$

where

$$\overline{Y} = \frac{\Sigma wY}{\Sigma w} \quad \text{and} \quad \overline{X} = \frac{\Sigma wX}{\Sigma w} \qquad \text{like } (16\text{-}16)$$

This new value of a and b gives us a more robust line. With it, we can start all over again [recalculating the deviations in (16-19)] and thus get an even better line. And continue to iterate.

To summarize:

1. We start by fitting the OLS line. [If you like, you can think of this as a special application of weighted least squares where all the weights are equal to 1 in (16-22) and (16-23). Of course, in this special case, these WLS formulas are exactly the same as the OLS formulas.]
2. We then measure $Y - \hat{Y}$, the deviation of each observation from the fitted line. These determine the set of weights (16-21) we then use in (16-22) and (16-23) to fit a more robust line.
3. With a new fitted line, we can then repeat step 2 as many times as we like. For example, the computer can keep iterating until there is no substantial improvement.

Of course, multiple regression is just as easy to biweight as simple regression.

G—ROBUST MEASURE OF SPREAD: THE IQR

Having derived various robust measures of center, it is now time to briefly mention robust measures of spread. When we examine the standard deviation s, we see that, like the sample mean, it is unfortunately sensitive to outliers. In fact, since s^2 involves *squared* deviations (which are very, very large for outliers), s is affected by outliers even more than $\overline{X}$ is.

In Chapter 2 we noted that the IQR was much more resistant to outliers than was s. It is therefore no surprise that the IQR is one of the most robust estimators of the population spread. (In fact, the IQR has already proved very useful, in (16-15).)

PROBLEMS

16-26 How is the trimmed mean $\overline{X}_{.25}$ related to the biweighted iterated mean $\overline{X}_{bi}$? Fill in the blanks:

a. Both techniques reduce the influence of observations further and further from the center: whereas ____ gives these outliers suddenly less weight, ____ gives them gradually less weight.

b. ____ is so complex to calculate that it really requires a computer.

c. When applied to regression, ____ transforms ordinary least squares (OLS) into ____, which is thereby made more ____.

16-27 In each of the samples below, which is the most stable (efficient) estimate—the sample mean, median, or 25% trimmed mean? Explain why, then calculate it.

a. A market researcher draws 12 observations from a normal population:

8.9	7.2	8.5	8.3	7.3	7.8
7.6	7.5	8.6	7.9	9.4	7.9

b. On New Year's day, suppose a random sample of 5 forecasters gave the following predictions of the unemployment rate in the coming year:

8.0% 7.4% 7.4% 8.3% 9.5%

Suppose also that the whole population of forecasters contains a few who make really extreme predictions.

c. An anthropologist measured the width (in centimeters) of 9 skulls from a Peruvian tribe. Unfortunately, his handwriting was so poor that the keypuncher occasionally had to guess at the digits as they were entered into the computer, as follows:

15.3 16.2 15.5 18.7
13.1 15.1 15.0 14.2 15.0

16-28 A firm specializing in home air filters wants to determine how effective a new and more expensive fan is. They try it out on 12 different days, along with the standard fan for comparison. The 12 improvements that the new fan made (in an index of pollen and dust pollution) turned out as follows:

105 105 125 97 99 103
97 113 102 90 101 −25

a. Find the median $\overset{\downarrow}{X}$, the mean $\overline{X}$, and the trimmed mean $\overline{X}_{.25}$.

b. Graph the data as 12 dots on the X-axis, and show the three statistics in part **a**.

c. This data was randomly drawn from a population symmetrically distributed around the center $c = 100$. Which of your answers in part **a** happened to be closest to this target?

16-29 Repeat Problem 16-28 for the following sample of 5:

91 104 140 108 104

16-30 Calculate a robust measure of *spread* for each of Problems 16-28 and 16-29.

***16-31** Calculate the biweighted mean for the sample in Problem 16-29.

***16-32** (Monte Carlo) The data in Problem 16-28 and Example 16-3 comes from a *mixed* population:

80% of the population are normally distributed around a mean $\mu = 100$ with standard deviation $\sigma = 10$. The remaining 20% are more widespread, with $\sigma = 50$ (but still the same mean, $\mu = 100$).

a. From this mixture, simulate a random sample of $n = 12$ observations. (*Hint*: To simulate each observation, first draw a random digit from Appendix Table I: if the digit is 1, . . . , 8, this means that you are sampling from the majority population with $\sigma = 10$; if the digit is 9 or 0, then you are sampling from the minority population with $\sigma = 50$. Then draw a random normal number Z from Appendix Table II, and calculate $X = \mu + Z\sigma$ to get the desired observation. Repeat 12 times to get all 12 observations. Incidentally, if you start at the top of Tables I and II, you will get the sample that appears in Problem 16-28.)

b. For this sample, find $\overset{\downarrow}{X}$, $\overline{X}$, and $\overline{X}_{.25}$. Which estimate happens to be closest to the target $\mu = 100$? Which is furthest?

c. Imagine parts **a** and **b** being repeated for many, many samples. Which of the three estimators would you guess gives the best overall performance (minimum MSE)? And the worst?

CHAPTER 16 SUMMARY

16-1 When a total is required, the mean is preferred to the other estimators discussed in this chapter, because only the mean is related to the total.

But what if we simply need a measure of central tendency? If the population has unknown shape, with possibly long thick tails, then there may be more stable (efficient) estimators than the sample mean—for example, nonparametric estimators such as the sample median, or robust estimators such as the trimmed sample mean.

16-2 The simplest nonparametric test is the sign test for a population median. It just uses the binomial distribution, where a "success" is defined as an observation "above the median" and consequently $\pi = .50$.

16-3 Using the same binomial logic as the sign test, a confidence interval for the population median can be constructed. We simply count off an appropriate number of observations on either side of the sample median.

16-4 Rank tests use more information than sign tests, and are usually more efficient. The simplest one is the Wilcoxon test that ranks the observations in two independent samples.

16-5 There is a very simple way to carry out a nonparametric test in many situations where the classical test seems unsatisfactory because of outliers (or some other form of non-normality): Just transform all measurements to ranks, and then perform the classical test on the ranks (instead of on the original measurements).

16-6 Independence of successive observations—a basic assumption of random sampling—can be tested by counting runs (that is, unbroken sequences of values above or below the median).

16-7 While one way of reducing the influence of outliers is to rank all the observations, another way is to chop off the outliers to get the trimmed mean. Or using a computer, we could give outliers less and less weight, to get the biweighted mean. These robust statistics are easily generalized to regression, in the form of biweighted least squares.

REVIEW PROBLEMS

In all problems after 16-34, calculate nonparametric instead of classical statistics.

16-33 How do nonparametric statistics (NPS) compare to classical statistics (CS) like t, ANOVA, and regression? Underline the correct choice in each bracket:

a. [NPS, CS] are based on averages, and therefore [appropriate, inappropriate] whenever a total is required.

b. [NPS, CS] are often based on medians or ranks.

c. [NPS, CS] are often easier to calculate, and sometimes called quick-and-dirty.

d. If you have prior knowledge that the distribution is normal, or nearly normal, you gain by exploiting this by using [NPS, CS].

e. [NPS, CS] are particularly useful for data that is ordered, for example from best to worst, without any actual numerical values.

f. [NPS, CS] are particularly appropriate when it is important for the actual level of confidence to equal the specified level of 95%, even when populations are very non-normal.

16-34 Underline the correct choice in each bracket:

a. The sign test is based on the [binomial, normal] distribution.

b. To test whether two populations are different, the sign test can be used if the two samples are [matched, independent].

c. In using ranks, the Wilcoxon test treats outliers in a compromise fashion—a compromise between [X, $\overline{X}$], which uses the numerical value of each outlier no matter how large, and [X, $\overline{X}$], which does not change even if the outlier is moved much farther out.

d. To see whether a series of hourly temperature readings has serial correlation, the [sign test, runs test, rank test] can be used. If the p-value for H_0 is relatively [high, low], it indicates there is indeed serial correlation.

16-35 A firm wished to test two different programs designed to improve the effectiveness of its sales staff. It therefore took a random sample of 8 salespersons who had been working in each program. The improvement that each salesperson showed during the course of the program was recorded on the following graph:

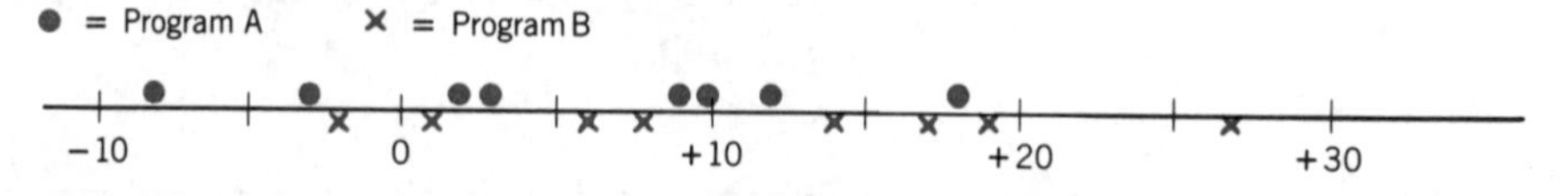

Calculate the p-value for each of the following null hypotheses:

a. Program A has a median improvement of zero.

b. Program B has a median improvement of zero.

c. The two programs are equally effective.

16-36 In view of its better performance in Problem 16-35, program B was being considered for widespread adoption. Calculate an appropriate confidence interval for the median improvement it would achieve in the population of the firm's entire sales staff.

16-37 Two samples of children were randomly selected to test two art education programs, A and B. At the end, each child's best painting was judged by an independent artist. In terms of creativity, the ranking was as follows:

Rank of Child	1	2	3	4	5	6	7	8	9	10	11	12	13	14
Art Program	B	A	B	B	B	A	B	B	A	B	A	A	A	A

State H_0 in words, and calculate its p-value.

16-38 A random sample of 10 pairs of twins was used in a certain study. In each pair, one twin was chosen at random for an enriched education program (E), and the other twin was given the standard program (S). At the end of the year, the performance scores were as follows:

Twin's Surname	*Jones*	*Able*	*Misak*	*Baker*	*Good*	*Lee*	*Berk*	*Wong*	*Rakos*	*Scott*
S Group	57	91	68	75	82	47	63	72	67	68
E Group	64	93	72	72	91	52	79	81	77	80

Is the enriched program really effective? To answer this, calculate:

a. An appropriate confidence interval (including a definition of the parameter).

b. An appropriate p-value.

16-39 A company recorded a sequence of 17 weekly sales (in thousands of dollars, for the first 4 months of 1985) as follows:

33, 26, 28, 24   28, 34, 28, 23   27, 29, 31, 32, 35   30, 32, 26, 31

a. Graph, and then calculate the p-value for the hypothesis of independent observations.

b. Can you validly test the hypothesis that the median meets the target value of 33? (Include a brief reason.) If so, calculate the p-value.

16-40 ***A Final Challenge: How Good Was Penicillin Initially?***

One of the pioneering randomized experiments in medicine evaluated the new penicillin drug streptomycin (Medical Research Council, 1948). A total of 107 tubercular patients were randomly assigned in a clinical trial: 52 to be given bed rest only (control), and 55 to be also given streptomycin (treatment). The degree of improvement after 6 months was observed for each patient, giving the following frequencies:

Improvement After 6 Months	*Treated Patients* *f*	*Control Patients* *f*
Considerable improvement	28	4
Moderate or slight improvement	20	13
No material change	2	3
Moderate or slight deterioration	5	12
Considerable deterioration	6	6
Death	4	14
	55	52

a. Should the physicians who evaluated the patients for degree of improvement have known which ones were on streptomycin? Why?

b. State H_0 in words.

c. Calculate the *p*-value for H_0, using an appropriate rank test. (*Hint:* To break the many ties that occur, see Problem 16-15).

d. Does this establish the value of streptomycin? Comment briefly.

CHAPTER 17

Chi-Square Tests
(Requires Chapter 9)

Doubt is the beginning, not the end, of wisdom.

ANONYMOUS

Chi-square (χ^2) provides a simple test based on the difference between observed and expected frequencies. Because it is so easy to understand and calculate, it is a very popular form of hypothesis testing. And it makes so few assumptions about the underlying population that it is commonly classified as a *non-parametric test*.

17-1 χ^2 TESTS FOR MULTINOMIALS: GOODNESS OF FIT

A—EXAMPLE

Let us test the null hypothesis that births in Sweden occur equally often throughout the year. Suppose the only available data is a random sample of 88 births, grouped into seasons of differing length. The observed frequencies O are given in Table 17-1.

How well does the data fit the null hypothesis (of no difference in the birth rate between seasons)? The notion of goodness of fit is developed in the following four steps (calculated in the last four columns of Table 17-1):

1. First consider the implications of the null hypothesis. H_0 means that every birth is apt to occur in any season with a probability proportional to the *length* of that season. For example, spring is defined to have 3 months, or 91 days; thus the probability of a birth occurring in the spring is $\pi = 91/365 = .25$. Similarly, all the other probabilities π are calculated in column (1).
2. Now calculate what the expected frequency in each season would be if the null hypothesis were true. For example, for spring we found $\pi = .25 = 25\%$, so that the expected frequency would be 25% of 88 = 22 births. Similarly, all the other frequencies[1] E are calculated in column (2):

$$\boxed{E = n\pi} \tag{17-1}$$

3. The question now is: "By how much does the observed frequency deviate from the expected frequency?" For example, in spring this deviation is 27 − 22 = 5. Similarly, all the other deviations $(O - E)$ are set out in column (3).
4. To get some idea of the collective size of these deviations, it is pointless to add them up, since their sum must always be zero—a problem we have met before. Once again, we solve it by squaring each deviation $(O - E)^2$. Then to show its relative importance, we compare each squared deviation with the expected frequency E in its cell, $(O - E)^2/E$, as shown in column (4). Finally, we sum the contributions from all cells, and obtain 6.16.

---

[1] Formula (17-1) is just a restatement of formula (4-13) for the mean of a binomial distribution. We should have $E \geq 1$ in each cell (more conservative authors say $E \geq 5$). If this condition is not met, then χ^2 should be used with considerable reservation. Or, cells can be redefined more broadly until this condition is met.

Note that we had a similar condition for the binomial: As suggested following (8-27), use of the normal approximation required at least 5 successes and 5 failures.

TABLE 17-1 Observed Frequencies of 88 ... and Subsequent χ^2 Calculations

Given Data		*4-S*			
		(1)	(2		
Season (Cell)	*Observed Frequency O*	*Probability (if H_0 true) π*	*Expe Frequ E =*		
Spring Apr–June	27	91/365 = .25	.25(8) = 22.0	27 − 22 = +5.0	5²/22 = 1.44
Summer July–Aug	20	.17	15.0	+5.0	1.67
Fall Sept–Oct	8	.167	14.7	−6.7	3.05
Winter Nov–Mar	33	.413	36.3	−3.3	.30
	$n = 88$	1.00✓	88✓	0✓	$\chi^2 \simeq 6.16$ p-value $\simeq .10$

This overall measure of deviation is called chi-square:

$$\textbf{chi-square, } \chi^2 \equiv \Sigma \frac{(O - E)^2}{E} \tag{17-2}$$

A large value of χ^2 indicates a large deviation from H_0, and consequently little credibility for H_0. To determine just how small this credibility is, the tail area or p-value can be determined from the χ^2 distribution in Appendix Table VII (just like the tail area was found from the t distribution in Table V).

Note that the four cell frequencies are not independent: Since $O_1 + O_2 + O_3 + O_4 = n$, any one of them may be expressed in terms of the others. For example, $O_4 = n - (O_1 + O_2 + O_3)$; thus, the last cell is determined by the previous three, and does not provide fresh information. Therefore, in this case χ^2 has only 3 pieces of information (degrees of freedom, d.f.). And in general, with r rows or cells,

$$\textbf{d.f.} = r - 1 \tag{17-3}$$

Since d.f. = 3, we scan along the third row of Appendix Table VII. We find that the observed χ^2 value of 6.16 is about the same as $\chi^2_{.10} = 6.25$. Thus

$$\text{p-value} \simeq .10 \tag{17-4}$$

At the customary 5% level, therefore, the null hypothesis (of the same birth rate in all seasons) cannot be rejected.

This example has shown how the χ^2 test can be applied to data counted off in several cells (such as seasons). This χ^2 test is sometimes called the *multinomial* test to indicate that it is an extension of the binomial, where data was counted off in two cells (such as male and female, or Democrat and Republican.)

B—χ^2 SCREENS, CONFIDENCE INTERVALS DESCRIBE

Continuing the example of Swedish births above, suppose that we gather a very large sample; in fact, *all* the births in Sweden in 1935 are shown in Table 17-2 (Cramer, 1946). With a little stretch of the imagination, this may be considered a random sample from an infinite conceptual population. χ^2 is calculated to be 128, which exceeds the last value in Table VII by so much that we conclude that the p-value $\ll .001$. At any reasonable level, H_0 is rejected.

At this point we must repeat the remarks about hypothesis testing made earlier in Appendix 10-3: Even before any data were gathered, we knew the hypothesis H_0 couldn't be exactly true. After all, would births have *exactly* the same probability throughout the year, to 100 decimal places or more? The main value of the χ^2 test, therefore, is not in rejecting H_0 which was already incredible, but rather as a routine screening test for telling us that we have gathered enough data to discern a departure from H_0.

To actually display the departure, confidence intervals are ideal. Let us continue to regard the 88,273 observed births as a very large sample from

TABLE 17-2 Observed Frequencies of 88,273 Swedish Births Classified by Season and Subsequent χ^2 Calculations

Given Data		*4-Step χ^2 Calculations*			
		(1)	(2)	(3)	(4)
Season	*Observed Frequency* O	*Probability (if H_0 true)* π	*Expected Frequency* $E = n\pi$	$(O - E)$	$(O - E)^2/E$
Spring Apr–June	23,385	.24932	22,008	1,377	86.16
Summer July–Aug	14,978	.16986	14,944	−16	.02
Fall Sept–Oct	14,106	.16712	14,752	−646	28.29
Winter Nov–Mar	35,804	.41370	36,519	−715	14.00
	88,273	1.0000✓	88,273✓	0✓	$\chi^2 = 128$ p-value $\ll .001$

an infinite conceptual population. Now consider P, the sample proportion of births observed in the first season, spring:

$$P = \frac{23{,}385}{88{,}273} = .265 \tag{17-5}$$

Next, use this to construct a 95% confidence interval for the corresponding population proportion (probability of spring births). From (8-27):

$$\pi = .265 \pm 1.96\sqrt{\frac{(.265)(.735)}{88{,}273}}$$

$$= .265 \pm .0029 \tag{17-6}$$

Now compare this with the probability of births in the spring if H_0 were true. Since spring was defined to have 91 of the 365 days of the year, we already found in Table 17-2 that

$$\text{null value } \pi_0 = \frac{91}{365} = .249 \tag{17-7}$$

Consider finally the ratio:

$$\frac{\pi}{\pi_0} = \frac{.265 \pm .0029}{.249}$$

That is,

$$\frac{\text{Actual births}}{\text{Expected births if } H_0 \text{ true}} = 1.06 \pm .01 \tag{17-8}$$

This is easy to interpret: In spring, births were about 6% above an "equal rate" pattern (more precisely, somewhere between 5% and 7% above, with 95% confidence).

As with any other confidence interval, we can immediately use (17-8) to test H_0. If the null hypothesis is true, then $\pi/\pi_0 = 1.00$. Since this value does not fall within the confidence interval (17-8), H_0 can be rejected, which confirms our earlier χ^2 hypothesis test.[2]

For completeness, we can construct confidence bands like (17-8) for the three other seasons too, and graph them all in Figure 17-1.

---

[2] Because the hypothesis test here is about *spring* births, it is not quite identical to our earlier hypothesis test, which considered births in *all* seasons. This subtle difference in fact is what the χ^2 test is explicitly designed to pick up (Wonnacott, 1977).

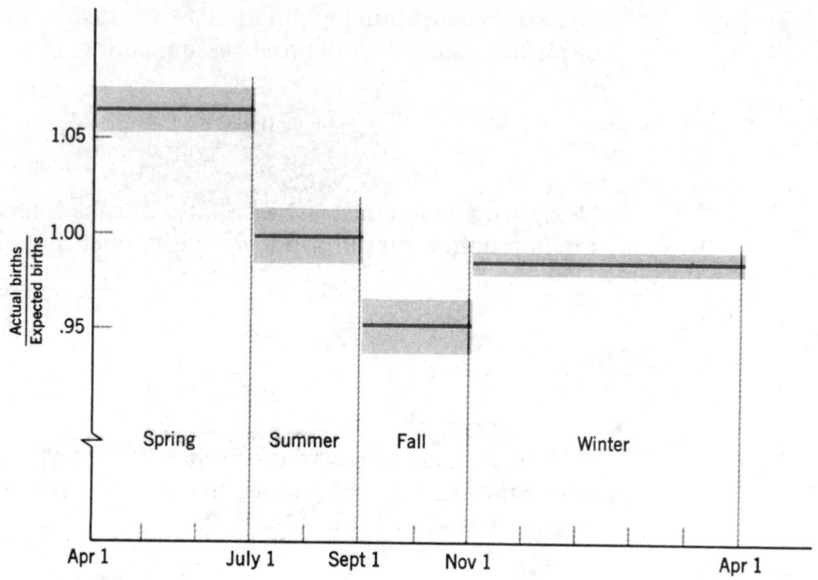

FIGURE 17-1
Ratio of actual births to expected births (if H_0 is true). Shading shows 95% confidence intervals.

PROBLEMS

17-1

Period of Day	*Number of Accidents*
8–10 A.M.	31
10–12 A.M.	30
1–3 P.M.	41
3–5 P.M.	58

This table classifies last month's accidents in a large steel plant into 4 equal time periods. Regarding it as a random sample,

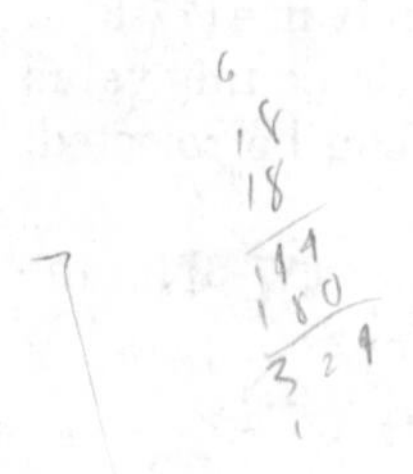

a. Find the p-value for H_0 (that accidents are equally likely to occur at any time of day).

b. Can you reject H_0 at the 5% error level?

c. Analyze in a more graphical way, as in Figure 17-1.

17-2 Parents of blood type AB will produce children of three different types: AA, AB, and BB. If the hypothesis of Mendelian inheritance is true, these three types will be born 25%, 50%, and 25% of the time in the long run. The following data gives the blood types of the 284 children born of 100 AB couples. What p-value does it yield for the Mendelian hypothesis?

Blood Type	*Number of Children*
AA	65
AB	152
BB	67

17-3 Throw a fair die 30 times (or simulate it with random digits in Table I).

a. Use χ^2 to calculate the p-value for H_0 (that it is a fair die).

b. Do you reject H_0 at the 5% level?

c. If each student in a large class carries out this test, approximately what proportion will reject H_0?

17-4 Repeat Problem 17-3 for an unfair die. (Since you do not have an unfair die available, use the table of random digits to simulate a die that is biased toward aces; for example, let the digit 0 as well as 1 represent the ace, so that the ace has twice the probability of any other face.)

17-5 Is there a better test than χ^2 for the die in Problem 17-4 that is suspected of being biased toward aces? If so, use it to recalculate Problem 17-4.

17-6 There are customarily 8 starting positions for a horse race, with position 1 being closest to the inside rail. It is suspected that a horse is more likely to win if it starts from a low-numbered position (near the inside rail). Here is typical data for 144 races:

Starting position	1	2	3	4	5	6	7	8
Number of times a horse in that position has won	29	19	18	25	17	10	15	11

a. State the null and alternative hypotheses.

b. Calculate χ^2 and the p-value for H_0.

c. Graph the number of wins Y against the starting position X.

d. Using regression, calculate the p-value for H_0. Is it sharper (smaller) than the p-value from the χ^2 test?

17-2 χ^2 TESTS FOR INDEPENDENCE: CONTINGENCY TABLES

A—EXAMPLE

Contingency means dependence, so a contingency table is simply a table that displays how one characteristic depends on another. For example, Table 17-3 shows how income is observed to depend on region in a sam-

TABLE 17-3 Observed Frequencies for 400 Families Classified by Region and Income, 1971

	i	1	2	3	4		
		Income ($000)				Total	P_j = Relative
j	Region	0–5	5–10	10–15	15–	Frequency	Frequency
1	South	28	42	30	24	124	.31
2	North	44	78	78	76	276	.69
Total Frequency		72	120	108	100	400	
P_i = Relative Freq.		.18	.30	.27	.25		

ple of 400 U.S. families in 1971. To test the null hypothesis of no dependence in the underlying population, χ^2 again may be used.

In Table 17-3 let π_{ij} denote the underlying bivariate probability distribution; for example, π_{41} is the probability that a family earns above $15 thousand, and is in the South. Let π_i and π_j similarly denote the marginal probability distributions. Then the null hypothesis of statistical independence may be stated precisely

$$H_0: \quad \pi_{ij} = \pi_i \pi_j \tag{17-9}$$

like (5-6)

To test how well the data fits this hypothesis, we set out the 4 steps in Table 17-4, analogous to the χ^2 calculations in Table 17-1:

1. First, work out the implications of H_0. To estimate π_i and π_j we use the proportions P_i and P_j calculated in the last row and column of Table 17-3. Substituting them into (17-9) yields the estimated probabilities P_{ij} for each cell as set out at the top of Table 17-4.[3]
2. Calculate the expected frequencies $E = nP_{ij}$.
3. Calculate the deviations $(O - E)$.
4. Square and divide by the expected frequencies; in other words, calculate $(O - E)^2/E$. Then sum to get an overall measure of discrepancy:

$$\text{chi-square for independence, } \chi^2 \equiv \Sigma\Sigma \frac{(O - E)^2}{E} \tag{17-10}$$

like (17-2)

[3] This step is very much like the fitting of each cell in 2-way ANOVA, except that here a probability is fitted by multiplying two component probabilities, whereas in ANOVA a *numerical* response is fitted by the *addition* of two component effects, as in (10-17). This analogy can be pushed further by taking logarithms, obtaining a *log-linear* model. To be absolutely correct, incidentally, the notation in Table 17-3 for P_i and P_j ought to be $P_{i.}$ and $P_{.j}$—just as we used $\bar{X}_{i.}$ and $\bar{X}_{.j}$ in Table 10-6.

TABLE 17-4 4-Step χ^2 Calculations

1. Assuming independence, estimate the bivariate probabilities $P_{ij} = P_i P_j$

					P_j
	.056	.093	.084	.077	.31
	.124	.207	.186	.173	.69
P_i	.18	.30	.27	.25	

2. Calculate the expected frequencies $E = nP_{ij}$

22.3	37.2	33.5	31.0
49.7	82.8	74.5	69.0

3. Calculate the deviations $(O - E)$

5.7	4.8	−3.5	−7.0
−5.7	−4.8	3.5	7.0

4. Calculate $(O - E)^2/E$

1.45	.62	.36	1.58
.65	.28	.16	.71

sum, $\chi^2 = 5.81$

We have written the Σ sign twice in (17-10) to indicate that we sum over the whole table (c columns and r rows). Then the degrees of freedom for this test are:[4]

$$\boxed{\text{d.f.} = (c - 1)(r - 1)} \tag{17-11}$$

Thus, for Table 17-4,

$$\text{d.f.} = (4 - 1)(2 - 1) = 3$$

Finally, the value $\chi^2 = 5.81$ calculated at the end of Table 17-4 can be converted to a p-value. Since d.f. = 3, we scan along the third row of Table

[4] The d.f. may be calculated from a general principle that is useful for many applications:

$$\text{d.f.} = (\text{\# cells}) - 1 - (\text{\# estimated parameters}) \tag{17-12}$$

To apply this, we have to know the number of estimated parameters (in this case, estimated probabilities). Consider first the c estimated column probabilities P_i. Once the first $(c - 1)$ are estimated, the last one is strictly determined, since $\Sigma P_i = 1$. Thus, there are only $(c - 1)$ independently estimated column probabilities, and by the same argument, only $(r - 1)$ row probabilities. Thus, from (17-12):

$$\begin{aligned}\text{d.f.} &= cr - 1 - [(c - 1) + (r - 1)]\\ &= (c - 1)(r - 1)\end{aligned} \qquad \text{(17-11) proved}$$

TABLE 17-5 χ^2 **Computed by MINITAB**

```
MTB > PRINT C1-C4

 ROW     C1     C2     C3     C4

   1     28     42     30     24
   2     44     78     78     76

MTB > CHISQUARE TEST ON TABLE IN COLUMNS C1-C4

EXPECTED COUNTS ARE PRINTED BELOW OBSERVED COUNTS

             C1         C2         C3         C4      TOTAL
    1        28         42         30         24        124
          22.32      37.20      33.48      31.00

    2        44         78         78         76        276
          49.68      82.80      74.52      69.00

TOTAL        72        120        108        100        400

CHISQ =   1.445 +    0.619 +    0.362 +    1.581 +
          0.649 +    0.278 +    0.163 +    0.710  =  5.807
DF = 3
```

VII. We find that the observed χ^2 value of 5.81 lies beyond $\chi^2_{.25} = 4.11$. Thus

$$p\text{-value} < .25 \tag{17-13}$$

This *p*-value is too high to reject H_0 at the customary 5% level. That is, at this level χ^2 fails to establish any dependence of income on region.

The calculations for χ^2 can become very tedious if the table is large, or if the independence of more than two factors is being tested. To show how helpful a computer can be, Table 17-5 gives the MINITAB input and output for the data in Table 17-3.

B—ALTERNATIVE TO χ^2: EXPLOITING NUMERICAL SCALES

Since the χ^2 test does not exploit the numerical nature of income, it misses the essential question: *How much* do incomes differ between regions?

This question can be answered by reworking the data in Table 17-3. Since income is numerical, we can calculate the mean income in the North ($\overline{X}_1$), and the South ($\overline{X}_2$). Then, as detailed in Problem 17-10, we can find the 95% confidence interval for the difference in the population mean incomes:

$$(\mu_1 - \mu_2) = (\overline{X}_1 - \overline{X}_2) \pm t_{.025}\, s_p \sqrt{\frac{1}{n_1} + \frac{1}{n_2}} \qquad \text{like (8-20)}$$

$$= (10.87 - 9.52) \pm 1.96\sqrt{27.3}\sqrt{\frac{1}{276} + \frac{1}{124}}$$

$$= 1.35 \pm 1.11 \text{ thousand dollars} \qquad (17\text{-}14)$$

That is, the North has a mean income that is $1350 ± $1110 higher than the South.

The secondary question of testing H_0 (no difference between regions) can be answered immediately: At the 5% level, H_0 now can be rejected, since 0 does not lie in the confidence interval (17-14). That is, there is a discernible difference between the two regions. This is a much stronger conclusion than we obtained from the χ^2 test following (17-13), where we failed to find a discernible difference between the two regions. The 2-sample t proved to be a more powerful test, because it takes into account the *numerical* nature of income, which the χ^2 test ignores.

Of course, if more than two regions were to be compared, we would use ANOVA instead of the two-sample t. But the conclusion would be generally the same: Any such test that fully exploits the numerical nature of the data will be more powerful than χ^2. Thus we conclude,

> **Numerical variables should be analyzed with tools (such as 2-sample t, ANOVA, regression, or their nonparametric equivalents) that exploit their numerical nature. The χ^2 test is appropriate if all the variables are categorical.** (17-15)

PROBLEMS

17-7 In a study of how occupation is related to education, the following random sample of 500 employed men was drawn in the United States in 1980.

	Occupation			
Education	*White Collar*	*Blue Collar*	*Services*	*Farm Work*
4 or more years of high school	194	146	27	10
Less than 4 years of high school	18	79	18	8

(constructed from the Stat. Abst. of U.S., 1981)

a. State H_0 in words.

b. Calculate χ^2 and the p-value for H_0.

c. For each occupation, graph the estimated proportion of better-educated workers, with its surrounding confidence interval.

17-8 The research division of a large chemical company tried each of three termite repellants on 200 wooden stakes driven into random locations. Two years later, the number of infected stakes was as follows:

	Treatment		
Infected?	T_1	T_2	T_3
Yes	26	48	18
No	174	152	182

Note that this experiment was designed to have exactly the same number of stakes (200) for each treatment. Thus the relative frequency for each treatment is 200/600 = 1/3, and does not really estimate any underlying population proportion. So the sampling differs from the simple random sample of Table 17-3.

Nevertheless, the standard χ^2 test still remains valid. When used this way, it is often called a *χ^2 test with fixed marginal totals*, or a *χ^2 test of homogeneity* (Are the various treatments homogeneous, i.e., similar in terms of infection rate?)

a. Calculate χ^2 and the p-value.

b. Are the treatments discernibly different at the 5% level?

17-9 A random sample of first marriages showed the following 5-year survival characteristics, by residence (simplified version of Balakrishnan, 1986)

	Place of Residence			
	Farm	*Small Urban*	*Large Urban*	*Totals*
Still Married	287	1124	2081	3492
Divorced or Separated	18	89	265	372
totals	305	1213	2346	3864

a. For each of the three places of residence, calculate and graph the survival rate.

b. State H_0 in words. What is its p-value?

c. Are the differences in survival rates statistically discernible at the 5% level?

17-10 Verify (17-14). (In Table 17-3, approximate the incomes from 0 to 5 by the cell midpoint 2.5. Continue for the other cells. In the last cell, which is open-ended and has no midpoint, use 17.5 as a rough approximation to the average income within the cell.)

17-11 In a survey for its advertisers, a newspaper chain randomly sampled 100 readers of each of its 3 major newspapers, with the following results:

	Newspaper		
Social Class	A	B	C
Poor	31	11	12
Lower Middle Class	49	59	51
Middle Class	18	26	31
Rich	2	4	6

a. State H_0 in words.

b. Calculate χ^2 and the p-value for H_0. Is the difference between newspapers discernible at the .001 level?

***17-12** **a.** Analyze Problem 17-11 in a way that exploits the ordered nature of social class: Since the four social classes are ordered from poor to rich, a reasonable strategy is to number them 1, 2, 3, 4 (call it a *social class score* if you like). With the 300 people all having their social class transformed into a numerical score, it is now possible to calculate the mean score for newspaper *A*, and compare it to the mean scores for newspapers *B* and *C* using ANOVA.

b. Did you find the difference between newspapers discernible at the .001 level? Is this ANOVA test better than χ^2 in this particular case?

CHAPTER 17 SUMMARY

17-1 χ^2 is a hypothesis test based on the difference between observed values and expected values (expected under the null hypothesis). In the simplest case, χ^2 can be applied to data sorted into several cells, according to a single factor such as season.

17-2 χ^2 can also be applied to data sorted according to two factors, to test their independence of each other. χ^2 tests are designed for purely categorical variables such as sex or nationality (while earlier procedures such as regression remain appropriate for *numerical* variables such as income or productivity).

REVIEW PROBLEMS

17-13 A random sample of 1367 university degrees earned in 1984 gave the following breakdown:

	Degree		
Sex	*Bachelors*	*Masters*	*Doctorates*
Male	534	144	22
Female	515	141	11

(constructed from the Stat. Abst. of U.S., 1987, p. 146)

a. State the null hypothesis in words.

b. Calculate χ^2 and the *p*-value for H_0.

c. For a more graphic alternative to χ^2, calculate the proportion of women in each of the 3 different degree categories. Include confidence intervals, and a graph.

17-14 According to the Mendelian genetic model, a certain garden pea plant should produce offspring that have white, pink, and red flowers, in the long-run proportions 25%, 50%, 25%. A sample of 1000 such offspring was colored as follows:

white, 21%; pink, 52%; red, 27%

a. Find the *p*-value for the Mendelian hypothesis.

b. Can you reject the Mendelian hypothesis at the 5% level?

17-15 In a study of how the burden of poverty varies among U.S. regions, a random sample of 1000 individuals in each region of the United States in 1979 yielded the following information on poverty (defined in 1979 as an income below $7400 for a family of 4 people, roughly).

Calculate the *p*-value for the null hypothesis that poverty is equally prevalent in all regions.

Incidence of Poverty by Region

	Northeast	*Midwest*	*South*	*West*
Poor	112	105	154	113
Not poor	888	895	846	887

(constructed from the Stat. Abst. of U.S., 1987, p. 442)

17-16 ***A Final Challenge: χ^2 Is More than a Test of H_0***

A random sample of 2000 adult Americans in 1985 would have typically yielded the following frequencies, classified by education and sex:

Education (Number of Schools Completed)	Sex	
	Male	*Female*
none (0)	84	101
primary (1)	202	203
secondary (2)	492	570
college (3)	214	134

(sample simulated from the U.S. population in Problem 5-20)

a. Calculate χ^2 and the p-value for H_0. Can you discern whether U.S. men and women have different educations (at level α = 5%)?

b. Take a detailed look at the table of discrepancies O–E in part **a**. Then write a short paragraph describing *how* U.S. men and women differ in education.

c. Choose the correct alternative:
The p-value in part **a** showed that H_0 had [a lot of, very little] credibility—something we [knew, did not know] even before collecting the data. However, a closer look at the calculation of the p-value—in particular the [table of discrepancies O–E, overall χ^2 value]—was very illuminating. This is similar to ANOVA or regression, where the [residuals $X - \hat{X}$ or $Y - \hat{Y}$, overall F value] can be very illuminating too.

d. For an alternative analysis, treat education numerically: X = 0, 1, 2, or 3 schools were completed, for each of $n_1 = 992$ males and $n_2 = 1008$ females. Use the two-sample confidence interval (8-20), and write a sentence describing how U.S. men and women differ in education.

Then calculate the p-value for H_0. Is the difference discernible at level $\alpha = 5\%$?

e. How is part **d** different from **a** and **b**?

CHAPTER 18

*Maximum Likelihood Estimation

(Requires Chapter 7)

We must believe in luck. For how else can we explain the success of those we don't like?

JEAN COCTEAU

The stars on Chapters 18, 19, and 20 indicate that they are a little more challenging. Readers who work their way through this material, however, will be amply rewarded: They will discover the philosophical foundations of modern statistics at the same time as they find practical solutions to important problems.

18-1 INTRODUCTION

In this chapter we will study a very powerful method for deriving estimates, called maximum likelihood estimation (MLE). To put it into perspective, we begin by reviewing some earlier estimation techniques.

A—METHOD OF MOMENTS ESTIMATION (MME)

The first principle of estimation that we used, back in Chapter 6, was the most obvious and intuitive one: estimate a population mean μ with the sample mean $\bar{X}$; estimate a population variance σ^2 with the sample variance s^2; and so on. This principle of estimating a population moment by using the equivalent sample moment is called *method of moments estimation* (MME). Often it works very well; but now we consider a case where it does not.

EXAMPLE 18-1

In World War II, the allies used sampling theory to measure German production very effectively (Wallis and Roberts, 1962). The Germans gave their rockets serial numbers from 1 to N. The problem for the allies was to estimate the size of the German arsenal; that is, how large was N?

To estimate this, captured German rockets were viewed as providing a random sample of serial numbers. To illustrate, suppose a total of 10 captured weapons had serial numbers as follows:

77, 30, 05, 39, 28, 10, 27, 12, 73, 49

The following sequence of questions will lead us to an estimate of N:

a. What is the sample mean $\bar{X}$?

b. For the population of serial numbers 1, 2, 3, . . . , N, what is the mean μ in terms of N?

c. Using the method of moments approach, set $\mu = \bar{X}$. Then solve for N.

d. Can you think of a better estimate?

SOLUTION

a. $$\bar{X} = \frac{77 + 30 + \ldots + 49}{10} = \frac{350}{10} = 35$$

b. The mean of the serial numbers 1, 2, 3, 4, 5, for example, is the middle number 3; formally, this is just (5 + 1)/2, the number midway between the last and the first. Similarly, for any set of serial numbers 1, 2, . . . , N, the mean is

$$\mu = \frac{N + 1}{2}$$

c.
$$\mu = \frac{N + 1}{2} = \overline{X}$$

Solving for N, the MME is:

$$N = 2\overline{X} - 1$$
$$= 2(35) - 1 = 69 \qquad (18\text{-}1)$$

d. When we look closely at the data, we see that N = 69 can be easily improved. The largest observation is 77, so that N must be at least this big:

$$N \geq 77$$

So N = 77 itself would clearly be a better estimate than the MME of 69.

B—MAXIMUM LIKELIHOOD ESTIMATION (MLE)

Example 18-1 illustrated what can go wrong with MME. A better way is needed to generate estimators in new and complex situations, and this is where statistics as a science stood about 1920. To fill this need, Maximum Likelihood Estimation (MLE) was developed by Sir Ronald Fisher (who also developed randomized control in experiments).

We will see how MLE provides a superior estimate in several situations, including Example 18-1 above. But first we will show that in some other more familiar situations, MLE provides the same estimate as the method of moments. For example, the MLE of a population proportion π is the sample proportion P. Thus MLE provides further justification for these familiar estimates.

18-2 MLE FOR SOME FAMILIAR CASES

A—EXAMPLE OF HOW MLE WORKS

Suppose that a shipment of radios is sampled for quality, and that 3 out of 5 are found defective. What should we estimate is the proportion π of defectives in the whole shipment (population)? Temporarily, try to forget the common sense method of estimating the population proportion π with the sample proportion $P = 3/5 = .60$. Instead, let us investigate an alternative method: consider a whole range of possible π that we might choose, and then try to pick out the one that best explains the sample.

For example, is $\pi = .1$ a plausible value for the population? If $\pi = .1$, then the probability of $S = 3$ defectives out of a sample of $n = 5$ observations would be given by the binomial formula (4-8):

$$\binom{n}{S}\pi^S(1-\pi)^{n-S} = \binom{5}{3}.1^3\,.9^2 \simeq .008 \tag{18-2}$$

In other words, if $\pi = .1$, there are only about 8 chances in a thousand of getting the actual sample that we observed.

Similarly, if $\pi = .2$, we would find from the binomial formula—or even better, from Table IIIb—that there are about 50 chances in a thousand of getting the sample that we observed. In fact, it seems quite natural to try out all values of π, in each case finding out how likely it is for such a population π to generate the sample that we actually observed. We simply read across Table IIIb, and so obtain the graph in Figure 18-1. In this situation, where the sample values $n = 5$ and $S = 3$ are fixed, and the only variable is the hypothetical value of π, we call the result the *likelihood function* $L(\pi)$:

$$L(\pi) = \binom{5}{3}\pi^3(1-\pi)^2 \tag{18-3}$$

From Table IIIb, where $n = 5$ and $S = 3$:

π	(0)	.1	.2	.3	.4	.5	.6	.7	.8	.9	(1.0)
$L(\pi)$	0	.008	.051	.132	.230	.312	.346	.309	.205	.073	0

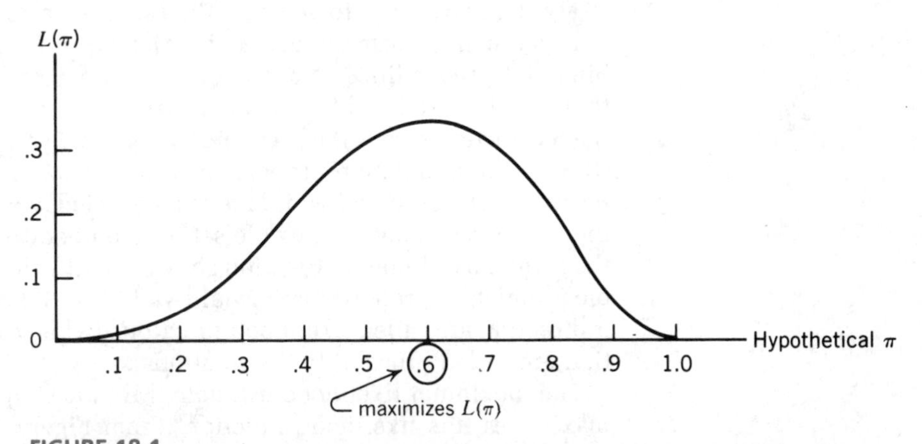

FIGURE 18-1
The likelihood function $L(\pi)$ copied down from Table IIIb and then graphed. It gives the likelihood that various hypothetical population proportions would yield the observed sample of 3 defectives in 5 observations.

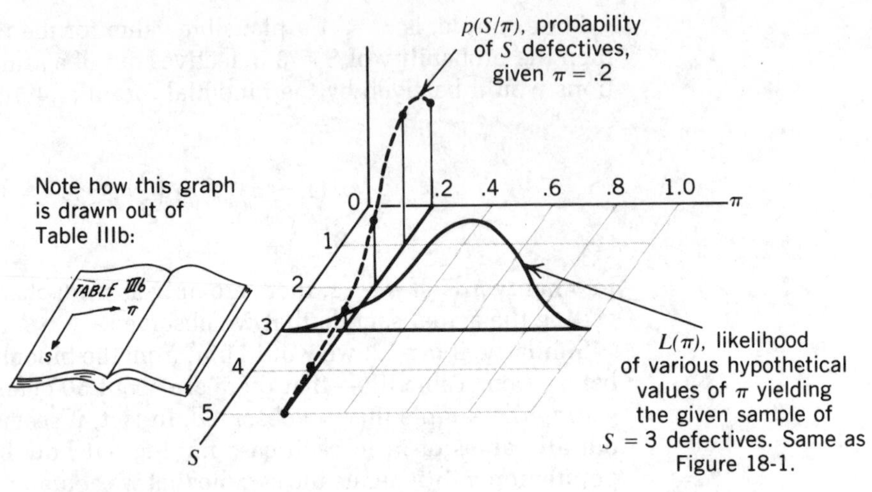

FIGURE 18-2
The binomial probabilities plotted against both S and π, for $n = 5$ observations.

In general, we similarly define:

The MLE is the hypothetical population value that maximizes the likelihood of the observed sample.	(18-4)

In other words, the MLE is the hypothetical population value that is more likely than any other to generate the sample we actually observed.

To show these same issues geometrically, in Figure 18-2 we graph the binomial probabilities as a function of both S and π. In Chapter 4, we thought of π fixed and S variable. For example, the dotted distribution in the S direction shows the probability of getting various numbers of defectives, if the population proportion were $\pi = .2$. But in this chapter, we regard S—the observed sample result—as fixed, while the population π is thought of as taking on a whole set of hypothetical values. For example, the solid curve in the π direction shows the likelihood that various possible population proportions π would yield S = 3 defectives. Slices in this π direction are called likelihood functions (whereas slices in the S direction are called probability distributions).

The *maximum likelihood estimate* (MLE) is simply the value of π that maximizes this likelihood function. From Figure 18-1 we see that this turns out to be $\pi = .60$—which coincides nicely with the common sense estimate $P = 3/5$.

B—MLE FOR A PROPORTION π IN GENERAL

We show in Appendix 18-2 that our result above was no accident, and that the maximum likelihood estimate of the binomial π is *always* the sample proportion P:

$$\boxed{\text{MLE of } \pi = P} \tag{18-5}$$

In Chapter 1, we appealed to common sense (the method of moments) in using the sample proportion to estimate the population proportion. Now we can add the more rigorous justification of maximum likelihood: a population with $\pi = P$ is more likely than any other to generate the observed sample.

C—MLE FOR THE MEAN OF A NORMAL POPULATION

Suppose we have drawn a random sample of 3 observations, say, X_1, X_2, X_3, from a parent population that is normal, with mean μ and variance σ^2. Our problem is to find the MLE of the unknown μ. Deriving the MLE with calculus would involve trying out all of the hypothetical values of μ; we illustrate this geometrically by trying out 2 typical values, μ_* and μ_0, as shown in the two panels of Figure 18-3.

First, in panel (*a*) we consider the likelihood of observing the sample X_1, X_2, X_3, if the population mean is μ_*. The probability (strictly speaking, the probability density) of observing X_1 is the arrow above X_1, which is quite large. So too is the probability of observing X_2. However, the probability of X_3 is very small because it is so distant from μ_*. Because they are randomly drawn, these sample values X_1, X_2, and X_3 are independent. Therefore, we can multiply their probabilities to get their joint probability—that is, the likelihood of this sample. Because of the very small probability of X_3, this likelihood is quite small.

On the other hand, a population with mean μ_0 as in panel (*b*) is more likely to generate the sample values. Since the X values are collectively closer to μ_0, the likelihood—derived by multiplying their probabilities together—is greater. Indeed, very little additional shift in μ_0 is apparently required to maximize the likelihood of the sample. It seems that the MLE of μ might be centered right among the observations X_1, X_2, X_3—that is, might be just the sample mean $\bar{X}$. In fact, this is proved in Appendix 18-2:

$$\boxed{\begin{array}{c}\textbf{For a normal population,}\\ \text{MLE of } \mu = \bar{X}\end{array}} \tag{18-6}$$

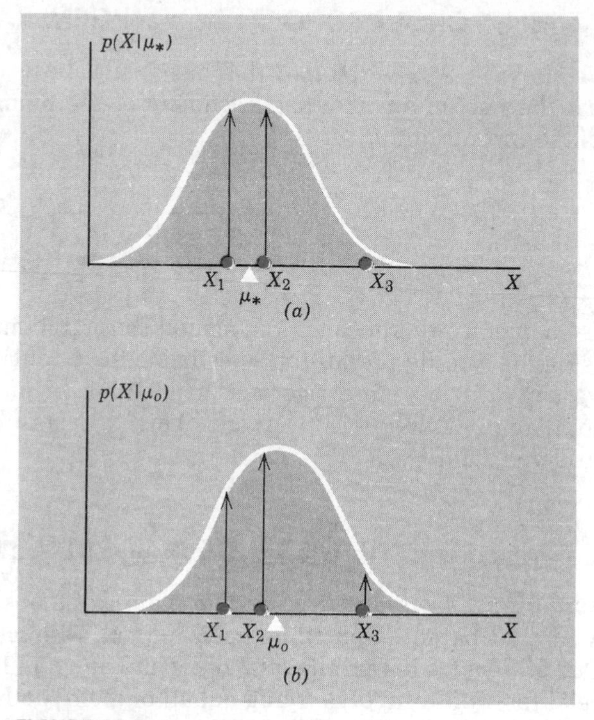

FIGURE 18-3
Likelihood for the mean μ of a normal population, based on a sample of three observations (X_1, X_2, X_3). (a) Small likelihood $L(\mu_*)$, the product of the three probabilities. (b) Larger likelihood $L(\mu_0)$.

D—MLE FOR NORMAL REGRESSION

Let us again assume the population shape is normal—this time, in the regression model:

$$E(Y) = \alpha + \beta X \qquad \text{(12-1) repeated}$$

Then our argument will be similar to the argument given above. Specifically, the MLE estimation of α and β requires selecting those hypothetical population values of α and β that are more likely than any others to generate the sample that we observed. For example, suppose we have observed the sample of three points shown in both panels of Figure 18-4.

First, let us try out the line shown in panel (a)—at first glance, a pretty bad fit for the three observed points. Temporarily, suppose that this were the true regression line; then the distributions of Y would be centered around it, as shown. The likelihood that they would generate the three observations in the sample is the product of the three probabilities (arrows above Y_1, Y_2, and Y_3). This likelihood seems relatively small, mostly

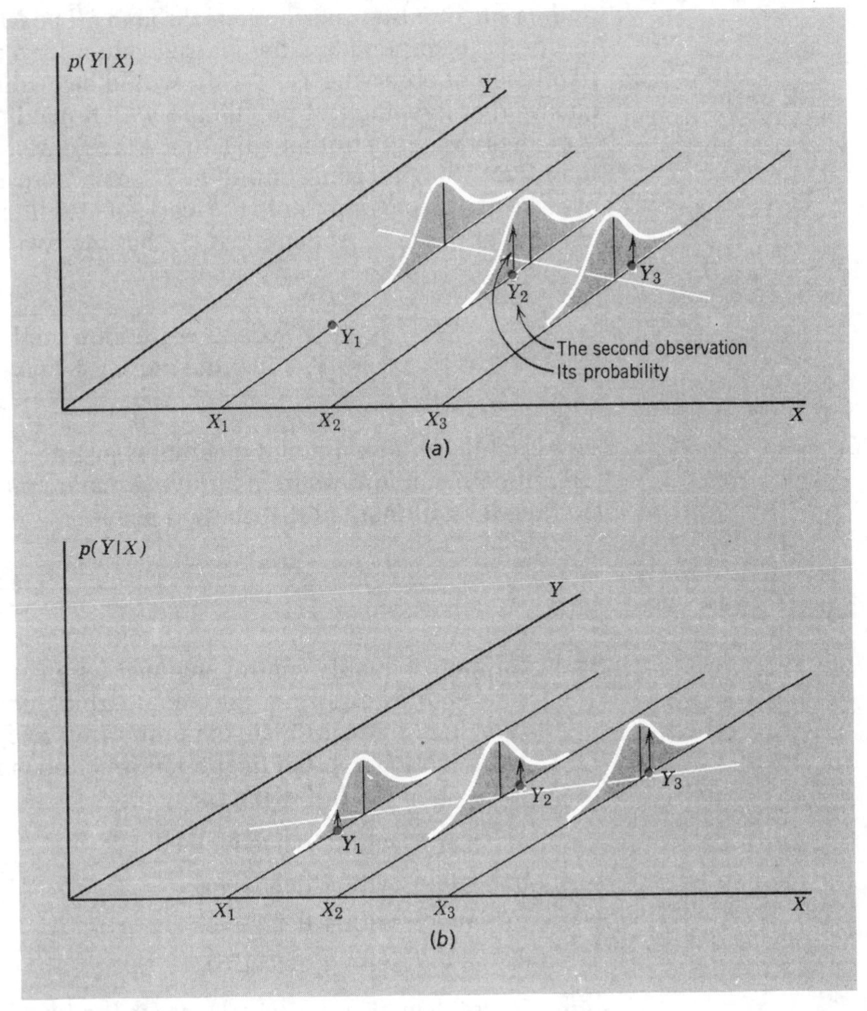

FIGURE 18-4
Likelihood for regression. (a) Small likelihood, the product of three probabilities. (b) Larger likelihood as the trial line comes closer to the three observed points.

because of the minuscule probability of Y_1. Our intuition that this is a bad estimate is confirmed; such a hypothetical population is not very likely to generate the given sample.

In panel (*b*) we show the same given sample, but now another hypothetical line. This line seems more likely to give rise to the sample we observed. Since the Y values are collectively closer to the hypothetical regression line, their probability is consequently greater.

The MLE technique speculates on possible populations (regression lines). How likely is each to give rise to the sample that we observed? Geometrically, our problem is to try them all out, by moving the population through all its possible values—that is, *by moving the regression line and its surrounding distributions through all possible positions.* Different positions correspond to different trial values for α and β. In each case, the likelihood of observing Y_1, Y_2, Y_3, would be evaluated. For our MLE, we choose that hypothetical population which maximizes this likelihood. It is evident that little further adjustment is required in panel (*b*) to arrive at the MLE. This procedure intuitively seems to result in a good fit; moreover, since it seems similar to the least squares fit, it is no surprise that we are able to prove in Appendix 18-2, that the two coincide:

In a normal regression model, MLE is identical to least squares. (18-7)

This establishes an important theoretical justification of least squares: It is the estimate that follows from applying maximum likelihood to a regression model with normal distribution shape.

PROBLEMS

18-1 Suppose a quality control engineer for an auto firm takes a random sample of n cars from the "population" coming off the assembly line, in order to estimate the proportion π of all cars with defective paint jobs. Graph the likelihood function, and show the MLE of π for each of the following cases:

a. $n = 8$, with 2 defectives.

b. $n = 8$, with 4 defectives.

c. $n = 2$, with 1 defective.

d. $n = 2$, with 0 defective.

18-2 In Problem 18-1, for which case is the likelihood function a parabola? For which cases is the MLE the sample proportion P?

18-3 In each of the following cases find the MLE and the MME:

a. For the mean of a normal population from which a sample yields the 4 observations: 17, 28, 92, 41.

b. For the proportion of defectives in a population from which a sample of 20 yields 8 defective.

c. For the slope in a normal regression population that yields a sample with these statistics:

$$\bar{X} = 10, \quad \bar{Y} = 56, \quad n = 15$$

$$\Sigma(X - \bar{X})^2 = 180 \quad \Sigma(Y - \bar{Y})^2 = 316 \quad \Sigma(X - \bar{X})(Y - \bar{Y}) = 45$$

18-3 MLE FOR THE UNIFORM DISTRIBUTION

So far, we have seen how MLE justifies some familiar estimates like P, $\overline{X}$, and least squares in regression. It is time to see how well it works in a less familiar case—the problem of estimating the number of German rockets in Example 18-1.

Recall that we are trying to estimate the population size N, with a sample of 10 serial numbers reproduced as dots in panel (a) of Figure

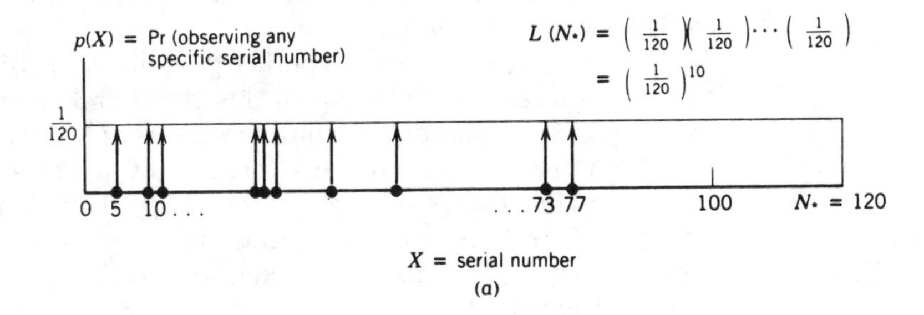

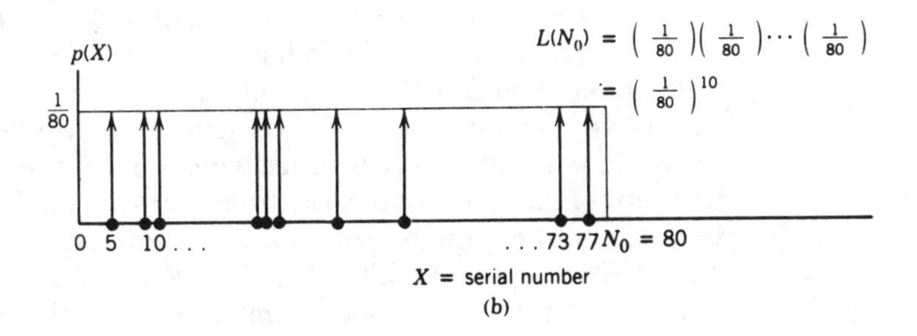

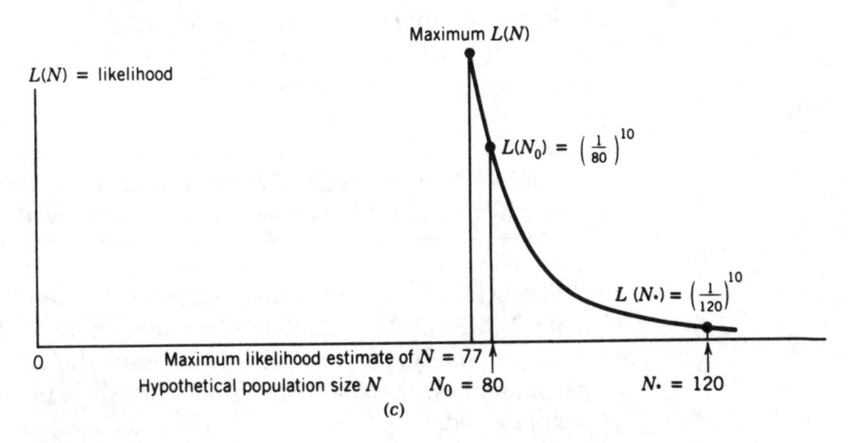

FIGURE 18-5
Likelihood for the uniform distribution. (a) Small likelihood, the product of 10 small probabilities. (b) Larger likelihood as the trial population N gets smaller. (c) The likelihood function plotted for these 2 values of N, and all others as well.

18-5. We speculate on various possible values of N, in each case calculating the likelihood of the given sample of 10 observations. In panel (*a*), for example, we show one possible value, $N_* = 120$. The rectangular or uniform distribution shows the probability of observing any specific serial number. (With 120 numbers, all equally probable, the probability of observing any one is 1/120.) The probability of each of the 10 blue observations is shown as usual by an arrow. Then the likelihood or joint probability of all 10 observations is the product[1] of these 10 probability arrows—namely, $(1/120)^{10}$. This likelihood $L(N_*)$ is then graphed as the small value in panel (*c*).

In panel (*b*), we consider another possible value of N—this time, $N_0 = 80$. The uniform distribution in this panel shows the probability of observing any of the now 80 equiprobable serial numbers. Because of this smaller range of serial numbers, there is now a greater probability of each; therefore, the arrows in panel (*b*) are larger than in panel (*a*). Thus their product—the likelihood of getting the sample we observed—is greater than in panel (*a*). This larger likelihood $L(N_0)$ is graphed as the higher value in panel (*c*).

If we reduce N even further, the 10 arrows would of course get even larger, as would their product—the likelihood $L(N)$. In other words, *up to a point*, smaller and smaller values of N result in larger and larger values of the likelihood function in panel (*c*).

However, for any value of N less than 77, $L(N)$ suddenly falls to zero, as shown in panel (*c*). It's easy to see why. If the entire population of rockets had serial numbers ranging, say from 1 to 75 (i.e., if $N = 75$), it would be impossible to get the rocket with serial number 77 that we actually observed. That is, the likelihood of this would be zero.

The maximum likelihood estimate is that value of N which is more likely than any other to generate the sample we observed—in other words, the value of N where the likelihood function $L(N)$ reaches a maximum. In panel (*c*) we see that this is $N = 77$, the largest value (serial number) that we observed.

The MLE of the largest value in a uniform distribution (of serial numbers) is the largest value observed in the sample.	(18-8)

The MLE of 77 is obviously superior to the Method of Moments Estimate (MME) of 69, calculated in Example 18-1. Whereas the MLE of 77 was more likely than any other to generate the sample we observed, in this particular case it was *impossible* for the MME of 69 to generate the sample we observed.

---

[1] In multiplying the 10 individual probabilities, we have assumed independence—that is, random sampling with replacement. Random sampling without replacement would still give approximately the same likelihood.

Although the MLE of 77 is in some sense the best single estimate (*point estimate*), in this case it is an extreme estimate: It's the lowest possible estimate of N that can be sensibly made. It would be much more informative to give the readers *the whole likelihood function* in panel (c), which shows that N must be at least 77, and there is relatively little likelihood that N is above 90 or 100.

PROBLEMS

18-4 Suppose a sample of 10 serial numbers of German rockets were as follows:

396, 576, 454, 519, 906, 964, 612, 26, 363, 162

What is the MME of total production? And the MLE?

18-5 The sample in Problem 18-4 was in fact a *simulated* sample drawn from the population 1, 2, 3, ... , 999. (We started at the beginning of Table I, drawing triples of digits.) The value of such a simulation is that since N is actually known ($N = 999$), we can judge how good any given estimate is.

a. In Problem 18-4, was MME or MLE closer to the target N?

b. Let everyone in the class do the same sort of simulation, and have the instructor graph the Monte Carlo distribution of the MME and MLE. Which is closer to the target on the whole? In what sense?

18-6 Continuing Problem 18-5:

a. Is the MME unbiased? Prove it.

b. Is the MLE unbiased? Prove it.

c. It can be shown that the bias of the MLE estimate can be removed if we blow it up by the factor $(n + 1)/n$. Calculate this unbiased estimate of N, for the sample in Problem 18-4.

d. It can be proved that the unbiased version of MLE in part (c) is very efficient:

$$\text{Efficiency of MLE relative to MME} = \frac{n+2}{3}$$

(Note that they are equally efficient for a sample size $n = 1$, because they coincide then.)

Now suppose in Problem 18-4, rather than the unbiased version of MLE based on $n = 10$ observations, the MME was used instead. To be equally accurate, how much larger would the sample have to be?

Repeat for $n = 1000$ observations.

18-4 MLE IN GENERAL

A—DEFINITION OF MLE FOR ANY POPULATION PARAMETER

Suppose a sample $(X_1, X_2, \ldots, X_n)$ is drawn from a population with probability function $p(X|\theta)$, where θ is the unknown population parameter we wish to estimate. If the sample is random (VSRS), then the X_i are independent, each with the probability function $p(X_i|\theta)$. Hence the joint probability function for the whole sample is obtained by multiplying:

$$p(X_1, X_2, \ldots, X_n|\theta) = p(X_1|\theta)p(X_2|\theta) \ldots p(X_n|\theta) \qquad (18\text{-}9)$$

But we regard the observed sample as fixed, and ask "Which of all the hypothetical values of θ maximizes this probability?" This is emphasized by renaming (18-9) the likelihood function $L(\theta)$, and the MLE is the hypothetical value of θ that maximizes this function.

B—THE ADVANTAGES OF MLE

MLE is a method of estimation with strong intuitive appeal: Since the MLE is the population value that is most likely to generate the observed sample, it is the population value that best "matches" the sample. In familiar situations it produces the familiar estimates, such as P for π, and $\overline{X}$ for μ. Its advantages, however, go far beyond these intuitively appealing ones, and include the following:

1. Where MLE is not the same as MME (method of moments estimation), then MLE is generally superior (as we saw in estimating N for the uniform distribution in Section 18-3).
2. MLE is very straightforward: Just write out the likelihood function, and maximize it. Even in very complex cases where a formula cannot be derived, powerful computers can nevertheless calculate a good numerical approximation.
3. As well as providing the MLE estimate, the whole likelihood function itself is useful to show the *range* of plausible values for the parameter (as we noted in estimating N at the end of Section 18-3, and will pursue in the next chapter).
4. MLE has many of the attractive properties described in Chapter 7. Specifically, under broad conditions, an MLE estimate has the following large-sample (asymptotic) properties. It is:

   i. *Unbiased.*

   ii. *Efficient,* with smaller variance than any other unbiased estimator. (However, this is only true if the parent population does have the specific shape—normal, uniform, or whatever—that is assumed in deriving the MLE. Thus, MLE may lack robustness in dealing with a population of unknown shape.)

iii. *Normally distributed* in its sampling distribution, with easily computed mean and variance. (That is, if we did a Monte Carlo study of how the MLE estimate varies from sample to sample, it would vary normally.) Thus, confidence intervals and tests are easy to carry out.

For example, we already have seen that the three asymptotic properties are all true for $\overline{X}$, the MLE of μ in a normal population. They are equally true for other MLE estimates too, in large samples.

However, in a small sample, MLE (like all the other estimators we have encountered so far) can often be improved upon, as we shall see in the next chapter.

C—CALCULATING THE MLE IN PRACTICE

If we take logs in (18-9), we reduce the product to a simpler sum:

$$\text{log likelihood} = \log p(X_1|\theta) + \log p(X_2|\theta) + \ldots$$

Since whatever maximizes likelihood must simultaneously maximize log likelihood, we can restate the MLE in more practical terms:

MLE is that value of θ that maximizes

log likelihood, $\mathcal{L}(\theta) \equiv \Sigma \log p(X_i|\theta)$ (18-10)

An example will illustrate how log likelihood simplifies finding the MLE, in sampling from any kind of population distribution.

EXAMPLE 18-2

The Poisson distribution has probability function

$$p(X|\theta) = \frac{e^{-\theta}\theta^X}{X!} \qquad (18\text{-}11)$$

To estimate the parameter θ, a small sample was observed: $X = 15$, 8, and 13.

Calculate how the log likelihood varies as θ varies from 5, 10, 15, 20, to 25. Approximately what is the MLE?

SOLUTION

We first calculate the log of the given probability distribution:

$$\log p(X|\theta) = \log \left[\frac{e^{-\theta}\theta^X}{X!}\right]$$

$$= -\theta + X \log \theta - \log X!$$

Thus,

$$\mathcal{L}(\theta) = \Sigma \log p(X_i|\theta) \qquad \text{(18-10) repeated}$$

$$= \sum_{i=1}^{n} (-\theta + X_i \log \theta - \log X_i!)$$

$$= -n\theta + (\Sigma X_i) \log \theta - \Sigma \log X_i!$$

For the given sample, $n = 3$ and $\Sigma X_i = 15 + 8 + 13 = 36$. The last term is $\Sigma \log X_i!$ which does not vary with θ, and so can be ignored. Thus

$$\mathcal{L}(\theta) = -3\theta + 36 \log \theta$$

As θ varies from 5, 10, 15, 20, to 25, we calculate this log likelihood $\mathcal{L}(\theta)$ essentially varies from 42.9, 52.9, 52.5, 47.8, to 40.9.

So $\mathcal{L}(\theta)$ peaks somewhere between $\theta = 10$ and $\theta = 15$, at about 12 or 13. That is, the MLE of θ is approximately 12.

PROBLEMS

18-7 The MLE of the regression slope β (when populations are normal) is just the OLS estimate $b = \Sigma xy/\Sigma x^2$. Does it satisfy asymptotic properties **i**, **ii**, and **iii** listed on page 576?

18-8 Is the MLE estimate of N in (18-8) unbiased? Asymptotically unbiased? (Hint: See Problem 18-6**c**.)

18-9 The waiting time X until the next telephone call arrives at a switchboard has an exponential distribution:

$$p(X) = \theta e^{-\theta X}, \qquad 0 \leq X$$

To estimate the parameter θ, a sample of 5 waiting times (in minutes) were observed: $X = 1.2, 7.5, 1.8, 3.7$, and 0.8.

a. Calculate how the log likelihood varies as θ varies from .1, .2, .3, .4, to .5.

b. Approximately what is the MLE of θ?

***c.** It can be proved that the mean of the population distribution is $\mu = 1/\theta$. Can you guess what the MLE of θ would be for a general sample $(X_1, X_2 \ldots X_n)$?

CHAPTER 18 SUMMARY

18-1 While simple methods of estimation are often adequate, more complex situations require a systematic and powerful method of deriving estimates—which maximum likelihood estimation (MLE) provides.

18-2 In many cases, MLE yields the same estimate as the one we have been using in earlier chapters. (For example, the MLE of the population proportion π is the sample proportion P.) This reassures us that MLE is a reasonable procedure. Even more important, the long list of valuable characteristics of MLE (given in Section 18-4) justifies these earlier estimates.

18-3 Estimating the largest number in a population of serial numbers is an example of a more complex situation when the naive method of moments fails to give a good estimate. Fortunately, MLE gives an excellent estimate—the largest serial number observed in the sample.

18-4 MLE has so many valuable characteristics that it is by far the most popular method of deriving estimates—especially in complicated situations, where computers can calculate good approximations.

REVIEW PROBLEMS

18-10

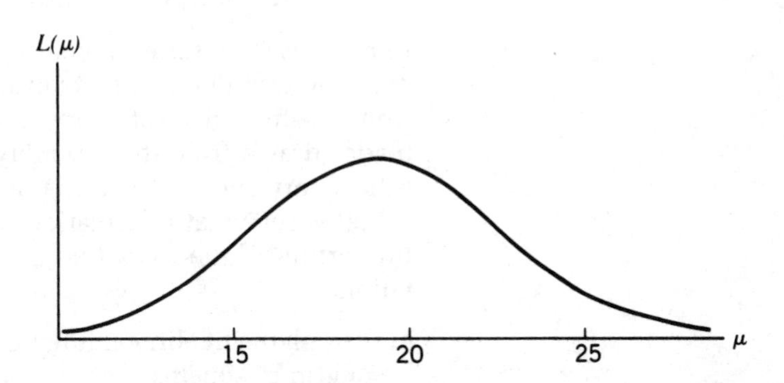

a. Given the likelihood function above, what is the MLE of μ?

b. The given likelihood function in fact is that of a random sample of 3 observations (X = 17, 22, and 18) from a normal population with $\sigma = 6$ and unknown mean μ. What principle does your answer in **a** therefore illustrate?

***c.** Using a computer and the formula (4-26) for the normal distribution, verify that the graph above really does represent the likelihood function in **b**.

18-11 In each of the following cases, calculate the MME and MLE, and state which is better (if they are different):

a. Quality Control randomly sampled six steel bolts from a new production run, and measured their hardness: 4.30, 4.38, 4.18, 4.20, 4.24, and 4.20. Assuming hardness is normally distributed, estimate the mean hardness for the whole run.

b. The same six bolts were tested to see whether their threads were milled with sufficient precision. Four were, but two were not and had to be discarded as defective. Estimate the proportion of defectives in the whole run.

c. As delegates arrived at a convention, they were given serial tags numbered 1, 2, 3, ... A brief walk in the corridor showed 5 tags, numbered 37, 16, 44, 87, 22. Assuming this is a random sample, estimate the total number of delegates.

d. The number of customer complaints at a large department store were carefully recorded for 10 randomly chosen days as follows:

22, 21, 14, 32, 15, 19, 21, 27, 16, 27

Assuming the daily number of complaints for all 310 working days in the year is normally distributed, estimate the total number of complaints for the year.

18-12 *A Final Challenge: For the Whole Story, Look at the Whole Likelihood Function*

In response to a series of complaints about its new model, a large manufacturer of chain saws examined the apparent source of the trouble—the tensile strength of the blade. A random sample of 10 blades drawn from the assembly line included 7 saws that were satisfactory and 3 that were not.

Let us see what information this sample provides about π, the proportion of the saws that are satisfactory in the whole population.

a. Graph the likelihood function (preferably on graph paper with a grid of squares).

b. For what value of π does the likelihood function peak? How is this π related to the sample proportion $P = 7/10$?

c. As well as the likeliest value, we need to know the range of *plausible* values of π. For example, what is the range where the likelihood is fairly large, say 15% or more of its peak value?

d. Alternatively, the range of plausible values of π can be expressed as a confidence interval for π. One way of constructing this (which will be justified in the next chapter) is to use the middle 95% of the area under the likelihood function. Using the grid of squares in **a**, roughly count off $2\frac{1}{2}$% of the area in each tail. What interval does this leave?

e. Finally, look up the classical 95% confidence interval for π in Figure 8-4.

f. Are the three answers in **c**, **d**, and **e** about the same? Then comment on whether this is a fair summary: "The plausible values of π vary roughly from 40% to 90%, with the wide range of uncertainty being due to the small sample size."

g. If Quality Control judges that the range of uncertainty in **f** should be halved before a decision can be made, how much larger must the sample be?

CHAPTER 19

*Bayesian Inference

(Requires Chapter 8)

Life is the art of drawing sufficient conclusions from insufficient premises.

SAMUEL BUTLER

In several places already (especially Chapters 9 and 13), it has become clear that prior belief about a parameter may play a key role in its estimation. Bayesian theory is the means of formally taking such prior information into account.

19-1 POSTERIOR DISTRIBUTIONS

A—CALCULATING POSTERIOR ODDS

The Bayesian theory introduced in Section 3-6 showed how to combine prior information with sample data, to produce posterior probabilities. Since this theory provides the basis for the next two chapters, we will review it, and then extend it.

EXAMPLE 19-1
TESTING A DOUBTFUL CONSIGNMENT

Over the past month, the Radex corporation has produced 200 truckloads of radios, now stored in its warehouse. Initially 44% of the radios were defective in the first 128 "bad" truckloads. After tightening up quality control, the company reduced the defective rate to 15% in the remaining 72 "good" truckloads.

Now suppose you have just been appointed purchaser for a large department store. Your first job is to make a decision on a truckload of radios your store has just received from Radex. You want to know if it's one of the bad truckloads—because if it is, you want to return it.

a. If the information above is all you have, what is the chance the truckload is bad?

b. To test the truckload, you draw a radio at random from it. If this sample radio turns out to be defective, what is the chance the truckload is bad?

SOLUTION

a. The solution is given in Figure 19-1. Its logic is exactly like Figure 3-10, if we keep clear that the "item" being tested and de-

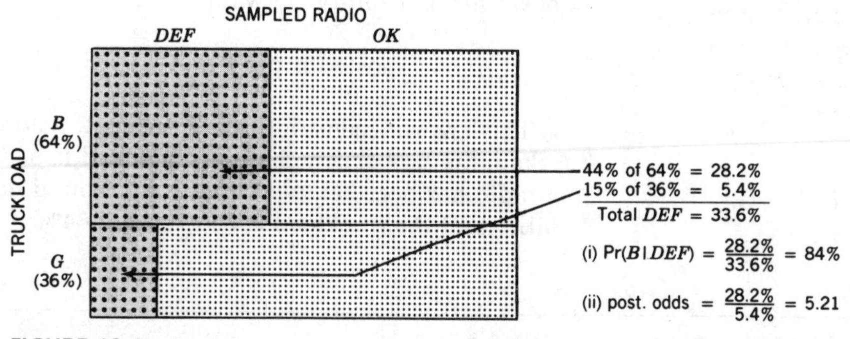

FIGURE 19-1
Bayes Theorem illustrated in a rectangular Venn diagram. Each of the 200 truckloads is shown as a dot, and those whose sampled radio would be defective are shaded in color. (Compare to Figure 3-10.) (i) Calculation of posterior probability (ii) Calculation of posterior odds.

cided on—the typical dot within the rectangle—is now a *truckload* (instead of a single car as in Figure 3-10). And the test now consists of sampling a radio (instead of taking a drive in the car with an expert mechanic).

Some brief notation will be helpful: Let

B = bad truckload $\quad$ DEF = sampled radio defective

G = good truckload $\quad$ OK = sampled radio satisfactory

There were 200 shipments of radios, of which 128 were bad (B) and 72 were good (G). Therefore,

$$\Pr(B) = \frac{128}{200} = .64$$

$$\Pr(G) = \frac{72}{200} = .36$$

These *prior* probabilities (before collecting any sample information) are shown in Figure 19-1 as the two horizontal slabs.

b. Now we are also told that in the bad shipments, 44% of the radios were defective—that is,

$$\Pr(DEF|B) = .44$$

Similarly, in the good shipments, only 15% were defective, that is,

$$\Pr(DEF|G) = .15$$

This information is shown in Figure 19-1 by the blue shading in each slab. The calculations in the margin give us eventually the *posterior* probability we want:

$$\text{posterior probability, } \Pr(B|DEF) = .84 \qquad (19\text{-}1)$$

This answer seems intuitively correct. Before any sample is taken, the probability that the truckload is bad is 64%. But once a radio has been sampled from it and found defective, the probability that the truckload is bad rises to 84%.

EXAMPLE 19-1
ALTERNATIVE SOLUTION, USING ODDS

a. The initial or prior *odds* for a bad truckload are just the *ratio* of bad truckloads to good truckloads:

$$\text{prior odds} = \frac{128}{72} = \frac{.64}{.36} \qquad \text{like (3-27)}$$

b. In Figure 19-1, we take the *ratio* of the two shaded regions (probabilities) to get the posterior odds for a bad truckload:

$$\text{posterior odds} = \frac{.64 \times .44}{.36 \times .15} = 5.21 \qquad (19\text{-}2)$$

If desired, we could recover the posterior probability:

$$\text{posterior probability} = \frac{\text{odds}}{\text{odds} + 1} \qquad \begin{array}{r}(19\text{-}3)\\ \text{like (3-28)}\end{array}$$

$$= \frac{5.21}{6.21} = .84 \qquad \text{(19-1) confirmed}$$

To clarify what we have done in the key equation (19-2), we express it in symbols:

$$\text{posterior odds} = \frac{\Pr(B)}{\Pr(G)} \times \frac{\Pr(DEF|B)}{\Pr(DEF|G)} \qquad (19\text{-}4)$$

To generalize, let θ_1 and θ_2 represent the two states that we are trying to discern (the kind of truckload B or G); and let X_1 represent the sample data (the sampled radio is defective.) Then the generalization of (19-4) is just:

$$\text{posterior odds} = \frac{p(\theta_1)}{p(\theta_2)} \times \frac{p(X_1|\theta_1)}{p(X_1|\theta_2)} \qquad (19\text{-}5)$$

Now the first ratio $p(\theta_1)/p(\theta_2)$ is just the *prior odds*, and the second is called the *likelihood ratio*. Thus (19-5) may be conveniently written as:

$$\boxed{\text{posterior odds} = \text{prior odds} \times \text{likelihood ratio}} \qquad (19\text{-}6)$$

This equation not only is easy to remember, it also shows an important philosophical point: In determining the final posterior odds, we must use both the prior odds and the sample information incorporated in the likelihood ratio. Another example will show how easy it is to use.

EXAMPLE 19-2

To provide early detection for a prevalent form of cancer, a test has been developed. In preliminary trials, its error rates were very small: Among

1000 patients with an early stage of this cancer, only 5 had an erroneous negative test result ("missed alarm"). Among 1000 perfectly healthy patients, only 20 had an erroneous positive test result ("false alarm"). In the population at large, only 1 in every 864 people have this cancer (in its early undetected stage).

Now my best friend has just heard she had a positive reaction. What are the odds she actually has this cancer (rather than a false alarm)?

SOLUTION

We start with the prior odds of 1 to 863—a very long shot. How will the likelihood ratio modify it?

For the likelihood ratio, we must find the likelihood of the observed sample result (positive reaction) under the two different states (cancerous and healthy):

$$\frac{995/1000}{20/1000} = \frac{995}{20} \simeq \frac{50}{1}$$

Then posterior odds = prior odds × likelihood ratio

$$= \frac{1}{863} \times \frac{50}{1} \tag{19-7}$$

$$= .058 \simeq \frac{1}{17}$$

So she can heave a sigh of relief. For every person in her shoes who has cancer, 17 do not.

In this surprising example, equation (19-7) illustrates again how the prior odds and the sample information contained in the likelihood ratio must both be taken into account. In this case, the prior odds of cancer are so tiny (1/863) that even an otherwise frightening sample result (a positive reaction) leaves the posterior odds of cancer small (1/17).

B—CALCULATING POSTERIOR PROBABILITIES

Let us express the fundamental relation (19-6) in more general terms of probability distributions instead of odds.

In calculating posterior probabilities, instead of the two states considered so far in calculating odds (like having cancer or not having it), let θ more generally represent any number of states. Then the posterior (conditional) probability distribution of θ, given the observed sample data X_1, is simply:

$$p(\theta|X_1) = \frac{p(\theta, X_1)}{p(X_1)} \qquad \text{like (3-17)}$$

When we re-express the numerator according to (3-18), we get

$$p(\theta|X_1) = \frac{1}{p(X_1)}\, p(\theta)p(X_1|\theta) \tag{19-8}$$

On the right side, let us look at the three factors one by one. Since the sample data X_1 has been observed, it is given and fixed for the discussion. This means that $p(X_1)$ is a fixed constant too. Next, $p(\theta)$ is the prior distribution incorporating all our prior knowledge about θ. Finally consider the last term $p(X_1|\theta)$; with X_1 fixed while θ varies, it is called the likelihood function as in (18-3).

If we let $\propto$ denote *equals except for a constant*, or *is proportional to*, then we can write out the formula (19-8) for probability distributions in words as,

$$\text{posterior distribution} \propto \text{prior distribution} \times \text{likelihood function}$$

or, more briefly,

$$\textbf{posterior} \propto \textbf{prior} \times \textbf{likelihood} \qquad \text{(19-9) like (19-6)}$$

This is *Bayes Theorem* for posterior distributions, and is illustrated in Figure 19-2. It will be used extensively in the next two sections.

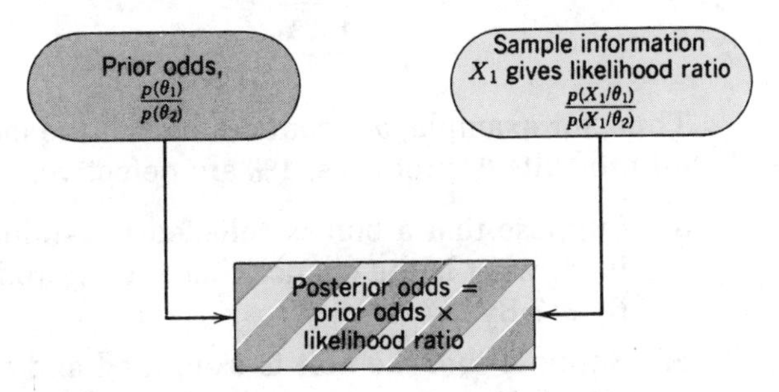

FIGURE 19-2
The logic of Bayes Theorem (compare to Figure 3-11).

PROBLEMS

19-1 A test has been developed to screen for a debilitating childhood disease that affects 620 per 100,000 children. Early trials of the test's reliability were very encouraging: Of 500 children with the disease who were tested, only 5 had an erroneous negative test result; of 2000 children free of the disease who were tested, only 50 had an erroneous positive test result.

To see how effective this test will be for large-scale testing of the whole population, calculate:

a. If a child has a positive reaction, what are the odds that he actually has the disease? And what is the probability?

b. If a child has a negative test reaction, now what are the odds that he has the disease? And what is the probability?

c. If the test for the disease had no error at all, what would be the probabilities in **a** and **b**?

19-2 You are in charge of the nationwide leasing of Q-cars, and discover that your service agent in Chicago has not been reliable: He has shortcut his servicing in the past about 1/10 of the time. Whenever such shortcutting occurs, the probability that an individual will cancel a lease increases from .2 to .5.

If an individual has canceled a lease, what are the odds that he or she received shortcut servicing? And what is the probability?

19-3 A factory has three machines (θ_1, θ_2, and θ_3) making bolts. The newer the machine, the larger and more accurate it is, according to the following table:

Machine	*Proportion of Total Output Produced by This Machine*	*Rate of Defective Bolts*
θ_1 (Oldest)	10%	5%
θ_2	40%	2%
θ_3 (Newest)	50%	1%
	100%✓	

Thus, for example, θ_3 produces half of the factory's output; and of all the bolts θ_3 produces, 1% are defective.

a. Suppose that a bolt is selected at random; Before it is examined, what is the chance that it was produced by machine θ_1? By θ_2? By θ_3?

b. Suppose that the bolt is examined and found to be defective; *after* this examination, what is the chance that it was produced by machine θ_1? By θ_2? By θ_3?

19-2 THE POPULATION PROPORTION π

A—EXAMPLE

Now we shall apply the general principle (19-9) to an example in which there are many, many states of nature θ, each one being a proportion π.

EXAMPLE 19-3

Let us consider a variation of the Radex problem in Example 19-1. Suppose now that the truckloads of radios are not just good or bad, but have a wide variety of proportions π of defective radios, as recorded in the first 3 columns of Table 19-1.

a. Graph this prior distribution of π.

b. Now suppose that you take a random sample of $n = 5$ radios out of the truckload you have received, in order to get sample evidence on π; and further suppose that 3 of these 5 turn out to be defective. Using (19-9), calculate the posterior distribution of π, and graph it.

c. Suppose that your department store will regard this truckload of radios as acceptable only if π is less than 25%. What is the probability of this:

i. Before the sample?

ii. After the sample?

SOLUTION

a. The prior distribution of π is given in the third column of Table 19-1, and graphed in Figure 19-3.

TABLE 19-1 Calculating the Posterior Distribution of a Population Proportion π

(a) Given Prior Distribution for π			(b) Calculations to Obtain Posterior Distribution		
(1) Proportion (Probability) Defective π	(2) Number of Shipments	(3) Relative Number of Shipments	(4) Likelihood of π (From Table IIIb, Given Sample $n = 5$, $S = 3$)	(5) Prior Times Likelihood (3) × (4)	(6) Dividing by .160, Yields Posterior
0%	2	.01	0	0	0
10%	30	.15	.008	.001	.01
20%	40	.20	.051	.010	.06
30%	42	.21	.132	.027	.17
40%	34	.17	.230	.039	.24
50%	26	.13	.313	.041	.25
60%	16	.08	.346	.028	.18
70%	8	.04	.309	.012	.08
80%	2	.01	.205	.002	.01
90%	0	0	.073	0	0
100%	0	0	0	0	0
	200	1.00✓		.160	1.00✓

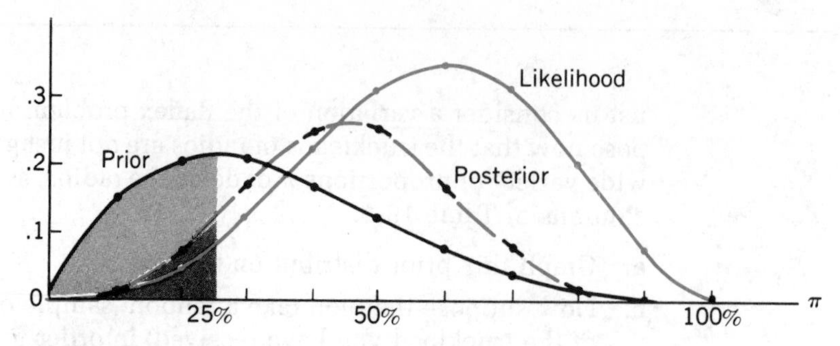

FIGURE 19-3
The prior distribution and likelihood function (based on sample information) are multiplied together to give the compromise posterior distribution of π.

b. To calculate the posterior distribution using (19-9), we will first need the likelihood function—that is, the likelihood of getting the 3 defectives that we observed in our sample of 5. This, of course, is given by the binomial formula, for a fixed $S = 3$, and various values of π. The easiest way to obtain it is to read Table IIIb horizontally along the row where $n = 5$ and $S = 3$ (obtaining the same likelihood function as in Figure 18-1). We record it in column (4) of Table 19-1, and graph it in Figure 19-3.

Now, following (19-9), we multiply the likelihood function in Table 19-1 by the prior distribution. This gives us the posterior distribution in column (5), except that it does not sum to 1. To achieve this, we divide all the probabilities in this column by .160 [just as we divided by $p(X_1)$ in the fundamental Bayesian Theorem (19-8)]. The result is the posterior distribution in the last column of Table 19-1, which we also graph in Figure 19-3.

c. In Figure 19-3 and Table 19-1 we see that $\pi < 25\%$ means a π value of 0, 10%, or 20%.

i. From column (3) of Table 19-1, the prior probability of less than 25% defectives is:

$$\Pr(\pi < 25\%) = .01 + .15 + .20 = .36$$

ii. From the last column of Table 19-1, the posterior probability is:

$$\Pr(\pi < 25\% | S = 3) = 0 + .01 + .06 = .07$$

Thus the sample, with its large proportion of defectives, has lowered the probability that this is an acceptable shipment from .36 to .07.

This example displays several features that will be found to be generally true:

1. In Figure 19-3 we see that the posterior distribution is a compromise, peaking between the prior distribution and the likelihood function.
2. If we had multiplied either the prior or the likelihood by some convenient constant, it merely would have changed the second-last column of Table 19-1 by the same constant. But the adjusted or "normed" values in the last column would be exactly as before. Accordingly:

Multiplying the prior or likelihood by a convenient constant does not affect the posterior. (19-10)

3. The problem as stated had discrete values for π (0, .1, .2, ...). However, this was just a convenient way of tabulating a variable π that really is continuous. So we have sketched all the graphs in Figure 19-3 as continuous.[1]

B—GENERALIZATION

To generalize Example 19-3, let us consider first the possible prior distributions for π. There is a whole family of distributions, called the β distributions, that serve as a convenient approximation for many of the priors that we might encounter in practice; and their formula is very simple:

$$\beta \text{ distribution for the prior, } p(\pi) \propto \pi^a(1 - \pi)^b \qquad (19\text{-}11)$$

This formula was deliberately chosen to be of the same form as the likelihood function (19-12) below, and is called the *conjugate* prior. This similarity will prove very convenient in the subsequent calculation of the posterior distribution.

In (19-11), the parameters a and b may be any numbers, although positive small integers are most common. For example, you can verify that the prior in column (3) of Table 19-1 is approximately the β distribution with $a = 1$ and $b = 3$:

$$p(\pi) \propto \pi(1 - \pi)^3$$

[1] Is it really legitimate to shift the argument back and forth between discrete and continuous models? For our purposes, yes. The essential difference between a discrete probability function and the analogous continuous probability density is simply a constant multiplier (the constant being the cell width, as shown in (4-14)). And constant multipliers do not really matter, as stated in (19-10), above.

Next, to generalize the likelihood function, consider a sample of n observations that results in S "successes" and F "failures" (where $F = n - S$, of course). The likelihood function then is given by the general binomial formula:

$$p(S|\pi) = \binom{n}{S} \pi^S(1 - \pi)^F \qquad \text{like (4-8)}$$

Since the sample has already been observed and only π is viewed as variable, we can write this more briefly as:

$$\text{likelihood } L(\pi) \propto \pi^S(1 - \pi)^F \qquad (19\text{-}12)$$

When the prior (19-11) is multiplied by the likelihood (19-12), we obtain the posterior:

$$\begin{aligned} p(\pi|S) &\propto \pi^a(1 - \pi)^b \pi^S(1 - \pi)^F \\ &\propto \pi^{a+S}(1 - \pi)^{b+F} \end{aligned}$$

The logic of this posterior is so simple and so useful that it is worth reviewing briefly:

$$\left.\begin{array}{ll} \textit{If} \text{ prior} & \propto \pi^a(1 - \pi)^b \\ \textit{and} \text{ likelihood} & \propto \pi^S(1 - \pi)^F \\ \textit{Then} \text{ posterior} & \propto \pi^{a+S}(1 - \pi)^{b+F} \end{array}\right\} \qquad (19\text{-}13)$$

Thus we see the real advantage of using a conjugate prior (19-11), of the same form as the likelihood (19-12). In (19-13) it greatly simplifies the derivation of the posterior distribution. In fact, all three distributions—prior, likelihood, and posterior—now have the same β function form. Furthermore, many such β functions are already tabulated, by reading *across* Table IIIb (ignoring the constant binomial coefficient, which does not really matter). This greatly reduces the computations, as the next example illustrates.

EXAMPLE 19-4

Referring back to Example 19-3, suppose Radex has much improved its quality control. In fact, the prior distribution has so improved that it now may be approximated with a β function with $a = 0$, and $b = 4$:

$$p(\pi) \propto \pi^0(1 - \pi)^4$$

Suppose, however, that the sample turns out the same way (3 defectives out of 5). Graph the prior, the likelihood, and the posterior.

SOLUTION

As already remarked in (19-10), we may ignore constants such as binomial coefficients, which do not depend on π.

First we extract each distribution from the appropriate row of Table III*b*. For example, the likelihood function is $L(\pi) \propto \pi^3(1-\pi)^2$, found in Table III*b*—under $n = 5$ and $S = 3$. The prior distribution is $p(\pi) \propto \pi^0(1-\pi)^4$, which we can also find in Table III*b*—under $n = 4$ and $S = 0$. Finally, the posterior distribution is given by (19-13) as:

$$p(\pi|S) \propto \pi^3(1-\pi)^6 \tag{19-14}$$

Again, we can find this in Table III*b*—under $S = 3$ and $n = 3 + 6 = 9$. These three distributions are copied down for easy reference:

π	0	.1	.2	.3	.4	.5	.6	.7	.8	.9	1.0
$L(\pi)$	0	.008	.051	.132	.230	.313	.346	.309	.205	.073	0
$p(\pi)$	1.00	.656	.410	.240	.130	.063	.026	.008	.002	.000	0
$p(\pi/S)$	0	.045	.176	.267	.251	.164	.074	.021	.003	.000	0

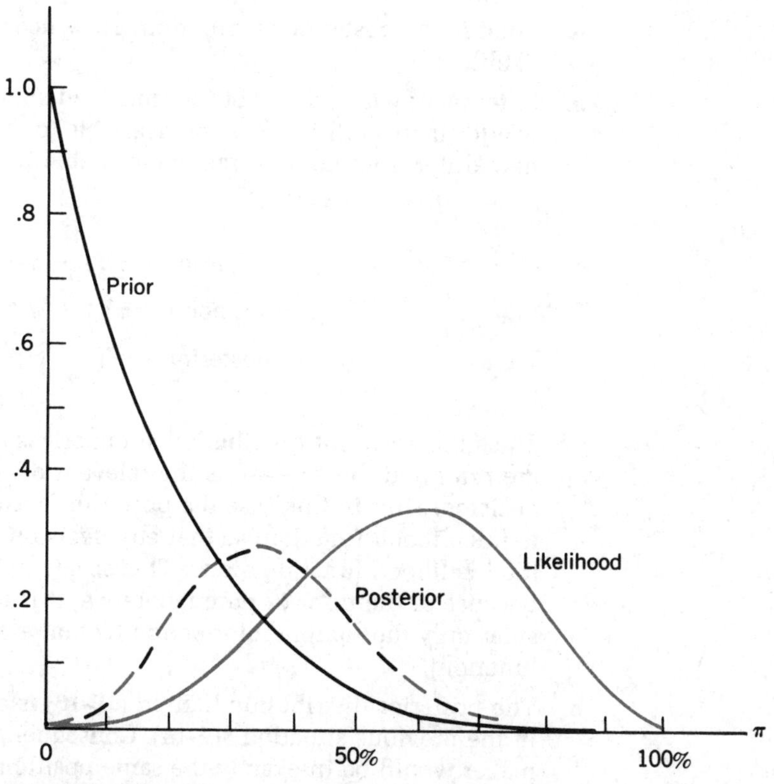

FIGURE 19-4
Different prior, hence different posterior, than in Figure 19-3.

The graphs of all three distributions are given in Figure 19-4. Note again that the posterior is a compromise, peaking between the prior and the likelihood.

C—THE PRIOR AS A QUASI-SAMPLE

The posterior formula (19-13) is very convenient not only for computations, but also to illustrate advantages of the Bayesian approach—as an example will illustrate:

EXAMPLE 19-5

In Example 19-4, suppose now our prior view is that all possible values of π are equally likely. That is, the prior distribution is completely flat, and thus might be called the *prior of pure ignorance*. It can be represented by a special β function, with $a = b = 0$:

$$p(\pi) \propto \pi^0(1 - \pi)^0 \tag{19-15}$$

Let us also suppose that a larger sample of $n = 9$ observations was taken, and had $S = 3$ defective radios.

a. What is the posterior distribution? How does it compare to the likelihood?

b. In terms of whether or not the truckload should be returned, how would the overall information available to the decision-maker here differ from the information available in Example 19-4?

SOLUTION

a.

$$\text{prior} \propto \pi^0(1 - \pi)^0$$

$$\text{likelihood} \propto \pi^3(1 - \pi)^6$$

Thus

$$\text{posterior} \propto \pi^3(1 - \pi)^6 \tag{19-16}$$

like (19-13)

Since the posterior distribution summarizes all the information—the prior and the data—it is the relevant distribution for making decisions. But in this case the posterior is exactly the same as the likelihood function, so that any decision should be based on the likelihood function alone. This seems intuitively correct: Because of the prior of pure ignorance, it is appropriate to consider only the sample information (contained in the likelihood function).

b. The posterior distribution here in (19-16) is exactly the same as in the previous situation (19-14). Consequently, the decision-maker would be in exactly the same position—absolutely no difference.

In Example 19-5, we combined a kind of informationless prior with a relatively large sample of 9 observations. On the other hand, in Example 19-4 we started with information in the prior, and a sample of 4 fewer observations. But in both cases, we got the same posterior distribution; and therefore the same decision about the shipment in the warehouse. So the prior in Example 19-4 may be thought of as providing exactly the same information as an extra 4 observations.

In terms of its impact on decision-making, we can therefore think of the prior distribution as equivalent to an additional sample—and so we call it a *quasi-sample.* In general, the prior distribution in (19-13) can be considered a quasi-sample of a successes and b failures, to be combined with the actual sample of S successes and F failures.

The concept of the quasi-sample makes the point of this chapter very clear: Ignoring prior information is like throwing away sample data.

D—CONFIDENCE INTERVALS

A Bayesian 95% confidence interval for π can be constructed by finding the interval that contains 95% of the posterior distribution. In this posterior distribution (19-13), the total number of "successes" is $(a + S)$—the quasi successes in the prior, plus the real successes in the sample. More precisely,

$$\left.\begin{aligned} \text{let} \qquad & S^* \equiv a + S + 1 \\ \text{and likewise,} \quad & F^* \equiv b + F + 1 \end{aligned}\right\} \qquad (19\text{-}17)$$

The extra 1 "success" and 1 "failure" are mathematical quirks, which, if you like, you can think of as a "bonus" for using this ingenious Bayesian technique. Then we naturally continue defining:

$$\left.\begin{aligned} n^* &\equiv S^* + F^* \\ P^* &\equiv \frac{S^*}{n^*} \end{aligned}\right\} \qquad (19\text{-}18)$$

In these terms, the Bayesian confidence interval is easily stated (and proved, in Appendix 19-2). It is just like the classical confidence interval, using P^* and n^* instead of P and n:

Bayesian 95% confidence interval:

$$\pi = P^* \pm 1.96 \sqrt{\frac{P^*(1 - P^*)}{n^*}} \qquad (19\text{-}19)$$

like (8-27)

Like the classical confidence interval, this formula requires S^* and F^* to be each at least 5.

EXAMPLE 19-6

In a sample taken from a shipment of radios, 6 were defective and 14 okay.

a. Calculate the 95% classical confidence interval for the proportion of defectives in the shipment.

b. Suppose the records of past shipments showed relatively few defectives, and could be approximated by the prior distribution

$$p(\pi) \propto \pi^1(1-\pi)^9$$

Calculate the 95% Bayesian confidence interval. How is it different from the classical?

SOLUTION

a. The sample proportion is $P = 6/(6+14) = .30$. Hence the 95% confidence interval is:

$$\pi = P \pm 1.96\sqrt{\frac{P(1-P)}{n}} \qquad \text{(8-27) repeated}$$

$$= .30 \pm 1.96\sqrt{\frac{.30(.70)}{20}}$$

$$= .30 \pm .20$$

b. To get the Bayesian 95% confidence interval, we first calculate:

$$\left.\begin{aligned} S^* &= S + a + 1 = 6 + 1 + 1 = 8 \\ F^* &= F + b + 1 = 14 + 9 + 1 = 24 \end{aligned}\right\} \qquad \text{(19-17) repeated}$$

Then

$$\left.\begin{aligned} n^* &= S^* + F^* = 8 + 24 = 32 \\ P^* &= \frac{S^*}{n^*} = \frac{8}{32} = .25 \end{aligned}\right\} \qquad \text{(19-18) repeated}$$

Hence the 95% confidence interval is:

$$\pi = P^* \pm 1.96\sqrt{\frac{P^*(1-P^*)}{n^*}} \qquad \text{(19-19) repeated}$$

$$= .25 \pm 1.96\sqrt{\frac{.25(.75)}{32}}$$

$$= .25 \pm .15$$

Because it exploits prior information, the Bayesian interval is centered better (at a compromise) and is more precise than the classical interval.

PROBLEMS

19-4 A proposed blood bank needed to estimate the proportion π of its blood donations that would be unsatisfactory (due to hepatitis, AIDS, or other reasons). The records of 24 similar banks showed their proportions π tended to be quite small, with a distribution roughly given by

$$p(\pi) \propto \pi(1 - \pi)^4$$

a. Graph this distribution.

b. In a random sample of 5 prospective donors from the neighborhood where this blood bank was proposed, 3 provided unsatisfactory blood. Show graphically how this evidence changes the range of plausible values of π.

c. Calculate the Bayesian 95% confidence interval for π. Show it on the graph in part **b.** Does it seem to cut about $2\frac{1}{2}$% from each tail of the posterior distribution?

19-5 In Problem 19-4, suppose a larger sample of 50 prospective donors was taken, with 30 providing unsatisfactory blood.

a. How would you expect the Bayesian 95% confidence interval to be different from:

i. The former answer in Problem 19-4?

ii. The classical 95% confidence interval?

b. Calculate the Bayesian and classical confidence intervals to confirm your expectations in **a.**

19-6 The manager of a newly opened franchise for auto brake relining wanted to estimate what proportion π of his customers would also need their steering aligned. If π was high enough, he planned to offer alignment as an additional service.

a. He randomly sampled 40 customers, and inspection showed 8 of them did indeed need alignment. What is the 95% confidence interval for π?

b. Fortunately, the experience of 86 other franchised shops was available to the manager on request. After eliminating the 11 shops that clearly serviced a different clientele from his own, the remaining 75 shops showed values of π ranging from .15 to

.63. In fact, a relative frequency histogram of these values of π showed it was approximated by the function $280\pi^3(1 - \pi)^7$.
What is the Bayesian 95% confidence interval for π?

19-3 THE MEAN μ IN A NORMAL MODEL

A—EXAMPLE

Once more, we shall apply the general principle (19-9), this time to estimate the mean μ in a normal model.

EXAMPLE 19-7

Steelco sells thousands of shipments of steel beams. Within each shipment, the breaking strengths of the beams are distributed normally around a mean μ, with standard deviation $\sigma = 17.3$. But μ changes from shipment to shipment because of poor quality control. In fact, suppose that when all shipment means μ are recorded in a bar graph, the result is Figure 19-5. That is, the distribution of μ is approximately normal, with mean $\mu_0 = 60$ and standard deviation $\sigma_0 = 10$. This is our prior information.

Now suppose we have received one specific shipment of beams from Steelco, and have to estimate its mean strength μ. (If μ is too low, we should return the shipment.) To estimate μ, we take a random sample of 12 beams from the shipment, and $\overline{X}$ turns out to be 70.

a. Sketch the likelihood function.

b. Sketch the posterior distribution obtained by multiplying the prior distribution of Figure 19-5 by the likelihood function.

c. Suppose that the shipment must be regarded as unsatisfactory if μ is less than 62.5. What would you say is the probability of this, as estimated from the sketched distributions:

  i. Before the sample was taken?

  ii. After the sample?

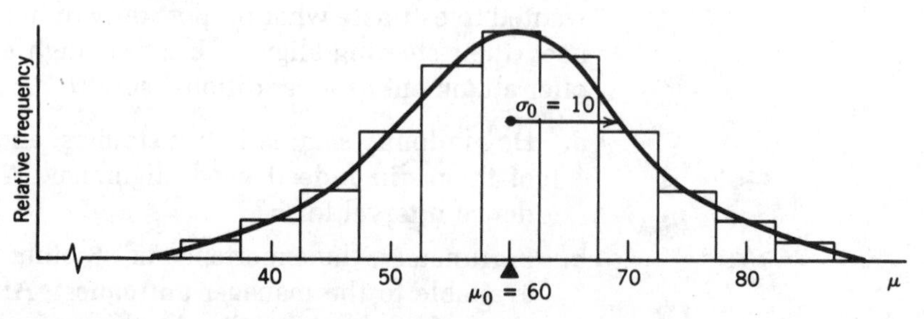

FIGURE 19-5
The distribution of shipment means is approximately normal.

SOLUTION

a. What is the likelihood of getting $\overline{X} = 70$? The distribution of $\overline{X}$ is normal, with standard error $\sigma/\sqrt{n} = 17.3/\sqrt{12} = 5.0$. Thus its equation is[2]:

$$p(\overline{X}|\mu) \propto e^{-\frac{1}{2}\left(\frac{\overline{X}-\mu}{5}\right)^2} \quad (19\text{-}20)$$

like (4-26)

where $\overline{X} = 70$, and μ is regarded as the variable. As usual, to emphasize its dependence on μ, we rename (19-20) the likelihood function:

$$L(\mu) \propto e^{-\frac{1}{2}\left(\frac{\mu-70}{5}\right)^2} \quad (19\text{-}21)$$

We recognize this likelihood as a normal curve, centered at 70 with a standard deviation of 5. We roughly sketch its graph in Figure 19-6*b*. [To do so, we recall from Figure 4-10 that a normal curve contains about 2/3 (68%) of its area within one standard deviation (in this case, 5 units) of its center, and 95% of its area within two standard deviations.]

b. The prior distribution in Figure 19-5 is similarly graphed in Figure 19-6*a*.

For the posterior distribution, we must multiply the prior times the likelihood. We do this for several values[3] of μ, to obtain several points on the posterior distribution. From them, we sketch the graph of the posterior distribution shown in Figure 19-6*c*.

c. **i.** Before the sample is taken, the probability that μ is below 62.5 must be estimated from the only available information—the prior. This probability, shown as the shaded area in Figure 19-6*a*, is approximately 60%.

ii. After the sample is taken, the best available information is the posterior. The desired probability, shown as the shaded area in Figure 19-6*c*, is approximately 10%.

In this example, the posterior seems to be distributed normally, which is no surprise, since it is the product of a normal prior and normal likelihood. (This is just like our previous example: the posterior distribution

---

[2] For simplicity, we have ignored the constant multiplier $1/\sqrt{2\pi}\,\sigma$ in the normal distribution, so we can plot it with a maximum value of 1. In view of (19-10), this will not essentially affect the posterior.

[3] For example, consider $\mu = 65$ shown in Figure 19-6. We read off the prior probability (.9) and likelihood (.6) from the first two graphs. Their product, $.9 \times .6 = .54$, is the desired posterior in the third graph.

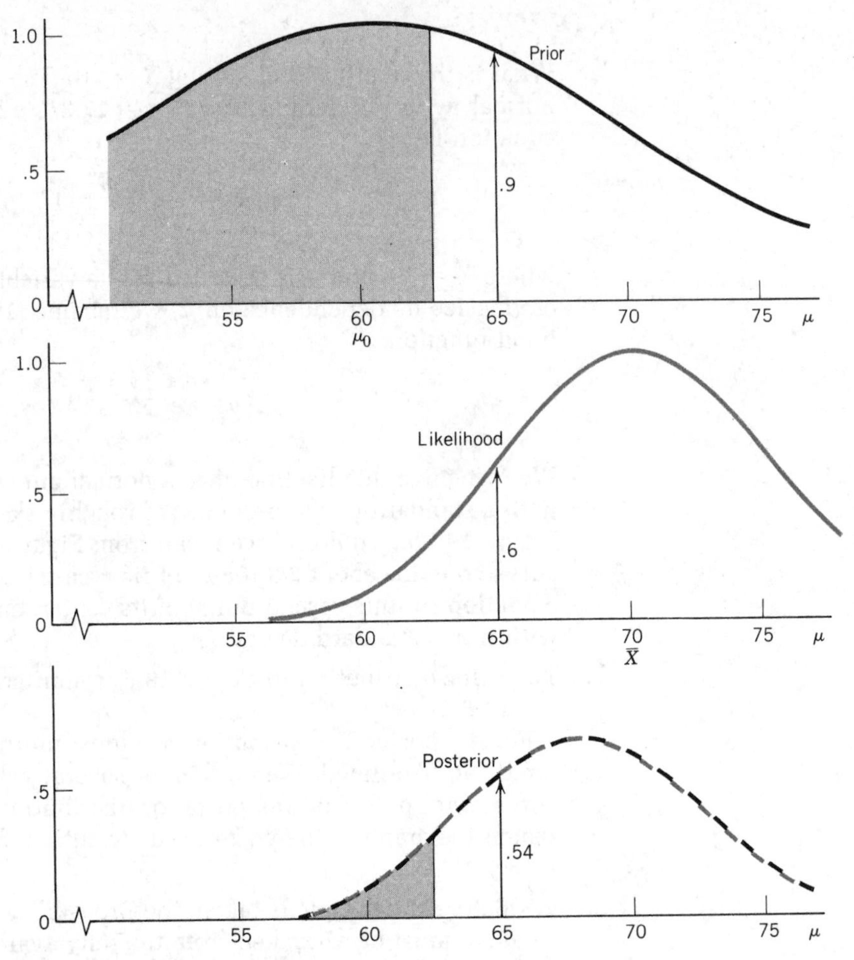

FIGURE 19-6
The prior distribution and likelihood function are multiplied to give the compromise posterior distribution of μ.

for π was a β-function, just like the prior and likelihood.) Again, we note that the posterior peaks between the prior and the likelihood, and that it is closer to the likelihood, the curve with the least variance. That is, the more concentrated curve, which accordingly provides the more precise and reliable information, has the greater influence in determining the posterior.

B—GENERALIZATION

The features of Figure 19-6 are generally true, and may be expressed with convenient formulas. We calculate the posterior distribution of μ from two pieces of information:

1. The *actual* sample centered at $\bar{X}$, which gives us the likelihood function.
2. The prior distribution, which is *equivalent* to additional sample information, called the quasi-sample.

The concept of the quasi-sample has already been encountered (in estimating π in Section 19-2). Of course, the prior distribution is not really a sample. But its effect on the posterior distribution is exactly equivalent to the effect of an additional sample with a certain number (n_0, say) of observations. And the quasi-sample will provide a nice intuitive way to understand and remember the formulas. (The proofs are given in Appendix 19-3).

The quasi-sample would, of course, be centered on the prior mean μ_0. But how many quasi-observations n_0 should we say it contains? That is, how heavily should we weight the quasi-sample when we combine it with the actual sample? The smaller the prior variance σ_0^2 (relative to σ^2), the more certainty or information is contained in the prior; consequently the larger n_0 will be:[4]

$$n_0 = \frac{\sigma^2}{\sigma_0^2} \tag{19-22}$$

When the n_0 quasi-observations centered at the prior mean μ_0 are combined with the n actual observations centered at $\bar{X}$, the overall posterior mean is the weighted average:

$$\text{Posterior mean} = \frac{n_0\mu_0 + n\bar{X}}{n_0 + n} \qquad \begin{matrix}(19\text{-}23)\\ \text{like } (2\text{-}7)\end{matrix}$$

Since the total number of observations is $n_0 + n$, the standard error is correspondingly reduced:[5]

$$\text{Posterior standard error} = \frac{\sigma}{\sqrt{n_0 + n}} \qquad \begin{matrix}(19\text{-}24)\\ \text{like } (6\text{-}7)\end{matrix}$$

---

[4] Of course, σ^2—the variance of the population from which we are sampling—is typically not known, so in practice we use the sample s^2 to estimate it. But we use σ^2 here to make the argument more transparent.

[5] Why doesn't σ_0^2 appear in this formula? Implicitly it does, because (19-22) defined n_0 in terms of σ_0^2.

Finally, when the prior is normal and the likelihood is normal (by the Normal Approximation Rule), then the posterior can be shown to be normal too. An example will illustrate these formulas.

EXAMPLE 19-8

Let us rework Example 19-7 with formulas instead of graphs.

a. Express the value of the prior distribution in terms of quasi-observations.

b. Calculate the posterior distribution.

c. Calculate the probability that μ is below 62.5:

  i. Before the sample is taken.

  ii. After the sample has been taken.

SOLUTION

a.

$$n_0 = \frac{\sigma^2}{\sigma_0^2} \qquad \text{(19-22) repeated}$$

$$= \frac{17.3^2}{10^2} = \frac{300}{100} = 3$$

That is, the prior distribution is equivalent to 3 observations.

b. The posterior is normal, with:

$$\text{Posterior mean} = \frac{n_0\mu_0 + n\overline{X}}{n_0 + n} \qquad \text{(19-23) repeated}$$

$$= \frac{3(60) + 12(70)}{3 + 12} = 68 \qquad \text{(19-25)}$$

$$\text{Posterior standard error} = \frac{\sigma}{\sqrt{n_0 + n}} \qquad \text{(19-24) repeated}$$

$$= \frac{17.3}{\sqrt{3 + 12}} = 4.5 \qquad \text{(19-26)}$$

c. **i.** Before the sample, we use the prior distribution. The standardized Z value is, therefore:

$$Z = \frac{\mu - \mu_0}{\sigma_0} = \frac{62.5 - 60}{10} = .25$$

Thus

$$\Pr(\mu < 62.5) = \Pr(Z < .25) = 1 - .401 = .599$$
$$= 60\%$$

ii. After the sample, we use the posterior distribution calculated in **b**. Then:

$$Z = \frac{62.5 - 68}{4.5} = -1.22$$

Thus

$$\Pr(\mu < 62.5) = \Pr(Z < -1.22) = .111$$
$$= 11\%$$

Note that the precise answers calculated from formulas in Example 19-8 correspond very nicely to the rough graphical answers that we found before in Example 19-7. Since the formulas are easier and more accurate, from now on we shall use them instead of graphs.

C—CONFIDENCE INTERVALS

Since the posterior distribution of μ is normal, 95% of its probability lies within ±1.96 standard deviations from its mean. This gives us:

Bayesian 95% confidence interval for a mean, assuming a normal prior:

$$\mu = \left(\frac{n_0\mu_0 + n\overline{X}}{n_0 + n}\right) \pm 1.96 \frac{\sigma}{\sqrt{n_0 + n}} \qquad (19\text{-}27) \text{ like } (8\text{-}9)$$

where, as always, $n_0 = \sigma^2/\sigma_0^2$. An example will illustrate:

EXAMPLE 19-9

For Example 19-8 calculate:

a. The classical 95% confidence interval.

b. The Bayesian 95% confidence interval.

SOLUTION

a.

$$\mu = \overline{X} \pm 1.96 \frac{\sigma}{\sqrt{n}} \qquad \text{like (8-9)}$$

$$= 70 \pm 1.96 \frac{17.3}{\sqrt{12}} = 70 \pm 10$$

b. Substitute (19-25) and (19-26) into (19-27):

$$\mu = 68 \pm 1.96(4.5) = 68 \pm 9 \qquad (19\text{-}28)$$

Because it exploits prior information, the Bayesian interval is centered better (at a compromise between $\overline{X} = 70$ and $\mu_0 = 60$), and is more precise than the classical interval.

PROBLEMS

19-7 Continuing Example 19-7, suppose the sample size is $n = 48$ instead of $n = 12$, but everything else is the same, namely: a normal prior with $\mu_0 = 60$, $\sigma_0 = 10$; and the n observations fluctuate with $\sigma = 17.3$, and have a mean $\overline{X} = 70$.

a. Graph the likelihood function, as well as the old prior.

b. Where does the likelihood function peak? What is this number called?

c. Graph the posterior also. Does the posterior peak between the prior and likelihood? Which is the posterior closer to? How much closer?

c. Calculate the classical and Bayesian 95% confidence intervals for μ, and comment on their difference.

19-8 Repeat Problem 19-7, if the sample size is $n = 2$.

19-9 From your experience in Problems 19-7 and 19-8, answer True or False; if False, correct it:

The Bayesian confidence interval is very similar to the classical when n is small. It is only when n grows large that the Bayesian confidence interval shows its real superiority to the classical.

19-10 An engineer was asked to estimate the mean breaking strength of a new shipment of cables. A large number of past shipments had varied considerably in their mean strength μ, which fluctuated around 3400 with a standard deviation of 100.

The engineer decided that this past record was so variable that further evidence was required, so he sampled the new shipment, obtaining the following 5 breaking strengths:

3600, 3300, 3500, 3700, 3900

a. What is the best estimate of the new shipment mean μ? What assumptions is it based upon?

b. Construct an interval around your estimate, wide enough so as to be 95% certain to contain the actual μ.

19-11 The value of wheat falls as its moisture content increases, as measured by the electrical conductivity of the wheat. Suppose the measured moisture value is distributed normally about the true value, with an error that has a standard deviation of only one-fifth of a percentage point.

Suppose that the loads of wheat that are brought to a grain elevator during a certain week have moisture contents m varying from 14% to 16%, roughly; specifically, the values of m are distributed normally about a mean of 15%, with a standard deviation of half a percentage point.

If one such load has a measured value of 13.8%, its true value m may be slightly different, of course. Specifically,

a. Find the Bayesian 95% confidence interval for m.

b. What is the probability that m is less than 14%?

19-4 THE SLOPE β IN NORMAL REGRESSION

Our treatment of the simple regression slope β will be very similar to the population mean μ in the previous section. We assume, for example, that the prior distribution of β is normal, with mean β_0 and standard deviation σ_0.

A sample of n observations (X,Y) gives further information about β, summarized by the estimate $b = \Sigma xy/\Sigma x^2$. To measure the reliability of b, we need σ (the standard deviation of the Y values about the line), and also σ_X (the standard deviation of the X values[6]). In fact, their ratio (σ/σ_X) plays the same role as σ formerly played for μ. Specifically, the amount of information in the prior is described by the size n_0 of the quasi-sample:

$$n_0 = \frac{(\sigma/\sigma_X)^2}{\sigma_0^2} \qquad \text{(19-29) like (19-22)}$$

[6] Of course, both σ and σ_X are typically unknown, and have to be estimated with s and s_X (just as σ was estimated with s in footnote 4 earlier).

When the n_0 quasi-observations centered at β_0 are combined with the n actual observations in the sample (from which b was calculated), the result is the weighted average (as proved in Appendix 19-4):

$$\textbf{Mean of the posterior distribution of } \beta = \frac{n_0\beta_0 + nb}{n_0 + n} \qquad \text{(19-30) like (19-23)}$$

Since the total number of observations is $n_0 + n$, and noting again that σ/σ_X plays the former role of σ,

$$\textbf{SE of the posterior distribution of } \beta = \frac{\sigma/\sigma_X}{\sqrt{n_0 + n}} \qquad \text{(19-31) like (19-24) and (12-6)}$$

When the prior and likelihood are normal, the posterior can also be shown to be normal. Then any desired probability can be calculated from the normal table, and a 95% confidence interval can be determined:

Bayesian 95% confidence interval for a regression slope, assuming a normal prior:

$$\beta = \left(\frac{n_0\beta_0 + nb}{n_0 + n}\right) \pm 1.96 \frac{\sigma/\sigma_X}{\sqrt{n_0 + n}} \qquad \text{(19-32)}$$

An example will illustrate:

EXAMPLE 19-10

Suppose that the prior distribution for a regression slope β is normal with a central value of 5.0 and a standard deviation of .50. In addition, suppose that a sample of 8 observations of (X,Y) are taken, and yield the following statistics:

$$\Sigma xy = 2100, \quad \Sigma x^2 = 350, \quad \text{residual } s = 12.7$$

To be more realistic than in our earlier examples, let us now suppose σ is unknown, so that s will replace σ where necessary, and correspondingly, $t_{.025}$ will replace 1.96. Then find:

a. The classical 95% confidence interval.

b. The Bayesian 95% confidence interval. How does it compare?

SOLUTION

a.

$$b = \frac{\Sigma xy}{\Sigma x^2} = \frac{2100}{350} = 6.0$$

Also, d.f. = n − 2 = 8 − 2 = 6, so that $t_{.025} = 2.45$. Thus the 95% classical confidence interval is

$$\beta = b \pm t_{.025} \frac{s}{\sqrt{\Sigma x^2}}$$
$$= 6.0 \pm 2.45 \frac{12.7}{\sqrt{350}}$$
$$= 6.0 \pm 1.7$$

b. In standard notation, the prior information is:

$$\beta_0 = 5.0$$
$$\sigma_0 = .50$$

In the sample, we estimate σ with s = 12.7, and σ_X with $s_X = \sqrt{\Sigma x^2/(n-1)} = \sqrt{350/7} = 7.1$. Hence the quasi-sample size (reflecting the strength of the prior) is:

$$n_0 = \frac{(\sigma/\sigma_X)^2}{\sigma_0^2} \qquad \text{(19-29) repeated}$$
$$\simeq \frac{(12.7/7.1)^2}{.50^2} \simeq 13$$

Because of the replacement throughout of σ by s, we need to replace 1.96 with $t_{.025}$ in the confidence interval. Since the total number of observations $n_0 + n = 13 + 8 = 21$, we have d.f. = 21 − 2 = 19, and hence $t_{.025} = 2.09$. Thus the Bayesian 95% confidence interval is

$$\beta = \frac{n_0\beta_0 + nb}{n_0 + n} \pm t_{.025} \frac{s/s_X}{\sqrt{n_0 + n}} \qquad \text{like (19-32)}$$
$$= \frac{13(5.0) + 8(6.0)}{13 + 8} \pm 2.09 \frac{12.7/7.1}{\sqrt{13 + 8}}$$
$$= 5.4 \pm 0.8$$

Because it exploits prior information, the Bayesian interval is centered better (at a compromise), and is more precise than the classical interval.

Bayesian techniques can easily be applied to multiple regression, too. The theory is basically the same, but the calculations are best left to a computer, of course.

PROBLEM

19-12 A consulting economist was given a prior distribution for a regression slope β (a marginal propensity to save) that was distributed normally about a mean of .20 with a standard deviation of .08. Calculate the Bayesian 95% confidence intervals for β as he successively gathers more data:

a. $n = 5$, $\Sigma xy = 5.0$, $\Sigma x^2 = 25$, $s = .36$

b. $n = 10$, $\Sigma xy = 8.0$, $\Sigma x^2 = 50$, $s = .28$

c. $n = 20$, $\Sigma xy = 15.0$, $\Sigma x^2 = 100$, $s = .31$

19-5 BAYESIAN SHRINKAGE ESTIMATES

A—PRIOR DISTRIBUTIONS: OBJECTIVE, SUBJECTIVE, AND NEUTRAL

In the examples so far in this chapter, the prior distribution has been based on empirical evidence as solid as the sample evidence on which the likelihood function is based. When we get such an empirical or *objective* prior, we are fortunate indeed.

Often, however, the prior distribution is not so clear-cut and may be based on the statistician's personal judgment. In principle, such a *personal* or *subjective* prior can be developed quite easily (as we discussed in Section 3-7). In practice, however, it requires considerable skill to develop a personal prior that is sufficiently free of prejudice.

If there seems to be no prior knowledge at all, even this can be formulated as an *informationless* or *neutral* prior. We shall now show how this will allow certain parts of the data (that classical statistics does not fully exploit) to help estimate the unknown parameter. The ingenious result is called a *Bayesian shrinkage estimate*, and we will see how nicely it resolves some of the dilemmas of classical estimation.

B—THE DILEMMA OF CLASSICAL ESTIMATION

As a concrete example, in Table 19-2 we repeat the data of Table 10-3. Suppose we need an estimate of μ_2, the long-run mean output of the second machine. What do we use?

The obvious estimate is $\bar{X}_2 = 56$, the *sample* mean of that machine. But what if H_0 is true (i.e., there is no difference in machines, so that all 15 observations come from the same population)? Then a better estimate would be the grand mean $\bar{\bar{X}} = 52$, based on all the data in Table 19-2.

TABLE 19-2 Production of 3 Machines (repeat of Table 10-3)

Machine 1	*Machine 2*	*Machine 3*
50	48	57
42	57	59
53	65	48
45	59	46
55	51	45
$\bar{X}_1 = 49$	$\bar{X}_2 = 56$	$\bar{X}_3 = 51$

Grand mean $\bar{\bar{X}} = 52$

$$F = \frac{65}{39.0} = 1.67$$

The problem in a nutshell is this: *We don't know which of these two estimates to choose because we don't know whether H_0 or H_A is true:* If H_0 is true (i.e., if there is no difference in machines), the better estimate is $\bar{\bar{X}} = 52$; but if H_A is true (and the machines do differ), then the better estimate is $\bar{X}_2 = 56$. The classical way out of this dilemma is to use the F test at some customary level, say 5%. In our example in Table 19-2, F was calculated to be 1.67. Since this falls short of the critical $F_{.05} = 3.89$, we cannot reject H_0; so we use the H_0 estimate of 52.

But imagine that Table 19-2 represented only one experiment in a whole sequence of possible experiments; and suppose the F values ranged continuously from 1.67 on up. Classical accept-or-reject theory would require us to use $\bar{\bar{X}}$ whenever F was less than $F_{.05} = 3.89$ (no matter how slightly) and $\bar{X}_2$ whenever F was above 3.89 (no matter how slightly). That is, our estimate could only take on two values ($\bar{\bar{X}}$ or $\bar{X}_2$), and would jump from one to the other because of a trivial change in the data (F changing, for example, from 3.88 to 3.90). This is clearly unsatisfactory. Instead, we should develop an estimate that changes *continuously* between $\bar{\bar{X}}$ and $\bar{X}_2$, depending on the strength of the sample message we get from F.

C—BAYESIAN SOLUTION IN GENERAL

To the extent that the F statistic is large, H_A is more credible; to the extent that F is small, H_0 is more credible. The Bayesian solution (derived in Wonnacott, 1981) makes this idea precise:

Bayesian shrinkage estimate (for $F \geq 1$):

Give H_0 a weight $\frac{1}{F}$ (19-33)

Give H_A the remaining weight $= 1 - \frac{1}{F}$

For $F < 1$, we would run into trouble if we tried to use (19-33): H_0 would get a weight of more than 1, and H_A would get a negative weight. Therefore to the above Bayesian estimate we must add the following guideline:

$$\text{For } F < 1: \quad \left.\begin{array}{l} \text{Give } H_0 \text{ a weight } = 1 \\ \text{Give } H_A \text{ a weight } = 0 \end{array}\right\} \tag{19-34}$$

To know when the Bayesian shrinkage estimate is appropriate, we must be clear on its basic assumption. It assumes the prior is vaguely distributed around the null hypothesis H_0; that is, values on either side of H_0 roughly seem equally likely. (For a more careful statement of assumptions and derivations, see Box and Tiao, 1973.)

Now let us see how the shrinkage formulas work in specific cases:

D—BAYESIAN SHRINKAGE ESTIMATES FOR ANOVA

For ANOVA, we saw that the null hypothesis H_0 used the grand mean $\overline{\overline{X}}$, and the alternative hypothesis H_A used the specific machine mean $\overline{X}_2$. If we denote the Bayesian estimate by BE, then (19-33) becomes:

Bayesian estimate of the typical (second) population mean in ANOVA:

$$\text{BE}(\mu_2) = \left(\frac{1}{F}\right)\overline{\overline{X}} + \left(1 - \frac{1}{F}\right)\overline{X}_2 \tag{19-35}$$

An example will show how the formula works, and how it can be interpreted graphically:

EXAMPLE 19-11

Recall that in Table 19-2, from a sample of $n = 5$ observations on each machine, the three machine means were 49, 56, and 51. The grand mean was $\overline{\overline{X}} = 52$, and the F statistic was 1.67.

a. Calculate the Bayesian estimate of the second machine mean, and also the first and third.

b. On a graph, contrast the Bayesian and classical estimates.

SOLUTION

a. The Bayesian estimate is a compromise between $\overline{\overline{X}} = 52$ and $\overline{X}_2 = 56$, with the weights determined by $F = 1.67$. When these numbers are substituted into (19-35), we obtain

$$\text{BE}(\mu_2) = \frac{1}{1.67}\overline{\overline{X}} + \left(1 - \frac{1}{1.67}\right)\overline{X}_2$$
$$= .60(52) + .40(56) = 53.6 \qquad (19\text{-}36)$$

The Bayesian estimate is thus a .60 − .40 compromise. For the other machines, the compromise is still .60 − .40, because the F statistic is still 1.67. Therefore,

$$\text{BE}(\mu_1) = .60(52) + .40(49) = 50.8$$
$$\text{BE}(\mu_3) = .60(52) + .40(51) = 51.6$$

b. As Figure 19-7 shows, Bayesian estimates are shrunk toward the grand mean $\overline{\overline{X}}$. So they are sometimes called *shrinkage* estimates.

E—BAYESIAN SHRINKAGE ESTIMATES FOR REGRESSION

We can also apply the basic Bayesian solution (19-33) to regression, provided once more our prior expectation is that the parameter is somewhere in the neighborhood of the null hypothesis.

Let us consider the simplest case, where the null hypothesis is $\beta = 0$. In other words, let us suppose the slope β is judged about as likely to be negative as positive, before we collect the sample. [This assumption that the prior distribution is centered at zero produces an estimate shrunk towards 0 in (19-37) below. If the prior distribution is centered at some other point, as it often is in regression, then the estimate should be shrunk toward that point, of course.]

When we substitute the null hypothesis ($\beta = 0$) and the alternative hypothesis (the classical estimate b) into (19-33), we obtain the compromise Bayesian estimate of the slope β:

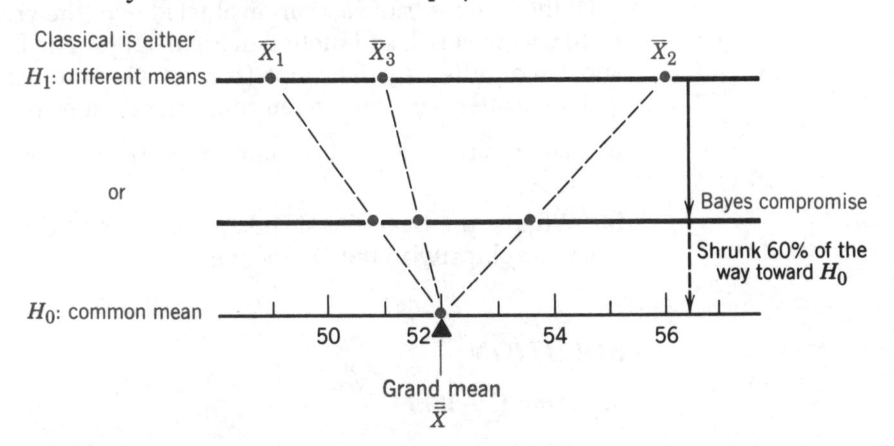

FIGURE 19-7
The Bayesian estimates are shrunk toward H_0. (In our example, with $F = 1.67$, there is a 60% shrinkage.)

$$\mathrm{BE}(\beta) = \left(\frac{1}{F}\right) 0 + \left(1 - \frac{1}{F}\right) b$$
$$= \left(1 - \frac{1}{F}\right) b \qquad (19\text{-}37)$$

where F is the customary F ratio for testing the null hypothesis:

$$F = t^2 = \left(\frac{b}{SE}\right)^2 \qquad (19\text{-}38)$$
(15-14) repeated

EXAMPLE 19-12

The Statistics 200 course at a large university has many sections, each taught by a different instructor. Every year, the students are all given a common final exam, and in each section the average mark is calculated—the students' performance Y. In turn, the students of that section fill out an evaluation form on how good they thought their instructor was—the instructor's popularity X. How is Y related to X?

It's not clear whether this is a positive or negative relationship. (If instructors who are judged good get this rating because they teach really well, then their students will do well and Y will be positively related to X. On the other hand, if instructors who are judged good get this rating primarily because they demand very little work, then their students will do badly and Y will be negatively related to X.) Thus the prior judgment is that β is about as likely to be positive as negative, so the Bayes compromise with 0 given in (19-37) is okay.

Of the hundreds of sections evaluated over the years, a random sample of 10 was selected, and plotted in Figure 19-8. The fitted least squares line showed a quite negative slope ($b = -2.4$)—due perhaps to the large degree of scatter, and subsequent high standard error (SE = 1.94).

a. What is the classical p-value for H_0 ($\beta = 0$, i.e., no relation of Y to X)?

b. What is the Bayesian shrinkage estimate of the slope β? Compare it graphically to the OLS slope.

SOLUTION

a. From (19-38),

$$F = \left(\frac{b}{SE}\right)^2 = \left(\frac{-2.4}{1.94}\right)^2 = 1.53$$

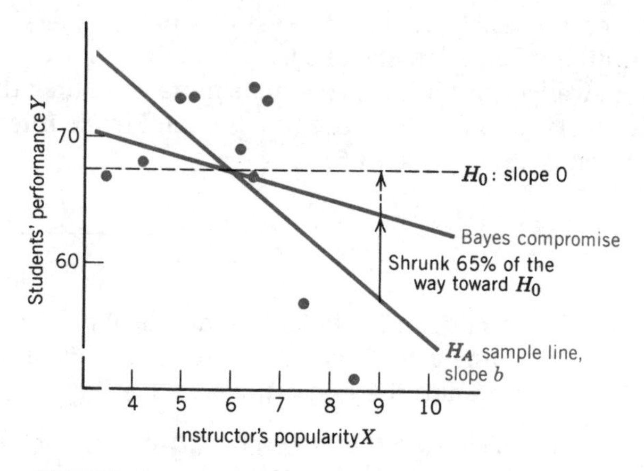

FIGURE 19-8
The Bayesian line is the least squares line shrunk toward H_0. (In our example, with $F = 1.53$, the shrinkage is 65%.)

We refer to Appendix Table VI, with F having d.f. = 1 and n − 2 = 8. The observed value F = 1.53 is close to $F_{.25} = 1.54$, so that we conclude:

$$\text{p-value} \simeq .25$$

b. Because H_0 had substantial credibility in part **a**, we expect the Bayes compromise slope to be shrunk substantially toward 0. Formula (19-37) gives it explicitly:

$$\begin{aligned} \text{BE}(\beta) &= \frac{1}{1.53}(0) + \left(1 - \frac{1}{1.53}\right)(-2.4) \\ &= .65(0) + .35(-2.4) \\ &= -.8 \end{aligned} \tag{19-39}$$

As shown in Figure 19-8, this means that the classical slope b is shrunk 65% of the way toward 0, from − 2.4 to −.8.

F—SOME OTHER APPROACHES

There are ways other than Bayesian shrinkage to modify classical estimates. They range from the very theoretical to the very practical, and are known by such names as *James-Stein estimation, ridge regression, cross validation,* and *minimum MSE.* All these modifications share a common goal of minimizing estimation error, and all produce roughly the same answer—the Bayesian shrinkage estimate given in (19-33). Since each of these philosophically different approaches yields much the same estimator, each tends to confirm the validity of the others, and in particular, the validity of Bayesian shrinkage.

As well as providing an estimate more valid than the classical, Bayesian shrinkage also gives a more precise confidence interval around it (as described in Appendix 19-5).

PROBLEMS

19-13 Recall that in Table 10-1, a sample of $n = 5$ observations from each machine gave 3 machine means: 49, 56, and 51. The grand mean was 52 and the F statistic was 8.3.

a. Calculate the Bayesian shrinkage estimates for the population means of all 3 machines.

b. On a graph, contrast the Bayesian shrinkage and classical estimates.

c. Comparing the graph in **b** to the graph in Figure 19-7

i. Which graph shows more shrinkage toward the null hypothesis value $\bar{\bar{X}}$?

ii. In which case was there more evidence that H_0 was true, as given by the classical test?

19-14 An experiment to compare three treatments was conducted. Eighteen rats were assigned at random, 6 to each of the 3 groups. Their lengths of survival (in weeks) after being injected with a carcinogen were as follows:

	T_1	T_2	T_3
	13	3	10
	9	6	7
	16	6	8
	7	5	12
	11	7	14
	10	9	9
Mean $\bar{X}$	11	6	10
$\Sigma(X - \bar{X})^2$	50	20	34

On a graph, contrast the classical and Bayesian shrinkage estimates of the mean survival time for the 3 treatments.

19-15 A random sample of 7 women showed a positive slope of blood cholesterol level on age. If the least squares slope was .024 with a standard error of .010, what is the Bayesian shrinkage slope?

19-16 The GMAT exam was given to a random sample of 5 men and an independent random sample of 5 women graduating from an East Coast university. The percentage scores obtained were:

Men:	73	61	60	70	76
Women:	71	85	72	93	84

For the difference between the male and female scores (average over the whole class), calculate the classical and Bayesian shrinkage estimates.

19-17 Suppose that a year after having taken the exam in Problem 19-16, the 5 men were again tested. The second test scores (along with the corresponding first test scores) were as follows:

First score:	73	61	60	70	76
Second score:	79	67	68	75	81

For the improvement in score (average for the whole graduating class of men), calculate the classical and Bayesian shrinkage estimates. What assumptions are you making for the latter?

19-6 CLASSICAL AND BAYESIAN ESTIMATES COMPARED

A classical estimate such as $\overline{X}$ or a least squares slope b is entirely based on the sample. The Bayesian estimate is a more subtle one that sees all shades of gray—a compromise between the sample and the prior distribution. If the prior is not known, but seems to be vaguely centered around the null hypothesis H_0, then a neutral prior will allow the F ratio of the sample to determine the degree of compromise (that is, the degree of shrinking toward H_0).

As the sample becomes larger and more reliable, there is a greater and greater relative weight placed on it, so that:

For large samples, the Bayesian estimate is practically the same as the classical estimate (based on the sample alone). (19-40)

In other words, if the sample is large, there is no need to derive the Bayesian estimate; the classical estimate will be similar, and easier. Thus the Bayesian estimate is primarily a *small-sample modification*.

For example, it would be foolish to ignore prior information in trying to guess an election if a sample contained only 15 voters. Yet it would be unnecessary to bother with prior information if the sample contained 1500 voters (as does the typical Gallup poll).

CHAPTER 19 SUMMARY

19-1 Bayesian statistics provide a whole new way of looking at estimation, as a combination of sample information *and* prior information. It is based on posterior probabilities, which are easily obtained from Bayes Theorem.

19-2 For a proportion π, the prior information can be regarded as a quasi-sample of a successes and b failures. They can then be combined naturally with the actual S successes and F failures in the sample.

19-3 For a mean μ, the prior information can be regarded as a quasi-sample of n_0 observations centered at μ_0 (the mean of the normal prior distribution). This can then be combined naturally with the n actual observations in the sample, to produce a compromise estimate between μ_0 and $\overline{X}$.

19-4 For a regression slope β, the prior information can similarly be regarded as a quasi-sample of n_0 observations. The same is true in multiple regression, where a computer is customarily used.

19-5 When the prior is vaguely distributed around the null hypothesis H_0, then the Bayesian estimate turns out to be the classical estimate shrunk toward H_0. The degree of shrinking is greatest when the sample F statistic is least (and consequently the p-value for H_0—the credibility of H_0—is greatest).

19-6 In large samples, the Bayesian estimate is practically the same as the classical estimate based on the sample alone. Thus the Bayesian modification is primarily for small samples

REVIEW PROBLEMS

19-18 A shipment of natural sponges is to be sampled to determine three characteristics:

1. The proportion π that are torn.
2. The mean weight μ.
3. The slope β of the graph of absorbency Y as a linear function of weight X.

Suppose, on the basis of past shipments, that the following priors are deemed appropriate:

1. $p(\pi) \propto \pi^3 (1 - \pi)^{12}$
2. μ is normal, with mean 150 and standard deviation 20.
3. β is normal, with mean 4.0 and standard deviation .50.

A sample of $n = 20$ sponges yielded the following statistics:

1. Sample proportion that are torn, $P = 10\%$.

2. For weight, $\overline{X} = 140$, $\Sigma(X - \overline{X})^2 = 22{,}800$.
3. For regression, $\Sigma(X - \overline{X})^2 = 22{,}800$, $\Sigma(X - \overline{X})(Y - \overline{Y}) = 114{,}000$, and residual $s = 53.4$.

Graph the posterior distribution and 95% confidence interval for

a. π
b. μ
c. β

19-19 a. Imagine an urn filled with chips, of which 2/3 are of one color and 1/3 of another. Peter has drawn 5 chips from the urn, and found that 4 were red and 1 was white. Paul has drawn 20 chips and found that 12 were red and 8 were white. *Without calculating,* guess who should feel more confident that the urn contains 2/3 red chips and 1/3 white chips, rather than the opposite?

This example (Tversky and Kahneman, 1974) illustrates how challenging it is to make an educated guess.

b. Let us see whether careful logic will help: To clarify the problem, assume there are two huge urns with millions of chips. The "largely red urn" contains twice as many red as white, while the "largely white urn" contains twice as many white as red. And an urn is chosen at random, so that the prior odds of picking the "largely red urn" are 1/1.

What would be the posterior odds after drawing:

i. 1 red chip?
ii. 4 red?
iii. 4 red and 1 white?
iv. 12 red and 8 white?

Was your guess in **a** correct, according to the last two answers?

c. To see what general lesson can be learned, write down the formula for the posterior probability after drawing r red chips, let us say, and *w* white chips. Then make the correct choice below:

In this problem, the posterior odds depend solely on:

i. The number of red chips drawn
ii. The *excess* number of red chips (in excess of the number of white)
iii. The *relative* number of red chips (proportion of red)

19-20 A statistician was asked to summarize what she knew about the proportion π of state senators who would favor higher gasoline taxes.

a. Before any sampling was done, her guess for π ranged generally on the low side—in fact, her personal prior distribution was

$$p(\pi) \propto \pi(1 - \pi)^3.$$

Graph this distribution.

b. A random sample of 6 senators turned out to have 5 in favor of higher gasoline taxes. Show graphically how this evidence changes the statistician's guess for π.

c. Construct the Bayesian 95% confidence interval for π. Show it on the graph in *b*. Does it seem to take in about 95% of the posterior distribution?

19-21 In testing out a new variety of hybrid corn, a small pilot experiment on $n = 100$ randomly selected plots found the average yield to be $\overline{X} = 115$ and $s = 21$.

a. Construct a 95% confidence interval for the mean μ.

b. Dr. C said that he would bet 95¢ to a nickel that the confidence interval in **a** covers the true mean μ.

Dr. B doubted that she would give such high odds. She had discussed the new variety with an expert who thought it would be at least as productive as the standard variety, whose record was well established: $\mu = 120$. Therefore, if she had to bet on the confidence interval, her odds would be in the neighborhood of 80¢ to 20¢.

Settle the dispute as well as you can.

c. Suppose the expert in *b* roughly quantified her knowledge by giving μ a normal prior distribution centered at 121, with a standard deviation of 3. What Bayesian confidence interval for μ would this give?

d. Suppose that instead of talking to the expert, they had gathered more data: Suppose 50 more plots had an average $\overline{X} = 121$ and $s = 20$.

Using all 150 observations, what is the best estimate of μ? What is the 95% confidence interval? (*Hint:* For all 150 observations, an elaborate calculation would show that $s \simeq 21$ still.)

e. How do the estimates in **c** and **d** compare?

19-22 ***A Final Challenge: What is Material Evidence?***

A cab was involved in a hit-and-run accident at night. Two cab companies, the green and the blue, operate in the city. A witness reports that the offending cab was blue, and legal action is brought against the Blue Cab Company. The court learns that, although the Green Cab Company owns 20 times as many cabs as the Blue Company, insurance records show that it is involved in only 10 times as many accidents, confirming the value of its stringent driver screening. Further, the court learns that on a test of ability to identify the color of cabs at night, the witness is correct on 80% of the identifications and incorrect on 20% (whether the cab is blue or green).

Suppose, for simplicity, that this is all the evidence available.

a. What is your best guess (in less than 30 seconds) for the odds that the responsible cab was indeed blue, as the witness claims.

b. Now calculate the odds carefully.

c. We won't embarrass you by asking how well you guessed in **a**. Instead, we will report what Tversky and Kahneman (1980) found in a similar problem: Most people guess around the likelihood ratio, .80/.20 = 4/1. That is, they implicitly ignore the prior. This creates a problem whenever ordinary people are asked to weigh uncertainties—as in a business conference or jury, say.

Suppose *you* were on a jury, for example, and had to decide this case. In which cases would you vote the Blue Cab Company is liable for the $50,000 damages:

i. Scenario above.

ii. Scenario above, simplified by a judge who rules that the prior odds must be disregarded because they are merely "base-rate data." Would this ruling make it easier or harder for you to make a fair verdict?

d. Suggest some possibly fairer alternatives to a simple "yes or no" judgment against the Blue Cab Company.

e. There is a lively dispute among lawyers over how much weight should be given "base-rate data" (prior odds, such as the ratio of cab accidents) relative to "case-specific information" (likelihood ratio, such as eyewitness reliability). Do you agree with the following view—and give your reasons:

> The distinction between what one can learn from case-specific as opposed to base-rate information is more imaginary than real. In terms of accurate fact finding, it is a difference that makes no difference. (Saks and Kidd 1986, p. 239.)

f. There is also a dispute among statisticians over how much weight should be given prior odds relative to the likelihood ratio, when the prior odds are subjective. Do you agree with the following view—and give your reasons:

> Bayesian inference is not a branch of Statistics: it is a new way of looking at the whole of Statistics. Its potential is enormous . . . . Lindley (1982).

CHAPTER 20

*Bayesian Decision Theory

(Requires Chapter 19)

Models don't make decisions. People do.
ANONYMOUS

In the last chapter we saw how Bayesian theory could be used in estimation. In this chapter we will see how useful it can be in making decisions.

20-1 MAXIMIZING GAIN (OR MINIMIZING LOSS)

In Example 19-7, we considered a shipment of beams. On the basis of the sample and prior information, we found a 10% probability of its being unsatisfactory ($\mu < 62.5$). Should it be returned or not? To make this decision, we also need to know the costs of a wrong decision. For example, if it's a good shipment but we err by deciding it is a bad one—and therefore return it—then we unnecessarily incur costly delays. On the other hand, if it is a bad shipment, but we erroneously decide it is a good one—and keep it—then the cost may be huge: A bridge using this inferior steel may collapse as a consequence.

Thus in this chapter we seek to develop a formal way of making the best decision by taking such losses into account. We begin with the simplest possible example.

EXAMPLE 20-1

John Nelson runs the refreshment concession at a football stadium, selling drinks and umbrellas. He is paid a flat fee of $100 a game, from which he must deduct his losses; these, in turn, depend on how badly he matches his merchandise with the weather. Suppose that he has just three possible options (actions, a):

$$a_1 = \text{sell only drinks}$$
$$a_2 = \text{sell some drinks, some umbrellas}$$
$$a_3 = \text{sell only umbrellas}$$

If he sells only drinks (a_1) and it rains, his loss is $70. If it shines, however, he just loses $10.

Similarly, if he chooses action a_2 or a_3, there will be other losses, and we can show them all in the following loss table:

TABLE 20-1 Loss Function $l(a,\theta)$

	Action		
State θ	a_1	a_2	a_3
θ_1 (Rain)	70	40	20
θ_2 (Shine)	10	40	60

Suppose further that the probability distribution (long-run relative frequency) of the weather is as follows:

TABLE 20-2 Probability Distribution of θ

State θ	$p(\theta)$
θ_1 (Rain)	.40
θ_2 (Shine)	.60

If he wants to minimize long-run losses, what is the best action for him to take? (As always, try to work this out before reading on; it will make the discussion much easier.)

SOLUTION

If he chooses a_1, what would his total loss be, in the long run? Equivalently, what would his average loss be? Let us call it $L(a_1)$. To calculate it, we simply weight each possible loss with its relative frequency, and obtain

$$L(a_1) = 70(.40) + 10(.60) = 34 \tag{20-1}$$

like (4-4)

Similarly, for each of his other actions, we again calculate his average loss:

$$L(a_2) = 40(.40) + 40(.60) = 40 \tag{20-2}$$

$$L(a_3) = 20(.40) + 60(.60) = 44 \tag{20-3}$$

All these calculations are summarized in Table 20-3. We see that the average loss $L(a)$ is a minimum at a_1. Thus the best action is to sell drinks only.

TABLE 20-3 Calculation of the Best Action *a*, Using the Prior Distribution $p(\theta)$

		Action		
$p(\theta)$	State θ	a_1	a_2	a_3
.40	θ_1 (rain)	70	40	20
.60	θ_2 (shine)	10	40	60
Average loss $L(a)$		34 ↑ minimum	40	44

Of course, this problem can be generalized to any number of states θ or actions a. For any action a that is taken, and any state θ that occurs, there is a corresponding loss[1] $l(a,\theta)$. Our decision is called a *Bayesian* decision if—as in the example above—we choose the action that minimizes average (expected) loss:

$$\textbf{Choose } a \textbf{ to minimize } L(a) \equiv \sum_{\theta} l(a,\theta)p(\theta) \qquad (20\text{-}4)$$

The probabilities $p(\theta)$, of course, should represent the best possible intelligence on the subject. For example, if the salesman cannot predict the weather, he will have to use the prior probabilities (.40 and .60) set out in Table 20-2; but if he can predict the weather by using a barometer, for example, then of course he should use the posterior probabilities that result from exploiting this sample information. An example will illustrate:

EXAMPLE 20-2

Suppose John Nelson in Example 20-1 has kept records of the local TV weather report: On rainy days it correctly predicts "rain" 90% of the time; on shiny days, it correctly predicts "shine" 70% of the time. (Note that the TV predictions are indicated with quotation marks.)

If the report predicts "rain," which of the three possible actions (a_1, a_2, or a_3) should he choose now?

SOLUTION

We first find the relevant posterior probabilities in Figure 20-1 (using tree reversal, as in Section 3-6.) The posterior probabilities of rain and shine (given the "rain" prediction) are circled in Figure 20-1*b* and are copied down as the first column of Table 20-4. Using these best possible probabilities, the analysis then proceeds just as it did in Table 20-3.

We conclude that his best action, once he has the forecast of "rain" (i.e., sample information), is to sell umbrellas only (action a_3).

The logic of calculating the best decision in general—*Bayesian decision theory*—is summarized in Figure 20-2. It combines a new element

[1] The formulation of the problem in terms of losses is perfectly general, since gains may be represented simply as negative losses. We choose to use loss rather than gain, however, since loss is more natural than gain in the context of this chapter.

The losses we consider are losses of money. Much more general and useful theory can be developed based on losses of intrinsic value called *utility*.

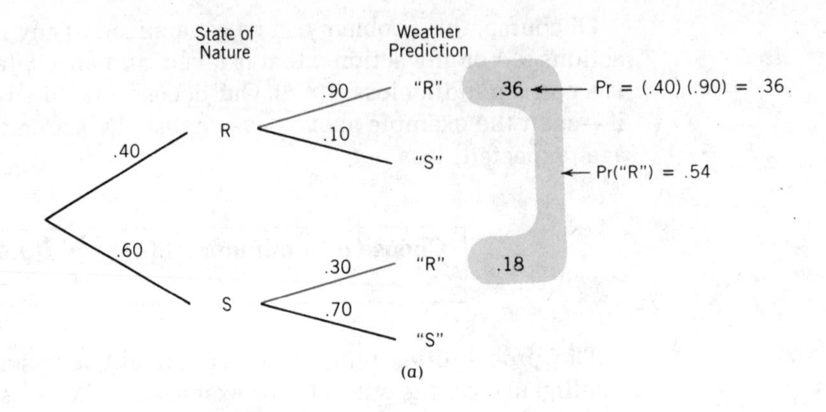

(a)

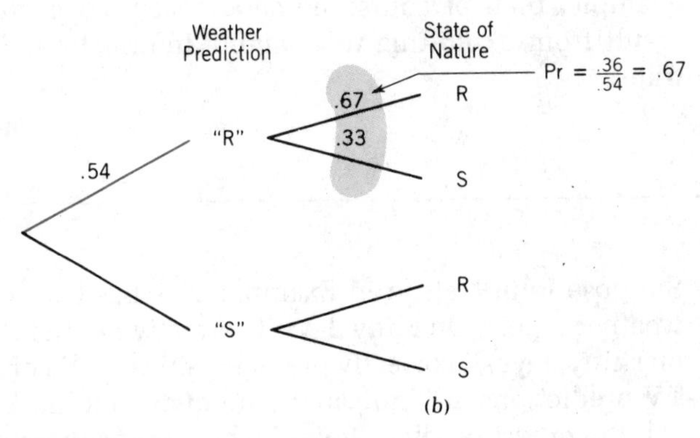

(b)

FIGURE 20-1
Calculation of the posterior probabilities by Bayes Theorem. (a) Original tree. (b) Reverse tree.

TABLE 20-4 Calculation of the Best Action a, Using the Posterior Distribution, $p(\theta|X_1)$

		Action		
$p(\theta\|X_1)$	θ	a_1	a_2	a_3
.67	θ_1	70	40	20
.33	θ_2	10	40	60
Average loss $L(a)$		50	40	33 ↑ minimum

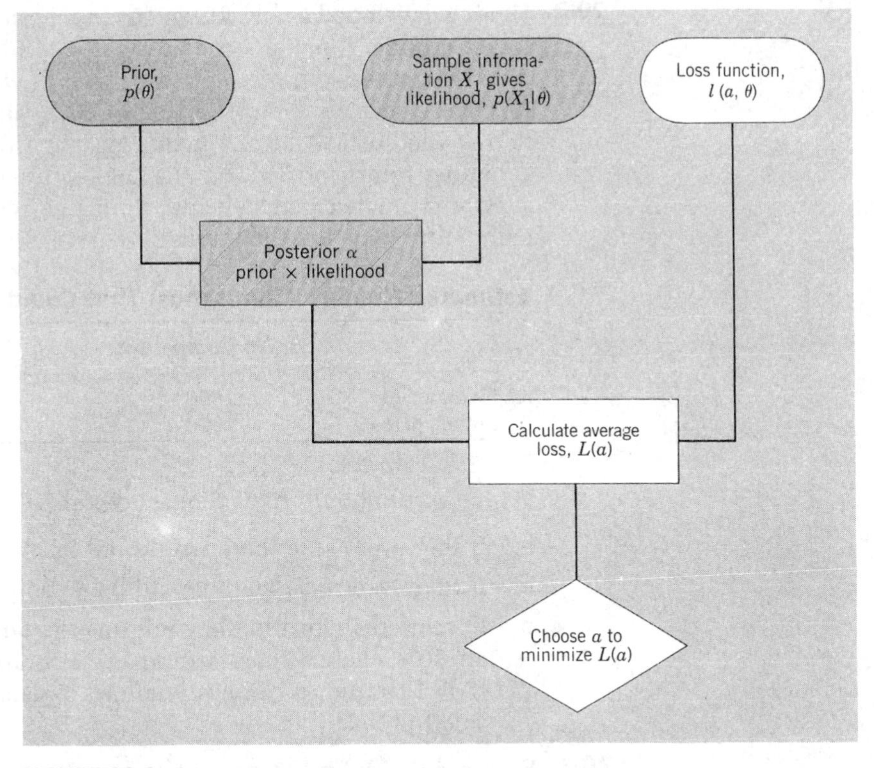

FIGURE 20-2
The logic of Bayesian decisions. The three given components—prior information, sample information, and the loss function—produce the best action a.

(the loss function) with the two elements (the prior and the sample) already studied in Chapter 19. It produces the decision that has the least possible long-run (average) loss.

PROBLEMS

20-1 Underline the correct alternative in brackets:

a. Bayesian decision theory is a technique for making the best decision. By "best," we mean the one that [protects us from bad luck the best, exploits possible good luck the best, weighs both good and bad luck in order to maximize expected profit].

b. When no current data is yet available for the states of nature, their prior probabilities alone [can still, cannot] be used to make a decision. When current data becomes available, then we can calculate the [prior, posterior, minimal] probabilities using [minimum expected loss, maximum expected profit, Bayes Theorem].

20-2 Having developed a new energy-saving thermostat to automatically lower a home's temperature at night, EMS Electronics had to decide its wholesale price. Two alternatives were suggested: (i) $50, to cover the manufacturing cost of $30, plus a return of $20 to defray the cost of development, etc., or (ii) $70, to give a more generous return of $40. At the higher price, however, a market survey estimated that demand would be reduced, especially if a competitor came on the market:

Estimated Number (Thousands) That Could be Sold

	If No Competitor	*If Competitor*
At lower price	1800	500
At higher price	1200	100

Which price should they choose to maximize their total return:

a. If they were sure there would not be a competitor?

b. If they were sure there would be a competitor?

c. If, more realistically, they felt unsure, but estimated there was an 80% chance there would be a competitor? (Assume that EMS Electronics can easily afford to gamble on this relatively small project.)

20-3 Suppose that John Nelson who is running the refreshment concession faces the following losses:

	Action		
State θ	a_1	a_2	a_3
θ_1 (Rain)	50	30	5
θ_2 (Shine)	15	30	35

a. If it rains 20% of the time and shines the remaining 80%, what is the best action?

b. Suppose that the local weather prediction has the following record of accuracy: Of all rainy days, 70% are predicted correctly to be "rain"; of all shiny days, 90% are predicted correctly to be "shine." What is the best action if the prediction is "rain"? If it is "shine"?

c. Is this summary True or False? If False, correct it: If John must decide before the weather report, he should choose the compromise a_2. However, if he can wait for the weather report, then he should choose a_3 if the report is "rain," or a_1 if the report is "shine." But this solution is obvious, without going to all the trouble of learning about Bayesian decisions.

d. How much is the weather report worth on average? This is called the Expected Value of Sample Information (EVSI). (*Hint:* What is the expected loss when "rain" is predicted? When "shine" is predicted? Overall? Then compare to the loss without prediction.)

If the weather report costs $2.50 each time, how much is its net worth on average—the Expected Net Gain from Sampling, (ENGS)?

20-4 The manager of a large grain elevator has to decide whether to sell his corn as feed for animals (action A) or for human consumption (action H). His losses depend on the corn's water content (determined after the decision has been made), according to the following loss table:

	Action a	
State θ	A	H
Dry	30	10
Wet	20	40

a. If his only additional information is that, through long past experience, his corn has been classified as dry 1/3 of the time, what should his decision be?

b. Suppose that he has developed a rough means of determining whether it is wet or dry—a method that is correct 3/4 of the time, regardless of the state of nature. What should his decision be if this method indicates his corn is "dry"? If it indicates "wet"?

***c.** As in Problem 20-3, find the EVSI (Expected Value of Sample Information).

20-2 POINT ESTIMATION AS A DECISION

A—THE BEST ESTIMATE DEPENDS ON THE LOSS FUNCTION

Recall that in Chapter 19 we combined the prior and sample information to create the posterior distribution. Then we could use the posterior distribution to construct a 95% confidence interval for the parameter θ.

Now we will use the posterior distribution for another purpose—to make a decision on a single *point* estimate θ. We will see that the loss function vitally affects what the point estimate should be. Although we learned in Chapter 7 that means and medians are often good point estimates for general scientific purposes, we will see that for *specific* decisions, we can often do better. An example will illustrate:

EXAMPLE 20-3

Professor Williams is to teach Economics 350 next quarter, and in ordering the texts, she faces a dilemma: If she orders too many, the excess must be returned—at a cost of $2 each for handling and postage; if she orders too few, there is an even bigger cost—each student who is missing a text must buy a temporary substitute costing $8 each.

Although Williams doesn't personally pay any of these costs, she would like to find the solution that would involve the least cost to everybody concerned. So she gathers whatever prior information she can: She finds that student enrollment in this course over the past 20 quarters has been quite stable, fluctuating between 40 and 80 with the following frequency distribution (grouped into cells of width 10).

Enrollment θ	*Relative Frequency* $p(\theta)$
40	10%
50	20%
60	40%
70	20%
80	10%
Total	100%

If she has to order the texts without any further information, then she will have to make a decision based on the above frequency distribution; it's the only information she has. Assuming the bookstore has a regulation that books must be ordered in multiples of 10, how many texts should she order?

SOLUTION

This problem is very similar to Example 20-1, with the possible actions $a_1, a_2 \ldots$ now being the number of texts to be ordered ($a_1 = 40$, $a_2 = 50$, and so on). For each of these actions, we first tabulate the loss function in Table 20-5.

This loss function reflects the costs of missing the target: When the estimated true enrollments are equal ($a = \theta$), note that there is a 0 loss. From there, the costs of missing the target in each column rise: $80 for each 10 books if actual enrollment turns out to be higher than estimated, and $20 for each 10 books, if it turns out to be lower.

Now we proceed exactly as in Example 20-1. If, for example, the estimate a_3 were chosen, we can calculate the expected loss:

$$L(a_3) = \$40(.10) + \$20(.20) + \cdots + \$160(.10) = \$40 \quad (20\text{-}5)$$

TABLE 20-5 Loss Function $l(a,\theta)$ Yields Average Loss $L(a)$

		Action a (Estimated Enrollment —i.e., Texts Ordered)				
$p(\theta)$	*State θ (Actual Enrollment)*	$a_1(40)$	$a_2(50)$	$a_3(60)$	$a_4(70)$	$a_5(80)$
.10	40	0	\$20	\$40	\$60	\$80
.20	50	\$80	0	\$20	\$40	\$60
.40	60	\$160	\$80	0	\$20	\$40
.20	70	\$240	\$160	\$80	0	\$20
.10	80	\$320	\$240	\$160	\$80	0
	Average loss $L(a)$	\$160	\$90	\$40	\$30 ↑ minimum	\$40

which is then recorded in the bottom margin. We similarly calculate the loss for each of the other actions. We then see that the minimum loss occurs at:

$$a_4\text{: order 70 texts} \tag{20-6}$$

Example 20-3 illustrated an important point. We did not select the mean (60) of the distribution $p(\theta)$, even though it was the median and mode too. The reason is that relatively heavy losses occurred on one side, as a glance at the numbers in, say, column a_3 will confirm. This pulled our best estimate off center.

The best (Bayesian) point estimate of θ depends upon the loss function as well as the distribution of θ. (20-7)

With the pressure created by an asymmetrical loss function now clear, we restrict ourselves in the rest of this section to symmetric loss functions.

B—SYMMETRIC LOSS FUNCTIONS

With a symmetric loss function, the best estimate often does turn out to be one of the familiar centers of the θ distribution—the mean, median, or mode. Figure 20-3 gives three symmetric loss functions, and shows that each leads the decision-maker seeking the best point estimate to a different center of the distribution. We can give a brief reason why (leaving the proofs for Problem 20-9).

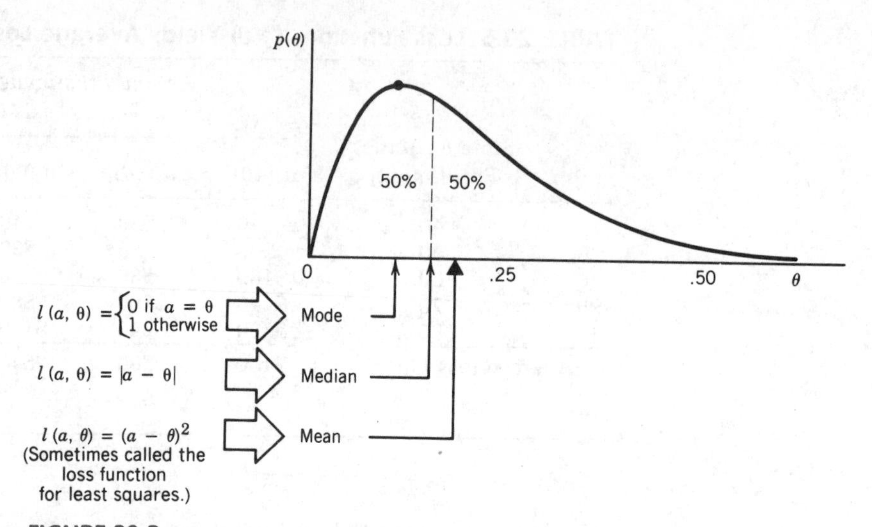

FIGURE 20-3
Different symmetric loss functions $l(a, \theta)$ lead to different central values of θ.

The 0-1 criterion means that "a miss is as good as a mile." Hitting the target exactly is all that counts. To maximize this chance, we go to the point where the distribution has the highest probability—the mode.

The least squares criterion listed last in Figure 20-3 is exactly the same criterion already used in least squares estimation. And you may recall from Section 11-3 that the least squares criterion always produces the mean.

The absolute value criterion is between the other two. It is therefore no surprise that the best estimate it produces is the median—the central measure that lies between the mode and the mean.

EXAMPLE 20-4

Suppose we are asked to estimate the proportion π of defective radios in a shipment, and we incur a cost of \$50 for every 1% we err in our estimate. For example, if we guessed 8%, and π turned out to be 13%, the error would cost us $5 \times \$50 = \$250$.

Suppose Figure 20-3 shows the posterior distribution of π (which, we suppose, has been derived from prior and sample information in the usual way.) What would be your best estimate of π, roughly?

SOLUTION

Since the loss function is essentially the absolute-value function, the estimate that minimizes cost is the *median* of the posterior distribution in Figure 20-3. This appears to be about $\pi = .15$.

PROBLEMS

20-5 A newsstand operator was in a dilemma about how many copies of the *Sunday Times* to order, since demand fluctuated from week to week. In fact, to help make an informed decision, over the past 100 weeks he kept records of sales:

Sales	*Relative Frequency*
20	10%
25	30%
30	20%
35	10%
40	10%
45	10%
50	5%
55	5%

Since the profit on each sale was $.40, he was tempted to order 55 papers every Sunday to be sure he never ran out. Every copy left unsold cost him an equal amount, however—$.40 in handling costs.

To maximize his net profit, how many should he order? (Assume it has to be a multiple of 5.)

20-6 In Problem 20-5, suppose the *Times* increased the profit to $1.20 (by lowering the wholesale price by $.80, so that the retail price and sales potential didn't change). And suppose handling cost remains at $.40.

a. Now what is the best number to order?

b. How much would this increase the average weekly retail sales?

20-7 Suppose that the steel beams manufactured by a new process have breaking strengths that are distributed normally about a mean of 220 with a standard deviation of 15. A beam is sampled at random to estimate its particular breaking strength θ, and it is measured with strain gauges. Five such independent measurements turned out to be 230, 245, 235, 255, 235. Past experience shows that such measurements have a standard deviation of 10, and are unbiased and normally distributed. What would you estimate is the breaking strength θ of this beam:

a. If the cost of estimation error is proportional to the error. For example, an estimate that is 4 times as far off is 4 times as costly.

b. If far-off estimates are more serious. For example, an estimate that is 4 times as far off is $4^2 = 16$ times as costly.

c. If far-off estimates are no more serious than a slightly off estimate, so that we can say "a miss is as good as a mile."

20-8 **a.** Suppose that the steel bars in a large shipment have the following distribution of breaking strengths:

Breaking strength θ	200	210	220	230	240	250
Relative frequency	.10	.30	.20	.20	.10	.10

You have just purchased a bar at random, and want an estimate a of its breaking strength θ. You consult three statisticians, who propose three estimates:

$$a_1 = \text{the mode of the distribution}$$
$$a_2 = \text{the median}$$
$$a_3 = \text{the mean}$$

Calculate each of these estimates.

b. Suppose the estimation error causes a loss proportional to the error:

$$l(a,\theta) = |a - \theta|$$

From Figure 20-3, which of the three estimates in part **a** is best (gives the minimum expected loss)?

To verify your answer, for the 6 possible values of θ and the 3 proposed values of a, tabulate $l(a,\theta)$. Then calculate which estimate a is best, as in Example 20-3.

c. Repeat, if the losses for large errors are especially heavy, now being proportional to the square of the error:

$$l(a,\theta) = (a - \theta)^2$$

d. Repeat, if the losses for large errors are no more than for small errors. Thus we can take the loss to be a constant value (say, 1 unit) no matter how large the error—and zero, of course, if there is no error at all:

$$l(a,\theta) = 0 \text{ if } a = \theta$$
$$= 1 \text{ otherwise}$$

***20-9** In Problem 20-8, we verified Figure 20-3 for one possible distribution of θ. Now prove Figure 20-3 is generally true, for any distribution of θ.

20-3 CLASSICAL AND BAYESIAN STATISTICS COMPARED

A—GENERAL

Now that we have finished the technical details, it is important to stand back for perspective, and see how the Bayesian methods of Chapters 19 and 20 fit in with the rest of the book. Let us begin with a brief review.

If we want to summarize sample data, classical statistics are appropriate (as in Chapters 1 to 18). For example, $\overline{X}$ along with the confidence interval constructed around it, provides an appropriate summary of the sample evidence.

If prior information is available, it can be incorporated with the data to give the improved posterior distribution and confidence interval (as in Chapter 19).

Finally, if a *decision* has to be reached, then the loss function is also essential (Chapter 20). We cannot possibly make a decision that minimizes losses (or equivalently, maximizes benefits) if we don't take into account what the losses are.

Of the three components—the data, prior distribution, and loss function—the data is usually the most solid and objective; it properly deserves the first 18 chapters of this text. The remaining two components are often subjective. Since decisions are made by humans, however, subjectivity will always be with us; and Bayesian analysis is a good way of dealing with it explicitly, rather than trying to sweep it under the rug.

B—SUBJECTIVE PRIORS AND LOSSES

When prior information is objective—as in Examples 20-1 or 20-3—there is of course no problem. Often an objective prior is not available, however, and a subjective prior must be used instead. Subjective priors are often not as difficult to reasonably define as one might expect. (Recall Section 3-7 where we showed how a subjective prior might be calibrated.) Nonetheless, specification of subjective priors remains one of the most controversial aspects of Bayesian analysis—because people have a very human tendency to exaggerate how good their guesses are (they tend to give subjective prior distributions too little variance[2]). Accordingly, it is important in any Bayesian analysis to give the reader not only the final posterior estimate, but also the two components—the prior and the sample data. If readers have a different prior, they will then be able to substitute it and come up with their own posterior. In fact, some authors give a range of several reasonable priors themselves in order to show the range of reasonable posteriors.

---

[2] We can protect ourselves against this kind of prejudice, by using "robust" Bayesian methods that encourage us to be broad-minded. In Section 19-3, for example, instead of using a normal prior, which is very nearly zero beyond three standard deviations, we could use a prior with heavier tails, which gives plausibility to a much wider range of parameter values. This would be a nice compromise between using a normal prior which is too concentrated, and an informationless prior which is too diffuse.

If there is no suitable prior, neither objective nor subjective, we can always use *informationless* or *neutral* priors that lead to shrinkage estimates. As we saw in Section 19-5, they are still better than falling back on classical statistics.

Losses are often subjective, too. How, for example, can we compare the loss of a limb with the loss of a million dollars? These questions are terribly difficult, but they *must* be answered by someone, somehow, in decisions such as how much to compensate workers for industrial accidents. Fortunately, statistical decision theory has a tool called *utility theory* for comparing things that at first glance seem incomparable (Raiffa, 1968). And surprisingly, economists are now developing methods of at least roughly approximating the most difficult loss of all to pin down: the loss of a human life (Bailey, 1980). Such developments greatly extend the applicability of this chapter on decisions.

Having dealt with the controversies of Bayesian decision theory in general, let us next see what they mean for the specific issues addressed in Chapters 19 and 20.

C—ESTIMATION

We have often emphasized the inadequacy of using a single point estimate to describe a population parameter. As early as Chapter 8, for example, we saw that an interval estimate was far more informative. Now we have seen that a posterior (Bayesian) interval estimate is even better because it incorporates prior information as well as the data. Of course, the most informative and detailed way of all to describe a population parameter is to show the whole posterior distribution. As computers take over the burden of computing and graphing, this is becoming a more and more viable alternative.

We must remember that as the sample becomes large enough (and hence swamps the prior) such posterior information reduces to the classical equivalent. For example, the posterior confidence interval reduces to the classical confidence interval; and the whole posterior distribution reduces to the classical likelihood function. (This is yet another reason to study classical statistics for 18 chapters.)

D—ESTIMATION AS A DECISION

While a population parameter is generally best described by a posterior confidence interval (or even better, by the whole posterior distribution) for specific decisions one often requires a specific point estimate—determined by the loss function. Ideally, this loss function should be applied to the posterior distribution. But in the face of more limited information, it may be applied to the prior (if no data exists), or to the classical likelihood function (if no prior exists, or the sample data are so plentiful that it swamps the prior). In short, the loss function should be applied to the best available distribution that describes the population parameter.

This allows us to put the classical technique of maximum likelihood estimation (MLE) into perspective. By using the likelihood function alone, MLE ignores any prior information; and by selecting the point where the likelihood function peaks (the mode), MLE implicitly uses the arbitrary 0-1 loss function. Accordingly, MLE should be viewed as a useful summary of sample data, rather than a guide for decision-making.

PROBLEMS

20-10 Answer True or False; if False, correct it:

a. Bayesian estimation combines sample data with a prior distribution and a loss function, whereas classical estimation uses only the data.

b. If the prior distribution is flat, then the posterior distribution coincides with the likelihood function.
If, in addition, the loss function is quadratic, then the Bayes estimate coincides with the MLE.

CHAPTER 20 SUMMARY

20-1 The best (Bayesian) decision is the one that minimizes total or average loss. It incorporates all three components of a decision: (1) the current data (as in classical statistics, Chapters 1 to 18), (2) the prior information, combined with the data to give the posterior distribution (as in Bayesian estimation, Chapter 19), and finally (3), the loss function (the new component).

20-2 For a specific decision, often a specific point estimate is needed (as opposed to the interval estimate, which is used for more general purposes of information). Various symmetric loss functions lead to various centers of the posterior distribution as the optimal point estimate—the mean, median, or mode. An asymmetric loss function, which penalizes an error in one direction more heavily than in the other, will naturally move the optimal point estimate off center.

20-3 When objective evidence is unavailable, the decision-maker's own subjective knowledge and values can be used for the prior distribution and loss function. This makes the personal nature of decision-making explicitly clear—and open to analysis and improvement.
As sample size grows and the data swamp the prior, Bayesian estimation approaches classical estimation. This is why 18 chapters were devoted to classical estimation, and why Bayesian statistics are called primarily a *small-sample technique*.

REVIEW PROBLEMS

20-11 Answer True or False; if False, correct it:

a. For an estimate V of a parameter θ, suppose the cost of missing the target is proportional to the size of the miss, $|V - \theta|$. Then the best estimate is the mean of the prior distribution of V.

b. The advantage of Bayesian over classical estimation is that Bayesian estimation does not require the specification of prior distributions, or losses.

20-12 ***A Final Challenge: What Is a Good Estimate?***

a. The sensitivity θ in a photographic process has the following prior distribution and likelihood function

θ	$p(\theta)$	$L(\theta)$
0	.10	.20
1	.10	.40
2	.20	.30
3	.20	.20
4	.30	.10
5	.10	.10

If θ is 2 or less the photographic process will be unsatisfactory. What is the chance of this,

i. If only the prior is known?

ii. If the data is available, so that the likelihood function is known too?

b. Find the best (least costly) point estimate V of the parameter θ:

i. If only the prior is known, and the cost of an error is proportional to its size, $|V - \theta|$.

ii. If the likelihood function is known too, and the cost is now proportional to the square of the error, $(V - \theta)^2$.

c. What is the MLE of θ? Would the MLE be better on average than the estimate V found in part **b(ii)**? How much better?

PART V

Special Topics For Business and Economics

CHAPTER 21

Decision Trees

(Requires[1] Chapter 3)

Two roads diverged in a yellow wood,
And sorry I could not travel both . . . .
ROBERT FROST

Decision trees, like probability trees in Chapter 3, are simply a graphic way to organize the calculations that will lead us to the best possible decisions in the face of uncertainty. We will see, for example, how a firm can weigh its risks in order to increase its profits, or how an investment portfolio might be selected to satisfy the twin goals of growth and security. As well as better business decisions that involve money, we will also see how to make better personal decisions that involve more subjective benefits.

---

hough Chapter 21 covers many of the same issues as Chapters 19 and 20, it is more ve and can be read independently.

21-1 THE BASIC TREE

A decision tree is like a probability tree in Chapter 3, with one important additional component: Decisions have to be made at various branchings of the tree.

A—EXAMPLE

Suppose the owners of BEA, a very large oil exploration company, hold a lease that must be either (1) sold now, (2) held for a year and then sold, or (3) exercised now. If they decide to exercise it, the cost of drilling will be 200K ($200,000) and will lead to one of the consequences (well types) listed in Table 21-1. (For example, reading along the first row, there is a 50% chance that the well will turn out to be dry, with a zero payoff.)

If they decide instead to sell their lease now, they can get 125K for it. Finally, if they decide to hold it for a year in a gamble that oil prices will rise, they face a risk: If this gamble fails—and they estimate that the chance of this is 90%—then they will take a slight loss; they will have to sell their lease for 110K. On the other hand, if this gamble succeeds and oil prices rise, they will be able to sell their lease for 440K.

Jack Moor, their vice president, has read somewhere that statistics will help make "wise decisions in the face of uncertainty," so he consults us to help determine the best strategy. What should we advise?

B—SETTING UP THE TREE

To outline the dilemma facing the BEA managers, we set up a tree, starting with their first decision: Should they sell now, sell in a year, or drill? This *decision fork* is shown as the square on the left in Figure 21-1, with the three lines coming from it representing the three possible alternatives that can be chosen.

Now we must work out the consequences of each of these three alternatives. The consequence of the first—the upper branch of the tree—is immediately seen to be 125K and we show this value with the "price tag" marked 125K.

The second branch of the tree is more complicated. If they sell their

TABLE 21-1 Possible Outcomes of Drilling[a]

Well Type	*Probability*	*Payoff*
Dry	.50	0
Wet	.40	400K
Gusher	.10	1500K

[a] It is assumed that drilling involves practically no time delay. And in the last column, the symbol K means $1000.

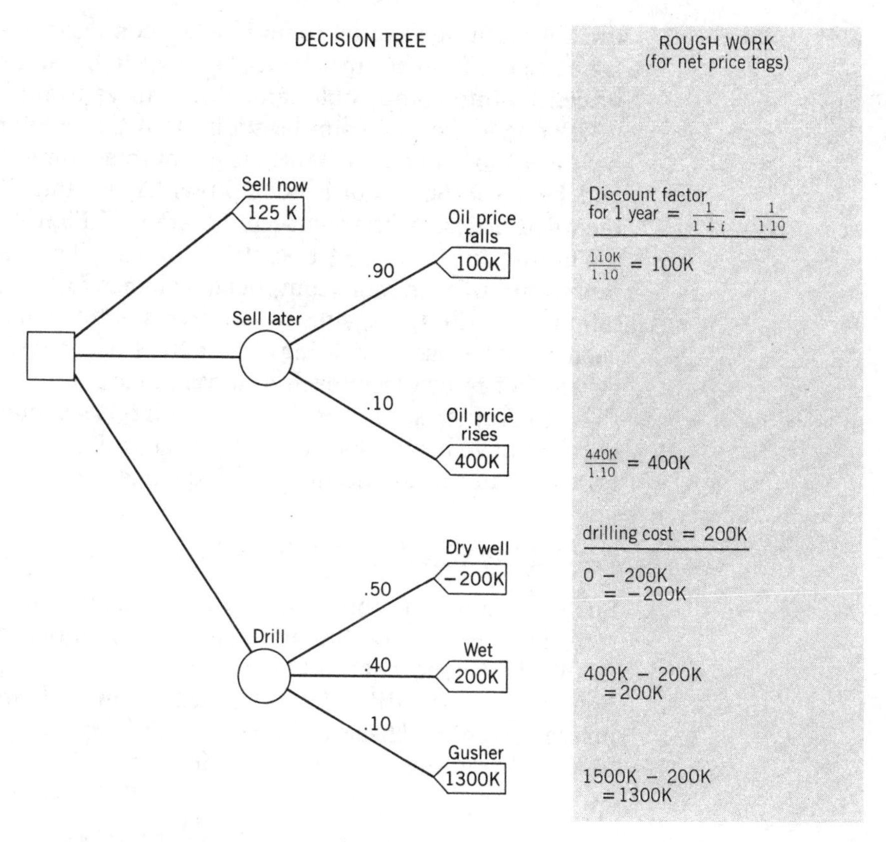

FIGURE 21-1
Setting up the decision tree.

lease a year from now, the price will be determined by chance (or at least, by something completely outside their control—the price of oil). This *chance fork* or *gamble* is shown as a circle to distinguish it from the *decision fork* on the left, which is shown as a square:

Decision forks are shown as squares, chance forks as circles.	(21-1)

The two possible outcomes branching from this "sell later" chance fork are marked with their probabilities, exactly as in the trees of Chapter 3.

How do we calculate the price tags for these two possible outcomes? Consider the first outcome, if the oil price falls. The sale would yield 110K next year. But at the prevailing interest rate $i = 10\%$, this 110K next year is worth only 100K this year. (The reason these two amounts have the same value is that you can take 100K this year, and by investing at the prevailing 10% interest rate, transform it into 110K next year.) Thus this discounted *present value* of 100K is entered in the price tag. [We must do this discounting in order to make a fair comparison with the earlier price tag of 125K (from selling the lease now). In other words, we must get all price tags into comparable terms (present values).]

Of course, we must similarly discount the value that we place on the next price tag, since the 440K we get in this case is also delayed a year—and hence is only worth 400K now. These and other calculations are recorded briefly in the right-hand margin of Figure 21-1.

Turning to the lowest branch of the tree, we encounter a circle that represents an even more complicated chance fork, representing the uncertainties of drilling. Again, the price tags are calculated in the margin: In each of these cases, a drilling cost of 200K has to be subtracted, in order to get the net return from each of these outcomes.

This completes our tree. The decision forks (squares) and chance forks (circles) have been laid out in sequence in Figure 21-1 so we can clearly follow them through to their consequences.

C—DERIVING THE BEST SOLUTION

So far, in setting up the decision tree, we have worked from left to right—recording on the way all the available information (appropriately adjusted in the right-hand column). Turning now to *solving* the decision tree in Figure 21-2, we will work *backwards* from right to left, with each step marked in color. These steps will be of two types: *averaging* each chance fork, and *pruning back* each decision fork:

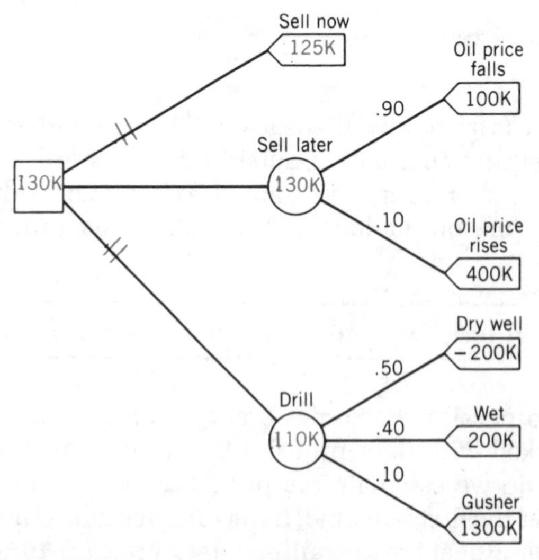

FIGURE 21-2
Solving the decision tree. We work backward, from right to left, averaging the chance forks (circles) and pruning the decision forks (squares). This simplifies the tree until it displays the best choice.

i. *Averaging each chance fork.* With the first alternative (sell now) having a price tag of 125K, for purposes of comparison how do we find a single price tag for the next alternative (sell later)? We take the *average* or *expected value* (EV), by weighting each outcome by its probability:

$$\text{EV of selling later} = .90(100\text{K}) + .10(400\text{K}) = 130\text{K} \tag{21-2}$$

This 130K is recorded in the "sell later" circle in blue.

Similarly, the expected value for the final alternative (drilling) is calculated to be

$$\text{EV of drilling} = .50(-200\text{K}) + .40(200\text{K}) + .10(1300\text{K}) = 110\text{K} \tag{21-3}$$

This 110K is similarly recorded in the "drill" circle in blue.[2]

It is worth briefly reviewing why this calculation of expected value can be applied in this case. Since BEA is a very large exploration company, we can imagine it gambling on a hundred such wells. Then:

About 50 would be dry, @ −200K each = 50(−200K)

About 40 would be wet, @ 200K each = 40(200K)

About 10 would be gushers, @ 1300K each = 10(1300K)

The average gain (expected value) per well is thus

$$\text{EV} = \frac{\text{total gain}}{100} = \frac{50(-200) + 40(200\text{K}) + 10(1300\text{K})}{100} = 110\text{K}$$

This is what justifies the calculation of expected value in (21-3).

---

[2] You may have noticed that there is an easier way of calculating this expected value of 110K. The procedure we used was to:

1. Subtract out the 200K drilling costs (in the right hand column) in order to get the *net* price tags (−200K, 200K, 1300K).
2. Average these.

A simpler computation is this:

1. Initially ignoring the 200K drilling costs, average the *gross* price tags (0, 400K, 1500K); this will yield 310K.
2. We can then subtract the 200K drilling cost to arrive at the same 110K result.

Equation (2-17) confirms that this is always true: We can subtract before *or* after averaging. We prefer to subtract before because the price tags shown in Figure 21-2 then give an accurate picture of the *range of risk;* and we shall see later in Section 21-3 that this may be very important.

ii. *Pruning back the decision fork.* The last step is to compare the three expected values—125K, 130K, and 110K. We simply slash off the inferior ones, which leaves the best policy (sell later); then we record its expected value (130K) in the decision square. This completes the decision, and clearly displays how it was derived.

D—DECISION-MAKING IN GENERAL

In Figure 21-3, we set out a more complicated tree. (Ignore the color for now.) Let us continue to suppose the decision-maker can easily afford to take risks (i.e., is *risk neutral* because of sufficient capital to finance gambles over and over, so that averaging out is relevant. For decision-makers

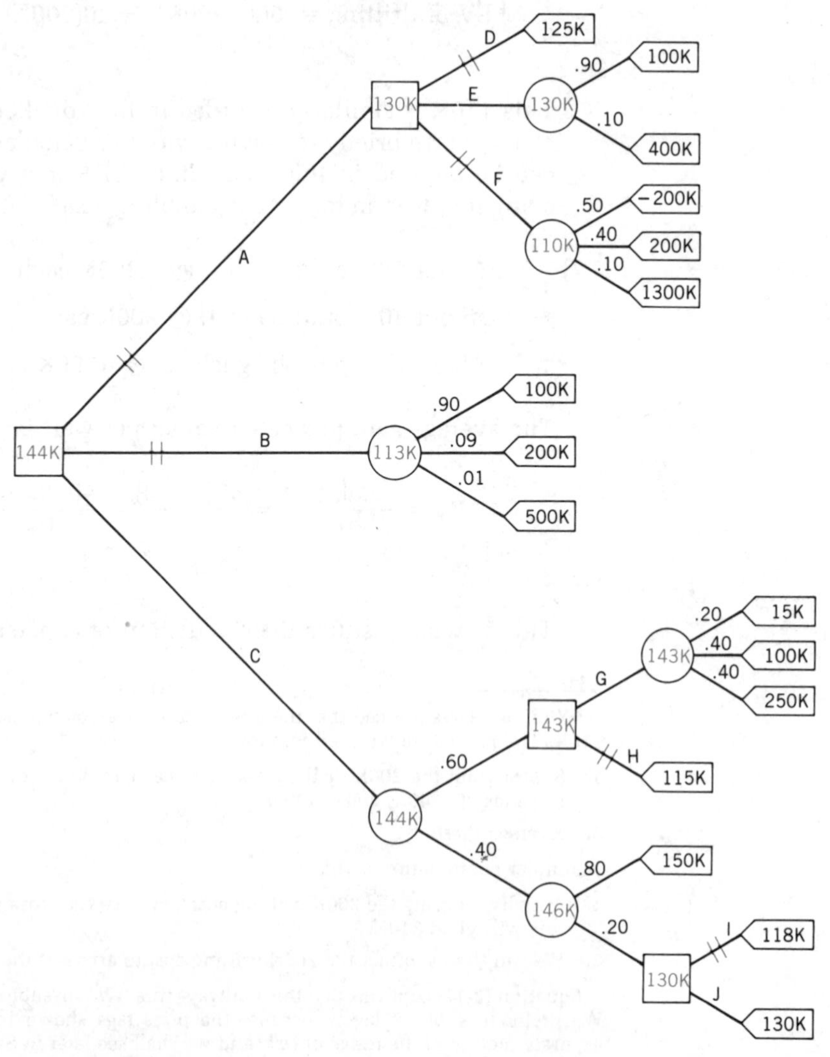

FIGURE 21-3
A more complicated tree.

who are risk averse, see Section 21-3). Then we can determine the best decision by working our way backwards through this tree, applying the following general rules:

1. Whenever we encounter a chance circle, we calculate the *average* (expected value) of this gamble, and record it in the circle. Having obtained this summary figure, we can then ignore the potentially confusing brush (all the branchings of the tree) to the right of this circle.
2. Whenever we encounter a decision square, we *prune* back (slash off) all inferior policies, leaving the best one recorded in the square. Once again, we can then ignore the brush to the right of this square.

The complete solution is shown in color in Figure 21-3. The question is: How would you explain this to a vice president who has never seen a decision tree before? You might describe your finding in this way:

Option C is the best, with an expected value of 144K, *provided* you play it right—like this:

1. Initially *choose option C*, which is a gamble. If its first outcome occurs (as it may, with a 60% chance), then you'll have to make another choice—between options G and H.
2. *Choose G*, which involves another gamble—this is a high risk one, but with an expected value of 143K.
3. When option C is initially chosen in step 1 above, suppose its *second*, rather than its first outcome occurs. That's good news: Your expected value has now risen to 146K; but you face another gamble. If *its* first outcome occurs, you're home free—with 150K. If its second outcome occurs, you must make another choice between options I and J. *Choose J*, which leaves you with 130K.

This analysis can be applied to a wide range of business problems. Notice that we haven't had to specify in any way in Figure 21-3 what sort of a business this is, or what sort of problems it faces. (We've only had to specify price tags and probabilities.) It might, for example, describe decision-making by an oil company. In fact, notice that the top branching (option A) in Figure 21-3 is just the decision BEA faced in Figure 21-2. Thus you can view Figure 21-3 as the problem BEA would have faced if it had introduced this form of decision-making one month earlier, say, before it had bought the exploration lease and when it had to decide between this lease and two other ways of spending its money (options B and C). In Figure 21-3, we now see that the purchase of the lease was a mistake; if we had introduced this analysis a month earlier, and chosen option C instead of the purchase of the lease (option A), we could have increased the company's expected earnings by 144K − 130K = 14K.

Alternatively, Figure 21-3 could describe an entirely different firm facing a sequence of risky decisions. For example, it could represent a retail firm deciding among three different levels of inventory, where the chance forks represent the uncertain sales that are expected to absorb this inventory.

PROBLEMS

In all the Problems in this section and the next, unless otherwise stated assume that decision-makers are wealthy enough to be risk neutral, that is, they can afford to go for the long-run average.

21-1 Karen Becker faced some major decisions on whether to expand her small riverside café. After careful thought, she found her decision tree reduced to the following (in thousands of dollars):

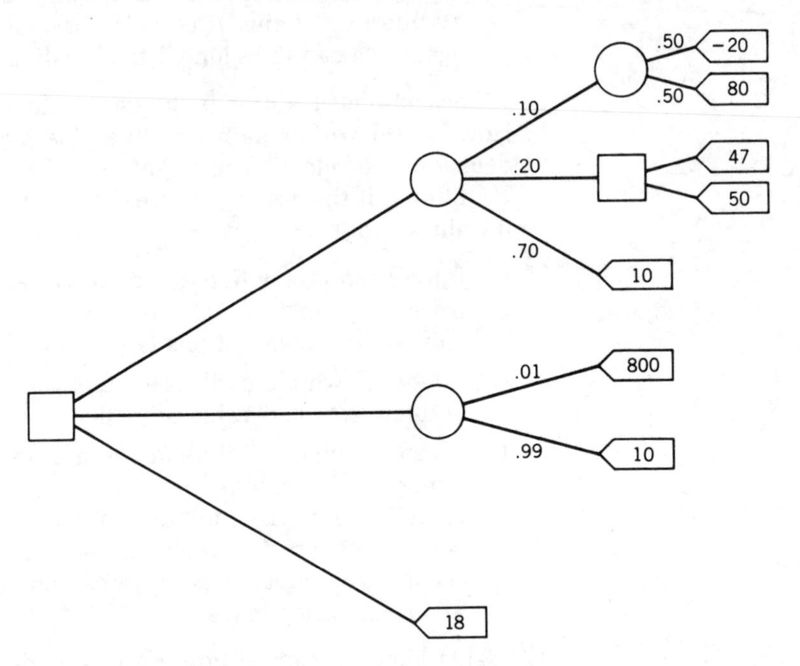

a. By averaging out and folding back, show her best strategy.

b. Suppose she is relatively poor and risk averse. Might that change her decision? Why?

21-2 A large oil corporation developed a very expensive new process for extracting oil from its shale fields in Colorado, and had to decide whether to go ahead with such a high-stakes game. The rough guess of the planning staff was that it would cost 200 million just to set up the plant; there was also a 60% chance the project would fail and they would lose their 200 million. Yet there was a 30% chance that it would work and produce a 100 million net profit (above their 200 million investment) and a 10% chance that it would work spectacularly and produce a whopping 1000 million net profit.

Assuming all these figures are present values (allowing for interest), should they go ahead with the plant?

21-3 In the 1960s, experimental work on the seeding of hurricanes at sea with silver oxide indicated it would probably reduce the force of the hurricane. Because of high risks, initially the seeding was entirely limited to experimental work on hurricanes that spent their life at sea. Before applying this research to huricanes that threatened the coast, the U.S. government had to face the possibility that seeding might sometimes make hurricanes worse rather than better, and so commissioned a formal decision analysis (Howard, 1972). The following table outlines the estimates of the various chances and losses involved:

Probabilities and Losses of Various Wind Changes Occurring in the 12 Hours Before Hurricane Landfall

Interval of Changes In Maximum Sustained Wind	*Approximate Midpoint of Interval*	*Consequent Damage ($1,000,000)*	*Probability that Wind Change Will be Within Interval*	
			If Seeded	*If Not Seeded*
Increase of 25% or more	+32%	336	.038	.054
Increase of 10% to 25%	+16%	191	.143	.206
Less than 10% change	0%	100	.392	.480
Reduction of 10% to 25%	−16%	47	.255	.206
Reduction of 25% or more	−34%	16	.172	.054

If the government was interested in minimizing long-run costs, would seeding be worthwhile? Work out the answer under two different assumptions:

a. The only cost of seeding was the cost of the operation—$250,000 for silver oxide and airplanes.

b. There was an additional cost of "government responsibility." If they seeded and the storm became worse, whether or not it was the fault of the seeding, they might be sued for damages, or suffer politically from a storm of criticism. Suppose this cost was considered roughly equivalent to an extra $168 million for the highest increase in wind (25% or more), an extra $57 million for a moderate increase in wind (10% to 25%), and an extra $5 million for very little change in wind (−10% to +10%).

21-4 Jack Campbell has just arrived at UCLA for a year's sabbatical leave from the University of Edinburgh. He needs a car but cannot decide which of the following three to choose:

i. He could lease a new Lasalle for 12 months at $300 per month, which includes insurance and all repairs.

ii. He could buy a new Renown for $6500, pay $500 insurance, and be free of repair bills because of the car's excellent warranty. At the end of 12 months, he expects he could sell it back to the dealer for $4200. Or better yet, there is a 30% chance his sister will be coming over to California, and would be happy to buy it from him for $4700.

iii. He could buy a 3-year-old Q-car from "Honest Ed" for $2500. The record of these cars is excellent—repair free, in fact—except for transmission trouble: Every year, 20% of them develop transmission trouble that is impossible to fix—it renders the car worthless. Furthermore, he would then have to lease a car for the remaining months at $400 per month. And his insurance of $500 would not be refundable at all.

Even if the car survived the twelve months, it would not command much of a resale price—about $800 on the used car market, or $1200 from his sister if she came over.

Jack doesn't mind taking a few risks, nor does he mind the extra wheeling and dealing required to deal with Honest Ed, his sister, or whomever. He heard you are taking a course in decision analysis, and wants your advice. Work out two answers:

a. Ignoring interest.

***b.** Assuming interest is 10% per year (and a rough approximation will do).

21-2 TESTING TO REVISE PROBABILITIES: BAYES THEOREM

A—EXAMPLE, WITH TEST INFORMATION ADDED

To return to the oil lease example in Figure 21-2, note again the drilling branch at the bottom of this diagram showing the high cost if a well turns out to be dry: The loss is 200K in drilling costs, with nothing in return. It would be ideal if we could wait to make the drilling decision *until after we knew* whether or not the well would be dry, and so avoid this waste.

In practice, we cannot know for sure without actually drilling the hole. However, suppose we can get a good idea from a preliminary seismic analysis that will determine the geological structure of the area in which we are drilling. There are 3 kinds of structure: no structure (N)—bad news; open structure (O)—better news; and closed structure (C)—most encouraging of all. Table 21-2 shows why N is bad news: From past records, geologists have found that most (70%) of the dry wells have been in this N structure, while most (60%) of the gushers have been in the C structure.

The cost of the seismic analysis to determine the geological structure is about 10K. Is it worth it? If so, how should the result be used?

B—SOLUTION: REVISED PROBABILITIES

Does Table 21-2 really give us useful information? It tells us, once we know the kind of well, the probabilities of various geological structures.

TABLE 21-2 Conditional Probabilities of Various Geological Structures for Each Type of Well

Given this Type of Well . . .	. . . These are the Probabilities of Various Kinds of Geological Structure		
	N	O	C
Dry	.70	.20	.10
Wet	.30	.40	.30
Gusher	.10	.30	.60

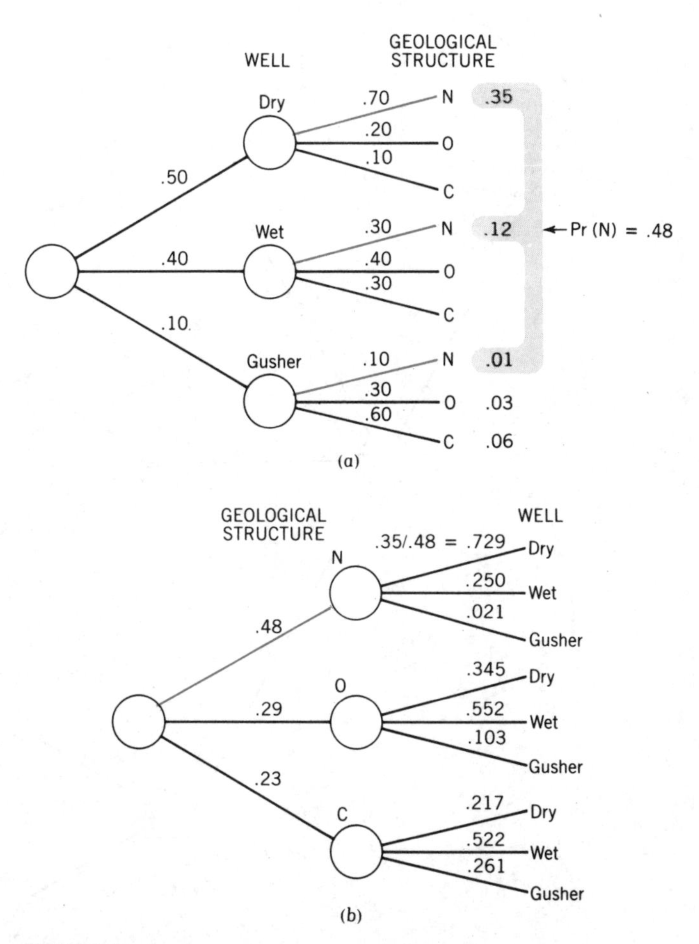

FIGURE 21-4

Bayes Theorem to revise probabilities. (a) Initial tree. (b) Reverse tree. These are not decision trees; they are Bayesian probability trees, which provide better probabilities to plug into the decision tree in Figure 21-5.

But we want information in the reverse order: Given (seismic) knowledge of the geological structure, what are the probabilities of various kinds of wells? Fortunately, this can be provided by the Bayesian tree reversal developed in Section 3-6 (Figure 3-9, for example). Figure 21-4 shows how it works in this case: Starting from the left in panel (a), we display the best information we have so far on the various kinds of well—the prior

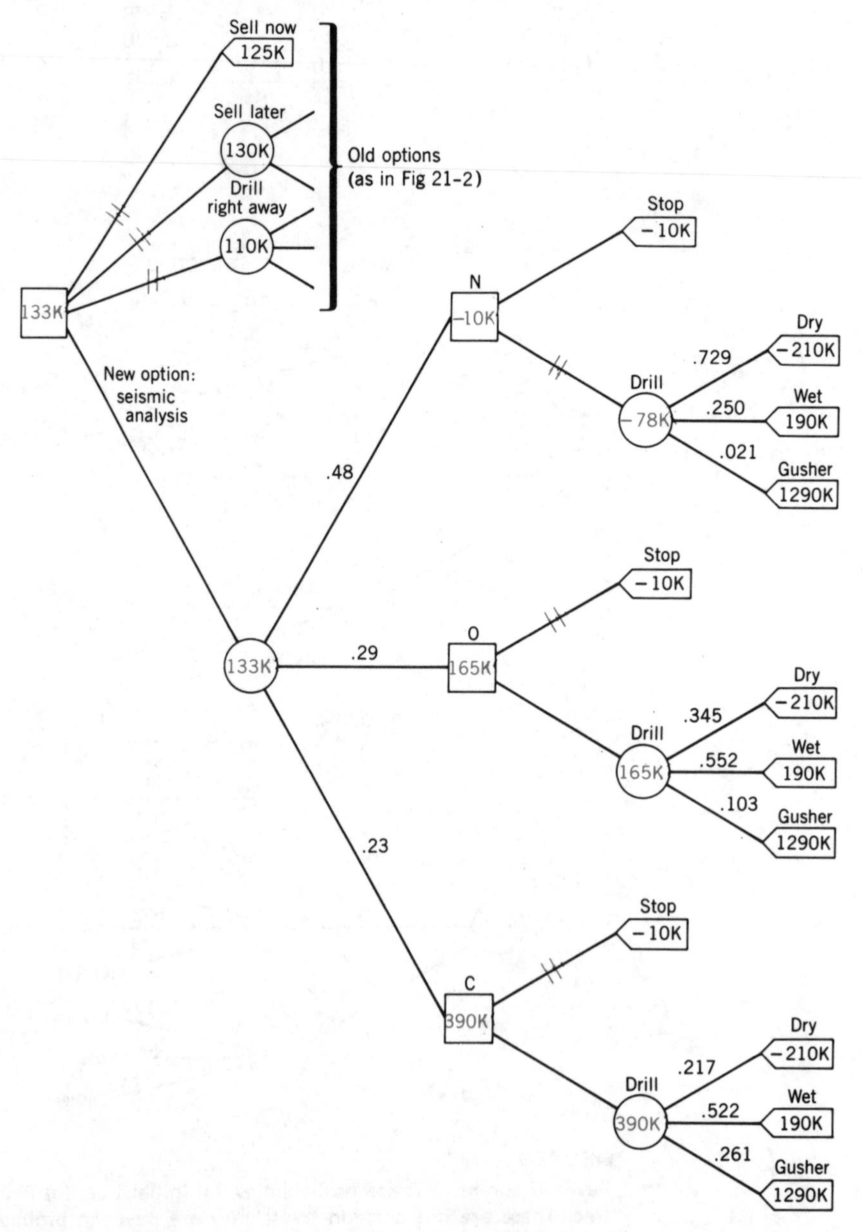

FIGURE 21-5
Drill decision (Figure 21-2) revised by seismic test results (from Figure 21-4b).

probabilities (.50, .40, .10, taken from Figure 21-2) that apply if we drill "blind," without first doing a seismic analysis. Moving to the right, we set out the three "branchings" (taken from the three rows in Table 21-2) that show the probability of each geological structure, once the type of well is known. Outlined on the extreme right is our calculation that there is a .48 probability of a N structure; this is reproduced in panel (b) as the first branch. Then the three branchings to the right give the desired *posterior* probabilities of various kinds of well, once the geological structure is known through our seismic analysis.

Panel (b) now provides exactly the information we need to describe our new "fourth option" (first doing a seismic analysis to find out the structure, and only then deciding on whether or not to drill). When it is plugged into Figure 21-2, we get the complete decision tree shown in Figure 21-5. Note that the right-hand price tags (for dry, wet, and gusher wells) are the same as before, except of course that now we must deduct the 10K cost of the seismic analysis. This 10K cost also appears in the 3 price tags marked "stop" that allow us to stop and not drill once we know the structure.

When we average out and prune back (shown in blue in Figure 21-5) we find that this new "fourth option" is worth 133K, and is now the best decision: We should begin with the seismic analysis of structure, and only then decide whether or not to drill.

C—WHAT IS THE SEISMIC ANALYSIS WORTH?

When we compare the new value of the tree (133K) with the old value (130K in Figure 21-2), we can calculate the net gain in the expected value of the enterprise due to the seismic analysis (or, in general, due to sampling of any sort):

$$\begin{aligned}&\text{Expected Net Gain from Sampling,}\\ &\text{ENGS} = 133\text{K} - 130\text{K}\\ &\quad\;\;\; = 3\text{K}\end{aligned} \tag{21-4}$$

Thus we see how sampling, processed by Bayes' Theorem, can improve decisions.

PROBLEMS

21-5 In Problem 21-2, suppose a small pilot plant was studied as a possible way to get valuable information. From past experience, it was guessed that with a cost of 40 million, a viable pilot plant could be built that would reasonably reflect the operation of the main plant itself, as follows: if the main plant works (or works spectacularly), the pilot plant has an 80% chance of working, and a 20% chance of failing; if the main plant fails, the pilot plant is sure to fail too, being smaller and cheaper.

a. Should they build the pilot plant?

b. A year later, having already invested 20 million in the pilot plant, the price of oil drops so that their gross profits (before paying for the pilot plant or the 200 million main plant) would be only 30% of their formerly estimated value. Now what should they do?

21-6 The Arvida Flour Mill was debating whether or not to change its packaging from a bag to a box. The increased cost would be 0.6¢ each, reducing the profit of each item from 5.3¢ down to 4.7¢. For this extra cost, however, Arvida would get a more convenient package, which, it was hoped, might improve sales: They guessed there was a 60% chance that sales would increase by 20%. (Otherwise, sales would remain unchanged.)

The planning horizon for Arvida was 5 years; beyond that, technology might change to make both boxes and bags obsolete. During that 5-year period, Arvida's projected sales were 15 million bags.

a. Is it worthwhile changing to a box?

b. In the past, Arvida has sometimes conducted a consumer survey to predict whether its sales would increase or not. This survey cost $10,000, and had a good record: Whether sales increased or not, there was a 75% chance of a correct prediction.

An intensive survey by a market research firm would cost $30,000, and increase the chances of a correct prediction from 75% to 90%. Should Arvida hire them? Or go with its own $10,000 survey? Or forget them both?

21-7 Replace Table 21-2 with the following "half-price" test that costs only 5K:

Conditional Probabilities of Various Geological Structures for Each Type of Well

Given this Type of Well . . .	*. . . These are the Probabilities of Various Kinds of Geological Structure*		
	N	O	C
Dry	.50	.30	.20
Wet	.40	.30	.30
Gusher	.20	.20	.60

a. Would you say this seismic test is better or worse than in Table 21-2?

b. Rework the decision tree in Figure 21-5, including as an option this half-price seismic test.

21-3 UTILITY THEORY TO HANDLE RISK AVERSION

A—THE LIMITATIONS OF EXPECTED MONETARY VALUE (EMV)

On the basis of Figure 21-5, Jack Moor recommends to BEA that it should proceed with the fourth option, worth 133K: Do a seismic analysis and then (unless the structure is N) drill for oil. But now suppose that Moor himself, rather than BEA, owns this lease. As an *individual* faced with exactly these same numbers, would he make the same decision?

His answer is *no way*—and he gives good reasons. True, if everything goes right he becomes a very rich man. (He ends up with a gusher netting 1290K.) But is it worth the risk? If everything goes wrong, he's wiped out. (He ends up having to pay for a seismic analysis and drilling a dry well that puts him 210K in debt.) He therefore opts for selling the lease and thus becomes just comfortably rich, for certain.

Clearly, this is a reasonable decision. Why then does he advise BEA to make an entirely different decision, and take a risk on drilling? The answer is that BEA can essentially ignore risk because, as a very large company, it is drilling hundreds of wells (or, equivalently, taking hundreds of other major decisions). True, some of these wells will be dry, but some will be gushers. As we saw in Figure 21-5, the average or expected value that BEA will earn on each well will be 133K, which is better than what it would get from selling.

In conclusion, it is appropriate for BEA to use the money price tags and the resulting calculations of *Expected Monetary Value* (EMV) in Figure 21-5. But these calculations are inappropriate for an individual who can only "spin the wheel once" and has a normal aversion to putting all his money (plus a lot he has to borrow) on the table. For such an individual, averaging these purely monetary price tags *must* be inappropriate, because it points to the wrong decision. This is our problem, then, in the rest of this chapter: to find a better set of price tags that reflect an individual's aversion to risk.

B—ALL DOLLARS DON'T HAVE THE SAME UTILITY

To confirm that individuals are typically averse to risk, and that EMV calculations are therefore inappropriate, consider the following question:

EXAMPLE 21-1

Suppose a generous friend offers you a once-in-a-lifetime gamble:

Option 1. On the flip of a fair coin, you get
$1,500,000 if heads, $0 if tails (21-5)

Alternatively, if you prefer, you can choose:

Option 2. $500,000 for certain (21-6)

Which option would you choose?

SOLUTION

Of course there is no "right" or "wrong" answer. Different people have different individual values that lead them to different but perfectly valid answers. Yet most people would prefer option 2, even though its expected monetary value is less:

$$\text{EMV of option 2} = \$500{,}000\ (1.0) = \$500{,}000 \tag{21-7}$$

whereas

$$\text{EMV of option 1} = \$1{,}500{,}000(.50) + 0(.50) = \$750{,}000 \tag{21-8}$$

The reason is simple: Most people value their first half-million more than their second or third. (Technically, we say that they have a declining marginal utility of money.) With the first $500,000 they can buy the important things—a home, a couple of cars, a good pension, and so on. With another $500,000, or even another $1,000,000, they can only buy less important things—a second house, several more cars, and so on. Why should they risk losing that first $500,000 in order to get just another $1,000,000?

Thus we conclude that everyone has a subjective valuation of money, called the "utility of money," and this depends on what money will buy (the first or second home, etc.). In Figure 21-6, we graph the utility of money for a typically risk-averse individual, say Jack Moor. The utility of the first half-million dollars is high, and is shown as the first vertical arrow. The additional (i.e., marginal) utility of the second or third half-million dollars is much less.[3] (To see just how a utility curve like this is derived, and why it is legitimate to then use it in decision analysis, see Raiffa, 1968)

C—DECISIONS BASED ON EXPECTED UTILITY

A wise decision is one that maximizes a person's happiness or satisfaction as measured by his utility function, rather than mere money. Thus, to solve a decision tree, the decision-maker must first convert each payoff on the right from dollars to utility—by reading utility values vertically off a

[3] Although we show just a limited range, and arbitrarily scale the *U* axis from 0 to 1 over this range, the utility curve continues to slowly rise on the right since human wants are never completely satisfied.

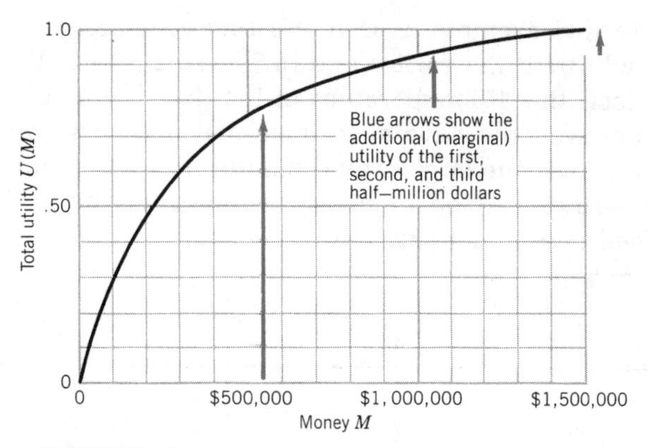

FIGURE 21-6
Jack Moor's utility of money.

graph reflecting personal values, such as Fig. 21-6. Then he proceeds as before, averaging out and folding back, to find the decision with highest expected utility. An example will illustrate:

EXAMPLE 21-2

Suppose the decision-maker is no longer the BEA Corporation, but instead is Jack Moor personally, with his utility function given in Figure 21-6. Also suppose the drilling option in Figure 21-1 is not available, so that the decision tree is the reduced version set out in Figure 21-7. Find Jack's optimal solution, that maximizes his expected utility.

SOLUTION

The money value of each outcome shown in Figure 21-7 is converted (using Figure 21-6) to utilities in Figure 21-8. These utilities, shown in special brackets, are then averaged out and folded back, to finally show the option with highest expected utility: the first option (sell now).

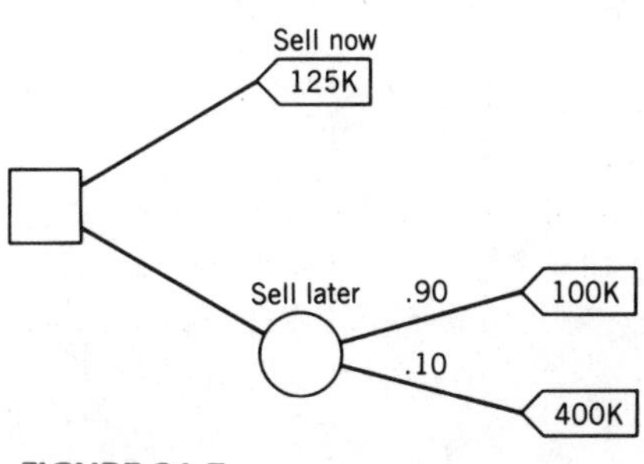

FIGURE 21-7
The decision tree set out in terms of money (reduced version of Figure 21-1).

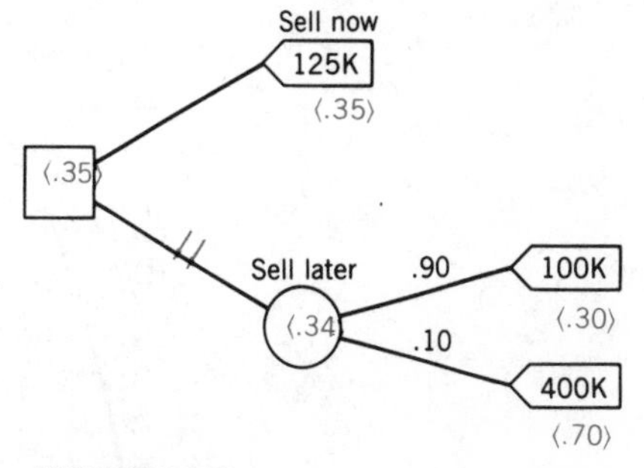

FIGURE 21-8
The decision tree converted to bracketed utilities, and solved.

In this example, it is interesting to compare the best decision ("sell now") with the earlier one in Figure 21-2 ("sell later"). The difference reflects the different values of the decision-makers. Specifically, in Jack Moor we now have a decision-maker who is risk averse, since he no longer has the large capital behind him that would enable him to go for long-run expected monetary value. Thus, he finds the risk-free choice ("sell now") more attractive.

PROBLEMS

21-8 Two forms of treatment are available for lung cancer—surgery or radiation—and they produce different survival patterns as roughly shown below (McNeil and others, 1978):

X = Additional Years of Life	Relative Frequency, $p(X)$	
	If Surgery	If Radiation
0	47%	23%
2	19%	48%
5	11%	10%
10	7%	6%
15	5%	5%
20	5%	5%
25	6%	3%

a. If patients want to maximize their life expectancy, which form of therapy should they choose? (This is the criterion traditionally recommended by doctors.)

b. A sample of 14 patients were probed with a series of questions that uncovered their utility of various lengths of life. The median patient had the following utility curve:

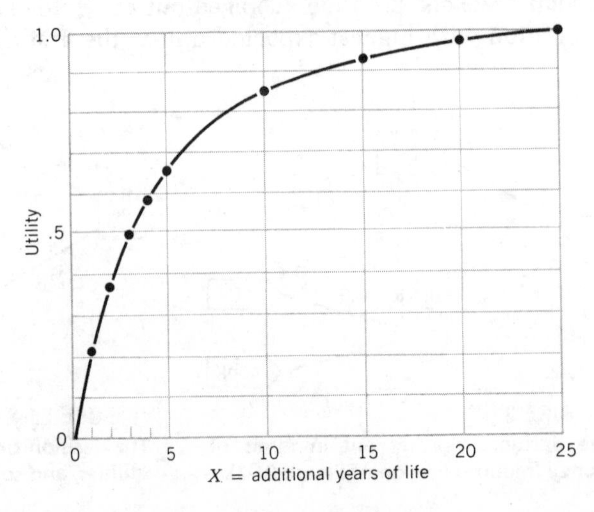

Now what is the best treatment for such a patient?

c. If you were a doctor, would you recommend surgery or radiation? Why?

d. Do you agree with the following conclusion of the authors (McNeil and others, 1978)? If not, why not?

> These results emphasize the importance of choosing therapies not only on the basis of objective measures of survival but also on the basis of patients attitudes.

21-9 Suppose a fire insurance policy costs $115 per year, and compensates the homeowner against the following losses. (Frequency is given as fires per 100,000 homes, annually. Data is hypothetical.)

Damage (in $000)	*Average Dollar Loss*	*Frequency*
Small fire (0–5)	$ 1,000	2100
Medium fire (5–20)	10,000	300
Major fire (20–60)	30,000	20
Beyond repair (60)	60,000	5

a. The owners of a mortgaged home always have to buy fire insurance. (The value of the house must be protected, or lenders will not provide mortgage money.) For someone who has just paid off the mortgage, however (and is thus free of all such restrictions imposed by lenders), is this insurance wise to keep?

b. Of all the income the insurance company receives from premiums, what proportion actually is paid out for fire losses? (The rest goes to administration costs and profit.)

c. Suppose the insurance company has a "$5000 deductible" option—they only pay damage after the first $5000. What percentage of their former losses would they have to pay out? If they passed that percentage on to the customer, what would the premium be instead of $115?

21-10 Suppose an insurance company insures against the $50 loss of a contact lens, in exchange for a premium of $12 per year. Its experience every year has been that 10% of its customers make one claim, and another 3% make two claims. (After that, the policy is cancelled.) Would you buy this insurance? Why or why not?

CHAPTER 21 SUMMARY

21-1 Decision problems can be graphed as a tree, with circles showing the chance forks, and squares showing the decision forks. For big companies that can average out their risk, the best decision can be found by using the criterion of expected monetary value (EMV). To calculate this, the circles (chance forks) are averaged out, and the squares (decision forks) are pruned back, to display the best choice.

21-2 Sample information, using Bayes Theorem, can reduce uncertainty and so improve the value of the enterprise.

21-3 For decisions that involve big risks relative to financial capacity, payoffs must be expressed in terms of utility, rather than money. In fact, utility is a versatile enough tool to allow us to compare *all* kinds of payoffs, not just money payoffs.

REVIEW PROBLEMS

21-11 When David Stein drives into the university each day, he has to choose a parking space. As the map shows, he can either turn right to the main parking lot P, where there is always plenty of space, or he can take his chances going directly ahead to the Business School B where he works.

There is a 30% chance he can find a spot in the small parking lot behind the Business School, or, failing that, he can always park at a meter at the front. If he feels adventurous, he can forgo feeding the meter the $4 it requires for the day, and chance getting a $15 parking ticket—which, he has noticed, occurs about a tenth of the time.

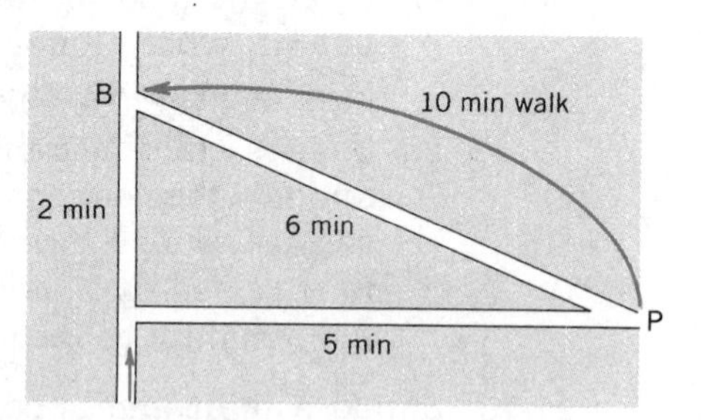

a. The times (in minutes) required for driving the various routes are marked on the map, as well as the 10 minute walk back from the parking lot P. If his time is worth $12 per hour, what is his best strategy? And how much does it cost?

b. Suppose he faces an additional penalty for not paying the meter: Half the cars that get a ticket also get towed away at a cost of $40 (on top of the $15 ticket), plus an hour of time.

Now what should he do? At what cost?

21-12 Susan Graham is wondering whether to borrow heavily to invest in real estate. When she sells after 12 months, she must pay off the loan, plus 10% interest. Tax laws allow her to reduce her taxes by one dollar for every two dollars spent on interest, so that only half of the interest paid is a genuine expense.

If the real estate rises in value, the increase in value will be a tax-free capital gain, but a profit is not assured. She estimates that for each $100,000 she invests, its possible values at year's end are:

Value at Year's End	*Capital Gain*	*Probability*
$125,000	$25,000	.30
$115,000	$15,000	.40
$105,000	$5,000	.10
$85,000	−$15,000 (loss)	.20

The investment opportunity allows only multiples of $100,000, and the bank will loan her a maximum of $500,000.

a. If Susan is risk-neutral, should she invest in this plan? If so, how much? Explain briefly.

b. In fact, she is not risk-neutral: Her utility curve is given in the table below. Given this attitude toward risk, what should Susan do?

Net Gain ($000)	*Utility*[a]	*Net Gain ($000)*	*Utility*	*Net Gain ($000)*	*Utility*
−100	0	0	0.60	100	0.80
−90	0.10	10	0.63	200	0.85
−80	0.19	20	0.66	300	0.89
−70	0.27	30	0.68	400	0.92
−60	0.33	40	0.70	500	0.95
−50	0.39	50	0.72	600	0.97
−40	0.44	60	0.74	700	0.99
−30	0.49	70	0.76	750	1.00
−20	0.53	80	0.77		
−10	0.57	90	0.79		

[a] If intermediate values are needed, use linear interpolation.

21-13 **a.** John Makeham's dream home has turned into a nightmare. Nine months ago, Regal Lumber contracted to supply all the lumber, precut and delivered for $40,000. However, because the price of lumber has increased since by 25%, Regal is now trying to back out. They offer to sell him the lumber for $50,000 or return his deposit of $5000, whichever he prefers.

If he now buys the lumber elsewhere, it will cost him $55,000 to have it precut to the specifications already built into the foundation. His lawyer advises him that, as soon as Regal has returned his $5000 deposit, he can then sue the company for the $15,000 difference he paid in excess of the contracted price. The chances of his winning the case, including his court costs, are estimated at 80%. If he loses, he will have to pay all the court costs of $10,000. His lawyer recommends that before he definitely decides on this risky option, he should consult a legal expert who, for a $4000 fee, could do extensive research and guarantee to let him know for sure whether or not he will win in court.

Since he has invested so much already in this house and lot, he feels he has to finish building it one way or another. Find his best course of action, assuming he is wealthy enough that he can easily absorb financial setbacks and therefore use expected monetary value as his criterion.

b. To what value would the legal expert have to reduce his fee in order for it to be a worthwhile buy? [This is sometimes called the Expected Value of Perfect Information, (EVPI).]

c. Find his best course of action, if he is risk-averse. In fact, suppose large costs are particularly worrisome, as indicated by his "disutility curve":

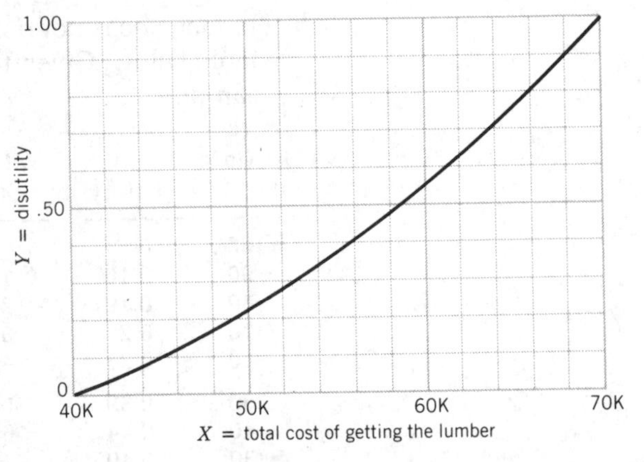

21-14 Suppose a very large company has an oil lease they could sell now for 250K, or else drill. Fortunately, to help them decide, they have not only a seismic test available, but also records of how the test and the subsequent drilling have turned out in hundreds of similar situations:

Bivariate Frequency Distribution for $n = 500$ Drillings

	Geological Structure		
Type of Well	N	O	C
Dry	170	80	30
Wet	30	40	30
Gusher	20	40	60

The test costs 20K and the drilling costs 300K. The expected returns are 2000K for a gusher, 500K for a wet well, and nothing of course for a dry well. What should they do?

21-15 Having developed a new quick-open can that keeps coffee fresher, a large food company now has to decide whether or not to market it. The marketing manager guesses that sales might roughly change 2%, 1%, 0, or −1%—with each of these possibilities being equally likely. After changeover costs, this would mean profit changes of \$75,000; \$30,000; \$−15,000; \$−60,000; respectively.

a. Is it worthwhile introducing the new can?

b. What would it be worth to be able to predict the market perfectly; that is, what is the Expected Value of Perfect Information (EVPI)?

c. A 6-month trial is suggested to get the reaction to the new can in Middletown—a small city, typical of the whole U.S. market, where the company has often tested new products. In fact, from past tests, the research staff guessed that the Middletown reaction will be closely related to U.S. sales, as outlined in the following table of probabilities:

Possible Change in U.S. Sales	*Reaction in Middletown*			*Total Probability*
	Favorable	*Neutral*	*Unfavorable*	
+2%	.8	.2	0	1.00
+1%	.6	.2	.2	1.00
0	.3	.4	.3	1.00
−1%	.1	.4	.5	1.00

i. If the trial costs \$40,000, is it worth it?

ii. If the trial costs \$10,000, is it worth it? If so, how should its results be used?

iii. At what price does the trial become too expensive?

21-16 ***A Final Challenge: A Question of Lifestyle***

John Ellwood grew up on a farm 15 years ago, has since become a successful accountant, and now has saved up \$100,000 (100K) to invest. As an alternative to a conservative investment portfolio of stocks and bonds, he would like to buy a farm because he and his wife would love living on it, working it, and raising their young family on it. But he realizes that a farm, especially a properly equipped large farm, is a big gamble (with four very uncertain components—weather, crop prices, interest rates, and government policy). So he estimates his chances as well as he can, and comes up with the following financial analysis of where he would be after 30 years (in 1990 prices).

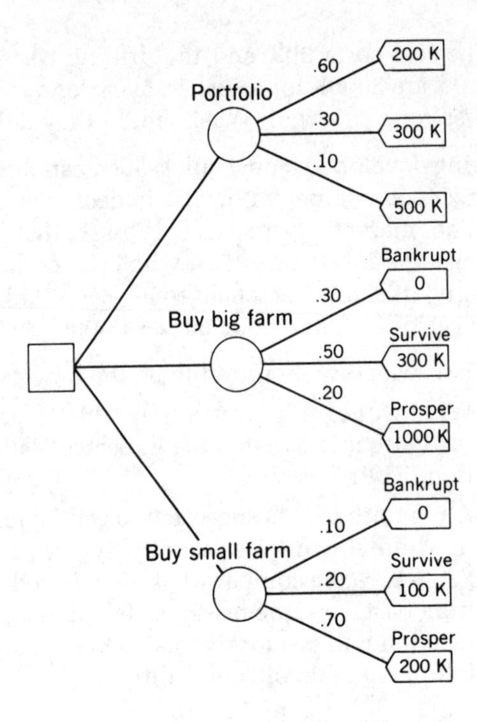

a. His friend Bill Wood tells John to use expected monetary value (EMV) as the criterion for choosing the best action. If he took this advice, what would John choose?

b. Another friend, Sue Doud, tells John he should discount huge sums of money appropriately, since later dollars are not as valuable as early dollars. That is, he should find his utility curve for money. To do this, Sue asked him several penetrating questions, from which John's utility function was constructed as follows:

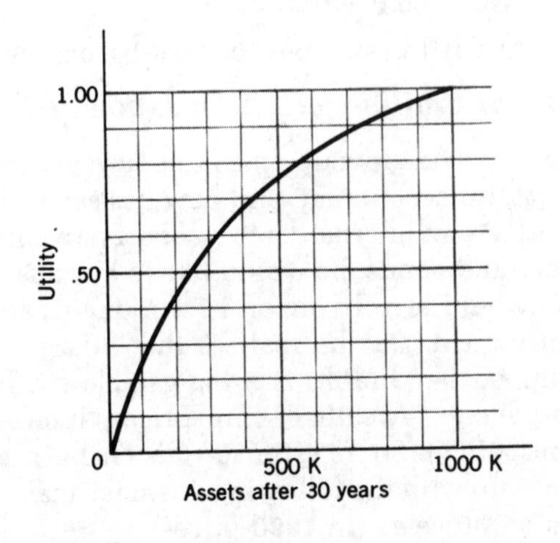

If John used expected utility as his criterion, as Sue suggested, what would he choose?

c. John asks you whose advice he should take, Bill's or Sue's? Or some other advice? What would you say?

CHAPTER 22

Index Numbers

(Requires Nothing Previous)

Inflation is like toothpaste. Once it's out, you can hardly get it back in again.

KARL-OTTO POHL

A *price index* is a single figure that shows how a whole set of prices has changed. For example, if we are asked what has happened to prices over the last 12 months, it is far simpler to reply that the overall price index has risen by 5%, say, rather than that the price of eggs is up 20%, the price of TVs is down 10%, and so on.

Similarly, if we wish to compare the quantity or output of industrial goods in the United States and Canada, it is convenient to state that the *industrial output index* of Canada is 8% that of the United States, rather than state that Canada produces, say, 9% of the U.S. output of autos, 2% of the U.S. output of aircraft parts, and so on.

22-1 PRICE INDEXES

A—PRICE RELATIVES

Let us develop a price index for food, assuming the national diet consists of just the three items listed in Table 22-1—steak, pepper, and bread—at prices initially denoted by P_o, and t years later by P_t. The price of steak, for example, has increased by the factor $3.00/2.20 = 1.36$. Customarily it is multiplied by 100 to get rid of the decimal point, and then it is called the *price relative:*

$$\text{Price relative} \equiv \frac{P_t}{P_o}(100) \tag{22-1}$$

How can we summarize the overall price trend with a single number? A natural suggestion is to average the price relatives for all items:

$$\text{Simple average} = \frac{136 + 100 + 120}{3} = 119$$

The problem with the simple average, of course, is that it gives pepper as much weight as bread or steak. We therefore must look for an index that gives a heavier weight to important items.

B—THE LASPEYRES AND PAASCHE INDEXES

A price index is intended to measure the overall increase in prices, so let us just see how much the average person's physical diet—the "basket of goods" quantities Q_o in Table 22-2—has increased in cost. The numbers along the first line of this table show that in 1980, this diet included 50 pounds of steak at a cost of \$2.20 per pound, for a total of \$110. Similarly, the expenditures on pepper and bread totaled \$4 and \$40, so that the total cost was \$154. In general terms:

$$\text{Initial cost} = \Sigma P_o Q_o \tag{22-2}$$

TABLE 22-1 Price Relatives for a Hypothetical Diet

	Given Prices		*Ratio*	*Price Relative*
Item	*1980* P_o	*1985* P_t	$\frac{P_t}{P_o}$	$\frac{P_t}{P_o}(100)$
Steak (per pound)	\$2.20	\$3.00	1.36	136
Pepper (per ounce)	\$2.00	\$2.00	1.00	100
Bread (per pound)	\$ .50	\$ .60	1.20	120

TABLE 22-2 From Prices and Quantities, the Laspeyres or Paasche Price Index Can Be Calculated

	Given Data				Laspeyres Price Index		Paasche Price Index	
	Prices		Quantities		Cost of 1980 Basket		Cost of 1985 Basket	
Item	1980 P_o	1985 P_t	1980 Q_o	1985 Q_t	In 1980 P_oQ_o	In 1985 P_tQ_o	In 1980 P_oQ_t	In 1985 P_tQ_t
Steak (lb)	\$2.20	\$3.00	50	40	\$110	\$150	\$ 88	\$120
Pepper (oz)	\$2.00	\$2.00	2	3	\$ 4	\$ 4	\$ 6	\$ 6
Bread (lb)	\$ .50	\$ .60	80	100	\$ 40	\$ 48	\$ 50	\$ 60
					\$154	\$202	\$144	\$186
			↑ 1980 basket of goods		Index = $\frac{\$202}{\$154}$ (100) = 131		Index = $\frac{\$186}{\$144}$ (100) = 129	

What would this same diet cost later? We merely use the later prices P_t instead of P_o:

$$\text{Later cost} = \Sigma P_t Q_o \tag{22-3}$$

The price index is calculated by comparing the costs in the two years, for *this fixed basket of goods:*

$$\boxed{\textbf{Laspeyres price index} \equiv \frac{\Sigma P_t Q_o}{\Sigma P_o Q_o}(100)} \tag{22-4}$$

$$= \frac{\$202}{\$154}(100) = 131$$

Note that the cost of pepper does influence the index very little indeed, since it was only \$4 in a budget totalling well over \$100.

The question naturally arises: Why do we use as weights the *initial* basket of goods; that is, why do we use weights Q_o in (22-4)? We could construct an equally valid index using the *later* basket of goods (given by Q_t). This gives us a slightly different answer:

$$\boxed{\textbf{Paasche price index} \equiv \frac{\Sigma P_t Q_t}{\Sigma P_o Q_t}(100)} \tag{22-5}$$

$$= \frac{\$186}{\$144}(100) = 129$$

Although there may be no theoretical reason for preferring one index to the other, there is a practical reason for using the Laspeyres index when indexing is done year after year: The Laspeyres index uses the same base weights Q_0 in all calculations, whereas the Paasche index has to use different weights Q_t every year.

Clearly, in applying the Laspeyres index, the selection of the base year becomes a crucial issue. For example, the index would become almost meaningless if the initial base period were a wartime year in which steak was rationed, and very little was consumed. In this case, steak would essentially disappear from the calculation of price indexes for the later peacetime period when it was an important item in consumption. Hence, great care must be taken that the base year is a reasonably typical one, free of disasters or other unusual events that distort consumption patterns.

C—FISHER'S IDEAL INDEX: THE GEOMETRIC MEAN

Recall that the ordinary mean (arithmetic mean) was defined by first adding all *n* items. We now define the *geometric mean* by first *multiplying* all *n* items—and then taking the *n*th root:

$$\text{Geometric mean} \equiv \sqrt[n]{X_1 X_2 \ldots X_n}$$

This is the mean that is appropriate in averaging ratios or factors of increase. A small digression will illustrate. Suppose the population of a suburb increased by a factor of 2 in the first decade, and by a factor of 8 in the second, so that the overall increase was 16 times:

	Population	*Increase Per Decade*
1950	1,000	
1960	2,000	2 times
1970	16,000	8 times
Increase overall		16 times

Does the arithmetic mean

$$\frac{2+8}{2} = 5$$

describe the typical increase per decade? The answer is no: If a fivefold increase occurred over two successive decades, the overall increase would be twenty-fivefold, not sixteen.

Instead, let us try the geometric mean:

$$\sqrt{(2)(8)} = 4$$

This is just right: If a fourfold increase occurred over two successive decades, the overall increase would be sixteenfold that actually did occur.

Now, consider the Laspeyres and Paasche indexes. Since they measure ratios, the geometric mean is the appropriate way to obtain their average too:

$$\boxed{\text{Fisher's ideal index} \equiv \sqrt{(\text{Laspeyres index})(\text{Paasche index})}} \qquad (22\text{-}6)$$

$$= \sqrt{(131)(129)} = 130$$

22-2 FURTHER INDEXES

A—QUANTITY INDEXES

A price index measures the increase in the price or "cost of living." Similarly, we could measure the increase in the *quantity* or "*standard* of living." For example, back in Table 22-2, notice that steak purchases went down while bread purchases went up. Overall, has the standard of living gone up or down? That depends on the relative importance of steak and bread in the consumer budget, which depends on the price of the two. That is, prices should be used as weights in calculating a quantity index, just as quantities were used as weights in calculating the price index. We thus obtain (using the sums already calculated in Table 22-2):

$$\text{Laspeyres quantity index} \equiv \frac{\Sigma Q_t P_o}{\Sigma Q_o P_o}(100) \qquad (22\text{-}7)$$

$$= \frac{144}{154}(100) = 94$$

$$\text{Paasche quantity index} \equiv \frac{\Sigma Q_t P_t}{\Sigma Q_o P_t}(100) \qquad (22\text{-}8)$$

$$= \frac{186}{202}(100) = 92$$

$$\text{Fisher's ideal index} \equiv \sqrt{(\text{Laspeyres index})(\text{Paasche index})} \qquad (22\text{-}9)$$

$$= \sqrt{(94)(92)} = 93$$

B—THE TOTAL COST INDEX

So far, we have defined both price and quantity indexes. It finally is possible to measure their combined effect, by seeing how much *total cost* increased (due to changes in *both* price and quantity):

$$\boxed{\textbf{Total cost index} \equiv \frac{\Sigma P_t Q_t}{\Sigma P_o Q_o}(100)} \tag{22-10}$$

$$= \frac{186}{154}(100) = 121$$

Now, if our indexes of price, quantity, and total cost are good indexes, they should satisfy the basic relation called the *factor-reversal test:*

$$\text{(price index)(quantity index)} = \text{total cost index} \tag{22-11}$$

For example, if the price index increases twofold and the quantity index increases threefold, then the total cost index should increase sixfold; if not, there is something peculiar about the price and quantity indexes we are using. Unfortunately, (22-11) often is *not* satisfied, as a simple calculation will show:[1]

$$\left.\begin{array}{ll} \text{Laspeyres indexes} & (131)(94) \stackrel{?}{=} 121 \\ & \text{No: } 123 > 121 \\ \text{Paasche indexes} & (129)(92) \stackrel{?}{=} 121 \\ & \text{No: } 119 < 121 \\ \text{Fisher's ideal indexes} & (130)(93) \stackrel{?}{=} 121 \\ & \text{Yes: } 121 \stackrel{\checkmark}{=} 121 \end{array}\right\} \tag{22-12}$$

It easily is proved (in Problem 22-5) that Fisher's ideal index *always* satisfies this factor-reversal test. This is one of the properties that justifies the name "ideal."

C—FURTHER ADVANTAGES OF FISHER'S IDEAL INDEX

We note in (22-12) that the Laspeyres indexes of price and quantity both are larger than the corresponding ideal indexes; thus their product is larger than it should be (i.e., larger than the cost index). This is not an isolated example; the Laspeyres indexes are too large in nearly all other cases as well, and it is interesting to see why. We shall give the reason in the case of the Laspeyres price index (leaving the quantity index as an exercise).

The key to the argument is the numerator, given in (22-4) as $\Sigma P_t Q_o$. We see that current prices are weighted by the old quantities. Thus, whatever goods currently have relatively high prices P_t and hence are not bought

[1] To be mathematically correct, we ought to express indexes with their decimal point included of course (i.e., without multiplying by the customary 100). For example, in (22-12), for the first equation we actually should write:

$$(1.31)(.94) \stackrel{?}{=} 1.21$$

very much, are nonetheless weighted with the old higher quantities Q_0, making the product P_tQ_0 too high. Hence the Laspeyres index overstates.

In a similar way, we may argue that the Paasche index understates. Consequently the ideal index, being the geometric mean between the Laspeyres and Paasche indexes, is preferred.

PROBLEMS

22-1

Item	Prices		Quantities (Per Person)	
	1970	1980	1970	1980
Flour (pound)	$ .25	$ .30	100	80
Eggs (dozen)	1.00	1.25	50	40
Milk (pint)	.30	.35	100	100
Potatoes (pound)	.05	.05	60	100

From the above hypothetical data, and using 1970 as the base year:

a. Calculate the three price indexes for 1980—Laspeyres, Paasche, and Fisher. Order them according to size. Is it the same order as in equation (22-12)?

b. Calculate the same three *quantity* indexes. Order them also according to size. Is it the same order as in equation (22-12)?

c. Calculate the total cost index, and verify which of the three indexes passes the factor-reversal test.

d. What difference to the various indexes would it make if all quantities were measured, not on a per person basis, but rather as total national consumption of the good? (That is, all figures in the last two columns would be 200 million times higher.)

22-2 **a.** For the data in Problem 22-1, calculate the price relatives for each good, and pick out the smallest and largest. Does the Laspeyres index lie between them? Does the Paasche index? The Fisher index?

b. Someone claims that the Laspeyres price index is just a weighted average of price relatives—the weight for each item being just the amount spent on it initially (P_0Q_0). Is this claim true for the data in Problem 22-1? Is it true in general?

22-3

Item	Prices				Quantities (Per Person)			
	1940	1950	1960	1970	1940	1950	1960	1970
Steak (pound)	$1.00	$1.20	$1.40	$1.20	40	50	70	50
Bread (pound)	.10	.20	.40	.20	80	100	110	100

From the above hypothetical data, answer the following questions:

a. Using 1940 as the base period, fill in the following table:

Type of Price Index	1950	1960	1970
Laspeyres			
Paasche			
Fisher			

b. Which of the three indexes is simplest to calculate and measure?

c. Fill in the following table:

Type of Price Index	1960 Index, Using 1950 Base	1970 Index, Using 1960 Base	Product of These 2 Indexes
Laspeyres			
Paasche			
Fisher			

Note that in 1970, both prices and quantities reverted to what they were in 1950; that is, during the 1960s, everything that happened in the 1950s was reversed. It therefore would be appropriate if the product of the two indexes, which measures the total change over the two decades, was 1.00 exactly. This *time-reversal test* is passed by which indexes?

22-4 Explain why:

a. The Paasche price index usually is an understatement.

b. The Paasche quantity index usually is an understatement.

*22-5 **a.** Prove that the Fisher indexes in general pass the time-reversal test stated in Problem 22-3c.

b. Prove that the Fisher indexes in general pass the factor-reversal test stated in (22-11).

22-3 INDEXES IN PRACTICE

A—PUBLISHED INDEXES

The U.S. Government publishes a wide variety of price indexes. The one most commonly called the "*cost of living*" is the *Consumer Price Index* (CPI) published monthly by the Bureau of Labor Statistics. A Laspeyres-type index, it traces the living costs of U.S. urban consumers. It includes food, rent and home ownership, energy, clothing, transportation, and medical care—each component having its own index published as well. The CPI is further broken down by region and even by city, making it altogether a very, very detailed report of consumer price changes. To complement the CPI, for primary commodities the *Producer Price Index* (PPI) is published, also in great detail.

For everything counted in the Gross National Product (GNP), the broadest possible index is required—the GNP implicit price deflator, sketched at the top of Figure 22-1. It is used to convert *money* GNP (in current dollars) into *real* GNP (in 1958 dollars) in Figure 22-1, as follows: The

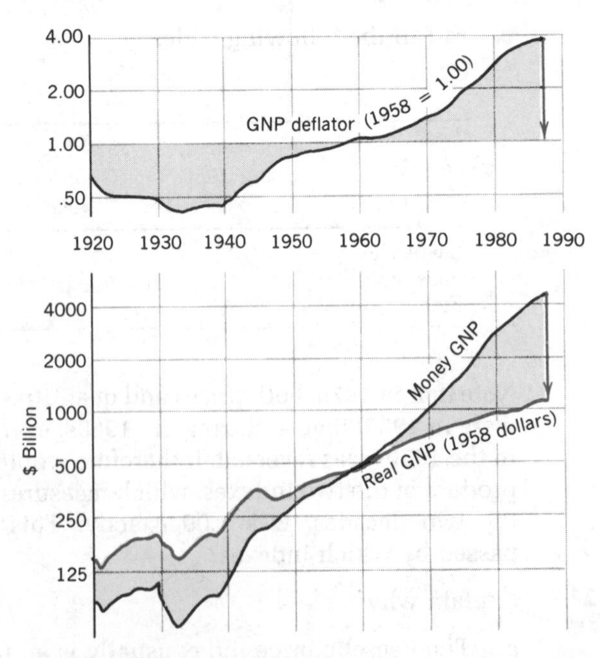

FIGURE 22-1
Deflation of U.S. money GNP, 1920–87. (based on Stat. Abst. of U.S., 1989)

steep curve is money GNP—the actual money paid on the nation's GNP every year. This reflects not only an increase in the physical quantity of goods and services produced but also an increase in their prices. Accordingly, we must divide money GNP with the GNP implicit price deflator to get the real (physical) GNP—the slowly rising curve in color.

B—WHAT'S REALLY HAPPENING TO THE COST OF LIVING?

There are several reasons why changes in the consumer price index (CPI), especially slow changes, cannot be taken too seriously:

1. Since only some of the items are sampled, and only in some of the stores, there is substantial sampling error—especially in the more finely divided components (such as the CPI for one city) where the sample size is small.
2. Actual transaction prices are sometimes difficult to determine, especially on items such as cars where the amount of discount from the list price varies with the skill of the buyer and many other factors.
3. As previously noted, the Laspeyres index used by the government tends to overstate price increases because it doesn't take into account the "partial escape from inflation" open to consumers—namely, their ability to substitute goods that have had a relatively low price increase for goods that have had a relatively high price increase.
4. A serious difficulty in calculating any index occurs because technology changes the basket of goods in ways that make comparisons of prices difficult. For example, suppose we want to compare prices in 1985 with prices in 1975. How do you deal with video cassette recorders, which were an important purchase in 1985, but weren't even available in 1975—at any price? Since the basket of available goods is thus changing, the base period cannot be too far distant in the past. Any extended index series generally involves a number of points in time at which base weights have been changed in recognition of the introduction of new products. In fact, there is some merit in changing the base every year, forming what is called a *chain index*.
5. A related problem of technology is that, even when data does exist, it often is not comparable. Televisions provide a good example. Suppose that we want to compare prices in 1977 with prices in 1947. Although TVs existed in 1947, they were not at all comparable with the 1977 models. To observe that their price has doubled may be of little consequence; if the increased size of screen, the addition of color, and so on have made a TV now "twice" as good, then isn't this twice the product for twice the price? Have prices changed at all? Unless quality adjustments are accounted for explicitly, such index calculations may not indicate the increase in the cost of living, but rather the increase in the cost of *better* living.

   The difficulty with quality judgments is that it is almost impossible to make them. Is the present TV set twice as good, or three times as good as the first model? Autos are another example. At one extreme there are some who are skeptical that the auto is really any better today than it was 30 years ago. On the other hand, we might look to specific improvements such as seat belts or disc brakes, with a view to making a quality adjustment for each. The question is: how much? One answer might be to look at each of the quality improvements that were first introduced as options (before they became standard equipment) and find out the extra price charged for each. But even this is not satisfactory. From either the producer's or consumer's point of view, the value of a car does not necessarily increase by the sum of a set of options that become standard equipment. For the producer, the cost of these optional items decreases when they become standard equipment, since they no longer require the special care and attention of custom items. For the consumer, there may be some items that he simply would not buy if they were options—hence he values them at less than their option price. (Indeed there may even be items—such as automatic transmission—that some buyers would prefer not to have, even if they were *free* options.)

It may be concluded, therefore, that adjustments for changes in product quality should be made; yet in practice they become extraordinarily difficult. Our example of auto improvements (initially priced as options) is perhaps the most conducive to cold calculation; yet even here, any estimate becomes very difficult to defend.

These various practical complications have led many observers to conclude that, in a world of rapidly changing products, small changes in the cost of living index on the order of, say, 1% or 2% may not mean much.

PROBLEMS

22-6 In a number of U.S. industries, wages now are tied to the CPI; that is, indexing in wage contracts ensures that wage rates automatically adjust for any increase in the CPI.

a. How are these justified?

b. Do you see any problem arising if such indexing becomes widespread for all (or most) wages? Can you suggest some solutions?

22-7 **a.** Would you prefer to spend an (after-tax) annual income of $10,000 by purchasing *entirely* out of the 1980 Sears catalog, or *entirely* out of the 1940 Sears catalog (with its lower prices, but more restricted selection of goods, which also are less up-to-date; and of course there will be many goods—like TVs—in the 1980 catalog that just are not available in the 1940 catalog). Assume that not only all goods but also all services (such as medical care and transatlantic trips) are included. In other words, would you prefer to spend your entire $10,000 on 1980 goods and services at 1980 prices, or on 1940 goods and services at 1940 prices?

b. Let us sharpen the answer to **a**: how much money do you think you would need to spend in the 1980 catalog in order to equal the satisfaction you would get by spending $10,000 in the 1940 catalog? This ratio of expenditure (1980 to 1940) might be called the "subjective" price index.

c. During this period, the U.S. Consumer Price Index actually rose from 42 to 246 (base = 1967). How does this compare with your answer in **b**? For your personal values, therefore, has the CPI overstated or understated price increases?

d. Repeat **a** to **c** for an income of $500,000 instead of $10,000.

22-8 Figure 22-1 used a *ratio scale*, where every doubling of *Y*—from 25 to 50 to 100 etc.—is conveniently represented by the same distance along the *Y*-axis. This makes it easy to answer some questions about the U.S. economy, for example:

a. The ratio scale works particularly well to show multiplication or division. For example, the fourfold increase in the GNP deflator from 1958 to 1985, and the corresponding fourfold reduction of money GNP, are equal distances in the graph—as shown by the two arrows.

Show this with arrows for the year 1970 as well. Then also for 1920.

b. When was the worst slump (proportionately) in real GNP? When was the greatest spurt?

c. Using the GNP deflator as a measure of inflation, which two decades had the highest inflation?

d. If real GNP had been measured in constant 1980 dollars instead of constant 1958 dollars, sketch what its graph would be.

e. Just as GNP was deflated, would it make sense to deflate the Dow-Jones average in Figure 2-18? What would this show about the performance of the real Dow-Jones average from 1965 to 1980?

CHAPTER 22 SUMMARY

22-1 A price index measures the change in price of a *fixed* basket of goods and services, and so is a measure of inflation. The Laspeyres index uses the *initial* basket, while the Paasche index uses the *present* basket. A subtle difference is produced, which the Fisher ideal index resolves by taking the geometric mean of these two.

22-2 A quantity index measures the change in the amount of physical goods and services consumed, and so is a measure of economic growth. It is calculated by interchanging price with quantity in the formula for the price index.

22-3 The U.S. Government publishes many indexes in great detail. Three of the most commonly quoted are the *Consumer Price Index* (CPI), the *Producer Price Index* (PPI), and the *GNP implicit price deflator*.

In constructing an index, there are many practical difficulties that limit its reliability: Sampling fluctuations have to be allowed for; list prices are discounted to an unknown extent; and changes in product quality and availability make it very difficult to define a "fixed" basket of goods.

REVIEW PROBLEMS

22-9 The following table gives the prices and quantities of a basket of goods chosen to be the basis for the price and quantity consumer indexes (hypothetical data):

	1980		*1990*	
Goods	Q_0	P_0	Q_t	P_t
Beans (16 oz. can)	40	$ .75	40	$ .80
Milk (quarts)	150	$ .60	100	$ .80
Gasoline (gal.)	200	$ 1.80	250	$ 2.00
Shoes (pair)	3.5	$ 40.00	4.0	$ 50.00
TV (color)	.05	$320.00	.10	$300.00

a. Calculate the 3 price indexes (Laspeyres, Paasche, Fisher).

b. Calculate the 3 quantity indexes.

c. Calculate the total cost index.

d. Confirm that the "factor-reversal" test (22-11) is true only for the Fisher index.

22-10 In each blank, write in one (*or more*) of "Laspeyres, Paasche, or Fisher."

a. The ______ price index is the price that the old basket of goods would cost today, compared to what it cost then.

b. The ______ price index is the price that today's basket of goods costs, compared to what it would have cost then.

c. The ______ index is usually higher than the ______ index, while the ______ index is invariably between them.

d. The ______ price index is invariably between the lowest and the highest price relative.

e. The ______ index passes the time reversal test and the factor reversal test.

f. The U.S. CPI is a kind of ______ price index.

22-11 a. The CPI rose 30% in the sixties, and again 113% in the seventies. How much did it rise over the 20-year period altogether?

b. Suppose the CPI rose 2% a year steadily. How much would it increase altogether after 50 years? After just 35 years?

22-12 ***A Final Challenge: Inflation in Historical Perspective.***

U.S. consumer price index (1967 = 100):

1920	1930	1940	1950	1960	1970	1980	1990(est)
60	50	42	72	89	116	247	390

a. In which decades was there inflation? Deflation (drop in the CPI)? In which decade was inflation greatest?

Would these questions be easier or harder to answer using a graph instead, as in Figure 22-1?

b. How much inflation in the CPI was there between 1970 and 1980? Does it roughly agree with the inflation in the GNP deflator in Figure 22-1?

c. The money income of the average U.S. household increased from $11,000 in 1970 to $22,000 in 1980. At the same time, the average household dropped in size from 3.14 to 2.76 people. What therefore was the approximate change during the 1970s

i. In real household income?

ii. In real per capita income?

CHAPTER 23

Sampling Designs
(Requires Chapter 8)

In earlier times they had no statistics, and so they had to fall back on lies. Hence the huge exaggerations of primitive literature—giants or miracles or wonders! They did it with lies and we do it with statistics; but it is all the same.

—STEPHEN LEACOCK

The simple random sampling of Chapters 6 and 8 is conceptually and computationally the most straightforward method of sampling a population. However, we can get estimates that have smaller variance (are more efficient) by *combining* random sampling with some special design features.

23-1 STRATIFIED SAMPLING

A—SIMPLIFIED EXAMPLE

Let us consider first an exaggerated example, where the benefits of stratified sampling are clearest. Suppose that a large population is known to be 60% urban, 40% rural, and that the problem is to estimate average income. Suppose that the unknown income levels are $10,000 for each urban worker and $5000 for each rural worker. Accordingly, the population earns a mean income:

$$\mu = 10{,}000(.6) + 5000(.4) = 8000 \qquad (23\text{-}1)$$

like (4-4)

How well would a simple random sample estimate μ? Three possible random samples of size 5 are displayed in the last three columns of Table 23-1. Because the samples are completely random, the number of urban and rural workers fluctuates; this in turn causes the sample mean $\bar{X}$ to fluctuate. Of course, occasionally we will be lucky, as in the very last column, where there are two "5 thousand" observations, that is, two rural workers. Then in this sample, the proportion of rural workers happens to be exactly the same as in the population, and $\bar{X}$ is dead on target.

But if we have prior knowledge of the proportion of urban and rural workers, why depend on luck? Surely it would be wise to design the sampling proportions to be exactly equal to the population proportions. This proportional sampling is shown in column (3); note that the result in

TABLE 23-1 Simple Random versus Stratified Sampling: an Oversimplified Example

Population			*Various Samples*				
			Stratified Samples		*Typical Simple Random Samples*		
Stratum	*Proportion* (1)	*Mean Income (in $1000 Units)* (2)	*(i) Proportional* (3)	*(ii) To Be Weighted* (4)	(5)	(6)	(7)
Urban	.60	10	10	10	10	5	5
			10		5	5	10
			10		10	5	10
					10	10	5
Rural	.40	5	5	5	10	5	10
			5				
Total	1.00	$10(.6) + 5(.4)$ $\mu = 8$					
		Sample Means	8√	$10(.6) + 5(.4)$ $\bar{X} = 8$√	9	6	8

this greatly oversimplified case is an estimate that is dead on target. In fact, this same favorable result is guaranteed with a sample of just one observation from each stratum, shown in column (4)—provided, of course, that instead of computing the ordinary mean, each observation is weighted according to the size of its stratum. This weighted or *stratified* sampling yields:

$$\overline{X}_s = 10{,}000(.6) + 5000(.4) = 8000 \tag{23-2}$$

which, of course, exactly coincides with μ in (23-1). This is the perfect estimator, dead on, with a sample of only two (the number of strata).

We emphasize that the reason we have been able to do so well is because the weights w_1 and w_2 (i.e., population proportions in each stratum) were *known*. For example, a source like the U.S. population census could be drawn upon for information on urban/rural proportions.

B—GENERAL CASE

Table 23-1 is contrived, of course, because each stratum is perfectly homogeneous. In practice, each stratum will have some variability, as we outline in Table 23-2. The mean and variance within the first stratum are denoted by μ_1 and σ_1^2, and so on. The most general stratified sample consists of drawing a sample of size n_1 from the first stratum, n_2 from the second, and so on, so that the total sample size $n = \Sigma n_i$.

Now the overall population mean is the weighted mean of the strata means μ_i:

$$\mu = w_1\mu_1 + w_2\mu_2 + \cdots \tag{23-3}$$

like (23-1)

where the weight w_i is the proportion of the population in the ith stratum. To estimate μ, it is natural to estimate each stratum mean μ_i with the *sample* mean $\overline{X}_i$ in that stratum. This produces the stratified sampling mean $\overline{X}_s$:

$$\boxed{\overline{X}_s \equiv w_1\overline{X}_1 + w_2\overline{X}_2 + \cdots} \tag{23-4}$$

like (23-3)

In words: We weight the *sample* means with the *correct* and *known* population weights. Using the rules for linear combinations in Chapter 5, we can show (in Problem 23-6) that $\overline{X}_s$ is an unbiased estimator:

$$\boxed{E(\overline{X}_s) = \mu} \tag{23-5}$$

like (6-5)

TABLE 23-2 Generalization of Table 23-1

	Population			Stratified Sample	
Stratum	*Proportion of Whole Population (Weight)*	*Mean*	*Variance*	*Sample Size*	*Sample Mean*
1	w_1	μ_1	σ_1^2	n_1	$\overline{X}_1 = \dfrac{\Sigma X_{1j}}{n_1}$
2	w_2	μ_2	σ_2^2	n_2	
⋮					
i	w_i	μ_i	σ_i^2	n_i	$\overline{X}_i = \dfrac{\Sigma X_{ij}}{n_i}$
⋮					
r	w_r	μ_r	σ_r^2	n_r	
	$\Sigma w_i = 1$	$\mu = \Sigma w_i \mu_i$ ↑		$n = \Sigma n_i$	$\overline{X}_s = \Sigma w_i \overline{X}_i$ ↑

Furthermore:

$$\text{var } \overline{X}_s = w_1^2 \text{ var } \overline{X}_1 + w_2^2 \text{ var } \overline{X}_2 + \cdots \qquad \text{like (5-22)}$$

$$= w_1^2 \frac{\sigma_1^2}{n_1} + w_2^2 \frac{\sigma_2^2}{n_2} + \cdots \qquad (23\text{-}6)$$

In practice, in each stratum the variance σ_i^2 is unknown and has to be estimated with the *sample* variance s_i^2, so that

$$\boxed{\text{var } \overline{X}_s \simeq w_1^2 \frac{s_1^2}{n_1} + w_2^2 \frac{s_2^2}{n_2} + \cdots} \qquad (23\text{-}7)$$

This leaves the problem of how the n_i are specified; that is, how many observations should be drawn from each stratum? Three common methods are given next.

C—PRESPECIFIED PROPORTIONAL STRATIFICATION

The most obvious way to choose n_i is to make the sample proportion exactly equal to the population proportion, as illustrated earlier in column (3) of Table 23-1:

Proportional sampling requires setting the n_i so that

$$n_i = w_i n \tag{23-8}$$

D—POST STRATIFICATION, AFTER SAMPLING

Suppose, as always, that we know the population weights w_i. For example, we might know that 70% of the population of a city is white and 30% black. In taking a house-to-house sample of 1000, we would like to use these population weights in (23-8) to fix our sample at 700 whites and 300 blacks. But we cannot. There is no way of knowing before we knock on a door whether the respondent will be a white or a black. So we have to knock on 1000 doors (i.e., take a simple random sample of 1000), and take whatever black and white proportion we happen to get. Suppose our sample turns out to include 680 whites and 320 blacks. We use the 680 white observations to calculate the mean ($\overline{X}_1$) and variance (s_1^2) for the whites; and similarly use the 320 black observations to calculate $\overline{X}_2$ and s_2^2 for the blacks. Then we use these sample means to estimate the population mean μ in (23-4) (noting, of course, that in this formula we use the *true* population weights .70 and .30, rather than the less accurate sample weights .68 and .32). This provides an estimate that is about as good as the prespecified proportional sampling in (23-8).

An example will show how effective this stratification can be:

EXAMPLE 23-1

When a shipment traveled via several railroads (or airlines, or other carriers), the freight charges were all recorded on a *waybill*. The total charge was customarily collected by the originating railroad, and later divided appropriately. The complete annual accounting of thousands of waybills became so expensive in time and money that a sampling scheme was tried—and found very successful (Neter, 1978).

Here is how it worked: Suppose, for example, that Railroad A took a simple random sample of 1000 of its 200,000 waybills. The amount X that it owed Railroad B on each waybill was calculated, and all 1000 of these observed debts to B were summarized with $\overline{X}$ = \$13.90 and s = \$18.71.

Since stratifying would improve accuracy, the population and sample were sorted according to the total charge T on the waybill. This gave the data in the table on the next page.

Estimate the total amount owed B, including a 95% confidence interval:

a. Use the simple random sample.

b. Use stratification after sampling.

Stratum Defined by the Total Charge T on the Waybill	Known Number of Waybills in Each Stratum of the Population	Number in Each Stratum of the Sample, n_i	Average Amount that B is Owed, $\overline{X}_i$	Standard Deviation s_i
$0 < T \le \$25$	104,000	540	\$ 4.20	\$ 4.50
$\$25 < T \le \$100$	68,000	330	\$18.70	\$12.10
$\$100 < T$	28,000	130	\$42.00	\$31.60
Totals	200,000	1000		

SOLUTION

a.

$$\text{var } \overline{X} = \frac{\sigma^2}{n} \simeq \frac{s^2}{n} \qquad \text{(6-6) repeated}$$

$$= \frac{18.71^2}{1000} = .35 \qquad \text{(23-9)}$$

Then the 95% confidence interval for μ is:

$$\mu = \overline{X} \pm 1.96 \text{ SE} \qquad \text{like (8-8)}$$

$$= 13.90 \pm 1.96\sqrt{.35} \qquad \text{(23-10)}$$

$$= 13.90 \pm 1.16$$

Finally, the *total* amount owed B is just the population size times the mean μ:

$$\text{Total} = 200{,}000\,(13.90 \pm 1.16)$$

$$= \$2{,}780{,}000 \pm \$232{,}000 \qquad \text{(23-11)}$$

b. We first need the population proportions w_i found from the second column of the given table:

$$w_1 = \frac{104{,}000}{200{,}000} = .52$$

Similarly, $w_2 = .34$ and $w_3 = .14$

Then we can calculate the stratified sample mean:

$$\overline{X}_s = w_1\overline{X}_1 + w_2\overline{X}_2 + \cdots \qquad \text{(23-4) repeated}$$

$$= .52\,(4.20) + .34\,(18.70) + .14\,(42.00)$$

$$= 14.42$$

Similarly, we can calculate its variance:

$$\text{var } \overline{X}_s \simeq w_1^2 \frac{s_1^2}{n_1} + w_2^2 \frac{s_2^2}{n_2} + \cdots \qquad \text{(23-7) repeated}$$

$$= .52^2 \frac{(4.50)^2}{540} + .34^2 \frac{(12.10)^2}{330} + .14 \frac{(31.60)^2}{130}$$

$$= .20$$

We note with satisfaction that this variance is about half the variance of $\overline{X}$ in (23-9). This illustrates the value of stratification.

To find the 95% confidence interval for μ, we follow the same steps as in **a**:

$$\mu = 14.42 \pm 1.96\sqrt{.20} \qquad \text{like (23-10)}$$

$$= 14.42 \pm .88$$

$$\text{Total} = 200{,}000\,(14.42 \pm .88)$$

$$= \$2{,}884{,}000 \pm \$176{,}000 \qquad \text{(23-12)}$$

That is, Railroad A would pay $2,884,000 to Railroad B, and both railroads could be assured this figure comes reasonably close to what a full and expensive accounting would disclose.

E—OPTIMAL STRATIFICATION

If we can allocate the sample sizes n_i in advance, can we improve upon proportional stratification? In the proportional approach (23-8), recall that we take more observations in stratum i if its size w_i is large—that is, if this stratum is a large part of the population. Now consider two other reasons for taking more observations in stratum i:

i. If σ_i is large—that is, if this stratum is highly varied, and hence requires a large sample to estimate $\overline{X}_i$ accurately. (Or, to restate: The smaller is σ_i, the smaller is the necessary sample. The limiting case is a stratum with very little variance, when only 1 observation is required—as shown already in column (4) of Table 23-1.)

ii. If the cost c_i of sampling each observation in this stratum is relatively low. That is, we should take more observations where they cost less. (We assume a simple model, where each observation within stratum i costs the same amount, c_i.)

If we have a fixed budget (an allowable cost C_o let us say), how can we get the most accurate estimate of μ? All three factors above (w_i, σ_i, and c_i) can be taken into account in a mathematical analysis that finally arrives at the appropriate formula:

Optimal sampling requires setting the sample size in stratum *i* at:

$$n_i = k\frac{w_i\sigma_i}{\sqrt{c_i}} \tag{23-13}$$

where the constant of proportionality k can be determined from the budget C_o and turns out to be:

$$k = \frac{C_o}{\Sigma w_i\sigma_i\sqrt{c_i}} \tag{23-14}$$

Generally, the variances σ_i^2 and the costs c_i are not known beforehand, so it is advisable to proceed in two stages:

1. After part of the sample has been taken on a simple random basis, the s_i observed so far may be used to estimate σ_i, and the costs incurred in the sampling so far may be used to estimate c_i.
2. These estimates are then used (along with prior information about w_i) in (23-13) to estimate the best n_i—that is, the best design for the rest of the sampling.

PROBLEMS

23-1 In the same kind of sampling scheme as Example 23-1, airline A took a simple random sample of 5000 of the 100,000 tickets purchased from it. (On each ticket, the passenger was carried by both airline A and airline B.) The amount X that airline A owed B on each ticket was calculated, and all 5000 were summarized with $\overline{X}$ = \$53.20 and s = \$108.00.

Stratification according to the total cost T of the ticket gave further detail:

Stratum Defined by the Total Cost T of the Ticket	Known Number of Tickets in Each Stratum of the Population	Number in Each Stratum of the Sample, n_i	Average Amount that B is Owed, $\overline{X}_i$	Standard Deviation s_i
$0 < T \leq \$100$	50,000	2470	\$ 16	\$ 32
$\$100 < T \leq \$250$	20,000	1020	\$ 29	\$ 51
$\$250 < T \leq \$500$	20,000	990	\$ 67	\$ 86
$\$500 < T$	10,000	520	\$251	\$202
Totals	100,000	5000		

Calculate the total amount owed B, including a 95% confidence interval:

a. Using the simple random sample.

b. Using stratification after sampling.

23-2 In Problem 23-1, suppose stratification *before* sampling had been planned, so that the sample sizes n_i *perfectly* reflected the population sizes:

Stratum	*Population Frequency*	*Prespecified Sample Frequency,* n_i	$\overline{X}_i$	s_i
$0 < T \leq \$100$	50,000	2500	\$ 15	\$ 35
$\$100 < T \leq \$250$	20,000	1000	\$ 29	\$ 62
$\$250 < T \leq \$500$	20,000	1000	\$ 63	\$ 75
$\$500 < T$	10,000	500	\$246	\$164
Totals	100,000	5000		

Now calculate the total amount owed B, including a 95% confidence interval.

23-3 A sample survey of TV watching habits was commissioned by a local TV station for its advertisers. Of the 1000 adults who were randomly selected to be mailed a questionnaire, 800 failed to respond. Rather than pursue all 800, a 10% subsample of 80 was randomly selected for a costly follow-up that persisted until all 80 finally responded.[1]

This can be regarded as a stratified sample, and here are the results for X = the number of hours of TV watched in the previous 7 days.

Stratum	$\overline{X}_i$	s_i	*Sample Size* n_i	*Approximate Population Proportion* w_i
Early responders	36	14	200	.20
Reluctant responders	11	8	80	.80

a. Calculate an unbiased estimate of the population mean μ.

b. If the survey team had decided to ignore the nonrespondents, what would their estimate have been? How useful would that answer be?

[1] In practice, there are always a few who never respond, and require special allowance. For simplicity, however, we ignore this problem here.

23-4 Referring to Problem 23-1, suppose the large tickets were more expensive to process—the cost for a ticket in stratum 1, 2, 3, and 4 averaged out to be $.25, $.36, $.64, and $1.00, respectively.

a. What was the cost of the stratified sampling in Problem 23-1?

b. For the same cost, what would the sample sizes be if optimal stratified sampling were used?

c. Then how much would the optimal design reduce the uncertainty (SE) of the estimate?

d. The three important tools we have studied in this case are:

i. *Random sampling* (simple random sampling).

ii. *Stratified* random sampling.

iii. *Optimal* stratified random sampling.

Briefly summarize the value of each successive level of sophistication.

23-5 Repeat Problem 23-4 for the data in Example 23-1. Assume the cost of sampling a waybill in stratum 1, 2, and 3 averaged out to be $.25, $.36, and $.64, respectively.

***23-6** Prove formulas (23-5) and (23-6).

23-2 OTHER SAMPLING DESIGNS

There are many other ways to improve upon simple random sampling, that can often be used along with stratified sampling. We will describe a few of the most helpful.

A—MULTISTAGE AND CLUSTER SAMPLING

When a population is expensive to sample because of high transportation costs, multistage sampling may provide a way to cut costs, as we illustrated already in Section 1-1. For a more detailed example, consider the three-stage sampling used by the U.S. Bureau of the Census in their Current Population Survey:

1. The United States is divided up roughly into 2000 areas, called primary sampling units (PSU), each one being a city or small group of contiguous counties. At the first stage, about 500 PSUs are randomly selected.
2. Each of these PSUs is divided up very roughly into 100 Enumeration Districts (ED). About 5 of these EDs are then randomly selected.
3. Each of these EDs is divided up very roughly into 100 Ultimate Sampling Units (USU). About 5 of these USUs are then randomly selected.

Each USU consists of roughly 10 people in a cluster of 3 or 4 households, and all of them are selected for the survey. When *all* of the people in the ultimate unit or cluster are selected like this, it is called *cluster sampling*. So the Current Population Survey may be called a multistage cluster sample or, more specifically, a *three-stage cluster sample*.

Like many other surveys, the Current Population Survey combines the ease of multistage sampling with the increased accuracy of stratified sampling. So the selection at each stage is not a *simple* random selection, but rather a random selection constrained by stratification (and whatever other sampling designs are being used). Some kind of random selection is essential, of course, to avoid bias.

It would be interesting to calculate the rough chance that *you* (if you are an adult American) will get selected in a given Current Population Survey. In Table 23-3 we see, for example, that about 500 out of the 2000 PSUs are chosen; then in each of these PSUs, about 5 out of the 100 EDs are chosen; and so on. Thus the chances you will be chosen are roughly $125{,}000/200{,}000{,}000 \simeq .0006$.

Clearly, multistage and cluster sampling provide great savings in transportation costs by concentrating the sampling in a few areas. Yet this same concentration produces less accuracy: To the extent that the people in a chosen area are "homogeneous"—have similar incomes, for example—only the first observation provides completely fresh information, while later observations just tend to repeat it. (But this cost is often small compared to the benefit, so that multistage and cluster sampling are very widely used.)

B—SYSTEMATIC SAMPLING

As an example, we may wish to draw a sample of 100 from a deck of 5000 computer cards. One straightforward way is to be *systematic*: Pull every 50th card. This method usually has about the same precision as simple random sampling, so those formulas may be used.

The only drawback of systematic sampling is that its precision may badly deteriorate if systematic fluctuations (*periodicities*) occur in the

TABLE 23-3 The Three Stages of Sampling Give the Rough Probability that You Will Be Selected for Next Month's Current Population Survey

At Each Stage, Sampling Selects . . .	*PSUs*		*EDs*		*USUs*		*People*		
$\frac{\text{Number sampled}}{\text{Number available}}$	$\frac{500}{2000}$	×	$\frac{5}{100}$	×	$\frac{5}{100}$	×	$\frac{10}{10}$	=	$\frac{125{,}000}{200{,}000{,}000}$

data (as would be the case, for example, if you sampled every seventh issue of the N.Y. *Times*, or sampled the density of traffic at 5 p.m. every Friday). If this is suspected as a possible problem, one could break the sample down into several subsamples that can be compared. To return to our example of computer cards, instead of one systematic sample of 100 cards, one could select 5 samples of 20 cards each (with each of these 5 samples beginning at a *randomly* chosen point at the beginning of the deck).

C—SEQUENTIAL SAMPLING

In sequential sampling, the sample size n is no longer fixed, but instead is revised as we accumulate sample information. The idea is to start with a small sample, and if the result is sufficiently clear, the job is done; but if the sample is ambiguous, a second, and perhaps even further stage of sampling is required until the ambiguity is resolved. This procedure is justified if the advantage of the expected smaller sample size outweighs the disadvantage of having to resume sampling several times.

PROBLEMS

23-7 Choose the correct alternative in each bracket:

a. In the last stage, multistage sampling often observes everyone in the final sampling unit—or, as it's called by the Current Population Survey, the [USU, PSU]. Then it is called [cluster, systematic] sampling.

b. Cluster sampling—and multistage sampling—work best when each cluster is relatively [heterogeneous, homogeneous].

c. When testing an hypothesis H_0 against an alternative H_1, [systematic, sequential] sampling allows you to exploit the early results to determine whether it is necessary to continue sampling. Thus the sample size n will be very short when the early results are [overwhelming, indecisive], and longer otherwise. So n must be regarded as a [random variable, fixed parameter].

The advantage of this kind of sampling is that the expected sample size will be [less, greater] than the sample size of the comparable simple random sample.

d. Systematic sampling [works best, may be disastrous] when there are unsuspected periodicities in the data. For example, to determine the average outgoing quality of automobiles from the Ford Ypsilanti plant, sampling each Friday afternoon would be [more biased, more fairly representative] than simple random sampling.

CHAPTER 23 SUMMARY

23-1 When a population has relatively large variability between strata, then stratified sampling is much more efficient than simple random sampling.

23-2 When a population has relatively little variability between clusters, then multistage cluster sampling can greatly cut down sampling costs with little corresponding loss in information.

There are many other convenient and ingenious variations of sampling as well—such as systematic sampling and sequential sampling.

REVIEW PROBLEMS

23-8 In each bracket, select the correct choice:

a. Stratified sampling is relatively effective when most of the variation occurs [between, within] strata. Similarly, cluster sampling is relatively effective when most of the variation occurs [between, within] clusters. Yet at some stage, [the first design, each design] requires random sampling as part of its procedure.

b. Stratified and multistage cluster sampling designs can be used together, often very effectively. Whether used together or alone, each design is intended to provide more information per budgeted dollar than [simple random sampling, optimal stratified sampling].

c. Stratified sampling yields an estimator of μ that is [biased, unbiased] and has [smaller, larger] variance than the simple random sampling estimate $\overline{X}$.

d. The crucial prior knowledge required in stratified sampling is to know [the variance σ_i^2, the relative size w_i] of each stratum.

23-9 In order to investigate student political attitudes, suppose you want a sample of students from your university. How could you take a simple random sample? A stratified sample? A multistage cluster sample?

23-10 Harry Roberts at Chicago has a rule (Roberts 1972, p 39) for saving time when he receives a mail questionnaire: He throws it in the wastebasket.

But if he receives a follow-up questionnaire, he answers it. Does this really do any good? Explain.

23-11 Ten days before the 1980 Presidential election, a Gallup poll of 600 men showed 51% were in favor of Reagan; and of 600 women,

42% were in favor of Reagan (ignoring third-party candidates, as usual). Construct an appropriate 95% confidence interval for:

a. The difference between men and women in the whole population.

b. The proportion of all adults (men *and* women) who were in favor of Reagan. Assume that women outnumbered men by about 52% to 48%—the 1978 voting figures. (*Hint:* The variance in each stratum is estimated from (6-20), with P substituted for π.)

23-12 *A Final Challenge: Using Past Performance to Estimate Inventory*

In order to estimate the total inventory of tires currently held, a company conducts a stratified sample of its dealers, stratified according to their inventory held the previous year. For a total sample size of $n = 1000$, the following data was obtained:

Stratum (Last Year's Inventory)	Population		Stratified Sample (Current Inventory)		
	Number of Dealers	Proportion w_i	Prespecified n_i	$\overline{Y}_i$	s_i^2
0–99	4,000	.20	200	105	1600
100–199	10,000	.50	500	180	2500
200–299	5,400	.27	270	270	2500
300–	600	.03	30	390	5600
Totals	20,000	1.00	1000		

a. Is the design a *proportional* stratified sample?

b. From this stratified sample, estimate the mean inventory μ, and hence the total inventory. Include a 95% confidence interval.

c. Compare this stratified sampling with the regression analysis in Problem 12-15. Then answer True or False, correct it:

i. Both methods involve the use of prior information (about last year's inventory X) to improve the estimate of this year's inventory Y.

ii. Stratified sampling can be applied to either a numerical stratification (e.g., size of inventory), or a categorical stratification (e.g., male/female); but regression can only be used for a numerical stratification.

iii. Stratified sampling does not require the assumption that the relation between X and Y is linear (which is required in regression analysis).

CHAPTER 24

Time Series

(Requires Chapter 15)

A religious sect is predicting that the world will end at 10 p.m. tonight. For more details, watch the news at eleven.

T.V. NEWS FLASH

There are two major categories of statistical information: cross section and time series. To illustrate, economists have often estimated the consumption function relating consumer expenditure to national income. Sometimes they use a detailed breakdown of the consumption of individuals at various income levels at one point in time (cross section); or they examine how total consumption is related to national income over a number of time periods (time series); or they may use a combination of the two.

In this chapter, we shall combine familiar techniques such as regression with some new methods to analyze time series. Although our examples will often use annual or quarterly data, the techniques are equally applicable to monthly data, weekly data, and so on.

24-1 TWO SPECIAL CHARACTERISTICS OF A TIME SERIES

Figure 24-1 shows a time series with a *trend*, a simple regression of wheat price against time. In earlier chapters, any such regression fit came with a warning: There are important characteristics of a time series that keep us from using this sort of simple trend line to forecast. We begin by considering two.

A—TIME SERIES HAVE SERIAL CORRELATION

One special pattern of time series is serial correlation—when each observation is statistically dependent on the previous ones. In Figure 24-1, for example, after years of low prices, next year's price is more likely to be low again.

This is more difficult to analyze than the customary regression models we have dealt with so far, where observations were independent. For example, suppose we have reached 1970 in Figure 24-1, and wish to forecast next year's price. It would be foolish indeed to use the fitted regression line (i.e., use arrow *a* to predict) because this would imply a sudden upward leap in price. It would be much better to ignore the fitted regression and simply draw in a freehand prediction such as arrow *b*, which assumes that next year's price will be the same as this year's. In this

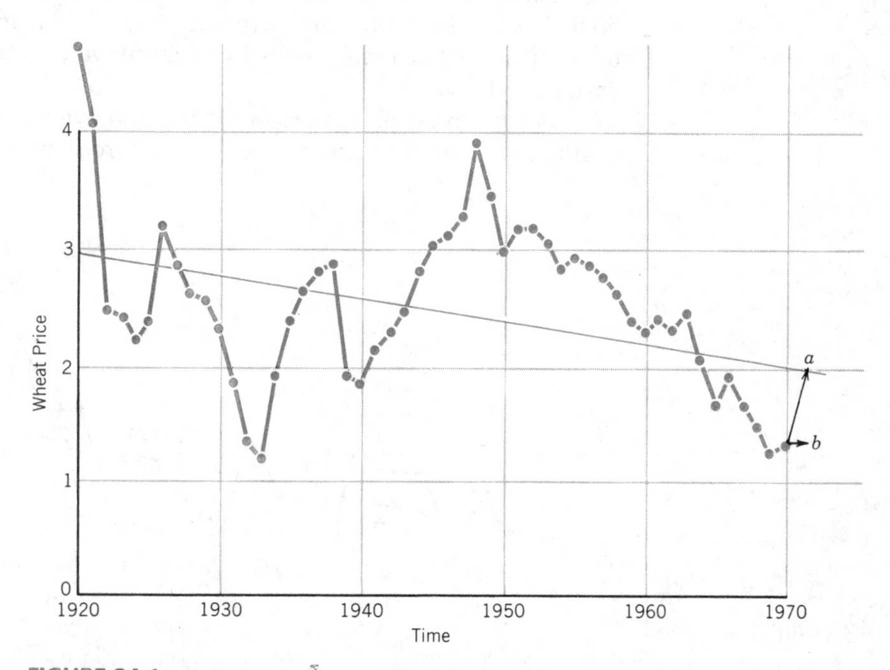

FIGURE 24-1
Serial correlation in a time series: When previous observations are low, the next tends to be low. (The price of wheat relative to the consumer price index, i.e., adjusted for inflation. From Simon, 1982).

chapter, we will see how we can do even better than either of these naive alternatives.

Since serial correlation can cause such difficulties, it is important to have a simple and routine test for whether or not it is present. This is provided by the Durbin-Watson test, which is customarily computed at the end of every regression, and which we return to later.

B—TIME SERIES OFTEN HAVE A SEASONAL PATTERN TOO

Another feature that occurs in many time series is *seasonal variation* (or monthly or other periodic variation). The quarterly data of Figure 24-2, for example, displays a seasonal pattern so strong that we can discern its main features at a glance: The fourth quarter of every year tends to be high, followed by a big drop in the next quarter.

To see why it is essential to take account of seasonal variation, we might ask: "Was observation F in the first quarter of 1966 disappointing?" (This might be important, for example, in evaluating a new government policy such as tax advantages to stimulate expenditures.) At first glance, it seems that F was indeed disappointing, since it was a big drop. But then we notice that it was not as big a drop as in the other first quarters. So we conclude that F reflects relatively good performance.

Other examples abound: In evaluating whether or not a government has been successful in increasing employment, the observation that employment has increased in the spring of 1980 would not be convincing evidence if, as part of a seasonal pattern, employment customarily rises every spring anyhow.

Thus when a series has seasonal variation, we must keep this in mind in evaluating a single observation—or in forecasting. For example, if we

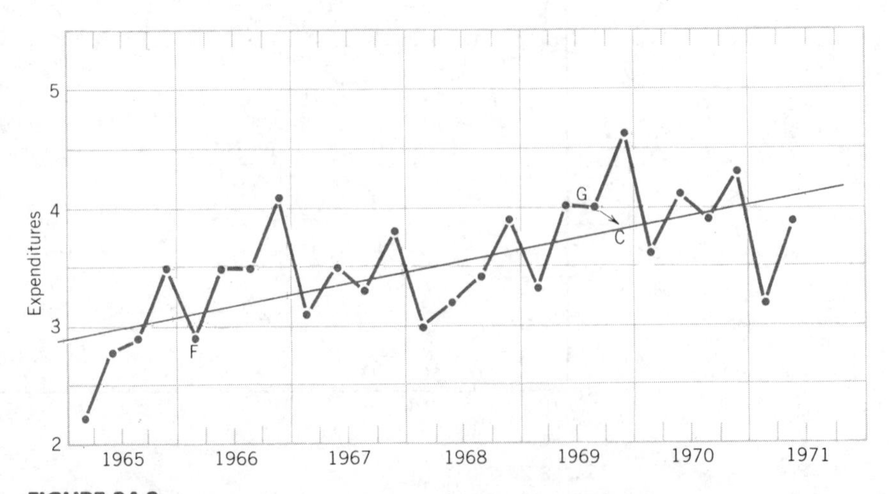

FIGURE 24-2
Seasonal variation in a time series—fourth quarter is always high (U.S. new plant and equipment expenditures, billions of dollars, for manufacturing durable goods).

have reached point G in 1969, it would be a mistake to forecast the next (fourth quarter) observation on the fitted regression line, that is, to follow arrow C down. This would ignore the large increase that has occurred in all the recent fourth quarters.

PROBLEMS

24-1 **a.** In Figure 24-1, consider each of the five years 1920, 1930, 1940, 1950 and 1960. Tabulate roughly the next year's prediction of wheat price, in two different ways:

i. Using the fitted regression curve.

ii. Using the simple rule: "Next year the same as this year."

b. For comparison, also tabulate what the next year's price actually was. Then for each of the two prediction methods, tabulate the errors and summarize them by squaring and averaging (MSE). Which prediction method works better? How much better?

24-2 Circle the correct choice in each bracket:

As Problem 24-1 showed, a mathematical technique such as least-squares [is always better, can be much worse] than a simple and more understandable technique.

The reason the high powered technique worked so [well, badly] is that it [is a robust technique that works well under many different assumptions, erroneously assumes the error terms are serially independent].

For time series that are measured more often than annually, such as quarterly or monthly, straight line prediction is particularly [appropriate, inappropriate].

24-2 DECOMPOSITION AND FORECASTING USING REGRESSION

In this section, we will use the familiar technique of multiple regression to illustrate two major objectives of time series analysis:

1. To *understand* the time series better, by *decomposing* it. That is, we estimate each of the patterns that make up the time series in order to get a picture of their relative importance. (The estimate of the seasonal pattern is also valuable for its own sake: We can use it for seasonal adjustment.)
2. To *forecast* future values from the observed past values of the time series.

If a time series followed only one of the patterns we have described above (trend, seasonal, or serial correlation), there would be few problems. In practice, however, it is typically a mixture of all three that is very difficult to unscramble. Consider again, for example, the quarterly data on capital expenditures shown in Figure 24-2. What combination of these three patterns can be perceived in this time series? We've already noted that there obviously appears to be some trend and some seasonal pattern. There is also some serial correlation, but precisely *how much* of each of these components is a mystery. Let's now solve that mystery.

A—TREND

Trend is often the most important element in a time series. It may be linear, as illustrated in Figure 24-2, growing at a *constant amount* over time. Or it may follow any of the nonlinear patterns discussed in Chapter 14; for example, it may be exponential, growing at a *constant rate* over time (in which case it would be linear on a log scale).

We will show how regression can be used to estimate trend in a way that will also capture the seasonal pattern described next.

B—SEASONAL PATTERN

There may be seasonal fluctuation in a time series for many reasons: A holiday such as Christmas results in completely different purchasing patterns. Or the seasons may affect economic activity; in the summer, agricultural production is high, while the sale of ski equipment is low. Or a seasonal pattern may result from tax laws; at the end of the year, people may buy or sell stocks simply to cash in their gains or losses for tax reasons.

To illustrate how regression can handle trend and seasonal patterns together, we take a really spectacular example—jewelry sales, as shown in Figure 24-3*a*. While there seems to be a slight upward trend (which we assume is linear for simplicity) the clearest pattern is a seasonal one, marked by the sharp rise in sales every fourth quarter because of Christmas.

These fourth quarter observations can be handled very easily with a dummy variable:

$$\left.\begin{aligned} Q_4 &= 1 \text{ if fourth quarter} \\ &= 0 \text{ otherwise} \end{aligned}\right\} \qquad \begin{aligned} &(24\text{-}1) \\ &\text{like } (14\text{-}2) \end{aligned}$$

Similarly, we can define dummy variables Q_2 and Q_3 for the second and third quarters. (The first quarter is left as the reference quarter, and so does not need a dummy variable. Thus, as always, the number of dummies will be 1 less than the number of categories.) These dummy variables

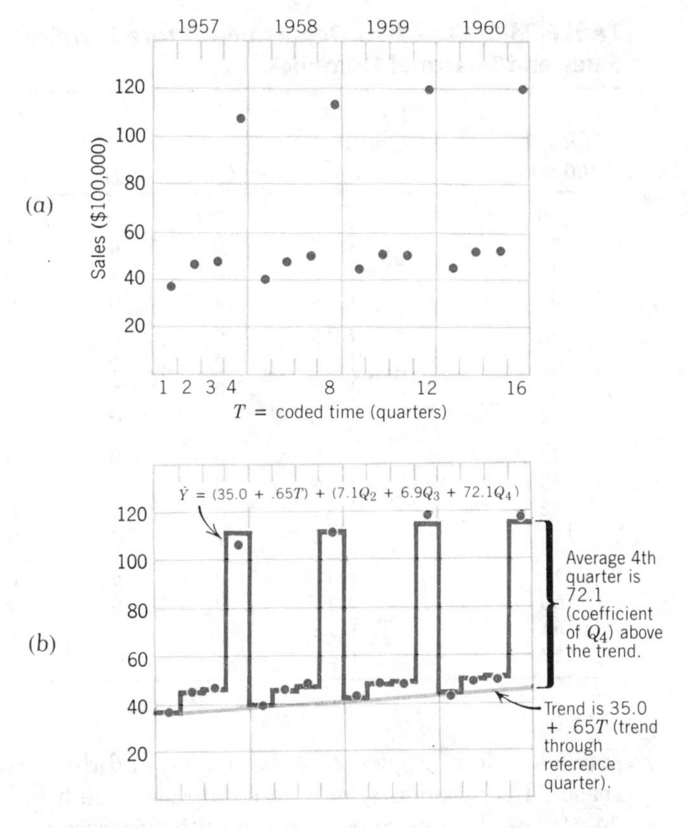

FIGURE 24-3
(a) Canadian jewelry sales. (b) Multiple regression of sales against time and seasonal dummies.

are tabulated in Table 24-1 along with the rest of the data ready to input to the computer. The computed least squares fit[1] turned out to be:

$$\hat{Y} = \underbrace{35.0 + .65T}_{\text{trend}} + \underbrace{7.1Q_2 + 6.9Q_3 + 72.1Q_4}_{\text{seasonal pattern}} \tag{24-2}$$

This is graphed as the jagged set of blocks in Figure 24-3*b*. Notice that we have used a technique that ensures the seasonal pattern is exactly the same every year; for example, each fourth quarter is the same amount (72.1) above the reference quarter (the first quarter).

Now we can decompose the original time series in the left-hand (un-

[1] For times series, ordinary least squares (OLS) can be improved upon. A technique called *generalized* least squares (GLS) allows for serial correlation and so is more efficient (as we explain in Section 24-6).

TABLE 24-1 Canadian Department Store Jewelry Sales and Seasonal Dummies

Sales, Y ($100,000s)		Time, T (Quarter Years)	Q_4	Q_3	Q_2
36	1957	1	0	0	0
44		2	0	0	1
45		3	0	1	0
106		4	1	0	0
38	1958	5	0	0	0
46		6	0	0	1
47		7	0	1	0
112		8	1	0	0
42	1959	9	0	0	0
49		10	0	0	1
48		11	0	1	0
118		12	1	0	0
42	1960	13	0	0	0
50		14	0	0	1
51		15	0	1	0
118		16	1.	0	0

shaded) side of Figure 24-4. Panels (*a*) and (*b*) show the fitted trend and seasonal components, in sum comprising the fitted regression (in Figure 24-3). The difference between the fitted regression and the observed dots (in Figure 24-3) is the residual series, reproduced in panel (*c*) of Figure 24-4. Thus the total jewelry sales series in panel (*d*) has been broken down into its three components in panels (*a*), (*b*), and (*c*).

With the trend and seasonal components captured by regression, this leaves the residual yet to be analyzed.

C—SERIALLY CORRELATED RESIDUAL

We have seen that, for any time period t, the difference between the least squares fit $\hat{Y}_t$ and the actual observed value Y_t is the *residual* term $\hat{e}_t$. Formally:

$$\text{Residual } \hat{e}_t = Y_t - \hat{Y}_t \tag{24-3}$$

For the time series we are analysing here, the residual in Figure 24-4*c* is so small that for many practical purposes it could be neglected. However, for most series the residual is substantial, and so we will examine in some detail how it should be treated. The model we use relates each e_t to its previous value e_{t-1} in a regression equation:

$$e_t = \rho e_{t-1} + v_t \tag{24-4}$$

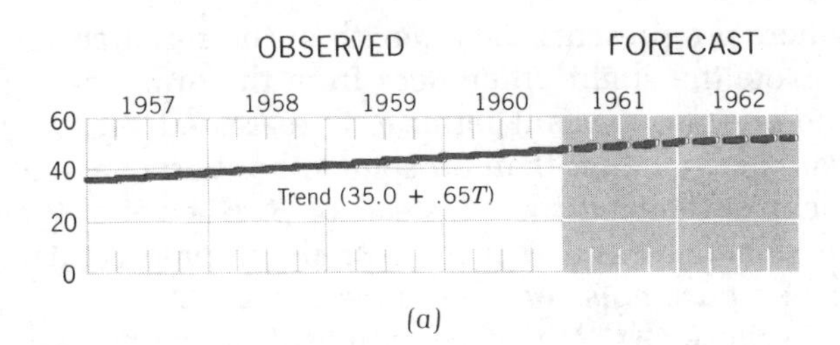

(a)

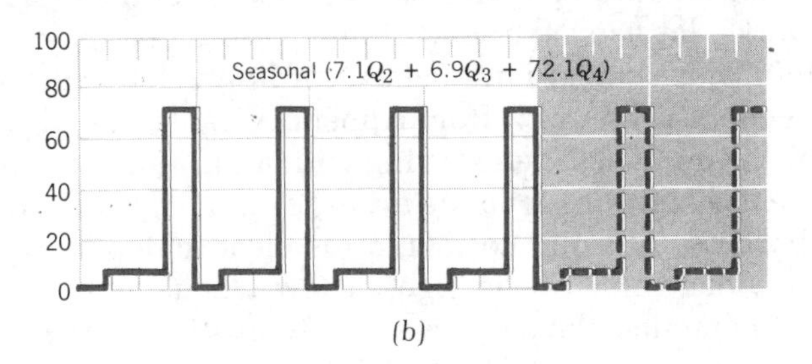

(b)

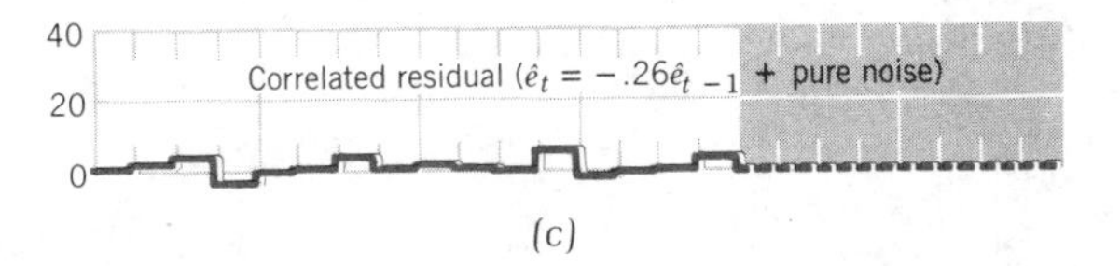

(c)

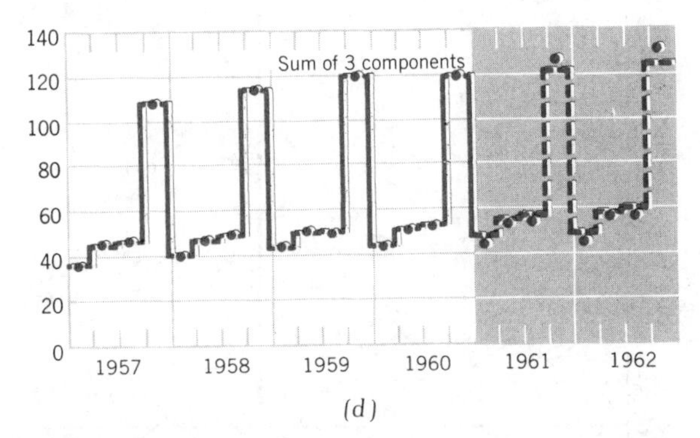

(d)

FIGURE 24-4
Decomposition of jewelry time series into its three components. On the right, each is projected with dashed lines into the gray future. (a) Trend component. (b) Seasonal component. (c) Residual. (d) Total (original) series of observed dots on the left is the sum of the three components above. On the right, compare the dashed-line forecast with the actual sales (as they eventually turned out) shown as dots.

where ρ represents the strength of the serial correlation.

Note the slight differences from the ordinary regression model (12-3): there is no constant term; e_t is regressed on its own previous (lagged) value e_{t-1}, rather than on some other variable; and the regression coefficient is denoted by ρ instead of β. But we still assume that the v_t are independent and, hence, entirely unpredictable. Thus they are often called *pure noise* or *white noise*.

Because (24-4) is a regression of e_t on its own previous values, it is called an *autoregression* as well as a *serial regression*. To illustrate how it works, let us construct a simple case where $\rho = 1$, and the white noise term v_t is standard normal. Accordingly, let us draw a sample of 20 independent values of v_t from Appendix Table II, and graph them in panel (*a*) of Figure 24-5. Then starting with an initial value of $e_0 = 5$, for example, we use (24-4) to generate $e_1, e_2, e_3, \ldots, e_{20}$ as shown in panel (*b*). The existence of serial correlation is clear: e_t tends to be high whenever the previous value e_{t-1} is high, or low whenever e_{t-1} is low.

In practice, the parameter ρ is typically less than 1. Its estimate r can be calculated by applying the OLS formulas to the residuals $\hat{e}_t$. For example,

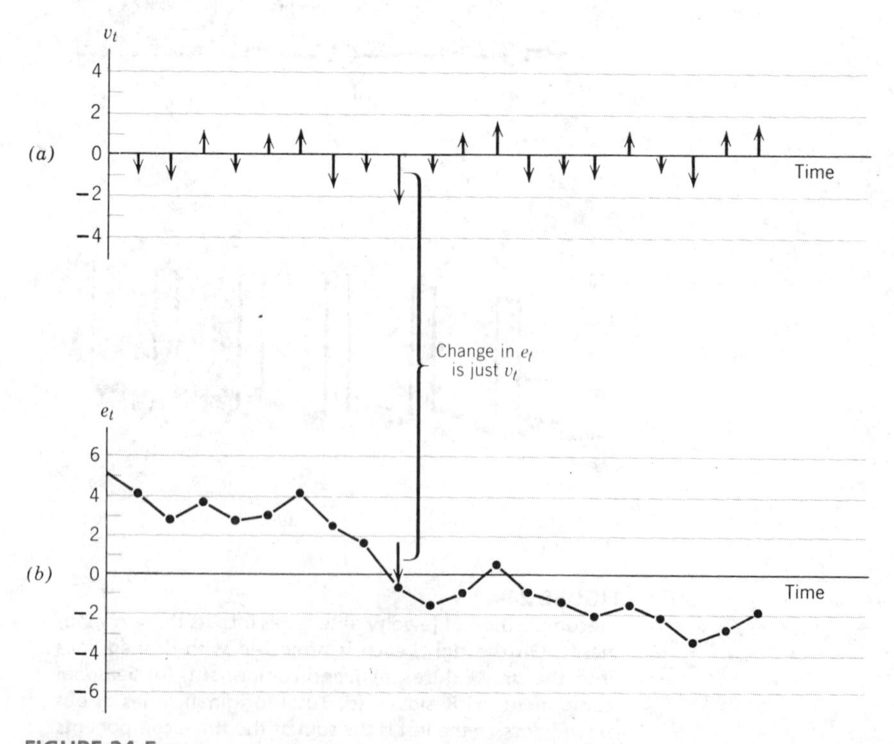

FIGURE 24-5
The construction of serially correlated e_t. (a) Independent v_t (white noise). (b) When $\rho = 1$, then $e_t = e_{t-1} + v_t$.

the autoregression used to estimate the residuals of jewelry sales data in Figure 24-4c was

$$\hat{e}_t = r\hat{e}_{t-1} \qquad (24\text{-}5)$$

estimates (24-4)

$$\hat{e}_t = -.26\hat{e}_{t-1} \qquad (24\text{-}6)$$

The details of (24-6) are given in Appendix 24-2, which also shows that r is essentially the correlation coefficient between $\hat{e}_t$ and $\hat{e}_{t-1}$. This is why we use the symbol r (and ρ), and call it the *serial correlation*. The Durbin-Watson test for serial correlation (also detailed in the same appendix) can be viewed essentially as just a test of whether r is discernibly different from 0.

The estimate $r = -.26$ in (24-6) shows that autocorrelation can be negative, as well as positive. In this case, values tend to change sign (positive values tend to be followed by negative ones, rather than tracking themselves over time—as they did when positively correlated in Figure 24-5. Inventory series may provide another example of negative serial correlation, if particularly large purchases for inventory result in overstocking, hence smaller purchases in the following period.)

Finally, let us consider the generalization of (24-4):

$$\boldsymbol{e_t = \rho_1 e_{t-1} + \rho_2 e_{t-2} + \cdots + \rho_k e_{t-k} + v_t} \qquad (24\text{-}7)$$

This could be called a multiple autoregression or, more commonly, a *k*th *order autoregression*.

D—FORECASTING

To review the decomposition of a time series such as jewelry sales into its components, we rewrite (24-3) as

$$Y = \hat{Y} + \hat{e}$$

When we substitute $\hat{Y}$ given in (24-2), the result is

$$\begin{array}{ccccc} \boldsymbol{Y = (35.0 + .65T)} & \boldsymbol{+} & \boldsymbol{(7.1Q_2 + 6.9Q_3 + 72.1Q_4)} & \boldsymbol{+} & \boldsymbol{(\hat{e})} \\ \textbf{Time series = trend} & \boldsymbol{+} & \textbf{seasonal} & \boldsymbol{+} & \textbf{residual} \end{array} \qquad (24\text{-}8)$$

Of course, this is just the equation form of the graphical breakdown of a time series into its components shown in the first three panels of Figure 24-4—with panel (d) showing the way they all add up. To forecast the time series, we simply forecast each component in the first three panels, and add them up[2] in panel (*d*). These forecast values are shown in gray.

While forecasting the first two components in panels (*a*) and (*b*) involve no problem, how do we forecast the third component (the serially correlated residual) with its more erratic pattern? The answer is just to use the autoregression fit:

$$\hat{e}_t = r\hat{e}_{t-1} = -.26\hat{e}_{t-1} \qquad \text{(24-9)}$$
(24-6) repeated

For example, the last $\hat{e}_t$ available was in the 16th quarter, and happened to be $\hat{e}_{16} = .5$. We can use this to forecast $\hat{e}_t$ in the next quarter:

$$\hat{e}_{17} = -.26\hat{e}_{16} = -.26(.5) = -.13 \qquad \text{like (24-9)}$$

With this in hand, we can forecast the next one again:

$$\hat{e}_{18} = -.26\hat{e}_{17} = -.26(-.13) = +.03$$
$$\hat{e}_{19} = -.26\hat{e}_{18} = -.26(.03) = -.01$$

Notice how this component, graphed in panel (*c*) of Figure 24-4, quickly dwindles away to zero in the future.

Turning finally to the forecast of the whole time series in panel (*d*), we wonder: With the benefit of hindsight, how well did it work out? Specifically, how close were the forecast values to the actual values we were later able to observe, which we continue to show as colored dots? We see that the forecast was very good for 1961, but not quite so good for 1962 because we were forecasting further into the future.

This is exactly what we would expect: The shorter the forecast, the better. Thus if funds and time are available, a forecast should be recomputed, to update it whenever new observations become available; specifically, the forecast for 1962 should be updated as soon as the 1961 figures become available.

While the regression analysis of this section has shown how a time series can be decomposed and used to forecast, more complex methods are often used in practice. Many of these have been developed *specifically*

[2] For example, by evaluating each of the three components in (24-8) we predict the 17th and 18th quarters to be:

Component	$T = 17$	$T = 18$
Trend		
$35.0 + .65T$	$35.0 + .65(17) = 46.05$	$35.0 + .65(18) = 46.70$
Seasonal		
$7.1Q_2 + 6.9Q_3 + 72.1Q_4$	Reference quarter = 0	Setting $Q_2 = 1$, $7.1(1) = 7.1$
Residual		
$-.26\hat{e}_{t-1}$	$-.26(.5) = -.13$	$-.26(-.13) = .03$
Total	45.92	53.83

for time series: In the next section, for example, we will look at a traditional decomposition that predates the computer, and in the following sections we will look at increasingly sophisticated forecasting techniques.

PROBLEMS

24-3 Given the following data on new car sales (in hundreds, *Statistics Canada*):

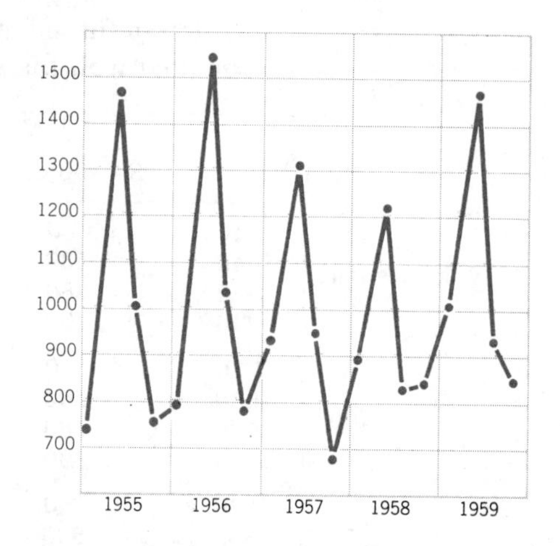

a. Fit a linear trend by eye.

b. Shift the linear trend in a parallel way so that it passes as close as possible to the first quarter (reference quarter) points. Then roughly estimate how much higher the second quarters rise, on average, above this reference line. Repeat for the third and fourth quarters. This produces an eyeball estimate of the seasonal component.

c. Graph your eyeball fit as a jagged set of blocks, as in Figure 24-3b.

d. If a trend-and-seasonal regression model like (24-2) was fitted, use your eyeball fit to roughly estimate what the coefficients would be.

24-4 (Seasonal Adjustment) The car sales from Problem 24-3 above were fitted with a regression equation like (24-2), and the computed seasonal component was $530\ Q_2 + 80\ Q_3 - 90\ Q_4$. If we tabulate this seasonal component S, we obtain the table below.

a. Calculate the mean of the seasonal series $\overline{S}$. Then tabulate the seasonal series in deviation form, $s = S - \overline{S}$. This gives us a seasonal series that fluctuates up and down *around zero*.

b. Subtract s from the original series of auto sales Y. This new series estimates how auto sales would move if there were no seasonal component, and so is called the *seasonally adjusted* series.

c. Graph the seasonally adjusted series on the figure in Problem 24-3 for comparison.

d. Comparing the second quarter of 1957 with the first quarter, what was the increase in:

i. Auto sales?

ii. Seasonally adjusted auto sales?

Which of these figures is more meaningful, in terms of indicating how well the auto industry fared in that quarter?

Year	*Auto Sales, Y*	*Seasonal, S*	*(a) Seasonal Deviations, s*	*(b) Seasonally Adjusted Auto Sales, Y − s*
1955	710	0		
	1440	530		
	980	80		
	740	−90		
1956	770	0		
	1530	530		
	1020	80		
	760	−90		
1957	920	0		
	1300	530		
	940	80		
	660	−90		
1958	890	0		
	1220	530		
	820	80		
	840	−90		
1959	1000	0		
	1470	530		
	930	80		
	850	−90		

24-5 a. Simulate a string of 10 serially correlated residuals e_t using Equation (24-4), with $\rho = .9$. Start with $e_o = 2$, say, and take v_t from Appendix Table II.

b. Graph e_t. Does it show random tracking like Figure 24-5?

25-6 Average weekly carloadings (in thousands, from Moody, 1975)

Year	*Quarter* 1	2	3	4
1968	508	566	550	544
1969	507	562	545	557
1970	499	550	523	513
1971	486	526	477	457

The data above were fitted with a multiple regression (for $T = 1, 2, \ldots 16$):

$$\hat{Y} = 533 - 4.7T + 56Q_2 + 33Q_3 + 32Q_4$$

a. Calculate the residual $\hat{e}_t$.

b. Graph $\hat{e}_t$ against $\hat{e}_{t-1}$, and then fit by eye a straight line through the origin; that is, roughly estimate r in the simple autoregression:

$$\hat{e}_t = r\hat{e}_{t-1}$$

c. Forecast Y_t into the next 4 quarters. Compare to the four actual values: 468, 514, 500, 511.

d. Seasonally adjust the time series Y_t (by subtracting the zero-average seasonal component, as in Problem 24-4). Then, for example, how did carloadings in the second quarter of 1971 compare (on a seasonally adjusted basis) to carloadings in the first quarter?

e. On one graph, show:

i. Y_t and seasonally adjusted Y_t^a, for 1970 and 1971.

ii. Projected $\hat{Y}_t$ and actual Y_t, for 1972.

24-3 TRADITIONAL RATIO TO MOVING AVERAGE

In this section we examine a traditional method of decomposing a time series and making seasonal adjustments. Although it predates the computer, in one form or another it is still commonly used. (The U.S. Bureau of the Census uses a variation called X-11ARIMA, for example, that provides short range forecasts as well as seasonal adjustment. For more information, as usual see the Encyclopedia edited by Kotz, Johnson and Read, 1982–88.)

This traditional decomposition of a time series Y assumes it has 4 components. These correspond *roughly* to the 3 components analyzed earlier in (24-8)—trend, seasonal, and residual—except that our earlier residual is now further broken down into a cyclical part C and a disturbance D. In other words, the components of a time series are:

$$\text{Trend, Seasonal, Cyclical, and Disturbance } (T, S, C, \text{ and } D) \quad (24\text{-}10)$$

The strategy for actually carrying out this decomposition, and then using it to seasonally adjust the time series, is summarized at the end of this section in Table 24-3. You may find it helpful to check off the various steps in this analysis as you progress through this section.

A—CAPTURING *T* AND *C* WITH A MOVING AVERAGE

The first step is to smooth the time series by averaging. Specifically, we average the first four quarters, then move on to average the next four quarters and so on—thus forming the *moving average* shown in column 3 of Table 24-2. However, since we want to center each average on a particular quarter—rather than leaving it stranded half-way between two quarters—we average again (this time as simply as possible, two at a time). Thus we obtain the *centered moving average M* in column 4. (As Appendix 24-3 shows, we could express this with a formula, and generalize.)

When M is graphed in Figure 24-6, we see that it is indeed much smoother than the original series, because it doesn't contain the large seasonal variation S. This seasonal fluctuation was removed because M averaged over all 4 quarters, so that each value of M contains in its average exactly one observation for each quarter (in particular, one of the very large second-quarter observations, and one of the very small fourth-quarter observations).

More generally, the M series smooths all the blips from the original series, whether they are generated by seasonal variation S or by the distur-

TABLE 24-2 Ratio-to-Moving-Average (Auto sales, from Figure 24-6)

(1) Time		(2) Sales Y	(3) Moving Average	(4) Centered Moving Average M	(5) Y/M	(6) Seasonal S Calculated	(7) Seasonal S Repeated	(8) Seasonally Adjusted $Y^a = Y/S$
1955	1	710					.91	780
	2	1440					1.39	1040
			968					
	3	980		975	1.01		.96	1020
			982					
	4	740		994	.74		.75	990
			1005					
1956	1	770		1010	.76	→ ave = .91	.91	850
			1015					
	2	1530		1018	1.50	1.39	1.39	1100
			1020					
	3	1020		1039	.98	.96	.96	1060
			1058					
	4	760		1029	.74	.75	.75	1010
			1000					
1957	1	920		990	.93		.91	1010
			980					
	2	1300		968	1.34		1.39	940
			955					
	3	940		951	.99		.96	980
			947					
	4	660		938	.70		.75	880
			928					
1958	1	890		913	.97		.91	980
			897					
	2	1220		920	1.33		1.39	880
			943					
	3	820		956	.86		.96	850
			970					
	4	840		1001	.84		.75	1120
			1032					
1959	1	1000		1046	.96		.91	1100
			1060					
	2	1470		1061	1.39		1.39	1060
			1063					
	3	930					.96	970
	4	850					.75	1130

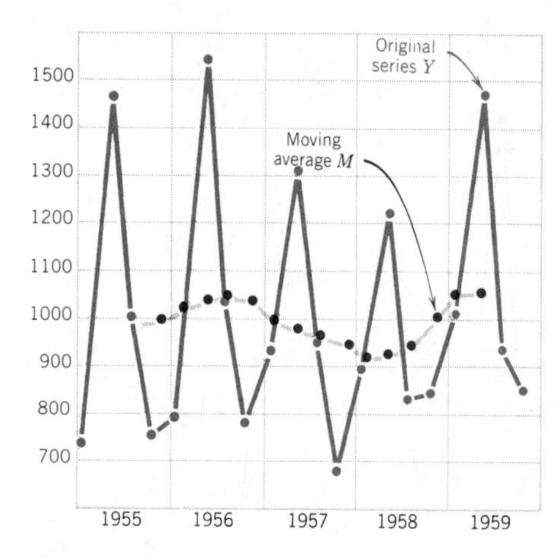

FIGURE 24-6
The moving average smooths out the series (auto sales, in hundreds, same as Problem 24-3).

bance D. With these components removed, the moving average M consists of the remaining components—trend T and cyclical C. We confirm from its wave-like pattern in Figure 24-6 that M does indeed capture the cyclical component C; and we notice that M also captures the trend T, which could be isolated by fitting a least squares regression line.

B—CAPTURING *S* AND *D* USING THE RATIO TO MOVING AVERAGE

With the moving average M defining trend T and cyclical C, we now turn to the task of analysing the remaining two components—seasonal variation S and disturbance D. Since S and D are the components that are included in the observed time series Y but are removed in calculating M, we could capture them by using either:

i. $Y - M$, the difference between the observed Y and the moving average M; or

ii. Y/M, the *ratio* of the observed Y to the moving average M, called the *ratio to moving average*. Traditionally, this is the method that is chosen; it is calculated in column 5 of Table 24-2, and is graphed in Figure 24-7*a*.

We can confirm that the ratio Y/M does indeed capture the seasonal effect: Every second quarter, this ratio substantially exceeds 1 because Y is substantially greater than M.

C—ISOLATING THE SEASONAL VARIATION *S*

The problem in Figure 24-7 is that Y/M in panel (*a*) gives us not only S, but also the disturbance D. How do we isolate S? The answer is to average

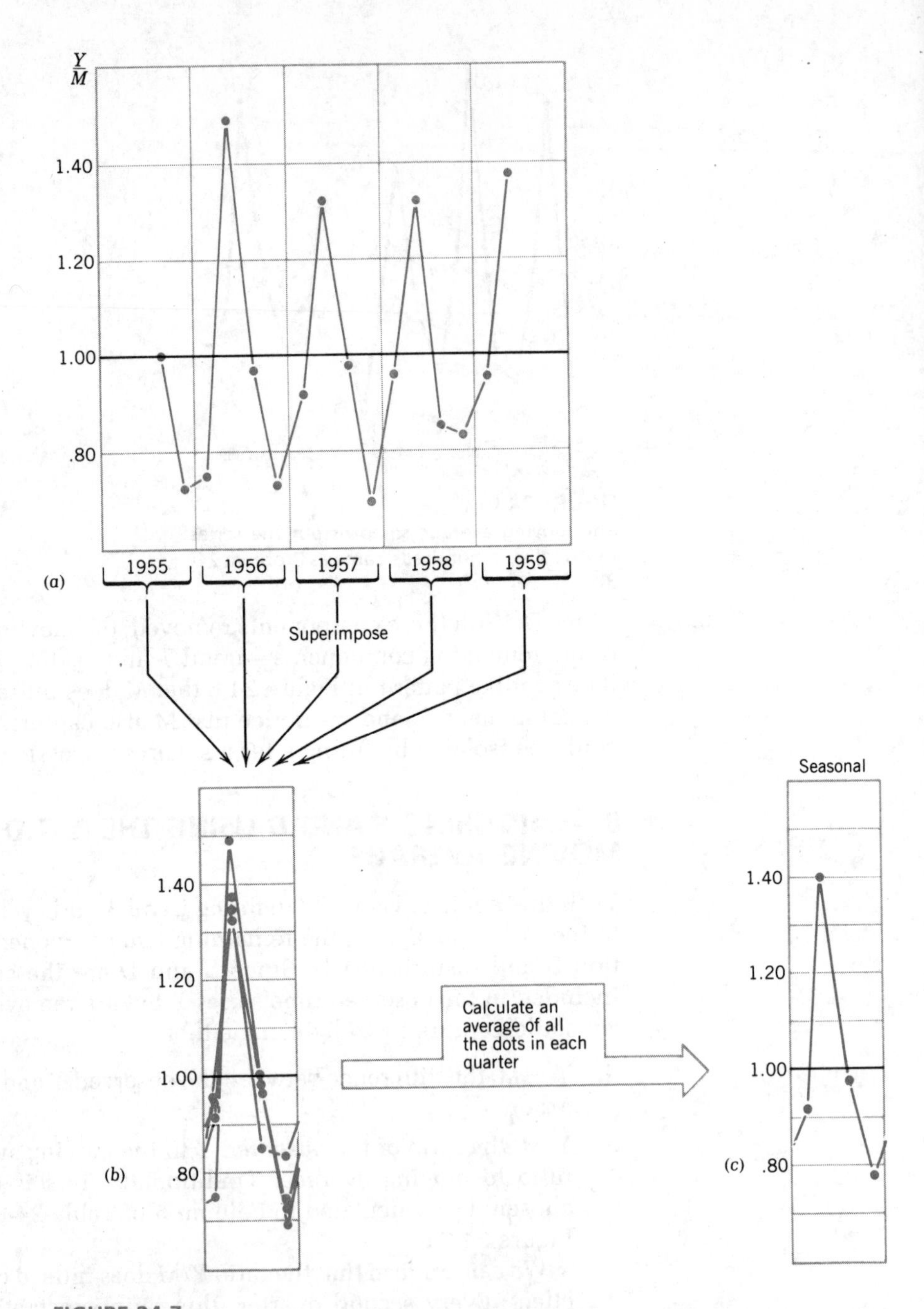

FIGURE 24-7
(a) Y/M = ratio to moving average, which captures the seasonal S and disturbance D. (b) Superimposing the yearly slices permits averaging to filter out the disturbance, leaving the seasonal in (c).

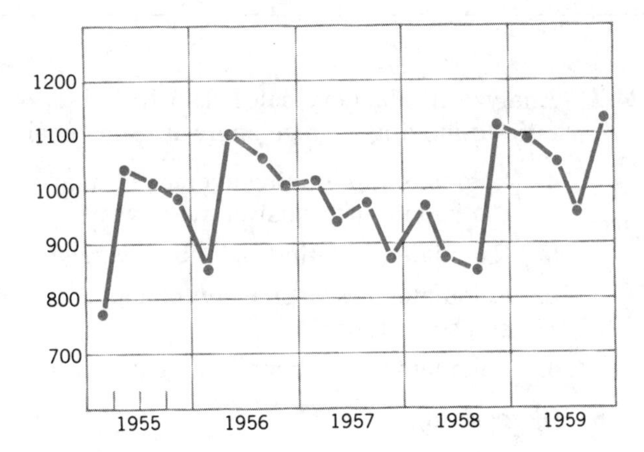

FIGURE 24-8
Seasonally adjusted series Y^a.

all the first quarter values of Y/M; then similarly, average all the second quarter values, and so on. To visualize this, imagine cutting panel (*a*) up into one year periods, superimposing them in panel (*b*), and finally averaging as shown in panel (*c*). (The actual numerical calculations are set out in column 6 of Table 24-2, and are recorded in full in column 7.)

D—USING *S* TO SEASONALLY ADJUST THE ORIGINAL *Y*

Once the seasonal component S has been calculated, it can be used to seasonally adjust (deseasonalize) the original time series Y. This is done simply by dividing Y by the seasonal pattern in column 7 of Table 24-2, recording the result in column 8. When we graph this adjusted series Y^a in Figure 24-8, we see that the clear-cut seasonal pattern in the original data Y (graphed in Problem 24-3) has now been eliminated.

To sum up: This ratio-to-moving-average approach is primarily used to decompose a time series—and, in particular, to isolate S, which is then used to seasonally adjust the original series. See Table 24-3.

TABLE 24-3 Summary of the Ratio-to-Moving-Average Decomposition

Time Series Y is Made Up Of:	
Trend T and Cyclical C	*Seasonal S and Disturbance D*
(A) T and C are captured in the moving average M	(B) S and D are captured by the ratio Y/M. (C) S is then isolated by averaging the yearly slices. (D) S can then be used to seasonally adjust Y: $Y^a = Y/S$

PROBLEMS

24-7 Analyze the jewelry sales data in Table 24-1, with the classical ratio-to-moving-average analysis. Specifically:

- **a.** Calculate the moving average (4 quarters). Does it smooth out the large fourth quarter every year?
- **b.** Calculate the ratio-to-moving average.
- **c.** Calculate the seasonal component S by averaging the series in **b** across all four years.
- **d.** Calculate the seasonally adjusted series, and graph it.

24-8 (Forecasting)

- **a.** Graph the moving average in Problem 24-7, part **a**, and extend it by eye another eight quarters. Roughly tabulate these extended values.
- **b.** Multiply the extended values of part **a** by the seasonal factor S found in Problem 24-7, part **c**, to obtain the *forecast* values. How do they compare to the values forecast with regression in Figure 24-4*d*?

24-9 Repeat Problem 24-7 for the carloading data of Problem 24-6.

24-4 FORECASTING USING EXPONENTIAL SMOOTHING

In this section we change gears. We concentrate on *forecasting* instead of decomposition, and accordingly we return to the approach of Section 24-2. In that context we assume—in the interests of simplifying a complex analysis—that trend and seasonal variation are not present. (For example, if we have a series of annual production figures, they cannot reveal any seasonal pattern.)

Nevertheless, the series will contain serial correlation, and we can forecast it using the approach already developed for a serially correlated residual. Specifically, we can use the *autoregressive model* that predicts Y_t as a linear combination of its previous values:

$$\hat{Y}_t = b_1 Y_{t-1} + b_2 Y_{t-2} + b_3 Y_{t-3} + \cdots \tag{24-11}$$

like (24-7)

where the coefficients $b_1, b_2, \ldots$ are estimated by least squares multiple regression.

How far back into the past should the autoregression (24-11) go? One solution is to let it go back indefinitely, with smaller and smaller weights that decline exponentially:

$$b_k = b\lambda^k, \qquad k = 1, 2, \ldots \text{ and } 0 < \lambda < 1 \tag{24-12}$$

Not only does this capture the sensible notion that more distant values should have less effect, it also turns out to be very convenient: As Appendix 24-4 shows, when we substitute (24-12) into (24-11), it reduces to a very simple form:

$$\boxed{\hat{Y}_t = (1 - \lambda)Y_{t-1} + \lambda\hat{Y}_{t-1}} \tag{24-13}$$

where the weight λ can be estimated by least squares. (The details are more complicated than in Chapter 11, but the principle is the same: Choose λ to minimize the squared errors that result from this fitting procedure.)

It is easy to interpret (24-13): To predict this year's sales, we just take a weighted average of last year's sales (Y_{t-1}), and the *prediction* ($\hat{Y}_{t-1}$) of last year's sales we made a year earlier. This formula is so easy it can be calculated on the back of an envelope. An example will illustrate:

EXAMPLE 24-1

A furniture salesman taking over a new territory was instructed to forecast each year's sales by the formula:

$$\begin{aligned}\text{Forecast sales} = {} & .30 \text{ (last year's sales)} \\ & + .70 \text{ (forecast of last year's sales)}\end{aligned}$$

[In other words, it had been estimated that λ in (24-13) was .70.] Suppose the forecast of last year's sales was 3.70 (million dollars). But the actual sales last year turned out to be 3.92.

a. What is the sales forecast for this year?

b. If this year's sales turn out to be 3.64, what would the forecast be for next year?

SOLUTION

a. Substitute appropriately into (24-13):

$$\text{Forecast} = .30(3.92) + .70(3.70) = 3.77$$

b. In (24-13) notice that t is now next year, and $t - 1$ is this year. Thus

$$\text{Forecast} = .30(3.64) + .70(3.77) = 3.73 \tag{24-14}$$

Of course, this forecast has been kept relatively simple because we have assumed that trend and seasonal components are not present. If they are, each component should be forecast, using essentially the same exponential smoothing developed above. Then they can be added together (just as in Figure 24-4), to provide a forecast of the overall time series. This is called a *Holt-Winters* forecast.

PROBLEMS

24-10 To forecast next week's sales of its bread, a bakery used an exponential smoothing formula with $\lambda = .40$:

$$\hat{Y}_t = .60\ Y_{t-1} + .40\ \hat{Y}_{t-1} \qquad \text{like (24-13)}$$

a. Last week's forecast was 24,200 while actual sales were 24,700. What is the forecast of this week's sales?

b. If this week's sales turned out to be 26,000, what is the forecast of next week's sales?

c. Continue making weekly forecasts, if actual sales continued on from 26,000 as follows:

25,800 24,800 23,700 23,600

24-5 FORECASTING USING BOX-JENKINS MODELS

In order to understand this increasingly popular but complex method of forecasting, we again keep the argument simple by initially assuming the time series is free of trend and seasonal components. Then an autoregressive model of the following form is appropriate:

$$Y_t = \beta_1 Y_{t-1} + \beta_2 Y_{t-2} + \cdots + \beta_p Y_{t-p} + u_t \qquad \text{(24-15) like (24-11)}$$

The potential number of lags p can be very large, of course. In the exponential smoothing technique of the previous section, we allowed an infinite number by locking in a rigid assumption of how the coefficients decreased exponentially into the past.

If we tried to avoid this restrictive assumption by a completely free fit of all the β parameters in (24-15), we would have too many parameters to estimate from a sample of relatively small size. The Box-Jenkins method is a compromise: It is a freer fit than exponential smoothing, yet it doesn't require all the parameters of a completely free fit of a long autoregression.

Specifically, the Box-Jenkins technique cuts Equation (24-15) off at a small number of lags—that is, includes only the most important recent lagged values. This means we cannot capture all of the serial correlation, so some remains in u_t. We could therefore model u_t with another autoregression (that is, a regression of u_t on its own previous values). It is more effective, however, to model u_t as a *moving average* of serially independent terms v_t (white noise):

$$u_t = \gamma_0 v_t + \gamma_1 v_{t-1} + \cdots + \gamma_q v_{t-q} \tag{24-16}$$

The moving average (24-16) might be more accurately called a "moving linear combination" since we don't require the coefficients to sum to 1, or even be positive. In fact, it is customarily written in a slightly different form:

$$u_t = v_t - \alpha_1 v_{t-1} - \alpha_2 v_{t-2} - \cdots - \alpha_q v_{t-q} \tag{24-17}$$

When this moving average (24-17) is substituted into the autoregression (24-15), we obtain a combination of an autoregression (AR) and moving average (MA) whose lengths are p and q, respectively:

ARMA (p,q) model:

$$Y_t = \beta_1 Y_{t-1} + \cdots + \beta_p Y_{t-p} + v_t - \alpha_1 v_{t-1} - \cdots - \alpha_q v_{t-q} \tag{24-18}$$

Although estimating the β and α parameters is complex, it can be done routinely with a computer package.

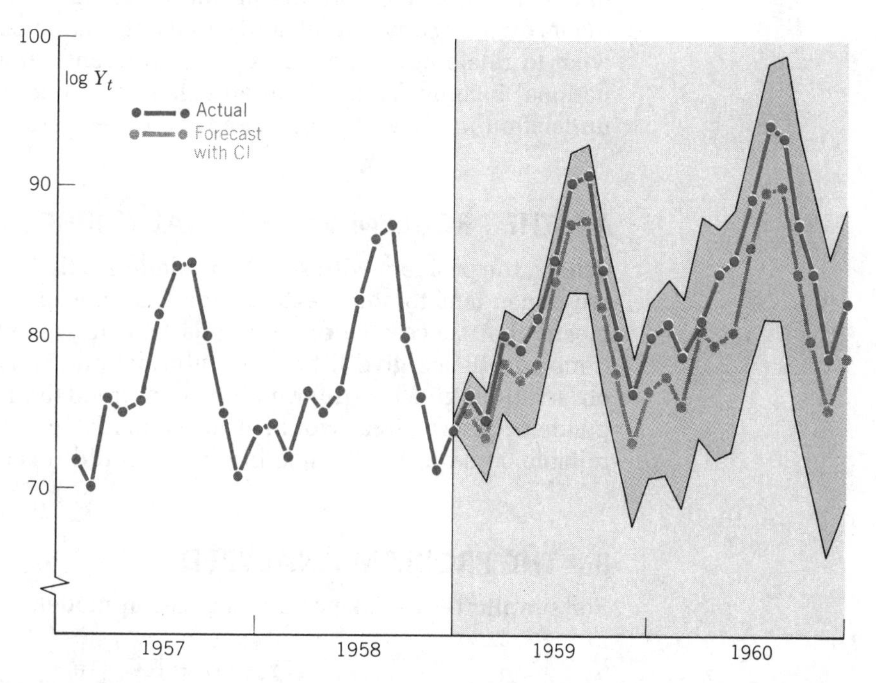

FIGURE 24-9
An example of a Box-Jenkins forecast, based on 120 months of data. The last 24 months are graphed, along with the gray forecast (and the 95% confidence interval around it) made in the last month, for the next 24 months into the future. Compare this forecast with the future series as it actually turned out, in blue. (Y_t = total number of international airline passengers; series G of Box and Jenkins, 1976.)

In practice, the Box-Jenkins model is even more complex. It also incorporates a seasonal component and a trend, and is known as a SARIMA model. Once its parameters are estimated, the model can be used for forecasting.

Although the details (Box and Jenkins, 1970) would fill a book, we do have space here to show just how well a SARIMA model can forecast. Figure 24-9 shows a computer forecast of airline passengers up to 24 months ahead (McLeod, 1982). It includes a 95% confidence band that of course grows vaguer as the forecast reaches further into the future.

*24-6 GENERALIZED LEAST SQUARES (GLS)

Again returning to our initial analysis of a time series in Section 24-2, recall that we used regression to estimate the trend and seasonal components, leaving a residual series to be analyzed for serial correlation. Unfortunately, a serially correlated residual mixed up in the original series will reduce the reliability of the regression. In this section we discuss this problem and suggest possible solutions.

A second objective is to extend our analysis. So far in this chapter we have concentrated on predicting *one* series, such as auto sales, by examining its own seasonal, trend, and serial correlation characteristics. Now we wish to relate auto sales to entirely different variables as well, such as national income. Thus our interest is not only in forecasting, but also in *understanding* how two or more time series variables may be related.

A—THE PROBLEM WITH SERIAL CORRELATION

Briefly, the problem with serial correlation is that successive observations are dependent to some extent. For example, positive serial correlation means that successive observations tend to resemble previous observations and hence give little new information. Thus n serially correlated observations give less information about trend (and seasonal) than n independent observations would. Consequently, our estimates will be less reliable, and our confidence intervals should reflect this.

B—THE PROBLEM ANALYZED

For simplicity, we take as our regression model,

$$Y_t = \alpha + \beta X_t + e_t \tag{24-19}$$

So far X_t has represented time itself, or seasonal dummies. Now let it represent *any* time series (or combination of series) deemed influential in determining Y_t. (Notice how this can take us, as we wish, beyond our earlier analysis of just one time series, to an analysis of how two or more time series are related.)

The residual e_t in (24-19) of course is assumed to be serially correlated, and for simplicity, we again take $\rho = 1$:

$$e_t = e_{t-1} + v_t \tag{24-20}$$

like (24-4)

where v_t is white noise (serially uncorrelated) as usual.

Now suppose that the true regression line (defined by α and β) is the one shown in panel (a) of Figure 24-10. Suppose further that the residual series $e_1, e_2, \ldots$ is given in panel (b)—the same one generated earlier in Figure 24-5. This produces the pattern of observations shown in panel (a): Once the observations are above the true regression, they tend to stay above it.

We immediately can see the difficulties that the serial correlation causes by observing in panel (a) how badly the estimated regression through this scatter fits the true regression: β is seriously underestimated. But in another sample we might have observed precisely the opposite pattern of residuals, with e_t initially taking on negative values, followed

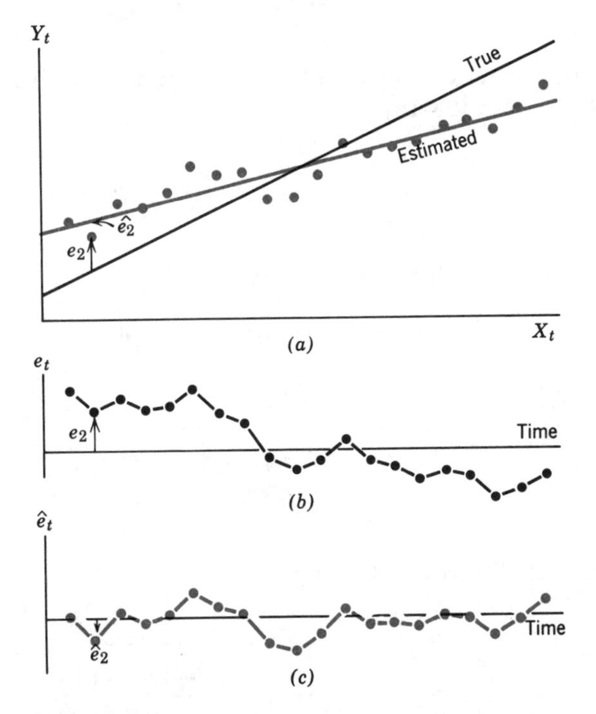

FIGURE 24-10
Regression with serially correlated residual. (a) True and estimated regression lines. (b) True residual (from Figure 24-5). (c) Estimated residual (around the estimated regression in panel (a)).

by positive ones. In this case, we would overestimate β. Since we are as likely to get an overestimate as an underestimate, the problem is therefore not bias. Rather, the problem is that estimates tend to be wide of the target—they have large variance.

Panel (c) of Figure 24-10 illustrates a second problem: Because serial correlation tends to produce a smooth series, the *estimated* residuals $\hat{e}_t$ tend to be smaller than the true residuals e_t. Thus the residual variance s^2 will be smaller than σ^2, and the subsequent confidence interval for β will be too narrow.

To sum up: Because of serial correlation, the OLS estimate of β is less reliable. But it has the illusion of being *more* reliable because autocorrelated data is smooth and yields smaller observed residuals.

C—FIRST DIFFERENCES

The remedy for serial correlation is to transform the data to a form that does satisfy the assumptions of OLS. Since (24-19) holds true for any time t, it holds for time $(t-1)$:

$$Y_{t-1} = \alpha + \beta X_{t-1} + e_{t-1} \tag{24-21}$$

We now can examine the change over time of our variables, by subtracting (24-21) from (24-19):

$$(Y_t - Y_{t-1}) = \beta(X_t - X_{t-1}) + (e_t - e_{t-1}) \tag{24-22}$$

Note from (24-20) that:

$$e_t - e_{t-1} = v_t \tag{24-23}$$

and define:

$$\left.\begin{aligned} \Delta Y_t &\equiv Y_t - Y_{t-1} \\ \Delta X_t &\equiv X_t - X_{t-1} \end{aligned}\right\} \qquad \begin{array}{r} (24\text{-}24) \\ \text{like } (24\text{-}23) \end{array}$$

Then (24-22) can be written:

$$\boxed{\Delta Y_t = \beta \Delta X_t + v_t} \tag{24-25}$$

where v_t is a white noise term with all the properties required by OLS. Thus, β may be estimated validly by OLS regression of ΔY_t against ΔX_t.

D—GENERALIZED DIFFERENCES: GENERALIZED LEAST SQUARES (GLS)

A more useful model for the serially correlated residual is:

$$e_t = \rho e_{t-1} + v_t \quad (24\text{-}26)$$

(24-4) repeated

where we no longer[3] insist that $\rho = 1$ as in (24-20); instead,

$$|\rho| < 1 \quad (24\text{-}27)$$

We continue to assume the linear regression model:

$$Y_t = \alpha + \beta X_t + e_t \quad (24\text{-}28)$$

(24-19) repeated

To estimate β, we difference the data in much the same way as before. Equation (24-28) is reexpressed for time $(t - 1)$ and is then multiplied by ρ:

$$\rho Y_{t-1} = \rho\alpha + \rho\beta X_{t-1} + \rho e_{t-1} \quad (24\text{-}29)$$

Subtracting (24-29) from (24-28):

$$(Y_t - \rho Y_{t-1}) = \alpha(1 - \rho) + \beta(X_t - \rho X_{t-1}) + (e_t - \rho e_{t-1}) \quad (24\text{-}30)$$

Now define the *generalized differences:*

$$\left.\boxed{\begin{aligned} \Delta Y_t &\equiv Y_t - \rho Y_{t-1} \\ \Delta X_t &\equiv X_t - \rho X_{t-1} \end{aligned}}\right\} \quad (24\text{-}31)$$

like (24-24)

Then (24-30) can be written:

$$\boxed{\Delta Y_t = \alpha(1 - \rho) + \beta \Delta X_t + v_t} \quad (24\text{-}32)$$

where v_t is again white noise, with all the properties required by OLS. Thus, after this transformation, we may regress ΔY_t against ΔX_t to estimate β. This technique is an example of *generalized least squares* (GLS).

---

[3] If $|\rho| \geq 1$ as in (24-20), a major theoretical problem arises because the residual e_t becomes "explosive"; that is, the variance of e_t increases over time without limit.

However, prior to this regression, one additional adjustment must be made to the data. The *first* observed values Y_1 and X_1 cannot be transformed by (24-31) since their previous values are not available; instead, the appropriate transformation is[4]:

$$\Delta Y_1 \equiv \sqrt{1-\rho^2}\, Y_1$$
$$\Delta X_1 \equiv \sqrt{1-\rho^2}\, X_1 \qquad (24\text{-}33)$$

The problem is, of course, that all of these transformations require a value for ρ, which is unknown. We have already seen one way to obtain an estimate r for ρ: We use OLS to fit

$$\hat{e}_t = r\hat{e}_{t-1} \qquad (24\text{-}34)$$

(24-5) repeated

Unfortunately, r has a bias, which can be seen from Figure 24-10: The estimated residuals $\hat{e}_t$ in panel (c) fluctuate around zero more (i.e., bounce back and forth across the baseline more) and hence have a smaller serial correlation r than do the true residuals e_t in panel (b). Thus r tends to underestimate ρ.

E—AN ALTERNATIVE METHOD TO ESTIMATE ρ

An alternative often used in practice to estimate ρ is to rearrange (24-30) into the following regression equation:

$$Y_t = \alpha(1-\rho) + \rho Y_{t-1} + \beta X_t - \beta\rho X_{t-1} + (e_t - \rho e_{t-1}) \qquad (24\text{-}35)$$

where $e_t - \rho e_{t-1} = v_t$ is again the white noise term. Accordingly, run this regression and estimate ρ from the coefficient[5] of Y_{t-1}. This can then be used in (24-31) and (24-33) to yield estimates of α and β.

---

[4] This transformation of the data is very important; without it, the regression (24-32) may be no better than OLS, and perhaps not even as good. And of course, the constant regressor (whose coefficient is α) also must be transformed. By analogy with (24-31) and (24-33), it becomes $(1-\rho)$ for $t = 2, 3, \ldots$ and $\sqrt{1-\rho^2}$ for $t = 1$.

The transformation (24-33) must be used with some care. It is appropriate if and only if the process (24-28) generating the residual has been going on undisturbed for a long time previous to collecting the data. In practice, however, the first observation sometimes is taken just after a war or some other catastrophe, which seriously disturbs the residual.

[5] Or, divide the coefficient of X_{t-1} by the coefficient of X_t, and change the sign. This second estimate of ρ can be averaged with the first to get an even better estimate. And if the two estimates of ρ are very different, it serves as a warning that the model may be poorly specified.

PROBLEMS

24-11 The daily closing prices of a stock form an interesting time series. If you took first differences, do you think you would get essentially white noise? Why?

CHAPTER 24 SUMMARY

24-1 Observations taken over time present special problems of serial correlation and seasonal variation.

24-2 Multiple regression can be used to decompose a time series. The seasonal component is easily estimated with dummies in regression—and at the same time, regression estimates trend. Any serially correlated residual that remains then requires special treatment as an autoregression.

Each of the time series components can be forecast, and then summed to provide a forecast of the original time series.

24-3 In the era before computers, decomposition of a time series started with a moving average to smooth the series. Then the ratio of the series to this moving average provided the seasonal component, plus a disturbance that could be averaged out.

When the series is divided by the seasonal pattern, we obtain a seasonally adjusted series that is often useful for its own sake.

24-4 An autoregression of Y_t on its own past values $Y_{t-1}, Y_{t-2}, \ldots$ is very useful for prediction. If we assume the coefficients exponentially decrease further and further into the past, we greatly simplify the model.

24-5 Box-Jenkins provides another, more flexible way to simplify the autoregression: After a few terms, the autoregression is chopped off, with the truncated part represented by a moving average.

***24-6** The OLS regression of Y_t against X_t is not fully efficient when the residuals are serially correlated. The remedy is to transform the regression equation by differencing, to produce *uncorrelated* residuals; then ordinary regression formulas can be used. This whole process is called Generalized Least Squares (GLS).

REVIEW PROBLEMS

24-12 Select the correct choice in each bracket:

a. Serial correlation in a time series means that the OLS fit is [particularly appropriate, inappropriate] as a forecast.

b. [Annual, Quarterly] economic series are often seasonally adjusted. Then the seasonally adjusted series [shows the actual historic record, may give a better idea of relative performance].

24-13 In which of the following series would you expect to find periodic patterns (such as the seasonal pattern in Figure 24-2)?

a. A sample of 100 monthly mean temperatures in Atlanta.

b. A sample of 500 hourly temperature readings in Atlanta.

c. Annual GNP growth from 1950 to 1985.

d. Quarterly GNP growth from 1950 to 1985.

24-14 ***A Final Challenge: Old Faithful Again***

Problem 12-18 showed how the interval till the next eruption of Old Faithful (Y) depended upon the duration of the last eruption (X).

But does Y also depend upon time? That very interesting question can be answered by a graph that plots the values of Y in serial order. Here are a couple of typical days (Denby and Pregibon 1987):

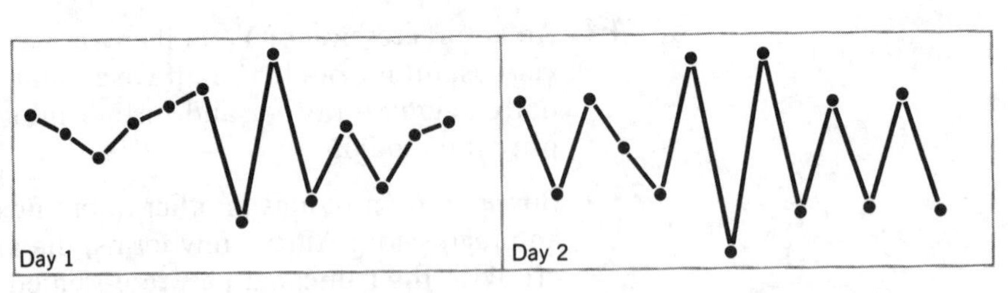

Note the fluctuation up and down suggesting negative serial correlation, which we can incorporate into our linear model:

$$Y_t = \alpha + \beta X_t + e_t \tag{24-36}$$

(24-19) repeated

and now

$$e_t = \rho e_{t-1} + v_t \tag{24-37}$$

(24-26) repeated

The regression technique (24-35) estimated ρ as $-.50$. Then GLS estimated α as 39, β as 8.2, and the standard deviation of v_t as 6.8 (Denby and Pregibon, 1987).

a. To predict Y_t, two equations were proposed:

$$\hat{Y}_t = 39 + 8.2X_t + (0 \text{ for } \hat{e}_t) \qquad (24\text{-}38)$$

like (24-36)

Or, substituting (24-37) into (24-36), we estimate:

$$\hat{Y}_t = 39 + 8.2X_t - .5\hat{e}_{t-1} + (0 \text{ for } \hat{v}_t) \qquad (24\text{-}39)$$

Which equation gives the better prediction? Why?

b. Specifically, suppose the last eruption lasted $X_t = 2$ minutes, and it was a surprising 10 minutes later than predicted by the linear equation, that is, $\hat{e}_{t-1} = 10$ minutes.

When would you predict the next eruption? How does this compare to the OLS prediction of 52.6 in Problem 12-18?

c. To tell the tourists an appropriate time to look for the next eruption, we need more than the "best prediction" in part **b**. We need to get them there *earlier*, as we saw in Problem 12-18 **f**, with an approximate prediction interval of, say, 90% accuracy:

$$Y_0 > \hat{Y}_0 - t_{.10}s$$

Substituting $t_{.10} = 1.3$ and $s = 6.8$, we get

$$Y_0 > \hat{Y}_0 - 8.8$$

Now use this to get a 90% prediction for the situation in **b**.

d. Suppose the eruption predicted in **c** occurred after an interval of 47 minutes, and lasted for 4.2 minutes. Did the tourists who came at the 90% prediction time catch it, or miss it?

Find the 90% prediction time for the *next* eruption.

e. Whenever a more complex model like this is used, it is wise to ask whether the added complexity—the time series wrinkle—is worthwhile. Answer with a brief essay (using the answer in Problem 12-18 as a basis for comparison, of course).

CHAPTER 25

*Simultaneous Equations

(Requires Chapter 13)

Whatever moves is moved by another.

ST. THOMAS AQUINAS

25-1 INTRODUCTION: THE BIAS IN OLS

Economic relationships are often more complicated than the techniques that we have introduced so far suggest. Specifically, seldom is a variable determined by a single relationship (equation). Instead, it is usually determined simultaneously with many other variables in a whole system of simultaneous equations. For example, the price of corn is determined simultaneously with the price of rye, the price of hogs, and so on.

As another illustration, consider a very simple model of national income using just two equations:

$$Y = \alpha + \beta X + e \tag{25-1}$$

$$X = Y + I \tag{25-2}$$

Equation (25-1) is the standard form of the consumption function that relates consumer expenditure Y to income X. The parameters of this function that must be estimated are α (the intercept) and β (the slope, or marginal propensity to consume). We assume that the error term is well-behaved: Successive values of e are assumed to be independent and identically distributed, with mean 0 and variance σ^2. Equation (25-2) states that national income is defined as the sum of consumption and investment I. (Since both sides of this equation are equal by economic definition, no error term appears in this equation—but the analysis remains the same in any case).

An important distinction must be made between two kinds of variables in our system. By assumption, I is determined *outside* the system of equations, so it is called *predetermined* (or *exogenous*). The essential point is that its values are determined elsewhere, and are not influenced by Y, X, or e. In particular, we emphasize that:

Because I is predetermined, I and e are statistically independent. (25-3)

On the other hand, X and Y are determined *within* the system and thus are influenced by I and e; they are often called mutually *dependent* (or *endogenous*). The two equations in this simultaneous system can be solved for the two dependent variables (the model is mathematically complete).

A diagram will be useful to illustrate the statistical difficulties encountered. To highlight the problems the statistician will face, let us suppose that we have some sort of omniscient knowledge, so that we know the true consumption function $Y = \alpha + \beta X$, as shown in Figure 25-1. And let us watch what happens to the statistician—a mere mortal—who does not have this knowledge but must try to estimate this function by observing only Y and X. Specifically, let us show how badly things will turn out if he or she estimates α and β by fitting a line by ordinary least squares (OLS). To find the sort of scatter of Y and X that he or she will observe, we must remember that all observations must satisfy both Equations (25-1) and (25-2).

Consider (25-1) first. Whenever e takes on a zero value, the observation of Y and X must fall somewhere along the true consumption function $Y = \alpha + \beta X$, shown in Figure 25-1. If e takes on a value greater than zero (say, +\$50 billion), then consumption is greater as a consequence and the observation of Y and X must fall somewhere along $Y = \alpha + \beta X + 50$. Similarly, if e takes on a value of -50, the statistician will observe a point on the line $Y = \alpha + \beta X - 50$. According to the standard assumptions, e is distributed about a zero mean. To keep the geometry simple, we further assume that e is equally likely to take on any value between $+50$ and -50. Thus the statistician will observe Y and X falling within this band around the consumption function, shaded in Figure 25-1.

Any observed combination of Y and X also must satisfy (25-2). What does this imply? This condition can be rewritten as:

$$Y = X - I \tag{25-4}$$

If I were zero, then Y and X would be equal, and any observation would fall on the 45° line where $Y = X$. Let us suppose that when I is determined by outside factors, it is distributed uniformly through a range of 100 to 250. If $I = 100$, then from (25-4) any observation of Y and X must fall along $Y = X - 100$, which is simply the line lying 100 units below the 45° line. Similarly, when $I = 250$, an observation of Y and X would fall along the line $Y = X - 250$. These two lines define the steeper band within which observations must fall to satisfy (25-2).

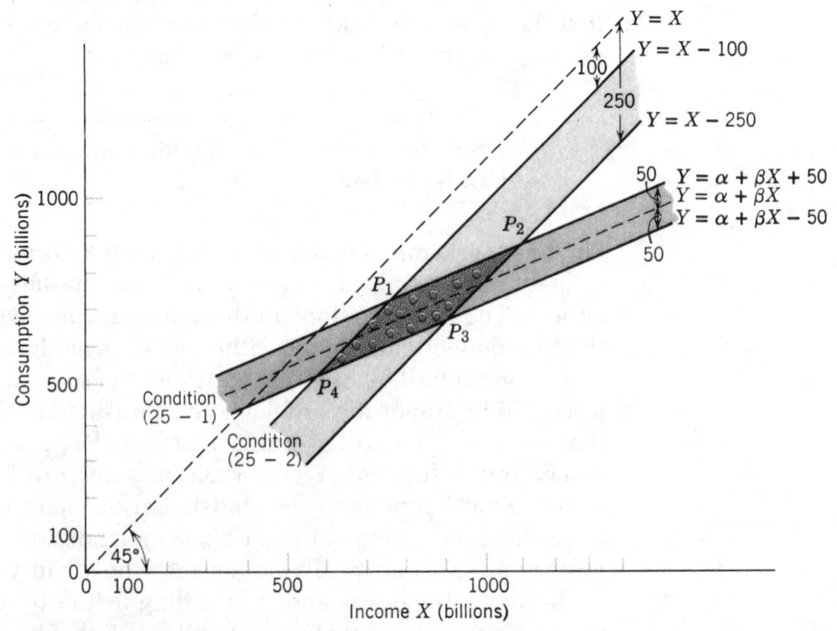

FIGURE 25-1
The consumption function, and the scatter of observed points around it.

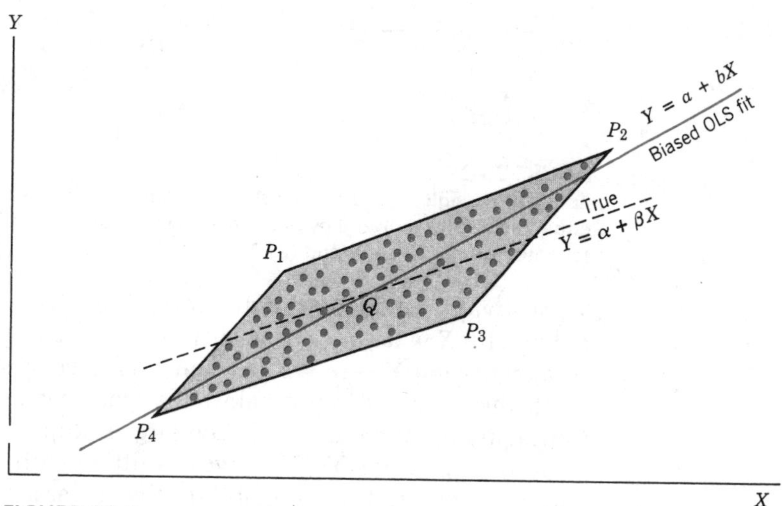

FIGURE 25-2
Inconsistent OLS fit of the consumption function.

Since any observed combination of Y and X must satisfy *both* conditions, all observations will fall within the parallelogram $P_1P_2P_3P_4$. To clarify, this parallelogram of observations is reproduced in Figure 25-2. When the statistician regresses Y on X using OLS, the result is shown as $Y = a + bX$. When this is compared with the true consumption function $Y = \alpha + \beta X$, it is clear that the statistician has come up with a bad fit; his estimate of the slope has an upward bias. What has gone wrong?

The observations around P_2 have "pulled" the estimating line above the true regression; similarly, the observations around P_4 have pulled the estimating line below the true regression. It is the pull on both ends that has tilted this estimated line. Moreover, increasing sample size will not help to reduce this bias. If the number of observations in this parallelogram is doubled, this bias will remain.[1] Hence, OLS is inconsistent; this technique that worked so well in a single-equation model clearly is less satisfactory when the problem is to estimate an equation that is embedded within a system of simultaneous equations.

The reason is evident: for the single-equation model, it was assumed in (12-3) that the expected value of e was 0 for every value of X (i.e., e was independent of X), and this is why OLS works so well. But in a simultaneous-equation model, this assumption no longer holds.

In an equation in a simultaneous system, regressors that are not predetermined are not independent of the error term *e*.	(25-5)

[1] With an increase in sample size, the reliability of b as an estimator will be increased somewhat, because its variance will decrease towards zero. However, its bias will not be reduced.

FIGURE 25-3
Contrast of single equations and simultaneous equations. (a) Single equations, easily analyzed by path analysis in Chapter 13. (b) Simultaneous equations (25-1) and (25-2).

To see why, note, for example, in Figure 25-2 how e is correlated positively with X: e tends to be positive (i.e., the observed point lies above the true regression $Y = \alpha + \beta X$) when X is large, and e tends to be negative (with the observed point below the true regression) when X is small.[2] Consequently, the OLS fit has too large a slope. The reason is intuitively clear: in explaining Y, OLS gives as little credit as possible to the error, and as much credit as possible to the regressor X. When the error and regressor are correlated, then some of the effect of the error is attributed wrongly to the regressor.

In conclusion, the problem is this: The single-equation technique of OLS is inconsistent in simultaneous equations. Perhaps a diagram will clarify just how simultaneous equations differ from single equations (even systems of single equations). In Figure 25-3, we see that the distinguishing feature of simultaneous equations is that the *mutually* dependent variables influence each other, as indicated by the arrows going *both* ways between X and Y in panel (*b*).

PROBLEMS

25-1 In the consumption model shown in Figure 25-1, suppose the true consumption function is $Y = 10 + .6X$ and the following combinations of Y, X, and I have been observed:

Y	X	I
46	60	14
31	45	14
61	75	14
58	80	22
43	65	22
73	95	22
70	100	30
55	85	30
85	115	30

[2] Note that the reason for this is precisely because of the second equation in the model: thus, in Figure 25-2, the observed points are not only determined by Equation (25-1), but they are also determined, or "pulled," by Equation (25-2). And it is this latter pull that results in the positive correlation of X and e.

a. Graph the true consumption function and the scatter of (X, Y) observations.

b. Regress Y on X using OLS, and graph the estimated consumption function. Is it unbiased?

25-2 A sociologist observes that the number of children available for adoption (Y_1) depends on the number of births (Y_2). At the same time, births depend on income (X) and on the number of children available for adoption.

a. Draw a schematic figure similar to Figure 25-3 illustrating these relationships.

b. Set up a system of two simultaneous equations showing how Y_1 and Y_2 are jointly determined.

25-2 THE REMEDY: INSTRUMENTAL VARIABLES (IV)

Since OLS is inconsistent, we now begin the search for an estimator that *is* consistent. The first step is to develop an important new device that will have very broad application.

A—THE COVARIANCE OPERATOR

The *covariance* of any two variables, V and Y say, is defined much like the variance:

$$\textbf{Covariance } s_{VY} \equiv \frac{\Sigma(V - \overline{V})(Y - \overline{Y})}{n - 1} \tag{25-6}$$

like (2-11), (5-10)

Just as the variance summarizes the variability of a variable, so the covariance is a single number that nicely summarizes the covariability or relation between two variables. To see how this concept of covariance can help us, consider the following familiar equation:

$$Y = \alpha + \beta X + e \tag{25-7}$$

If we express all variables in deviation form, then the constant conveniently drops out[3]:

$$(Y - \overline{Y}) = \beta(X - \overline{X}) + (e - \overline{e}) \tag{25-8}$$

[3] To prove this, we simply take averages in (25-7):

$$\overline{Y} = \alpha + \beta\overline{X} + \overline{e} \qquad \text{like (2-19)}$$

When we subtract this from (25-7), then (25-8) follows.

We now select another variable V, and to both sides of (25-8) we do the following three things:

1. multiply by $(V - \overline{V})$,
2. sum from 1 to n,
3. divide by $n - 1$.

The result is the following equation in covariances:

$$\boxed{s_{VY} = \beta s_{VX} + s_{Ve}} \tag{25-9}$$

Notice how we have transformed the equation relating variables (25-7) to the equation relating covariances (25-9). This transformation is called *applying the covariance operator* to (25-7), or *taking covariances with respect to V*.

So far, these are only mathematical manipulations. The question is: How can they help us to estimate the unknown target β?

B—THE INSTRUMENTAL VARIABLE ESTIMATE OF β

Let us solve (25-9) for the unknown parameter β by dividing through by s_{VX}:

$$\frac{s_{VY}}{s_{VX}} = \beta + \frac{s_{Ve}}{s_{VX}} \tag{25-10}$$

If the last term is small enough to be negligible and drops out, we have an estimate of β—s_{VY}/s_{VX}. Since this estimate depends upon the variable V that was *instrumental* in obtaining it, we name it accordingly:

Instrumental Variable (IV) estimator of β:

$$b_V \equiv \frac{s_{VY}}{s_{VX}} \tag{25-11}$$

Finally, let us substitute (25-11) back into (25-10):

$$\boxed{b_V = \beta + \left(\frac{s_{Ve}}{s_{VX}}\right)} \tag{25-12}$$

The bracketed term represents the error in using b_V to estimate the target β. If this error is large, b_V will be a bad estimate; if it is small, b_V will be a good estimate. Thus we will look for an instrumental variable V that will make this bracketed error term small—that is, will make its numerator small and its denominator large.

Requirements of a good instrumental variable V	
1. To make s_{Ve} small, V should be uncorrelated with the error e ($s_{Ve} \to 0$).[4] If it is, the estimate is consistent.	(25-13)
2. To make s_{VX} large, V should be highly correlated to X.	

To sum up. It doesn't matter where (25-7) comes from. That is, it doesn't matter whether it is one equation in a simultaneous system—like (25-1)—or if it is the one equation in a single equation model—like (12-3). In either case, we can take covariances of all variables in this equation with respect to V, to get the covariance equation (25-9). This in turn yields the IV estimator (25-11) which is a good estimator if conditions (25-13) are satisfied. To illustrate when this IV estimator (25-11) is a good estimator and when it is not, we next consider three cases.

C—APPLYING THE IV ESTIMATOR (25-11)

Case 1: On a single equation. Return to the simple situation in Chapter 12 where there was no problem of simultaneous equations: (25-7) was a single equation relating Y to X. If we try to estimate β by using this new technique, we have to select an instrumental variable. What could be better than X itself? [It perfectly satisfies the second condition in (25-13), because X is perfectly correlated with itself. And the first condition is discussed below.] When we thus use X as the instrumental variable V, (25-11) becomes:

$$b_X = \frac{s_{XY}}{s_{XX}} \tag{25-14}$$

But this is just the OLS estimate[5] b. Thus:

For the equation $Y = \alpha + \beta X + e$, OLS is equivalent to using X as an instrumental variable (IV).	(25-15)

[4] For V and e to be uncorrelated means that the *population* covariance σ_{Ve} is 0; that is, the sample covariance s_{Ve} approaches 0 as $n \to \infty$.

[5] To prove this, we write:

$$b_X \equiv \frac{s_{XY}}{s_{XX}} = \frac{\Sigma(X - \bar{X})(Y - \bar{Y})/(n-1)}{\Sigma(X - \bar{X})^2/(n-1)} = \frac{\Sigma xy}{\Sigma x^2} \equiv b$$

Moreover, the first condition in (25-13) tells us that OLS—or equivalently, using X as an IV—requires that:

For consistency, X must be uncorrelated with the error e. (25-16)

This requirement was indeed guaranteed by our OLS model in Chapter 12. [In (12-3), we required the expected value of e to be zero for *every* value of X. Thus, when X was large, for example, there was no tendency for e to be positive (or negative). That is, the correlation of X and e was 0.]

Case 2: In a simultaneous system, a mutually dependent variable gives an inconsistent estimate. Now suppose the equation we are estimating is—like (25-1)—part of a simultaneous system of equations. If we calculate the estimator (25-14) using X as an instrument—that is, if we apply OLS to this equation—the result is an inconsistent estimator, because (25-16) is violated—specifically, by (25-5). This confirms our earlier conclusion that OLS was inconsistent in Figure 25-2.

Case 3: In a simultaneous system, a predetermined variable gives a consistent estimate. If using X as the instrumental variable (i.e., OLS) is not consistent in a simultaneous system, what *would* be? The second requirement in (25-13) is still that the instrumental variable be highly correlated with X. So we had better stick to a variable that is relevant, that is, one of the variables in the system.

Why not use I instead of X as the instrumental variable? In fact, it passes with flying colors because, according to (25-3), it is uncorrelated with e. Thus we obtain a consistent IV estimator of the slope β:

$$b_I = \frac{s_{IY}}{s_{IX}} \tag{25-17}$$

In the next section, we will generalize this same issue—finding the best IV—to more complicated situations.

PROBLEMS

25-3 **a.** Use the data in Problem 25-1 to actually calculate the consistent IV estimate (25-17) of the consumption slope β. How far off the target $\beta = .6$ is it?

b. Explain why this small sample was a lucky one. What would you expect if your small sample is less lucky?

25-4 For the consumption model in this chapter, suppose the covariance table (also called the covariance *matrix*) of X, Y, and I has been computed for a sample of $n = 50$ observations:

$$\begin{bmatrix} s_{XX} & s_{YX} & s_{IX} \\ s_{XY} & s_{YY} & s_{IY} \\ s_{XI} & s_{YI} & s_{II} \end{bmatrix} = \begin{bmatrix} 130 & 100 & 30 \\ 100 & 80 & 20 \\ 30 & 20 & 10 \end{bmatrix}$$

a. Calculate the estimate of the consumption slope β (i) using X as the IV, and (ii) using I as the IV.

b. Which of the estimates in part **a** are biased? How much?

25-5 Consider the multiple regression model:

$$Y = \beta_0 + \beta_1 X_1 + \beta_2 X_2 + e \qquad \text{(13-2) repeated}$$

a. If you take covariances using the instrumental variable X_1, what equation do you get? If you take covariances using X_2 as an instrument, what equation do you get?

b. Outline how you would use these two equations to estimate β_1 and β_2.

c. To estimate β_1 and β_2, which is better—the IV estimates obtained from **b**, or the OLS estimates obtained from (13-5) and (13-6)?

25-3 TWO STAGE LEAST SQUARES (2SLS)

A—INTRODUCTION

As we saw in our simple two-equation system, it is desirable, if possible, to use as instrumental variables only those predetermined variables that explicitly appear in our model—that is, which appear in at least one of the equations in the system. It is evident that neither this approach, nor any other, entirely overcomes our difficulties; the decision on which variables may be used as instrumental variables merely is pushed onto the researcher who specifies the model and, in particular, the predetermined variables that are included. Specification of the model remains arbitrary to a degree, and this gives rise to some arbitrariness in statistical estimation. But this cannot be avoided. We can only conclude that the first task of specifying the original structure of the model is a very important one, since it involves a prior judgment of which variables are "close to" X and Y, and which variables are relatively "far away."

Now let us consider more complicated and typical systems. We will denote the predetermined or exogenous variables (such as investment) by $X_1, X_2, \ldots,$ and the mutually dependent or endogenous variables (such as income and consumption) by $Y_1, Y_2, \ldots.$ For the system to be complete, there must be as many equations as there are dependent variables.

For example, to determine 4 dependent Y variables, 4 equations would be required[6]:

$$Y_1 = \gamma_2 Y_2 + \gamma_3 Y_3 + \beta_1 X_1 + \beta_4 X_4 + \beta_6 X_6 + e \qquad (25\text{-}18)$$

$$Y_2 = \cdots$$

$$Y_3 = \cdots$$

$$Y_4 = \cdots$$

For simplicity, we explicitly showed only the first equation. Once we show how to estimate it, every other equation can be similarly estimated.

It is customary to specify that some of the coefficients are zero. For example, in (25-18) β_2, β_3, β_5, and γ_4 have been specified as zero, so that the terms in X_2, X_3, X_5, and Y_4 do not appear. This specification keeps each equation of manageable length (or *identified*, as we will show in Problem 25-8).

B—CHOOSING INSTRUMENTAL VARIABLES

In (25-18), what can we use as instrumental variables (IV)? To find variables that are highly correlated with the regressors—the second requirement in (25-13)—we might try the regressors themselves (Y_2, Y_3, X_1, X_4, and X_6). No problem is involved in using X_1, X_4, and X_6; because they are predetermined, (25-3) means that they satisfy the first requirement in (25-13). But unfortunately, Y_1, Y_2, and Y_3 are mutually dependent (i.e., determined by the predetermined X variables and the errors) and so are correlated with the error e; thus Y_2 and Y_3 violate this first requirement. One of the most ingenious solutions involves two simple steps:

1. First *purge* Y_2 and Y_3 of their dependence on e, so that they will satisfy the first requirement in (25-13).
2. Apply them, along with X_1, X_4, and X_6, as our instrumental variables.

These two stages—known as *Two Stage Least Squares* (2SLS)—in fact work well, as we will now show in detail.

C—FIRST STAGE

To purge Y_2 of its dependence on e, we regress it on all the exogenous X variables in the system,[7] obtaining the OLS fitted value:

---

[6] For simplicity, in (25-18) we have omitted the constant term, because it drops out when the covariance operator is applied. Then it can easily be estimated after everything else, using an equation like (13-7).

[7] Strictly speaking, when Theil (1957) introduced 2SLS, he specified the whole system of equations. However, the actual form of the other equations in the system doesn't matter. So statisticians applying 2SLS often just use whatever exogenous variables are reasonably relevant and available in the data bank, without specifying exactly what the system is.

$$\hat{Y}_2 = b_0 + b_1X_1 + b_2X_2 + \cdots \tag{25-19}$$

Since each exogenous X variable is independent of e, their linear combination $\hat{Y}_2$ will also be independent[8] of e. Therefore, $\hat{Y}_2$ (and similarly $\hat{Y}_3$) can be used as instrumental variables for consistent estimation.

D—SECOND STAGE

For the second stage, we just apply all 5 instruments—$\hat{Y}_2$, $\hat{Y}_3$, and of course X_1, X_4, and X_5. For example, using $\hat{Y}_2$ as an IV on (25-18) yields

$$s_{\hat{Y}_2Y_1} = \gamma_2 s_{\hat{Y}_2Y_2} + \gamma_3 s_{\hat{Y}_2Y_3} + \beta_1 s_{\hat{Y}_2X_1} + \beta_4 s_{\hat{Y}_2X_4} + \beta_6 s_{\hat{Y}_2X_6} + s_{\hat{Y}_2e}$$

while using $\hat{Y}_3$ as an IV yields

$$s_{\hat{Y}_3Y_1} = \gamma_2 s_{\hat{Y}_3Y_2} + \cdots \qquad + s_{\hat{Y}_3e}$$

Thus, each such application of an IV to the equation (25-18) will give us this sort of estimating equation—for a total of 5 such equations, which can then be solved for estimates of the 5 unknown parameters $\gamma_2, \gamma_3, \ldots$. (Since the last terms $s_{\hat{Y}_2e}$, etc. approach zero, they can be disregarded.)

PROBLEMS

25-6 Suppose the following equations were set up as a simple macroeconomic model of the United States. Altogether 2 mutually dependent Y variables were simultaneously determined by 3 predetermined X variables:

$$Y_1 = \gamma_2Y_2 + \beta_1X_1 + \beta_2X_2 + e$$
$$Y_2 = \gamma_1Y_1 + \beta_3X_3 + e$$

Outline how you would estimate:

a. The first equation.

b. The second equation.

25-7 (The Identification Problem) Now consider a smaller simultaneous system than Problem 25-6, with 2 mutually dependent Y variables and just 1 predetermined X variable:

[8] Not quite independent. Since the b coefficients in (25-19) are not absolute constants, but are estimates depending slightly on e, $\hat{Y}_2$ depends slightly on e too. But with larger and larger sample size n, this problem disappears. So we still obtain a consistent estimate.

$$Y_1 = \gamma_2 Y_2 + e$$

$$Y_2 = \gamma_1 Y_1 + \beta_1 X_1 + e$$

	Y_1	Y_2	X_1
	38	8	21
	27	15	17
	31	10	20
	21	18	14
	20	15	12
	43	6	24
Averages	30	12	18

a. Using the data above, derive the 2SLS estimate of the coefficient γ_2 in the first equation.

b. Using 2SLS on the second equation, set up the appropriate estimating equations for γ_1 and β_1—in symbols and numbers. Why can't you solve these for γ_1 and β_1? (The original equation $Y_2 = \gamma_1 Y_1 + \beta_1 X_1 + e$ is therefore called *unidentified*.)

25-8 (The Identification Problem in General) In Problem 25-7 part **b**, the equation was unidentified because it had two parameters that had to be estimated (two variables on the right side), yet there was only one predetermined variable (X_1) in the system of equations. In a sense, the equation was "too long" for the available data to handle. And this may be proved to be more generally true: *If the number of parameters to be estimated in an equation*[9] *exceeds the number of exogenous variables (appearing anywhere in the system), then the equation cannot be estimated, and is therefore called unidentified.*

Using this principle, decide which equations are not identified in the following system containing 5 mutually dependent Y variables and 3 predetermined X variables: (For simplicity, we represent each coefficient with an asterisk, rather than a Greek symbol.)

$$Y_1 = * \; Y_3 + * \; X_1 + * \; X_3$$

$$Y_2 = * \; Y_1 + * \; Y_3 + * \; Y_4 + * \; X_1 + * \; X_3$$

$$Y_3 = * \; Y_4 + * \; X_2$$

$$Y_4 = * \; X_1 + * \; X_2 + * \; X_3$$

$$Y_5 = * \; Y_1 + * \; Y_2 + * \; Y_3 + * \; Y_4$$

[9] We continue to ignore the constant term, which is recovered when all other estimation is complete.

CHAPTER 25 SUMMARY

25-1 OLS is biased when the error is correlated with the regressor; then some of the effect of the error term gets mistakenly attributed to the regressor. This bias occurs commonly in systems of simultaneous equations when mutually dependent variables appear as regressors.

25-2 A consistent estimate can be obtained using an instrumental variable (IV) that is highly correlated with the regressor, yet uncorrelated with the error term.

25-3 Two Stage Least Squares (2SLS) is a popular way to obtain consistent estimates in simultaneous equations: The first stage calculates the most effective IVs; the second stage applies them.

REVIEW PROBLEMS

25-9 Circle the correct choice in each bracket:

a. In a system of mutually dependent variables, a regression equation may be badly biased if [IV, OLS] is used. This is because the error term is [correlated, uncorrelated] with the regressors. And OLS, in attributing as much as possible of the response to the regressors, attributes [some, none] of the error to the regressors.

b. An instrumental variable should be [highly correlated, uncorrelated] with the regressors, and [highly correlated, uncorrelated] with the error term.

c. OLS and 2SLS are both special cases of instrumental variables: OLS uses [mutually dependent variables, the regressors themselves] as IV, while 2SLS uses [mutually dependent variables, linear combinations of the predetermined variables] as IV.

25-10 ***A Final Challenge: The Consumption Function Again***

For the consumption model in this chapter—equations (25-1) and (25-2)—suppose the covariance matrix of X, Y, and I has been computed for a sample of $n = 30$ observations:

$$\begin{bmatrix} s_{XX} & s_{YX} & s_{IX} \\ s_{XY} & s_{YY} & s_{IY} \\ s_{XI} & s_{YI} & s_{II} \end{bmatrix} = \begin{bmatrix} 340 & 290 & 50 \\ 290 & 250 & 40 \\ 50 & 40 & 10 \end{bmatrix}$$

a. Find a consistent estimate for β, the marginal propensity to consume.

b. Estimate β using OLS on the consumption equation (25-1). Is this estimate consistent too? Is this OLS estimate higher or lower than the estimate in **a**? Is this typical of what to expect from Figure 25-2?

c. The first column of the covariance matrix is the sum of the last two columns. Is this just a fluke, or is this always true of the consumption model, no matter what data are gathered? Prove your answer one way or the other.

APPENDIXES

APPENDIX TO SECTION 2-2

CAREFUL APPROXIMATION OF THE MEDIAN

To illustrate how a median can be approximated quite accurately from grouped data, consider the distribution of heights in Table 2-2. A graph will clarify where the first 50% of the observations lie.

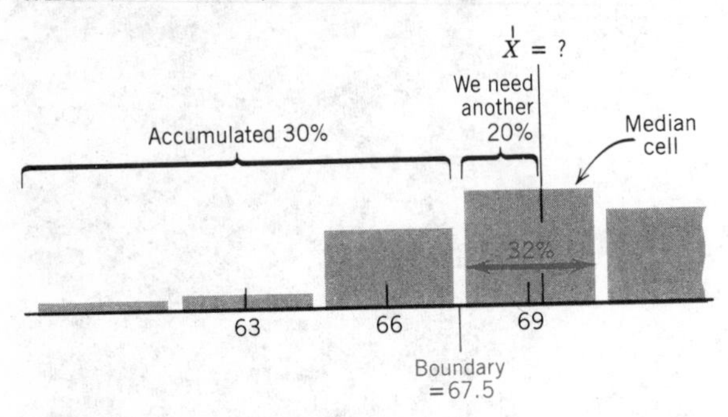

Recall that 30% of the observations were accumulated to the left of the median cell. To get the median, we must therefore pick up another 20% of the observations. Since the median cell includes 32% of the observations, we move 20/32 of the way through it. Starting at the cell boundary 67.5, and remembering that the cell width is 3, we therefore approximate the median as:

$$X \simeq 67.5 + \left(\frac{20}{32}\right) 3$$

$$= 69.4 \text{ inches}$$

Any other percentile can be approximated the same way. For example, you can similarly verify the lower and upper quartile values of 66.8 and 71.9.

APPENDIX TO SECTION 2-5

EFFECTS OF A LINEAR TRANSFORMATION: PROOFS

We will prove the two parts of Equation (2-19)—first the mean and then the variance. To establish the mean, we start with the definition for the new mean $\overline{Y}$:

$$\overline{Y} \equiv \frac{1}{n}[Y_1 + Y_2 + \cdots]$$

$$= \frac{1}{n}[(a + bX_1) + (a + bX_2) + \cdots]$$

$$= \frac{1}{n}[na + b(X_1 + X_2 + \cdots)]$$

$$= a + b\overline{X}$$

Next, to establish the variance, we start with the definition (2-11) for the new variance s_Y^2:

$$s_Y^2 \equiv \frac{1}{n-1}\{(Y_1 - \overline{Y})^2 + (Y_2 - \overline{Y})^2 + \cdots\}$$

$$= \frac{1}{n-1}\{[(a + bX_1) - (a + b\overline{X})]^2 + [(a + bX_2) - (a + b\overline{X})]^2 + \cdots\}$$

$$= \frac{1}{n-1}\{[b(X_1 - \overline{X})]^2 + [b(X_2 - \overline{X})^2] + \cdots\}$$

$$= \frac{b^2}{n-1}\{(X_1 - \overline{X})^2 + (X_2 - \overline{X})^2 + \cdots\}$$

$$= b^2 s_X^2$$

Thus $s_Y = |b| s_X$ (2-19) proved.

APPENDIX TO SECTION 3-7

PROBABILITY AS AXIOMATIC MATHEMATICS

Historically, probability theory was set up on a proper axiomatic basis by the Russian mathematician Kolmogoroff in the 1930s. Of course, Kolmogoroff's axioms and theorems were much more rigorous than the extremely simple version that we now set out in this appendix, to illustrate the spirit of the axiomatic approach.

AXIOMS

A_1: $\Pr(e) \geq 0$ for every point e.

A_2: $\Pr(e_1) + \Pr(e_2) + \cdots + \Pr(e_N) = 1$

where N is the total number of points in the sample space.

A_3: $\Pr(E) = \Sigma \Pr(e)$

where the sum extends over all those points e that are in E.

Then the other properties are theorems that can be proved from these axioms. For example:

THEOREMS T_1: $0 \le Pr(E)$

T_2: $Pr(E) \le 1$

T_3: $Pr(\bar{E}) = 1 - Pr(E)$

Proofs According to axioms A_1 and A_2, $Pr(E)$ is the sum of terms that are positive or zero, and is therefore itself positive or zero; thus theorem T_1 is proved.

To prove T_3, we start with axiom A_2:

$$\underbrace{Pr(e_1) + Pr(e_2)}_{\text{Terms for } E} + \underbrace{\cdots + Pr(e_N)}_{\text{Terms for } \bar{E}} = 1$$

that is, $$Pr(E) + Pr(\bar{E}) = 1$$

from which T_3 follows.

In T_1, we proved that every probability is positive or zero. In particular, $Pr(\bar{E})$ is positive or zero; substituting this into the equation above finally ensures that:

$$Pr(E) \le 1 \qquad T_2 \text{ proved}$$

APPENDIX TO SECTION 4-2

EASIER FORMULA FOR σ^2: PROOF

To confirm (4-6), we begin with the definition of variance:

$$\sigma^2 \equiv \Sigma(x - \mu)^2 p(x) \qquad \text{(4-5) repeated}$$
$$= \Sigma(x^2 - 2\mu x + \mu^2)p(x)$$

and, noting that μ is a constant:

$$\sigma^2 = \Sigma\, x^2 p(x) - 2\mu\, \Sigma\, xp(x) + \mu^2\, \Sigma\, p(x)$$

Since $\Sigma\, xp(x) = \mu$ and $\Sigma\, p(x) = 1$,

$$\sigma^2 = \Sigma\, x^2 p(x) - 2\mu(\mu) + \mu^2(1)$$
$$= \Sigma\, x^2 p(x) - \mu^2 \qquad \text{(4-6) proved}$$

APPENDIX TO SECTION 4-3

BINOMIAL FORMULA: PROOF

The derivation of the binomial formula (4-8) will be a lot easier to follow if we split our page, showing on the left an example, and on the right the generalization. The example will be a familiar one—tossing a coin $n = 5$ times. We suppose the coin is somewhat biased, coming up heads (H) with probability $\pi = .60$, and tails (T) with probability $1 - \pi = .40$. Let us calculate the probability of the event shown in white below—that is, the probability that the number of heads $S = 3$.

We begin by looking at just one of the many ways we could get $X = 3$: We could get the 3 heads first, followed by 2 tails. In other words, we could get the sequence

$$\underbrace{HHH}_{3}\ \underbrace{TT}_{2}$$

or, in general, the sequence

$$\underbrace{HH \cdots H}_{s \text{ times}}\quad \underbrace{TT \cdots T}_{(n-s) \text{ times}}$$

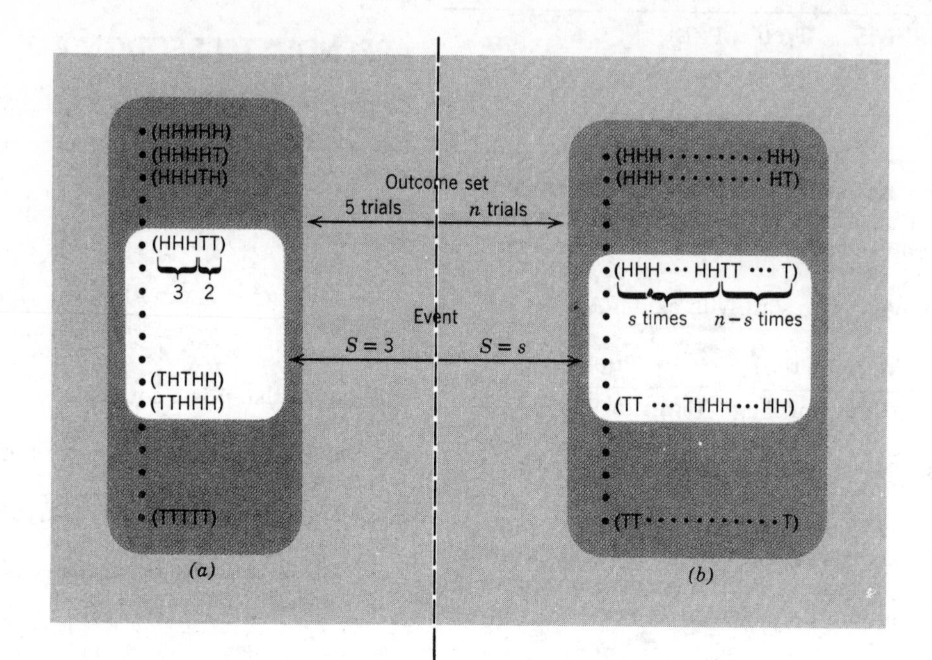

It has probability

$$(.60)(.60)(.60)(.40)(.40) = (.60)^3(.40)^2$$

where the simple multiplication is justified by the *independence* of the trials.

But there are many other ways we could get exactly 3 heads in 5 tosses. For example, we might get the sequence (*THTHH*), which has a probability

$$(.40)(.60)(.40)(.60)(.60) = (.60)^3(.40)^2$$

This is the same probability as before, because we are multiplying together exactly the same numbers as before. (The different order doesn't matter.) In fact, all sequences in the event $S = 3$ will have this same probability.

So the final question is, how many such sequences are there in the white region of the Figure? That is, how many ways are there to get exactly 3 heads? The answer: the number of different ways that three *H*'s and two *T*'s can be arranged. This number of ways is denoted by $\binom{5}{3}$, and can be calculated from

$$\binom{5}{3} = \frac{5!}{3!2!} = 10 \qquad (4\text{-}1A)$$

(as we will show at the end of the appendix)

It has probability

$$\pi \cdot \pi \cdot \cdot \cdot (1 - \pi) \cdot (1 - \pi) \cdot \cdot \cdot = \pi^s(1 - \pi)^{n-s}$$

and, in general,

$$\binom{n}{s} = \frac{n!}{s!(n - s)!}$$

To summarize, the event

$$(S = 3)$$

includes

$$\binom{5}{3} = 10$$

outcomes, each with probability

$$(.60)^3(.40)^2 = .035$$

Hence its probability is:

$$p(3) = \binom{5}{3}(.60)^3(.40)^2$$
$$= 10(.035) = .35$$

To finish our proof, we must finally show where formula (4-1A) comes from. In how many ways can we arrange five distinct objects, designated H_1, H_2, H_3, T_1, T_2? We have a choice of 5 objects to fill the first position, 4 the second, and so on; thus the total number of arrangements is:

$$5 \cdot 4 \cdot 3 \cdot 2 \cdot 1 = 5! \qquad \text{(4-2A)}$$

But this is not quite the problem at hand; in fact we cannot distinguish between H_1, H_2, and H_3—all of which appear as H. Thus many of the separate and distinct arrangements counted in (4-2A) cannot be distinguished, and appear as a single arrangement (e.g., $H_1\ H_2\ H_3\ T_1\ T_2$ and $H_2\ H_3\ H_1\ T_1\ T_2$ and many others appear as the single arrangement *HHHTT*). Thus (4-2A) involves serious overcounting. How much?

We overcounted $3 \cdot 2 \cdot 1 = 3!$ times because we assumed in (4-2A) that we could distinguish between H_1, H_2, and H_3, when in fact we could not. (3! is simply the number of distinct ways of rearranging H_1, H_2, and H_3). Similarly, we overcounted $2 \cdot 1 = 2!$ times because we assumed in (4-2A) that we could distinguish between T_1 and T_2, when in fact we could not. When (4-2A) is deflated for overcounting in both these ways, we have:

$$\frac{5!}{3!2!} \qquad \text{(4-1A) proved}$$

In general, the event

$$(S = s)$$

includes

$$\binom{n}{s}$$

outcomes, each with probability

$$\pi^s(1 - \pi)^{n-s}$$

Hence its probability is:

$$\boxed{p(s) = \binom{n}{s}\pi^s(1 - \pi)^{n-s}}$$

Thus (4-8) is proved.

APPENDIX TO SECTION 4-4

CALCULUS FOR CONTINUOUS DISTRIBUTIONS

For continuous random variables, sums are replaced by integrals—the limiting sum in calculus. Thus, for example, probability is the area under the curve p(x), and is calculated as the integral:

$$\Pr(a \leq X \leq b) = \int_a^b p(x)\,dx \qquad \text{like (4-12)}$$

Similarly, the mean and variance are calculated as integrals:

$$\mu = \int_{\text{all } x} xp(x)\,dx \qquad \text{like (4-4)}$$

$$\sigma^2 = \int_{\text{all } x} (x - \mu)^2 p(x)\,dx \qquad \text{like (4-5)}$$

All the theorems that we state about discrete random variables then are equally valid for continuous random variables, with summations replaced by integrals.

PROBLEMS

4-2A Suppose that a continuous random variable X has the probability distribution:

$$p(x) = 3x^2 \qquad 0 \le x \le 1$$
$$= 0 \qquad \text{otherwise}$$

a. Calculate $\Pr(0 \le X \le .5)$, and show it on the graph of $p(x)$.

b. Find the mean, median, and mode. Show them on the graph. Are they in the order you expect?

c. Find σ, and show it on the graph. Is it a typical deviation in the sense of (2-15)?

4-3A Repeat Problem 4-2A for each of the following distributions defined on the interval 0 to 1. [Called Beta distributions, they are all polynomials of the form $x^a(1 - x)^b$]:

i. $p(x) = 6x(1 - x)$

ii. $p(x) = 12x^2(1 - x)$

iii. $p(x) = 105x^4(1 - x)^2$

APPENDIX TO SECTION 5-3

INDEPENDENT IMPLIES UNCORRELATED: PROOF

To prove (5-12), we are given that X and Y are independent. According to (5-6), this means that for all x and y,

$$p(x, y) = p(x)p(y)$$

We substitute this into the definition of the covariance (5-10):

$$\sigma_{X,Y} \equiv \sum_x \sum_y (x - \mu_X)(y - \mu_Y)p(x, y)$$
$$= \sum_x \sum_y (x - \mu_X)(y - \mu_Y)p(x)p(y)$$

When we sum over y, we can take out as a common factor whatever does not depend on y (i.e., whatever depends on x alone):

$$\sigma_{X,Y} = \sum_x (x - \mu_X)p(x) \sum_y (y - \mu_Y)p(y)$$

The right-hand sum over y is zero—since every weighted sum of deviations is zero. [The proof would be like (2-9).] Thus

$$\sigma_{X,Y} = 0$$

That is, X and Y are uncorrelated, and (5-12) is proved.

APPENDIX TO SECTION 5-4

LINEAR COMBINATIONS: PROOFS

$$E(X + Y) = E(X) + E(Y)? \qquad (5\text{-}16)$$

To prove this additive property for E, we start with the formula (5-9), noting that $g(X, Y) = (X + Y)$ in this case. Thus,

$$E(X + Y) = \sum_x \sum_y (x + y)p(x, y)$$
$$= \sum_x \sum_y xp(x, y) + \sum_x \sum_y yp(x, y)$$

We rewrite the first term, so we can use the definition of the marginal distribution (5-4):

$$\sum_x \sum_y xp(x, y) = \sum_x x\left[\sum_y p(x, y)\right]$$
$$= \sum_x x[p(x)]$$
$$= E(X)$$

Similarly, the second term reduces to $E(Y)$, so that:

$$E(X + Y) = E(X) + E(Y)\checkmark$$

This completes the proof of (5-16). The proof for the weighted sum (5-17) is similar.

Finally, we must prove (5-18):

$$\text{var}(X + Y) = \text{var}\,X + \text{var}\,Y + 2\,\text{cov}(X, Y)?$$

To prove this formula, it is time to simplify our proofs by using brief notation—that is, by using E(W) rather than the awkward $\Sigma wp(w)$, or the even more awkward $\sum_x \sum_y w(x, y)p(x, y)$. In this new notation, the variance of $S = X + Y$ is defined as:

$$\text{var } S \equiv E(S - \mu_S)^2$$

Substitute for S, and μ_S given by (5-16):

$$\begin{aligned}\text{var } S &= E[(X + Y) - (\mu_X + \mu_Y)]^2 \\ &= E[(X - \mu_X) + (Y - \mu_Y)]^2 \\ &= E[(X - \mu_X)^2 + (Y - \mu_Y)^2 + 2(X - \mu_X)(Y - \mu_Y)]\end{aligned}$$

According to (5-17), this linear combination of several terms can be averaged term by term. Thus,

$$\begin{aligned}\text{var } S &= E(X - \mu_X)^2 + E(Y - \mu_Y)^2 + 2E(X - \mu_X)(Y - \mu_Y) \\ &= \text{var } X + \text{var } Y + 2 \text{ cov } (X, Y) \checkmark\end{aligned}$$

This completes the proof of (5-18). The proof of the weighted sum (5-19) is similar.

APPENDIX TO SECTION 6-3

THE CENTRAL LIMIT THEOREM

Mathematicians call the Normal Approximation Rule by a different name—the *Central Limit Theorem*. Each of these three words deserves some explanation:

i. It is a *theorem*, that is, it can be proved in general. The standard proof (Lindgren, 1976) requires two assumptions: *Random* sampling, from a population that has a *finite* variance (i.e., terribly extreme values are not too probable). In practice, the requirement of finite variance is nearly always met. Unfortunately, the requirement of randomness often is not.

ii. It is a *limit* theorem, that is, its conclusion is carefully stated in the form of a limit as follows: The probability that the standardized sample mean $(\overline{X} - \mu)/(\sigma/\sqrt{n})$ falls in a given interval converges in the limit to the probability that the standard normal variable Z falls in that interval.

iii. It is *central*, in the sense that it describes how $\overline{X}$ concentrates around its central value, the target μ.

APPENDIX TO SECTION 6-4

CONTINUITY CORRECTION: GRAPHICAL EXPLANATION

In the figure below, we show the actual discrete distribution of P with bars, centered at the possible values of P: 0, 1/15, 2/15, ... The exact probability we want is the sum of all the shaded bars, from 11/15 on up ("more than 10 boys").

To approximate this sum with the normal curve as closely as possible, we should start the normal curve at the same place as those bars start. Since the first bar is *centered* at 11/15, it *starts* at $10\frac{1}{2}/15$, and this is precisely our continuity correction (c.c.):

$$\Pr\left(P > \frac{10\frac{1}{2}}{15}\right) = .061 \quad \text{(6-15) proved}$$

The probability of .061 obtained with c.c. compares very favorably with the exact answer of .059 (obtained from a tedious evaluation of all the shaded bars using the binomial formula).

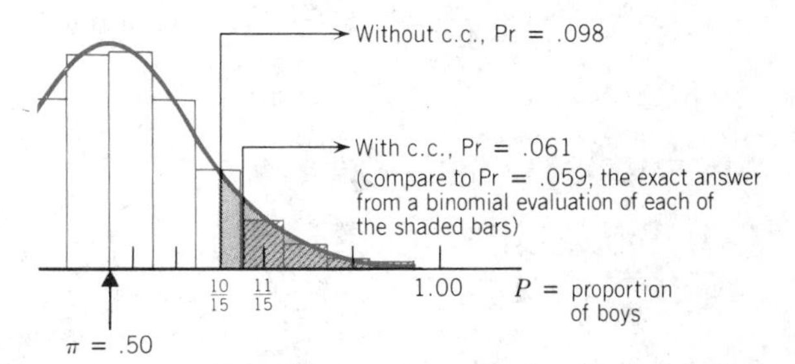

APPENDIX TO SECTION 7-2

STANDARD ERROR OF $\check{X}$

A general large–sample formula for the standard error of the sample median for *any* continuous population can be derived:

$$\operatorname{var} \overset{|}{X} \simeq \frac{1}{4n[p(\nu)]^2} \qquad (7\text{-}1A)$$

where n is the sample size, and $p(\nu)$ is the height of the population probability density at the median ν.

For example, the symmetric Laplace distribution has density

$$p(x) = \frac{1}{\sqrt{2}\sigma} e^{-\sqrt{2}\left|\frac{x-\mu}{\sigma}\right|}$$

This differs from the normal curve (4-26) primarily because the negative exponent is not squared, and consequently the curve does not drop off so fast in the tails. To get var $\overset{|}{X}$, symmetry assures us that $\nu = \mu$, and so $p(\nu)$ reduces to $p(\mu) = 1/\sqrt{2}\sigma$. Thus (7-1A) yields

$$\operatorname{var} \overset{|}{X} \simeq \frac{1}{4n(1/\sqrt{2}\sigma)^2}$$

$$= \frac{2\sigma^2}{4n} = .50\frac{\sigma^2}{n} \qquad \text{(7-7) confirmed}$$

By a similar argument, we can confirm var $\overset{|}{X}$ for the normal distribution given earlier: From (4-26), $p(\nu) = 1/\sqrt{2\pi}\,\sigma$, and thus

$$\operatorname{var} \overset{|}{X} \simeq \frac{1}{4n(1/\sqrt{2\pi}\sigma)^2}$$

$$= \frac{2\pi\sigma^2}{4n} = 1.57\frac{\sigma^2}{n} \qquad \text{(7-5) confirmed}$$

APPENDIX TO SECTION 7-4

CONSISTENCY: CAREFUL DEFINITION

The precise definition of consistency involves a limit statement:

> **V is defined to be a consistent estimator of θ, if for any positive δ (no matter how small),**
>
> $$\Pr(|V - \theta| < \delta) \to 1 \quad \text{as } n \to \infty \qquad (7\text{-}2A)$$

This is seen to be just a formal way of stating that in the limit as $n \to \infty$, it eventually becomes certain that V will be as close to θ as we please (within δ).

To be concrete, in Example 7-4 we show that the sample proportion P is a consistent estimator of π; for this case, (7-2A) therefore becomes:

$$\Pr(|P - \pi| < \delta) \to 1 \quad \text{as } n \to \infty \qquad (7\text{-}3A)$$

Stated informally, (7-3A) means that it eventually becomes certain that P will get as close to π as we please (within δ). In fact, (7-3A) is the precise statement of the law of large numbers (3-2).

As (7-15) states (and advanced texts prove), if the MSE approaches zero, then V is consistent. But the definition (7-2A) is broad enough that V can be consistent in other cases as well. An example will illustrate. Consider an estimator V with the following sampling distribution:

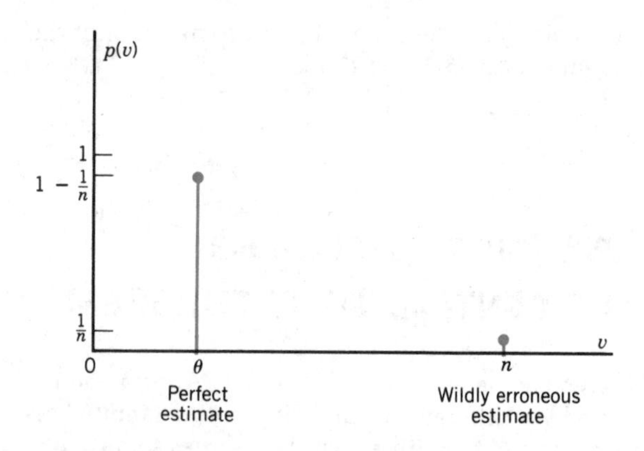

As n increases, note how the distribution of V becomes increasingly concentrated on its target θ while the probability of getting an erroneous estimate becomes smaller and smaller (as $1/n$ decreases). Thus, V is a consistent estimator according to the definition (7-2A).

But now let us consider the MSE of V:

$$\begin{aligned}
\text{MSE} &= E(V - \theta)^2 \\
&= \Sigma(v - \theta)^2 p(v) \\
&= 0^2\left(1 - \frac{1}{n}\right) + (n - \theta)^2\left(\frac{1}{n}\right) \\
&= n - 2\theta + \frac{\theta^2}{n}
\end{aligned}$$

As $n \to \infty$, this MSE does not approach zero (in fact, it behaves much worse—it approaches infinity!) In conclusion, then, we have found an estimator V that is consistent, even though its MSE does not tend to zero.

PROBLEM

7-1A Prove formula (7-11), that MSE = variance + bias^2.
[*Hint:* First prove a generalization of (4-6),

$$E(X - a)^2 = \sigma^2 + (a - \mu)^2$$

Then put the estimator V in the role of X, and the target θ in the role of a.]

APPENDIX TO SECTION 8-3

THE STANDARD ERROR OF $(\bar{X}_1 - \bar{X}_2)$: PROOF

The difference $(\bar{X}_1 - \bar{X}_2)$ is a linear combination of two random variables that are independent (since the two samples are assumed independent). Its variance can therefore be found from the general formula (5-22):

$$\text{var}(aX + bY) = a^2 \text{ var } X + b^2 \text{ var } Y$$

Substitute $X = \bar{X}_1$, $Y = \bar{X}_2$, $a = 1$ and $b = -1$.

$$\text{var}(\bar{X}_1 - \bar{X}_2) = 1^2 \text{ var } \bar{X}_1 + (-1)^2 \text{ var } \bar{X}_2$$

$$= \text{var } \bar{X}_1 + \text{var } \bar{X}_2$$

For single samples, we already know the variances:

$$\text{var } \bar{X} = \text{SE}^2 = \frac{\sigma^2}{n} \qquad \text{like (6-6)}$$

Thus

$$\text{var}(\bar{X}_1 - \bar{X}_2) = \frac{\sigma_1^2}{n_1} + \frac{\sigma_2^2}{n_2}$$

$$\text{SE} = \sqrt{\frac{\sigma_1^2}{n_1} + \frac{\sigma_2^2}{n_2}}$$

When this is substituted into (8-17), we obtain the desired confidence interval (8-18).

APPENDIX TO SECTION 8-5

CONFIDENCE INTERVAL FOR π: DERIVATION OF GRAPH

To see why Figure 8-4 works, let us return to first principles, and see how a deduction can be turned around into an induction.

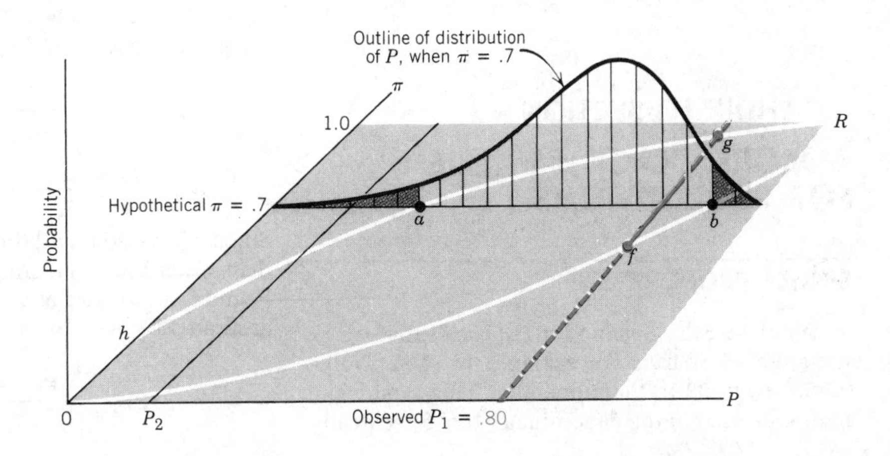

Our deduction of how the estimator P is distributed for a sample size $n = 20$ and $\pi = .7$ for example, is shown in the figure above. The range *ab* marks off the central chunk that contains 95% of the probability. Similarly, for every other possible value of π, the distribution of P determines the two critical points like *a* and *b*. When they are all joined, they make up the two white curves enclosing the 95% *probability band*.

This deduction of how the statistic P is related to the population π is now turned around to draw a statistical inference about π from a given sample P. For example, if we observe a sample proportion $P_1 = 16/20 = .80$, then the 95% confidence interval for π is defined by the interval *fg* contained within this probability band above P_1:

$$.55 < \pi < .95 \qquad \text{(8-28) proved}$$

Whereas the (deduced) probability interval is defined in the horizontal direction of the P axis, the (induced) confidence interval is defined in the vertical direction of the π axis.

To see why this works, suppose, for example, that the true value of π is .7. Then the probability is 95% that a sample P will fall between *a* and *b*. *If and only if it does* (e.g., P_1) will the confidence interval we construct bracket the true $\pi = .7$. We therefore are using an estimation procedure that is 95% likely to bracket the true value of π, and thus yield a correct statement. But we must recognize the 5% probability that the sample P will fall beyond *a* or *b* (e.g., P_2); in this case, our interval estimate will not bracket $\pi = .7$, and our conclusion will be wrong.

APPENDIX TO SECTION 9-2

A MORE EXACT *p*-VALUE FOR PROPORTIONS

SINGLE PROPORTION

In calculating the p-value for H_0, recall that we assume that H_0 is true. For example, in (9-22) we assumed $\pi_0 = .02$ in the numerator. This same value should be used in the denominator too. Specifically, $\pi_0 = .02$ should be used to get the *exact* value of the standard error—instead of just extracting an approximate value for SE from the confidence interval (9-21).

With this exact value of the SE, we can use the normal instead of the t distribution (even when the sample size is a lot smaller than the $n = 500$ given in this case). So we write explicitly,

$$z = \frac{\text{estimate} - \text{null hypothesis}}{\text{exact SE}} \qquad \text{like (9-14)}$$

$$\boxed{z = \frac{P - \pi_0}{\sqrt{\dfrac{\pi_0(1 - \pi_0)}{n}}}} \qquad \text{(9-1A)}$$

$$= \frac{.042 - .02}{\sqrt{\dfrac{.02(.98)}{500}}} = 3.51$$

The normal table then gives the more exact p-value of .0002.

For a final refinement, we could use the continuity correction, which gives $P = 20.5/500$, consequently $z = 3.35$, and finally $p \simeq .0004$.

TWO PROPORTIONS

The comparison of *two* proportions can be treated similarly. The customary null hypotheses is H_0: $(\pi_1 - \pi_2) = 0$, that is, π_1 and π_2 are equal. Then their common value can be estimated by pooling the sample proportions P_1 and P_2, obtaining:

$$\boxed{P = \frac{n_1P_1 + n_2P_2}{n_1 + n_2}} \qquad \text{(9-2A)}$$

Since P is based on *all* the data, it is a better estimate than either P_1 or P_2 alone. When P is used instead of P_1 and P_2 in the formula (8-29), the result is the more accurate SE,

$$\text{SE} = \sqrt{\frac{P(1 - P)}{n_1} + \frac{P(1 - P)}{n_2}}$$

This improved SE can then be used in the z ratio:

$$z = \frac{\text{estimate}}{\text{SE}} = \frac{(P_1 - P_2)}{\sqrt{\frac{P(1-P)}{n_1} + \frac{P(1-P)}{n_2}}} \qquad \text{(9-3A)}$$

APPENDIX TO SECTION 10-1

BREAKDOWN OF TOTAL SS: PROOF

Let us begin with a concrete example. In Table 10-1, the third observation in the second column (58) is greater than the grand mean (52). This total deviation can be broken down into two parts, noting that the second column mean is 56:

(58 − 52)	=	(58 − 56)	+	(56 − 52)
total deviation	=	deviation within column	+	deviation between this column and others

That is,

$$6 = 2 + 4$$

In words: the given observation is 6 better than the grand average—2 better than its column average, which in turn is 4 better than the grand average.

The generalization starts with the typical observation X_{it}:

$$(X_{it} - \overline{\overline{X}}) = (X_{it} - \overline{X}_i) + (\overline{X}_i - \overline{\overline{X}})$$

This equation must always be true, because the two occurrences of $\overline{X}_i$ cancel on the right side. Now let us interchange the order on the right-hand side, then square both sides, and finally sum over all i and t:

$$\sum_i \sum_t (X_{it} - \overline{\overline{X}})^2 = \sum_i \sum_t (\overline{X}_i - \overline{\overline{X}})^2 + 2 \sum_i \sum_t (\overline{X}_i - \overline{\overline{X}})(X_{it} - \overline{X}_i) + \sum_i \sum_t (X_{it} - \overline{X}_i)^2$$

On the right the first term can be reduced:

$$\underbrace{\sum_{t=1}^{n} \sum_{i=1}^{c} (\overline{X}_i - \overline{\overline{X}})^2}_{\text{independent of } t} = n \sum_{i=1}^{c} (\overline{X}_i - \overline{\overline{X}})^2$$

Furthermore, the next term (cross product) vanishes:

$$2 \sum_{i=1}^{c} (\overline{X}_i - \overline{\overline{X}}) \underbrace{\sum_{t=1}^{n} (X_{it} - \overline{X}_i)}_{\substack{\text{This is 0, because the algebraic sum} \\ \text{of deviations about the mean is always 0}}} = 0$$

With these two simplifications, we thus obtain our goal—Equation (10-14):

$$\sum_i \sum_t (X_{it} - \overline{\overline{X}})^2 = n \sum_i (\overline{X}_i - \overline{\overline{X}})^2 + \sum_i \sum_t (X_{it} - \overline{X}_i)^2$$

$$\text{total SS} = SS_A + SS_E$$

APPENDIX TO SECTION 10-2

TWO-WAY ANOVA, BREAKDOWN OF TOTAL SS: PROOF

This may be proved just like one-factor ANOVA in Appendix 10-1. We begin with the similar identity:

$$(X_{ij} - \overline{\overline{X}}) = (X_{ij} - \hat{X}_{ij}) + (\overline{X}_{i\cdot} - \overline{\overline{X}}) + (\overline{X}_{\cdot j} - \overline{\overline{X}})$$

where

$$\hat{X}_{ij} = (\overline{X}_{i\cdot} - \overline{\overline{X}}) + (\overline{X}_{\cdot j} - \overline{\overline{X}}) + \overline{\overline{X}}$$
$$= \overline{X}_{i\cdot} + \overline{X}_{\cdot j} - \overline{\overline{X}}$$

By squaring and summing and noting how all the cross-product terms drop out, a little rearranging finally gives us our goal—Equation (10-18):

$$\sum_{i=1}^{a}\sum_{j=1}^{b}(X_{ij}-\overline{\overline{X}})^2 = b\sum_{i=1}^{a}(\overline{X}_{i\cdot}-\overline{\overline{X}})^2 + a\sum_{j=1}^{b}(\overline{X}_{\cdot j}-\overline{\overline{X}})^2 + \sum_{i=1}^{a}\sum_{j=1}^{b}(X_{ij}-\hat{X}_{ij})^2$$

$$\text{total SS} = SS_A + SS_B + SS_E$$

APPENDIX TO SECTION 10-3

ANOVA IS MUCH MORE THAN JUST TESTING H_0

If ANOVA were only used for testing the null hypothesis that the population means are equal ($\mu_1 = \mu_2 = \mu_3 = \ldots$) then it would be of limited use. One reason is that a mathematically exact null hypothesis, like all mathematical models, is practically never *exactly* true in the real world. For example, *even before we collected the data* in Table 10-1, it would be a safe bet that the three machines won't have long-run means μ_i that are *exactly* equal (to 100 decimal places or more).

Fortunately, ANOVA is valuable for more important things than hypothesis testing, such as:

1. Two-factor ANOVA (or 3- or 4-factor ANOVA) can be used as a screening device to distinguish between the indiscernible and discernible factors. For the discernible factors, confidence intervals can then be constructed from the information in the ANOVA table.
2. ANOVA provides a conceptual framework for generating a lot of useful information. For example, the first column of the ANOVA Table 10-8 shows the relative contribution of the three sources to the overall variability (total SS)—an important decomposition in its own right, regardless of how the statistical tests turn out in the last column. The residuals in Table 10-7 also show us many things: A single residual that is exceptionally large indicates a machine-operator combination that doesn't fit the model very well (or perhaps was mistakenly recorded). Certain patterns of residuals may indicate that the whole model needs to be improved, as we discuss in the context of regression in Section 14-5.

ANOVA tables have therefore become a traditional way to report research results in the literature—a statistical "language" we have to learn in order to communicate.

APPENDIX TO SECTION 11-1

LINES AND PLANES

LINES

The definitive characteristic of a straight line is that it continues forever in the same constant direction. The figure below makes this idea precise. In moving from one point P_1 to another point P_2, we denote the horizontal distance by ΔX (where Δ is the Greek letter *D*, for difference) and the vertical distance by ΔY. Then the slope is defined as

$$\text{Slope} \equiv \frac{\Delta Y}{\Delta X} \tag{11-1A}$$

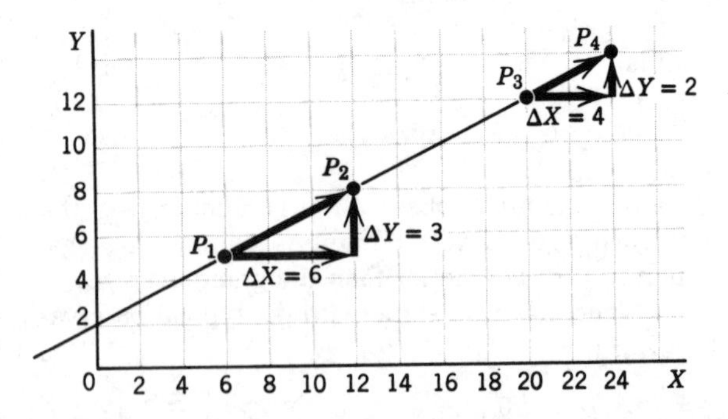

Slope is a concept useful in engineering as well as mathematics. For example, if a highway rises 12 feet over a distance of 200 feet, its slope is 12/200 = 6%. The characteristic of a *straight* line is that the slope remains the same everywhere:

$$\boxed{\frac{\Delta Y}{\Delta X} = b \text{ (a constant)}} \tag{11-2A}$$

For example, the slope between P_3 and P_4 is the same as between P_1 and P_2, as calculation will verify:

$$P_1 \text{ to } P_2: \quad \frac{\Delta Y}{\Delta X} = \frac{3}{6} = .50$$

$$P_3 \text{ to } P_4: \quad \frac{\Delta Y}{\Delta X} = \frac{2}{4} = .50 \qquad \text{(11-3A)}$$

A very instructive case occurs when X increases just one unit: then (11-2A) yields

$$\boxed{\text{When } \Delta X = 1, \quad \Delta Y = b} \qquad \text{(11-4A)}$$

In words, "b is the increase in Y that accompanies a unit increase in X," which agrees with the regression interpretation (11-8).

It is now very easy to derive the equation of a line if we know its slope b and any one point on the line. Suppose the one point we know is the Y intercept—the point where the line crosses the Y axis, at height a, let us say. As the figure below shows, in moving to any other point (X, Y) on the line, we may write

$$\text{Slope, } \frac{\Delta Y}{\Delta X} = \frac{Y - a}{X - 0} \qquad \text{(11-5A)}$$

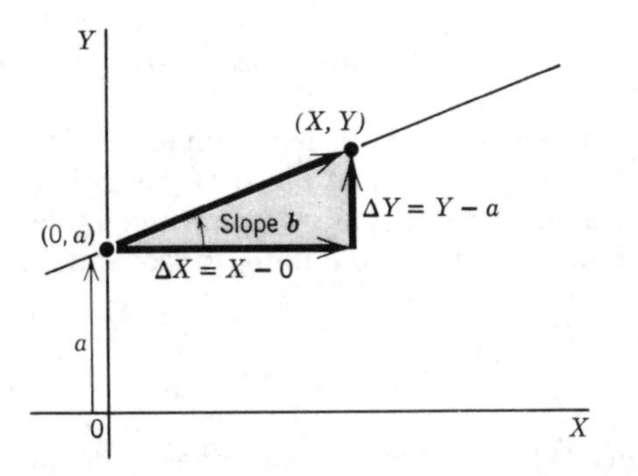

For the line to be straight, we insisted in (11-2A) that this slope must equal the constant b:

$$\frac{Y - a}{X - 0} = b$$

$$Y - a = bX$$

$$\boxed{Y = a + bX} \qquad \text{(11-6A)}$$

This is the required equation of a line (11-1).

PLANES

The figure below shows a plane in the 3-dimensional (X_1, X_2, Y) space. Let L_1 denote the line where this plane cuts the X_1Y plane. Then we may think of the plane as a roof made of rafters parallel to the line L_1 and having the same slope b_1. That is, for every foot we move in the X_1 direction, the rafter rises vertically in the Y direction by b_1 feet.

Equally well, of course, we may think of the plane as a grid of rafters parallel to the line L_2 on the X_2Y plane, with slope b_2.

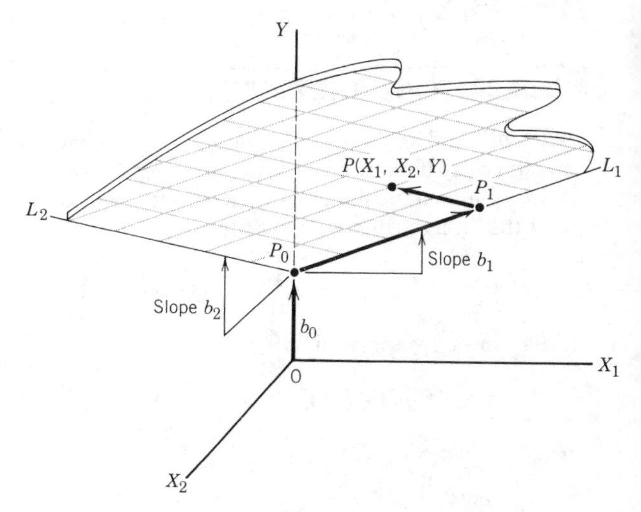

It is now very easy to derive the equation of a plane. Referring to the figure, let us start at the Y intercept, the point P_0 at height b_0. Let us move to the typical point P with coordinates (X_1, X_2, Y), in two steps: (1) we move along the line L_1 to the intermediate point P_1; and from there (2) we move parallel to L_2 to reach the final height Y at P.

1. Just as (11-6A) gives the height as a function of X, likewise we find the height of P_1 on L_1 as a function of X_1:

$$b_0 + b_1X_1 \qquad \text{(11-7A)}$$

2. For our final move from P_1 to P, note that our intercept has now become $b_0 + b_1X_1$ as given above. Note also that we will be moving along a grid line (rafter) parallel to L_2, with slope b_2. Applying (11-6A) to this case,

$$Y = (b_0 + b_1X_1) + b_2X_2$$

$$\boxed{Y = b_0 + b_1X_1 + b_2X_2} \qquad (11\text{-}8A)$$

This is the required equation of a plane (13-4).

APPENDIX TO SECTION 11-2

LEAST SQUARES FORMULAS: PROOFS

REEXPRESSING THE CRITERION

We will find the proofs in the next two chapters much easier if we invest a little time now to express $\hat{Y}$ in a mathematically more convenient form. Recall that the straight line we are fitting is

$$\hat{Y} = a + bX \qquad (11\text{-}6A) \text{ repeated}$$

This can be reexpressed as

$$\hat{Y} = (a + b\overline{X}) + b(X - \overline{X})$$

That is,

$$\boxed{\hat{Y} = a_* + bx} \qquad (11\text{-}9A)$$

where

$$a_* = a + b\overline{X} \qquad (11\text{-}10A)$$

$$x = X - \overline{X} \qquad (11\text{-}11A)$$

(11-4) repeated

This reexpression (11-9A) just uses the deviation form $(x = X - \overline{X})$, and as a consequence a must be replaced by a_*. Then the least squares criterion takes the form:

$$\text{minimize } \Sigma[Y - (a_* + bx)]^2 \quad \text{like (11-2)}$$

This sum of squares will be denoted by $S(a_*, b)$, as a reminder that it is a function of a_* and b. Thus our problem is to select the values of a_* and b that minimize:

$$\boxed{S(a_*, b) \equiv \Sigma(Y - a_* - bx)^2} \qquad (11\text{-}12A)$$

As a_* and b vary—that is, as various straight lines of the form (11-9A) are tried out—then $S(a_*, b)$ will vary too. Those values of a_* and b that make $S(a_*, b)$ a minimum give us the least squares line.

FINDING THE LEAST SQUARES VALUES OF a_* AND b

Minimizing $S(a_*, b)$ requires setting its partial derivatives equal to zero. So we first set the partial derivative with respect to a_* equal to zero:

$$\frac{\partial}{\partial a_*}\Sigma(Y - a_* - bx)^2 = \Sigma 2(Y - a_* - bx)^1(-1) = 0$$

Dividing through by -2:

$$\Sigma(Y - a_* - bx) = 0 \qquad (11\text{-}13A)$$

Rearranging:

$$\Sigma Y - na_* - b\Sigma x = 0 \qquad (11\text{-}14A)$$

Now we see why the deviation form x is so useful. Since the positive and negative deviations exactly cancel, their sum is zero [as shown in Table 11-2, for example, or Equation (2-9) in general]. In other words:

$$\Sigma x = 0 \qquad (11\text{-}15A)$$

Thus (11-14A) greatly simplifies: The term in b drops out, and we can solve for a_*:

$$\boxed{a_* = \frac{\Sigma Y}{n} = \overline{Y}} \qquad (11\text{-}16A)$$

Returning to $S(a_*, b)$ in (11-12A), we must also set its partial derivative with respect to b equal to zero:

$$\frac{\partial}{\partial b}\Sigma(Y - a_* - bx)^2 = \Sigma 2(Y - a_* - bx)^1(-x) = 0$$

Dividing through by −2:

$$\Sigma x(Y - a_* - bx) = 0 \quad (11\text{-}17A)$$

Rearranging:

$$\Sigma xY - a_*\Sigma x - b\Sigma x^2 = 0$$

Noting again that $\Sigma x = 0$, we can solve easily for b:

$$\boxed{b = \frac{\Sigma xY}{\Sigma x^2}} \quad (11\text{-}18A)$$

REEXPRESSING THE SOLUTION

Let us solve (11-10A) for the original intercept a:

$$a = a_* - b\overline{X}$$

Substituting (11-16A),

$$\boxed{a = \overline{Y} - b\overline{X}} \quad (11\text{-}6) \text{ proved}$$

Finally, let us reexpress b. We shall use the deviation form for Y as well as X; in other words, let

$$y = Y - \overline{Y} \quad (11\text{-}4) \text{ repeated}$$

That is, $Y = y + \overline{Y}$, which we can substitute into equation (11-18A):

$$b = \frac{\Sigma x(y + \overline{Y})}{\Sigma x^2} \quad (11\text{-}19A)$$

We now reexpress the numerator (noting that $\overline{Y}$ is a constant and can therefore be taken outside the summation):

$$\Sigma x(y + \overline{Y}) = \Sigma xy + \overline{Y}\Sigma x$$
$$= \Sigma xy$$

since $\Sigma x = 0$ according to (11-15A). Consequently, the solution for b simplifies to

$$\boxed{b = \frac{\Sigma xy}{\Sigma x^2}} \quad (11\text{-}5) \text{ proved}$$

PROBLEM

11-1A If the regression equation is lengthened to include another regressor, we obtain the *multiple* regression equation:

$$\hat{Y} = b_0 + b_1X_1 + b_2X_2$$

Show that the least squares values of b_0, b_1, and b_2 must satisfy the three equations given in (13-5) to (13-7).

APPENDIX TO SECTION 12-2

THE MOMENTS OF *b*: PROOFS AND DISCUSSION

Although (11-5) may be the easiest formula for calculating b, the easiest formula for understanding the nature of b is the equivalent formula in Appendix 11-2 that uses Y values in their original, rather than deviation, form:

$$b = \frac{\Sigma xY}{\Sigma x^2} \quad (11\text{-}18A) \text{ repeated}$$

To appreciate what this means, we write out explicitly the sum in the numerator:

$$b = \frac{1}{\Sigma x^2}[x_1Y_1 + x_2Y_2 + \cdots] \quad (12\text{-}1A)$$

That is,

$$b = w_1Y_1 + w_2Y_2 + \cdots \quad (12\text{-}2A)$$

where the coefficients or weights are:

$$w_1 = \frac{x_1}{\Sigma x^2} \qquad w_2 = \frac{x_2}{\Sigma x^2} \cdots \quad (12\text{-}3A)$$

Since each x is a constant (in our example, a specific level of fertilizer fixed by the experimenter), each w coefficient is also a constant. Thus, we have established the important conclusion:

***b* is a weighted sum (linear combination) of the random variables $Y_1, Y_2, \ldots, Y_n$**	(12-4A)

EXPECTED VALUE

Since b is a linear combination, we can find its expected value term by term, according to (5-17):

$$E(b) = w_1E(Y_1) + w_2E(Y_2) + \cdots \quad (12\text{-}5A)$$

Now for each term, substitute (12-1) into (12-5A):

$$E(b) = w_1(\alpha + \beta X_1) + w_2(\alpha + \beta X_2) + \cdots$$
$$= \alpha(w_1 + w_2 + \cdots)$$
$$+ \beta(w_1X_1 + w_2X_2 + \cdots) \quad (12\text{-}6A)$$

To simplify the first set of brackets, substitute the value of each of the w coefficients given in (12-3A):

$$(w_1 + w_2 + \cdots) = \frac{x_1 + x_2 + \cdots}{\Sigma x^2}$$

The sum of all the positive and negative deviations x in the numerator is zero, according to (2-9). Thus

$$(w_1 + w_2 + \cdots) = \frac{0}{\Sigma x^2} = 0 \quad (12\text{-}7A)$$

To simplify the last set of brackets in (12-6A), again substitute the value of each of the w coefficients given in (12-3A), and also express each $X = x + \bar{X}$ (since $x \equiv X - \bar{X}$):

$$(w_1X_1 + w_2X_2 + \cdots)$$
$$= \frac{x_1(x_1 + \bar{X}) + x_2(x_2 + \bar{X}) + \cdots}{\Sigma x^2}$$
$$= \frac{(x_1^2 + x_2^2 + \cdots) + (x_1 + x_2 + \cdots)\bar{X}}{\Sigma x^2}$$
$$= \frac{(\Sigma x^2) + 0\bar{X}}{\Sigma x^2} = 1$$

Consequently (12-6A) can be written

$$E(b) = \alpha(0) + \beta(1) = \beta \quad (12\text{-}8A)$$

Thus we have proved that b is an unbiased estimate of β.

VARIANCE

Our model (12-2) assumed that the variables $Y_1, Y_2, \cdots$ were independent. So the variance of their linear combination will simply be the sum of variances, according to (5-22):

$$\text{var}(b) = \text{var}(w_1Y_1 + w_2Y_2 + \cdots)$$
$$= w_1^2 \text{ var } Y_1 + w_2^2 \text{ var } Y_2 + \cdots \quad (12\text{-}9A)$$

Our model (12-2) also assumed that each Y_i has the same variance σ^2. Thus (12-9A) becomes:

$$\text{var}(b) = w_1^2\sigma^2 + w_2^2\sigma^2 + \cdots$$
$$= (w_1^2 + w_2^2 + \cdots)\sigma^2 \quad (12\text{-}10A)$$

To simplify what is in brackets, we again write out the meaning of each w given in (12-3A):

$$(w_1^2 + w_2^2 + \cdots) = \left(\frac{x_1}{\Sigma x^2}\right)^2 + \left(\frac{x_2}{\Sigma x^2}\right)^2 + \cdots$$
$$= \left(\frac{1}{\Sigma x^2}\right)^2 (x_1^2 + x_2^2 + \cdots)$$
$$= \left(\frac{1}{\Sigma x^2}\right)^2 (\Sigma x^2) = \left(\frac{1}{\Sigma x^2}\right)$$

Substitute this into (12-10A):

$$\text{var}(b) = \left(\frac{1}{\Sigma x^2}\right)\sigma^2$$

That is,

$$SE = \frac{\sigma}{\sqrt{\Sigma x^2}} \quad (12\text{-}4) \text{ proved}$$

THE GAUSS-MARKOV THEOREM

In (12-4A) we saw that the OLS estimate b is a linear combination of $Y_1, Y_2, \ldots$, and in (12-8A) we saw that it was unbiased. If we look at other possible estimates in this same class—unbiased linear estimates—it is impossible to find one that is more efficient than OLS (i.e., that has smaller variance). This result, known as the Gauss-Markov Theorem, is illustrated below; it is one more reason why OLS is popular.

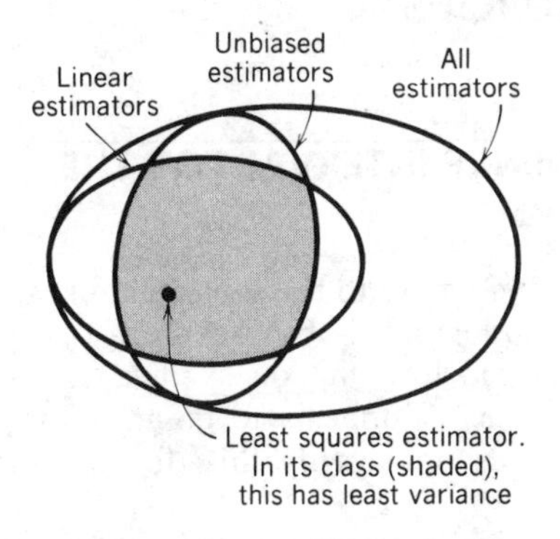

PROBLEMS

12-1A Suppose that the experimenter of Example 11-1 was in a hurry to analyze his data, and so drew a line joining the first and last points. We shall denote the slope of this line by b_1.

a. Calculate b_1 for the data in Table 11-1.

b. Write out a formula for b_1 in terms of X_1, Y_1, X_7, Y_7.

c. Is b_1 a linear estimator?

d. Is b_1 an unbiased estimator of β?

e. Without doing any calculations, can you say which has a larger SE, b_1 or the OLS estimator b?

f. Verify your answer in part **e** by actually calculating the SE of b_1 and of b for the data of Example 11-1. (Express your answer in terms of the unknown error variance σ^2.)

12-2A In Problem 12-1A, we considered the two extreme values, X_1 and X_7. Now let us consider an alternative pair of less extreme values—say X_2 and X_6. We shall denote the slope of this line by b_2. Like b_1, it can easily be shown to be linear and unbiased.

a. Calculate the SE of b_2. How does it compare with the SE of b_1?

b. Answer True or False; if False, correct it: b_1 has a smaller SE than does b_2, which illustrates a general principle: The more a pair of observations are spread out, the more "statistical leverage" they exert, hence the more efficient they are in estimating the sample slope b.

APPENDIX TO SECTION 12-3

A ONE-SIDED OR TWO-SIDED TEST?

SIMPLEST CASE, IMPLIED BY WORDING OF THE QUESTION

In regression, we again encounter the issue first raised in Chapter 9: Should we use a one- or two-sided test (or p-value, or confidence interval)? Sometimes the answer may be found in the way the question is worded. For instance, in Example 12-3, the null hypothesis was that "yield *does not increase* with fertilizer." This implies the alternative hypothesis is that yield *does* increase with fertilizer—that is,

$$H_1: \quad \beta > 0$$

Since this is a one-sided hypothesis, the one-sided p-value was appropriate.

On the other hand, in Example 12-2, the null hypothesis was that "yield is unrelated to fertilizer." This implies the alternative hypothesis that yield is related to fertilizer in either a positive or negative way. Thus we may write this alternative hypothesis as:

$$H_1: \quad \beta > 0 \text{ or } \beta < 0$$

that is,

$$H_1: \quad \beta \neq 0$$

Since this is a two-sided hypothesis, the two-sided

test based on the two-sided confidence interval is appropriate.

Thus, just as in Chapter 9, the wording of the question typically provides the key. Phrases like: Y is "unrelated to" or "unaffected by" X suggest that a two-sided test is appropriate. On the other hand, phrases like: X "raises," "lowers," "improves," or "decreases" Y, suggest that a one-sided test is required.

SUBTLE CASE, REQUIRING *A PRIORI* REASONING

The problem is that we are often *not* given the question, but have to phrase it ourselves. Should we use a one- or two-sided approach? The answer depends on prior theoretical reasoning. To illustrate, suppose we wish to investigate the effect of wages W on the national price level P, using the simple relationship,

$$P = \alpha + \beta W$$

On theoretical grounds, it may be concluded a priori that if wages affect prices at all, this relation will be a positive one. In this case, H_0 is tested against the one-sided alternative:

$$H_1: \ \beta > 0$$

On the other hand, as an example of a case in which such clear prior guidelines do not exist, consider an equation explaining saving. How does it depend on the interest rate? It is not clear, on theoretical grounds, whether this effect is a positive or a negative one. Since interest is the reward for saving, a high interest rate should provide an incentive to save, leading us to expect the interest rate to affect saving positively. But if individuals save in order to accumulate some target sum (perhaps for their retirement, or to buy a house), then the higher the interest rate, the more rapidly any saving will accumulate, hence the less they need to save to reach this target. In this case, interest affects saving negatively. If it is not clear which of these two effects may dominate, it is appropriate to test H_0 against the two-sided alternative:

$$H_1: \ \beta \neq 0$$

APPENDIX TO SECTION 12-4

CONFIDENCE INTERVALS ABOVE X_0: PROOFS

CONFIDENCE INTERVAL FOR THE MEAN μ_0

We refer once more to the sampling distribution of $\hat{Y}_0$ shown in Figure 12-5*b*. Sometimes $\hat{Y}_0$ is too high, sometimes too low, but on average, it seems just right. That is, $\hat{Y}_0$ appears to be an *unbiased* estimator. Let us now verify this; that is, show that $E(\hat{Y}_0) = \mu_0$.

In the theoretical approach that follows, it is convenient—as in Appendix 11-2—to use the deviation form $x = X - \bar{X}$. Then the fitted line has the form:

$$\hat{Y} = a_* + bx \qquad \text{(12-11A) like (11-9A)}$$

In particular, when x is set at a specific level x_0

$$\hat{Y}_0 = a_* + bx_0 \qquad \text{(12-12A)}$$

For the true regression line, there is a corresponding form denoted with Greek symbols:

$$E(Y) = \alpha_* + \beta x \qquad \text{(12-13A)}$$

Then

$$\mu_0 = E(Y_0) = \alpha_* + \beta x_0$$

We have already shown that b fluctuates around β with variance $\sigma^2/\Sigma x^2$. Similarly, we could show that a_* fluctuates around α_* with variance σ^2/n. [According to (11-16A), $a_* = \bar{Y}$, so this variance is just the formula (6-6) for sample means.] Furthermore, b and a_* are uncorrelated (as proved in advanced texts such as Wonnacott, 1981). This zero correlation in fact is an important reason for using the deviation form x.

The prediction $\hat{Y}_0$ in (12-12A) fortunately is a linear combination of these two variables (estimates) b and a_* (with coefficients 1 and x_0). Thus the theory of linear combinations can be applied. From (5-17),

$$
\begin{aligned}
E(\hat{Y}_0) &= E(a_* + bx_0) \\
&= E(a_*) + x_0 E(b) \\
&= \alpha_* + x_0 \beta \\
&= \mu_0
\end{aligned}
$$

Thus $\hat{Y}_0$ is indeed an unbiased estimator of μ_0.

With the mean of $\hat{Y}_0$ thus determined, we now turn to its variance. First, note from (5-22) that

$$
\begin{aligned}
\text{var}(\hat{Y}_0) &= \text{var}(a_* + bx_0) \\
&= \text{var}\, a_* + x_0^2\, \text{var}\, b \\
&= \frac{\sigma^2}{n} + x_0^2 \frac{\sigma^2}{\Sigma x^2} \\
&= \sigma^2 \left[\frac{1}{n} + \frac{x_0^2}{\Sigma x^2}\right] \qquad \text{(12-14A)}
\end{aligned}
$$

$$
\text{SE of } \hat{Y}_0 = \sigma \sqrt{\frac{1}{n} + \frac{x_0^2}{\Sigma x^2}}
$$

To make a 95% confidence interval, as usual we substitute s for σ, and use $t_{.025}$ to compensate:

$$
\mu_0 = \hat{Y}_0 \pm t_{.025}\, \text{SE}
$$

That is,

$$
\mu_0 = (a_* + bx_0) \pm t_{.025}\, s \sqrt{\frac{1}{n} + \frac{x_0^2}{\Sigma x^2}}
$$

While this is the formula for the deviation form x, it can be easily seen that it translates back into the original X values, as follows:

$$
\mu_0 = (a + bX_0) \pm t_{.025}\, s \sqrt{\frac{1}{n} + \frac{(X_0 - \bar{X})^2}{\Sigma(X - \bar{X})^2}}
$$

This completes our derivation of (12-19).

PREDICTION INTERVAL FOR A SINGLE OBSERVATION Y_0

We must now make an assumption we haven't needed before, that the individual Y values are scattered *normally* about the population regression line.

With x expressed in deviation form, the best prediction of a single observed Y_0 is again the point on the estimated regression line above x_0.

As already noted, an *interval* estimate for Y_0 requires (1) the variance (12-14A) reflecting the errors in estimating the fitted regression *plus* (2) the variance σ^2 reflecting the fluctuation in an individual Y observation. Adding these both together, we obtain:

$$
\sigma^2 \left(\frac{1}{n} + \frac{x_0^2}{\Sigma x^2}\right) + \sigma^2 = \sigma^2 \left(\frac{1}{n} + \frac{x_0^2}{\Sigma x^2} + 1\right)
$$

Except for this larger variance, the prediction interval for Y_0 is the same as the confidence interval for μ_0 given earlier:

$$
Y_0 = (a + bX_0) \pm t_{.025}\, s \sqrt{\frac{1}{n} + \frac{(X - X_0)^2}{\Sigma x^2} + 1}
$$

This completes our derivation of (12-20).

APPENDIX TO SECTION 13-2

SOLUTION OF A SET OF SIMULTANEOUS LINEAR EQUATIONS

To illustrate, let us take the pair of estimating equations in Table 13-2:

$$
16{,}500 = 280{,}000 b_1 + 7000 b_2 \qquad (1)
$$

$$
600 = 7000 b_1 + 400 b_2 \qquad (2)
$$

To solve a set of simultaneous equations, we eliminate one unknown at a time. To eliminate the first unknown b_1, we match its coefficient in equations (1) and (2), by multiplying equation (2) by 40:

$$
24{,}000 = 280{,}000 b_1 + 16{,}000 b_2 \qquad (3)
$$

When equation (1) is subtracted from (3), b_1 is indeed eliminated:

$$
7500 = 9000 b_2
$$

$$
b_2 = \frac{7500}{9000} = .833 \qquad (4)
$$

With b_2 solved, we can use it to solve for the other unknown b_1. We substitute equation (4) back into (1):

$$16{,}500 = 280{,}000b_1 + 7000(.833)$$

$$b_1 = \frac{10{,}667}{280{,}000} = .0381 \qquad (5)$$

Thus equations (4) and (5) are the required solution.

APPENDIX TO SECTION 13-5

DIRECT PLUS INDIRECT RELATION: PROOF

We will prove in general that the total relation of Y to X_1 (i.e., the simple regression coefficient of Y against X_1) is equal to the direct plus the indirect relation, as set out in (13-41). We begin with the first estimating equation (13-5) for the multiple regression of Y against X_1 and X_2:

$$\Sigma x_1 y = b_1 \Sigma x_1^2 + b_2 \Sigma x_1 x_2$$

If we divide this equation by Σx_1^2, we get:

$$\left(\frac{\Sigma x_1 y}{\Sigma x_1^2}\right) = b_1 + b_2 \left(\frac{\Sigma x_1 x_2}{\Sigma x_1^2}\right)$$

The bracketed expression on the left is the simple regression coefficient of Y against X_1—that is, the *total* relation. The bracketed expression on the right is the simple regression coefficient of X_2 against X_1, denoted b. Thus the whole equation may be written as the required equation (13-41):

$$\text{Total relation} = b_1 + b_2 b$$

APPENDIX TO SECTION 14-4

LOG REGRESSION HANDLES A MULTIPLICATIVE ERROR TERM

Earlier in Chapter 14, we said nothing about population models or error terms; we simply showed how various equations can be fitted. Standard assumptions about the error term would have justified the regression procedure, and there was no point in repeating the obvious.

However, an exception now occurs in log regression, where we must make a different assumption about the error term. For example, when we estimate exponential growth, we are assuming that the original population model has an error u that appears in the following *multiplicative* form:

$$P = \gamma e^{\beta x} u \qquad \text{like (14-23)}$$

Taking logs:

$$\log P = \log \gamma + \beta X + \log u$$

Letting $\log P \equiv Y$, $\log \gamma \equiv \alpha$, and $\log u \equiv e$, our population model takes the familiar form:

$$Y = \alpha + \beta X + e$$

Note how the log transformation has made the error term additive, as required. If we make the other usual assumptions about e (independence and constant variance), then this becomes the standard regression model (12-3).

PROBLEM

14-1A In each model in Problem 14-21, what form should the error take in order for your transformation to reduce the model to the standard linear form?

APPENDIX TO SECTION 15-1

CORRELATION IN CHAPTER 15 AGREES WITH CHAPTER 5

The correlation defined in Chapter 15 is the same correlation ρ that we met in Chapter 5. To see exactly why, let us begin with the equation that calculates the correlation for the whole population of N individuals:

$$\rho = \frac{\sum^N xy}{\sqrt{\sum^N x^2 \sum^N y^2}} \qquad \text{like (15-2)}$$

To reexpress this, we can write out the deviations explicitly: $x = X - \mu_X$, and $y = Y - \mu_Y$, where, of course, μ_X and μ_Y are population (rather than sample) means. Let us also divide by N in the numerator, and again in the denominator to compensate:

$$\rho = \frac{\frac{1}{N}\sum^N (X - \mu_X)(Y - \mu_Y)}{\sqrt{\frac{1}{N}\sum^N (X - \mu_X)^2 \frac{1}{N}\sum^N (Y - \mu_Y)^2}}$$

We recognize the numerator as the covariance σ_{XY} given in (5-10), and the denominator as $\sqrt{\sigma_X^2\sigma_Y^2}$. Thus ρ takes on the familiar form we have met already:

$$\rho = \frac{\sigma_{XY}}{\sigma_X\sigma_Y} \qquad \text{(5-13) repeated}$$

APPENDIX TO SECTION 15-2

ANOVA AND r^2: PROOFS

BREAKDOWN OF TOTAL SS

The proof of (15-10) is very similar to the proof in Appendix 10-1. We just square both sides of (15-8), and sum:

$$\begin{aligned}\Sigma(Y - \overline{Y})^2 &= \Sigma[(\hat{Y} - \overline{Y}) + (Y - \hat{Y})]^2 \\ &= \Sigma(\hat{Y} - \overline{Y})^2 + 2\Sigma(\hat{Y} - \overline{Y})(Y - \hat{Y}) \\ &\quad + \Sigma(Y - \hat{Y})^2 \qquad \text{(15-1A)}\end{aligned}$$

To prove the second-last sum is zero, once more the deviation form used in Appendix 11-2 will be useful:

$$\hat{Y} = a_* + bx \qquad \text{(15-2A)}$$
(11-9A) repeated

from (11-16A),

$$= \overline{Y} + bx$$

Thus

$$\hat{Y} - \overline{Y} = bx \qquad \text{(15-3A)}$$

Substitute this into the second-last sum in (15-1A); this term then becomes

$$2\Sigma bx(Y - \hat{Y})$$

Ignoring the constant $2b$, we obtain:

$$\Sigma x(Y - \hat{Y}) = \Sigma x(Y - (a_* + bx))$$

from (11-17A),

$$= 0$$

With its second-last sum reduced to 0, (15-1A) becomes:

$$\Sigma(Y - \overline{Y})^2 = \Sigma(\hat{Y} - \overline{Y})^2 + \Sigma(Y - \hat{Y})^2 \qquad \text{(15-4A)}$$
(15-9) proved

If we substitute (15-3A) into the middle term of this, we obtain another useful form:

$$\Sigma(Y - \overline{Y})^2 = b^2\Sigma x^2 + \Sigma(Y - \hat{Y})^2 \quad (15\text{-}5A)$$

(15-10) proved

r^2 IS THE COEFFICIENT OF DETERMINATION

To prove (15-16), we begin by expressing b in terms of r. To do so, we divide equation (15-1) by (15-2), obtaining:

$$\frac{b}{r} = \frac{\sqrt{\Sigma y^2}}{\sqrt{\Sigma x^2}}$$

Solve for b:

$$b = r\frac{\sqrt{\Sigma y^2}}{\sqrt{\Sigma x^2}} \quad (15\text{-}6A)$$

Incidentally, if we divide numerator and denominator by $\sqrt{n-1}$, we obtain the equivalent form:

$$b = r\frac{\sqrt{\Sigma y^2/(n-1)}}{\sqrt{\Sigma x^2/(n-1)}} = r\frac{s_Y}{s_X} \quad (15\text{-}7A)$$

(15-7) proved

Now we substitute (15-6A) into the fundamental ANOVA relation (15-5A):

$$\Sigma(Y - \overline{Y})^2 = r^2 \Sigma y^2 + \Sigma(Y - \hat{Y})^2$$

The solution for r^2 is:

$$r^2 = \frac{\Sigma(Y - \overline{Y})^2 - \Sigma(Y - \hat{Y})^2}{\Sigma y^2} \quad (15\text{-}8A)$$

We can reexpress the numerator using (15-4A). And the denominator, by definition, is $\Sigma y^2 \equiv \Sigma(Y - \overline{Y})^2$. Thus

$$r^2 = \frac{\Sigma(\hat{Y} - \overline{Y})^2}{\Sigma(Y - \overline{Y})^2}$$

$$= \frac{\text{explained SS}}{\text{total SS}} \quad (15\text{-}16) \text{ proved}$$

= coefficient of determination

RESIDUAL VARIANCE IS REDUCED BY r^2

To prove (15-17), note first that the *coefficient of indetermination* (the complement of r^2) is:

$$1 - r^2 = \frac{\text{unexplained SS}}{\text{total SS}}$$

To convert SS to MS (variance), divide both numerator and denominator by $n - 1$. Then in the denominator we get s_Y^2, the total variance of Y. In the numerator we almost get s^2, the residual variance (the slight difference is that s^2 should have a divisor of $n - 2$ rather than $n - 1$). Thus

$$1 - r^2 \simeq \frac{s^2}{s_Y^2}$$

That is,

$$s^2 \simeq (1 - r^2)s_Y^2 \quad (15\text{-}17) \text{ proved}$$

APPENDIX TO SECTION 18-2

MLE FOR SOME FAMILIAR CASES: PROOFS

MLE FOR A PROPORTION π

Given a sample where S successes were observed in n trials, the likelihood function is given by the binomial formula,

$$L(\pi) = \binom{n}{S}\pi^S(1 - \pi)^{n-S}$$

The reader who has carefully learned that π is a fixed population parameter may wonder how it can appear in the likelihood function as a variable. This is simply a mathematical convenience. The true value of π is, in fact, fixed. But since it is unknown, in MLE we let it range through all of its possible or hypothetical values; in other words, we treat it like a variable.

To find the maximum of $L(\pi)$, we therefore set its derivative equal to zero:

$$\frac{dL(\pi)}{d\pi} = \binom{n}{S} [\pi^S(n - S)(1 - \pi)^{n-S-1}(-1) + S\pi^{S-1}(1 - \pi)^{n-S}] = 0$$

Divide by $\binom{n}{S} \pi^{S-1}(1 - \pi)^{n-S-1}$ to obtain:

$$-\pi(n - S) + S(1 - \pi) = 0$$

$$-n\pi + S = 0$$

$$\pi = \frac{S}{n} = P$$

We could easily confirm that this is a maximum (rather than a minimum or inflection point). Actually, this derivation assumed that $0 < S < n$. When $S = 0$, the proof does not even require calculus: When $S = 0$, then $L(\pi) = (1 - \pi)^n$, which is clearly a maximum at the end-point $\pi = 0$. Similarly, when $S = n$, then $L(\pi) = \pi^n$, which is clearly a maximum at the other end-point, $\pi = 1$. Thus we have proven (18-5) valid in all possible cases.

MLE IS IDENTICAL TO LEAST SQUARES IN A NORMAL REGRESSION MODEL

To simplify, the proof below is for simple regression; but the argument may be easily generalized to cover multiple regression as well. Suppose that we have a sample of n points, rather than just 3. Because Y_1, for example, is assumed normally distributed, its probability (density) is given by (4-26) as:

$$p(Y_1) = \frac{1}{\sqrt{2\pi}\sigma} \exp\left[-\frac{1}{2}\left(\frac{Y_1 - \mu}{\sigma}\right)^2\right]$$

where exp[ ] is just a more convenient way of writing the exponential function $e^{[\ ]}$.

Now μ, the mean of Y_1, is given by (12-1) as:

$$\mu = \alpha + \beta X_1$$

Substituting this yields:

$$p(Y_1) = \frac{1}{\sqrt{2\pi}\sigma} \exp\left[-\frac{1}{2}\left(\frac{Y_1 - (\alpha + \beta X_1)}{\sigma}\right)^2\right]$$

In terms of the geometry of Figure 18-4, $p(Y_1)$ is the arrow above Y_1. The probability of Y_2 is similar, except that the subscript 2 replaces 1 throughout, and so on, for all the other observed Y values.

The independence of the Y values justifies multiplying all these probabilities together to find their joint probability (that is, the probability they would all occur, given α and β):

$$p(Y_1, Y_2, \ldots, Y_n|\alpha, \beta) = \frac{1}{\sqrt{2\pi}\sigma} \exp\left[-\frac{1}{2}\left(\frac{Y_1 - (\alpha + \beta X_1)}{\sigma}\right)^2\right] \times \frac{1}{\sqrt{2\pi}\sigma} \exp\left[-\frac{1}{2}\left(\frac{Y_2 - (\alpha + \beta X_2)}{\sigma}\right)^2\right] \times \cdots$$

Recall that the observed Y's are given. We are speculating on various values of α and β. To emphasize this, we call this the likelihood function $L(\alpha,\beta)$. At the same time, using the familiar rule for exponents (namely, $e^a e^b = e^{a+b}$), this product can be reexpressed by summing exponents:

$$L(\alpha,\beta) = \left(\frac{1}{\sqrt{2\pi}\sigma}\right)^n \exp -\frac{1}{2\sigma^2}\sum^n [Y_i - (\alpha + \beta X_i)]^2$$

Now we ask, what values of α and β produce the largest L? The only place α and β appear is in the exponent; moreover, maximizing a function with a negative exponent involves minimizing the magnitude of the exponent. Hence the MLE estimates are obtained by choosing the α and β that

$$\text{Minimize } \Sigma[Y_i - (\alpha + \beta X_i)]^2$$

The selection of maximum likelihood estimates of α and β to minimize this is identical to the selection of least squares estimates α and β to minimize (11-2). That is, MLE and least squares yield identical estimates and (18-7) is proved.

COROLLARY: MLE FOR THE MEAN OF A NORMAL POPULATION

In the special case of regression where $\beta = 0$, then every Y comes from the *same* population centered at α. That is, we have a sample of n observations from one population. The MLE will still be the least squares estimate, of course, which we found in (11-9) was just $\overline{Y}$. Thus we have proved (18-6):

In a normal population,

$$\text{MLE of population mean} = \overline{Y}$$

PROBLEM

18-1A To prove the MLE is identical to least squares in a normal *multiple* regression model, how would the proof have to be changed?

APPENDIX TO SECTION 19-2

BAYESIAN CONFIDENCE INTERVAL FOR π: PROOF

BASIC STATISTICAL ARGUMENT

Note that in Figure 19-3 or 19-4, the posterior distribution is approximately normal. This will be true in general, especially when S^* and F^* are each greater than 5. This normal approximation means that 95% of the probability lies within ±1.96 standard deviations of the mean. To prove (19-19), therefore, we need only show:

$$\text{Posterior mean} = P^*$$

$$\text{Posterior variance} \simeq \frac{P^*(1 - P^*)}{n^*}$$

CALCULUS PREREQUISITE

The key result we need from integral calculus is:

$$\int_0^1 \pi^u(1 - \pi)^v \, d\pi = \frac{u!\, v!}{(u + v + 1)!} \qquad \text{(19-1A)}$$

The proof could be carried out by mathematical induction, when u and v are positive integers. (If other u and v are of interest, see a text in advanced calculus.)

PROOF CARRIED OUT

Let us express the posterior distribution in terms of the convenient symbols S^* and F^*. According to (19-17), $a + S = S^* - 1$ and $b + F = F^* - 1$, so that the posterior can be written as:

$$p(\pi|S) \propto \pi^{S^*-1}(1 - \pi)^{F^*-1} \qquad \text{(19-2A) like (19-12)}$$

i. First, let us find out what the constant of proportionality is, in (19-2A). We substitute $u = S^* - 1$ and $v = F^* - 1$ into (19-1A):

$$\int_0^1 \pi^{S^*-1}(1 - \pi)^{F^*-1} \, d\pi = \frac{(S^* - 1)!(F^* - 1)!}{(S^* + F^* - 1)!}$$

We should divide (19-2A) by this, to make $p(\pi|S)$ a proper probability distribution with a total probability (integral) of 1:

$$p(\pi|S) = \frac{(S^* + F^* - 1)!}{(S^* - 1)!\,(F^* - 1)!} \pi^{S^*-1}(1 - \pi)^{F^*-1}$$

ii. The mean is easily found:

$$E(\pi) \equiv \int_0^1 \pi p(\pi|S) \, d\pi$$

Substitute $p(\pi|S)$:

$$E(\pi) = \frac{(S^* + F^* - 1)!}{(S^* - 1)!\,(F^* - 1)!} \int_0^1 \pi \pi^{S^*-1}(1 - \pi)^{F^*-1} \, d\pi$$

If we temporarily ignore the large expression outside the integral, we can concentrate on the integral itself:

$$\int_0^1 \pi^{S^*}(1 - \pi)^{F^*-1} \, d\pi$$

This can be evaluated by substituting $u = S^*$ and $v = F^* - 1$ into (19-1A):

$$\int_0^1 \pi^{S^*}(1 - \pi)^{F^*-1} \, d\pi = \frac{S^*!\,(F^* - 1)!}{(S^* + F^*)!}$$

When we substitute this into $E(\pi)$, many of the

factorials cancel out, leaving the desired conclusion:

$$E(\pi) = \frac{S^*}{S^* + F^*} = P^*$$

iii. To calculate the variance, it would be easiest to first calculate $E(\pi^2)$, and then use

$$\sigma^2 = E(\pi^2) - [E(\pi)]^2 \quad \text{like (4-35)}$$

The details are left as an exercise. They would finally establish the desired conclusion:

$$\sigma^2 = \frac{P^*(1 - P^*)}{n^* + 1} \simeq \frac{P^*(1 - P^*)}{n^*}$$

APPENDIX TO SECTION 19-3

POSTERIOR DISTRIBUTION OF μ IN A NORMAL MODEL: PROOF

We will show that the posterior distribution of μ is normal, with the mean and standard error as claimed in (19-23) and (19-24). Denoting by K_1, K_2, . . . the unimportant constants that do not involve the unknown μ, we use the normal formula (4-26) to give us the two basic components:

Prior: $$p(\mu) = K_1 \exp\left[-\frac{1}{2}\left(\frac{\mu - \mu_0}{\sigma_0}\right)^2\right]$$

Likelihood: $$p(\overline{X}|\mu) = K_2 \exp\left[-\frac{1}{2}\left(\frac{\overline{X} - \mu}{\sigma/\sqrt{n}}\right)^2\right]$$

Recall that posterior = (prior) × (likelihood)

$$= K_1 K_2 \exp\left[-\frac{1}{2}\left[\left(\frac{\mu - \mu_0}{\sigma_0}\right)^2 + \left(\frac{\overline{X} - \mu}{\sigma/\sqrt{n}}\right)^2\right]\right]$$

Let us consider in detail the exponent, which may be rearranged as a quadratic function of μ:

$$-\frac{1}{2}\left[\mu^2\left(\frac{1}{\sigma_0^2} + \frac{n}{\sigma^2}\right) - 2\mu\left(\frac{\mu_0}{\sigma_0^2} + \frac{n\overline{X}}{\sigma^2}\right) + K_3\right]$$

From (19-22), we substitute n_0/σ^2 for $1/\sigma_0^2$:

$$-\frac{1}{2}\left[\mu^2\left(\frac{n_0 + n}{\sigma^2}\right) - 2\mu\left(\frac{n_0\mu_0 + n\overline{X}}{\sigma^2}\right) + K_3\right]$$

$$= -\frac{1}{2}\left(\frac{n_0 + n}{\sigma^2}\right)\left[\mu^2 - 2\mu\left(\frac{n_0\mu_0 + n\overline{X}}{n_0 + n}\right) + K_4\right]$$

$$= -\frac{1}{2}\left(\frac{1}{\sigma^2/(n_0 + n)}\right)\left[\mu - \left(\frac{n_0\mu_0 + n\overline{X}}{n_0 + n}\right)\right]^2 + K_5$$

Ignoring K_5, this exponent has the form

$$-\frac{1}{2}\frac{1}{b^2}[\mu - a]^2$$

in which—by analogy with the exponent in (4-26)—we recognize that μ has a normal distribution with mean a and standard deviation b. That is:

$$\text{Mean} = \frac{n_0\mu_0 + n\overline{X}}{n_0 + n} \quad \text{(19-23) proved}$$

$$\text{SE} = \sigma/\sqrt{n_0 + n} \quad \text{(19-24) proved}$$

APPENDIX TO SECTION 19-4

POSTERIOR DISTRIBUTION OF β IN NORMAL REGRESSION: PROOF

We assume a normal prior, and a normal likelihood (which is approximately true if n is large, or exactly true if the Y observations are distributed normally about the line). Then we can appeal to the normal model already derived in Section 19-3. Into (19-22), (19-23), (19-24) we substitute:

β for μ

b for $\bar{X}$

σ/σ_x for σ

and of course,

β_0 for μ_0

σ_0 for σ_0

Then we obtain (19-29), (19-30), (19-31), as required.

APPENDIX TO SECTION 19-5

BAYESIAN SHRINKAGE CONFIDENCE INTERVALS

We have seen how a Bayesian shrinkage estimate uses all the data—not just the estimate itself, but also its measure of reliability F. This has two advantages: (1) better point estimates, as already noted; (2) reduced variability of these estimates, which we will discuss now.

When F is reasonably large ($F \geq 3$, say), the variance of the estimate is reduced by the same shrinkage factor $1 - (1/F)$ that is used for the estimate itself. Consequently, the SE (standard error) of the estimate is reduced by the square root $\sqrt{1 - (1/F)}$:

Bayesian shrinkage (if $F \geq 3$): Shrink the SE by the factor $\sqrt{1 - (1/F)}$ (19-3A)

PROBLEMS

19-1A Contrast the classical and Bayesian shrinkage 95% confidence intervals, calculated for each of the following problems (in each case, calculate $F = t^2$ to determine the amount of shrinkage towards zero):

a. Problem 19-15.

b. Problem 19-16.

c. Problem 19-17.

19-2A In each case in Problem 19-1A, when is the Bayesian confidence interval narrower than the classical?

APPENDIX TO SECTION 24-2

SERIAL CORRELATION AND THE DURBIN-WATSON TEST

ESTIMATING ρ

In the autoregression (24-5), an estimate r for ρ can be computed with the usual least squares regression formula. Since residuals have 0 mean, they are already in deviation form and can therefore be substituted into (11-5) directly, which gives:

$$r = \frac{\sum_{t=2}^{n} \hat{e}_{t-1}\hat{e}_t}{\sum_{t=2}^{n} \hat{e}_{t-1}^2} \quad \text{(24-1A)}$$

Because of the shift of one time period, both sums had to start at $t = 2$, not $t = 1$. For the jewelry sales in Figure 24-4, these two sums can be calculated in the usual tableau:

	Given		*Regression Calculations*	
t	$y =$ *residual* $\hat{e}_t$	$x =$ *lagged residual* $\hat{e}_{t-1}$	$xy = \hat{e}_{t-1}\hat{e}_t$	$x^2 = \hat{e}_{t-1}^2$
1	.4			
2	.6	.4	.24	.16
3	1.2	.6	.72	.36
4	−3.7	1.2	−4.44	1.44
5	− .2	−3.7	.74	13.69
6	·	−.2	·	·
·	·	·	·	·
·	·	·	·	·
			−10.5	41.0

$$r = \frac{-10.5}{41.0} = -.26 \quad \text{(24-6) proved}$$

r IS APPROXIMATELY THE CORRELATION COEFFICIENT

Let us calculate the correlation between $x = \hat{e}_{t-1}$ and $y = \hat{e}_t$:

$$\text{corr} = \frac{\sum_{t=2}^{n} \hat{e}_{t-1}\hat{e}_t}{\sqrt{\sum_{t=2}^{n} \hat{e}_{t-1}^2 \sum_{t=2}^{n} \hat{e}_t^2}} \qquad \text{(24-2A) like (15-2)}$$

In the denominator, the second sum is the same as the first, except for the first and last term (because t and $t-1$ are one unit apart). That is:

$$\sum_{t=2}^{n} \hat{e}_t^2 \simeq \sum_{t=2}^{n} \hat{e}_{t-1}^2$$

When this is substituted into (24-2A), we obtain (24-1A). That is, in an autoregressive equation the regression coefficient is essentially the correlation coefficient.

THE DURBIN-WATSON TEST

The Durbin-Watson statistic to test for $\rho = 0$ is defined as:

$$DW \equiv \frac{\sum_{t=2}^{n} (\hat{e}_t - \hat{e}_{t-1})^2}{\sum_{t=1}^{n} \hat{e}_t^2} \qquad \text{(24-3A)}$$

If there is serial correlation, then $\hat{e}_t$ will tend to track $\hat{e}_{t-1}$, and the numerator of DW—and hence DW itself—will be small. Hence small values of DW define the region for establishing serial correlation (i.e., rejecting H_0) as tabulated in Appendix Table IX.

Another useful view is obtained by expanding the numerator of (24-3A):

$$DW = \frac{\sum_{t=2}^{n} \hat{e}_t^2 - 2\left(\sum_{t=2}^{n} \hat{e}_t\hat{e}_{t-1}\right) + \sum_{t=2}^{n} \hat{e}_{t-1}^2}{\sum_{t=1}^{n} \hat{e}_t^2}$$

Note that the first and last terms are each approximately equal to the denominator. Moreover, when the middle term in brackets is matched with the denominator, it gives approximately the serial correlation r in (24-1A). Thus:

$$\boxed{DW \simeq 2 - 2r}$$

This makes it clear that if the serial correlation increases (r rises towards 1), then DW falls towards zero.

APPENDIX TO SECTION 24-3

MOVING AVERAGES IN GENERAL

In Table 24-2, we first averaged 4 quarters at a time, and then in order to center, averaged 2 at a time. The net effect was to average over 5 time periods, with each end getting half weights. Thus, the moving average M can be written with the formula:

$$M(Y_t) = \frac{Y_t + Y_{t+1} + Y_{t-1} + .5Y_{t+2} + .5Y_{t-2}}{4}$$

That is, M is the average of the nearby values. We could easily generalize to any number of values and different weights:

$$M(Y_t) = a_0Y_t + a_1Y_{t+1} + a_{-1}Y_{t-1} + \cdots + a_kY_{t+k} + a_{-k}Y_{t-k}$$

where $\Sigma a_i = 1$. The weights a_i typically decrease so that more distant values count less—until finally, beyond a distance of k quarters, they don't count at all.

Although moving averages are most commonly used on seasonal data, they can be used for annual data without any seasonal component. They still accomplish the goal of every average: In averaging out the fluctuations, the average smooths the time series.

PROBLEM

24-1A
a. If we average 4 at a time, and then 2 at a time, prove that the resulting moving average is the one given in the first equation above.

b. Similarly, calculate the formula for the overall moving average:

  i. If we average 4 at a time, and then again 4 more at a time.

  ii. If we average 4 at a time once more (for the third time).

APPENDIX TO SECTION 24-4

EXPONENTIAL SMOOTHING: PROOF

To establish (24-13), substitute (24-12) into (24-11):

$$\hat{Y}_t = b\lambda Y_{t-1} + b\lambda^2 Y_{t-2} + b\lambda^3 Y_{t-3} + \cdots$$

As an aside, notice that since this applies for any time period t, we can set $t = t - 1$, and thus get

$$\hat{Y}_{t-1} = b\lambda Y_{t-2} + b\lambda^2 Y_{t-3} + b\lambda^3 Y_{t-4} + \cdots$$

Returning now to the first equation, note that it appears to be impossible to estimate, because it is an infinite series. However, we can greatly simplify it by rewriting it:

$$\hat{Y}_t = b\lambda Y_{t-1} + \lambda(b\lambda Y_{t-2} + b\lambda^2 Y_{t-3} + \cdots)$$

The expression in brackets turns out to be $\hat{Y}_{t-1}$ given in the second equation. Thus:

$$\hat{Y}_t = b\lambda Y_{t-1} + \lambda \hat{Y}_{t-1}$$

If we require the weights to add to 1, then the first weight must be the complement of the second weight λ; that is:

$$\hat{Y}_t = (1 - \lambda)Y_{t-1} + \lambda \hat{Y}_{t-1} \quad \text{(24-13) proved}$$

APPENDIX TO SECTION 24-5

FORECASTING USING BOX-JENKINS MODELS

In this appendix, we will continue the ARMA model of Section 24-5, showing how it can be used to forecast, and how it can include trend and seasonal components.

FORECASTING

Since (24-18) is true for any t, it is true for $t + 1$:

$$Y_{t+1} = (\beta_1 Y_t + \beta_2 Y_{t-1} + \cdots) + (v_{t+1} - \alpha_1 v_t - \alpha_2 v_{t-1} - \cdots)$$

To get the forecast value $\hat{Y}_{t+1}$, we substitute the extimated coefficients $(b_1, b_2, \ldots, a_1, a_2, \ldots)$ for their unknown targets $(\beta_1, \beta_2, \ldots, \alpha_1, \alpha_2, \ldots)$. We also substitute the residuals from the estimation process $(\hat{v}_t, \hat{v}_{t-1}, \ldots)$. Finally, we must estimate the future disturbance v_{t+1}; since it is pure noise and perfectly unpredictable, we can only estimate it with its mean value 0. Thus:

$$\hat{Y}_{t+1} = b_1 Y_t + b_2 Y_{t-1} + \cdots + 0 - a_1 \hat{v}_t - a_2 \hat{v}_{t-1} - \cdots$$

To forecast another period ahead, of course it would be best to use the actual Y_{t+1} if it were available, and recalculate all the estimates $b_1, b_2, \ldots, a_1, a_2$, and so on. But if Y_{t+1} is not available, its estimate above can be used instead to obtain

$$\hat{Y}_{t+2} = b_1 \hat{Y}_{t+1} + b_2 Y_t + \cdots + 0 - a_1(0) - a_2 \hat{v}_t - \cdots$$

and so on.

TREND HANDLED BY DIFFERENCING: ARIMA MODELS

For a series that has an increasing trend, it is natural to consider the change in the series:

$$\Delta Y_t \equiv Y_t - Y_{t-1}$$

If the trend is linear, this difference will remove it. Then we fit the appropriate ARMA (p, q) model to the new ΔY_t series.

The original series Y_t may be called the *integrated* series (in order to distinguish it from the differenced series ΔY_t). Thus the whole model is called an ARIMA model (Auto Regression, Integrated, Moving Average). If differencing is applied d times successively (to remove a polynomial trend of degree d), then the model is called an ARIMA (p, d, q) model.

SEASONAL INCLUDED TOO: SARIMA MODELS

To handle seasonal variation, let us consider what all the winter (first) quarters would look like in a series like Figure 24-2. Being all winter values, they would form a subseries without the ups and downs of seasonal variation (which occur only as we pass from season to season). Thus we could handle them with an ARIMA model (p_s, d_s, q_s) say.

Similarly, all the spring (second) quarters could be fitted with a second ARIMA model, and so on. [To keep the number of parameters small, this estimation is often constrained so that it will generate only one set of coefficients $(b_1, b_2, \ldots, a_1, a_2, \ldots)$ for all four quarters.]

From this seasonal fitting, there will be estimated pure noise terms $\hat{v}_t$. Strung together as a new time series, they can be fitted with another ARIMA model (p, d, q). The whole model then is called a *Seasonal* ARIMA, or more formally, a SARIMA $(p, d, q) \times (p_s, d_s, q_s)_4$ model.

In practice, to keep the complexity down to a reasonable level, the SARIMA model is often specified to include very few parameters. For example, a $(0, 1, 1) \times (0, 1, 1)_4$ model is common—or, for monthly data, a $(0, 1, 1) \times (0, 1, 1)_{12}$ model. Such a model is closely related to the exponential smoothing discussed in Section 24-4.

TABLES

TABLE I Random Digits (Blocked merely for convenience)

39 65 76 45 45	19 90 69 64 61	20 26 36 31 62	58 24 97 14 97	95 06 70 99 00
73 71 23 70 90	65 97 60 12 11	31 56 34 19 19	47 83 75 51 33	30 62 38 20 46
72 20 47 33 84	51 67 47 97 19	98 40 07 17 66	23 05 09 51 80	59 78 11 52 49
75 17 25 69 17	17 95 21 78 58	24 33 45 77 48	69 81 84 09 29	93 22 70 45 80
37 48 79 88 74	63 52 06 34 30	01 31 60 10 27	35 07 79 71 53	28 99 52 01 41
02 89 08 16 94	85 53 83 29 95	56 27 09 24 43	21 78 55 09 82	72 61 88 73 61
87 18 15 70 07	37 79 49 12 38	48 13 93 55 96	41 92 45 71 51	09 18 25 58 94
98 83 71 70 15	89 09 39 59 24	00 06 41 41 20	14 36 59 25 47	54 45 17 24 89
10 08 58 07 04	76 62 16 48 68	58 76 17 14 86	59 53 11 52 21	66 04 18 72 87
47 90 56 37 31	71 82 13 50 41	27 55 10 24 92	28 04 67 53 44	95 23 00 84 47
93 05 31 03 07	34 18 04 52 35	74 13 39 35 22	68 95 23 92 35	36 63 70 35 33
21 89 11 47 99	11 20 99 45 18	76 51 94 84 86	13 79 93 37 55	98 16 04 41 67
95 18 94 06 97	27 37 83 28 71	79 57 95 13 91	09 61 87 25 21	56 20 11 32 44
97 08 31 55 73	10 65 81 92 59	77 31 61 95 46	20 44 90 32 64	26 99 76 75 63
69 26 88 86 13	59 71 74 17 32	48 38 75 93 29	73 37 32 04 05	60 82 29 20 25
41 47 10 25 03	87 63 93 95 17	81 83 83 04 49	77 45 85 50 51	79 88 01 97 30
91 94 14 63 62	08 61 74 51 69	92 79 43 89 79	29 18 94 51 23	14 85 11 47 23
80 06 54 18 47	08 52 85 08 40	48 40 35 94 22	72 65 71 08 86	50 03 42 99 36
67 72 77 63 99	89 85 84 46 06	64 71 06 21 66	89 37 20 70 01	61 65 70 22 12
59 40 24 13 75	42 29 72 23 19	06 94 76 10 08	81 30 15 39 14	81 83 17 16 33
63 62 06 34 41	79 53 36 02 95	94 61 09 43 62	20 21 14 68 86	94 95 48 46 45
78 47 23 53 90	79 93 96 38 63	34 85 52 05 09	85 43 01 72 73	14 93 87 81 40
87 68 62 15 43	97 48 72 66 48	53 16 71 13 81	59 97 50 99 52	24 62 20 42 31
47 60 92 10 77	26 97 05 73 51	88 46 38 03 58	72 68 49 29 31	75 70 16 08 24
56 88 87 59 41	06 87 37 78 48	65 88 69 58 39	88 02 84 27 83	85 81 56 39 38
22 17 68 65 84	87 02 22 57 51	68 69 80 95 44	11 29 01 95 80	49 34 35 86 47
19 36 27 59 46	39 77 32 77 09	79 57 92 36 59	89 74 39 82 15	08 58 94 34 74
16 77 23 02 77	28 06 24 25 93	22 45 44 84 11	87 80 61 65 31	09 71 91 74 25
78 43 76 71 61	97 67 63 99 61	80 45 67 93 82	59 73 19 85 23	53 33 65 97 21
03 28 28 26 08	69 30 16 09 05	53 58 47 70 93	66 56 45 65 79	45 56 20 19 47
04 31 17 21 56	33 73 99 19 87	26 72 39 27 67	53 77 57 68 93	60 61 97 22 61
61 06 98 03 91	87 14 77 43 96	43 00 65 98 50	45 60 33 01 07	98 99 46 50 47
23 68 35 26 00	99 53 93 61 28	52 70 05 48 34	56 65 05 61 86	90 92 10 70 80
15 39 25 70 99	93 86 52 77 65	15 33 59 05 28	22 87 26 07 47	86 96 98 29 06
58 71 96 30 24	18 46 23 34 27	85 13 99 24 44	49 18 09 79 49	74 16 32 23 02
93 22 53 64 39	07 10 63 76 35	87 03 04 79 88	08 13 13 85 51	55 34 57 72 69
78 76 58 54 74	92 38 70 96 92	52 06 79 79 45	82 63 18 27 44	69 66 92 19 09
61 81 31 96 82	00 57 25 60 59	46 72 60 18 77	55 66 12 62 11	08 99 55 64 57
42 88 07 10 05	24 98 65 63 21	47 21 61 88 32	27 80 30 21 60	10 92 35 36 12
77 94 30 05 39	28 10 99 00 27	12 73 73 99 12	49 99 57 94 82	96 88 57 17 91

TABLE **II** **Random Normal Numbers, $\mu = 0$, $\sigma = 1$ (Rounded to 1 Decimal Place)**

.5	.1	2.5	-.3	-.1	.3	-.3	1.3	.2	-1.0
.1	-2.5	-5	-.2	.5	-1.6	.2	-1.2	.0	.5
1.5	-.4	-.6	.7	.9	1.4	.8	-1.0	-.9	-1.9
1.0	-.5	1.3	3.5	.6	-1.9	.2	1.2	-.5	-.3
1.4	-.6	.0	.3	2.9	2.0	-.3	.4	.4	.0
.9	-.5	-.5	.6	.9	-.9	1.6	.2	-1.9	.4
1.2	-1.1	.0	.8	1.0	.7	1.1	-.6	-.3	-.7
-1.5	-.5	-.2	-.1	1.0	.2	.4	.7	-.4	-.4
-.7	.8	-1.6	-.3	-.5	-2.1	-.5	-.2	.9	-.5
1.4	.2	.4	.8	.2	-.7	1.0	-1.5	-.3	.1
-.5	1.7	-.1	-1.2	-.5	.9	-.5	-2.0	-2.8	-.2
-1.4	-.2	1.4	-.6	-.3	-.2	.2	.8	1.0	-.9
-1.0	.6	-.9	1.6	.1	.4	-.2	.3	-1.0	-1.0
.0	-.9	.0	-.7	1.1	-.1	1.1	.5	-1.7	.4
1.4	-1.2	-.9	1.2	-.2	-.2	1.2	-2.6	-.6	.1
-1.8	-.3	1.2	1.0	-.5	-1.6	-.1	-.4	-.6	.6
-.1	-.4	-1.4	.4	-1.0	-.1	-1.7	-2.8	-1.1	-2.4
-1.3	1.8	-1.0	.4	1.0	-1.1	-1.0	.4	-1.7	2.0
1.0	.5	.7	1.4	1.0	-1.3	1.6	-1.0	.5	-.3
.3	-2.1	.7	-.9	-1.1	-1.4	1.0	.1	-.6	.9
-1.8	-2.0	-1.6	.5	.2	-.2	.0	.0	.5	-1.0
-1.2	1.2	1.1	.9	1.3	-.2	.2	-.4	-.3	.5
.7	-1.1	1.2	-1.2	-.9	.4	.3	-.9	.6	1.7
-.4	.4	-1.9	.9	-.2	.6	.9	-.4	-.2	-.1
-1.4	-.2	.4	-.6	-.6	.2	-.3	.5	.7	-.3
.2	.2	-1.1	-.2	-.3	1.2	1.1	.0	-2.0	-.6
.2	.3	-.3	.1	-2.8	-.4	-.8	-1.3	-.6	-1.0
2.3	.6	.6	-.7	.2	1.3	.1	-1.8	-.7	-1.3
.0	-.3	.1	.8	-.6	.5	.5	-1.0	.5	1.0
-1.1	-2.1	.9	.1	.4	-1.7	1.0	-1.4	-.6	-1.0
.8	.1	-1.5	.0	-2.1	.7	.1	-.9	-.6	.6
.4	-1.7	-.9	.2	-.7	.3	-.1	-.2	-.1	.4
-.5	-.3	.2	-.7	1.0	.0	.4	-.8	.2	.1
.3	-.5	1.3	-1.2	-.9	.1	-.5	-.8	.0	.5
1.0	3.0	-.6	-.5	-1.1	1.3	-1.4	-1.3	-3.0	.5
-1.3	1.3	-.6	-.1	-.5	-.6	2.9	.5	.4	.3
-.3	-.1	-.3	.6	-.5	-1.2	-1.2	-.3	-.1	1.1
.2	-.9	-.9	-.5	1.4	-.5	.2	-.4	1.5	1.1
-1.3	.2	-1.2	.4	-1.0	.8	.9	1.0	.0	.8
-1.2	-.2	-.3	1.8	1.4	.6	1.2	.7	.4	.2
.6	-.5	.8	.1	.5	-.4	1.7	1.2	.9	-.3
.4	-1.9	.2	-.5	.7	-.1	-.1	-.5	.5	1.1
-1.4	.5	-1.7	-1.2	.8	-.7	-.1	1.0	-.8	.2
-.2	-.2	-.4	-.8	.3	1.0	1.8	2.9	-.8	-.1
-.3	.5	.4	-1.5	1.5	2.0	-.1	.2	.0	-1.2
.4	-.4	.6	1.0	-.1	.1	.5	-1.3	1.1	1.1
.6	.7	-1.1	-1.4	-1.6	-1.6	1.5	1.3	.7	-.9
.9	-.9	-.1	-.5	.5	1.4	.0	-.3	-.3	1.2
.2	-.6	.0	-.5	-.9	-.4	-.5	1.7	-.2	-1.2
-.9	.4	.8	.8	.4	-.3	-1.1	.6	1.4	1.3

TABLE III(a) Binomial Coefficients $\binom{n}{s}$

n	s = 0	1	2	3	4	5	6	7	8	9	10
0	1										
1	1	1									
2	1	2	1								
3	1	3	3	1							
4	1	4	6	4	1						
5	1	5	10	10	5	1					
6	1	6	15	20	15	6	1				
7	1	7	21	35	35	21	7	1			
8	1	8	28	56	70	56	28	8	1		
9	1	9	36	84	126	126	84	36	9	1	
10	1	10	45	120	210	252	210	120	45	10	1
11	1	11	55	165	330	462	462	330	165	55	11
12	1	12	66	220	495	792	924	792	495	220	66
13	1	13	78	286	715	1287	1716	1716	1287	715	286
14	1	14	91	364	1001	2002	3003	3432	3003	2002	1001
15	1	15	105	455	1365	3003	5005	6435	6435	5005	3003
16	1	16	120	560	1820	4368	8008	11440	12870	11440	8008
17	1	17	136	680	2380	6188	12376	19448	24310	24310	19448
18	1	18	153	816	3060	8568	18564	31824	43758	48620	43758
19	1	19	171	969	3876	11628	27132	50388	75582	92378	92378
20	1	20	190	1140	4845	15504	38760	77520	125970	167960	184756

Note: $\binom{n}{s} = \frac{n(n-1)(n-2)\cdots(n-s+1)}{s(s-1)(s-2)\cdots 3\cdot 2\cdot 1}$; $\binom{n}{0} = 1$; $\binom{n}{1} = n$.

For coefficients missing from the above table, use the relation:

$\binom{n}{s} = \binom{n}{n-s}$, e.g., $\binom{20}{11} = \binom{20}{9} = 167960$.

TABLE III(b) Individual Binomial Probabilities $p(s)$

n	s	π = .10	.20	.30	.40	.50	.60	.70	.80	.90
1	0	.900	.800	.700	.600	.500	.400	.300	.200	.100
	1	.100	.200	.300	.400	.500	.600	.700	.800	.900
2	0	.810	.640	.490	.360	.250	.160	.090	.040	.010
	1	.180	.320	.420	.480	.500	.480	.420	.320	.180
	2	.010	.040	.090	.160	.250	.360	.490	.640	.810
3	0	.729	.512	.343	.216	.125	.064	.027	.008	.001
	1	.243	.384	.441	.432	.375	.288	.189	.096	.027
	2	.027	.096	.189	.288	.375	.432	.441	.384	.243
	3	.001	.008	.027	.064	.125	.216	.343	.512	.729
4	0	.656	.410	.240	.130	.063	.026	.008	.002	.000
	1	.292	.410	.412	.346	.250	.154	.076	.026	.004
	2	.049	.154	.265	.346	.375	.346	.265	.154	.049
	3	.004	.026	.076	.154	.250	.346	.412	.410	.292
	4	.000	.002	.008	.026	.063	.130	.240	.410	.656
5	0	.590	.328	.168	.078	.031	.010	.002	.000	.000
	1	.328	.410	.360	.259	.156	.077	.028	.006	.000
	2	.073	.205	.309	.346	.313	.230	.132	.051	.008
	3	.008	.051	.132	.230	.313	.346	.309	.205	.073
	4	.000	.006	.028	.077	.156	.259	.360	.410	.328
	5	.000	.000	.002	.010	.031	.078	.168	.328	.590
6	0	.531	.262	.118	.047	.016	.004	.001	.000	.000
	1	.354	.393	.303	.187	.094	.037	.010	.002	.000
	2	.098	.246	.324	.311	.234	.138	.060	.015	.001
	3	.015	.082	.185	.276	.313	.276	.185	.082	.015
	4	.001	.015	.060	.138	.234	.311	.324	.246	.098
	5	.000	.002	.010	.037	.094	.187	.303	.393	.354
	6	.000	.000	.001	.004	.016	.047	.118	.262	.531
7	0	.478	.210	.082	.028	.008	.002	.000	.000	.000
	1	.372	.367	.247	.131	.055	.017	.004	.000	.000
	2	.124	.275	.318	.261	.164	.077	.025	.004	.000
	3	.023	.115	.227	.290	.273	.194	.097	.029	.003
	4	.003	.029	.097	.194	.273	.290	.227	.115	.023
	5	.000	.004	.025	.077	.164	.261	.318	.275	.124
	6	.000	.000	.004	.017	.055	.131	.247	.367	.372
	7	.000	.000	.000	.002	.008	.028	.082	.210	.478
8	0	.430	.168	.058	.017	.004	.001	.000	.000	.000
	1	.383	.336	.198	.090	.031	.008	.001	.000	.000
	2	.149	.294	.296	.209	.109	.041	.010	.001	.000
	3	.033	.147	.254	.279	.219	.124	.047	.009	.000
	4	.005	.046	.136	.232	.273	.232	.136	.046	.005
	5	.000	.009	.047	.124	.219	.279	.254	.147	.033
	6	.000	.001	.010	.041	.109	.209	.296	.294	.149
	7	.000	.000	.001	.008	.031	.090	.198	.336	.383
	8	.000	.000	.000	.001	.004	.017	.058	.168	.430

TABLE **III(b)** (continued)

		π								
n	s	.10	.20	.30	.40	.50	.60	.70	.80	.90
9	0	.387	.134	.040	.010	.002	.000	.000	.000	.000
	1	.387	.302	.156	.060	.018	.004	.000	.000	.000
	2	.172	.302	.267	.161	.070	.021	.004	.000	.000
	3	.045	.176	.267	.251	.164	.074	.021	.003	.000
	4	.007	.066	.172	.251	.246	.167	.074	.017	.001
	5	.001	.017	.074	.167	.246	.251	.172	.066	.007
	6	.000	.003	.021	.074	.164	.251	.267	.176	.045
	7	.000	.000	.004	.021	.070	.161	.267	.302	.172
	8	.000	.000	.000	.004	.018	.060	.156	.302	.387
	9	.000	.000	.000	.000	.002	.010	.040	.134	.387
10	0	.349	.107	.028	.006	.001	.000	.000	.000	.000
	1	.387	.268	.121	.040	.010	.002	.000	.000	.000
	2	.194	.302	.233	.121	.044	.011	.001	.000	.000
	3	.057	.201	.267	.215	.117	.042	.009	.001	.000
	4	.011	.088	.200	.251	.205	.111	.037	.006	.000
	5	.001	.026	.103	.201	.246	.201	.103	.026	.001
	6	.000	.006	.037	.111	.205	.251	.200	.088	.011
	7	.000	.001	.009	.042	.117	.215	.267	.201	.057
	8	.000	.000	.001	.011	.044	.121	.233	.302	.194
	9	.000	.000	.000	.002	.010	.040	.121	.268	.387
	10	.000	.000	.000	.000	.001	.006	.028	.107	.349
11	0	.314	.086	.020	.004	.000	.000	.000	.000	.000
	1	.384	.236	.093	.027	.005	.001	.000	.000	.000
	2	.213	.295	.200	.089	.027	.005	.001	.000	.000
	3	.071	.221	.257	.177	.081	.023	.004	.000	.000
	4	.016	.111	.220	.236	.161	.070	.017	.002	.000
	5	.002	.039	.132	.221	.226	.147	.057	.010	.000
	6	.000	.010	.057	.147	.226	.221	.132	.039	.002
	7	.000	.002	.017	.070	.161	.236	.220	.111	.016
	8	.000	.000	.004	.023	.081	.177	.257	.221	.071
	9	.000	.000	.001	.005	.027	.089	.200	.295	.213
	10	.000	.000	.000	.001	.005	.027	.093	.236	.384
	11	.000	.000	.000	.000	.000	.004	.020	.086	.314
12	0	.282	.069	.014	.002	.000	.000	.000	.000	.000
	1	.377	.206	.071	.017	.003	.000	.000	.000	.000
	2	.230	.283	.168	.064	.016	.002	.000	.000	.000
	3	.085	.236	.240	.142	.054	.012	.001	.000	.000
	4	.021	.133	.231	.213	.121	.042	.008	.001	.000
	5	.004	.053	.158	.227	.193	.101	.029	.003	.000
	6	.000	.016	.079	.177	.226	.177	.079	.016	.000
	7	.000	.003	.029	.101	.193	.227	.158	.053	.004
	8	.000	.001	.008	.042	.121	.213	.231	.133	.021
	9	.000	.000	.001	.012	.054	.142	.240	.236	.085
	10	.000	.000	.000	.002	.016	.064	.168	.283	.230
	11	.000	.000	.000	.000	.003	.017	.071	.206	.377
	12	.000	.000	.000	.000	.000	.002	.014	.069	.282

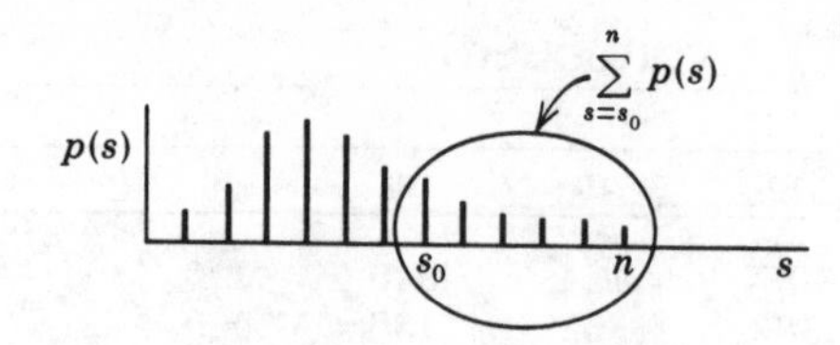

TABLE **III(c)** Cumulative Binomial Probability in Right-Hand Tail

n	s_0	π .10	.20	.30	.40	.50	.60	.70	.80	.90
2	1	.190	.360	.510	.640	.750	.840	.910	.960	.990
	2	.010	.040	.090	.160	.250	.360	.490	.640	.810
3	1	.271	.488	.657	.784	.875	.936	.973	.992	.999
	2	.028	.104	.216	.352	.500	.648	.784	.896	.972
	3	.001	.008	.027	.064	.125	.216	.343	.512	.729
4	1	.344	.590	.760	.870	.937	.974	.992	.998	1.000
	2	.052	.181	.348	.525	.687	.821	.916	.973	.996
	3	.004	.027	.084	.179	.312	.475	.652	.819	.948
	4	.000	.002	.008	.026	.062	.130	.240	.410	.656
5	1	.410	.672	.832	.922	.969	.990	.998	1.000	1.000
	2	.081	.263	.472	.663	.812	.913	.969	.993	1.000
	3	.009	.058	.163	.317	.500	.683	.837	.942	.991
	4	.000	.007	.031	.087	.187	.337	.528	.737	.919
	5	.000	.000	.002	.010	.031	.078	.168	.328	.590
6	1	.469	.738	.882	.953	.984	.996	.999	1.000	1.000
	2	.114	.345	.580	.767	.891	.959	.989	.998	1.000
	3	.016	.099	.256	.456	.656	.821	.930	.983	.999
	4	.001	.017	.070	.179	.344	.544	.744	.901	.984
	5	.000	.002	.011	.041	.109	.233	.420	.655	.886
	6	.000	.000	.001	.004	.016	.047	.118	.262	.531
7	1	.522	.790	.918	.972	.992	.998	1.000	1.000	1.000
	2	.150	.423	.671	.841	.937	.981	.996	1.000	1.000
	3	.026	.148	.353	.580	.773	.904	.971	.955	1.000
	4	.003	.033	.126	.290	.500	.710	.874	.967	.997
	5	.000	.005	.029	.096	.227	.420	.647	.852	.974
	6	.000	.000	.004	.019	.062	.159	.329	.577	.850
	7	.000	.000	.000	.002	.008	.028	.082	.210	.478
8	1	.570	.832	.942	.983	.996	.999	1.000	1.000	1.000
	2	.187	.497	.745	.894	.965	.991	.999	1.000	1.000
	3	.038	.203	.448	.685	.855	.950	.989	.999	1.000
	4	.005	.056	.194	.406	.637	.826	.942	.990	1.000
	5	.000	.010	.058	.174	.363	.594	.806	.944	.995
	6	.000	.001	.011	.050	.145	.315	.552	.797	.962
	7	.000	.000	.001	.009	.035	.106	.255	.503	.813
	8	.000	.000	.000	.001	.004	.017	.058	.168	.430

TABLE **III(c)** (continued)

n	s_0	π .10	.20	.30	.40	.50	.60	.70	.80	.90
9	1	.613	.866	.960	.990	.998	1.000	1.000	1.000	1.000
	2	.225	.564	.804	.929	.980	.996	1.000	1.000	1.000
	3	.053	.262	.537	.768	.910	.975	.996	1.000	1.000
	4	.008	.086	.270	.517	.746	.901	.975	.997	1.000
	5	.001	.020	.099	.267	.500	.733	.901	.980	.999
	6	.000	.003	.025	.099	.254	.483	.730	.914	.992
	7	.000	.000	.004	.025	.090	.232	.463	.738	.947
	8	.000	.000	.000	.004	.020	.071	.196	.436	.775
	9	.000	.000	.000	.000	.002	.010	.040	.134	.387
10	1	.651	.893	.972	.994	.999	1.000	1.000	1.000	1.000
	2	.264	.624	.851	.954	.989	.998	1.000	1.000	1.000
	3	.070	.322	.617	.833	.945	.988	.998	1.000	1.000
	4	.013	.121	.350	.618	.828	.945	.989	.999	1.000
	5	.002	.033	.150	.367	.623	.834	.953	.994	1.000
	6	.000	.006	.047	.166	.377	.633	.850	.967	.998
	7	.000	.001	.011	.055	.172	.382	.650	.879	.987
	8	.000	.000	.002	.012	.055	.167	.383	.678	.930
	9	.000	.000	.000	.002	.011	.046	.149	.376	.736
	10	.000	.000	.000	.000	.001	.006	.028	.107	.349
11	1	.686	.914	.980	.996	1.000	1.000	1.000	1.000	1.000
	2	.303	.678	.887	.970	.994	.999	1.000	1.000	1.000
	3	.090	.383	.687	.881	.967	.994	.999	1.000	1.000
	4	.019	.161	.430	.704	.887	.971	.996	1.000	1.000
	5	.003	.050	.210	.467	.726	.901	.978	.998	1.000
	6	.000	.012	.078	.247	.500	.753	.922	.988	1.000
	7	.000	.002	.022	.099	.274	.533	.790	.950	.997
	8	.000	.000	.004	.029	.113	.296	.570	.839	.981
	9	.000	.000	.001	.006	.033	.119	.313	.617	.910
	10	.000	.000	.000	.001	.006	.030	.113	.322	.697
	11	.000	.000	.000	.000	.000	.004	.020	.086	.314
12	1	.718	.931	.986	.998	1.000	1.000	1.000	1.000	1.000
	2	.341	.725	.915	.980	.997	1.000	1.000	1.000	1.000
	3	.111	.442	.747	.917	.981	.997	1.000	1.000	1.000
	4	.026	.205	.507	.775	.927	.985	.998	1.000	1.000
	5	.004	.073	.276	.562	.806	.943	.991	.999	1.000
	6	.001	.019	.118	.335	.613	.842	.961	.996	1.000
	7	.000	.004	.039	.158	.387	.665	.882	.981	.999
	8	.000	.001	.009	.057	.194	.438	.724	.927	.996
	9	.000	.000	.002	.015	.073	.225	.493	.795	.974
	10	.000	.000	.000	.003	.019	.083	.253	.558	.889
	11	.000	.000	.000	.000	.003	.020	.085	.275	.659
	12	.000	.000	.000	.000	.000	.002	.014	.069	.282

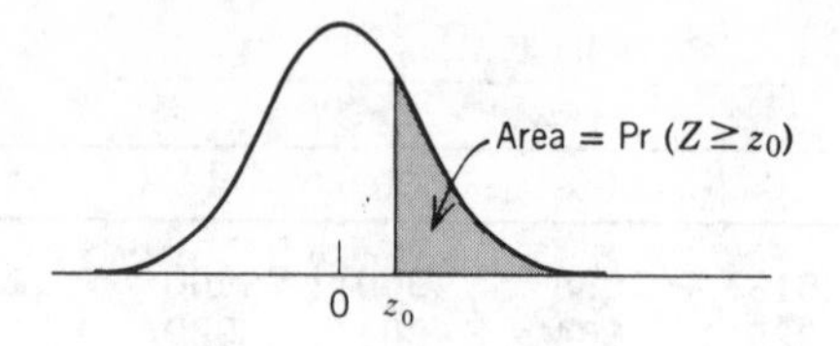

TABLE IV Standard Normal, Cumulative Probability in Right-Hand Tail (For Negative Values of z, Areas are Found by Symmetry)

Z_0	NEXT DECIMAL PLACE OF Z_0									
	0	1	2	3	4	5	6	7	8	9
0.0	.500	.496	.492	.488	.484	.480	.476	.472	.468	.464
0.1	.460	.456	.452	.448	.444	.440	.436	.433	.429	.425
0.2	.421	.417	.413	.409	.405	.401	.397	.394	.390	.386
0.3	.382	.378	.374	.371	.367	.363	.359	.356	.352	.348
0.4	.345	.341	.337	.334	.330	.326	.323	.319	.316	.312
0.5	.309	.305	.302	.298	.295	.291	.288	.284	.281	.278
0.6	.274	.271	.268	.264	.261	.258	.255	.251	.248	.245
0.7	.242	.239	.236	.233	.230	.227	.224	.221	.218	.215
0.8	.212	.209	.206	.203	.200	.198	.195	.192	.189	.187
0.9	.184	.181	.179	.176	.174	.171	.169	.166	.164	.161
1.0	.159	.156	.154	.152	.149	.147	.145	.142	.140	.138
1.1	.136	.133	.131	.129	.127	.125	.123	.121	.119	.117
1.2	.115	.113	.111	.109	.107	.106	.104	.102	.100	.099
1.3	.097	.095	.093	.092	.090	.089	.087	.085	.084	.082
1.4	.081	.079	.078	.076	.075	.074	.072	.071	.069	.068
1.5	.067	.066	.064	.063	.062	.061	.059	.058	.057	.056
1.6	.055	.054	.053	.052	.051	.049	.048	.047	.046	.046
1.7	.045	.044	.043	.042	.041	.040	.039	.038	.038	.037
1.8	.036	.035	.034	.034	.033	.032	.031	.031	.030	.029
1.9	.029	.028	.027	.027	.026	.026	.025	.024	.024	.023
2.0	.023	.022	.022	.021	.021	.020	.020	.019	.019	.018
2.1	.018	.017	.017	.017	.016	.016	.015	.015	.015	.014
2.2	.014	.014	.013	.013	.013	.012	.012	.012	.011	.011
2.3	.011	.010	.010	.010	.010	.009	.009	.009	.009	.008
2.4	.008	.008	.008	.008	.007	.007	.007	.007	.007	.006
2.5	.006	.006	.006	.006	.006	.005	.005	.005	.005	.005
2.6	.005	.005	.004	.004	.004	.004	.004	.004	.004	.004
2.7	.003	.003	.003	.003	.003	.003	.003	.003	.003	.003
2.8	.003	.002	.002	.002	.002	.002	.002	.002	.002	.002
2.9	.002	.002	.002	.002	.002	.002	.002	.001	.001	.001

Z_0	DETAIL OF TAIL ($._{2}135$, FOR EXAMPLE, MEANS .00135)									
2.	$._{1}228$	$._{1}179$	$._{1}139$	$._{1}107$	$._{2}820$	$._{2}621$	$._{2}466$	$._{2}347$	$._{2}256$	$._{2}187$
3.	$._{2}135$	$._{3}968$	$._{3}687$	$._{3}483$	$._{3}337$	$._{3}233$	$._{3}159$	$._{3}108$	$._{4}723$	$._{4}481$
4.	$._{4}317$	$._{4}207$	$._{4}133$	$._{5}854$	$._{5}541$	$._{5}340$	$._{5}211$	$._{5}130$	$._{6}793$	$._{6}479$
5.	$._{6}287$	$._{6}170$	$._{7}996$	$._{7}579$	$._{7}333$	$._{7}190$	$._{7}107$	$._{8}599$	$._{8}332$	$._{8}182$
	0	1	2	3	4	5	6	7	8	9

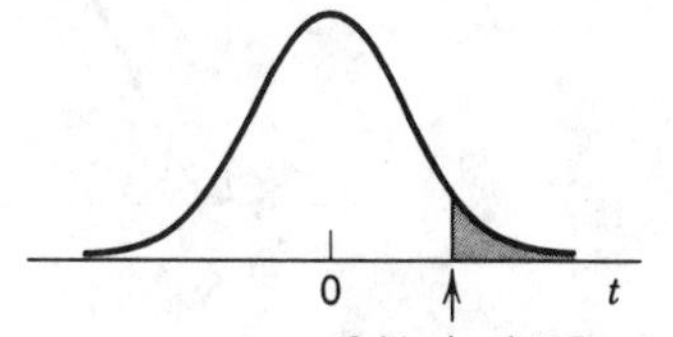

Critical point. For example: $t_{.025}$ leaves .025 probability in the tail.

TABLE V t Critical Points

d.f.	$t_{.25}$	$t_{.10}$	$t_{.05}$	$t_{.025}$	$t_{.010}$	$t_{.005}$	$t_{.0025}$	$t_{.0010}$	$t_{.0005}$
1	1.00	3.08	6.31	**12.7**	31.8	63.7	127	318	637
2	.82	1.89	2.92	**4.30**	6.96	9.92	14.1	22.3	31.6
3	.76	1.64	2.35	**3.18**	4.54	5.84	7.45	10.2	12.9
4	.74	1.53	2.13	**2.78**	3.75	4.60	5.60	7.17	8.61
5	.73	1.48	2.02	**2.57**	3.36	4.03	4.77	5.89	6.87
6	.72	1.44	1.94	**2.45**	3.14	3.71	4.32	5.21	5.96
7	.71	1.41	1.89	**2.36**	3.00	3.50	4.03	4.79	5.41
8	.71	1.40	1.86	**2.31**	2.90	3.36	3.83	4.50	5.04
9	.70	1.38	1.83	**2.26**	2.82	3.25	3.69	4.30	4.78
10	.70	1.37	1.81	**2.23**	2.76	3.17	3.58	4.14	4.59
11	.70	1.36	1.80	**2.20**	2.72	3.11	3.50	4.02	4.44
12	.70	1.36	1.78	**2.18**	2.68	3.05	3.43	3.93	4.32
13	.69	1.35	1.77	**2.16**	2.65	3.01	3.37	3.85	4.22
14	.69	1.35	1.76	**2.14**	2.62	2.98	3.33	3.79	4.14
15	.69	1.34	1.75	**2.13**	2.60	2.95	3.29	3.73	4.07
16	.69	1.34	1.75	**2.12**	2.58	2.92	3.25	3.69	4.01
17	.69	1.33	1.74	**2.11**	2.57	2.90	3.22	3.65	3.97
18	.69	1.33	1.73	**2.10**	2.55	2.88	3.20	3.61	3.92
19	.69	1.33	1.73	**2.09**	2.54	2.86	3.17	3.58	3.88
20	.69	1.33	1.72	**2.09**	2.53	2.85	3.15	3.55	3.85
21	.69	1.32	1.72	**2.08**	2.52	2.83	3.14	3.53	3.82
22	.69	1.32	1.72	**2.07**	2.51	2.82	3.12	3.50	3.79
23	.69	1.32	1.71	**2.07**	2.50	2.81	3.10	3.48	3.77
24	.68	1.32	1.71	**2.06**	2.49	2.80	3.09	3.47	3.75
25	.68	1.32	1.71	**2.06**	2.49	2.79	3.08	3.45	3.73
26	.68	1.31	1.71	**2.06**	2.48	2.78	3.07	3.43	3.71
27	.68	1.31	1.70	**2.05**	2.47	2.77	3.06	3.42	3.69
28	.68	1.31	1.70	**2.05**	2.47	2.76	3.05	3.41	3.67
29	.68	1.31	1.70	**2.05**	2.46	2.76	3.04	3.40	3.66
30	.68	1.31	1.70	**2.04**	2.46	2.75	3.03	3.39	3.65
40	.68	1.30	1.68	**2.02**	2.42	2.70	2.97	3.31	3.55
60	.68	1.30	1.67	**2.00**	2.39	2.66	2.92	3.23	3.46
120	.68	1.29	1.66	**1.98**	2.36	2.62	2.86	3.16	3.37
∞	**.67** $= z_{.25}$	**1.28** $= z_{.10}$	**1.64** $= z_{.05}$	**1.96** $= z_{.025}$	**2.33** $= z_{.010}$	**2.58** $= z_{.005}$	**2.81** $= z_{.0025}$	**3.09** $= z_{.0010}$	**3.29** $= z_{.0005}$

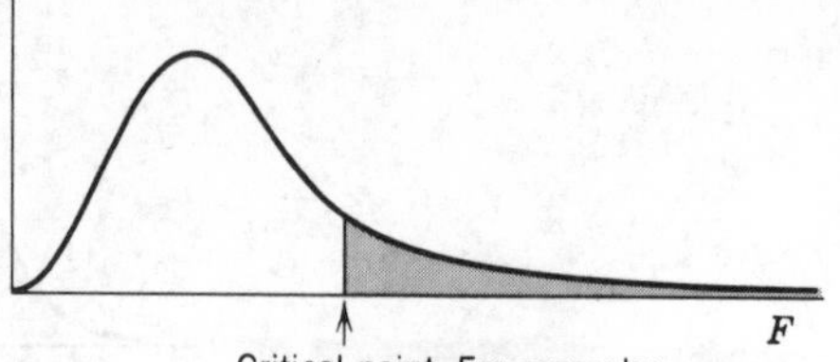

Critical point. For example: $F_{.05}$ leaves 5% probability in the tail.

TABLE VI *F* Critical Points

Degrees of freedom for denominator		Degrees of freedom for numerator: 1	2	3	4	5	6	8	10	20	40	∞
1	$F_{.25}$	5.83	7.50	8.20	8.58	8.82	8.98	9.19	9.32	9.58	9.71	9.85
	$F_{.10}$	39.9	49.5	53.6	55.8	57.2	58.2	59.4	60.2	61.7	62.5	63.3
	$F_{.05}$	161	200	216	225	230	234	239	242	248	251	254
2	$F_{.25}$	2.57	3.00	3.15	3.23	3.28	3.31	3.35	3.38	3.43	3.45	3.48
	$F_{.10}$	8.53	9.00	9.16	9.24	9.29	9.33	9.37	9.39	9.44	9.47	9.49
	$F_{.05}$	18.5	19.0	19.2	19.2	19.3	19.3	19.4	19.4	19.4	19.5	19.5
	$F_{.01}$	98.5	99.0	99.2	99.2	99.3	99.3	99.4	99.4	99.4	99.5	99.5
	$F_{.001}$	998	999	999	999	999	999	999	999	999	999	999
3	$F_{.25}$	2.02	2.28	2.36	2.39	2.41	2.42	2.44	2.44	2.46	2.47	2.47
	$F_{.10}$	5.54	5.46	5.39	5.34	5.31	5.28	5.25	5.23	5.18	5.16	5.13
	$F_{.05}$	10.1	9.55	9.28	9.12	9.10	8.94	8.85	8.79	8.66	8.59	8.53
	$F_{.01}$	34.1	30.8	29.5	28.7	28.2	27.9	27.5	27.2	26.7	26.4	26.1
	$F_{.001}$	167	149	141	137	135	133	131	129	126	125	124
4	$F_{.25}$	1.81	2.00	2.05	2.06	2.07	2.08	2.08	2.08	2.08	2.08	2.08
	$F_{.10}$	4.54	4.32	4.19	4.11	4.05	4.01	3.95	3.92	3.84	3.80	3.76
	$F_{.05}$	7.71	6.94	6.59	6.39	6.26	6.16	6.04	5.96	5.80	5.72	5.63
	$F_{.01}$	21.2	18.0	16.7	16.0	15.5	15.2	14.8	14.5	14.0	13.7	13.5
	$F_{.001}$	74.1	61.3	56.2	53.4	51.7	50.5	49.0	48.1	46.1	45.1	44.1
5	$F_{.25}$	1.69	1.85	1.88	1.89	1.89	1.89	1.89	1.89	1.88	1.88	1.87
	$F_{.10}$	4.06	3.78	3.62	3.52	3.45	3.40	3.34	3.30	3.21	3.16	3.10
	$F_{.05}$	6.61	5.79	5.41	5.19	5.05	4.95	4.82	4.74	4.56	4.46	4.36
	$F_{.01}$	16.3	13.3	12.1	11.4	11.0	10.7	10.3	10.1	9.55	9.29	9.02
	$F_{.001}$	47.2	37.1	33.2	31.1	29.8	28.8	27.6	26.9	25.4	24.6	23.8
6	$F_{.25}$	1.62	1.76	1.78	1.79	1.79	1.78	1.77	1.77	1.76	1.75	1.74
	$F_{.10}$	3.78	3.46	3.29	3.18	3.11	3.05	2.98	2.94	2.84	2.78	2.72
	$F_{.05}$	5.99	5.14	4.76	4.53	4.39	4.28	4.15	4.06	3.87	3.77	3.67
	$F_{.01}$	13.7	10.9	9.78	9.15	8.75	8.47	8.10	7.87	7.40	7.14	6.88
	$F_{.001}$	35.5	27.0	23.7	21.9	20.8	20.0	19.0	18.4	17.1	16.4	15.8
7	$F_{.25}$	1.57	1.70	1.72	1.72	1.71	1.71	1.70	1.69	1.67	1.66	1.65
	$F_{.10}$	3.59	3.26	3.07	2.96	2.88	2.83	2.75	2.70	2.59	2.54	2.47
	$F_{.05}$	5.59	4.74	4.35	4.12	3.97	3.87	3.73	3.64	3.44	3.34	3.23
	$F_{.01}$	12.2	9.55	8.45	7.85	7.46	7.19	6.84	6.62	6.16	5.91	5.65
	$F_{.001}$	29.3	21.7	18.8	17.2	16.2	15.5	14.6	14.1	12.9	12.3	11.7
8	$F_{.25}$	1.54	1.66	1.67	1.66	1.66	1.65	1.64	1.63	1.61	1.59	1.58
	$F_{.10}$	3.46	3.11	2.92	2.81	2.73	2.67	2.59	2.54	2.42	2.36	2.29
	$F_{.05}$	5.32	4.46	4.07	3.84	3.69	3.58	3.44	3.35	3.15	3.04	2.93
	$F_{.01}$	11.3	8.65	7.59	7.01	6.63	6.37	6.03	5.81	5.36	5.12	4.86
	$F_{.001}$	25.4	18.5	15.8	14.4	13.5	12.9	12.0	11.5	10.5	9.92	9.33
9	$F_{.25}$	1.51	1.62	1.63	1.63	1.62	1.61	1.60	1.59	1.56	1.55	1.53
	$F_{.10}$	3.36	3.01	2.81	2.69	2,61	2.55	2.47	2.42	2.30	2.23	2.16
	$F_{.05}$	5.12	4.26	3.86	3.63	3.48	3.37	3.23	3.14	2.94	2.83	2.71
	$F_{.01}$	10.6	8.02	6.99	6.42	6.06	5.80	5.47	5.26	4.81	4.57	4.31
	$F_{.001}$	22.9	16.4	13.9	12.6	11.7	11.1	10.4	9.89	8.90	8.37	7.81

DEGREES OF FREEDOM FOR DENOMINATOR		DEGREES OF FREEDOM FOR NUMERATOR										
		1	2	3	4	5	6	8	10	20	40	∞
10	$F_{.25}$	1.49	1.60	1.60	1.59	1.59	1.58	1.56	1.55	1.52	1.51	1.48
	$F_{.10}$	3.28	2.92	2.73	2.61	2.52	2.46	2.38	2.32	2.20	2.13	2.06
	$F_{.05}$	4.96	4.10	3.71	3.48	3.33	3.22	3.07	2.98	2.77	2.66	2.54
	$F_{.01}$	10.0	7.56	6.55	5.99	5.64	5.39	5.06	4.85	4.41	4.17	3.91
	$F_{.001}$	21.0	14.9	12.6	11.3	10.5	9.92	9.20	8.75	7.80	7.30	6.76
12	$F_{.25}$	1.56	1.56	1.56	1.55	1.54	1.53	1.51	1.50	1.47	1.45	1.42
	$F_{.10}$	3.18	2.81	2.61	2.48	2.39	2.33	2.24	2.19	2.06	1.99	1.90
	$F_{.05}$	4.75	3.89	3.49	3.26	3.11	3.00	2.85	2.75	2.54	2.43	2.30
	$F_{.01}$	9.33	6.93	5.95	5.41	5.06	4.82	4.50	4.30	3.86	3.62	3.36
	$F_{.001}$	18.6	13.0	10.8	9.63	8.89	8.38	7.71	7.29	6.40	5.93	5.42
14	$F_{.25}$	1.44	1.53	1.53	1.52	1.51	1.50	1.48	1.46	1.43	1.41	1.38
	$F_{.10}$	3.10	2.73	2.52	2.39	2.31	2.24	2.15	2.10	1.96	1.89	1.80
	$F_{.05}$	4.60	3.74	3.34	3.11	2.96	2.85	2.70	2.60	2.39	2.27	2.13
	$F_{.01}$	8.86	5.51	5.56	5.04	4.69	4.46	4.14	3.94	3.51	3.27	3.00
	$F_{.001}$	17.1	11.8	9.73	8.62	7.92	7.43	6.80	6.40	5.56	5.10	4.60
16	$F_{.25}$	1.42	1.51	1.51	1.50	1.48	1.48	1.46	1.45	1.40	1.37	1.34
	$F_{.10}$	3.05	2.67	2.46	2.33	2.24	2.18	2.09	2.03	1.89	1.81	1.72
	$F_{.05}$	4.49	3.63	3.24	3.01	2.85	2.74	2.59	2.49	2.28	2.15	2.01
	$F_{.01}$	8.53	6.23	5.29	4.77	4.44	4.20	3.89	3.69	3.26	3.02	2.75
	$F_{.001}$	16.1	11.0	9.00	7.94	7.27	6.81	6.19	5.81	4.99	4.54	4.06
20	$F_{.25}$	1.40	1.49	1.48	1.46	1.45	1.44	1.42	1.40	1.36	1.33	1.29
	$F_{.10}$	2.97	2.59	2.38	2.25	2.16	2.09	2.00	1.94	1.79	1.71	1.61
	$F_{.05}$	4.35	3.49	3.10	2.87	2.71	2.60	2.45	2.35	2.12	1.99	1.84
	$F_{.01}$	8.10	5.85	4.94	4.43	4.10	3.87	3.56	3.37	2.94	2.69	2.42
	$F_{.001}$	14.8	9.95	8.10	7.10	6.46	6.02	5.44	5.08	4.29	3.86	3.38
30	$F_{.25}$	1.38	1.45	1.44	1.42	1.41	1.39	1.37	1.35	1.30	1.27	1.23
	$F_{.10}$	2.88	2.49	2.28	2.14	2.05	1.98	1.88	1.82	1.67	1.57	1.46
	$F_{.05}$	4.17	3.32	2.92	2.69	2.53	2.42	2.27	2.16	1.93	1.79	1.62
	$F_{.01}$	7.56	5.39	4.51	4.02	3.70	3.47	3.17	2.98	2.55	2.30	2.01
	$F_{.001}$	13.3	8.77	7.05	6.12	5.53	5.12	4.58	4.24	3.49	3.07	2.59
40	$F_{.25}$	1.36	1.44	1.42	1.40	1.39	1.37	1.35	1.33	1.28	1.24	1.19
	$F_{.10}$	2.84	2.44	2.23	2.09	2.00	1.93	1.83	1.76	1.61	1.51	1.38
	$F_{.05}$	4.08	3.23	2.84	2.61	2.45	2.34	2.18	2.08	1.84	1.69	1.51
	$F_{.01}$	7.31	5.18	4.31	3.83	3.51	3.29	2.99	2.80	2.37	2.11	1.80
	$F_{.001}$	12.6	8.25	6.60	5.70	5.13	4.73	4.21	3.87	3.15	2.73	2.23
60	$F_{.25}$	1.35	1.42	1.41	1.38	1.37	1.35	1.32	1.30	1.25	1.21	1.15
	$F_{.10}$	2.79	2.39	2.18	2.04	1.95	1.87	1.77	1.71	1.54	1.44	1.29
	$F_{.05}$	4.00	3.15	2.76	2.53	2.37	2.25	2.10	1.99	1.75	1.59	1.39
	$F_{.01}$	7.08	4.98	4.13	3.65	3.34	3.12	2.82	2.63	2.20	1.94	1.60
	$F_{.001}$	12.0	7.76	6.17	5.31	4.76	4.37	3.87	3.54	2.83	2.41	1.89
120	$F_{.25}$	1.34	1.40	1.39	1.37	1.35	1.33	1.30	1.28	1.22	1.18	1.10
	$F_{.10}$	2.75	2.35	2.13	1.99	1.90	1.82	1.72	1.65	1.48	1.37	1.19
	$F_{.05}$	3.92	3.07	2.68	2.45	2.29	2.17	2.02	1.91	1.66	1.50	1.25
	$F_{.01}$	6.85	4.79	3.95	3.48	3.17	2.96	2.66	2.47	2.03	1.76	1.38
	$F_{.001}$	11.4	7.32	5.79	4.95	4.42	4.04	3.55	3.24	2.53	2.11	1.54
∞	$F_{.25}$	1.32	1.39	1.37	1.35	1.33	1.31	1.28	1.25	1.19	1.14	1.00
	$F_{.10}$	2.71	2.30	2.08	1.94	1.85	1.77	1.67	1.60	1.42	1.30	1.00
	$F_{.05}$	3.84	3.00	2.60	2.37	2.21	2.10	1.94	1.83	1.57	1.39	1.00
	$F_{.01}$	6.63	4.61	3.78	3.32	3.02	2.80	2.51	2.32	1.88	1.59	1.00
	$F_{.001}$	10.8	6.91	5.42	4.62	4.10	3.74	3.27	2.96	2.27	1.84	1.00

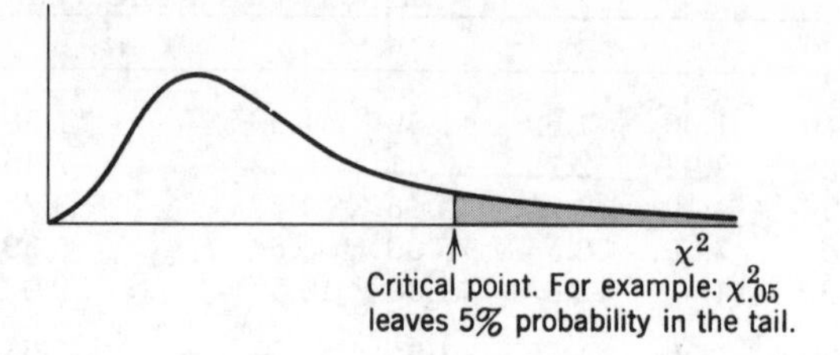

Critical point. For example: $\chi^2_{.05}$ leaves 5% probability in the tail.

TABLE VII χ^2 Critical Points

d.f.	$\chi^2_{.25}$	$\chi^2_{.10}$	$\chi^2_{.05}$	$\chi^2_{.025}$	$\chi^2_{.010}$	$\chi^2_{.005}$	$\chi^2_{.001}$
1	1.32	2.71	3.84	5.02	6.63	7.88	10.8
2	2.77	4.61	5.99	7.38	9.21	10.6	13.8
3	4.11	6.25	7.81	9.35	11.3	12.8	16.3
4	5.39	7.78	9.49	11.1	13.3	14.9	18.5
5	6.63	9.24	11.1	12.8	15.1	16.7	20.5
6	7.84	10.6	12.6	14.4	16.8	18.5	22.5
7	9.04	12.0	14.1	16.0	18.5	20.3	24.3
8	10.2	13.4	15.5	17.5	20.1	22.0	26.1
9	11.4	14.7	16.9	19.0	21.7	23.6	27.9
10	12.5	16.0	18.3	20.5	23.2	25.2	29.6
11	13.7	17.3	19.7	21.9	24.7	26.8	31.3
12	14.8	18.5	21.0	23.3	26.2	28.3	32.9
13	16.0	19.8	22.4	24.7	27.7	29.8	34.5
14	17.1	21.1	23.7	26.1	29.1	31.3	36.1
15	18.2	22.3	25.0	27.5	30.6	32.8	37.7
16	19.4	23.5	26.3	28.8	32.0	34.3	39.3
17	20.5	24.8	27.6	30.2	33.4	35.7	40.8
18	21.6	26.0	28.9	31.5	34.8	37.2	42.3
19	22.7	27.2	30.1	32.9	36.2	38.6	32.8
20	23.8	28.4	31.4	34.2	37.6	40.0	45.3
21	24.9	29.6	32.7	35.5	38.9	41.4	46.8
22	26.0	30.8	33.9	36.8	40.3	42.8	48.3
23	27.1	32.0	35.2	38.1	41.6	44.2	49.7
24	28.2	33.2	36.4	39.4	32.0	45.6	51.2
25	29.3	34.4	37.7	40.6	44.3	46.9	52.6
26	30.4	35.6	38.9	41.9	45.6	48.3	54.1
27	31.5	36.7	40.1	43.2	47.0	49.6	55.5
28	32.6	37.9	41.3	44.5	48.3	51.0	56.9
29	33.7	39.1	42.6	45.7	49.6	52.3	58.3
30	34.8	40.3	43.8	47.0	50.9	53.7	59.7
40	45.6	51.8	55.8	59.3	63.7	66.8	73.4
50	56.3	63.2	67.5	71.4	76.2	79.5	86.7
60	67.0	74.4	79.1	83.3	88.4	92.0	99.6
70	77.6	85.5	90.5	95.0	100	104	112
80	88.1	96.6	102	107	112	116	125
90	98.6	108	113	118	124	128	137
100	109	118	124	130	136	140	149

TABLE VIII Wilcoxon Rank Test (Two Independent Samples)

The one-sided p-value corresponding to the rank sum *W* of the smaller sample, ranking from the end where this smaller sample is concentrated. For $n_1 \geq 6$, see equation (16-10).

Smaller Sample Size $n_1 = 2$

W	$n_2 = 2$	3	4	5	6	7	8	9	10	11	12	13	14	15
3	.167	.100	.067	.048	.036	.028	.022	.018	.015	.013	.011	.010	.008	.007
4	.333	.200	.133	.095	.071	.056	.044	.036	.030	.026	.022	.019	.017	.015
5		.400	.267	.190	.143	.111	.089	.073	.061	.051	.044	.038	.033	.029
6			.400	.286	.214	.167	.133	.109	.091	.077	.066	.057	.050	.044
7				.429	.321	.250	.200	.164	.136	.115	.099	.086	.075	.066
8					.429	.333	.267	.218	.182	.154	.132	.114	.100	.088
9						.444	.356	.291	.242	.205	.176	.152	.133	.118
10							.444	.364	.303	.256	.220	.190	.167	.147
11								.455	.379	.321	.275	.238	.208	.184

Smaller Sample Size $n_1 = 3$

W	$n_2 = 3$	4	5	6	7	8	9	10	11	12	13	14	15
6	.050	.029	.018	.012	.008	.006	.005	.003	.003	.002	.002	.001	.001
7	.100	.057	.026	.024	.017	.012	.009	.007	.005	.004	.004	.003	.002
8	.200	.114	.071	.048	.033	.024	.018	.014	.011	.009	.007	.006	.005
9	.350	.200	.125	.083	.058	.042	.032	.024	.019	.015	.012	.010	.009
10	.500	.314	.196	.131	.092	.067	.050	.038	.030	.024	.020	.016	.013
11		.429	.286	.190	.133	.097	.073	.056	.044	.035	.029	.024	.020
12			.393	.274	.192	.139	.105	.080	.063	.051	.041	.034	.028
13			.500	.357	.258	.188	.141	.108	.085	.068	.055	.046	.038
14				.452	.333	.248	.186	.143	.113	.090	.073	.060	.050
15					.417	.315	.241	.185	.146	.116	.095	.078	.065
16					.500	.388	.300	.234	.184	.147	.120	.099	.082
17						.461	.364	.287	.228	.182	.148	.122	.102
18							.432	.346	.277	.224	.182	.150	.125
19							.500	.406	.330	.268	.220	.181	.151

Smaller Sample Size $n_1 = 4$

W	$n_2 = 4$	5	6	7	8	9	10
10	.014	.008	.005	.003	.002	.001	.001
11	.029	.016	.010	.006	.004	.003	.002
12	.057	.032	.019	.012	.008	.006	.004
13	.100	.056	.033	.021	.014	.010	.007
14	.171	.095	.057	.036	.024	.017	.012
15	.243	.143	.086	.055	.036	.025	.018
16	.343	.206	.129	.082	.055	.038	.027
17	.443	.278	.176	.115	.077	.053	.038
18		.365	.238	.158	.107	.074	.053
19		.452	.305	.206	.141	.099	.071
20			.381	.264	.184	.130	.094
21			.457	.324	.230	.165	.120
22				.394	.285	.207	.152
23				.464	.341	.252	.187
24					.404	.302	.227
25					.467	.355	.270
26						.413	.318
27						.470	.367

Smaller Sample Size $n_1 = 5$

W	$n_2 = 5$	6	7	8	9	10
15	.004	.002	.001	.001	.000	.000
16	.008	.004	.003	.002	.001	.001
17	.016	.009	.005	.003	.002	.001
18	.028	.015	.009	.005	.003	.002
19	.048	.026	.015	.009	.006	.004
20	.075	.041	.024	.015	.009	.006
21	.111	.063	.037	.023	.014	.010
22	.155	.089	.053	.033	.021	.014
23	.210	.123	.074	.047	.030	.020
24	.274	.165	.101	.064	.041	.028
25	.345	.214	.134	.085	.056	.038
26	.421	.268	.172	.111	.073	.050
27	.500	.331	.216	.142	.095	.065
28		.396	.265	.177	.120	.082
29		.465	.319	.218	.149	.103
30			.387	.262	.182	.127
31			.438	.311	.219	.155
32			.500	.362	.259	.185

TABLE IX Critical Points of the Durbin-Watson Test for Autocorrelation

This table gives two limiting values of critical D (D_L and D_U), corresponding to the two most extreme configurations of the regressors; thus, for every possible configuration, the critical value of D will be somewhere between D_L and D_U:

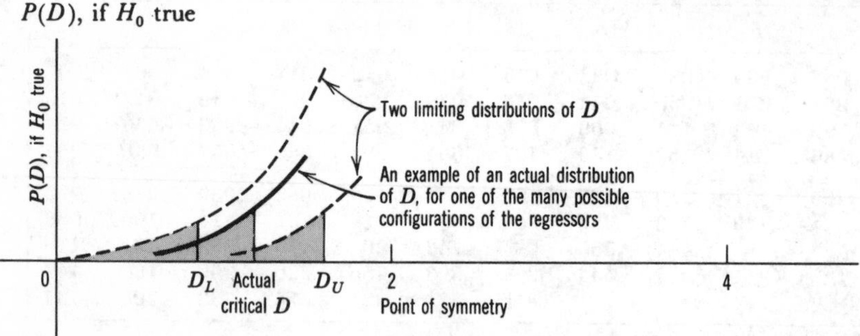

As an example of a test for positive serial correlation, suppose that there are $n = 15$ observations and $k = 3$ regressors (excluding the constant) and we wish to test $\rho = 0$ versus $\rho > 0$ at the level $\alpha = .05$. Then if D falls below $D_L = .82$, reject H_0. If D falls above $D_U = 1.75$, do not reject H_0. If D falls between D_L and D_U, this test is indecisive.

To test for negative serial correlation ($\rho = 0$ versus $\rho < 0$), the right-hand tail of the distribution defines the critical region. The symmetry of the distribution permits us to calculate these values very easily. With the same sample size, number of regressors, and level α as before, our new critical values would be $4 - D_L = 4 - .82 = 3.18$, and $4 - D_U = 4 - 1.75 = 2.25$. Accordingly, if D falls beyond 3.18, reject H_0. If D falls short of 2.25, do not reject H_0. If D falls between 2.25 and 3.18, this test is indecisive.

SAMPLE SIZE = n	PROBABILITY IN LOWER TAIL (LEVEL, α)	k = NUMBER OF REGRESSORS (EXCLUDING THE CONSTANT) 1		2		3		4		5	
		D_L	D_U	D_L	D_U	D_L	D_U	D_L	D_U	D_L	D_U
15	.01	.81	1.07	.70	1.25	.59	1.46	.49	1.70	.39	1.96
	.025	.95	1.23	.83	1.40	.71	1.61	.59	1.84	.48	2.09
	.05	1.08	1.36	.95	1.54	.82	1.75	.69	1.97	.56	2.21
20	.01	.95	1.15	.86	1.27	.77	1.41	.68	1.57	.60	1.74
	.025	1.08	1.28	.99	1.41	.89	1.55	.79	1.70	.70	1.87
	.05	1.20	1.41	1.10	1.54	1.00	1.68	.90	1.83	.79	1.99
30	.01	1.13	1.26	1.07	1.34	1.01	1.42	.94	1.51	.88	1.61
	.025	1.25	1.38	1.18	1.46	1.12	1.54	1.05	1.63	.98	1.73
	.05	1.35	1.49	1.28	1.57	1.21	1.65	1.14	1.74	1.07	1.83
40	.01	1.25	1.34	1.20	1.40	1.15	1.46	1.10	1.52	1.05	1.58
	.025	1.35	1.45	1.30	1.51	1.25	1.57	1.20	1.63	1.15	1.69
	.05	1.44	1.54	1.39	1.60	1.34	1.66	1.29	1.72	1.23	1.79
60	.01	1.38	1.45	1.35	1.48	1.32	1.52	1.28	1.56	1.25	1.60
	.025	1.47	1.54	1.44	1.57	1.40	1.61	1.37	1.65	1.33	1.69
	.05	1.55	1.62	1.51	1.65	1.48	1.69	1.44	1.73	1.41	1.77
80	.01	1.47	1.52	1.44	1.54	1.42	1.57	1.39	1.60	1.36	1.62
	.025	1.54	1.59	1.52	1.62	1.49	1.65	1.47	1.67	1.44	1.70
	.05	1.61	1.66	1.59	1.69	1.56	1.72	1.53	1.74	1.51	1.77
100	.01	1.52	1.56	1.50	1.58	1.48	1.60	1.46	1.63	1.44	1.65
	.025	1.59	1.63	1.57	1.65	1.55	1.67	1.53	1.70	1.51	1.72
	.05	1.65	1.69	1.63	1.72	1.61	1.74	1.59	1.76	1.57	1.78

REFERENCES

Anderson, T. W. (1958), *An Introduction to Multivariate Analysis*. New York: Wiley.

Anderson, T. W., and S. L. Sclove (1978), *Statistical Analysis of Data*. Boston: Houghton-Mifflin.

Anscombe, F. J. (1973), "Graphs in Statistical Analysis," *American Statistician*, 27, pp. 17–21.

Arkes, H. R., and K. R. Hammond (1986) (eds.), *Judgment and Decision Making: An Interdisciplinary Reader*. Cambridge: Cambridge University Press.

Bailey, Martin (1980), *Reducing Risks to Life*. Washington: American Enterprise Institute.

Balakrishnan, T. R., K. V. Rao, E. Lapierre-Adamcyk, K. J. Krotki (1987), "A Hazard Model Analysis of Marriage Dissolution in Canada," *Demography* 24, No. 3, pp. 395–406.

Berger, James O. (1985), *Statistical Decision Theory and Bayesian Analysis, 2nd ed*. New York: Springer-Verlag.

Bickel, P. J., and J. W. O'Connell (1975), "Sex Bias in Graduate Admissions: Data from Berkeley," *Science* 187, February, pp. 398–404.

Blau, P. M., and O. D. Duncan (1967), *The American Occupational Structure*. New York: Wiley.

Bostwick, Burdette E. (1977), *Finding the Job You've Always Wanted*. New York: Wiley.

Box, G. E. P., W. G. Hunter, and J. S. Hunter (1978), *Statistics for Experimenters*. New York: Wiley.

Box, G. E. P. and G. M. Jenkins (1970), *Time Series Analysis: Forecasting and Control*. San Francisco: Holden-Day.

Box, G. E. P., and G. C. Tiao (1973), *Bayesian Inference in Statistical Analysis*. Reading, MA: Addison-Wesley.

Brownlee, K. A. (1965), *Statistical Theory and Methodology in Science and Engineering*. New York: Wiley.

Campbell, S. K. (1974), "Flaws and Fallacies in Statistical Thinking." Englewood Cliffs, NJ: Prentice-Hall.

Choldin, H. M. (1978), "Urban Density and Pathology," *Annual Review of Sociology*, Vol. 4, pp. 91–113.

Choldin, H. M., and D. W. Roncik (1976), "Density Population Potential and Pathology," *Review of Public Data Use*, July, pp. 19–30.

Cleveland, W. S. (1985), *The Elements of Graphing Data*. Monterey, CA: Wadsworth.

Clopper, C. J., and E. S. Pearson (1934), "The Use of Confidence or Fiducial Limits Illustrated in the Case of the Binomial," *Biometrika* 26, p. 404.

Colton, T., and R. C. Buxbaum (1977), "Motor Vehicle Inspection and Motor Vehicle Accident Mortality," in Fairley and Mosteller (1977), pp. 131–142.

Conner, J. R., K. C. Gibbs, and J. E. Reynolds (1973), "The Effects of Water Frontage on Recreational Property Values," *Journal of Leisure Research* 5, pp. 26–38.

Conover, W. J. (1980), *Practical Nonparametric Statistics*, 2nd ed. New York: Wiley.

Consumer Reports (1976), "Is Vitamin C Really Good for Colds?" *Consumer Reports*, February 1976, Vol. 41, No. 2, pp. 68–70.

Cramer, H. (1946), *Mathematical Models of Statistics*. Princeton, NJ: Princeton University Press.

Crichton, Michael (1968), *A Case of Need.* New York: Signet.

Daniel, Cuthbert, and F. S. Wood (1971), *Fitting Equations to Data.* New York: Wiley.

Dean, Joel (1941), "Statistical Cost Functions of a Hosiery Mill," *Journal of Business.*

Denby, L., and D. Pregibon (1987), "An Example of the Use of Graphics in Regression," *American Statistician* 41, pp. 33–38.

Fadeley, R. C. (1965), "Oregon Malignancy Pattern Physiographically Related to Hanford, Washington, Radioisotopic Storage," *Journal of Environmental Health* 27, pp. 883–897.

Fairley, W. B., and F. Mosteller (eds.) (1977), *Statistics and Public Policy.* Reading, MA: Addison-Wesley.

Fisher, F. M. (1980), "Multiple Regression in Legal Proceedings," *Columbia Law Review* 80, pp. 702–736.

Freedman, David A. (1986), "A Case Study in Nonresponse: Plaintiff vs California State Board of Equalization," *Journal of Business and Economics* 4, pp. 123–124.

Freedman, D., R. Pisani, and R. Purvis (1978), *Statistics.* New York: Norton.

Freedman, J. L. (1975), *Crowding and Behavior.* New York: Viking Press.

Gallup, George H. (1976), "What Mankind Thinks About Itself," *Reader's Digest,* October 1976, pp. 25–31.

Gandz, Jeffrey (1985), *Perfect International Inc.,* Case #9-85-C038, University of Western Ontario Business School, London, Canada.

Gilbert, J. P., B. McPeek, and F. Mosteller (1977), "Statistics and Ethics in Surgery and Anesthesia," *Science* (18 November), pp. 684–689.

Glick, N. (1970), "Hijacking Planes to Cuba: An Updated Version of the Birthday Problem," *American Statistician,* February, pp. 41–44.

Gourou, Pierre (1966), *The Tropical World, Its Social and Economic Conditions and Its Future Status.* New York: Wiley.

Haupt, A., and T. T. Kane (1978), *Population Handbook.* Washington, DC: Population Reference Bureau.

Hooker, R. H. (1907), "The Correlation of the Weather and Crops," *Journal of the Royal Statistical Society* 70, pp. 1–42.

Howard, R. A. (1972), "The Decision to Seed Hurricanes," *Science* 176, June.

Huff, Darrell (1954), *How to Lie with Statistics.* New York: Norton (paperback).

Huff, Darrell (1957), *How to Take a Chance.* New York: Norton (paperback).

Jones, K. L., D. W. Smith, A. P. Streissgrath, and N. C. Myrianthopoulos (1974), "Outcome in Offspring of Chronic Alcoholic Women," *Lancet* (1 June), pp. 1076–1078.

Katz, D. A. (1973), "Faculty Salaries, Promotions, and Productivity at a Large University," *American Economic Review* 63, pp. 469–477.

Kendall, M. G., and C. A. O'Muircheartaigh (1977), *Path Analysis and Model Building* (Tech. Bulletin 414), World Fertility Survey.

Kennel, J. H., D. K. Voos, and M. H. Klaus (1979), "Parent–Infant Bonding," Chapter 23 in J. Oxofsky, *Handbook of Infant Development.* New York: Wiley.

Klaus, M. H., R. Jerauld, N. C. Kreger, W. McAlpine, M. Steffa, and J. H. Kennel (1972), "Maternal Attachment," *New England Journal of Medicine,* 2 March.

Kotz, S., N. L. Johnson, and C. B. Read (eds.) (1982–88), *Encyclopedia of Statistical Sciences,* Vols. 1–9, New York: Wiley.

Langbein, L. I. (1980), *Discovering Whether Programs Work*. Santa Monica, CA: Goodyear.

Lave, L. B., and E. P. Seskin (1977), "Does Air Pollution Shorten Lives?" in Fairley and Mosteller (1977), pp. 143–160.

Lefcoe, N. M., and T. H. Wonnacott, "The Prevalence of Chronic Respiratory Disease in Four Occupational Groups," *Archives of Environmental Health* 29, September, pp. 143–146.

Light, R. J., and Pillemer, D. B. (1984), *Summing Up: The Science of Reviewing Research*. Cambridge: Harvard University Press.

Lindgren, B. W. (1976), *Statistical Theory*. New York: MacMillan.

Lindley, D. V. (1982), *Bayesian Inference*, in *Encyclopedia of Statistical Sciences*, edited by N. L. Johnson and S. Kotz, Vol. 1, pp. 197–204. New York: Wiley.

Marey, E. J. (1885), *La Methode Graphique*. Paris.

McLeod, A. I. (1982), personal communication.

McNeil, B. J., R. Weichselbaum, and S. G. Pauker (1978), "Fallacy of the Five Year Survival in Lung Cancer," *New England Journal of Medicine* 229, December, pp. 1397–1401.

Medical Research Council (1948), "Streptomycin Treatment of Pulmonary Tuberculosis," *British Medical Journal*, Vol. 2, p. 769.

Meier, Paul (1978), "The Biggest Public Health Experiment Ever: The 1954 Field Trial of the Salk Poliomyelitis Vaccine," in Tanur and others (1978), pp. 3–15.

Miksch, W. F. (1950), "The Average Statistician," *Colliers* (17 June), pp.

Moody, (1975), *Moody's Transportation Manual*.

Moore, David S. (1979), *Statistics: Concepts and Controversies*. San Francisco: Freeman.

Mosteller, F., and J. W. Tukey (1977), *Data Analysis and Regression: A Second Course in Statistics*. Reading, MA: Addison-Wesley.

Neter, John (1978), "How Accountants Save Money by Sampling," in Tanur and others (1978), pp. 249–258.

Ng, Y-K. (1975), *Welfare Economics*. London: MacMillan.

Peacock, E. E. (1972), quoted in *Medical World News*, September 1, 1972, p. 45.

Pearson, E. S. and N. W. Please (1975), "Relation between the Shape of Population Distribution and the Robustness of Four Simple Test Statistics," *Biometrika* 62, pp. 223–241.

Pindyck, R. S., and D. L. Rubinfeld (1976), *Econometric Models and Economic Forecasts*. New York: McGraw-Hill.

Raiffa, H. (1968), *Decision Analysis*. Reading MA: Addison-Wesley.

Raiffa, H. (1982), *The Art and Science of Negotiation*. Cambridge, MA: Belknap/Harvard.

Roberts, H. V. (1974), *Conversational Statistics*. Palo Alto, CA: Scientific Press.

Rosenzweig, M., E. L. Bennett, and M. C. Diamond (1964), "Brain Changes in Response to Experience," *Scientific American* (February), pp. 22–29.

Ryan, T. A., B. L. Joiner, and B. F. Ryan (1985), *Minitab Handbook, 2nd ed.* North Scituate, MA: Duxbury Press.

Saks, M. J., and R. F. Kidd (1986), "Human Information Processing and Adjudication: Trial by Heuristics," in *Judgment and Decision Making: An Interdisciplinary Reader*, edited by H. R. Arkes and K. R. Hammond, pp. 213–242. Cambridge: Cambridge University Press.

Schunk, G. J., and W. L. Lehman (1954), "Mongolism and Congenital Leukemia," *Journal of the American Medical Society* (May).

Schwarz, H. (1978), "The Use of Subjective Probability Methods in Estimating Demand," in Tanur and others (1978), pp. 259–267.

Simon, J. L. (1981), *The Ultimate Resource*. Princeton, NJ: Princeton University Press.

Simon, J. L. (1986), *Theory of Population and Economic Growth*. Oxford: Basil Blackwell Ltd.

Slonim, M. J. (1966), *Sampling in a Nutshell*. New York: Simon and Shuster (paperback).

Snecedor, G. W., and W. G. Cochran (1967), *Statistical Methods*, 6th ed. Ames, IA: Iowa State University Press.

Sprent, P. (1988), *Taking Risks: The Science of Uncertainty*. London: Penguin.

Statistical Abstract of the United States: 1987. See U. S. Bureau of the Census (1986).

Tanur, J. M., F. Mosteller, W. H. Kruskal, R. F. Link, R. S. Pieters, G. R. Rising, and E. L. Lehman (eds.) (1978), *Statistics: A Guide to the Unknown, 2nd ed.* San Francisco: Holden-Day.

Tufte, E. R. (1974), *Data Analysis for Politics and Policy*. Englewood Cliffs, NJ: Prentice-Hall.

Tufte, E. R. (1983), *The Visual Display of Quantitative Information*. Cheshire, CN: Graphics Press.

Tukey, J. W. (1977), *Exploratory Data Analysis*. Reading, MA: Addison-Wesley.

Tversky, A., and D. Kahneman (1974), "Judgment Under Uncertainty: Heuristics and Biases," *Science*, 185, pp. 1124–1131.

U. S. Bureau of the Census (1986), *Statistical Abstract of the United States: 1987* (107th edition). Washington, DC: U. S. Government Printing Office.

U. S. Department of Transportation (1981), National Highway Traffic Safety Administration, *National Accident Sampling System Report on Traffic Accidents and Injuries for 1979*. Washington, DC: U. S. Government Printing Office.

U. S. Surgeon-General (1979), *Smoking and Health, a Report of the Surgeon-General*. U. S. Department of Health, Education, and Welfare. Washington, DC: U. S. Government Printing Office.

Van de Geer, J. P. (1971), *Introduction to Multivariate Analysis for the Social Sciences*. San Francisco: Freeman.

Wainer, H. (1984), "How to Display Data Badly," *American Statistician* 31, pp. 137–147.

Wallis, W. A., and H. V. Roberts (1956), *Statistics: A New Approach*. New York: Free Press. Abbreviated paperback appears as *The Nature of Statistics* (1962).

Wonnacott, Paul (1984), *Macroeconomics*, 3rd ed. Homewood, Ill: Irwin.

Wonnacott, P., and R. J. Wonnacott (1986), *Economics*, 3rd ed. New York: McGraw-Hill.

Wonnacott, T. H., and R. J. Wonnacott (1977), *Introductory Statistics for Business and Economics, 2nd ed.* New York: Wiley.

Wonnacott, T. H., and R. J. Wonnacott (1981), *Regression: A Second Course in Statistics*. New York: Wiley.

Zeisel, H., and H. Kalven (1978), "Parking Tickets and Missing Women: Statistics and the Law," in Tanur and others (1978), pp. 139–149.

ANSWERS TO ODD-NUMBERED PROBLEMS

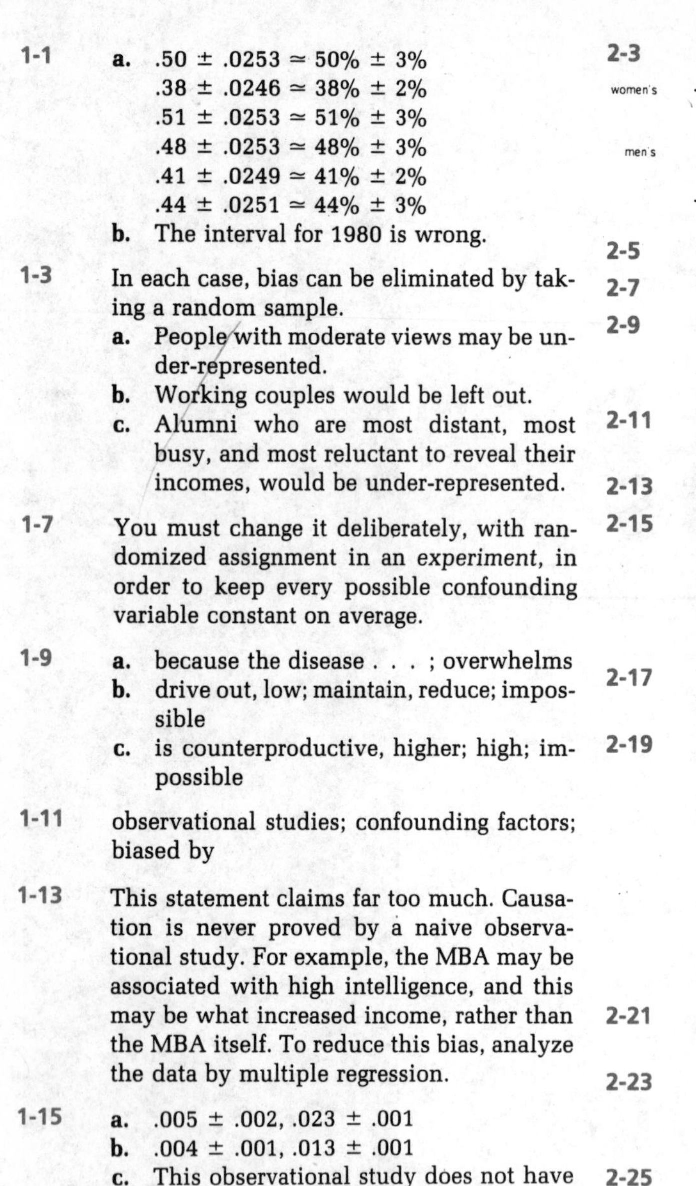

1-1
- **a.** $.50 \pm .0253 \simeq 50\% \pm 3\%$
  $.38 \pm .0246 \simeq 38\% \pm 2\%$
  $.51 \pm .0253 \simeq 51\% \pm 3\%$
  $.48 \pm .0253 \simeq 48\% \pm 3\%$
  $.41 \pm .0249 \simeq 41\% \pm 2\%$
  $.44 \pm .0251 \simeq 44\% \pm 3\%$
- **b.** The interval for 1980 is wrong.

1-3 In each case, bias can be eliminated by taking a random sample.
- **a.** People with moderate views may be under-represented.
- **b.** Working couples would be left out.
- **c.** Alumni who are most distant, most busy, and most reluctant to reveal their incomes, would be under-represented.

1-7 You must change it deliberately, with randomized assignment in an *experiment*, in order to keep every possible confounding variable constant on average.

1-9
- **a.** because the disease . . . ; overwhelms
- **b.** drive out, low; maintain, reduce; impossible
- **c.** is counterproductive, higher; high; impossible

1-11 observational studies; confounding factors; biased by

1-13 This statement claims far too much. Causation is never proved by a naive observational study. For example, the MBA may be associated with high intelligence, and this may be what increased income, rather than the MBA itself. To reduce this bias, analyze the data by multiple regression.

1-15
- **a.** $.005 \pm .002$, $.023 \pm .001$
- **b.** $.004 \pm .001$, $.013 \pm .001$
- **c.** This observational study does not have any obvious biases (like problem 1-13, for example). So it suggests (although it cannot prove) that seatbelts reduce the chance of injury.

1-17
- **a.** $66.8\% \pm 0.3\%$ **c.** No
- **b.** $6.1\% \pm 0.2\%$

2-1
- **a.** She was obligingly reporting everything over 65—the maximum acceptable hardness—as 65 or less.
- **b.** The outlier on the extreme right.

2-3

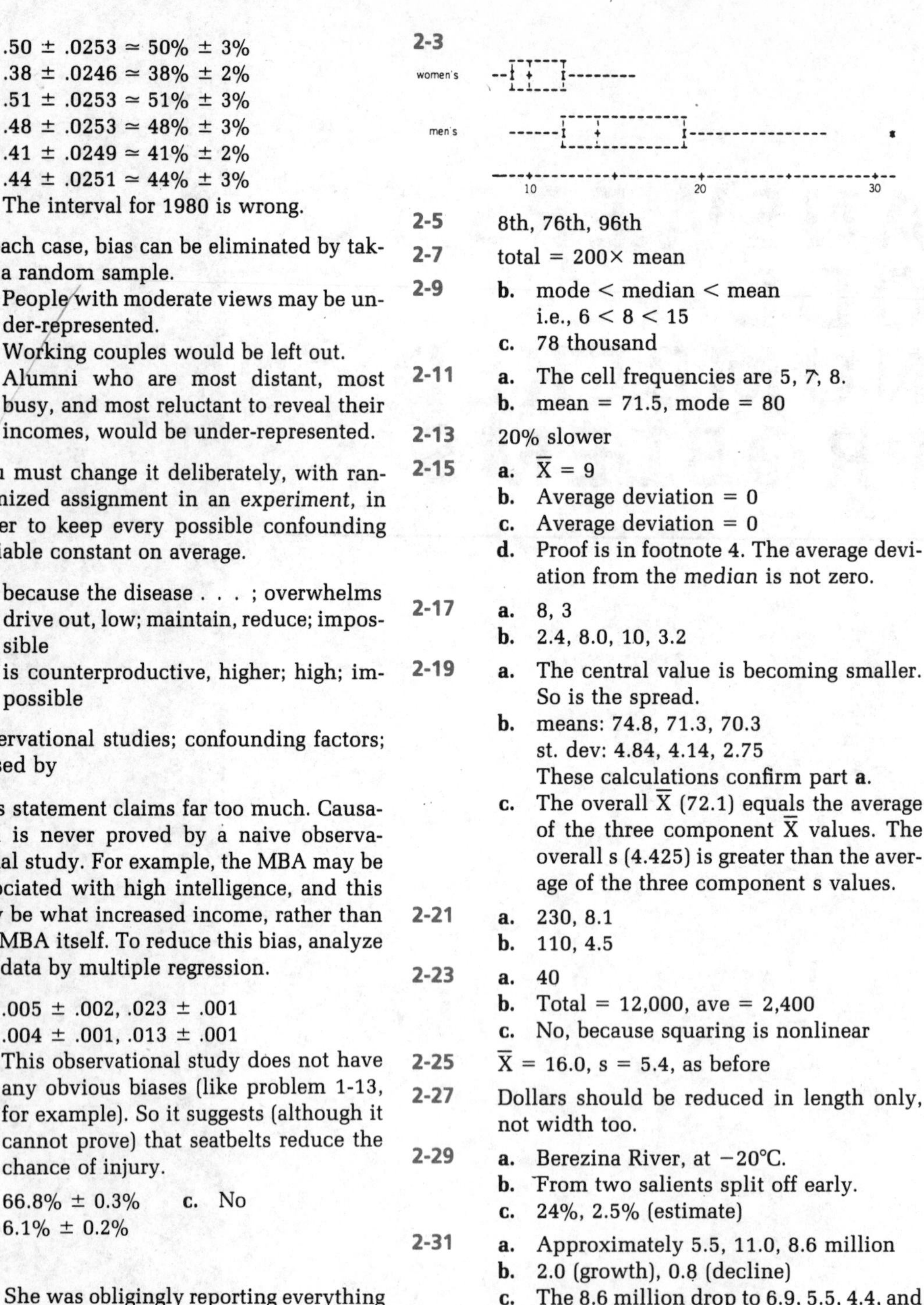

2-5 8th, 76th, 96th

2-7 total = 200× mean

2-9
- **b.** mode < median < mean
  i.e., $6 < 8 < 15$
- **c.** 78 thousand

2-11
- **a.** The cell frequencies are 5, 7, 8.
- **b.** mean = 71.5, mode = 80

2-13 20% slower

2-15
- **a.** $\overline{X} = 9$
- **b.** Average deviation = 0
- **c.** Average deviation = 0
- **d.** Proof is in footnote 4. The average deviation from the *median* is not zero.

2-17
- **a.** 8, 3
- **b.** 2.4, 8.0, 10, 3.2

2-19
- **a.** The central value is becoming smaller. So is the spread.
- **b.** means: 74.8, 71.3, 70.3
  st. dev: 4.84, 4.14, 2.75
  These calculations confirm part **a**.
- **c.** The overall $\overline{X}$ (72.1) equals the average of the three component $\overline{X}$ values. The overall s (4.425) is greater than the average of the three component s values.

2-21
- **a.** 230, 8.1
- **b.** 110, 4.5

2-23
- **a.** 40
- **b.** Total = 12,000, ave = 2,400
- **c.** No, because squaring is nonlinear

2-25 $\overline{X} = 16.0$, $s = 5.4$, as before

2-27 Dollars should be reduced in length only, not width too.

2-29
- **a.** Berezina River, at −20°C.
- **b.** From two salients split off early.
- **c.** 24%, 2.5% (estimate)

2-31
- **a.** Approximately 5.5, 11.0, 8.6 million
- **b.** 2.0 (growth), 0.8 (decline)
- **c.** The 8.6 million drop to 6.9, 5.5, 4.4, and finally 3.5 after four generations.
- **d.** More useful to suggest what will happen *if* present trends continue.

2-33 One possible answer: $34\frac{4}{16}$, $2.65/16 \simeq 3/16$.

2-35 a. $7.75
b. $7.27
c. Dollar-cost average is always lower.
d. 20 shares per quarter, to now get the *higher* price on average.

2-37 a. approximately 3.0
b. 4.44
c. approximately 4.0
d. 60th to 65th percentile

2-39 a. 44.2, 35.6
b. 2210 thousand mi^2

2-41 a. 47 b. 104

3-1 a. long-run relative frequency
b. throw it many times
c. select the last few December days for the past 10 years, for example
d. .07

3-3 a. .50 (by symmetry)
b. relative frequency
c. relative frequency; or by reasoning from the symmetry of the dice, $8/36 = 22\%$

3-5 a. $.48 = 48\%$
b. $.432 \simeq 43\%$

3-7 a. $.255 \simeq 25\%$
b. $.091 \simeq 9\%$

3-9 a. .96 b. .74

3-11 a. .999
b. .998

3-13 a. .52 b. .17
c. .40 d. .33
e. .77

3-15 a. 7.2% b. 7.0%
c. 7.5%

3-17 a. .875 b. .50
c. .57 d. .75

3-19 Absurd, of course. The conditional probability of another passenger carrying on a live bomb is one in a million, no matter what he himself carries on with him.

3-21 a. 26% b. 26%
c. yes

3-23 a. 7.2% b. 13.6%
c. no

3-25 5.6%

3-27 a. .25 b. .57

3-29 a. 50% b. 23%
c. 38%
d. The chance first goes down and then goes up again, of course.

3-33 all valid

3-35 a. .06 b. .12
c. .68

3-37 a. 11.2% b. 43%

3-39 a. .18 b. .62
c. .38 d. .36
e. .24 f. True

3-41 a. 3.8% b. 12%

3-43 a. $\frac{365}{365} \times \frac{364}{365} \times \frac{363}{365} \simeq .992$

b. $\frac{365}{365} \times \frac{364}{365} \times \frac{363}{365} \times \cdots \times \frac{336}{365} \simeq .294$

c. $1 - .294 = .706$

d. We ignored Feb. 29, assumed all days are equally likely, and assumed no twins.

3-45 a. True b. True
c. False. *A* and *B* are *independent* . . .
d. False. . . . will be ½.

4-1

a.

x	p(x)
0	1/8
1	3/8
2	3/8
3	1/8

b.

y	p(y)
1	2/8
2	4/8
3	2/8

4-3

a.

x	p(x)
0	1/8
1	3/8
2	3/8
3	1/8

b. 1.50
c. .75

4-5

a.

x	p(x)
0	.072
1	.104
2	.176
3	.648

b. .824

4-7 a. 62.0, 9.5

b. 80%, 20%
c. 70

4-9 If he doesn't mind taking risks, he should not cancel. This would minimize his expected loss at $24,500.

4-11 .44

4-13 **a.** 3.00, 1.22
b. 2.40, 1.39

4-15 **a.** .121
b. Shots have a constant probability of success.
c. Revise it upwards.

4-17 **a.** .125 **b.** 10

4-19 **a.** .055 **b.** .044
c. .949 **d.** .103
e. .475 **f.** .950
g. .682 **h.** .006

4-21 **a.** .045 **b.** .212

4-23 **a.** .773 **b.** .773
c. Assume I am a driver drawn at random; and that all four tires, sharing the same conditions, wear out at the same time.
More realistically, front tires generally wear out sooner, so the chance of all 4 tires lasting 50,000 miles is *less* than .773.

4-25 **a.** 37.0 **b.** 8.4
c. 28.6

4-27 **a.** 2.4 **b.** $36
c. .767, .233

4-29 **a, b, e** are true, because they have linear transformations.

4-31 **a.** First, what's it worth to *you* (V)?
b. $4800 **c.** $4400

4-33 **b.** Yes, it is a parabola, because it is the product of two linear factors.
c. True, so long as $(L + V)/2 < H$

4-35 **a.** 60% **b.** 65%
c. 73%

4-37 **a.** mean = 1.90 (or slightly more)
median = 2, mode = 2, st. dev. = 1.29
For growth, the mean is needed.

4-39 **a.** 71% **b.** $.99^7 = 93\%$
c. 4.20, 1.30

4-41 .9999

4-43 **a.** .035
b. Yes, we would question the hypothesis of "no effect."

4-45 **a.** **i** No, his revenue averages only $687/week.
ii No, he is even less help now.
b. $88/week (86.72 is better)

5-1 **a.** .07, table similar
b. p(x) = .08, .19, .54, .19
p(y) = .29, .37, .34
c. No, they are dependent.
d. $\mu_X = 1.84, \sigma_X = .82$

5-3 Yes, it agrees of course.

5-5

x	1	2	3
p(x|Y = 1)	.17	.66	.17

Since this conditional distribution does not equal the unconditional (marginal) distribution, X and Y are not independent.

5-7 **b.**

x	p(x)
0	.008
1	.096
2	.384
3	.512

y	p(y)
0	.008
100	.064
200	.160
300	.256
400	.512

And p(x) is the same as in Problem 4-4, of course.
c. 2.40, $320
d. no

5-9 **a.** 16.17 **b.** 6.6
c. 6145 **d.** 1.288, 23.3, no

5-11 **a.** 2.33, .56, .75
b. 1.83, .81, .90
c. 4.17, 1.36, 1.17
d. Means and variances do add. But standard deviations do not.

5-13 **a.** For part **c**, $\rho = 0$, and X and Y are independent.
For part **d**, $\rho = 0$, yet X and Y are not independent.
b. (1) True (2) False

5-15 **a.** 1.20, 1.42, 1.50
b. .0585, .153
c. If self-reported happiness is believable, **i** and **ii** are true. **iii** Last sentence is

false: Education does not necessarily cause the greater happiness. (In an observational study, confounding factors may be the cause.)

5-17 **b.** E(X) = 30, var (X) = 60
E(Y) = 25, var (Y) = 40
c. $\sigma_{X,Y} = 20$
d. E(S) = 55, var (S) = 140
e. E(W) = 38, var (W) = 66.4
f. E(D) = 5, var (D) = 60
g. Not very good. In an observational study like this, confounding factors may cause the difference in income.

5-19 i **b** (200), then **c** (118), finally **a** (110)
ii **b** (5.9), then **c** (6.7), finally **a** (9.5)

5-21 **a.** p(x|z) = .085, .213, .489, .213
b. p(x|z) is indeed different so X is dependent on Z.
c. 1.83
d. 1.72, so females have less education on average.
e. E(X) is the (weighted) average of the two conditional means (with weights 47% and 53%, to be precise).

5-23 **a.** 19.1 ($000) **b.** 14.25
c. 8.7 **d.** 13.83

5-25 **a.** 30 year old females have completed 2.03 schools on average, compared to 2.09 for males.
b. For age 45, 1.84 vs 1.92
For age, 70, 1.41 vs 1.47
c. At each age level, females have completed about .06 fewer schools on average than males.
d. Surprisingly larger, more, less; still be somewhat less than men's; multiple regressions.

5-27 RCE, OS, RCE, OS, multiple regression

5-29 **b.** $\mu = 9.65$, $\sigma = 7.5$
c. mode = 2.5 (or 0, if finer detail were given). Median is in between the mode and mean.

5-31 The ABC poll gave a biased view of the whole country, since it relied only on volunteer calls. So of course the polls did not agree.

5-33

a.	b.
1000	.026
974	.009
965	.019
947	.022
926	.053
877	.133
760	.288
541	.521
259	.803
51	1.000

b. i Correction: . . . the *second* decade
ii Improvement: . . . *from age 30 to age 90.*
c. i About $19 ii about $54
d. i .049 ii .926 iii .053

5-35 **a.**

x	0	1	2	3
p(x)	.512	.384	.096	.008

b. $\mu = .60$, $\sigma^2 = .48$
c. $13.88

5-37 **a.** about 5 people
b. about 293 people
c. only 32%
d. There are so many non-diabetics that even the small error rate of 2% produces relatively many "false alarms."

5-39 **a.** 2, 1, 4, 700
b. no
c. yes

6-1 **a.** $1,475,000
b. Assumed nonresponse bias is small.
c. $96,000

6-3 **c.** $\mu = 4.5$
d. $\overline{X}$ is indeed closer to μ than many of the individual observations.

6-5 **a.** True
b. Correction: SE of only $\sigma/\sqrt{n}$

6-7 **a.** .010 thousand = $10
b. .031 thousand = $31

6-9 **a.** $30,000, $1800, normal
b. .047

6-11 **a.** .047
b. <.00048
c. ≈ 0 (z = −6.67)

6-13 **a.** 34, 8
b. .000048

- **c.** Assumed the 50 mufflers were a random sample from the year's given record.

6-15 twice

6-17 .038 ≃ 4% (wcc, .056)

6-19 .007

6-21
- **a.** .472 (wcc, .658; and binomial answer of .656 is best of all)
- **b.** .954 (wcc, .964)
- **c.** 1.000 (wcc, 1.000)

6-25
- **a.** half as much: 5%, 2½%, ½%
- **b.** $N \geq 50n$

6-27
- **a.** $\mu = .769$, $\sigma = 1.31$
- **b.** .233 ≃ 23% (wcc, .271)

6-31
- **b.** The results should indeed be like Figure 6-11.

6-33 equally

6-35
- **a.** ⅕%
- **b.** Yes, random selection ensures that it is indeed unbiased and representative.

6-37
- **a.** .251 ≃ 25%
- **b.** .00048 ≃ .05%

6-39 .001 (wcc, .003)

6-41 .869 ≃ 87%

6-43
- **a.** 5.26 cents per dollar bet
- **b.**
  - **i** .548 ≃ 55%
  - **ii** .603 ≃ 60%
  - **iii** .722 ≃ 72%

7-1
- **a.** True
- **b.** Interchange μ and $\overline{X}$
- **c.** If we *quadruple* the sample size, . . .
- **d.** True

7-3 64%

7-5
- **a.** True
- **b.** Are you sure you have analyzed it efficiently? If not, maybe it would be wiser to spend $99,000 collecting the data and $1,100 analyzing it.

7-7
- **a.** .000308
- **b.** .000182, 69% more efficient
- **c.** .000156, 97% more efficient
- **d.** True, as part **a** showed.

7-9 Gauge C, with MSE = 50

7-11 MSE = .131, in between the two surveys in Problem 7-10.

7-13
- **a.** $\pi(1-\pi)/n$, consistent
- **b.** $\dfrac{1+\pi(1-\pi)(n-4)}{(n+2)^2}$, consistent
- **c.** Consistency doesn't help, but efficiency does.
- **d.** For $\pi = 0, .1, .2, \ldots$, rel. eff. = 0, 84%, 118%, 134%, 142%, 144%, 142%, on down.
- **e.** P* is preferred if π is anywhere near 1/2.

7-15
- **a.** Scale A, with MSE = .0001
- **b.** True

7-17
- **a.** They are slightly different
- **b.** Average first (method **ii**)
- **c.** Zero bias

7-19
- **a.** 1.6%; 1.8%
- **b.** 800,000; 900,000

8-1
- **a.** $\overline{X}$, μ, random
- **b.** $\sigma/\sqrt{n}$, standard error SE
- **c.** 2, μ
- **d.** about 50 times, would not
- **e.** wider

8-3 T = 9,990,000 ± 2,120,000 (better, ±2,030,000)

8-5 True

8-7
- **a.** 99.8 ± 67.9
- **b.** 5000 ± 3400
- **c.** yes

8-9 66.0 ± 3.8

8-11
- **a.** $\mu_M - \mu_W = 5.0 \pm 5.8$
  That is, the men at the university earn 5.0 (±5.8) thousand dollars more than the women, on average. Or equivalently,
  $\mu_W - \mu_M = -5.0 \pm 5.8$
  That is, women earn 5.0 (±5.8) less than men.
- **b.** It fails to show discrimination on two counts: (1) This is an observational study, and whatever differences exist may be due to confounding factors such as men having better qualifications, more experience, etc. (2) We're not even sure a difference exists in the population; the confidence interval includes $\mu_1 - \mu_2 = 0$ (i.e., no difference).

8-13
- **a.** Alcoholism in the mothers causes a drop of 21 ± 14 IQ points, on average, *if*

this had been a randomized study (which of course would be unethical).

b. The confounding factors that were not matched remain as a possible source of bias.

8-15 **a.** $\Delta = 3.00 \pm 1.35$
b. There is good evidence that an interesting environment stimulates the growth of the cortex in rats, increasing its weight by about 5% (±2%).

8-17 **a.** $0 < \pi < .45$
b. $.01 < \pi < .30$
c. $.04 < \pi < .22$, or $\pi = .10 \pm .08$
d. $\pi = .10 \pm .042 \simeq .10 \pm .04$

8-19 **a.** $\pi_1 - \pi_2 = .07 \pm .077 \simeq 7\% \pm 8\%$
b. $\pi_1 - \pi_3 = -.17 \pm .079 \simeq -17\% \pm 8\%$

8-21 **a.** 28.5, 71.0, 46.2 (per 100,000)
b. We estimate the vaccine reduces the polio rate from 71 to 28 cases per 100,000—a reduction of 43 cases per 100,000 (with 95% confidence, a reduction of 43 ± 14).
c. **i** An observational study like this would have confounded the effects of volunteering and vaccination.
ii And since volunteering is a substantial effect (an estimated 25 cases per 100,000) it would seriously bias the estimated effect of the vaccine (downwards by about 25 cases per 100,000).

8-23 **b.** $.43 \pm .0251 \simeq 43\% \pm 3\%$
$.35 \pm .0241 \simeq 35\% \pm 2\%$
c. $-.08 \pm .0348 \simeq 8\%$ drop $\pm 3\%$
$.03 \pm .0344 \simeq 3\%$ rise $\pm 3\%$
d. small, did not stand out; large, did, value, distinguish between, mostly sampling "noise"

8-25 **a.** 13.0 ± 21.4
b. It does not show this, for the same two reasons as in Problem 8-11.

8-27 The claim should not be modified, but discarded. This observational study very likely is badly biased. Perhaps the 50¢ per hour wage differential is due not to the right-to-work laws, but to some confounding factor such as the South being more rural, more anxious to reduce unemployment, etc.

8-29 **a.** $\mu = 44.2 \pm 5.5$ (± 5.3 better)
b. Total = 16,800 ± 2,100

8-31 **a.** 90.4% ± 0.9%
96.2% ± 1.1%
91.3% ± 1.4%
84.3% ± 2.0%
b. 11.9% ± 2.3%
c. This observational study may be badly biased by confounding factors such as age at marriage, city size, etc.

9-1 **i** $\Delta = -4.0 \pm 5.8$, indiscernible
ii $\mu_2 - \mu_1 = 13 \pm 21$, indiscernible
iii $\pi_2 - \pi_1 = -45\% \pm 9\%$, discernible

9-3 **a.** $\Delta = 2.0 \pm 8.5$ (\$000)
b. no **c.** no **d.** no
e. H_0: $\Delta = 0$ cannot be rejected

9-5 **i** $p < .10$ ($t = 1.93$)
ii $p \simeq .10$ ($t = 1.40$)
iii $p \ll 10^{-8}$ ($t = -10.2$)

9-7 I, α. II, β. α, β.

9-9 **a.** H_0: the proportion of defectives is unchanged, that is, $\pi = .10$
H_A: the proportion of defectives is worse, that is, $\pi > .10$
b. Reject H_0 if $P > 14\%$ (.140, exactly).
c. Reject all but the first and third shipments.

9-11 25 times bigger, so $n = 2500$

9-13 **a.** No, do not reject H_0
b. We would follow common sense, because the classical test is narrow-minded, and arbitrarily sets $\alpha = .05$
c. Since $\overline{X} = 1245$ exceeds the new critical value of 1235, we reject H_0. So the problem in **a** was indeed inadequate sample size.
d. Since $\overline{X} = 1201$ exceeds the new and very stringent critical value of 1200.5, we reject H_0. Therefore we find the increase of 1 unit "statistically significant."

The stated conclusion is true, and shows another problem with classical testing.

9-15 α would likely decrease, and consequently β would increase. (Where some doubt remains, maybe juries should be given a third choice—life imprisonment).

9-17 a. H_A: $\pi = .30$
b. $.149 \simeq 15\%$

9-19 a. $\overline{X}_c = 8.664$
b. yes, reject H_0
c. $\beta = .74, .09, .00$ (for $\mu_A = 8.6, 8.8, 9.0$)
d. $\simeq .01$

9-21 a. $\alpha = .13$ (wcc, .11)
b. $\beta = .500, .176, .043, .008$ (wcc, .540, .203, .052, .010)
d. Power is just OCC flipped upside down.

9-23 a. $\pi_{75} - \pi_{72} = .03 \pm .0355 \simeq .03 \pm .04$
b. .096
c. No, not discernible.

9-25 a. $\mu > 14{,}084$
b. .032
c. Yes, is discernible.

9-27 Type I error is to leap off the tracks if no train is coming. Type II error is to continue walking if a train is indeed coming—much more serious.

9-29 a. H_0: $\pi = .29$
b. $p \simeq 0$ ($t = -10.4$. But $z = -8.16$ is better)
c. definitely reject H_0

10-1

Source	SS	df	MS	F	p
Fert.	312	2	156	9.0	<.01
Residual	156	9	17.3		
Total	468	11			

10-3

Source	SS	df	MS	F	p
Cities	24,390	3	8,130	4.94	<.05
Residual	26,310	16	1,644		
Total	50,700	19			

10-5 $F = \dfrac{310}{34.0} = 9.1$, $p < .001$

10-9

Source	SS	df	MS	F	p
Hours	18	2	9	3.6	<.25
Men	78	2	39	15.6	<.05
Residual	10	4	2.5		
Total	106	8			

10-11

Source	SS	df	MS	F	p
Fert.	608	2	304	51.7	<.001
Seeds	183	1	183	31.1	<.001
Blocks	261	3	87	14.8	<.001
Residual	100	17	5.88		
Total	1152	23			

10-13 San Diego is higher on average by:
a. 45 ± 54 ($000) or ± 62
b. 45 ± 80 ($000)

10-15 a.

Source	SS	df	MS	F	p
Varieties	54	2	27.0	4.5	<.10
Soils	186	2	93.0	15.5	<.05
Residual	24	4	6.0		
Total	264	8			

b. $\mu_A - \mu_B = -3.00 \pm 7.45$
$\mu_A - \mu_C = 3.00 \pm 7.45$
$\mu_B - \mu_C = 6.00 \pm 7.45$
c. He seems to have succeeded—B's yield in loam (31) is much better than any other yield in the table. This means the assumption of additivity is suspect, and so is the analysis in parts **a** and **b**.

10-17 a. False: . . . an *acceptable* hypothesis, while . . . a *rejected* hypothesis.
b. False: The *sample* mean . . . with expectation μ and approximate standard deviation 10.
c. False: . . . the *true but unknown* population mean μ.

10-19 a. i $\pi_M - \pi_W = .023 \pm .024$
ii $\pi_M - \pi_W = -.045 \pm .032$
iii $\pi_M - \pi_W = .097 \pm .018$
b. The hypothetical population of all those students with the same sorts of qualifications, who might have applied.
c. The only faculty with discernibly different rates is Science, where women have a *higher* admission rate. The reason women have a discernibly lower admission rate in the whole school is that they tend to apply to the tougher faculty—not sex discrimination. For more detail, see Problem 1-18.

10-21 a. $\pi_H - \pi_L = .10 \pm .18$
b. $t \simeq z = 1.06$, $p \simeq .145$
c. We estimate the 3-month survival rate is

better for high concentration of oxygen than for low—better by 10 ± 18 percentage points, with 95% confidence (statistically indiscernible).

10-23 $\mu = 186 \pm 53.3$

10-25 **a.** Type I error, Pr = α
b. Type II error, Pr = β

10-27 **a.** 2-sided $p < .10$ ($t = 2.17$)
b. $p < .10$ ($F = 4.70$)
c. Same answer, same assumption of independent *random* samples from normal populations with equal variances.

10-29 **a.** True
b. True

10-31 Not fair at all. Some confounding factor, such as ambition or intelligence, may be producing much of the higher incomes of college graduates.

11-1 **a.** $\hat{Y} = 59 + 7.0X$
b.

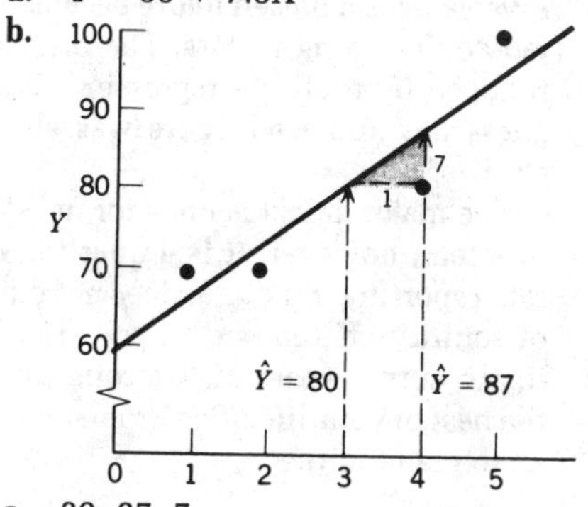

c. 80, 87, 7

11-3 **a.** $\hat{Y} = 119 + 9.0X$
b. 164, 119
c.

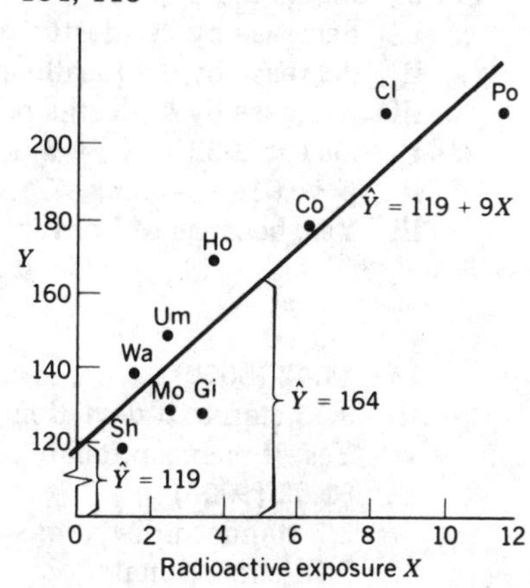

d. Since this is an uncontrolled observational study, it does not provide proof. (Other evidence, however, shows radiation is harmful).

11-5 **a.** mean **b.** normal
c. easy **d.** OLS, LOWESS, curve

11-7 **a.** $P = 30 + .50R$
c. It only estimates roughly how they are *related*. Causation cannot be inferred from an observational study.

12-3 **a.** When the two points are 4 times as far apart, we get 4 times the accuracy.
b. $SE = \sigma/\sqrt{\Sigma x^2}$, and the denominator was increased 4 times.

12-5 **a.** $\hat{S} = -.78 + .142X$
b. $\beta = .142 \pm .169$
d. Only $\beta = .50$ is rejected

12-7 **a.** $\hat{S} = -.24 + .081X$
b. $\beta = .081 \pm .085$
d. Only $\beta = .5$ is rejected

For Problem 12-6:
a. $\beta = 0, \beta > 0$
b. $p < .05$ ($t = 3.02$)
c. $\beta > .018$
d. Reject H_0

12-9 **b.** 15.0 ± 3.9, 39.0 ± 2.5
63.0 ± 1.7, 87.0 ± 2.5
c. This band contains far fewer than 95% of the points.

12-11 **a.** $\beta = 800 \pm 490$
b. Is discernible, since 800 exceeds ±490.
c. \$9,200 ± \$14,800 (very roughly, since income is not normally distributed)
d. No, since this is just an observational study. Perhaps men with higher education also tend to have more ambition, and this may be what produces the higher income.

12-13 $p = .003$ ($t = z = 2.76$)

12-15 **a.** $\hat{Y} = 0.7 + 1.266X$
c. $\mu_Y = 229 \pm 45$
d. $\mu_Y = 140 \pm 117$
e. The confidence interval is centered better, and narrower

12-17 **b.** $\alpha = 0.7 \pm 57.4$

13-1 **a.** The graph shows two lines, nearly parallel, with slope of about .18
b. +.18 approximately
c. −.7 approximately
d. $\hat{Y} = 2.5$

13-3 **a.** 15, .8 per inch **b.** 66

13-5 **a.** four equally spaced and parallel lines with slope of −.13
b. decrease of .13 percentage points
c. decrease of .034 percentage points
d. 1.4 percentage points

13-7 the simple regression formula $b = \dfrac{\Sigma x_1 y}{\Sigma x_1^2}$

13-9 **a.**

SE	(.046)	(.010)
95% CI	(±.15)	(±.032)
t ratio	(−2.8)	(−3.4)
p	(<.05)	(<.025)

b. We are assuming the 6 years represent a random sample from a large hypothetical population (which is pretty far fetched).
c. change in real income, X_2
d. Keep it, on both prior and statistical grounds.

13-11 **a.** $3.30 less, per front foot
b. $ .67 higher, per front foot
c. *For the same kind of lot,* the price was up by $1.50 per front foot, per year.

13-13 **a.** 10.14 **b.** .36
c. 10.50 **d.** 9.66
e. 9.66 **f.** −2.08

13-15 **a.** False: . . . a year with *above*-average rainfall would *tend to* produce above average yield.
b. Could be improved: In view of the positive multiple regression coefficient, it would improve the crop to irrigate, *assuming* **i** irrigation acts like rain water, **ii** the level of water is not near the saturation point where further water would hinder rather than help, **iii** temperature is the only important confounding factor that needs to be allowed for in the multiple regression, etc.

13-17 **a.** 3.38
b. 3.22
c. Increase yield by 3.38 (making the same assumptions as in Problem 13-15b).
d. 3.22, −.208

a.

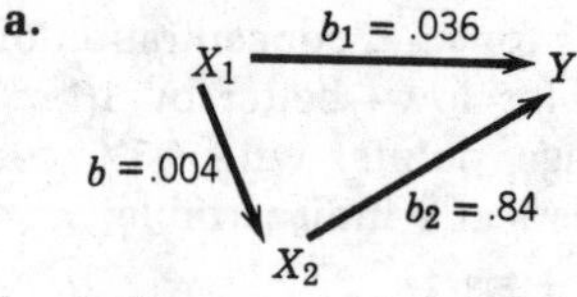

b. .039
c. The simple regression fits the data as well as any single line possibly can (though not as well as the 3 separate lines).
d. Yes, yes—and that is the great virtue of randomization.

a. .26 children fewer (on average)
b. .07 children fewer
c. .16 children fewer
d. .069 children more

b. .490, .303, .304
c. **i** decrease of .030
ii increase of .912

Five years is a biased figure because of omitted confounding factors. The bias could be reduced by multiple regression. We would *guess* the unbiased figure was about 3 instead of 5.

The major defect is not a formal statistical problem, however. It is a question of accurate reporting. Smoking does not cut 3 years of senility off the *end* of your life. It more likely cuts 3 years of vigorous living from the *best* of your life. (See Problem 13-24**d** for an explanation).

a. 100 (deaths per 10,000). This is a very good prediction.
b. 91 (deaths per 10,000)
c. **i** decrease by 29 (deaths per 10,000)
ii decrease by 0.4 (deaths per 10,000)
iii decrease by 4 (deaths per 10,000)
d. **i** .041 ± .032
ii $p < .010$ ($t = 2.5$)
iii Yes, because of **i** or **ii**

a. **i** 74.42 ($000)
ii 3.15 standard deviations. Yes, it is exceptional.
iii 81.62 ($000) 2.7 standard deviations. Still exceptional.

b. i $H_0: \beta = 0$
p = .251 (t = .67). No real evidence of sex discrimination.
ii Not fair, since causation cannot be concluded from an observational study with many factors still uncontrolled (such as ambition, etc.).

14-3 **a.** -39 ± 3.5, -9.0 ± 4.3, -350 ± 90, -380 ± 104, -180 ± 106
b. Age and cigarette smoking, 350 ml lower
c. 30 ml higher **d.** 39 ml lower
e. 180 ml lower
f. 4.6 years, important variables omitted

14-5 **a.** Two parallel lines, 10.6 units apart.
b. i 10.6 ii 1.39
d. Simple regression line would be steeper—biased by omitting D.

14-7 **a.** No, about the same admission rates (if anything, women have a slightly higher admission rate).
b. Yes

14-9 **a.** i 61 ii 70 iii 73
b. 61, 70, 73, same as in part **a**.
c. One-factor ANOVA. The response is yield, and the factor is fertilizer type.
d. $\hat{Y} = 61 + 9\,D_A + 12\,D_B$

14-11 **a.**

Additive		*Interactive*	
70	80	74	77
55	65	53	67
65	75	68	73

b. Additive, both sexes.

14-13 **a.** For large I, the expected yield would surely curve down (negative term in I^2).
b. $p < .001$ (t = −3.75) so that H_0 has little credibility and **a** is confirmed.
c. Maximum at I = 4.0, but irrigate much less if expensive.
d. 4.5

14-15 **a.** Grain production seems to have risen more slowly than population.
b. Grain is up 24%, population is up 21%, so grain increased more.

14-17 Yes, if the model is multiplicative instead of additive.

14-19 $\log Q = \log \beta_0 + \beta_1 \log K + \beta_2 \log L$
Regress $Y = \log Q$ against $X_1 = \log K$ and $X_2 = \log L$

14-21

	Response	*Regressors*
a.	Y	X, X^2, X^3
b.	Y	$T, \sin\left(\frac{2\pi T}{12}\right)$
c.	Log Y	T
d.	Log Y	T, X
e.	Y	X, T, X^2, T^2, XT

f. We have to compute least squares estimates by brute force.

14-23 **b.** Four parallel but unequally spaced lines.

14-25 **a.** race, dummy variables
b. just categorial factors, suitable
c. X and X^2 and X^3 as the regressors
d. can, measured; unit, constant
e. cannot, some omitted confounding factors. . .

14-27 **a. b.**

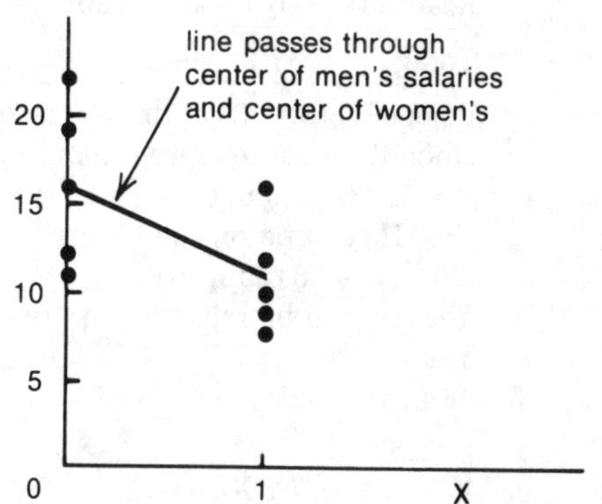

c. $\hat{Y} = 16.0 - 5.0X$
d. $\beta = -5.0 \pm 5.8$
Women earn on average $5,000 (±$5,800) less than men.
e. Same
f. No. To measure discrimination, men and women with the same qualifications should be compared.

14-29 False: After holding constant many (*but not all*) other variables, women made $2,400 less than men. Therefore, $2,400 is our *best feasible measure*.
In conclusion, the $2,400 figure may be due to discrimination, or it may be due to some more subtle difference between men and women not measured in this study.

14-31 Such severe rounding makes the coefficient easy to state and interpret, but it also loses some information and hence probably weakens the t ratio.

15-1 a. $.787 \simeq 79\%$
b. $-.05 < \rho < .96$, approx.
c. H_0: $\rho = 0$ is acceptable, that is, no proven relation.

15-3 a. .450
b. $-.62 < \rho < .91$, approx.
c. $\hat{Y} = .165 + .405X$
$\beta = .405 \pm 1.476$
e. i No, because of **(c)**
ii No, because of **(b)**

15-5 a. $\hat{Y} = 1.15 + .0232X$
b.

Source	SS	df	MS	F	p
Regression	5.73	1	5.73	44.6	<.001
Residual	6.17	48	.129		
Total	11.9	49			

Reject H_0 ($\beta = 0$) at the 5% error level, since its p-value is less than 5%.
c. $\beta = .0232 \pm .0070$
Yes, H_0 can be rejected.
d. $.50 < \rho < .81$, approx.
Yes, H_0 can be rejected.
e. Yes
f. 48%, yes; 52%, yes

15-7 a. r = .57
b. $\hat{X}_2 = 24 + .61\ X_1$
c. 79, 48.4
d. mean = 73, about the same as 79 in **c**
e. mean = 43, about the same as 48 in **c**
f. True with a minor qualification: The pilots who scored very well or very badly on the first test X_1 *tended* to be closer to the average on the second test X_2.

15-9 a. In this observational study, the effect of criticism (or praise) cannot be distinguished from the natural regression toward the mean.
b. The proper way to compare criticism with praise (or nothing), is with a *randomized* experimental design.

15-11 a. R = .92
b. r = .92, the same

15-13 **a** with **e**; **b** with **c** and **d**.

15-15 a.

X_1	X_2
−2	2
−1	−1
0	−2
1	−1
2	2

r = 0
b. No
c. $SE_1 = 1.25$, $SE_2 = 1.06$
d. You can simply drop off the X_2 term.

15-17 r = 1.00

15-19 a. True
b. False: $\sigma^2_{\hat{Y}} = \sigma^2_{\hat{X}}$
c. True
d. True
e. False: . . . the predicted X score is 75

15-21 c. $r = \sqrt{1(.50)} = .71$
d. $\hat{Y} = 70$
e. $\hat{X} = 65$

15-23 a. True
b. False: Profits altogether are as extreme in 1985 as in 1984.
c. True
d. False: . . . the best single prediction of its 1985 profit would be 9.5% (on the *regression* line).

15-25 a. True
b. False: . . . if the correlation is near 1.
c. False: . . . *many but not all* confounding factors . . .
d. True
e. False: One *advantage* of multiple regression is that it can . . .

15-27 a.

CI	.09 ± .02	−.24 ± .10	2.61 ± 1.61
t	9.0	−4.8	3.18
p	<.0005	<.0005	<.001
r	.54	−.32	.22

b. 32 minutes, 27.4 minutes
c. The second prediction error was smaller—only 54% as big.
d. Yes. [The prediction errors with and without regression are in the ratio (squared) of $(Y - \hat{Y})^2/(Y - \bar{Y})^2 = 5.4^2/10.0^2 = .29$. For all 200 patients, we likewise obtain $\Sigma(Y - \hat{Y})^2/\Sigma(Y - \bar{Y})^2 = 1 - R^2 = 1 - .72 = .28$. So this one patient in part **c** was typical.]

16-1 **a.** $.109 \simeq 11\%$
b. $.344 \simeq 34\%$

16-3 **a.** $.035 \simeq 4\%$
b. $.062 \simeq 6\%$
c. $.004 \simeq 4/10\%$

16-5 $.968 \simeq 97\%$

16-7 **a.** $67 \leq \nu \leq 76$
$63 \leq \nu \leq 69$
$3 \leq \nu \leq 7$
b. $.930 = 93\%$

16-9 **a.** Yes, approximately normal
b. The nonparametric CI is likely wider
c. $67.8 \leq \mu \leq 74.2$, indeed narrower

16-11 **a.** $\overset{|}{X} = 15$
b. 99.8% (wcc, 99.4%)
c. $12 \leq \nu \leq 19$ (wcc, $10 \leq \nu \leq 23$)

16-13 .033

16-15 .028

16-17 **b.** $p < .25$ ($t = -.84$)

16-19 **b.** $p < .025$ ($t = 2.73$)
c. p-value is sharper (smaller) than earlier, because more information (ranking) was used.

16-21

Wilcoxon two-sample test	Kruskal-Wallis 1-factor ANOVA
Wilcoxon paired-sample test	Friedman 2-factor ANOVA

16-23 $r = .70$, not discernibly different from 0

16-25 $p = .006$ (wcc, .011)

16-27 **a.** For a normal distribution, the best estimate is $\overline{X} = 8.1$
b. Because of possible outliers, the best estimate is $\overline{X}_{.25} = 7.9\%$ or perhaps $\overset{|}{X} = 8.0\%$.
c. Because of possible outliers, the best estimate is $\overline{X}_{.25} = 15.18$

16-29 **a.** 104, 109.4, 105.3
c. $\overset{|}{X} = 104$

16-31 105.13

16-33 **a.** CS, appropriate **b.** NPS
c. NPS **d.** CS
e. NPS **f.** NPS

16-35 **a.** $p = .145$ (sign test), or $p < .10$ (Approximate Wilcoxon, with $t = 1.84$)
b. $p = .035$ (sign test), or $p < .01$ (Approx. Wilcoxon, with $t = 3.43$)
c. $p < .25$ (Approx. Wilcoxon, with $t = 1.05$)

16-37 H_0: programs A and B are equally effective. $p < .05$ (Approx. Wilcoxon, with $t = 2.07$)

16-39 **a.** $p = .152 \simeq 15\%$ (wcc, .221)
b. We cannot *a priori* expect a time series like this to be a random sample. And the test in part **a** does nothing to allay our fears. We therefore won't assume it is safe to proceed with a test for ν.

17-1 **a.** $\chi^2 = 12.65$, $p < .01$
b. Yes, reject H_0

17-3 **c.** about 5% (the error level α)

17-5 **a.** Instead of χ^2, use the proportion of aces P. To calculate the p-value, standardize:

$$Z = \frac{P - 1/6}{\sqrt{\frac{(1/6)(5/6)}{30}}}$$

c. much greater than 5% (the power of the test)

17-7 **a.** education and occupation are independent
b. $\chi^2 = 53$, $p \ll .001$

17-9 **a.** proportions surviving are .94, .93, .89
b. survival is independent of residence, $p < .001$ ($\chi^2 = 19.7$)
c. yes, discernible

17-11 **a.** newspaper and class are independent
b. $\chi^2 = 20.6$, $p < .005$, not discernible at level .001

17-13 **a.** degree and sex are independent
b. $\chi^2 = 3.25$, $p < .25$
c. $\pi_1 = 49\% \pm 3\%$
$\pi_2 = 49\% \pm 6\%$
$\pi_3 = 33\% \pm 16\%$

17-15 $\chi^2 = 14.0$, $p < .005$

18-1 MLE = .25, .50, .50, 0

18-3 **a.** $\overline{X} = 44.5$ **b.** $P = .40$
c. $b = .25$

18-5 **a.** MME, just the luck of the draw
b. MLE, in the sense of MSE (mean squared error), for example.

18-7 yes

18-9
a. −13.0, −11.0, −10.5, −10.6, −11.0
b. about .3, or a little more
c. $1/\overline{X}$, in this case, .33

18-11
a. MME = MLE = $\overline{X}$ = 4.25
b. MME = MLE = P = 33%
c. MME = 64, MLE = 44 is better (in MSE sense)
d. MME = MLE = 6634

19-1
a. .247, .198 ≃ 20%
b. .000064, .000064
c. 1 and 0, respectively

19-3
a. .10, .40, .50
b. .28, .44, .28

19-5
a. a lot narrower than in Problem 19-4, and a little narrower than the classical CI. Also centered better.
b. Bayesian: $\pi = .56 \pm .13$
Classical: $\pi = .60 \pm .14$

19-7
a. normal, mean = 70, st. dev. = 2.5
b. at $\overline{X}$ = 70, the MLE
c. the posterior is 16 times closer to the likelihood, which has 16 times as much information.
d. Classical: $\mu = 70 \pm 4.9$
Bayesian: $\mu = 69.4 \pm 4.7$ (almost the same)

19-9 False. . . . n is *large*. It is only when n is *small* that . . .

19-11
a. m = 13.97 ± .36
b. 56%

19-13
b. The Bayesian estimates are shrunk 12% of the way to H_0 (52).
c. **i** Figure 19-7
ii the same, Figure 19-7

19-15 Shrinkage slope = .020, we assumed *a priori* that the population slope β was as likely to be − as +.

19-17 classical estimate = 6.0, shrinkage estimate = 5.96 (for this, we assumed *a priori* that the population improvement was as likely to be − as +)

19-19
a. Most people guess that Peter has better evidence.
b. **i** 2 **ii** $2^4 = 16$
iii $2^{4-1} = 8$ **iv** $2^{12-8} = 16$
So Peter's posterior odds in **iii** are not as strong as Paul's in **iv**.
c. Posterior odds = 2^{r-w}, so **ii** is correct.

19-21
a. $\mu = 115 \pm 4.2$
b. Each is making a correct inference; it's just that Dr. B knows more.
c. $\mu = 117.0 \pm 3.4$
d. $\mu = 117.0 \pm 3.4$
e. practically the same

20-1
a. weighs both good and bad luck . . .
b. can still, posterior, Bayes Theorem

20-3
a. $L(a_1) = 22$ is min.
b. if "rain," $L(a_3) = 15.9$ is min.
if "shine," $L(a_1) = 17.7$ is min.
c. False. Action a_1 is best when "shine" is predicted, and *also* when no prediction is possible. Action a_3 is best when "rain" is predicted. Action a_2 is never best.
d. 4.7

20-5 30

20-7
a. 238.4 **b.** 238.4
c. 238.4

20-11
a. F: . . . Then the best estimate is the *median* of the *posterior* distribution of V.
b. F: . . . *Bayesian* estimation *exploits* prior distributions and losses.

21-1
a. Choose the top option, with expected value of 20K.
b. To avoid risk, she might be wise to choose the bottom option (the "sure thing").

21-3
a. Seed, at an expected cost of 94.3 million.
b. Still seed, at an expected cost of 110.8 million.

21-5
a. The pilot plant would be best, to net 64 million.
b. Stop and keep losses to 20 million. It is pointless to complete the pilot plant.

21-7
a. slightly worse
b. This half-price test is useless. So use the better seismic test again.

21-9
a. For homeowners who are risk averse, some form of insurance is wise to protect them from severe losses.

b. 52%
c. 38%, $43.60

21-11 a. Go to B, and if there is no room in the small lot, park at a meter without feeding it and risk a fine. Expected daily cost is $1.85 (or if we ignore the time to return home, $1.45)
b. Go to B, and if there is no room in the small lot, park at a meter. But now pay the meter. Expected daily cost is $3.60. (If we ignore the time to return home, the solution is to go to B, and if there is no room in the small lot, go over to P. Expected daily cost is then $2.64)

21-13 a. He should buy elsewhere and sue, without consulting the legal expert. Then expected cost is $45,000.
b. to $3,000 or less (EVPI = $3,000)
c. He should get expert legal advice; if it's encouraging, buy elsewhere and sue; if not, buy from Regal. Then expected disutility is about .13

21-15 a. Yes the new can would increase expected profit by 7.5K
b. EVPI = 19K
c. i not worth it
ii not worth it
iii 9.4K

22-1 a. 120.8, 120.0, 120.4
same order: PPI < FPI < LPI
b. 88.0, 87.4, 87.7
same order: PQI < FQI < LQI
c. cost index = 105.6
only Fisher's indexes pass
d. no difference

22-3 a.

133.3	183.3	133.3
133.3	175.3	133.3
133.3	179.3	133.3

b. LPI is simplest to calculate, and more important, it is simplest to measure: It does not require new quantity measurements every year (Q_t), but just initially (Q_0).

c.

137.5	74.6	102.6
134.0	72.7	97.4
135.7	73.7	100.0

The time reversal test is passed only by Fisher's Index.

22-9 a. 117, 115, 116
b. 115, 113, 114
c. 132

22-11 a. 177%
b. 169%, 100%

23-1 a. $5,320,000 ± $300,000
b. $5,230,000 ± $220,000

23-3 a. 16 hours
b. 36 hours, which may be worse than useless.

23-5 a. $337
b. 220, 322, 260
c. SE = .39, a reduction of 13%
d. Earlier steps save more. Thus stratification reduces the SE by 24%, and sampling itself helps enormously.

23-7 a. USU, cluster
b. heterogeneous
c. sequential, overwhelming, random variable, less
d. may be disasterous, more biased

23-11 a. 9% ± 6%
b. 46.3% ± 2.8%

24-1 b. MSE ≃ 2.8 and 0.7, so the simple rule has only ¼ as much MSE.

24-3 d. See Problem 24-4

24-5 b. Yes, it does show random tracking.

24-7 If you use a computer package (which we highly recommend), you will get slightly different answers for Problems 24-7 and 24-9, due to the minor refinements the computer can easily make.
Starting at the third quarter of 1957:
a. Centered M = 58.0, 58.5, 59.0, 60.0, . . . , which does indeed smooth out the large fourth quarter
b. .776, 1.812, .644, .767, . . .
c. .763, 1.816, .654, .768, repeated
d. Starting now at the first quarter: 55, 57, 59, 58, . . .

24-9 Starting at the third quarter of 1968;
a. Centered M = 542, 541, 540, 541, . . . , which is indeed smooth

b. 1.015, 1.006, .939, 1.039, . . .
c. 1.009, 1.011, .944, 1.050, and repeated
d. Starting now at the first quarter: 538, 539, 545, 538, . . .

24-11 Essentially white noise, because any pattern would make somebody who found it enormously rich.

24-13 **a.** Strong seasonal component each *year*
b. Strong periodic component each *day*
c. No periodic component
d. Likely a seasonal component each *year*.

25-1 **b.** $\hat{Y} = -1.5 + .744X$, which is biased.

25-3 **a.** $\hat{Y} = 10 + .60X$, which is perfectly on target.
b. This is a lucky sample, because the errors e_i exactly cancel.

25-5 **a.** $s_{X_1Y} \simeq \beta_1 s_{X_1X_1} + \beta_2 s_{X_1X_2}$
$s_{X_2Y} \simeq \beta_1 s_{X_2X_1} + \beta_2 s_{X_2X_2}$
b. Solve the two equations for the two unknowns, β_1 and β_2.
b. They are the same, since the equations in part **(a)** are just the estimating equations (13-5) and (13-6)—except for the constant divisor n − 1.

25-7 **a.** $\hat{Y}_1 = -2.09\ Y_2$
b. Using $\hat{Y}_1$ as an IV (where $\hat{Y}_1 = 1.99\ X_1$):
$s_{\hat{Y}_1Y_2} \simeq s_{\hat{Y}_1Y_1}\ \gamma_1 + s_{\hat{Y}_1X_1}\ \beta_1$
i.e., $-38.6 \simeq 80.8\ \gamma_1 + 40.6\ \beta_1$
Using X_1 as an IV:
$s_{X_1Y_2} \simeq s_{X_1Y_1}\ \gamma_1 + s_{X_1X_1}\ \beta_1$
i.e., $-19.4 = 40.6\ \gamma_1 + 20.4\ \beta_1$
But this is just the first equation restated (multiplied by 1/1.99).

25-9 **a.** OLS, correlated, some
b. highly correlated, uncorrelated
c. the regressors themselves, linear combinations of the predetermined variables

4-3A

	i	ii	iii
a.	.50	.31	.23
b.	.50	.600	.625
	.50	.614	.636
	.50	.667	.667
c.	.22	.20	.16

12-1A **a.** .067 **b.** $b = \dfrac{Y_7 - Y_1}{X_7 - X_1}$
c. yes **d.** yes
e. b_1 has larger SE than OLS, by the Gauss-Markov Theorem.
f. $.00236\sigma$, $.00189\sigma$

14-1A **a.** +e, where e has mean 0
b. +e, where e has mean 0
c. ×u, where u has median 1
d. ×u, where u has median 1
e. +e, where e has mean 0
f. +e, where e has mean 0, and compute OLS by brute force.

18-1A The argument is the same, if we replace $(\alpha + \beta X)$ everywhere by $(\beta_0 + \beta_1X_1 + \beta_2X_2 + \ldots)$

19-1A **a.** .024 ± .026, .020 ± .023
b. −13 ± 12, −10.9 ± 11.1
c. 6.00 ± 1.52, 5.95 ± 1.52

GLOSSARY OF COMMON SYMBOLS

SYMBOL	MEANING	REFERENCE
	ENGLISH LETTERS	
a	number of columns in ANOVA, or	Tables 10-4a, 10-8a
	regression intercept	Figure 11-4, (11-6)
ANOVA	analysis of variance	(10-14), (10-18)
b	number of rows in ANOVA, or	Table 10-8a
	regression slope	Figure 11-4, (11-5)
cov	covariance, $= \sigma_{XY}$	(5-10), (5-18)
d.f.	degrees of freedom	(2-16), (8-12), (13-14)
D	difference in two paired observations	(8-24), Table 8-3
e	error term in regression	(12-3)
E	event (also F, G, etc.)	(3-6)
$\overline{\text{E}}$	not E	(3-14), (3-15)
E( )	expected value, $= \mu$	(4-32), (5-9), (5-17)
F	variance ratio	(10-15)
H_0	null hypothesis	(9-9), (19-33)
H_A	alternative hypothesis	(9-10), (19-33)
$L(\ )$	likelihood function, or	(18-3), (18-4)
	average loss	(20-4)
MLE	maximum likelihood estimate	(18-4), (18-10)
MSD	mean squared deviation	(2-10), (2-21)
MS	mean square	Tables 10-4a, 10-8a
n	sample size	(6-7), (8-11)
n_0	quasi-sample size	(19-22), (19-29)
N	population size	(6-24)
O	observed value	Table 17-1
OLS	ordinary least squares	(11-2)
$p(x)$	probability distribution	(4-2), (5-4)
$p(x, y)$	joint probability distribution	(5-2)
P	sample proportion	(6-12), (8-27), (8-29)
$\Pr(E)$	probability of event E	(3-2), (3-7)
$\Pr(E\|F)$	conditional probability	(3-17)
r	simple correlation	(15-2), (15-6)
r^2	coefficient of determination	(15-16), (15-17)
R	multiple correlation, or	(15-27)
	number of runs	(16-12)
R^2	coeff. of multiple determination	(15-28)
$\overline{R}^2$	R^2 corrected for d.f.	(15-29), (15-30)
s	standard deviation	(2-13), (2-14)
s^2	variance of sample, or	(2-11), (2-12)
	residual variance	Table 10-8, (12-7)
s_p^2	pooled variance of samples	(8-21), (10-5)
s_X^2	variance of X values in regression	(12-6), (15-7)
s_Y^2	variance of Y values in regression	(15-7), (15-17)
S	number of successes	(4-8), Table 4-3

SE	standard error	(6-7), (8-15), (12-8)
SS	sum of squares (variation)	(10-14), (10-18)
t	t variable	(8-15), (9-16), (9-18)
var	variance, $= \sigma^2$	(4-5), (5-18)
w	bisquare weights	(16-13), (16-21)
W	Wilcoxon test statistic	(16-9)
X	random variable, or	(4-2), Figure 4-1
	regressor in original form	(11-4)
x	realized value of X, or	Figure 4-1
	regressor in deviation form	(11-4)
$\overline{X}$	sample mean	(2-4), (6-9), (8-11)
$\overset{\mid}{X}$	sample median	(2-2)
Y	response in regression	(12-2)
$\hat{Y}$	fitted value of Y	(11-1), (12-20)
Z	standard normal variable	(4-16), (4-23), (6-11)

MATHEMATICAL SYMBOLS

$\propto$	is proportional to
$\equiv$	equals, by definition
$\simeq$	approximately equals
$>$	is greater than
*	optional section or problem
Σ	sum of

GREEK LETTERS ARE RESERVED FOR POPULATION PARAMETERS

α	probability of type I error, or	Figures 9-4, 9-6
	population regression intercept	Figure 12-2, (12-12)
β	probability of type II error, or	Figures 9-6, 9-9
	population regression slope	Figure 12-2, (12-10)
Δ	population mean difference	(8-24)
θ	any population parameter	(7-1), (18-10), (19-8)
μ	population mean	(4-4), (4-28), (8-11)
μ_0	regression mean at X_0, or	(12-19), Figure 12-6
	mean of prior distribution, or	(19-23), Figure 19-5
	null population mean	(9-9)
ν	population median	(16-2), (16-5)
π	population proportion	(8-27), (8-29), (19-19)
ρ	population correlation	(5-13), Figure 15-4
σ^2	population variance	(4-5), (5-18)
σ_{XY}	population covariance	(5-10), (5-18)
χ^2	chi-square variable	(17-2), (17-10)

INDEX OF EXAMPLES AND PROBLEMS

Letters in bold refer to Examples (**E**), Figures (**F**), Problems (**P**), and Tables (**T**).

INDEX

Printed and bound in Singapore by Arico Printers Pte Ltd

Where to Find It: A guide to Basic Confidence Intervals

PROBLEM	SOLUTION NAME	95% CONFIDENCE INTERVAL	EQUATION	WORKED EXAMPLE	PROBLEM EXERCISE
	MEANS				
Estimating one mean	t	$\mu = \bar{X} \pm t_{.025}\,\text{SE}$ $= \bar{X} \pm t_{.025}\dfrac{s}{\sqrt{n}}$	(8-15) (8-11)	Example 8-2	Problem 8-7
Comparing two means (a) independent samples	2-sample t	$\mu_1 - \mu_2 = (\bar{X}_1 - \bar{X}_2) \pm t_{.025}\, s_p \sqrt{\dfrac{1}{n_1} + \dfrac{1}{n_2}}$	(8-20)	Example 8-3	Problem 8-11
(b) paired observations	paired t	$\Delta = \bar{D} \pm t_{.025}\dfrac{s_D}{\sqrt{n}}$	(8-24)	Example 8-4b	Problem 8-15
Comparing k means	ANOVA	$\mu_1 - \mu_2 = (\bar{X}_1 - \bar{X}_2) \pm \sqrt{(k-1)\,F_{.05}}\; s\sqrt{\dfrac{1}{n_1} + \dfrac{1}{n_2}}$ $\mu_1 - \mu_3 = (\bar{X}_1 - \bar{X}_3) \pm$ etc.	(10-25)	Example 10-4	Problem 10-13
	PROPORTIONS				
Estimating one proportion	Normal approximation	$\pi = P \pm 1.96\sqrt{\dfrac{P(1-P)}{n}}$	(8-27)	Example 1-1	Problem 8-17
Comparing two proportions	Normal approximation	$\pi_1 - \pi_2 = (P_1 - P_2) \pm 1.96\sqrt{\dfrac{P_1(1-P_1)}{n_1} + \dfrac{P_2(1-P_2)}{n_2}}$	(8-29)		Problem 8-19
Comparing k proportions	Chi-square χ^2	test: $\chi^2 = \Sigma\dfrac{(O-E)^2}{E}$	(17-2)	Table 17-1	Problem 17-1
	RELATIONS (REGRESSION)				
Response to one factor (a) numerical factor	Simple regression	$\beta = b \pm t_{.025}\dfrac{s}{\sqrt{\Sigma x^2}}$	(12-10)	Example 12-1	Problem 12-5
(b) categorical factor	ANOVA, or dummies	$\beta = b \pm t_{.025}\text{SE}$ where the standard error (SE) is found from the computer output	(10-25) (14-14)		Problem 14-9
Response to k factors (a) all factors numerical	Multiple regression		(13-13)	Example 13-3	Problem 13-9
(b) some factors categorical	Multiple regression (dummies)		(14-8)	Example 14-1	Problem 14-3
Nonlinear response	Transformation		(14-19) (14-31)	Table 14-2 Table 14-3	Problem 14-13 Problem 14-21

(cont'd)

SOME MODERN ALTERNATIVES

Any unknown parameter	Bootstrap	Figure 8-5		Example 8-5	Problem 8-22
To make a one-sided claim	one-sided CI	for example, $\mu > \overline{X} - z_{.05}SE$	(9-31)	Example 9-9	Problem 9-25
Nonnormal population	nonparametric CI	$X_{(3)} \leq \nu \leq X_{(7)}$	(16-5)	Figure 16-2	Problem 16-5
Vague prior knowledge	Bayesian shrinkage	shrink estimate by $(1 - 1/F)$ shrink SE by $\sqrt{1 - 1/F}$	(19-33) (19-3A) Appendix	Example 19-11	Problems 19-13, 19-1A